Palm OS Programming
The Developer's Guide

SECOND EDITION

Palm OS Programming
The Developer's Guide

Neil Rhodes and Julie McKeehan

Beijing · Cambridge · Farnham · Köln · Sebastopol · Tokyo

Palm OS Programming: The Developer's Guide, Second Edition
by Neil Rhodes and Julie McKeehan

Copyright © 2002, 1999 O'Reilly & Associates, Inc. All rights reserved.
Printed in the United States of America.

Published by O'Reilly & Associates, Inc., 101 Morris Street, Sebastopol, CA 95472.

Editor:	Troy Mott
Production Editor:	Linley Dolby
Cover Designer:	Edie Freedman
Interior Designer:	Melanie Wang

Printing History:

January 1999:	First Edition.
January 2002:	Second Edition.

Library of Congress Cataloging-in-Publication Data

Rhodes, Neil, 1962-.
    Palm OS programming / by Neil Rhodes & Julie McKeehan.-- 2nd ed.
        p. cm.
    ISBN 1-56592-856-3
    1. PalmPilot (Computer)--Programming. 2. Palm OS. I. McKeehan, Julie. II. Title.

QA76.8.P138 R555 2001
005.26'8--dc21   2001045921

ISBN: 978-1-565-92856-5
[LSI]   [2013-03-29]

Table of Contents

Part II.   Programming a Palm Application

Preface

By almost anybody's standard of measure, the Palm OS and Palm handhelds are wildly successful. Everybody loves them: users buy them faster than any other handheld, product reviewers give them awards, and programmers, once they find the platform, never want to leave.

How do we account for this phenomenon? What makes the Palm handheld such a great device? Simple. It's really fast, it's cheap, it does almost anything you ask it to, and it fits in your shirt pocket. Combine all that with the loyalty of its users and one of the most ardent developer followings seen since the glory days of the Macintosh, and you have all the elements of a whirlwind success. If you are a programmer, the question you should really be asking yourself right now is, "What do I need to know to join in the fun?" To find out, keep reading.

What's New in This Edition

We've added some new material in this edition based on changes to the OS and comments from readers. The major additions are as follows:

- We have added a tutorial that walks a C programmer new to the Palm OS through the creation of a small application. This step-by-step tutorial covers the installation and use of both CodeWarrior and PRC-Tools.
- We have added a chapter containing a comprehensive discussion of the Memory Manager APIs.
- We have greatly expanded discussions about forms and form objects. We tell you about the UI and give examples for every type of form and form object available in the Palm OS.

- We have changed how we create our resources. Rather than using Constructor and PilRC based on the development environment, we use PilRC in all cases. The PilRC text format is cross-platform and easy to display in a book.
- We have updated the conduit chapter to reflect the newer Conduit Development Kit. We have removed coverage of Basemon conduits and expanded material on Generic conduits. We have also added more material on conduit installers.

Minor changes can be found everywhere. We have updated every chapter to reflect changes in Palm OS versions up to and including Version 4.0. We have also expanded coverage of many topics and added new material throughout.

The Source Code Web Site

The source code we discuss in this book is available at our web site. We use this approach because it is much easier to keep the code current to released versions of the Palm OS and other development tools. Our web site is located at:

http://www.calliopeinc.com/palmprog2/

Additionally, we will keep an up-to-date online version of the tutorial found in Chapter 4 on our web site. It will be current with any newer versions of CodeWarrior, PRC-Tools, and the Palm OS SDK.

Using Code Examples

This book is here to help you get your job done. In general, you may use the code in this book in your programs and documentation. You do not need to contact us for permission unless you're reproducing a significant portion of the code. For example, writing a program that uses several chunks of code from this book does not require permission. Selling or distributing a CD-ROM of examples from O'Reilly books does require permission. Answering a question by citing this book and quoting example code does not require permission. Incorporating a significant amount of example code from this book into your product's documentation does require permission.

We appreciate, but do not require, attribution. An attribution usually includes the title, author, publisher, and ISBN. For example: *Palm OS Programming: The Developer's Guide, Second Edition*, by Neil Rhodes and Julie McKeehan (O'Reilly). Copyright 2002 O'Reilly & Associates, Inc., ISBN 978-1-5659-2856-5.

If you feel your use of code examples falls outside fair use or the permission given here, feel free to contact us at *permissions@oreilly.com*.

Whom This Book Is for: C/C++ Programmers

If you know C and want to write applications for Palm OS devices, this is the book for you. It doesn't matter if you own a Palm and are an avid user or if you are only now thinking about getting one. You can be a starving student who wants to mess around with a Palm device in your spare time using free development tools or a programmer in a Fortune 500 company who has just been told to write an application for the 5,000 units the company is deploying in the field next month.

We have tried to make sure that there is useful information for everyone from beginning Palm programmers to those of you who are more advanced.

We'll use only C for most of the book, but since the Generic conduit framework requires C++, we'll switch to that in Chapter 16.

What This Book Is About and How to Read It

This book shows you how to create a Palm application and a conduit. It assumes that you have the Palm OS documentation (available at *http://www.palmos.com/dev*) and know where to find things in it. Before showing you how to create an application, we spend some time explaining the development environments, the UI, and what makes for a successful handheld application.

Here is a summary of what we cover:

Part I, *Overview of the Palm OS*, gives you the big picture. You learn about the handhelds, their history, what makes them great devices, the development environments, and the right way to design a Palm application.

Chapter 1, *The Palm Solution*
We happily admit that this chapter is unabashedly partisan. Would you want someone who doesn't like the Palm OS telling you about it? We also describe what makes this handheld platform successful and the philosophy behind the handheld design. We touch on how these factors, in turn, influence application design.

Chapter 2, *Technical Overview and Development Environments*
We describe the choices in development environments and the range of languages you can use. We cover everything from simple forms-based environments that use languages like Visual Basic to full-blown environments that require C.

Chapter 3, *Designing a Solution*

We discuss the use of all of the forms and form objects in the Palm OS. We then venture onto the topic of handheld UI design and philosophy. This includes everything from how the intended audience shapes the content of applications to a careful look at some well-designed forms and dialog boxes. We then show you the UI of the Sales application, what each form does, and why we designed it the way we did.

Part II, *Programming a Palm Application*, covers everything you need to know in order to code a Palm OS application. We describe its structure, memory restrictions, data design, and other material from the API that you need to know. Each chapter includes descriptions and sample code for the Sales application or other samples. We start the section with a tutorial to get people new to the Palm OS up and running.

Chapter 4, *Tutorial*

This chapter shows someone brand new to the Palm how to install and use CodeWarrior or the GNU Compiler Collection (GCC) to get a simple Palm OS application up and running. We use a step-by-step approach that shows a new-comer how to create, download, and debug a simple application.

Chapter 5, *Structure of an Application*

We take you through the whole cycle of a Palm application, from the time the user launches it to the moment it quits.

Chapter 6, *Memory Manager*

Memory on the Palm is unusual and takes some explanation to understand. We describe how memory is used and the restrictions on it that will affect your applications.

Chapter 7, *Debugging Palm Applications*

In this chapter, we turn to the crucial topic that is the bane of every program-mer's existence—debugging. We show you how to figure out what's wrong with your code and review the various tools that are available to help.

Chapter 8, *Resources and Forms*

This chapter describes how to create the three types of forms (forms, dialog boxes, and alerts) that are available in the Palm OS.

Chapter 9, *Form Objects*

We describe every form object within the Palm OS. We discuss any restrictions, behaviors, and what is involved in adding them to a form in an application.

Chapter 10, *Databases*

We explain the unique way the Palm OS creates data structures and stores data on a Palm handheld. We show you how to add data to an application.

Chapter 11, *Menus*

We explain menus and the items in them. You learn how to create them, where to put them, and how to add Graffiti shortcuts.

Chapter 12, *Extras*

We show how to add support for Find and the Exchange Manager (beaming).

Chapter 13, *Communications*

We describe the various communication protocols supported on the Palm OS. These include serial, TCP/IP, and IrDA. We implement serial and TCP/IP in two sample applications.

Part III, *Designing Conduits*, covers conduits. Just as we created a Palm application, we do the same for a conduit. This section includes everything from a complete description of the parts of a conduit to their development platforms and code walk-throughs. Unlike the other three parts, these chapters build on each other and should be read in order.

Chapter 14, *Getting Started with Conduits*

We start once again with the bigger picture. After we describe all the general things you need to know about conduits, we turn to code. We show you how to install and remove a conduit and get you to the point where you have a working conduit shell.

Chapter 15, *Moving Data to and from the Handheld with a Conduit*

We explain how to create a conduit that moves data between the handheld and the desktop.

Chapter 16, *Two-Way Syncing*

We show you a conduit that uses full-blown data syncing with the exchange of data depending on where it has last been modified. We also describe various logic problems you encounter with a device that can synchronize data on multiple desktops.

Part IV, *Appendixes*, includes some resources that will come in handy.

Appendix A, *Where to Go from Here*

This appendix lists Palm developer resources.

Appendix B, *Sales Source Code*

This appendix contains a complete listing of the source code for the Sales application, the Palm OS sample application we develop in this book.

Appendix C, *PilRC Manual*

This appendix contains the manual for PilRC, Version 2.8 for those programmers who wish to use this development environment.

How to Read This Book

There are a couple of different approaches people take to reading a programming book:

- The skip-through-and-read-what's-interesting approach
- The cover-to-cover approach
- The in-front-of-a-computer-trying-to create-your-own-application approach

The Skip-Through Approach

If you choose this approach, view Part I as background information. The section is more essential for beginners to the Palm OS platform than for old-timers. Chapter 1 is a general orientation that helps newcomers understand handhelds. If you already know what development environment you are using, then you can easily skip Chapter 2. Chapter 3 is the most essential in that it gives you an overview of the Palm OS UI and teaches you a lot about designing handheld applications. We also describe the UI of the Sales application.

You can skip around Part II or read its chapters in order. In either case, don't wait too long to read Chapter 7 on debugging. No matter what, read this chapter before you try to create your own project.

Part III won't make much sense unless you read it in order. Each chapter builds on the previous chapter.

The Cover-to-Cover Approach

We didn't write the book in this order, but it seemed like the right progression at the time. Feel free to read from the beginning to the end.

The In-Front-of-a-Computer Approach

Anxious-to-get-started types should read the tutorial (Chapter 4) and the debugging chapter (Chapter 7) before taking too deep a plunge into creating an application. Otherwise, far be it from us to try and slow you down. Get to it!

Conventions Used in This Book

We use a couple of conventions worth noting:

Italic
> Used for URLs and filenames

Constant width
> Used for code, routines, parameters, functions, events, attributions, and macros

---

Constant width italic
> Used for variables

Constant width bold
> Used to indicate code entered by the user and to emphasize specific lines of code in code samples

This icon indicates a tip or hint.

This icon indicates a warning. Examples, known bugs, or other kinds of problems are discussed in this type of note.

How to Contact Us

Please address comments and questions concerning this book to the publisher:

> O'Reilly & Associates, Inc.
> 101 Morris Street
> Sebastopol, CA 95472
> (800) 998-9938 (in the United States or Canada)
> (707) 829-0515 (international/local)
> (707) 829-0104 (fax)

There is a web page for this book, which lists errata, examples, or any additional information. You can access this page at:

> *http://www.oreilly.com/catalog/palmprog2/*

To comment or ask technical questions about this book, send email to:

> *bookquestions@oreilly.com*

You can also send email to us, the authors:

> *neil@pobox.com* (Neil Rhodes)
> *julie@pobox.com* (Julie McKeehan)

For more information about books, conferences, Resource Centers, and the O'Reilly Network, see the O'Reilly web site at:

> *http://www.oreilly.com*

Versions of Tools

We use a lot of tools in this book. Our web site will contain information on the most current versions of all of these tools. Chapter 4 discusses the versions of Code-Warrior and PilRC used in this book.

Whom We Need to Thank

We would like to thank some very helpful people who offered technical reviews of our work. They are Peter Easton, Scott Johnson, Dave Lippincott, Ray Marshall, Brian Mathis, and Steve Palmen. Special thanks go to Richard Burmeister for his technical review. These folks made this a better book by critiquing our writing and catching mistakes through which you would otherwise have had to suffer.

We discuss the UI of several applications in Chapter 3. The creators of those applications kindly gave us permission to dissect their work. Howard Tomlinson, the creator of Bejeweled, Alexander Hinds who wrote WordSmith, and last and most importantly C. E. Steuart Dewar who wrote DateBk4 and Datebook+, all allowed us to use their work to teach you about designing handheld applications. You should know that we made no attempt to review the applications as wholes. On the contrary, we ripped apart each application and discussed the UI out of context so as to show you a neat trick or a less-than-perfect design choice. Even though they knew that this was happening to their creations, they let us proceed. Such generosity and willingness among colleagues are much appreciated by us. Advice on what applications to use in this chapter also came from the recommendations of a couple of folks at PalmGear (the best place to find Palm OS stuff on the Internet, *http://www.palmgear.com*). They helped us find the perfect applications to discuss. Our thanks to Ken Wright and Jonathan Reimann—great job, guys.

We would also like to thank all of our friends and colleagues at Palm and within the Palm community. Writing a book about Palm OS programming can be done without a great programmer community, but it is not nearly as fun.

We are grateful for the enduring patience of our children Nicholas, Alexander, Nathaniel, and Michael through the writing of this, our seventh book.

Overview of the Palm OS

The Palm Solution

Palm has single-handedly defined the handheld market. Its operating system has dominated since it raced to the front of the pack of contenders six years ago. This is true even in the face of repeated handheld salvos launched by software giants such as Microsoft and Apple, and hardware giants such as Hewlett Packard and Compaq. Competitors have repeatedly attempted to penetrate this market and failed. The question that you have to ask yourself is, what did Palm figure out that others didn't? How did Palm at first succeed and continue to succeed even when so many others failed? The answer is easy to say but takes the rest of the chapter to explain. The simple truth is that they understood the magic formula—they figured out what customers really needed in a handheld and how much they were willing to pay. Wait, don't just gloss over this last sentence. Mull it over a bit and let it influence your thinking about your own software development ideas and how you evaluate the Palm OS.

How Palm Succeeded

Over the last five years, the market for handhelds has changed dramatically in many ways. The customer base has significantly broadened—there are early adopters, loyal followers, and business enterprise users, mixed with growing numbers of less-sophisticated general consumers. All of these folks are buying handhelds to organize differing aspects of their lives and they have enormously varying tolerances for difficulty and desires for the latest cool features. As of mid-2001, Palm and its licensees have sold more than 13 million handhelds and they control close to 80 percent of the market. This is a lot of people using a lot of handhelds.

This is all great news if you want to write software for the Palm OS platform. There are lots of potential customers. Whether you are developing consumer software, or enterprise software for thousands to tens of thousands of units, or a vertical application for a particular niche market, the Palm OS/device combination will work for you. It will, that is, if you pay attention to the key features that have made it successful.

The Magic Formula

So, here are those key features. Here are the elements of Palm's magic formula to a successful handheld:

- Easy to carry
- Inexpensive
- Expandable (both for a user and a developer)
- Effortlessly connects with a desktop computer
- Works great and is simple to use

Every feature matters—you can't take one out of the mix and still have the same successful handhelds. So, while you may see some of these features incorporated into competing handhelds, you don't see all of them. As a result, it is clear to us that Palm continues to understand the handheld market better than its competitors and will continue to be far more successful. So, pay attention to the whole list of features. Likewise, notice how competing handhelds differ (later on we will look at some of the key differences). As you will see, Palm handhelds are great devices not because of one particular feature, but because of the combination of features.

We are telling you this because the magic formula has enormous implications for your software. If you want to develop for this platform, then it is crucial for you to understand what has made it successful. You need to design your applications to function in harmony with the platform. We tell you in detail what makes this a great platform so that you know how to write software that works with it. We want you to attack the design of your application with the same magic formula that Palm used to define the platform and continues to use to innovate it. Design does not happen in a vacuum. If you ignore the features and characteristics that make Palm a success, your application will bomb.

Let's start with the beginning of the story, before looking at the current situation.

Why Palm Succeeded Where So Many Failed

Not everybody knows that the PalmPilot was hardware born out of software, and not even system software, at that. Its origins are in Graffiti, the third-party handwriting-recognition software developed for Newton and other Personal Digital Assistants (PDAs).

In 1994, Palm came out with some handwriting-recognition software that promised accuracy and speed of recognition for PDAs at the price of a little bit of shorthand. Many industry experts thought such software was doomed to fail, as it required too much work from the user. They were proved wrong. Speed and accuracy were more important—Graffiti was able to offer enough to compensate for the relatively minor work required to learn the new strokes.

No One Would Make a Good Enough Device

Buoyed by its success with Graffiti and frustrated by other companies' inabilities to get the platform right, Palm decided to create its own handhelds. The result was the release of the Pilot 1000 in mid-1996. It, followed by the Pilot 5000, rapidly made headway. So popular was this product that with the release of its next device 18 months later, the company topped the one-million-unit mark and clearly dominated the market.

Elements in the Magic Formula

It would be good to stop at this point and examine why this company succeeded when so many other companies failed. How was it able to produce a successful handheld? It wasn't experience in hardware design—companies like Apple, Casio, and Hewlett-Packard clearly had more. It wasn't the breadth of features—Windows CE and Newton devices had more. It wasn't the price—Texas Instruments' Avigo was cheaper. So what did the Palm offer that all these other companies weren't providing? The answer was in the combination of features. *It was a small, inexpensive handheld that worked great.* These original units fit in a pocket easily, cost substantially less than most of the competitors' products, and did tasks that handhelds were uniquely qualified to do (like provide address books and calendars). Wait, wait, some of you might be stuttering, What about the list of features, the processor speed, the amount of memory, and the pixel depth of color screens? Nope, those things weren't compelling ingredients in the success story.

So, let's return to the list of key features and discuss them relative to the current situation of the handheld world. Also, let's look at the features, not in order of their importance, but in terms of how easy they are to understand. (As you will see, size is pretty easy to figure out, defining "works great" is a different kettle of fish.)

Easy to Carry

Palm OS devices are small—they fit in a hand or a pocket. This was true six years ago and is still true today. Palm devices fit in anyone's pocket—whether it is the biggest device, the Palm VIIx, or a smaller one such as a Handspring Visor Edge. This is enormously important in understanding the success of the Palm. Other handhelds were made that didn't fit in a pocket and they bombed. In Table 1-1 you can see the footprint of some Palm OS devices to see what these magic dimensions are.

Table 1-1. Palm OS device dimensions

Device	Height (in.)	Width (in.)	Depth (in.)	Weight (oz.)
Original PalmPilot	4.7	3.2	0.7	5.7
Palm m100	4.7	3.2	0.7	4.4
Palm Vx	4.5	3.1	0.4	4
Handspring Visor	4.8	3.0	0.7	6.1
Handspring Visor Edge	4.7	3.1	0.4	4.8
Palm VIIx	5.3	3.3	0.8	6.7
Palm m505	4.5	3.1	0.5	5.1
Palm IIIc	5.1	3.2	0.7	6.8
HandEra 330	4.7	3.2	0.7	5.9
Sony CLIE	4.8	2.8	0.8	6.5

Each of these devices differs in some features and remains the same in others. What should be most striking, however, is that very little tolerance exists for size variation. Try putting a Palm VIIx into your pocket. You will find that it is just barely comfortable (some people would say it isn't!), while a device like the Visor Edge fits easily. Notice though that the difference between these two devices is about only 2 ounces in weight, 0.6 inches in length, and 0.4 inches in depth. When you look at such dimensions on a chart or in a product review they may seem insignificant, but when you feel each device in your pocket, such tiny changes make a huge difference. The first crucial point is that a small, objective difference in size creates a great, subjective difference in the quality of user experience.

The designer of the first Palm device, Jeff Hawkins, and the rest of the PalmPilot team, walked around with variously sized mock-up wood boards in their hands and pockets. These smart people knew an incredibly important rule—make it comfortable to hold and carry or no one will want it. Five million cool features will not make a normal person lug a log around all day.

Palm knows that a device bigger than a Palm VIIx won't fit in most pockets, and would defeat the advantage of being a handheld, so Palm does not make anything bigger. The right handheld has to be the right size and there's little room for error (as some other handheld makers have learned). Indeed, the trend at Palm in creating devices is not towards adding features, but reducing size. The newest devices from Palm and other licensees are getting smaller.

Look at the history of cell phones for a similar lesson in the importance of device size. Cell phones are getting smaller as well.

Now, this raises an interesting point concerning other handhelds. A few years ago, other handheld makers commonly made much bigger devices (so they could pack those features in). Now, by looking at the current crop of Pocket PC devices, we can see that others have learned something about the size rule from Palm. What it seems the contenders have learned is that you can't make a handheld *bigger* than the largest dimensions. By comparing these units with Palm's new products (see Table 1-2 and Table 1-3), you can see that Palm is pushing the size envelope to the smallest possible and that Pocket PC makers are pushing it to the largest possible.

Table 1-2. Pocket PC 2000 and 2001 handheld dimensions

Pocket PC device (intro date)	Height (in.)	Width (in.)	Depth (in.)	Weight (oz.)
Compaq IPAQ H3150 (1/2001)	5.11	3.28	0.62	5.8
HP Jornada 525 (4/2001)	5.2	3.1	0.7	8
Casio Cassiopeia E-125 (9/2000)	5.2	3.3	0.8	9

Table 1-3. Palm and licensee 2000 and 2001 handheld dimensions

Palm OS devices (intro date)	Height (in.)	Width (in.)	Depth (in.)	Weight (oz.)
Palm m505 (4/2001)	4.5	3.1	0.5	5.1
Palm m500 (4/2001)	4.5	3.1	0.4	4
Handspring Visor Edge (3/2001)	4.7	3.1	0.4	4.8

Notice that these Pocket PCs are only about as small as the biggest Palm devices, and aren't even close in size to the slimmer handhelds.

Inexpensive

Moving from size to cost, we encounter another item that has always been important in Palm's success: the price of the units is quite modest compared with other choices. This was true five years ago when a Palm device was half the cost of that of its competitors and it is still true today when Palm devices, whether made by Palm or a licensee, are still much cheaper. (See Table 1-5, which contains a vast array of comparisons.)

We believe that low entry price is a critical part of the equation of a successful handheld. Early adopters will buy whatever new gadget they want, *regardless of price*—they are by definition gadget fanatics who have to have the latest toys. Mainstream consumers who start using a new electronic device—be it a cell phone, VCR, DVD player, or handheld—seriously consider price. Users debating between a handheld purchase of a couple hundred bucks probably won't compare it to the possibility of buying a notebook computer instead (around $1000). Once the price of a handheld nudges into the $600 to $800 range then the jump to a notebook computer doesn't look so large. Furthermore, there are many new customers who will consider a couple hundred dollars to try out a new device and who won't even stop to look at a device over the magic $500 amount.

Price matters. So the real question becomes, what is the price point that justifies the utility of a handheld? Palm and its licensees set that threshold much lower. This strategy puts handhelds in a lot more hands.

Expandable

Palm devices are simple, but are designed to be expandable. This was true from the very first Palm device to the current models. Let's look at hardware and then software to see what this means.

Hardware Expandability

Palm devices come with very few types of built-in hardware features. While hardware features have changed over the last six years, this has been not so much an addition of features as an improvement of the existing ones. See Table 1-4.

Table 1-4. Palm hardware features

Feature	Early units	Current units
ROM/Flash RAM	512K	2 MB
RAM	128K	8 MB
Screen type	Black and White	Grayscale and color
Infrared	No	Yes
Connection type	Serial	USB and serial

There are Palm OS devices that have bar code scanners, modems, MP3 players, and memory sticks; they are just not on every device. Likewise, you can buy modems, cell phone attachments, keyboards, and Global Positioning System (GPS) add-ons for a Palm handheld. From this, it is easy to see that Palm's strategy is to have this minimal set of basic features and encourage licensees and other hardware device makers to offer optional device enhancements.

There has also been quite a bit of hardware differentiation for expandability among the Palm OS licensees: Handspring has their Springboard modules, Sony devices have MemoryStick expansion, Handera supports CompactFlash cards, and Palm's m500 and m505 support MultiMedia cards and Secure Digital (SD) cards.

Software Expandability

Palm has used the same strategy with software. The original Palm Computing built-in applications included Date Book, Address, To Do list, Memo Pad, Calculator, and Password Protection. Palm added a new built-in application for expenses to the PalmPilot and a built-in mail application to the PalmPilot Pro. That's a list of six software applications that expanded to eight. Compare this with a standard list of

Pocket PC applications and you will see a different strategy at work. Rather than trying to provide all of the customers' possible needs themselves, Palm has depended upon others to expand what's available. They focused on creating an OS and offering development tools that made the device attractive to developers.

The result of this strategy is over 10,000 Palm OS applications (as of mid-2001). While no one would deny that this range of software and hardware comes in part from Palm's success in defining the handheld space, it is also true that the software and devices have, in turn, made Palm successful.

Developing for the Platform

From the beginning, Palm has had several advantages that have made it an easier platform for which to write software. These include:

- A free Software Development Kit (SDK)
- Lots of documentation
- Support in many different formats (email, conferences, knowledge bases, etc.)
- A vibrant developer community

Because of decisions like these, the Palm OS continues to rapidly acquire developers—to the tune of 1,000 per week. All these people, whether they create mainstream software, vertical applications, or cool device add-ons, are an essential part of the Palm economy.

Expandability and the future

More is coming in the future for the Palm OS and its devices. Bluetooth, or short-range radio networking, will become quite important in the near to mid-term future for the Palm OS. Unlike infrared, which requires a short range (within 1 meter) and a line of sight (you have to point the infrared devices at each other), Bluetooth can work over longer ranges (on the order of the size of a conference room), and can work without directly pointing two devices at one another.

You might wonder how such a technology can be useful to Palm. Here is an example: a Bluetooth cell phone could be kept in a backpack or purse. A Bluetooth headset could transmit a voice to or from the cell phone and the user. The Bluetooth-enabled Palm OS device could communicate with the phone to ask it to dial. The device could also use the phone to do TCP/IP.

Currently, of course, you can use a headset, but it has to be connected to the phone with a wire. You can also use a Palm OS device to dial the phone or to do TCP/IP over the phone connection. Again, you either have to use a wire or infrared (which requires careful holding to make sure the connection isn't broken).

Expandability allows users to accomplish different tasks

Palm has made their platform expandable because they know different users want to accomplish different tasks with their handhelds. Rather than trying to create one handheld that can accommodate everyone's every possible need, Palm has created an OS that can run on a range of handhelds and support a variety of applications. Palm added a small number of applications that accomplish common tasks easily and quickly. More importantly, it has created an open OS that allows developers to write software and lets users do more specialized tasks. It has also encouraged hardware designers to specialize in different kinds of Palm OS devices and hardware add-ons.

Effortlessly Connects to a Desktop Computer

Another one of the key features of a handheld is that it does not function independently. People want to use it in conjunction with their desktop computers. They also want it to work perfectly and easily.

Indeed, one of the necessary features that makes the handheld so useful—its small size—means that it simply can't do some tasks or have some hardware features. As a result it is absolutely dependent on a desktop computer to provide what it lacks.

What Palm OS Devices Don't Have and Why

Almost more important than what Palm OS devices have is what they lack. Palm OS devices do not have keyboards, full text recognition, or powerful processors.

Now, reflect for a moment on why this is so. Adding any of these features requires changing the magic combination of speed, size, and price that has made the Palm devices so popular.

 Palm has announced that the next version of the OS (we'll call it 5.0, even though it may not actually ship as that number) will work on ARM processors, rather than the current 68K processors. This will provide more processing power. ARM processors, although somewhat more expensive than the current 68K processors, are very battery-efficient.

A Keyboard

Designing a device with a keyboard is a double problem: it radically affects the size and it changes the types of things a user will attempt to do. If there is a keyboard, a user will expect to be able to enter text easily. But in order to handle extensive data input, you need a system that can support that type of activity, a processor capable of handling it, and screen that is big enough and clear enough to display it. Once you have both a system and a fast enough processor, the price has crept so high that users go get laptops instead; for just a few dollars more, they get a lot more capability.

By removing both the keyboard and any real way of handling text input in quantity, Palm kept its focus on the kind of device it was providing. Palm's strategy was to deliberately create a device that was an extension of a desktop computer. Think of the handheld as a "tentacle" (using the metaphor of the creator of the Palm, Jeff Hawkins) reaching back to the desktop. It is a window onto the data that resides on the desktop. Having this sort of window is so useful because it can be taken anywhere. Palm figured out that to be taken anywhere, it has to fit almost anywhere. So, absolutely, positively no keyboard.

Text-Recognition Software

Besides removing the keyboard, Palm did away with supporting true text recognition. Palm knew from Apple Computer's hard lesson with the Newton (painfully broadcast across the pages of Doonesbury comic strips) that the recognition algorithms were just not good enough five years ago (and still aren't today). Apple ended up with frustrated people who spent far too much time trying to get their Newtons to recognize what they wrote. Instead, Palm made the nervy choice to ask users to spend a few minutes learning the stroke requirements of Graffiti.

No doubt Apple had many focus group meetings where it asked legions of users the question, "Is it important to you that a handheld device be able to recognize your handwriting?" If faced with this question, users probably universally said yes, it was very important. Palm decided to figure out what users actually wanted instead of what they *said* they wanted—not always the same thing. Users, it turns out, would rather spend a few minutes learning to write a "T" like "7" than spend three times as much money and have a device take a staggeringly long time at even the most simple tasks.

A Powerful Processor

Palm OS devices run on small, inexpensive processors (competitors would, no doubt, call them antiquated, twerpy little processors that can't do anything fast). Even though the newest Palm OS devices have more memory, the processor still remains quite diminutive and the clock speed is downright pokey (see Table 1-5). This is especially true when you compare a Palm OS device to a Pocket PC device, which is built around the ARM processor (an order of magnitude more CPU power than in current Palm OS devices).

So, let's examine the implications of this one difference, a fast versus a not-so-fast processor. First, there is the expense issue—fast processors cost more (result—Pocket PC devices are double to triple the price of Palm OS devices). Second, two simultaneously important and disastrous things happen when a faster, more expensive processor is thrown on a handheld. Since the processor is more expensive, device makers feel compelled to add additional features to justify the cost. Because they can add more features, device makers also end up tasking the processor to its limits with greater software and hardware challenges. Just as you would expect, Hewlett-

Packard, Compaq, and Casio have stepped up to this challenge by offering customers their newest Pocket PC devices with great backlit color screens, lots of built-in software that allow the user to do everything from surfing web pages to editing and creating word processing documents, sending email, playing MP3s, and sucking the battery dry before the sun goes down. Yep, these devices have itty-bitty battery life. But this gets into the next important feature: "works great and is simple to use."

 This also raises the interesting issue of the well-known fact that the Palm is moving to the ARM processor in its next device transition (slated for 2002). We predict they will solve the battery problem—you won't see battery-sucking devices like the current crop of competitors.

Works Great and Is Simple to Use

Now, we are into very subjective stuff and we are the first to admit it. When we say a handheld has to "work great and be simple to use" many of you may justifiably want a much more exact description of what this means—how the various combinations of features that go into the creation of a particular handheld translate into a great user experience. We would be the first to admit that how you compare and measure things like great backlit color screens against long battery life is notoriously open to debate. Whether the presence of a cool MP3 player or the ability to look at web pages is more important than the price is debatable.

It would be great to see about five years into the future when it will be obvious which were the right choices for today's customers. We could all pontificate about how we knew all along that *this* set of features and device options were the golden ones. Barring the presence of a rift in the time-space continuum, however, we are forced to guess. So, we will tell you about our guesses and Palm's guesses. We will tell you what Palm thinks "works great and is simple to use" means. These guesses have led to design decisions in the Palm OS and on Palm OS devices that will determine how you develop for this platform. Stated most generally, what Palm means when it says "works great and is simple to use" is that usability matters more than looks, and simple common features that work well are more important than lots of built-in choices. Quintessential handheld tasks better be easy to do and faster than lightning.

Let's see how these general ideas translate into current day device and OS decisions. First, let's examine the battery life issue, which we file under the category of "usability matters more than looks."

Battery Life

Palm OS devices, whether built by Palm or by its licensees, last a long time between battery changes or recharging. This is a big deal at Palm. Look, for example, at Palm's color m505 (a new device as of May 2001). Reviewers have said its screen isn't as clear as those of Pocket PC color devices. But the m505 has a much longer battery life than the color Pocket PC devices. This is an important difference and one you should not gloss over—it will dramatically affect how people use each device.

People use a computer differently if they expect it to last weeks instead of days. Palm is betting this is a crucial difference, and we agree. Most people can take their Palm unit on a trip (whether on business for a week or rock climbing for 10 days) without worrying about the charging mechanism or extra batteries.

With an 8–12 hour rated life, a Pocket PC owner will learn to carry spare batteries or power cables (much like a notebook computer user). These differences in battery life are across-the-board differences between Palm units and Pocket PCs as you can see from Table 1-5, which shows some comparisons of screen color, processor speed, and battery life.

It should be obvious from Palm's devices that long battery life is an important part of a great user experience. As you can see, it is more important than many other features. It's more important than having the best color screen and more important than having a backlit screen with which you can navigate a pitch black cave. To be a great handheld, a device has to run for a long time. There is more to it than this, however. To be a great handheld, a device has to perform certain quintessential "handheld" tasks very simply and faster than lightning.

Table 1-5. Pocket PC and Palm OS device battery life and specifications

Device type	Manufacturer's claimed battery life	Battery type	Display type	Backlit display	Processor speed
Pocket PC					
Casio Cassiopeia E-125	8 hours	Lithium ion	Color	Yes	150 MHz
Compaq iPAQ H3650	12 hours	Lithium polymer	Color	Yes	206 MHz
Compaq iPAQ H3150	14 hours	Lithium polymer	Grayscale	Yes	206 MHz
HP Jornada 525	8 hours	Lithium ion	Color	Yes	133 MHz
HP Jornada 545	8 hours	Lithium ion	Color	Yes	133 MHz
HP Jornada 548	8 hours	Lithium ion	Color	Yes	133 MHz
Palm OS					
Palm IIIc	14 days	Lithium ion	Color	Yes	20 MHz
Palm m505	21 days	Lithium polymer	Color	No	33 MHz
Palm m500	21 days	Lithium polymer	Grayscale	Yes	33 MHz
Handspring Visor Prism	14 days	Lithium ion	Color	Yes	33 MHz
Handspring Visor Edge	28 days	Lithium ion	Grayscale	Yes	33 MHz
Sony CLIE PEG-N710C	15 days	Lithium polymer	Color	No	33 MHz

When you further compare them with the Palm units that run on standard AAA batteries instead of rechargeable ones, the differences become even greater (see Table 1-6).

Table 1-6. Palm OS devices with alkaline batteries

Device type	Rated battery life	Battery type	Display type	Backlit display	Processor speed
Palm VIIx	2–4 weeks	2 AAA	Grayscale	Yes	20 MHz
Palm m100, 105	4.3 weeks	2 AAA	Grayscale	Yes	16 MHz
Handspring Visor	6–8 weeks	2 AAA	Grayscale	Yes	16 MHz
HandEra 330	4–8 weeks	4 AAA	Grayscale	Yes	33 MHz

Common Handheld Tasks Are Simple and Fast

Let's start by explaining that a quintessential handheld task is *one that a handheld user is going to do all the time.*

A perfect example is setting an appointment. Imagine I have to set an appointment for one week from tomorrow. I am on the phone right now with the dentist and the receptionist is telling me to bring my kid in at 2 P.M. a week from tomorrow. That task had better be easy to do and fast. To accomplish this on my Palm m505 takes about 10–15 seconds (taking the device from my pocket, turning the unit on with the button push that opens the Date Book, making three quick taps, and inputting the appointment text *Nick's dentist appt.* in the correct appointment timeslot).

Here is another example. I want to call someone and I need her phone number. Looking that up is also quite easy; it only takes a few seconds. To accomplish this, I switch on my Palm handheld and open to Address with the press of one button. Then, I write the first letter of her last name. At that point, most likely, the name will be on-screen along with the phone number. (I can keep writing letters to narrow the choices.)

Both of these are quintessential handheld tasks. The way the handheld is designed, the buttons it has, and the application it uses all revolve around this idea of optimizing the user's experience with common tasks. This idea has enormous implications for you as a software designer.

Designing Applications for Palm Devices

Here are the elements of that magic formula again:

- Easy to carry
- Inexpensive
- Expandable (both for a user and a developer)
- Effortlessly connects with a desktop computer
- Works great and is simple to use

You, as a software designer, are responsible for adding to the expandability of the platform by creating software applications that work great and are simple to use. Part of this task is up to you and we can help you with the rest.

Here are our jobs:

Your job

Come up with the great application idea (if you don't already have one).

Our job

Help you understand what's involved in making a good idea into a Palm application that is simple to use and fast. We tell you about good Palm OS design. We also tell you what belongs in the handheld application and what belongs in the conduit. We give you some design guidance and tell you where to find information in this book.

Essential Design Elements

We spent so much time discussing what makes Palm OS handhelds successful so that you would understand the design philosophy behind a Palm OS application. We do this in part, because handheld software is not like desktop software (any of you desktop software designers will have a bunch of bad design habits that you need to ruthlessly crush). These are the essential elements for which every Palm application needs to be designed:

- Small screen size
- Limited text input on the handheld
- Seamless syncing to a program on a desktop computer
- Small in size, simple in design, fast as lightning (at least for common tasks)

But there is all the difference in the world between listing these elements and knowing how to design an application that uses them. Let's address each point in turn.

Designing for a small screen size

The size of the standard Palm OS screen is a mere 160×160 pixels in a 6×6 cm area. As its history has shown, the form factor of Palm devices is absolutely essential. It's small so people can take it anywhere easily. You should assume that this screen size is here to stay. Unlike some other handhelds that have changed size this way and that, Palm devices will keep this form factor for some time. While you might expect to see some integrated devices with a different screen size, these will be for very specific uses and won't necessarily pertain to the design of most Palm OS applications. However, although the size will probably remain constant, you may see the number of pixels in that area increasing (for higher resolution). An example of this is the Sony Clie with its crisp, clear 320×320 pixel screen.

The data you present in an application needs to be viewable in the 6×6 cm area. Because the area is so small, you will need to break data into parts. While keeping the data in logical groups and relying on different views to show each element will help, you will undoubtedly need to iterate your design several times to get it right.

Look at how the Date Book handles the presentation of appointments, for example. If the user has many appointments in a small period of time, that portion of the day is shown. The user doesn't have to scroll through large gaps or look at lots of blank areas. The application shapes the way the data is presented to accommodate a small screen.

Start the design process by mocking up a couple of screens of data. See if the data falls into logical groups that fit nicely in the small area. If you are requiring your users to scroll back and forth continuously, rethink the organization. Here is the first rule to remember: *the screen size drives the design—not the other way around.*

If you are making the user horizontally and vertically scroll through blank areas continually, redo your design. Trying to display too much data can require the user to do too much scrolling; too little data can require flipping between too many views. You have to find the right balance.

Limiting text input on the handheld

HotSync and wireless technology make text input far less necessary on the handheld. The small screen size and lack of a keyboard make text entry difficult. All this leads to an ironclad truth for you to remember: a Palm handheld is not a manual text input device. The user has a nice desktop computer that contains many good things to facilitate text entry: keyboards, big screens, and fast processors. A Palm handheld has none of these things. These facts lead to another rule in designing for the Palm OS: *data is entered on the desktop and viewed on the handheld.*

Obviously, we are not excluding all data entry or even trying to limit some types. For example, the application we create in this book is an order entry application. In this case, the handheld user is not required to enter text, but instead picks items from lists. This works nicely because picking things is easy, while entering text is hard. It is also clear that there are some obvious places where users need to enter data on their handheld, such as in the To Do list. Apart from effortless data entry, you should steer your user toward adding data on the desktop.

 Symbol's SPT 1500 provides a great example of effortless data entry on a large scale. With this device, the user has a way to enter data (via the bar code reader) quickly and easily while not sitting at a desktop.

Where your application does allow the user to input something, you will need to support the system keyboard, Graffiti input, cut, copy, paste, and undo in the standard manner as outlined in the documentation. Likewise, you need to support any shortcuts to text entry that the Palm OS documentation describes.

Seamless syncing

The bold stroke of providing a convenient cradle and an easy-to-manage connection with the desktop has been crucial to Palm's success. Palm engineers designed these handhelds to exist in a symbiotic relationship with another computer. As a result, an enormously important part of your application is the conduit—this is code that runs as part of the HotSync process on the desktop and transfers information to and from the handheld. In a symbiotic relationship, both organisms rely on each other for something, and both provide something to the other, just as in our Palm OS application and our desktop conduit.

The conduit will handle communication between the handheld and the outside world. The handheld portion of the application will do the following:

- Offer the user data viewing anytime and anywhere
- Allow the user to somewhat modify the data or arrange it differently
- Do tasks with as few taps as possible

Syncing commonly occurs between the handheld and a corresponding application on the desktop, but syncing is not limited to this model. Here are other scenarios for syncing:

- A conduit can transfer data to and from the handheld and corporate database that exists on a remote server.
- A user might fill out a search form on the handheld that the conduit would read and use to perform a web search. The search result would then be transferred back to the handheld for the user to view.
- A conduit could sync the Address Book to a web-based Personal Information Manager (PIM). Thus, while the data may reside far away, the web-based storage ensures that this information is available to a user who travels anywhere in the world.

Making the application small

The handheld portion of the application needs to take up as little space and memory as possible. There isn't much heap space and storage to go around (this was true in 1998 when we wrote the first edition, and is still true in 2001). To end up with a good design, you must be absolutely ruthless about this. Trim the size and keep the number of tasks your handheld application performs to a bare minimum.

Later, we will talk about ways to optimize your application programmatically. For now we simply want to get your thinking clear about the tasks of the handheld application and the conduit.

Making the application fast

Handheld users measure time differently than desktop computer users. One is moving; one is sitting still. Handheld users are usually doing more than one thing—whether that is talking on the phone or walking through a store with a list. Contrast this with the desktop user who is sitting at a desk and will most likely be there for a long time.

The desktop user will wait patiently for an application to launch, in contrast to the handheld user who is on the move. If you make the handheld user wait a minute before your program is ready to use, you won't keep that user. Speed is absolutely critical. This is true not only at application launch time but throughout its use. If you make that process too slow or require flipping through too many screens, your user will give up. The Palm is a lively little machine, so don't bog it down with slow applications.

Always remember that there are enormous problems when attempting to do things on a handheld that you could do easily on a desktop computer. It has a pip-squeak processor with no more power than a desktop machine in the mid-1980s. As a result, you should precalculate as much as possible on the desktop. The stack space is so abysmally small that you have to be careful of recursive routines or large amounts of stack-based data. The dynamic memory is so paltry that your global variable space must be limited and large chunks of data can't be allocated in the dynamic heap.

If that were not enough, the amount of storage space is tiny. For that reason, your desktop portion of the application needs to pay attention to which data the user really needs in this sync period. In our order entry application, we should download data only on customers whose information the salesperson is going to use in the near future. Customers who won't be visited in this time period should be left out.

Rather than bemoaning the sparseness of your programming options, you should keep two things in mind: (1) it's a great programming challenge to create a clean, quick handheld application under these conditions and (2) the very existence of these conditions is why Palm devices are outselling everything else around. If you design for the device instead of beating your head against the wall for what you can't do, you'll end up with an application that millions of people might want.

 Look, you can scream all day about the slow processor and the tiny application heap, but it won't help. (If you aren't screaming now, you will be after you do some development or talk to a veteran Palm programmer.) We just gave you very good reasons for the processor speed and the small amount of memory. Your job is to write great applications in spite of these limitations. Anybody can write a great application with tons of processing power and vast heaps of memory. You get to do more with less.

User Interface Guidelines

The documentation that comes from Palm contains user interface (UI) guidelines. These docs cover much of what you need to know. Follow them. What the docs don't tell you, we do. Follow our advice.

Designing your application to behave like the built-in applications can also be a good idea. For example, if you have an application that needs to display records similar to Address Book, then copy the format used in the Address application (including the location of items). Palm has provided the source code to the built-in applications because it wants to facilitate your use of them. Mimic them wherever it makes sense.

The guidelines also discuss the display of different views in your application, navigating between views, and how to convey information to the user. Not surprisingly, the guidelines also emphasize the importance of speed and optimization in your application. You should also check Palm's web site for system updates and the release of new Palm devices.

Elements in a Palm Application

Now that you know something about designing a Palm application, let's describe its two components. After that we will look at how they communicate with each other.

The two-part solution

Most Palm solutions are composed of a handheld application and desktop conduit:

The handheld portion
> This is the portion that resides on the handheld and allows the user to view and manipulate data. Part II of this book deals with the creation of this application.

The conduit portion
> Here you have code that handles syncing the data with a desktop application. Part III shows you how to create this part.

The handheld portion has an icon that is displayed in the application list. Users will usually use the Palm Install Tool from a Windows or Macintosh machine to install your application (it installs the application on the next synchronization).

HotSync Overview

When a user puts a Palm OS device in its cradle and presses the HotSync button, the handheld application begins communicating with the desktop conduit. For example, the Address Book has a built-in conduit that synchronizes the address book information on the handheld with the address book information in the Palm desktop PIM. If a new entry has been made in either place, it is copied to the other. If an entry has been modified in either place, it is copied to the other. If an entry has been deleted in one place, it is usually deleted in the other.

Third parties provide other conduits that replace the Address conduit so that the device's address book synchronizes with other PIMs (Microsoft Outlook, for example). You'll usually want to write a conduit for your application's database that will upload and download information in a manner appropriate for your application.

For example, the Expense conduit reads the expense information from the handheld, fills in a spreadsheet based on the information, and then deletes the information from the handheld. From a user's point of view, this is ideal: they get their information in the standard, easy-to-use form of a spreadsheet on the desktop. The Palm OS application doesn't have to worry about creating reports; its only purpose is recording expense information.

If you don't want to write your own conduit, then a backup conduit is provided. It backs up any database marked to use the backup conduit.

In Conclusion

In this chapter, we have described Palm devices, the circumstances that governed their design, and the history of Palm's success with this combination. Then, we discussed application design in light of the devices' history, design, and future directions. Last, we discussed the important elements in a Palm application and gave you some rules to help you start thinking about application design.

Now it's time to look more closely at development environments for the Palm. We tell you what is out there and how good it is. Following that, we turn to UI and design issues. As you read further, remember the magic formula and what applies most to you—applications are fast, simple, and small.

## CHAPTER 2

Technical Overview and Development Environments

This chapter deals with the what and how of the Palm OS and its features. First, we describe what you're programming for—the relevant aspects of the Palm OS. Then we show you how to do it—the available development environments. By the time we are through, you should have a good idea of the range of applications you can create for the Palm OS, the coding requirements, and which development environment you want to use.

Let's start with a piece of good news—there is a development environment for programmers of all types. Whether you are a C++ master or a Visual Basic newcomer, the popularity of the Palm platform means there is an environment for you to use.

Palm OS Overview

Developing for the Palm OS is in some ways similar to other platforms and in other ways strikingly different. Two important similarities are as follows:

- Applications are event-driven.
- You can use anything from C++, to standard C code, to assembler, to scripting.

Differences tend to center around features crucial to the device size and purpose. These include how the Palm OS handles:

- Memory requirements
- Application and data storage
- Connectivity of the device to the desktop

Most importantly, you should remember that the relationship between the device and the OS is extremely tight. Further, everything has been built on the premise that the handheld is an extension, not a miniature version, of the desktop. It specializes in ensuring that mobile tasks are simple and fast.

Interaction Between an Application and the OS

First, let's examine this tight interaction of the OS and the applications on the hand-held. The Palm OS runs on top of a preemptive multitasking kernel. One task runs the UI, while other tasks handle things like monitoring input from the stylus. The UI permits only one application to be open at a time. Thus, when your application is open, it (more or less) has control of the entire screen.

Because applications run within the single-user interface thread and can't, themselves, be multithreaded, the multitasking provided by the kernel is for the operating system's use only, and isn't available to you.

Memory

Memory is handled in an unusual fashion (discussed in detail in Chapter 6). The RAM on a Palm OS device is used for two purposes:

Dynamic memory allocation
> This is memory your application or the system needs while it is running. It also includes the stack your application requires. On a reset, this memory is cleared. This portion of memory is analogous to RAM in a traditional OS.

Permanent storage
> This includes downloaded applications as well as data that the user will view, create, and/or edit. To-dos, names and phone numbers, memos, and all the other data for built-in applications also use this memory. On a reset, it is not cleared. This portion of memory is analogous to files on a hard disk in a traditional OS. Memory used for storage of records is discussed in Chapter 10.

For both kinds of memory, allocation is done as chunks. The permanent storage holds databases, with related chunks kept in a single database. For example, all the memos are stored (each as a separate chunk or database record) in a single database. Another database holds all records from the Address application. A database that has been copied to the desktop is stored with a *.pdb* extension—often called *PDB* files.

Unlike in a traditional desktop operating system, data and code are not copied from permanent storage to dynamic memory; they are used in-place. For example, when your code executes, it is executing in-place from the permanent storage. Since the permanent store itself is in RAM, it can be read by the CPU like any other RAM. Similarly, data can be read (and displayed) directly from storage.

Palm has been careful to protect permanent storage against accidental overwrites. Palm reasoned that users would be unhappy if one bug in a single application caused all their data to be lost. So while the permanent storage can be read like any other RAM, it is write-protected by the device. In order to write to specific chunks within permanent memory, you have to use the operating system's mechanism, which includes a check against attempts to write to places outside the chunk.

Events

A Palm OS application is event-driven; everything it does is an event. Events arrive, like `penDownEvent` or `keyDownEvent`, and your application responds to them. Some events are handled by your application; others are handled by the operating system. Once your application gets started, it enters an event loop, repeatedly getting, then handling event after event. The loop continues until the user launches another application, which causes your application to quit. Events are covered in Chapter 5.

Resources

An application on the Palm OS is a resource database that contains many different resources. A resource is simply a database record that has a type and an ID. Stored within these resources are the guts and skin of your application. On the desktop, these resource databases have *.prc* extensions. You'll often find them referred to as *PRC files*. We discuss resources in Chapter 8.

Examples of the types of things stored in resources are as follows:

- Your code
- UI elements
- Text strings
- Forms
- Icons

The UI elements that appear on the Palm device are initialized based on the contents found in these resources. Because the initialization is not embedded within your code, you can change the appearance of your application (for instance, to localize it for another language) without modifying the code itself. Another advantage is that you can use visual editors to display and edit the UI portions of your application. Such editors allow you to tweak the look or presentation of data easily without recompiling and redownloading your application.

Forms and Controls

The Palm OS has built-in support for various controls and for managing forms. Forms are similar to windows on a desktop operating system. Because of the simpler UI on the Palm OS, only one form is active even though several forms may be displayed. Form objects are dealt with in Chapter 9.

The Palm OS provides a rich API for forms that includes many UI elements (form objects). Some of these form objects are as follows:

- Checkboxes
- Radio buttons
- Push buttons

- Pickers (pop-up lists)
- Lists (one column)
- Tables (multicolumn)
- Scrollbars
- Static text labels
- Editable text fields
- Menus

Because these elements are stored as resources rather than in your code, you can create a prototype of your application very quickly. The simplicity of adding the UI elements and the variety of them that are available makes it easy to try out various application designs.

Communications

The Palm OS supports a variety of communication methods. As communicating is an essential aspect of the Palm's success, you should expect this area of the OS to be critical in both current and future applications. Current communication protocols are as follows:

- Serial communication.
- TCP/IP with a socket interface.
- Infrared. Low-level infrared support is via Infrared Data Association (IrDA) protocols.
- A higher-level object exchange is provided that allows exchanging information between Palm devices and other devices using an industry-standard object exchange. This object exchange currently runs over IrDA and over the Short Messaging Service (SMS) supported by GSM cell phones. It will be supported over Bluetooth and may be supported over other transports in the future. Communications protocols are covered in Chapter 13.

Miscellaneous

The Palm OS has various other APIs for features such as:

Strings
There are APIs for searching within strings, copying, and converting to and from numbers.

Date and time
Support is provided for converting from native time format (minutes since midnight, January 1, 1904) to printable format, and to separate day/month/etc. In addition, there are APIs that allow the user to select a day or a time.

Alarms

> Your application can set an alarm for a particular date and time. Your application is then notified when that date and time are reached (even though it may not be running at the time).

Find

> The Palm OS provides a device-wide Find that allows the user to search for a string anywhere within the device. Each application does its part by searching for the specified string within its own databases.

With all these features, you can see that the Palm OS provides a solid base for rich and varied applications. Text and the presentation of content are supported by a wide variety of tools that aid in the visual display of information.

 The subsystems of the Palm OS are called managers and the naming convention for functions designate the managers in which they reside. For example, all Memory Manager routines begin with Mem. All Database Manager routines begin with Dm. All Form Manager routines begin with Frm. We discuss each manager and its naming abbreviations in later chapters.

Conduit Overview

The second part of the Palm application is the desktop connection. Because a Palm device acts as an extension of the desktop, it is crucial that information be easily exchanged. Conduits are the mechanisms for doing this (see Figure 2-1).

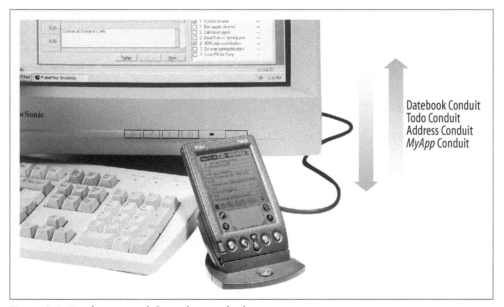

Datebook Conduit
Todo Conduit
Address Conduit
MyApp Conduit

Figure 2-1. Conduits control the exchange of information

A conduit is code on the desktop that is called during a HotSync to manage the flow of information between databases on the handheld and the desktop. Conduits register the database or databases for which they are responsible. Note that each database should have only one conduit responsible for it. Conduits are created using the Conduit Development Kit (CDK) for Windows or Mac OS.

Applications that do not have a conduit portion use a system-provided one instead. This conduit is used for backups and is part of HotSync. This backup conduit copies the application data or database from the device and stores it as a file. You specify that you'd like a database to be backed up when you create a database. Think of this as the "If you can't afford an attorney, one will be appointed for you at no charge" conduit—the last resort.

During a HotSync session, the backup conduit is called for databases that have been marked as needing backup. At this point, it copies each record from the database and copies database header information into a file. This file can then be used to restore the state of the device (including applications) if necessary. For example, if the user has to replace a handheld it takes only a sync to restore it to the previous handheld's state.

More sophisticated conduits do more than this basic copying of information. They can read or write specific information to or from the device. For example, a conduit for a sales application might handle the downloads of new price lists, overwriting any existing price list that has expired. It might also be responsible for uploading a database of sales orders.

The most sophisticated conduits are those that synchronize records on the handheld with information on the desktop. Good examples of these include conduits that synchronize the Date Book records with various desktop PIMs like Outlook or Lotus Organizer. These synchronization conduits usually work by using the unique ID of a record and tracking when a particular record has been changed.

Handheld Development Environments

As we said earlier, the good news is that there are many different development tools available for Palm programming. There is everything from a collection of tools that let you write C code to polished forms-based packages that require only modest amounts of scripting. From this gamut of choices, you should be able to pick the right tool for the type of application you want to create. Before we discuss the advantages and disadvantages of each choice, however, we describe each environment.

For the development of the handheld portion of your Palm application, you can write code on Windows, Unix, or Macintosh platforms. Palm's official development environment, CodeWarrior, is available for both Windows and Macintosh. Unix and Windows programmers have access to a free set of tools—PRC-Tools based on the GNU C compiler, or GCC—and there are packages for Windows-based form development. Last, but not least, programmers can use 68K assembler or other languages.

device while you develop. Because it can load a ROM image from disk, it usefully emulates different versions of the Palm OS. Figure 2-5 shows how POSE appears on your monitor.

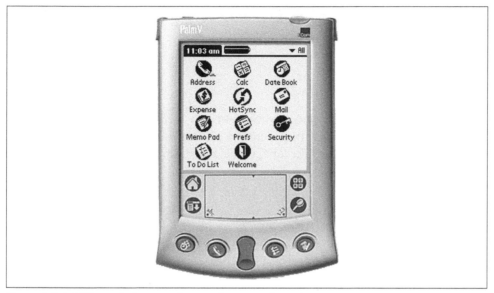

Figure 2-5. POSE in a desktop window emulating a Palm V device

 Of course, final testing of your application should take place with actual Palm OS devices. (We feel like the folks who write warning labels on ladders for reckless fools who need to be told that standing on the top step is dangerous.) If we hadn't seen this problem—programmers writing and testing an application only on POSE—we wouldn't be telling you something that seems this obvious. Do not ship an application having tested it only on the emulator.

ROMs

There are ROM images that you can use with POSE. There are both release ROMs, as shipped in actual devices, as well as debugging ROMs, to which have been added, among other things, extra debugging code that does sanity checking of parameters.

Palm OS documentation

All the documentation for the Palm OS can be found on Palm's web site. There are numerous FAQs, tech notes, and white papers. This documentation is updated frequently.

Palm OS SDK

The SDK is available as a separate download at Palm's developer web site. Depending on the release schedule of CodeWarrior, Palm may have a newer SDK than the one that ships with the CodeWarrior product.

Conduit Development Kit (CDK)
    This is the SDK for creating conduits for Mac OS and/or Windows.

Alternative Development Environments

The following sections describe several useful alternative development environments for the Palm OS.

Java

There are two different full Java environments, as well as two Java-like environments. Keep in mind, however, that there is a definite overhead to using Java (interpreters and garbage collection take time, virtual machines take storage space).

Sun KVM

Sun's approach to Java is to provide a way to write Java applications that will run across multiple platforms. Since the Java 2, Standard Edition is too large to run on small devices like those running the Palm OS, Sun has defined Java 2, Micro Edition (J2ME), a subset of the standard edition with new class libraries.

Sun has defined *configurations*: APIs targeted at classes of devices with related characteristics and limitations (memory, speed, and so on). The configuration for Palm devices is the Connected Limited Device Configuration (CLDC), which targets devices like PDAs, cell phones, and two-way pagers.

There are also *profiles*, which are more specific. There are two profiles of interest for Palm OS devices: the PDA profile (which, at the time of this writing, was not yet defined) and the Mobile Information Device Profile (MIDP). MIDP applications are called "MIDlets" and can run on any CLDC configuration with the MIDP profile.

Sun has a version of the CLDC configuration and MIDP APIs for the Palm OS at *http://java.sun.com/products/midp/palmOS.html*.

IBM VisualAge Micro Edition

This product uses a slightly different approach than Sun's write-once run-anywhere strategy. Instead of a portable API across different platforms, VisualAge provides native access to all of the Palm OS. You call the same APIs that a C programmer would call. It provides support for using Java as an alternative programming language, as opposed to Sun's approach, which views Java not just as a language, but as a portable platform.

The product comes in two versions: The individual version is free, while the Collaborative package, which includes a team repository and version-based collaborative tools, costs $99.

The VisualAge IDE runs on either Windows or Linux. It's a very mature IDE (the same one that's used for their desktop Java development). Tools provided include the following:

- Source-level debugger.
- IDE with source-level debugger.
- Palm OS JAR file, providing access to Palm OS APIs.
- J9 Java Virtual Machine.
- Base class libraries. One library is a beta version of the Connected Limited Device Configuration that allows cross-platform development; the other library is an IBM-specific cross-platform library.

Full information can be found at *http://www.embedded.oti.com/palm/*.

Jump

This novel environment allows you to write your application in a subset of Java using a Palm class library and your favorite Java development environment. Jump then compiles the resulting Java *.class* files into Motorola 68K code. Jump includes a very small runtime library that provides crucial Java support, such as garbage collection.

This development environment is free and source code is provided. Jump is the brainchild of Greg Hewgill and you can get it from *http://www.hewgill.com/*. A newer version, Jump2, is available from *http://sourceforge.net/projects/jump/*.

Waba

Waba defines a subset of the Java language (no longs, doubles, exceptions, or threads). You use your favorite Java development environment to compile this Java subset to a Java *.class* file. Waba includes a virtual machine (VM) that implements a subset of the Java opcodes (it leaves out those having to do with longs, doubles, exceptions, and threads). This stripped-down VM is small and fairly fast.

The Waba SDK also includes a class library. You can use the class library directly on the Palm OS or on top of the standard Java class library, thereby allowing you to develop your application using the Waba class library on the desktop, and use the same code for your final application on the Palm OS.

The standard version is found at *http://www.wabasoft.com*. A souped-up version of this SDK is found at *http://www.superwaba.org*.

A tool has been written to allow apps using the Waba API to be used with Jump. That way, an application is completely self-contained (rather than requiring a separate VM) and faster. It can be found at *http://www.wabajump.org*.

PocketStudio

This Windows development environment is Pascal-based and is similar to Borland Delphi. In fact, it is aimed at existing Delphi programmers who are familiar with Object Pascal (an object-oriented extension to standard Pascal).

This environment offers complete access to all Palm OS APIs. Like CodeWarrior and PRC-Tools, its a true compiler that creates 68K code (rather than something that's interpreted on the handheld). The environment can create standard applications, shared libraries, and so on.

At the time this book was written (July 2001), the product was in beta. For further information, see *http://www.pocket-technologies.com*.

Pocket C

You can do on-board handheld development using Pocket C. You wouldn't want to develop large programs with it, but you can write small C applications without the need for any other machine. If you're a Pocket C user, you'll need to either get very good at Graffiti or invest in a portable keyboard!

Pocket C is shareware ($18.50) and is available at *http://www.orbworks.com/PalmOS/*.

Assembler SDK (ASDK)

This SDK allows development of applications written in Motorola 68K assembler. It includes Pilot Assembler (PILA). To us this would be sheer agony, but apparently some developers enjoy writing applications in assembly language. You certainly can't beat the price—it's free.

For more information, see Darren Massena's web site (*http://www.massena.com*).

Pocket Smalltalk

Pocket Smalltalk is a development environment that allows you to write your application using Smalltalk. It includes a VM. The development environment is written in Squeak (*http://www.squeak.org*), an open source Smalltalk environment available for just about any platform. Thus, the Pocket Smalltalk IDE runs on just about any platform. Pocket Smalltalk is free and it comes with source code.

Of course, just as with Java, this comes with the overhead of a garbage-collecting VM; some applications might be willing to pay the price, but others probably can't afford it.

High-Level Forms Development

Palm devices are so numerous and applications so popular that there are even a couple of third-party development environments specifically for creating specialized forms-based Palm applications.

Satellite Forms

Satellite Forms, by Puma Technology, is an environment for creating very sophisticated Palm OS applications. In Satellite Forms, your application consists of a number of database tables and forms. Each form is tied to a specific table. UI elements on a form can be tied to fields from the table. For example, a checkbox will display the value of a Boolean field; tapping the checkbox will automatically update the field.

Instead of using C/C++ code, you control the actions of the application in one of two ways:

- You specify a set of built-in actions that occur when the user taps a control. For instance, when a button is pressed, you could request (among many choices) that a new form be opened or that you return to the previous form.

- You specify custom code that you want executed. The code is created using a scripting language that is very similar to Visual Basic.

The application comes with a number of built-in controls as well as a library of routines. Satellite Forms also has an extension mechanism that allows you to write C code for your own new controls and new libraries (imagine, for instance, a library of financial routines or a new UI control).

Satellite Forms has an ActiveX control that is connected to a HotSync conduit. You can use the ActiveX control during HotSync to copy any table to, or from, the Palm device. The tables are stored on the desktop as DBX files (standard dBase files), which can be easily integrated with any database.

As of the writing of this book, the price tag for Satellite Forms was $795 (plus license fees for the runtime engine). You have a couple of limitations, as well. It only runs on Windows and applications you create require a runtime library on the Palm device. There is also a charge to license the runtime library, which can make it very expensive to deploy applications built with Satellite Forms. There is a demo version (which limits the number and size of the tables you create, and doesn't allow the creation of new projects) available at the company's web site (*http://www.pumatech.com*).

There are certain things that can't be done in Satellite Forms. For example, you don't have direct control of events, you can't specify your own menu items, and text fields have maximum lengths. It may be quite difficult to create a very specialized UI (although the extension mechanism does allow a lot of flexibility).

AppForge

AppForge (*http://www.appforge.com*) is fairly new to the game of Palm development, first shipping in late 2000. For a newcomer, it is quite impressive. It uses Microsoft's Visual Basic as a development environment, with AppForge-specific elements (*ingots*) added as well. There is a runtime library (338 KB), but no runtime license fee.

For Visual Basic programmers, this is the easiest migration to Palm OS programming.

You write Visual Basic code to deal with your UI and with your data. There are functions that can read or write records from a database. These functions work on databases on the handheld and on the desktop directly with PDB files. That way, you can test and debug your application on the desktop. Thus, you can be testing your UI and your data-handling code simultaneously.

To use AppForge, you must already have Microsoft Visual Basic (which runs about $100). AppForge itself comes in different versions with different prices:

Personal
> This version can create handheld applications. At the time this book was written, it was selling for $20.

Standard
> This version includes a conduit that will automatically sync your handheld database using ODBC. It also includes a signature capture ingot, and support for TrueType fonts. It costs $299.

Professional
> This version includes wireless support, symbol bar code–scanning support, and a library that allows you to call other applications or shared libraries. It costs $695.

Pendragon Forms

This Windows application provides an easy way to create simple multipage forms that contain text fields, checkboxes, radio buttons, and so on. Pendragon Forms also provides a conduit that automatically uploads information into databases.

Pendragon Forms is $149 and, nicely enough, there is no runtime fee necessary for deploying applications. See *http://www.pendragon-software.com* for further details.

NS Basic

NS Basic (*http://www.nsbasic.com*) is a Windows IDE in which you create Palm applications using Basic. You create forms visually, and drag from a palette of UI widgets. It also provides signature capture support and Symbol barcoding support.

NS Basic costs $100. There is a 86 KB runtime engine, but there's no runtime fee. You can distribute the runtime separately or integrate it into your application.

Unfortunately, the product has no source-level debugging, and there's no conduit provided (although, of course, you can write your own).

 While this book is primarily for C and C++ programmers, we included information about different development environments because, like most Palm programmers, we don't use just one environment exclusively. Different types of projects lend themselves more readily to different types of environments—use what works.

Handheld Development Recommendations

Now that you have a good idea of the choices for creating applications for Palm devices, it's time to figure out which is right for you. It should not be surprising that Windows programmers have the most flexibility; Macintosh and Unix folks have none. Let's look at the Macintosh, Unix, and then Windows choices in order.

Developing Using Mac OS

CodeWarrior for Palm OS is currently the only way to do development on Mac OS 9 and under. The good news is that CodeWarrior for Palm OS started on the Macintosh, so you can be assured that it's a robust, elegant product.

If you use Mac OS X, you have the option of using PRC-Tools.

Developing Using Unix

You'll be using PRC-Tools for your development environment. This isn't really a disadvantage, however. If you are accustomed to twiddling around with Unix in the first place, then the slightly more complex setup of PRC-Tools (e.g., the need to use makefiles) won't even get a twitch out of you. Plus, it's free.

Developing Using Windows

You have quite a bit of choice, as every environment we have discussed is available on Windows. Let's try to eliminate some of the options by focusing on what might factor into your decisions:

Assembly programming
    If programming in assembly is your cup of tea, then ASDK is for you.

C/C++ programming
    If you are an ardent C programmer, use CodeWarrior or PRC-Tools. If you are an occasional or hobbyist programmer, then PRC-Tools is probably your best choice, given its attractive sticker price. While it is more flexible, it is also more difficult to use (it requires familiarity with makefiles and command lines).

For greater usability, we suggest that you go with CodeWarrior. The project-based IDE can make development much easier.

Forms-based script development

If price is an important factor, then we think Pendragon Forms is a good low-cost way to create simple forms for inputting data. If we were writing a simple survey-type application on a tight budget, this would be our tool of choice.

AppForge and Satellite Forms are both industrial-strength development environments that we'd recommend for applications that need to go beyond creating simple forms.

Switching Platforms

If you are changing development platforms, there are a few issues for you to consider. CodeWarrior is compatible across platforms, as projects and files can be moved from Macintosh to Windows and vice versa. You also have cross-platform compatibility between Windows and Unix if you are using PRC-Tools. The only thing to watch for is line break conventions—they are different on the two operating systems.

Metrowerks Constructor uses Mac OS resource forks. (If you're not familiar with Mac OS resource forks, now is not the time to learn.) While this creates no problem for the Mac OS, Windows is another matter. A Windows project requires two separate files for your Constructor resource files, one for the data fork and one for the resource fork. This can cause some confusion on Windows, since both these files are visible. Additionally, in order to get these two separate files created, you have to copy Constructor files using a floppy; copying over the network won't work.

If you have a resource file on the Mac, *foo.rsr*, then on Windows, you'll have two files: one is empty and named *foo.rsr*, the other is in a subdirectory called *Resource.frk* and is also named *foo.rsr*. The latter file contains all the resource information.

You can download a Macintosh resource converter, *DropRsr*, from *http://www.metrowerks.com/pda/palm/extras/Utilities/*. It will convert the resource fork of a file to the data fork and vice versa.

Switching development environments

Switching from CodeWarrior to GCC or vice versa is possible, but there's a large stumbling block. The source code is not much of a problem, even though there are some differences between the two C/C++ compilers. The resources are a different matter, since Constructor stores its resources in a binary format that's very different from the text format used by PilRC. The simplest and easiest approach is to use the PilRC text format for all of your resources, whether you're using GCC or CodeWarrior.

We ported PilRC to make it a CodeWarrior plug-in (for both Mac OS and Windows) in order to address this resource-incompatibility problem. See *http://www.calliopeinc.com/pilrcplugin* for more details and the latest version.

We use PilRC format for all the resources in this book, and actually use it for all our resource creation these days (giving up the GUI of Constructor for the simplicity of text files).

One added bonus for us is that text formats are much simpler to display in a book than a succession of screenshots from Constructor.

Conduit Development

If you are creating a conduit for your Palm application, you need to do so on Macintosh or Windows using Palm's Conduit SDK. The Conduit SDK comes with the following:

- Header files
- Libraries
- DLLs
- Frameworks
- Source code for sample conduits

What Is a Conduit?

Under Windows, a conduit is a dynamic link library (DLL) that is called when a HotSync occurs. An install DLL is provided for you to register your conduit with HotSync. On Mac OS, a conduit is a shared library.

Conduits have access to databases on the Palm OS. The Sync Manager handles the complexities of communication; it is not your concern. You simply call routines to read and write records in the database. The Sync Manager handles the communication protocol.

Using C/C++

In order to develop conduits for Windows, use a compiler that can generate 32-bit DLLs (the compilers supported by Palm are Visual C++ 6.0 or Metrowerks CodeWarrior for Windows). For Mac OS, you can use any development environment that has the ability to create shared libraries (CodeWarrior for Mac OS is a likely candidate).

C++ classes that simplify creating a synchronization conduit are provided by Palm (Generic Conduit Framework). These C++ classes are the basis of a number of sample conduits. As your application's syncing needs differ from what is provided by the Generic Conduit Framework, the C++ classes become less useful, and you might wish to consider reverting to the underlying C/C++ Conduit Manager API to make things work properly.

Using Java

Presently, Java conduits work only on Windows. Conduits written in Java can take advantage of Java Database Classes (JDBC) for easy interaction with database engines. The sample code that is part of the Conduit SDK, Java SyncSuite, uses JDBC to interact with an Oracle database.

In Conclusion

You should now have a good idea of which development environment you want to use to write your Palm OS applications. You should also know enough about the features in the Palm OS and the devices to make intelligent decisions about the types of applications that you can create for Palm devices. Next, we discuss UI issues in more detail.

## CHAPTER 3

Designing a Solution

Now that you know about the features of the Palm OS and you have figured out what development environment you are going to use, it is time to design a new application. To do this, you need to know what the Palm OS provides by way of UI elements. Second, you need a description of how and where these elements are used in an application. To this end, we show you several forms, dialog boxes, and alerts; we discuss what works and what doesn't, so that you can intelligently design your own projects.

From this discussion of UI elements, we move to the more general discussion of key issues that need to be addressed in the design of any Palm OS application. We cover everything from what OS versions you should support to determining what tasks an application should accomplish.

From this general overview, we move to a concrete example: the UI of the Sales application. This is the sample application that we are going to create and then dissect in this book. We show you its design, what actions the user performs, how we prototyped it, and the design complications we encountered. Once we've covered the handheld portion of the application, we turn to a description of its conduit.

Throughout this discussion, keep in mind the important principles you learned in Chapter 1 about the design of a Palm OS device. Remember also that a Palm application needs to work great and be simple to use. This means that quintessential handheld tasks must be simple to do and faster than lightning. A good application also has to take into account the small screen size, limited memory, and limited processor ability.

With these application goals in mind, examine the UI elements that Palm OS gives you and the principles of design we recommend. If you fit your application within this model, all it needs is a great idea. If you don't, your application will be lackluster, bloated beyond recognition, confusing, and a waste of a great idea.

User Interface Elements in the Palm OS

The Palm OS provides you with an abundance of UI elements. In what follows, we give you a description of these elements. We also show you some common examples of each type and, where relevant, give you guidelines on its placement and use. (Later chapters show you how to create them and implement them in your code.)

Alerts

Figure 3-1 shows a typical alert. It is simply a modal dialog box that displays a title, a message, an icon, and one or more buttons. You are responsible for setting the text of the title, the message, and the button(s). You also specify the type of alert. It can be any of the following types (arranged from mildest in consequence to most severe):

Notification
> This has an "i" icon. The alert provides the user with some information (for example, that an action can't be completed). No data loss has occurred.

Question
> This has a "?" icon. The alert asks the user a question and asks the user to confirm an action or choose from possibilities.

Warning
> This has a "!" icon. It asks the user if the action is really intentional. Data loss could occur if the action is completed. The Memo Pad uses a question alert for deleting memos, since the user can choose to save an archive on the PC (thus the data is not lost). However, the system uses a Warning dialog box when the user chooses to delete an application, since after the delete, the application is completely gone. Figure 3-1 shows a warning alert.

Error
> This has a stop sign icon. This alert tells the user that an error occurred as a result of the last action.

Figure 3-1. A warning alert

Forms

A form is a general-purpose container for one or more other UI elements. A form can contain buttons, lists, tables, controls, and icons. It can also have a menu bar associated with it. Forms come in two basic flavors: modal and modeless. These forms have different characteristics, as shown in Table 3-1.

Table 3-1. Form characteristics

Characteristic	Modal	Modeless
Width	Full width of the screen	Full width of the screen
Height	Less than full height; usually as short as possible	Full height
Alignment	Bottom of the screen	Fills the screen
Title	Centered in a solid titlebar	Left justified
Frame	2 pixels on all sides	None

Modal forms are generally used for dialog boxes and alerts. Modeless forms are used for data entry and as the main form of the application. Figure 3-2 contains three different forms from the built-in applications to give you an idea of the variability they can have.

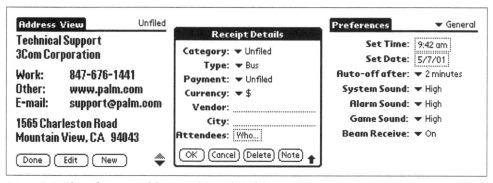

Figure 3-2. Three forms: modeless, modal, and modeless

When creating any form in an application, make sure to provide a form title. This title can include the application name. Every application has at least one form, but most often has more.

Menus, Menu Items, and Menu Bars

Menus, menu items, and menu bars are related to one another. A menu bar contains one or more menus. A menu contains one or more menu items. Menu items often have Graffiti shortcuts associated with them. Figure 3-3 contains an example of a menu bar with two menus in it. We discuss these features in detail in Chapter 10.

Placement

The only control you have over menu placement is in which order they appear within the menu bar. As a rule of thumb, follow the order of menus used by the built-in applications. The menu order for forms with editable text is Record, Edit, Options. Place menu items within a menu using a similar ordering strategy.

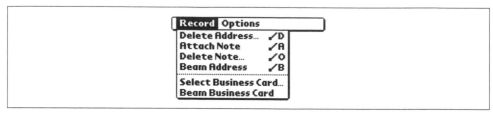

Figure 3-3. A menu bar with two menus; the first menu has six items (plus a separator bar)

Tables and Lists

Tables and lists are used for similar purposes. Use tables when you want to display multiple columns of editable data and use lists when you need to display a single column of noneditable data. Lists are used for unchanging data and tables are useful for data to be edited in place (text and numbers, for example). Vertical scrolling is automatic in lists, but not in tables. We discuss this further in the section "Tables" in Chapter 9. Figure 3-4 contains an example of two lists on the left and a table on the right. As you can see in Figure 3-4, tables are made to support different types of data.

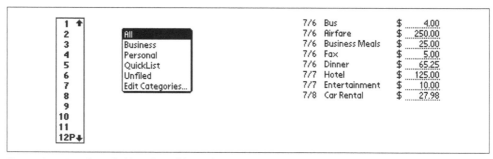

Figure 3-4. Two lists (left) and a table (right)

Placement

Placement rules for tables and lists are hard to generalize. Where they are placed within a form depends on their functions. Make sure you don't try to squeeze too much information into too small a space (a temptation hard to avoid in tables).

Buttons

A button is a tappable object with a label. The label is surrounded by a rounded rectangle. An action occurs when the button is tapped. Figure 3-5 contains some examples of buttons. Note that a button with an ellipsis (...) in the label indicates that a new form will appear when the button is tapped.

Figure 3-5. Buttons from various applications

Placement

When placing buttons within a form, there are a few general rules to keep in mind (see Figure 3-6 for examples and layout details of buttons):

- Buttons can be used in any form. Button text is centered within all buttons.

- Group buttons together by function (for example, OK and Cancel). Note that "together" does not mean too close together. If you can, allow for finger tap acceptance in selecting one button from the other (lots of people, including us, use fingers instead of the stylus to tap a button, but fingers are not as precise).

- Leave 2 pixels above and 3 pixels below the button text and button edge, and 5 pixels (minimum) to the left and right of the text and the frame.

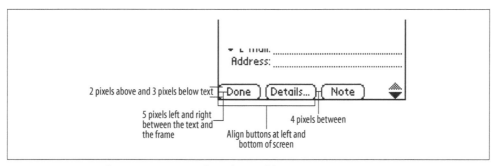

Figure 3-6. Button placement in a main form from Address

In modeless forms:

- Buttons should align with the left and bottom of the screen; leave no space.

- Buttons should have 4 pixels of space between each other.

In modal forms:

- Leave 4 pixels of space between the button frame and the left/right and bottom edges of the form (see Figure 3-7).

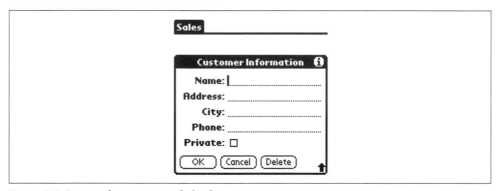

Figure 3-7. Button placement in a dialog box

Checkboxes

A checkbox represents an on (checked) or off (unchecked) state for items. Checkboxes can be grouped together and tend to allow for multiple choices (as opposed to push buttons, which indicate exclusive selection). They can have a text label associated with them. Tapping anywhere on the box or label toggles the on/off state of the checkbox. Figure 3-8 shows examples of checkboxes.

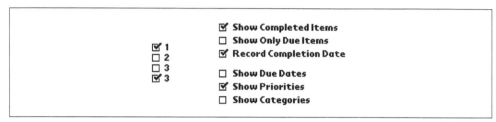

Figure 3-8. Checkboxes

Command Toolbar

The command toolbar is a new addition as of OS 3.5. Earlier versions of the OS displayed a command line briefly at the bottom of the screen; in the 3.5 OS, a command toolbar is displayed instead (see Figure 3-9). In either case, the user has the ability to enter the shortcut letter once the command line or toolbar is displayed. Either disappears in a few seconds if the user takes no action.

Figure 3-9. Two different command toolbars as found in OS 3.5 and later

The user can tap on the icons in the toolbar (which are context sensitive) as an alternative to entering the shortcut letter. The context is based on the user's task. For example, if a field is being edited when the command stroke is used, then the icons on the toolbar should include paste. If text in a field is selected, the icons should include cut and copy as well. If a form is being displayed, then the icons should offer beaming and other appropriate choices.

You can add your own custom icons to the toolbar, but no more than four can easily be displayed at one time. In designing the bitmap for your own custom icon, keep with the look and feel of the built-in ones. Table 3-2 shows these built-in system bitmaps and the actions associated with them.

Table 3-2. Command toolbar icons and system bitmap names

Icon	Action/bitmap	Icon	Action/bitmap
🗑	Delete record Bitmap: `BarDeleteBitmap`	✂	Cut selection Bitmap: `BarCutBitmap`

Table 3-2. Command toolbar icons and system bitmap names (continued)

Icon	Action/bitmap	Icon	Action/bitmap
	Beam record Bitmap: `BarBeamBitmap`		Copy selection Bitmap: `BarCopyBitmap`
	Show Security dialog box Bitmap: `BarSecureBitmap`		Paste Clipboard contents Bitmap: `BarPasteBitmap`
	Show Info dialog box Bitmap: `BarInfoBitmap`		Undo last action Bitmap: `BarUndoBitmap`

Fields

These UI objects are for user data entry. Fields have the following important characteristics:

- They have one or more lines of text.
- They are either editable or noneditable. Customarily, editable fields display with underlining, while noneditable fields have no underlining. (You aren't forced to follow this tradition, but you will probably confuse your users if you don't.)
- They are selectable.
- They should support Cut, Copy, and Paste (including the Graffiti commands).
- They can have a maximum number of characters.
- OS 3.5 or later supports double-tapping for word selection and triple-tapping for entire line selection.
- They can support various stylistic characteristics such as left or right justification, fonts, and underlining.

Figure 3-10 contains examples of fields.

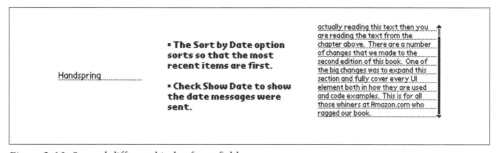

Figure 3-10. Several different kinds of text fields

Placement

Fields are often the central element in a form. For the most part, fields should be left-justified to some other UI element (like a label) or expanded to take up all the horizontal space in the form (minus the pixels for a possible scrollbar).

Form Bitmap

A bitmap is a graphic element. These bitmap objects can be grouped into families containing multiple versions of a bitmap in 1-, 2-, 4-, 8-, and 16-bit pixel depths. In cases where no bitmap in a family exists for the screen depth, the next-lower depth from the family is used instead. Figure 3-11 contains examples of bitmaps.

Figure 3-11. Two bitmaps

Gadgets

This is a custom UI object that you can use to make almost anything. Gadgets are good for simple or complicated uses. A gadget is just an empty frame; it is up to you to handle all the drawing and taps on the object. A great example of a gadget comes from the Date Book application (see Figure 3-12); it was created to handle the display of custom appointment times.

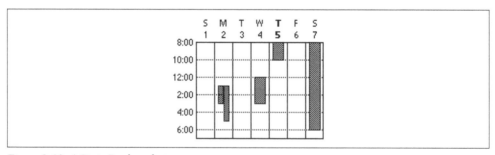

Figure 3-12. A Date Book gadget

Graffiti Shift Indicator

This shows the current Graffiti shift state: punctuation, symbol, uppercase shift, or uppercase lock (see Table 3-3). This indicator should be in any form that allows text entry.

Table 3-3. Graffiti Shift Indicator symbols

Symbol	Meaning	Symbol	Meaning	Symbol	Meaning
●	Punctuation	↑	Uppercase shift	あ	Used for Japanese
＼	Symbol	⬆	Uppercase lock	ｱ	Used for Japanese

Graffiti Shift Indicator placement

The Graffiti Shift Indicator should be near the right-hand side of the form. It is not necessarily the rightmost element, however, as Figure 3-13 shows. Scrollbars or scroll arrows are often placed in that position.

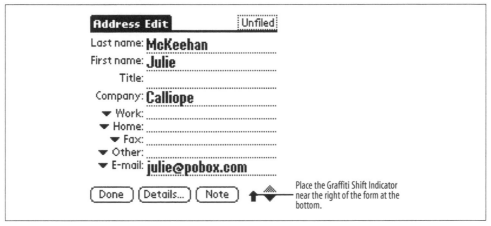

Figure 3-13. Graffiti Shift Indicator

Label

A label is a noneditable text object. In most cases the label is bold to distinguish it from editable text. Label text generally ends with a colon (:). Labels can be used in forms or dialog boxes and can be changed dynamically. A label is to the left of the item it labels; it is right-justified with other labels. See Figure 3-14 for an example.

Figure 3-14. Labels

Pop-up Trigger

When the user taps on the pop-up trigger, it displays a pop-up list, as shown in Figure 3-15. The trigger is a combination of a graphic object (the arrow) and a text label. The text that shows in the trigger is the currently selected text from the list. The trigger's horizontal size will expand and contract with the width of the text in the text label.

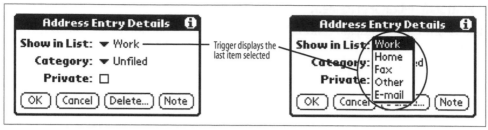

Figure 3-15. Pop-up trigger

Push Button

These nifty little UI objects have inherited the role held by radio buttons in many UIs. A push button represents an on/off state. As a rule, push buttons are grouped so that only one of the group can be selected at a time. Selecting a push button inverts that button and deselects the previously selected button. They are rectangular. See Figure 3-16 for examples of push buttons.

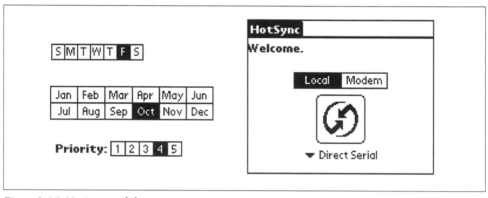

Figure 3-16. Various push buttons

Placement

Push buttons should always be aligned horizontally so they touch each other.

Repeating Button

These work like buttons, but there is a repeating action while the button is held down. The ubiquitous small scroll arrows found in many applications (Figure 3-17) are a common manifestation of this UI object. You can use repeating buttons as scroll arrows to scroll vertically in applications like Address Book, or to scroll horizontally as Date Book does with either days, weeks, or years.

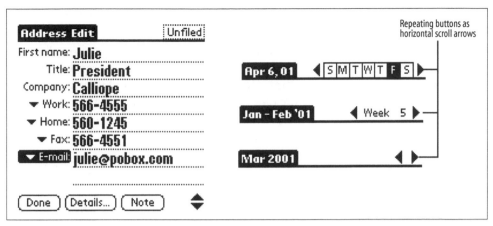

Figure 3-17. Repeating buttons as scroll arrows

Scrollbar

This object is often used for scrolling text, lists, tables, and fields. It allows one-line scrolling, page scrolling, and direct navigation to a particular location. Scrollbars are not available prior to Palm OS 2.0. Figure 3-18 contains scrollbars.

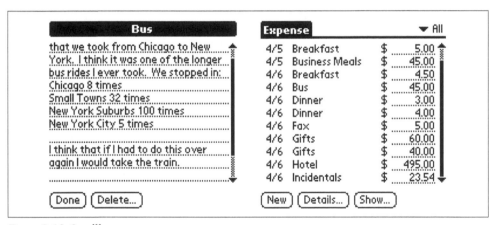

Figure 3-18. Scrollbars

Placement

The scrollbar's vertical height should match that of the object to which you are attaching it. Its horizontal width is 7 pixels. Scroll bars are always placed on the right-hand side of the object. Align the scrollbar with the rightmost edge of the form.

Selector Trigger

When a selector trigger is tapped, a dialog box pops up to allow the user to edit the value. The appearance of a selector trigger is notable as it is always surrounded by a gray (dotted) rectangle. The width of the rectangle changes to compensate for whatever text it is displaying.

Use a selector trigger for data that can be represented in a small text area, but that needs a separate dialog to edit. Good examples of selector triggers can be found in Date Book. The Details dialog contains settings for Time, Date, and Repeat—all selector triggers. For example, tapping the time trigger brings up a dialog to allow easy time scheduling (see Figure 3-19). Tapping the date trigger brings up a calendar view.

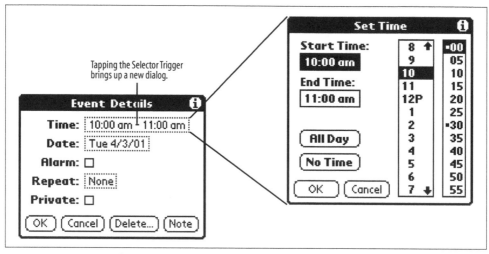

Figure 3-19. Various selector triggers in Date Book

Sliders

As of OS 3.5, sliders are supported UI objects. A slider (see Figure 3-20) displays a value that falls within the minimum and maximum range available. There are two types of sliders:

Regular sliders
> These do not update until the user finishes moving it.

Feedback sliders
> These update continuously as the user moves them.

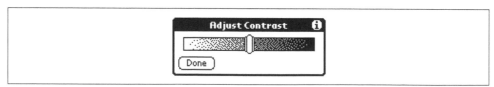

Figure 3-20. A feedback slider

Designing with a Particular User in Mind

Now we are going to turn to more general issues of design. First, we are going to explore how the audience and expected use of an application can shape how it is designed. To this end we will compare three applications: the built-in Date Book, Datebook+, and DateBk4.

Comparing Date Book, Datebook+, and DateBk4

The application, DateBk4, by Pimlico Software (*http://www.pimlicosoftware.com*) has been extremely popular with Palm users through several revisions. It is so well liked that Handspring is shipping a simpler version of the application, called Datebook+, on all Handspring Visors. This situation allows us a unique opportunity to study one type of application (the scheduling type) that has been designed for different audiences. The built-in Date Book and Datebook+ are designed for everybody. DateBk4 is for sophisticated Palm power users. Both Datebook+ and DateBk4 are intended to offer the Palm user more useful alternatives to the built-in Date Book application.

Why DateBk4 and Datebook+?

The author of DateBk4 and Datebook+, C. E. Steuart Dewar, has graciously allowed us to use his applications as Palm UI teaching tools. His work is a great choice because:

- It has been designed for more than one audience.
- DateBk4 has previous versions (so its design and features have been subjected to user feedback and revisions).
- DateBk4 is very popular and therefore, by definition, must be useful to many real Palm users. (This is a important criteria for judging the UI of any application!)

We'll show you the design decisions the authors of each application made for their audiences. We'll explain the issues that influenced their choices, which design rules they violated and why, and in general tell you what we think. In the instances where we might disagree with design choices, we offer you some other alternatives to consider.

To better understand the choices made, let's first compare the built-in Date Book's main form with that of DateBk4 and Datebook+. DateBk4 and Datebook+ (to a lesser extent) each offers an integrated Date Book with Address, To Do list, and Memo Pad. Figure 3-21 compares the main forms of DateBk4, Datebook+, and the built-in Date Book. For the purposes of this discussion, we are going to focus on some of the most interesting design issues that these three similar applications present. Please note that these are not product reviews and in no way attempt to cover everything interesting or useful about each application.

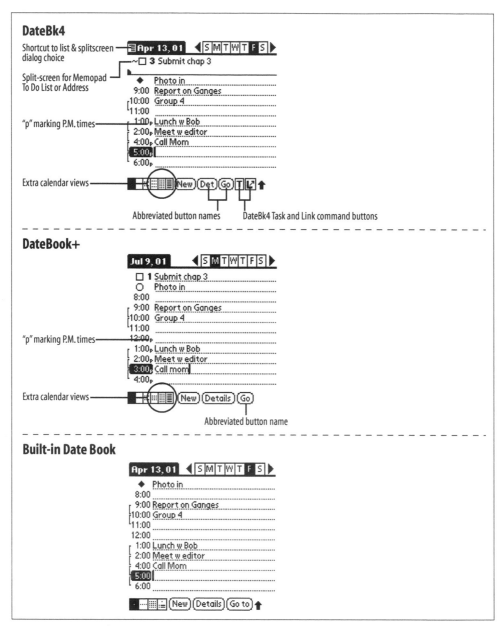

Figure 3-21. DateBk4's main screen as compared to Datebook+ and to the built-in Date Book

DateBk4's Extra Features

As you should have expected, DateBk4 has the most complicated main form of the three, while Datebook+ is only a little more complicated than the built-in Date Book. To get at the important design issues, let's start with a quick explanation of the features found in DateBk4 (and sometimes Datebook+) that are not found in the built-in application. If you look at DateBk4's main form, you see that it has several additions. Let's move from the top down. Where Datebook+ shares a feature we will also note it.

Menu icon

In DateBk4 there is an icon in the top lefthand corner (see Figure 3-22) that offers a shortcut to a list where users may choose to do several things, such as:

- Toggle the split-screen (on/off)
- Choose Address, Memo, or To Do list to display
- Do a refined Find
- Select a Category
- Show recent items
- Edit the display preferences

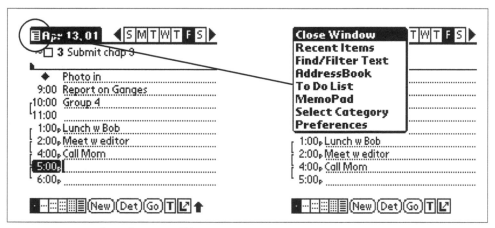

Figure 3-22. DateBk4's shortcut pulldown menu

Split display and time information

There is a split-level display directly below the days of the week push buttons that shows a view of To Do list, Memo, and Address items. There are similar time of day displays with DateBk4's addition of a small "p" by P.M. time slots.

Buttons and their views

At the bottom of the view is a series of buttons, some like those of Date Book and others unique to DateBk4. Datebook+ has some of these buttons in common with DateBk4. Two of the push buttons are additional ways to view calendar information along with the standard day, week, and month views. Next, there are three command buttons: New, Det (short for Details), and Go (short for Go To), which are similar to the command buttons in Date Book. New and Det each perform a different set of actions, however. Datebook+ has these same command buttons, but only the Go To button has been shortened to Go.

Buttons unique to DateBk4

Last of all, there are two uniquely shaped buttons specific to DateBk4 that are labeled T and L/. The T button stands for template; this is the app's way to let the user set up a template for a typical action. For example, if a user always has a 2-hour editor meeting, it can be saved as a template. On the day it occurs, the user:

- Taps the time where the appointment should be placed
- Taps the T button
- Taps the item in the list and thereby assigns the appointment to that slot (see Figure 3-23)

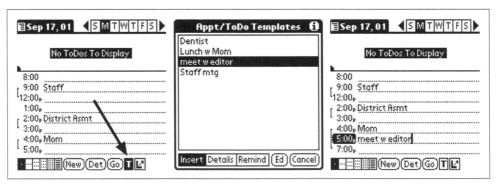

Figure 3-23. DateBk4's templates

Datebook+ has this same functionality, but it is available through the New menu with the Create Template menu item instead of through a button on the main form. (This is one important difference that we will discuss shortly.)

The L/ button allows the user to "link" an appointment or a To Do item to an Address, Memo, or To Do item and access that information with a single tap. For example, the user has a dentist appointment coming up and keys the event to the Address Book entry for the dentist (see Figure 3-24). Tapping on the event brings up that entry.

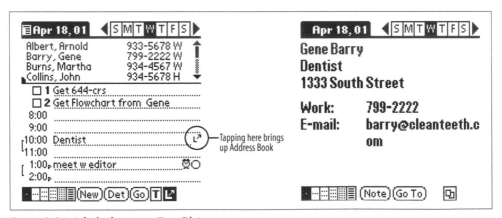

Figure 3-24. A linked entry in DateBk4

Why the Designs of Date Book, Datebook+, and DateBk4 Differ

These are the important differences between the main forms of DateBk4, Datebook+, and Date Book. Of course, there are many other differences in menus and various options that we will not be looking at now. Instead, we are going to focus on the issues that drove the design choices in these main forms. These issues are crystallized within the answers to a few very important questions:

- Who is the user?
- What are the most important aspects of an application?
- What should be sacrificed when there is no way to have it all—features, Palm UI guidelines, or what?

Who is the user?

At first glance, it should be obvious that DateBk4 is a more feature-rich and complex piece of software than either of the other two choices. The author of DateBk4 will tell you this application is not for novices; it is intended for power users. Indeed, the main way to get a hold of a copy is via the Internet and a Palm software site (*http://www.palmgear.com*). This is not something one would expect a novice computer user to be able to do easily. So, here is the important question such an assumption generates: "Given this audience, is the additional complexity warranted?" Another way to address this problem is to ask: "Within the Palm UI model, how do you design an application for power users?" "Is it option-rich or is it still a clean, simple design not much different from a standard Palm application?"

Thankfully, within the diverse Palm world we get to observe various programmers answering these questions quite differently. We then, in turn, get to watch customers tell us which choices work well and which ones flop. What is important for you to know is that you, like the author of DateBk4, should intentionally make this choice. Decide who your users are, what they want, and then design the UI of the application to match. DateBk4, with its multitude of objects and options in the main form assumes that its users will accept more clutter for the sake of convenience and flexibility. This leads us to our next issue of discussion—that of deciding on the most important aspects of an application. By way of introduction to this issue, it is time to introduce you to Palm's version of the famous 80/20 rule and its influence on the design of an application.

The 80/20 Rule

Palm UI philosophy has it own variation of the 80/20 rule:

> Eighty percent of the users of an application will only use about 20 percent of the features. Therefore, design an application so that those features are simple to do and as fast possible (and maybe all the application does). Everything else about the application must be designed around these tasks. If a feature gets in the way, throw it out.

This rule comes in many variations and forms, but it was first incorporated into the design philosophy of Palm handheld applications by Rob Haitani (the original designer of Date Book) and frequently discussed in his now-famous talk "The Zen of Palm" at annual Palm Developer Conferences.

With this rule in mind, let's look at the audiences and tasks of these three applications.

Date Book: The Most Important Aspects of an Application

The Date Book author has designed the application to make scheduling simple, unique events as quick as possible. The screen is fairly empty of extraneous detail, which makes it easier for users to successfully tap on the objects (users don't always hit what they aim for on such a small screen).

Date Book tasks and times

Look at each of the following increasingly complex tasks. Notice that the length of time they take to accomplish increases or becomes impossible with the complexity of the task (the tasks most important to Date Book are emphasized):

1. *Scheduling an appointment for today* takes only a few seconds. The user taps on the appointment time and writes in the information.

2. *Scheduling an appointment for one week from tomorrow*, takes a few extra taps and about 10 seconds.

3. *Scheduling an ongoing appointment*, on the first of the month for a year, takes about a minute.

4. Scheduling an appointment for late tomorrow night (11 P.M.) requires several experimental taps and is slightly difficult to figure out for a new user.

5. Scheduling a frequently repeating event (for example, lunch with Dad) at variable times takes as long every time. Each instance of the event takes the same length to create as the original.

6. Scheduling an appointment that is connected to a To Do list (for example, Matt's birthday party) is impossible. The user has to go to the To Do list independently and write a list there.

7. Scheduling an appointment that is connected automatically to a name card that will appear at the same time as the appointment is impossible. The user has to go to the Address Book independently and look up whatever name is connected to the event.

How the 80/20 rule was implemented within Date Book's design

Obviously, the author of Date Book believes that the first three tasks are the ones that fit the 80/20 rule for Date Book's users. He made each of those tasks as easy and fast as possible. The side effect of this easiness is that other tasks may be harder or even impossible.

Datebook+: The Most Important Aspects of an Application

If you look at the initial main form of Datebook+, you will find little difference from that of the original Date Book. The most obvious differences are the addition of the small "p" by P.M. times and the extra calendar views. What people think of these small changes is also, we discovered, open to quite a difference of opinion.

The "p" for P.M.

The "p" beside P.M. appointments (see Figure 3-25) generated some heated controversy in our UI discussions. While one of us really loved it, the other hated it. So, here are our two points of view. The pro argument for its placement is that it is very easy to lose track of the time of day when you are looking at a field of time slots. Having that tiny "p" icon is just the trick for a quick orientation. The con argument is that the lost 4 pixels of writing room are not worth the cost of the display; the space would be better used showing more appointment information. Furthermore, the user can probably figure out the time by looking at the context (if the screen is showing appointments from 11 to 7, those before 12 are A.M., and the others are P.M.). Finally, the argument goes, users can scroll up or down quickly if they are still unsure of the time.

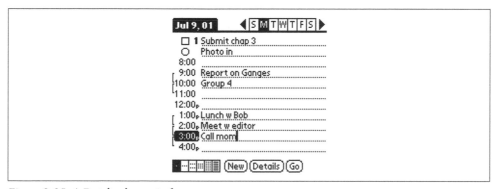

Figure 3-25. A Datebook+ main form

 We discussed our differing UI opinions here so you realize that sometimes a design choice will please one group of users at the cost of annoying another. Try to maximize the number of happy people while minimizing the number of mad ones. The author of DateBk4 tried to have the best of both worlds by making the "p" an option the user could choose to display or hide. The downside of this, of course, is it makes for more complex preferences (we will discuss these shortly).

Extra calendar views

Fitting more calendar views into the main form seems like a fine idea if they are useful. Whether they are used enough to justify their presence on the main form is a question best answered through lots of user testing. If they are as helpful as the other "standard" buttons then their presence is justified. Obviously, the people at Handspring and all the users of DateBk4 think these extra calendar views are worth the loss of pixel space—it is made up for in Datebook+ by shortening the name of the Go To button to Go. Such a tiny change seems more than reasonable to us for the addition of the extra access to the calendar views.

Datebook+ tasks and times

Now, look at the same set of tasks we examined for Date Book and let's see how long they take in Datebook+. Notice that it is the fifth and sixth events that differ significantly. (The most important tasks are emphasized):

1. *Scheduling an appointment for today* takes only a few seconds. The user taps on the appointment time and writes in the information. (No difference in time.)

2. *Scheduling an appointment for one week from tomorrow*, takes a few extra taps and about 10 seconds. (No difference in time.)

3. *Scheduling an ongoing appointment*, on the first of the month for a year, takes about a minute. (No difference in time.)

4. Scheduling an appointment for late tomorrow night (11 P.M.) requires several experimental taps and is slightly more difficult to figure out for beginning users and takes slightly longer than it does for Date Book users.

5. *Scheduling a frequently repeating event* (for example, lunch with Dad) at variable times takes very little time. Each repeat instance of the original event takes only a couple of taps and a few seconds to schedule.

6. *Scheduling an appointment that is connected a To Do list* (for example, Matt's birthday party) is possible. The user has to tap the New button and select a To Do list item, which is then displayed at the top of the Datebook+ view (see Figure 3-26). Each new To Do item requires the same number of steps to create, but you don't have to switch out of the application to see them.

7. Scheduling an appointment that is connected automatically to a name card is impossible. The user has to go to Address independently.

Figure 3-26. A Datebook+ To Do list

How the 80/20 rule was implemented within Datebook+'s design

The first three tasks are also the most important ones in Datebook+. This is not to exclude the fifth task—scheduling a frequently occurring, but nonrepeating task is also very important. This task requires a small amount of setup (slightly less than a standard repeating task) and then is easier and faster than any new event. The sixth task is possible in Datebook+, but it requires some work for each new item (you have to tap the To Do item in the new button over and over).

We could ask at this point, what—if anything—did the author have to sacrifice to make these extra tasks either possible or easier to do? (This is certainly the question you should ask yourself, each time you modify a feature to add additional functionality.) The answer is he traded complexity from one place to another. Date Book users hit the New button and they get the Time screen, which allows them to schedule a late night or untimed appointment quickly. Datebook+ users tap the new button and they get a list of five items the last of which takes them to the Time screen (thus, it is slightly harder to make a new unscheduled or late night event).

 Yes, we know that a user can simply write the time in the Graffiti area and the Set Time dialog box comes up in either Date Book or Datebook+. This does not discount the aforementioned problem for general users. Writing in the Graffiti area and expecting Date Book to launch to the Set Time dialog box—while a neat feature—is certainly not obvious. Such jewels should always be added to an application, but don't depend on them to carry the UI for a task.

You might well ask: "Was this the correct choice to make?" Our answer is, "It depends on your user." To be sure, trading complexity in such ways can well be the correct solution. It can also represent the designer's inability to "just say no" to one more feature and can be evidence of a truly awful handheld application design. It was certainly a well thought out choice on the part of Datebook+'s author. You, likewise, should make such decisions just as thoughtfully. Like Datebook+, if you are going to make this choice, do it because it will make life easier for your users and be aware of the sacrifice you are making.

DateBk4: The Most Important Aspects of an Application

Now it's time to look at the date book for power users. One glance is enough to see that this application is different. The screen is more crowded: there are buttons and icons all over the place. It is clearly more difficult to use and it is far more likely that the user might accidentally tap on the wrong thing. Let's see what this complexity gives us.

DateBk4 tasks and times

Here are the same set of tasks we examined for the other two applications. Some of the simpler tasks take longer to accomplish, but the more complex ones take less time or are now possible. Notice that it is the fifth, sixth, and seventh events that differ significantly. (The differences in the tasks are emphasized):

1. Scheduling an appointment for today takes only a few seconds. The user taps on the appointment time and writes in the information. (This task is no different.)

2. Scheduling an appointment for one week from tomorrow, takes a few extra taps and about 10 seconds. (This task is no different.)

3. Scheduling an ongoing appointment, on the first of the month for a year, takes about a minute. *This task usually takes about the same length of time. It can, however, be slightly quicker in some scheduling scenarios due to DateBk4's different Change Repeat dialog box as you can see in Figure 3-27.*

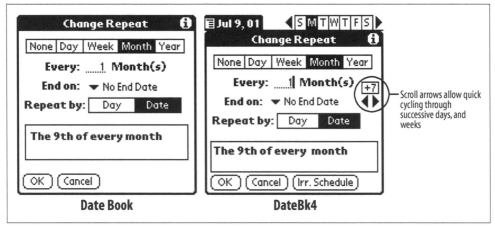

Figure 3-27. Date Book and DateBk4 Change Repeat dialog boxes

4. Scheduling an appointment for late tomorrow night (11 P.M.) *is both more difficult (takes longer) and easier, depending on the approach the user takes.*

   It takes longer to schedule a late night event when the user creates this appointment by tapping the New button:
   - DateBk4 contains a long list of items to choose between. One item (Appointment) takes the user to a more complex Set Time dialog box (see Figure 3-28).
   - Date Book's New button takes the user directly to the Set Time dialog box.

   It is quicker when the user writes in the Graffiti area:
   - DateBk4 immediately takes users to a Set Time dialog box that doesn't require the user to scroll to select P.M. times (see Figure 3-28).
   - Date Book takes the user to the Set Time dialog box and requires scrolling.

5. Scheduling a frequently repeating event (for example, lunch with Dad) at variable times *takes very little time and is significantly easier in DateBk4*. Each new instance of the original event takes only a couple of taps and a few seconds to schedule.

This is because the "T" button on the bottom of the form allows the user to precisely set up just this sort of event using templates.

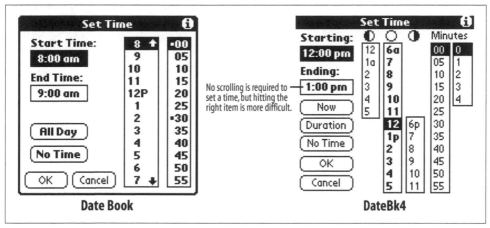

Figure 3-28. Date Book and DateBk4 Set Time dialog boxes

6. Scheduling an appointment that is connected a To Do list (for example, Matt's birthday party) requires a tap of the New button and selecting one item from a long list. *This is about as easy to accomplish as it is in Datebook+, and it is not possible in Date Book.*

7. *Scheduling an appointment that is connected automatically to a name card is possible and fairly easy to do.* The user taps the event to link and selects the "L" button at the bottom of the screen. Later on, tapping the small icon to the far right of the event brings up the relevant information in the Address Book (see Figure 3-29).

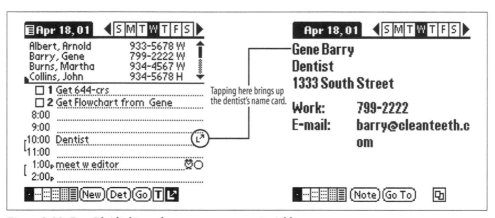

Figure 3-29. DateBk4 linking of an event to a name in Address

How the 80/20 rule was implemented within DateBk4's design

Looking at our list of tasks, we can tell that the author of DateBk4 is not overly concerned with the 80/20 rule. In fact, it doesn't seem to be the force driving the design of the application. Something else is—the issue of who the user is and what that user expects *to be able to accomplish with this application.* Power users want to be able to do lots of things. The designer of this application is catering to that set of users. His choices are based on offering flexibility and speed instead of simplicity and speed. In DateBk4, doing some simple things simply is not as important as having the flexibility to schedule events and appointments in a variety of ways. Simple dialog boxes give way to more complex dialog boxes and, in some cases, make tasks easier and in some cases harder. Menus have lots of items in them and buttons become so plentiful that names have to be shortened to the point of obscurity.

We want you to consider what situations and set of users might *appropriately* drive a handheld application designer to makes these choices. DateBk4's author is intimately aware of Palm's UI guidelines and has chosen to violate them to accomplish other goals. If you are going to do the same thing you better have good reasons. Herein lies an important lesson to learn about design—violate UI design rules only when:

1. You know what the rules are. (Ignorance is no excuse.)

2. It is very worthwhile for other reasons (it's also a good idea if you can get real users to agree with you).

What Should Be Sacrificed?

Now, it is time to discuss the last important design issue that we raised when we started discussing these three scheduling applications. What should you do when you have a clear conflict between desires—you want to add a feature but it will make for a more complex screen or slower completion times, and so on, and so on. To elucidate this issue we can look at some more examples of where DateBk4 swerves from simplicity and some reasons why. We discuss these further situations because you will likely encounter these very types of problems in your own application design. We think you can learn from DateBk4's choices and, in a few instances, where we would redesign it. In either case, you need to remember that one solution will not necessarily make sense for all audiences. As a rule of thumb, the more general the audience, the simpler the solution should be.

Other than this, all bets are off. Indeed, something DateBk4's designer, C. E. Steuart Dewar said (in our discussion about these applications) sums up the problem nicely:

> Obviously not all people need a calendar program on their Palm that is more powerful than the one they typically run on their desktop—but apparently many do. My attitude is that if you want a simple, clean, efficient date book application, use the built-in date book—it's there, it's free, and it's more than adequate for most users. So if you want to move beyond that, then you are presumably willing to make the investment to learn a more functional application. And a more functional application by definition is *always* going to be more complex and difficult to learn. No matter how hard you try,

you will never get the controls for a nuclear power station to be as simple as the controls on your toaster.

So, while wishing to make nuclear power station controls as simple as those of a toaster, let us proceed....

DateBk4's pop-up common task list

This list (see Figure 3-30) offers a combination of interesting UI problems. First, this is a list acting a lot like a menu. But this is not the standard way to access a menu on the Palm OS—menus are accessed by way of the Menu button or by tapping on the title (OS 3.5 or later). Second, this list is accessed via the tiny little icon up in the left corner; tapping it is the only way the user knows something is up there. Using a list as menu substitute certainly violates UI.

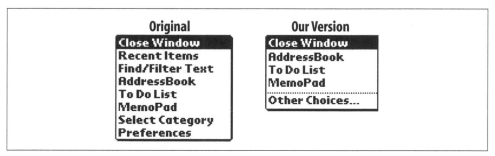

Figure 3-30. Redesigned pseudomenu

This immediately raises the issue of whether this list should be changed into a menu. The con for such a move is that it could be argued that these actions occur too frequently to hide away in a menu (invoking the 80/20 rule as justification). After all, the designer put that little icon up in the corner because no other good option seemed to be available. Furthermore, it is convenient to be able to switch split views between To Do list, Address Book and Memo Pad (or nothing) with just two taps.

If you find such an argument persuasive and want to leave the icon/list that acts like a menu, then the length of the list is another issue. It is very long and possibly contains items that shouldn't be there. The items with which we have the most trouble are Recent Items, Find/Filter Text, Select Category, and Preferences.

Selecting Recent Items allows the user to see the last ten items accessed in both Memo Pad and Address Book. Selecting Find/Filter Text allows the user to filter what is displayed in the split-screen window. Select Category allows the user to set the category of items displayed in the split-screen window. Preferences contains choices for the split-screen display.

Our question is whether these actions are so common that they should be put in the same list with the others. Our assumption is they are not (now, it's our turn to invoke the 80/20 rule) and as a result we don't want to see them in this list. We want them hidden in a menu.

A possible second critique has to do with the ordering of the list. We would rather have seen the applications that can be displayed in the split screen show up directly below the Close Window choice (see our redesign in Figure 3-30). We do like putting the Close Window choice first, however, as this easily allows the user to get rid of the split screen with two quick taps or open it with one tap. Upon reflection, we think putting the other choices in this menu adds unnecessary clutter. Show us some evidence that these actions are frequent and we would reevaluate our position, however.

The split display

The split display's UI poses some interesting issues. Allowing the complete hiding of the window and the ability to choose which of the built-in applications to display are clever and useful touches (though complex). Allowing the user more than one way to change the proportions of the split is also helpful (see Figure 3-31). It can be changed in a preference and by dragging the split divider bar (though the icon showing the drag spot is vague).

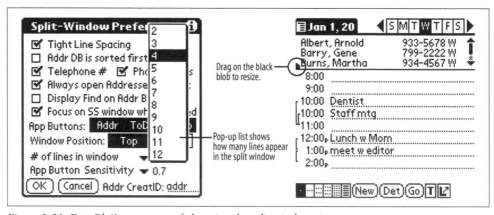

Figure 3-31. DateBk4's two ways of changing the split window size

This leaves the interesting question of whether access to and manipulation of data from other applications is part of the Palm OS UI model. Admittedly, it can be useful to have this kind of access. For example, its nice to be able to see the name and telephone number of your 3 P.M. appointment (and change it if necessary). All in all, we like this feature for sophisticated users and would happily tolerate the complexity to keep it.

Button action and common activity

The New button is no different in design than that found in the original Date Book. What happens when the user taps it is a different story. In Date Book, tapping the New button brings up the Set Time dialog box shown at the left of Figure 3-32. In DateBk4, tapping the New button brings up a list on the right that contains a massive number of "new" choices.

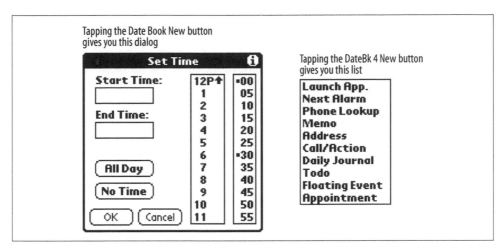

Tapping the Date Book New button gives you this dialog

Set Time

Start Time:

End Time:

All Day

No Time

OK   Cancel

12P↑
1
2
3
4
5
6
7
8
9
10
11

•00
05
10
15
20
25
•30
35
40
45
50
55

Tapping the DateBk 4 New button gives you this list

Launch App.
Next Alarm
Phone Lookup
Memo
Address
Call/Action
Daily Journal
Todo
Floating Event
Appointment

Figure 3-32. The choices produced by the New button in Date Book and DateBk4

The different actions of the New button in these applications demonstrate an important design issue. Each application is attempting to determine "the most useful" action desired by its user when this button is tapped. In Date Book, the Set Time dialog box is presented because the designer assumes that the user wants to set a long appointment, one with no time, or an unusual time. If a standard appointment were needed, the user would have simply gone to that time slot and written something on that line. *This solution is designed for a general, often beginning user.*

Date Book is trying to minimize the number of taps required to do any of these frequent, but unusually timed, activities. For example, imagine I want to set a 3:15 dentist appointment; it takes four quick taps to set it up (time required: about 5 seconds).

To accomplish this same activity in DateBk4, a beginning user (not the intended audience, to be sure) must hunt through the long New list, and then through five possible time lists (time required: about 10 seconds if no wrong choices are made). As we mentioned earlier, DateBk4 is aimed at flexibility instead of simplicity. Once again the nature of the user (a power user who wants to be able to do lots of stuff) is driving the design of this application.

It is also important to know that this issue primarily affects new users. Sophisticated Palm users know to just write "315" in the Graffiti area to set an appointment at 3:15. Thus, you can see that a power user will not be hindered by a design choice in DateBk4.

Abbreviating button names—hitting the screen-size wall

Another unusual choice the designer made was to abbreviate the Details and Go To buttons. Using Go for Go To seems acceptable, but using Det as an abbreviation of Details requires some explanation. With this button, the designer of DateBk4 hit against the wall of screen size—he simply ran out of pixels. There was no way to fit everything on the bottom of the form.

You should both sympathize with the designer and consider the issue carefully as we promise that you too will hit the screen-size wall. Here's what to do about it. In cases where your application is destined for a general audience, don't use abbreviations like Det for Details. In a more vertical application, you have more latitude. In either case, try hard to come up with a simple solution before shortening names of common Palm UI names (for example, New, Go To, Details). In the case of DateBk4, we don't mind the shortening of Go To to Go, but Det for Details is tough to look at without wincing.

 No, we don't have a great alternative to offer. For power users, Det is probably OK. We would have been tempted to lose that last calendar view to make room for the full spelling, but we can already hear the users screaming about how useful that view is and how they wouldn't want to lose it. (Even though this is all adjustable via Preferences.) We would probably go this route anyway. The only thing we can tell you with certainty is, don't try this abbreviation on a general audience.

Buttons that don't look like buttons

This leaves the T and L/ command buttons to discuss. Once again this is an issue of space and the designer of DateBk4 is out of room. While we can all readily agree these should have been standard command buttons (in a traditional rounded rectangle), that is not an alternative if they are going to be at the bottom of the form. The choices are: keep the feature in a type of form object, lose the feature to some other place (like a menu), or drop the functionality altogether.

Power users will not want to lose the functionality these buttons provide and so the designer of DateBk4 went with strangely shaped buttons (not quite push buttons, not quite icons). We would suggest that as the screen resolution on Palm devices gets better it will be easier to address such issues with more icon-like choices. Until then, square buttons are better than round ones that violate command-button design rules.

Preference dialog boxes

One way that DateBk4 tries to address the complexity issue is by giving the user lots of Preference choices. Figure 3-33 contains the Options menu and just two of the Preference dialog boxes that are items in that menu. As you can see, the user of DateBk4 has enormous flexibility in terms of how items are displayed and used. Views, time zones, durations, and categories can all be changed. A word of caution is in order, however. Before presenting this much choice to a user, make sure it is both warranted and necessary. DateBk4's designer has more license than many designers given his intended audience. Even so, this is a complex set of forms that we wouldn't want to see in many applications. Wherever possible make some of these choices yourself. Where it's not possible, try and organize items by logical user categories.

We have been told that a redesign for DateBk4's Preferences is planned in some later release. As a result, these views may look different in a version that you have.

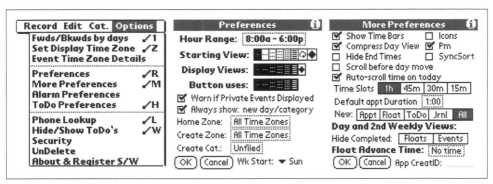

Figure 3-33. Menus and Preference dialog boxes in DateBk4

We would rather have seen tabbed panels within Preferences. One for displays, one for time information, one of alarms, and so on. But this choice itself raises another dilemma the application designer faces, which is the tradeoff between nicely spaced dialog boxes and making the application larger.

Dialog boxes, and especially the code associated with them, take up space in a Palm application. A Palm user often asks the question of whether a particular application is worth the space it takes up on his handheld. The desktop user, coversely, rarely considers this.

The problem is that each additional form makes the application larger. Two preference dialog boxes crammed with options (as is typical of DateBk4) might take up, say, 1.5 KB of space in an application. Take those same two dialog boxes and pretty them up into five nicely laid-out dialog boxes and the application might grow by 1 or 2 KB. While one such choice will probably not cause your application to be too big, twenty such choices might start to matter.

Who Is Your User?

As you can see, your audience determines a lot about your application. If you have a general audience in mind, then design a simple, clean handheld application. If you have an application targeted at a particular group of people, then take into account their special needs. Following the 80/20 rule is essential when you choose which tasks will be simple and quick. This is true whether you are catering to a general audience or to one that craves flexibility and power.

We want to thank the author of DateBk4 and Datebook+, C. E. Steuart Dewar, at Pimlico Software, for so graciously allowing us to put his applications under the microscope. It is not easy to voluntarily let someone be critical of your work. (Just ask us what we think of computer book critics!) The point of this process is to help you with your own application design. This lets you see what a popular application—one that has gone through many revisions—and a simpler variation of it look like.

The Well-Designed Form

Now that you have seen some examples of the UI objects available on the Palm OS, and seen how the audience of an application can affect its design, it is worthwhile to show you some well-designed and not-so-well–designed forms. We will also point out important placement rules that agree with Palm's own guidelines along the way.

Here are the important optimization rules to use when designing your forms:

- The quintessential handheld tasks your application provides should drive the design.
- Minimize the number of taps and time to complete frequent actions (follow the 80/20 rule).
- Minimize screen clutter by hiding infrequent actions in menus and other forms.
- Provide command buttons for common multistep activities.
- Minimize switching screens for common tasks.
- Be clever in implementing unique aspects of the application.

In these next sections, we will show you some forms that in some ways follow these placement rules and in some ways that violate them. You should keep these optimization rules in mind as we look at their designs.

The To Do List—A Well-Designed Main Form

We are looking at the To Do list as an example of a well-designed main form of a built-in application (Figure 3-34).

Some of the essential features of any main form of an application are:

- It uses the entire screen or in other words, it is modeless.
- It has a title (tapping on the title in OS 3.5 or later should display the menu bar).
- If it has buttons, they are aligned to the very bottom of the screen.

The To Do list certainly fulfills these criteria. It also minimizes the number of taps needed to complete common actions. For instance, changing the priority of an item takes two taps and creating a new item takes only one tap. It minimizes screen clutter by hiding infrequently used actions in the Details dialog box and in menus. It

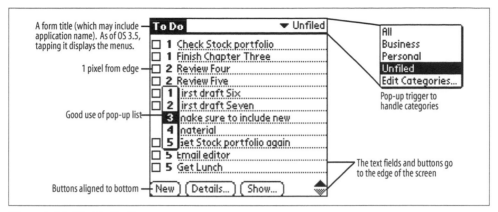

Figure 3-34. The To Do list

minimizes switching screens by making sure that the most frequently used activities happen in the main form. For example, changing the priority of item doesn't require going to another screen. It has no command buttons for common multistep activities, but that is primarily due to the simplicity of the application.

The Security Application—A Not-So-Well–Designed Form

It is not only third-party applications that sometimes choose the wrong form objects for tasks. We threw in this next example to show you that even the folks at Palm can occasionally make designs that can be improved. The Security application contains the main form shown in Figure 3-35.

Figure 3-35. The Security application

The Privacy setting of records is controlled by a selector trigger, when it should plainly have been a set of push buttons. This application begs for push buttons with only three possible, mutually exclusive choices. See Figure 3-36 for our suggested re-design.

Other than this change, there is not a lot to this application. It performs a simple task that doesn't require much in the way of complication. Perhaps another minor adjustment that could be made if it did not compromise performance would be to put a small descriptive information area to explain what each of the terms Show, Hide and Mask mean for the display of records. It might look similar to the descriptive area found in the Change Repeat dialog box of the Date Book application. Tapping a selection causes a description of the action to appear below. Figure 3-37 demonstrates this.

Figure 3-36. The redesigned Security application

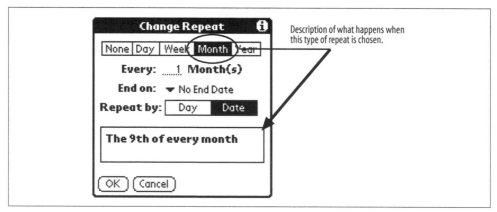

Figure 3-37. The Change Repeat dialog box

The Date Book—A Well-Designed Dialog Box

The Date Book has many clever features, which include the Details dialog box for an item (see Figure 3-38). With just one tap, the user can adjust the time, date, set an alarm, repeat the event, and perform various other activities. Most of the items rely on selector triggers to hide information from the user until she is ready to use it.

Here are some of the most important features that together are the hallmark of any well-designed dialog box:

- It is as short as possible without scrunching items too closely together. A good dialog box usually leaves the form or application title visible as a point of reference for the user. This is for those times when the user is interrupted in the middle of the task and needs some context to complete the activity later.

- It has a good balance of labels and editable information. Selector triggers are great for dialog boxes. With one tap, the user can get to a screenful of selectable items quickly, make a choice, and complete the task faster than entering a handful of Graffiti characters in a field.

- It provides online help. It can't hurt to give as much help as necessary. The user can look at it or ignore it.

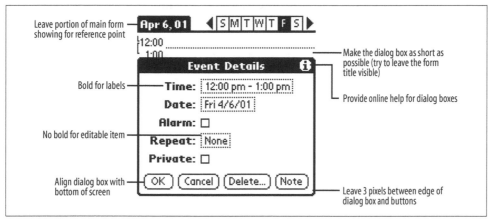

Figure 3-38. The Date Book Details dialog box

WordSmith—A Well-Designed Dialog Box

The next dialog box comes from a document editing application called WordSmith (*http://www.bluenomad.com*). There is a command button labeled Font on the main form. When it is tapped it gives the user the dialog box shown in Figure 3-39.

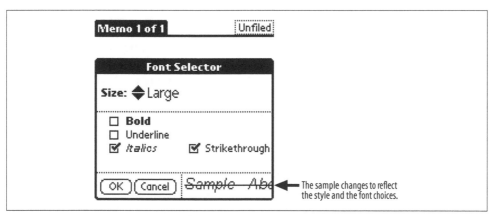

Figure 3-39. WordSmith's Font Selector dialog box gives immediate style feedback

The nice touch in this dialog box is that it gives the user font size and style feedback with every choice. If the large font is chosen, then the sample at the bottom right changes to show that font. Bold, italic, underline, strikethrough, and other font sizes reflect similar changes. This is a well-designed dialog box because it doesn't make the user guess what the effect will look like, but rather gives a clear example of it.

Small things like this in an application's UI give the user real pleasure. While simple enough to do, these are also the kinds of things that get left out all too often.

There is one change we would have made in the Font Selector dialog box. The control for the size choices is a selector trigger and we think it should be a set of three push buttons instead. Since there are only these three mutually exclusive size choices, this is an ideal situation for push buttons.

The Address Application—A Well-Designed Alert

There are many kinds of alerts. The best ones are those that give you important information or tell you how your actions are affecting your data. An alert should only show up when necessary. A good example of this can be found in the Address application. In Address, when you mark an entry as private in the Details dialog box, the application will give you an alert if you don't have Preferences set to hide Private records (see Figure 3-40).

Figure 3-40. Address application alert when a record is marked Private

Users expect things to happen when they do things. If nothing is going to happen, you need to let them know. In this case, the user has marked a record Private, but the Security application has not been set to hide Private records. (Pre-3.0 OS changed these in the Preferences dialog box.) When it is set to hide, the record vanishes and the user understands what effect the action has had. In our earlier case, the application displays an alert letting the user know why the record is still visible.

Bejeweled—A Really Well-Designed Alert

Now we want to discuss an application that offers a really nice use of alerts. It is called Bejeweled (*http://www.astraware.com*). Besides its nice alerts, it has a stunning color interface for color Palm OS devices. This is a game that involves moving jewel like objects around the screen. The first time the user runs the game and attempts an illegal move the application posts the alert shown in Figure 3-41.

Using contextual alerts like this is a great way to help your less-experienced users. It doesn't force them to learn all the rules of your application before using it. Instead, it

Figure 3-41. Bejeweled's Hint alert

waits until something is done incorrectly and displays an alert; it tells the user how to do the action correctly when the information is useful. It is also not annoying the way some alerts can be (appearing each time you do something to trigger it). This alert appears once and then doesn't bug you any more. This is a great idea.

Indeed, this is an example of an application with something unique added to its interface. Many people want to play a new game immediately, learning the absolute minimum beforehand. The designers of Bejeweled have taken this common human game trait into account in the design of their game.

Taking Advantage of the Unique Elements in an Application

Your design needs to take advantage of unique elements in your application. Saying such a thing, however, doesn't go very far towards your understanding of what we mean. (This is one of those vague design generalities we always find annoying in other people's books.) So we are going to explain what we mean by giving you some examples. These are applications that have, in one way or another, thought about their users and their actions and incorporated something that enhances that user experience.

Great hinting

Our first example comes again from the game Bejeweled. As we said, this is a swapping game that comes in either a nice grayscale or a pretty color version. Figure 3-42 shows a grayscale example of the main form. The lovely unique detail that this game offers is its method of hinting. If it has been a while since the user has made a move (about 15 to 20 seconds) then a jewel will sparkle briefly. The sparkle means the jewel is next to another jewel that can be swapped for a winning move.

This is a great hint because it fits with the theme of the game, it is unobtrusive enough that you can ignore it, and it makes you feel virtuous while you're using the hint/cheat (you had to look around for the sparkle).

Anticipating the user's needs

Our next example comes from Address. In a New Contact when the user is filling in a company, from the initial letter, Address anticipates a match to an existing company (see Figure 3-43). If the anticipation is correct, the user is done with that entry. If it is incorrect then additional letters overwrite the guess.

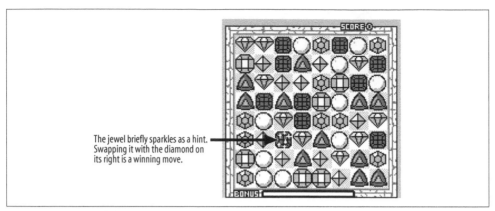

Figure 3-42. Bejeweled's Sparkle hint

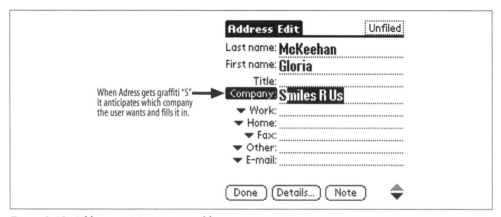

Figure 3-43. Address anticipates a possible company entry

Hidden tricks that save time

This next example also comes from Address. If you hold the Address hard button down for one second then Address beams your business card to another device. It will even switch on the device and open the application if necessary. This is a great time-saving touch. It shows that someone actually spent some time thinking about how people often exchange personal information (by swapping business cards in a hurry) and tried to make that as quick and easy as possible.

How to enter an odd appointment time

The Date Book application offers a nice time-saving feature to its users as well. It is in answer to the problem of what to do when the user wants to add an appointment at an odd time, say 11:55. The solution to this problem is quite sweet. The user opens Date Book and then writes 1155 into the numerical portion of the Graffiti area. Date Book immediately opens to the Set Time dialog box with the "Start Time" filled in with 11:55.

Other Design Issues

Most applications contain a certain number of core user interface elements. Even the simplest application will, at the very least, need a form and some controls. Most applications go well beyond the minimal number of features and have multiple menus, forms, and dialog boxes. You will have to decide about these forms, as well as the types of screens (black and white, grayscale, color, pixel depth) that you will support. There are also OS versions to support or ignore. Finally, and most importantly, there are a couple of gotchas that commonly get programmers from the desktop world. Let's look at these first.

Gotchas from the Desktop

There are two common problems that desktop programmers stumble upon when they enter the handheld world: what to do about passwords and where to put the Exit button. Thankfully, we can tell you exactly what to do about both of these situations.

Handling passwords on a handheld

In the desktop world, it is common to present a dialog box in which the user enters a password where the actual letters or digits in the password are obscured with asterisks (*) or other symbols. *You must not obscure a password on a Palm handheld.* Instead, show the actual letters and digits the user enters in the dialog box (see Figure 3-44).

Figure 3-44. Entering a password in the Security application Password dialog box

You also need to show the actual letters and digits in any verification dialog boxes and in an initial dialog box that you present to allow access to your application (that has been password protected). There are two good reasons for this absolute rule:

1. The practice of obscuring passwords came about on the desktop because someone might well be looking over your shoulder at the screen when you need to enter the code. (It is kind of hard to pick up a desktop computer or hunch over enough to cover the screen.) This situation does not exist on the handheld; a user can easily move or shield the entire screen to hide what is being entered.

2. The second reason is even more important. Graffiti, as nice as it is, is not perfect. It is common enough to enter a letter and have something unexpected show up on the screen. It would be bad manners indeed to obscure a password field thereby making it impossible for a user to know what digit has been messed up.

 Do not obscure password fields. This is an absolute rule—don't even think about violating it!

Hey, where's the Exit button?

You can always tell a new handheld user or programmer because he is constantly hunting around for the Exit (or Quit) button in an application. Handheld applications don't have them. While it may take awhile to get used to, the UI for moving from one application to the next is to simply start another application. Turning the handheld off is just as straightforward: push the power button. No matter how counter intuitive this may feel, this is the UI. So applications don't have Exit buttons. Once again, this is a strongly held rule of the Palm OS—don't violate it.

Design Issues

When you sit down to design your application, you'll need to ask yourself the following questions and come up with some reasonable answers to them:

What tasks does the application accomplish?
> Obviously, this is a question one would ask about any application on any platform. That doesn't make it any less relevant here. You need to lay out as clearly as possible what the user can do with your application—what quintessential handheld tasks the user can perform. Just as importantly, you should have a clear idea of tasks that the user can't do.

> The essence of the Palm OS and the handheld is speed and accessibility. Eliminating a possible feature because it ruins either of these is something to be proud of and is terribly difficult to do in this era of "kitchen sink" applications.

What forms does the application have?
> There is at least a startup form that the user sees when tapping the application icon. Each dialog box (other than an alert) or other data view is also a new form. A good rule of thumb is that you will have one form for every view of data. Forms add up fast when you count this way.

What menus does the application have?
> Commonly, you will support the Record, Edit, and Option menus. They will be similar to those found in the built-in applications and include the same menu items. Custom menus are also often a part of the application.

What alerts does the application have?

Alerts give information, ask questions, issue warnings, and report errors. As we have seen, they can also anticipate when the user needs help and offer timely suggestions at opportune times.

What is the structure of the application's database or databases?

The database is where you store information that is displayed on the handheld. You need to decide how many databases you will need, how the records are ordered, and what is stored in each record.

What versions of the OS will you support?

You need to decide what versions of the Palm OS you are targeting. As we write this, there are six important versions: 1.0, 2.0, 3.0, 3.1, 3.5, and 4.0.

 We think, as of Spring 2001, that fewer than 1 percent of the Palm OS devices in use were running the 1.0 version of the OS and fewer than 5 percent were running 2.0. Our recommendation is not to worry about compatibility with the Palm 1.0 or 2.0 OS. Of course, your particular situation may dictate that you support the earlier versions of the OS.

Here are the major changes in those operating systems:

Palm OS 2.0

This OS includes many new APIs, some changed APIs, support for TCP/IP (on ≥ 1 MB devices), support for scrollbars, and support for IEEE Floating Point (32-bit floats, 64-bit doubles).

Palm OS 3.0

This OS includes added support for infrared (devices include IR ports), additional sound support, additional font support, progress manager, and possible unique device IDs.

Palm OS 3.1

This OS includes modified character encoding to match that of Windows exactly. This OS version is important because the Handspring Visor (which can't be upgraded) uses it.

Palm OS 3.5

This OS includes color support and notification.

Palm OS 4.0

This OS includes telephony, attention, expansion cards, and extended Exchange Manager beyond IR.

What does the conduit do?

If all you want to do is save the handheld data to the desktop as a backup, use the backup conduit. If the user needs to look at or edit the data on the desktop, or if the user needs to transfer data from the desktop to the handheld, then you need to design a conduit and determine what it can and can't do with data. You must determine what data will be transferred, whether data will be uploaded, downloaded, or synchronized, and what application on the desktop the user will use to view the data.

How the Sample Applications Are Useful

Some of you may be wondering how useful the Sales application will be to you. Does it show you how to use all the APIs? Does it contain the essential components of most Palm applications? Here are some answers. The Sales application uses much of the Palm API and, to that extent, offers a broad treatment. Because it isn't an exact clone of the built-in apps, you will see some new design issues and code. You also get to see our reasoning behind the design choices we make. The application implements databases, beaming, menus, dialog boxes, and Find. Another crucial component is the detailed description of its conduit. We hope that much of what is mystifying about conduits is clarified in our descriptions and the code we create.

We also cover some Palm OS features in smaller sample applications. We handle tables, serial, and TCP/IP in this manner. Indeed, we try to show an implementation of most UI objects in at least one sample application. Our objective was to treat the easiest issues lightly and spend much more time on the most difficult or important ones. Our examples are created with this goal in mind.

Here are some of the important coding tasks you will be able to do in your own applications when you have worked through our examples:

- Create forms, menus, alerts, and dialog boxes in a Palm application.
- Create and use most UI objects in the Palm OS.
- Create multiple databases; add, delete, and modify records in those databases as necessary.
- Support Find.
- Support Exchange.

User Interface of the Sales Application

The sample application we are creating is a forms-based application that will be used to record orders. This application is for a person who sells toys to stores. These are the activities we want the salesperson to be able to accomplish in the application:

- Create a new order for a customer.
- Delete an order.
- Delete or modify items in an order.
- Beam a customer to another device.
- Modify, delete, or create a new customer.

The Sales Application Customer List

The user starts the application and picks a customer from a list.

The Customer list

This is the startup form of the application. It is a list of all the customers that our salesperson normally sells toys to during that selling period. The user can tell which customers already have orders because those who still need orders are in bold.

We admit that bolding an item to indicate status is a subtle, if not obscure, design element. Its presence is reasonable when you remember the audience of this application. The same user will use it daily for taking orders. The bolding of an item in a constantly used application may be warranted, while it may not be in a more general purpose application. In any case, a user who doesn't know what the bold is for is not hurt—it's just a shortcut for the experienced user.

When a name is selected from the Customer list (see Figure 3-45), the Order form for that customer is opened.

Figure 3-45. Picking a customer from a list

For the rare occasion that the salesperson may want to create a new customer while out in the field, we provide this capability on the handheld. On Palm devices with IR capability, the salesperson might also want to beam customer information. Both these actions are handled in this form as part of the Customer list record menu (see Figure 3-46).

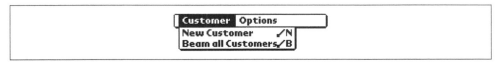

Figure 3-46. Customer menu in the Customer list form

New Customer

When the user selects New Customer, the Customer Information dialog box you see in Figure 3-47 is shown.

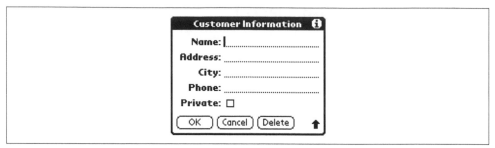

Figure 3-47. Customer Information dialog box

 A nicety that you should always provide where possible is the correct case as a default for an entry area. As you can see in Figure 3-47, we have initial uppercase set for the customer's name. We do the same thing for the Address and City fields (initial uppercase would be bad for an email field).

Note that customer records can be labeled Private. When a user selects either of these options and the Preferences are set to View All Records, we put up a dialog box explaining why that customer is still visible (see Figure 3-48).

We put up the dialog box to prevent confusion on the user's part when all records are viewable. This is a good example of explaining logical, but unexpected, results.

Figure 3-48. Explanation of Private Records checkbox

The user clearly expects something to happen when selecting the Private or Masked checkbox. If Preferences are set to Mask Records, the record disappears from view and the Customer list is shown with a Masked item where our new customer would be alphabetically (Figure 3-49).

 Remember to add the locking icon in forms that display masked records. This is modeled on the behavior of the built-in applications.

If Preferences have been set to Hide Private Records, the record disappears from view when the user taps OK.

Figure 3-49. Customer list with a Masked customer displayed

Beam All Customers/Send All Customers

The Beam All menu item provides a quick way for the salesperson to transfer all the customer information to another device. When Beam All Customers is selected, the user gets the message shown in Figure 3-50. The person receiving the customers also gets status information.

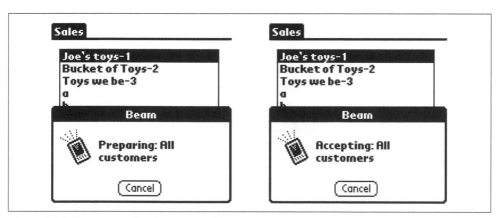

Figure 3-50. The status when beaming and receiving customers

If the Palm device is not capable of sending (pre-4.0 OS), the user never sees the item in the Customer menu. An alternative would have been to tell users they can't send on a non-send-capable device—we like our way better.

The Order Form

Once a customer is tapped on, the user is shown the individual Order form. Most of the activity in the application happens here.

Creating items

The most important activity is adding items to the order. This is done by selecting toys and adding them to the customer's order. Figure 3-51 shows an empty Order and one that has several items in it.

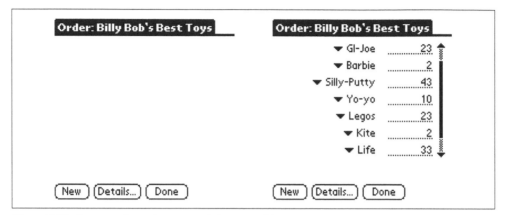

Figure 3-51. A new order and one containing several items

The name on this form is worth noting. First, we show the name of the customer along with the form name (Order). While not necessary, it certainly takes no extra space and we can imagine instances where the salesperson is later reviewing orders and forgets which customer she is looking at.

As you can see, each item in the order is a selector trigger and text field entry combination. Figure 3-52 shows the item listed by category. First, the user selects a category (if the current category is wrong) and then selects one of the toys in it.

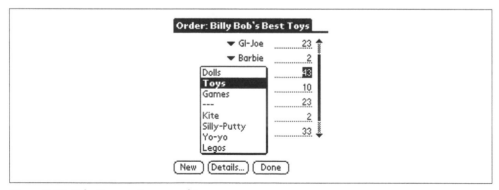

Figure 3-52. Selecting a category and toy

Once an order is complete, the salesperson closes it and moves on to another customer. Orders can be revisited, if necessary. As there is only one order per customer, selecting that customer from the list automatically takes the user back to the order.

Ideally, a customer should be able to have more than one order associated with the Customer form. In a real-life application, we would certainly add that functionality. For the purposes of this book, however, the extra programming doesn't add much new to our explanation of the Palm OS. We leave it as an additional exercise for eager readers.

Another way to add items to an order

Because this is the crucial form in the application, it is important to make the process of order entry as quick and easy as possible. Certainly the salesperson can simply select the New command button and a new item will be added to the screen. One of the ways to make our user's job easier is to make items easier to add. To this end, we provide a hidden feature. If nothing is selected in the order and the user writes in the number field, we immediately provide a new item in the order with that number filled in the number field (see Figure 3-53).

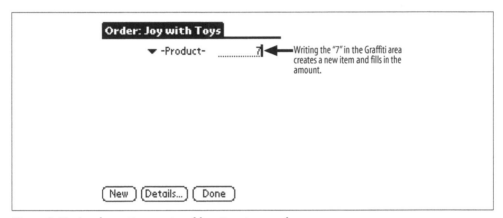

Figure 3-53. An alternative way to add an item to an order

 A really slick design on a device with a bar code scanner would be to add UPC support. Then our salesperson could simply scan in the UPC tags of items the customer wants in the order.

Modifying an item in an order

The user can modify an item by tapping on the part of it that needs changing. If the toy is wrong, a new toy can be selected.

Adding duplicate items to an order

While our list of toys is relatively small, we can imagine a situation where the salesperson has a huge inventory from which to choose. Whenever a list is long enough, it raises the possibility of duplicate items being ordered. This raises a design issue for our application. We decided that the correct design would assume that duplicate entries were either errors or intended as amendments to the original entry. We designed our application accordingly and the user sees the dialog box shown in Figure 3-54 if a duplicate item is added to an order.

Figure 3-54. Dialog box shown for a duplicate product

Notice also that we tell the user what item is duplicated and give the choice of canceling the item or adding more of the item to the original. If the choice is to add to the existing order, we correctly add in the new amount.

Deleting an item in an order

Deleting the item can be done in two ways. The quick way is to select Delete Item in the Record menu (see Figure 3-55).

Figure 3-55. Deleting from the Record menu

If the user failed to first select an item, we give a dialog box reminder prompting an item's selection (Figure 3-56). Otherwise, we show the user a confirmation dialog box just to make sure the delete request was valid.

It's difficult to say whether it's better to require a user to constantly confirm deletion requests or to allow the accidental deletion of items. Two points that drove our decision were the smallness of the Palm screen and the real likelihood that the user would be mobile when selecting items. Remember, there are only a couple of pixels of space between Delete Customer and Delete Item in the Record menu. If you give the user no warning before deleting an item, you can easily turn a mistap into a terrible mistake.

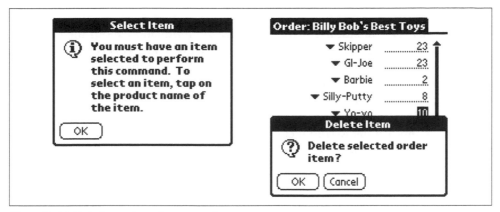

Figure 3-56. Deleting an item from an order

The user can also enter the Graffiti command and write "D" or select the Delete icon on the Command toolbar to delete an item (see Figure 3-57).

Figure 3-57. Deleting an item from an order using the Command toolbar

Another way to delete an item is by selecting the Details button, which brings up the Details dialog box. A deletion confirmation dialog box is also shown. A fourth way is not to specify a product: when a different row is tapped, an item with no product is removed.

Changing Customer Information

To change information about a customer, the user selects Customer Details in the Record menu (see Figure 3-58). The Delete Customer menu item is used to get rid of the customer entirely. (We talk more about why this information is handled here in "Design Trade-offs in the Sample Application," later in this chapter.)

There are two different Details forms: one for the customer and one for the item. They have different user interfaces. When you follow the logic of the Palm UI and look at the number of times a user is likely to do either of these tasks, you will understand our positioning of each of these choices.

Customer details

Customer details is the form in which you change information about the customer or, secondarily, delete the customer entirely (see Figure 3-58). This is not something we commonly expect the user to want to do. Indeed, this is information that is primarily entered and maintained on the desktop. We allow editing to give the user flexibility, not because we think this form will be edited very often. The user is more likely to look at this form to get the customer's telephone number than to change it. As access is through the Record menu, this form is difficult to get to, and it may be hard for the user to remember its location. This is OK if it allows better access for a more frequent activity. It does—to the Item details form.

Figure 3-58. Customer information

Order details

Every customer has a detail screen associated with the order, as well. In this form, the user can do three things (from most frequent to least):

- Delete the item from the order.
- Change the quantity of the item being ordered.
- Change the type of item being ordered.

The activity most likely to occur is the deletion of an item because the item amount or type can also be changed in the order itself (see Figure 3-59). As this is a more common activity than viewing information about the customer, this form is easier to get to for the user.

Deleting the Customer

If the user selects the Delete Customer menu item, a confirmation dialog box is shown (see Figure 3-60). We provide the user with an option to archive the customer information on the PC, as opposed to deleting it completely from both the handheld and the PC.

Figure 3-59. The Item details screen

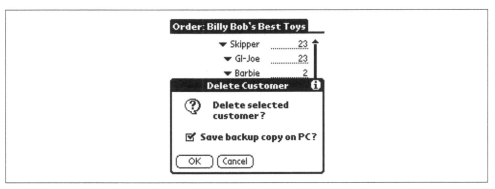

Figure 3-60. Deleting a customer

Beaming the Customer

The user can also beam information about a single user. Selecting the Beam Customer menu item takes care of this. On 4.0 OS devices we display a Send Customer menu item as well (see Figure 3-61 for a comparison).

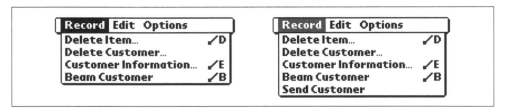

Figure 3-61. The Record menu on 3.0 and 4.0 devices

Edit and Options Menus

Last, but not least, we offer Edit and Options menus in our application with the standard Graffiti shortcuts (see Figure 3-62).

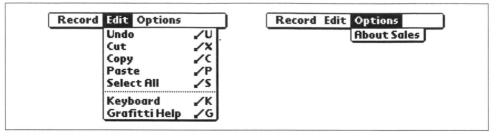

Figure 3-62. Sales application Edit and Options menus

Designing the Sales Application

Now you have seen the application in its final form. We have also discussed some of the design decisions that we had to make while creating the various forms and dialog boxes. There were other decisions, however, that occurred even before the intricate details of each form could be decided. Our very first task was to prototype the application.

Clarify the Tasks

Our prototype design was a mock-up of the basic views that we wanted to have in the application. We came up with those views by listing the actions we wanted the user to be able to do and the order and frequency in which we thought they would be used. Our strategy was to optimize the application so that the more frequent the action, the fewer steps it took to complete. We also wanted to emulate the design of the built-in applications wherever possible.

The Start Screen

The first and most important view to create is the start screen—what your user sees when the application is launched. In the Sales application, the place to start seemed straightforward—with a list of the salesperson's customers. This is a list that can be modified on the handheld, but would ordinarily be created on the desktop. The desktop application should be clever about culling customers from the list if the salesperson isn't visiting them on this trip. It might also want to display the customers either alphabetically or by visit (as the salesperson prefers).

Design Trade-offs in the Sample Application

As with any design, we made some modifications that changed the look and functionality of this application. We think it will be useful to you to explain how we made these decisions.

Adding items to an order

There are a couple of things to notice about the design that we ended up with for this action (see Figure 3-63). When the user taps on the customer name, an order form immediately presents itself. As this is the most common action, we focused on minimizing the steps necessary to complete it. In our final design, we managed to eliminate one of the steps required to take an order. Look at the two possible designs in Figure 3-63, and you will see where we saved a step. The example on the left requires the user to first select the customer name and then tap the New Order button below the list (two actions). The example on the right brings the order forward with one fewer action.

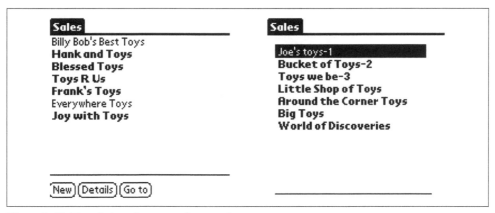

Figure 3-63. Two designs for new order creation

The trade-off here affects two things. We can make an order easier to create (our solution) or make customers easier to create and edit. For us the choice is obvious; we assume that the salesperson rarely adds new customers or modifies old ones. This is the standard list of customers that our user always deals with when selling toys. In a world where customers came and went more often, we might have chosen differently.

Where to put customer information

The next design issue we tackled was how the user accesses, modifies, and deletes customer information. Menu items or buttons could go either in the Customer list or in the Order form. Both choices carry their own sets of advantages and disadvantages. Before showing you the logic of our choices, back up and look again at what we want the user of the Palm device to be able to do:

- Create a new customer.
- Beam or send a customer list.
- Beam or send a single customer.
- Modify a customer.
- Delete a customer.

In a desktop application, we are certain that all of these activities would be put in the same menu. On the handheld, we weren't so sure they should be kept together. After some consideration, we chose to put creating a new customer and beaming a customer list in the Customer list form because these are the only two general customer items. Every other action has to do with a particular customer, whether that is creating an order, changing the customer's information, or deleting the information from the unit.

Creating a new customer

Clearly, the time when a user is going to create a new customer is in the Customer list. The right user interface for this is a menu item, not a button. This is an infrequent action, so we don't want to waste valuable screen real estate with a button for it. In our solution, getting to the Customer Information form (where new customers can be added) takes three taps: one to display the menu bar, one to choose the Customer menu, and one to select the New Customer menu item. This is a reasonable number of steps for such an infrequent action.

Beaming or sending a list of customers

Our users might share customers with each other; we wanted to give them an easy way of sending customer information to each other (we chose not to support beaming orders, though). The menu item was our way of doing this. It takes three taps to accomplish this task.

Deleting a customer

You could place this item in the Customer list form or in the Order details form. If you put it in the menu of the Customer list form, as we did in an earlier version of this application, you need a way for the user to select which customer to delete. The user selects Delete Customer from the Customer menu and a dialog box is displayed with a list of customers from which the user can select one to delete.

However, there's a faster way that requires fewer taps (and no new list picks). Within the Palm UI model, you commonly delete an item while you are viewing it (for example, in the built-in Address and Memo Pad applications as shown in Figure 3-64). Notice that you start with a list of items and select one to display it. Only at this point can you use a Record menu item to delete the name or memo you are viewing.

Likewise, in our application the customer is selected from a list and then, while viewing the order form, the user can delete that client.

A desktop application would not be designed this way. Single-clicking on a customer from the list would select it. At that point, the Delete menu item would delete it, while the Open menu item (or, as a shortcut, a double-click) would open the Order form for the customer. However, the Palm OS is not a desktop OS.

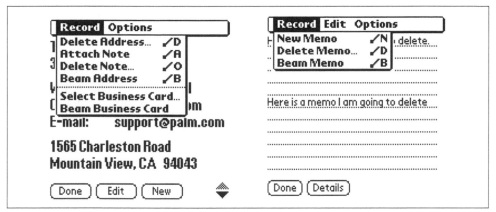

Figure 3-64. How the built-in Address and Memo Pad applications handle actions

 In the first edition, we went on to say here that "Double-taps aren't part of the idiom. Users of a Palm OS device expect a single tap to make an action occur." Well things have changed a bit with OS 3.5. While editing an item like a string of text, single tap now means insert cursor; double tap means select word; and triple tap means select line. How does this affect your UI decisions? While text is multi-tappable, applications are still usually navigated with single taps. For now, while not manipulating text, single tapping should still make actions occur.

You might ask why this model has been adopted. The design makes sense when you realize that the initial items in the startup list are "hot." If you touch them, something happens immediately to switch you to another form. The Palm model is attractive because it cuts down on the number of steps required to complete the most common actions. Each of these very common actions takes a smaller number of steps because list items are hot:

- Viewing a name in the Address application requires pushing the built-in Address button and tapping the name in the list.

- Opening a memo requires pushing the built-in Memo Pad button and tapping the appropriate memo.

- Creating a new order for a customer requires opening the application and tapping a customer's name.

Designing for a Small Screen

One of the biggest challenges you face as a handheld application designer is how to fit data in the screen space on a Palm device. In the Sales application, this challenge happens when we are trying to figure out the right way to select a toy. We assume that there are more toys than would fit on one list on the screen. One approach might have been to have one long scrolling list—the least favorable solution. Toys, like many other types of items, naturally fall into obvious groups. We chose to take advantage of this by first putting the toys into categories.

Table 3-4 contains three ways that we could have organized the items. Our solution was to go with a category organization. This makes things like special sales promotional items easy to handle. A fast-food restaurant might use a similar approach for taking orders. In both cases, the customer is going to go through categories in certain obvious groupings.

Organizing things alphabetically is another possibility, but one that doesn't make as much sense for our application. Neither the customer nor the salesperson is likely to think about the toys in this way.

Organizing the items by number might have been a good choice from the salesperson's point of view. It is not uncommon to memorize part numbers of items you work with all the time; however, where this organization strategy breaks down is from the customer's point of view. The customer is not necessarily going to request items by number. We imagine the customer thinks in terms of the store's shelves that are themselves organized by category. Our strategy is to match the customer's organizational model. Doing so minimizes the number of steps required to add an item to the order (less category switching).

Table 3-4. Ways of categorizing toys

By category	Alphabetically	By item number
Games	**A–C**	**001–99**
Acquire	Aardvark Arnie	1–Aardvark Arnie
Mousetrap	Absolute Terror Tim	2–Jane Sit and Spit
Monsterwalk	Acquire	3–Pretty Patty
Siege Towers	Chubby Bunny	4–Zebra with Baby
Dolls	**D–H**	**100–199**
Aardvark Arnie	Glow in the Dark Pumpkin	101–Marbles by the 100s
Jane, Sit and Spit	Halloween Princess	102–Ball and Jacks
Zebra with Baby	Happy Bunny PlayAlong	104–Glowing Glop
Action Figures	**I–P**	**200–299**
Absolute Terror Tim	Jane, Sit and Spit	200–Siege Towers
Chubby Bunny	Monsterwalk	201–Acquire
Daredevil Dan	Mousetrap	202–Moustrap
Sissy Sunny	Pretty Patty	203–Monsterwalk
Promotional	**Q–Z**	**900–999**
Glow in the Dark Pumpkin	Siege Towers	900–Glow in the Dark Pumpkin
Halloween Princess	Sissy Sunny	901–Halloween Princess
Halloween Pirate	Zooming Eyes	903–Happy Bunny PlayAlong

Designing the Databases

Once you have figured out how to organize the data, your next big decision is to determine the number of databases you should use. We settled on four databases in the Sales application; they are customers, products, orders, and categories.

Customers

The customer database contains the information about the customers. Each customer record contains five items:

Customer ID
> This is a unique customer code assigned at corporate headquarters. If a new customer is created on the handheld, it is assigned a temporary negative customer ID. Corporate headquarters is responsible for assigning a permanent ID after a HotSync.

Name, Address, City, and Phone
> These are each strings.

The order in the database is the order in which they are displayed in the list. New customers are added at the beginning. There are at least two possible ways to reasonably organize the customer database—alphabetically or by visit order (the first name is the first customer the salesperson visits, the second name is the second visit, and so on).

Products

The product database contains information about each of the toys that can be ordered by the customer. Each product record contains:

Product ID
> This is an integer, assigned by corporate headquarters.

Price
> This is a number; a cent amount that we can store as an integer rather than as a floating point number of dollars.

Name
> This is a string.

Category number
> This is a number. It is a value from 0 to 15 used as an index into the category database. Instead of storing the category number as a separate piece of data directly in the record, we use the category feature of the database manager to store it. Doing so saves a small amount of space and gives us a pedagogical excuse to discuss this feature of databases.

Orders

The order database contains records for each of the salesperson's orders. The order database does not contain records for customers with no orders. Each order record contains:

Customer ID
> This is included in order to match a customer to an order.

Number of items ordered
> This is an integer. It is the quantity of each item that was ordered.

Items
> This is an array of items where each item contains a product ID and a quantity.

We considered having the customer's order be part of the customer database, but decided to separate them as a precursor to providing multiple orders for each customer in the future.

Categories

There's a Category UI that we don't implement in the Sales application. It is inappropriate to our application because it is a mechanism for allowing the storing of editable category names. The Category UI displays categories at the top-right and items are stored within these categories. The Category UI provides a mechanism for editing the category names. This is the feature we wish to restrict in our application—products come from the desktop and are unchangeable.

We didn't want to hardcode the category names into the application either, as product lists have been known to change. We chose to store the information in the application info block of the products database instead. This way we can modify it during a sync.

The categories are stored sequentially as null-terminated strings. The order of the categories matches the category numbers used in the products database—record 0 of this database contains the name of category 0. For example, if we want to know the name of category 4, we go to the fifth record in the category database.

Designing the Conduit

A conduit is a desktop application made in a desktop development environment. It uses HotSync synchronization to connect the desktop to the handheld. Conduits are responsible for the transfer of data to and from the handheld and the desktop. The user views the data using some application (a spreadsheet, for example, for viewing expense report items). The conduit needs to make sure that this desktop application has the data it needs to handle processor-intensive tasks. Before looking at the design of the Sales application conduit, let's examine this issue of off-loading processor-intensive tasks.

Processor-Intensive Tasks

Here is another design rule to remember: use the conduit to transfer the data, moving processor-intensive tasks onto the PC and off of the handheld. If you can't move tasks, you should almost always get rid of them.

Palm devices are noted for being both fast and cheap—two of the key features that have made them so popular. One of the reasons they are cheap is they have little bitty processors that don't have much horsepower. Your job as a good application designer is to avoid taxing the handheld's processing abilities. Don't turn it into a slow device—there are already plenty of those around. This means that you may end up making design decisions about your database that don't make sense from a desktop database designer's point of view, but do make sense when you take into account the desktop's superior processing abilities. Here is an example.

We were involved in porting an application from another handheld platform (with a fast processor) to the Palm platform. This is an application that keeps track of a bunch of vending machines: when they need filling, what products go in what slots, how much money is collected, and so on. The Account screen provides a summary of the machines that belong in that account (an account could have many machines or just a few). The Machine screen provides a summary of items for that particular machine. In the original platform, as we entered an Account screen at runtime, we'd run through the database, summarizing and totalling (for instance, we'd total how many machines needed to be serviced for an account, along with how many total machines an account had).

When we began our port of the application to the Palm platform, this way of handling the task no longer made sense. The time hit the user would endure when opening a Machine or Account screen was too long. So we bit the bullet and moved the summarizing and totalling to the desktop application. This information is now stored in the account database. The price we had to pay is duplicate data in every account (upping by a small amount the size of our databases). It was worth it, however, to have a zippy Account screen that instantly displayed information about machines.

The built-in Expense application provides another useful example. Let's approach the issue from the point of view of a question.

Q: *What feature is missing from the Expense application?*

A: There is no expense total.

Why? you might ask. We think it is to avoid an unnecessary processing task that doesn't really provide the user with necessary information. Totals are things a user will care about back at the office when sitting calmly at a desktop computer, not when he is rushing from a cab through an airport to catch a flight.

The moral of the story is not to make users pay for processor-intensive tasks if there is any way to avoid it. Sometimes that means keeping functionality, but moving the processing elsewhere (as in our ported vending machine application); sometimes that means not offering a feature in the first place (as in the Expense application with no total).

 Tasks that may be fast on the handheld, but can't be implemented well for other reasons should also be moved to the desktop. For example, think of subtotalling a list of figures in an expense report. This task is easy to do on a big screen using a mouse and a combination of keys to select and total the figures. It is much harder to do on a tiny screen (you can't see many of the items at one time), where data is close together (it's easy to hit the wrong figure), and selecting is complex (items are hot and tapping does something). Desktop applications and handheld ones should complement each other and extend functionality in ways that neither could handle alone—they should not duplicate features.

Design of the Sales Application Conduit

Our Sales application conduit handles the following tasks during a HotSync:

- Opening and closing the sales, customer, and product databases on the Palm device
- Iterating through the records in the databases on the handheld
- Uploading customer orders from the handheld to the desktop
- Downloading the product database from the desktop to the handheld
- Comparing customer records so that only modified records are synced
- Appropriately adding, deleting, and modifying customer records on the handheld and on the desktop
- Converting the data in the application's database records to a text-delimited file that can be read into a database on the desktop computer.

The conduit also needs to be installed and uninstalled. With a commercial application, this process should be handled automatically, invisible from the user.

 Use an installer program to automate the installation and uninstallation of the conduit; (we tell you about this in "Registering and Unregistering" in Chapter 14).

Design Summary

By now, you should have a good feel for how to design a Palm application and conduit. We showed you the Palm OS UI objects and a range of applications in which they are implemented. We talked about important placement and performance rules and showed you some well-designed forms, dialog boxes, and alerts. Last of all, we covered the Sales sample application that we will be building over the course of this book. We discussed the design decisions we faced and the choices that we made. We tried wherever possible to remember these important rules for designing for a Palm application:

Keep it clean
> Minimize screen clutter by hiding infrequent actions.

Keep it fast
> Minimize the number of taps to complete frequent actions (the 80/20 rule).

Make it easy
> Provide command buttons for common multistep activities.

Be clever
> Take advantage of the unique aspects of your application to make for a better user experience.

Now it's time to take everything you have learned and apply it. It's time to write some code.

## PART II

Programming a Palm Application

In this chapter:
- POSE
- CodeWarrior
- PRC-Tools
- Installing a PRC on the Handheld
- Installing PRC on POSE
- Modifying the Sample Application

CHAPTER 4
Tutorial

You have learned all about development environments, design issues, and the Palm platform and now it's time to put all that knowledge to work. With our help, you are going to create, build, and download a simple Palm OS application. The good and bad news is that we are going to walk you through this process step by step. It's good news because a good programmer, new to the platform, can often use just this type of help. It's bad news because it involves telling you how to use a bunch of different tools and development environments that have their own release cycles that will most likely be obsolete within six months.

The software tools discussed here are those current as of mid-2001. Each discussion of a tool will include its version number. As newer versions of tools are made and installation procedures change, we'll update the relevant sections of this chapter online.

Thus, the first thing you should do before reading the printed version of this chapter is to go to our web site (*http://www.calliopeinc.com/palmprog2/*) to see whether there are newer instructions.

There are two things you need to do in this chapter:

1. Read about how to install and run the Palm OS Emulator (POSE) and how to run your application on it.

2. Choose an environment and read our tutorial for it. The two development environments you can choose between are CodeWarrior and PRC-Tools. Read the material in that tutorial and feel free to ignore the other. Each tells you how to:

   - Build an executable Palm application (a PRC file)
   - Make changes to the application (in both the source code and the resources)
   - Rebuild the application

The development platforms that are covered in our discussion of POSE and each tutorial are shown in Table 4-1.

Table 4-1. Development tools and platforms

	Windows 95/NT	Mac OS	Unix
POSE	✓	✓	✓
CodeWarrior	✓	✓	
PRC-Tools	✓	✓ (Mac OS X)	✓

We will always cover each platform in the following order: Windows, Mac OS, and Unix. This chapter won't cover how to use the debuggers from these environments; that's covered in Chapter 7.

POSE

POSE emulates the hardware of a number of different Palm OS devices: Pilot 1000, Pilot 5000, Palm III, Palm IIIx, Palm V, Palm Vx, Palm VII, Palm VIIx, Palm IIIc, Palm m500, Palm m505, Symbol 1700, Handspring Visor, Handspring Prism, HandEra TRGPro, and HandEra 330.

Everybody should read and follow the instructions for POSE. First, we will show you how to install it, then how to run it. We'll be discussing POSE Version 3.2.

Getting and Installing POSE

The first thing to do is to download and install POSE. The instructions are slightly different for Unix, because you need to build it from the sources.

On Windows and Mac OS you can download the latest version of POSE from *http://www.palmos.com/dev/tech/tools/emulator/*.

On Unix, things are a bit more complicated. You'll need to build POSE from the source code. Before you can do this you need to get the FLTK toolkit.

1. Download the FLTK toolkit (*fltk-1.0.11-source.tar.gz*) from *http://www.fltk.org*.

2. Uncompress it:

   ```
   tar -zxf fltk-1.0.11-source.tar.gz
   ```

3. Build FLTK:

   ```
   cd fltk-1.0.11
   ./configure
   make
   make install
   ```

4. Download POSE at *http://www.palmos.com/dev/tech/tools/emulator/emulator-src-32.tar.gz*.

5. Extract the sources:

   ```
   tar -zxf emulator-src-32.tar.gz
   ```

6. Configure and build the POSE sources (instructions are in the file, *Docs/_Building.txt*):

```
cd Emulator_Src_3.2/BuildUnix
./configure
make
```

7. Install POSE into */usr/local/bin/pose*:

```
make install
```

Emulator Skins

You'll also want to install Emulator Skins for your platform. Skins are pictures of actual devices used to provide a more faithful representation of the device. Here are the steps:

1. Download the latest Emulator Skins file and uncompress it. It'll create a directory named something like *Skins 1.7*.

2. Move that *Skins 1.7* directory into the proper place to ensure that POSE finds the skins when it needs them:

Windows and Mac OS
> Make a directory within the POSE directory called *Skins*. Move the *Skins 1.7* directory into this newly created *Skins* directory. POSE looks for its skins recursively within the *Skins* directory.

Unix
> Create a *Skins* directory in your home directory, and place the *Skins 1.7* directory within that newly created directory.

POSE and ROM Images

You can get ROM images for POSE from the Internet or from an actual device.

Palm-branded product ROMs require registration and signed license agreements. You can register at *http://www.palmos.com/dev/*.

Handspring ROMs require registration and faxed license agreements. You can get further information from *http://www.handspring.com/developers/*.

Retrieving ROM from a Handheld

Before you get a copy of your particular handheld's ROM, make sure that POSE can use that type. If the handheld from which you are obtaining the ROM isn't in the earlier list, POSE will refuse to use the resulting ROM image.

To retrieve a ROM image you need to do a couple of things. First, you'll need to install the ROM Transfer application (part of the POSE distribution) onto your handheld using the standard desktop installation procedure. You will then see the form shown in Figure 4-1 when you run the application on your device.

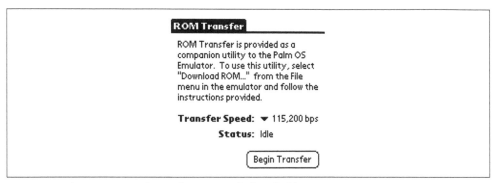

Figure 4-1. The ROM Transfer application on the handheld

Follow the instructions on the device and tap the Begin Transfer button. Now, you'll need to initiate the process on the desktop as well. (See the following instructions for the appropriate platform.)

In Windows:

1. Run Palm OS Emulator. You'll see the initial dialog box (see Figure 4-2).

2. Click on the Download button to display the Transfer ROM dialog box shown in Figure 4-3.

3. Follow the directions in this dialog box.

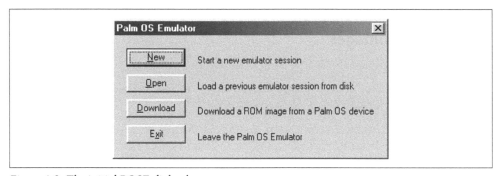

Figure 4-2. The initial POSE dialog box

In Mac OS, POSE transfers ROMs using a serial connection. Since modern Mac OS computers don't have serial ports, you'll need either:

- A serial PC card (like those available from *http://www.socketcom.com*).

- A USB-serial adapter (like the Keyspan USB PDA Adapter from *http://www.keyspan.com*). The PalmConnect® USB-serial adapter works only with the HotSync application, and can't be used by POSE.

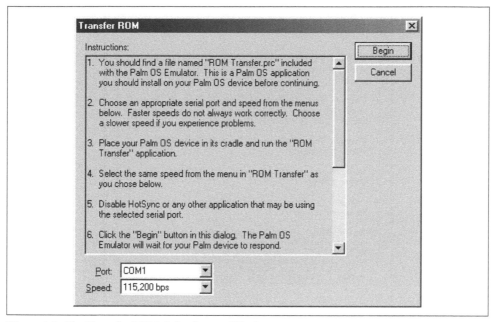

Figure 4-3. The Transfer ROM dialog box on Windows

Now do the following:

1. Run Palm OS Emulator on your Macintosh. You'll see the New Session dialog box (see Figure 4-4). Press Cancel.

2. Choose Transfer ROM from the File menu. The Transfer ROM dialog box (shown in Figure 4-5) will describe all the steps needed to transfer the ROM.

Figure 4-4. The initial dialog box shown on Mac OS

In Unix:

1. Run the Emulator and you'll see the initial POSE window.

2. Right-click on the window to display a menu. From that menu, choose Transfer ROM. Follow the instructions shown in the resulting Transfer ROM dialog box.

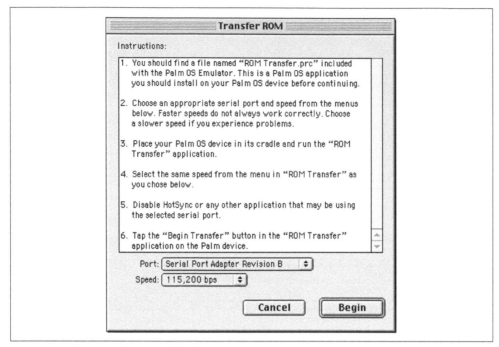

Figure 4-5. The Transfer ROM dialog box on Mac OS

Creating a New POSE Session

Now that you've downloaded a ROM image you can use it.

1. Close Palm OS Emulator, and reopen it.

2. Create a New Session (Windows and Mac OS: click the New button; Unix: right-click and choose New).

   You'll see the New Session dialog box (see Figure 4-6). From this dialog box, you'll need to change the ROM file (change to the one you just downloaded). The Device pop up will change automatically to reflect the devices for which this ROM is valid. The Skin is a picture of the actual device (though all that it affects is the visual look of the Emulator).

3. Choose a RAM Size of 2048K (you don't want the size larger than actual devices you'll be targeting).

4. Tap OK, and the Emulator will display a picture of a Palm device that is booting up. Then it will show the main screen (see Figure 4-7).

5. You can tap on the screen with your cursor just as you would with a stylus. Tap on the hardware buttons as well. You can enter characters with both the Graffiti system, and with the desktop's keyboard.

In Windows and Unix the menu for POSE is available by right-clicking on the POSE window. On the Macintosh the menus are in the menu bar.

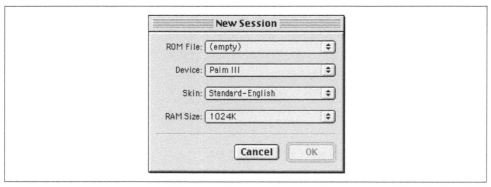

Figure 4-6. The New Session dialog box

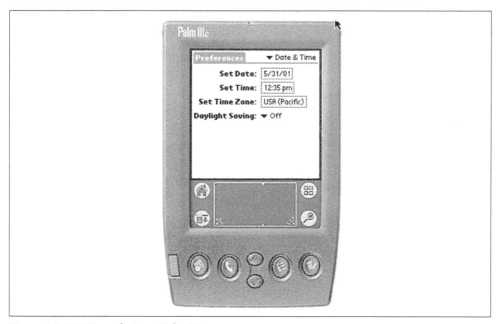

Figure 4-7. POSE emulating a Palm IIIc

Now it is time to choose which tutorial you wish to read through. This first one is for CodeWarrior (Windows, Mac OS). If you'll be using PRC-Tools, skip to "PRC-Tools" on page 119.

CodeWarrior

This first tutorial goes through CodeWarrior. As most Palm OS application development takes place in CodeWarrior, it seemed like a good place to start. Here is what the tutorial describes:

- What CodeWarrior includes (which tools you install and use)

- How to install and use the newest 4.0 SDK from Palm with CodeWarrior
- How to install a PilRC plug-in
- How to use some stationery (OReilly Starter) that we provide, which makes creating a new project much easier
- The various settings in CodeWarrior
- Creating a new project
- Making a PRC file
- A quick walkthrough of the CodeWarrior IDE
- Using Constructor to create resources

What CodeWarrior Includes

We're discussing CodeWarrior for Palm OS Platform 7.0, the current release in mid-2001. When you install CodeWarrior, it will put these tools on your computer:

CodeWarrior IDE
> This is a project-based Integrated Development Environment (IDE).

Constructor for Palm OS
> This is a graphical resource editor.

Palm OS Emulator (3.0a7)
> This is not the latest version of POSE; see "Installing PRC on POSE" later in this chapter for information on getting the latest version.

Palm OS 3.5 SDK
> This software development kit (SDK) includes header files, libraries, examples, and documentation. It can be used to create applications that run on any earlier version of the OS as well. It can't be used, however, to access any 4.0-specific APIs (see the next section, "Installing 4.0 SDK," for information).
>
> The header files and libraries are kept in *Metrowerks\CodeWarrior for Palm OS Platform 7.0\Palm OS 3.5 Support*.

Palm OS 3.5 SDK Stationery
> These are the starting points of projects for creating applications. These stationery projects are kept in *Metrowerks\CodeWarrior for Palm OS Platform 7.0\ Stationery\Palm OS 3.5*.

Handspring SDK
> A separate SDK includes the headers and documentation for using Handspring-specific APIs.

If you do a Thrill Seekers install of CodeWarrior, it'll also install the PilRC plug-in. This allows you to use PilRC files to specify your resources. However, the version of the plug-in is 2.6, which is not the latest. See the later section "Installing PilRC Plug-in," for information on how to get the latest version.

Installing 4.0 SDK

In order to use 4.0-specific APIs, you need to use the 4.0 SDK. As with the other SDKs, you can always use the 4.0 SDK to develop applications that will work with an earlier OS—just don't use the new 4.0 APIs. In general, you'll want to use the latest SDK available.

The 4.0 SDK can be downloaded from the Palm OS web site: *http://www.palmos.com/dev/tech/tools/sdk40.html*.

For Windows or Mac OS, the SDK is available as an executable installer. It installs the SDK in the appropriate locations within the CodeWarrior folder.

Installing additional examples

While the SDK will include the minimum necessary to compile projects (headers, libraries, and updated tools), you'll also want to have the example files as well as the documentation. To get these you need to download the documentation and examples from Palm's web site (*http://www.palmos.com/dev/*). Once you have done so, follow these steps:

1. Uncompress the documentation and move it to the *Palm Documentation* folder. Name it *Palm OS 4.l0 Docs*.
2. Uncompress the examples folder and move it to the *CodeWarrior Examples* folder. Name it *Palm OS 4.0 SDK Examples*.

The naming conventions for the 4.0 SDK have changed slightly from that used by previous SDKs. Rather than putting the SDK version number as part of the folder name, the folder name is now generic. As things stood, when a new SDK came out, projects had to be modified in order to reflect the new folder name. By using a generic name, future changes to new SDKs are as simple as removing the old folder and replacing it with a new one.

The headers and libraries in a subfolder of the CodeWarrior folder called *Palm OS Support*. The stationery is kept in a *Palm OS Application* subfolder within the *Stationery* folder.

Installing PilRC Plug-in

We will be using PilRC to create resources in this book. We use PilRC rather than Constructor because:

- *.rcp* text files can easily be displayed in the book.
- They are cross-platform. They work with both CodeWarrior (Mac OS and Windows) and with PRC-Tools.
- We like them—we find it much easier to work with text files. For example, source code control and finding differences between two versions of a file are easier to do with text.

The latest version of the PilRC plug-in can always be downloaded from *http://www. calliopeinc.com/pilrcplugin.html*.

The current version as of this writing is 2.8. (Look on the web site for the most recent version.) Install it by moving it to:

- Mac OS: *Metrowerks CodeWarrior:CodeWarrior Plugins:Compilers*
- Windows: *Metrowerks\CodeWarrior for Palm OS Platform 7.0\Bin\Plugins\ Compiler*

Installing OReilly Stationery

We know our job is to make things as simple as possible for you. As a result, we imagine that when you create a new CodeWarrior project you would like it to be as easy as can be expected. The stationery that ships with CodeWarrior is too complicated for our tastes. We find that using this default stationery as a starting point causes us to spend a fair amount of time removing functionality we don't want before we can even begin adding our own code.

So, presto, we have made life easier. We've created some new, very simple stationery that has the correct structure of a Palm OS application. Of course, it doesn't actually *do* very much, but that way it's easier to use as the basis of a new application. A bonus feature is that our stationery has been set up already to use the PilRC plug-in. You can:

1. Download this stationery from *http://www.calliopeinc.com/stationery.html*.
2. Install it by moving it to *Metrowerks\CodeWarrior for Palm OS Platform 7.0\ Stationery\Palm OS Application* (or *Metrowerks CodeWarrior:(Project Stationery): Palm OS Application for Mac OS*).

CodeWarrior Setup

Now, it is time to set the various settings in CodeWarrior. In order for you to do this, you need to run it. Launch it according to your platform and then continue reading.

In Windows, run CodeWarrior using Start → Program Files → CodeWarrior for Palm OS Platform 7.0 → CodeWarrior IDE. In Mac OS, launch *CodeWarrior IDE 4.1*.

Launching POSE automatically

Changing a couple of settings will make using CodeWarrior much more handy. The first change is to enable CodeWarrior to launch POSE automatically. You need to do the following:

1. Inform CodeWarrior of the location of POSE. Choose Edit → Preferences to open the IDE Preferences dialog box.
2. At the left side, choose the Palm Connection Settings panel (see Figure 4-8). For the Target, select Palm OS Emulator.

---

3. Select Choose to specify the location of POSE. If you'd like CodeWarrior to automatically launch POSE every time CodeWarrior is started, check Always launch emulator.

4. Click OK to dismiss the dialog box.

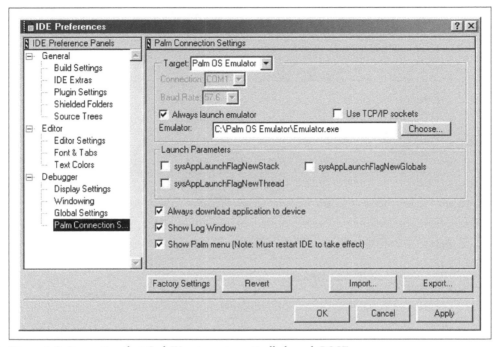

Figure 4-8. Requesting that CodeWarrior automatically launch POSE

If you checked Always launch emulator, then from now on, CodeWarrior will automatically start POSE. If you haven't checked it, you can still cause CodeWarrior to launch POSE by choosing Palm → Launch Emulator.

Multifile searching

It's also very handy to set up CodeWarrior's multifile search to allow easy searching of the headers and Palm OS examples.

1. Select the Multifile Search dialog box with the Search → Find in Files menu item.

2. Click on the In Files project tab.

3. Add the 4.0 SDK header files to the list of files to search by dragging the *Palm OS Support* folder (from Windows Explorer or the Finder) to the File Set area of the dialog box (see Figure 4-9).

4. Click the Save This Set button and name the set *Palm 4.0 Includes* (Figure 4-10).

5. In a similar fashion, create a new file set containing the contents of the *Palm OS 4.0 Examples* folder. Name it *Palm 4.0 Examples*.

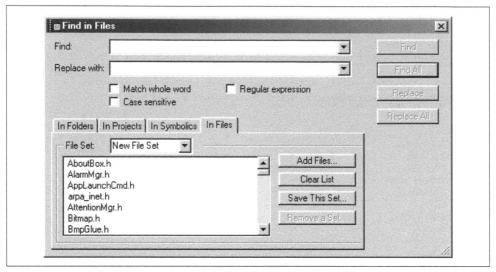

Figure 4-9. Find in Files dialog box with Palm OS Support files dragged in

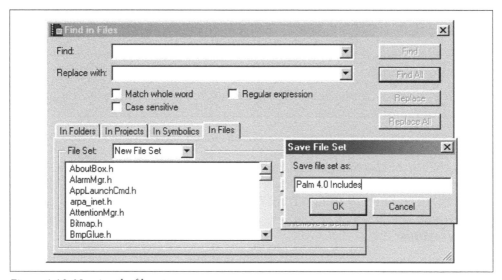

Figure 4-10. Naming the file set

Once you've created these file sets, it'll be easy to search for text in the headers, or examples by using the Find in Files dialog box and choosing the appropriate file set.

Creating a New Project

To create a new project in CodeWarrior:

1. Choose File → New.
2. Select Palm OS Application from the Project tab.

3. Give your project a name, and a location (see Figure 4-11). Then, click OK.

   If Palm OS Application Stationery doesn't appear in the list of projects, you haven't installed the 4.0 SDK. (See "Installing 4.0 SDK" earlier in this chapter for instructions.)

4. Select OReillyStarter as the project stationery (see Figure 4-12). Click OK; CodeWarrior will duplicate the project, along with all the files in the project and name it *MyProject*.

   If OReillyStarter doesn't appear in the list of stationery, you haven't installed it. (See the earlier section, "Installing OReilly Stationery," for instructions.)

5. Once you've created the new project, the project window will be displayed (see Figure 4-13).

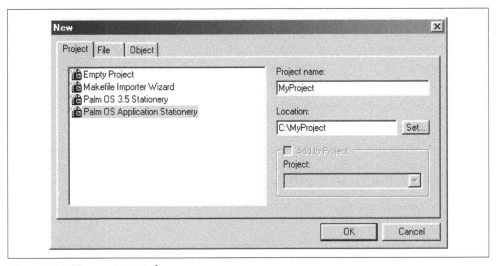

Figure 4-11. New project window

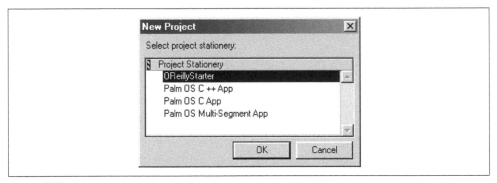

Figure 4-12. Selecting the project stationery

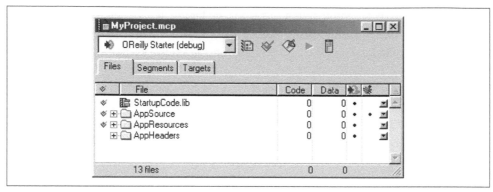

Figure 4-13. The MyProject window

Making a PRC

Now that you have CodeWarrior up and running and a brand new skeleton project to work with, it is time to practice making the project. CodeWarrior will do the following when you select Project → Make:

- Compile all needed source files and link them together.
- Use PilRC to compile the resource file.
- Run the PalmRez PostLinker to combine the code and the resources into a PRC file. If you have installed and used the *OReilly Stationery* it creates a PRC named *OreillyStarter.prc* in the (*CW Debug*) directory.

That's it—you should now have a working project and a PRC file that you can download to a device.

If you already know how to use CodeWarrior or you want to continue straightaway with the tutorial, go directly to "Installing a PRC on the Handheld" on page 128.

The next two sections deal with various settings and tools in CodeWarrior that you can read about now or later as you prefer.

CodeWarrior IDE

We want to tell you a little more about the CodeWarrior IDE. We will just provide a brief introduction to the major parts of the IDE. To get the most out of this very full-featured environment, we recommend reading the documentation, including *Getting Started with Palm OS*, *Targeting Palm OS Platform*, and *IDE User Guide*.

CodeWarrior is project-based, where a project contains one or more targets. A target is a set of files sharing common build settings. A project can contain multiple targets. For example, a project might have a release target and a debug target, each with different build settings.

The Project window

The Files panel of the Project window (see Figure 4-14) displays the files in the project organized into groups. Double-clicking on a group opens that group. Double-clicking on a file opens the file. Table 4-2 shows the columns of information.

Table 4-2. Columns in the CodeWarrior MyProject window

Column	What it is
✅	The checkmark indicates that the file needs to be recompiled.
File	Filename.
Code	Size of the code (if this is a source file and has been compiled).
Data	Size of the data (if the file is a source file and has been compiled).
🔹	The • indicates the file is in the current target.
🔸	The • indicates the file is enabled for source-level debugging.
▼	The header files included by the file (if the file has been compiled).

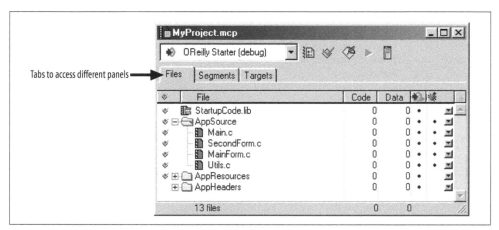

Figure 4-14. The Files panel of the project window

The second panel is the Segments panel (accessed by clicking on the Segments tab). It is used to organize your source files into multiple segments. This is only needed if you have a large application (in which your code exceeds 64 KB). The *Targeting Palm OS Platform* manual discusses how to modify a target to support multiple segments.

The third panel is the Targets panel (click on the Targets tab), which displays all the targets for the project.

At the top left of the project window is a pop up that allows you to change the current target.

The Project Settings dialog box

The Project Settings dialog box sets all the various build options for the current target. You can bring up that dialog box either by tapping on the leftmost button at the top of the project window, or by choosing Edit → *Target* Settings.

There are a number of useful panels in this dialog box. Table 4-3 contains an extremely brief description of how you'll use them when doing Palm OS development.

Table 4-3. CodeWarrior Project Settings panels

Panel name	What it does
Target Settings	This panel controls the name of the target and the location of the final output PRC file.
Access Paths	This panel controls where CodeWarrior will search for include files. If you specify a directory, CodeWarrior will search in that directory, and in any subdirectories.
68K Target	This panel controls the output that the linker creates.
	The filename specified here must match the Mac resource files specified in the PalmRez Post Linker panel.
C/C++ Language	This panel allows you to control exactly how the C and C++ compiler are used. You can turn on the C++ compiler by checking Activate C++ Compiler. The prefix file is CodeWarrior's answer to command-line *#defines*. Specify a prefix file here and it will be automatically included at the very beginning of any C or C++ source file.
PalmRez Post Linker	This panel controls how the PRC file will be built. Here, you specify the name of the PRC file that is generated (output file), along with the type, creator ID, attributes, and database name of the application.

Constructor for Palm OS

Constructor is a graphical resource editor that was originally developed by Metrowerks. It has since been turned over to Palm and is now developed by them. It can be used to create resources graphically when using CodeWarrior (see Figure 4-15). Notice also that it is a separate application that edits resource files (of extension *.rsrc* or *.rsr*). These files can then be added to your project.

If you want to use Constructor you can look at the *Constructor for Palm OS* documentation that's part of the Palm OS SDK. It covers Constructor's use in detail.

At this point you should know everything necessary to start using CodeWarrior for a Palm Project. You should have done the following:

- Created a sample Palm OS simple application using OReilly Stationery
- Compiled it to create a brand new PRC file named *OreillyStarter.prc*

You should also know about CodeWarrior's IDE and the benefits of PilRC versus Constructor.

You are done with CodeWarrior, skip to "Installing a PRC on the Handheld" on page 128. That section is the next step in your tutorial. The following tutorial uses PRC-Tools to duplicate the same steps we just did in the CodeWarrior tutorial.

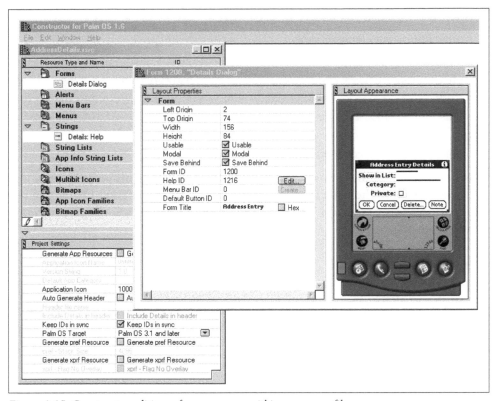

Figure 4-15. Constructor editing a form resource within a resource file

PRC-Tools

This tutorial shows you how to use PRC-Tools to create a simple Palm OS application. It is the second of two possible tutorials that you can read through. The PRC-Tools development environment has a great price (it's free) and it's well loved by many a C programmer. Just like CodeWarrior, we have made sure that you can use it in conjunction with the source code and examples in the rest of the book easily (all the code has been compiled within both environments).

Here is what this PRC-Tools tutorial describes:

- What PRC-Tools includes (which tools you install and use).
- How to install PRC-Tools (this includes instructions first for Windows and then for Unix). *This is by far the most complicated portion of this tutorial.*
- How to use a sample project (OReilly Starter)—a useful starting point.
- How to create a new project.
- How to make a PRC file.

What PRC-Tools Includes

The most important elements are:

GNU Compiler Collection (GCC)
    This compiles C/C++ code to Motorola 68K. It also functions as a linker.

Build-PRC
    This builds a PRC file from the code and the resources.

GDB
    This is a source-level debugger.

This next section of the tutorial deals with installing PRC-Tools on Windows. Use it, or skip ahead to the Unix section ("Installing on Unix" on page 126) if you use that platform. After we cover installation for both platforms, we will deal with creating a project.

Installing on Windows

The official distribution location for PRC-Tools is *http://prc-tools.sourceforget.net*. Our instructions are for installing PRC-Tools 2.1, pre-3, the latest version at the time this book was written. Installing PRC-Tools on Windows requires several steps, which we've outlined in the following sections.

Installing Cygwin shell and utilities

Cygwin is a Unix-like shell and set of commands that runs on Windows. The PRC-Tools relies on Cygwin in order to run.

1. To get Cygwin, go to *http://sources.redhat.com/cygwin/* and download *setup.exe*.

2. Create a directory for *setup.exe* (perhaps *C:\CygwinInstall*). This will also be a local packages directory, in which the many different packages that make up Cygwin will be downloaded.

3. Run *setup.exe*. When it asks the type of install, choose Install from Internet (see Figure 4-16). Go to the next dialog box.

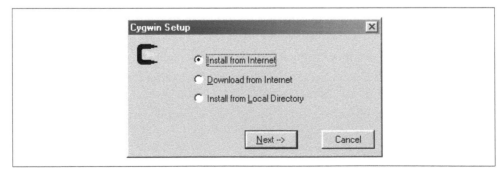

Figure 4-16. The Cygwin type of install

4. When it asks the local package directory, leave it at the default setting (see Figure 4-17). This is the same directory containing *setup.exe*. Go to the next panel.

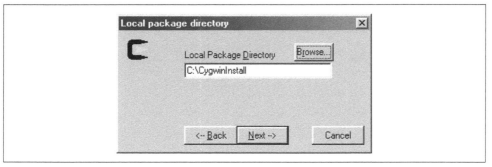

Figure 4-17. Specifying the local package directory

5. When it asks for the root directory, leave it at the default, or choose a different destination (see Figure 4-18). Also, specify DOS as the Default Text File Type. Go to the next dialog box.

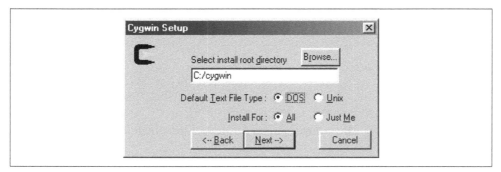

Figure 4-18. Specifying the root directory

6. When it asks about your connection, you'll need to choose appropriate values, depending on whether you're behind a firewall (see Figure 4-19). Go to the next dialog box.

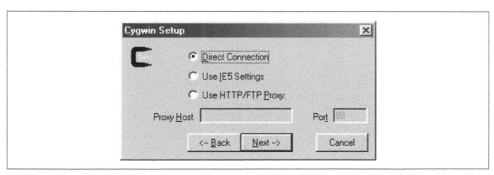

Figure 4-19. Specifying the type of connection

7. When it asks for a download site, choose a close site (see Figure 4-20). Go to the next panel.

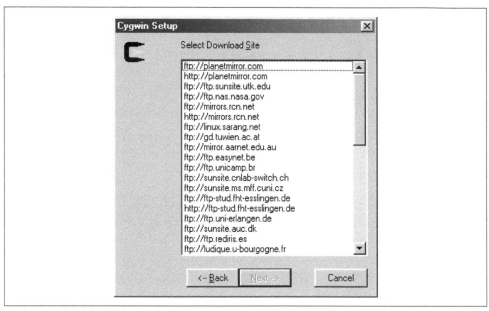

Figure 4-20. Choosing a site from which to download

8. Now it is installation time. When the installer asks which packages to install (see Figure 4-21), your best bet is to just leave it alone. If you'd like a somewhat reduced install (85 MB), however, you can install just the following files:

ash	ctags	gawk	m4	pcre	vim
autoconf	cygrunsrv	gcc	make	regex	w32api
automake	cygwin	gdb	man	sed	which
bash	dejagnu	gperf	mingw	sh-utils	zlib
binutils	diff	grep	mt	tar	
bison	expect	groff	ncurses	tcltk	
bzip2	file	gzip	opengl	termcap	
clear	fileutils	inetutils	openssh	texinfo	
cpio	findutils	less	openssl	textutils	
crypt	flex	login	patch	time	

You can probably get by with even fewer packages, but we haven't tested it with a smaller set. To choose not to install a package, click on the version number until it changes to Skip. Go to the next panel.

9. The Setup application will chug away and install everything you've chosen. When it's complete, a dialog box will appear asking whether you'd like to create a desktop icon and/or add it to the Start menu (see Figure 4-22). At the very least, choose to add it to the Start menu.

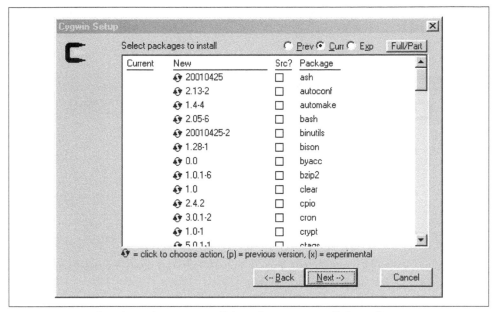

Figure 4-21. Deciding the packages to install (best choice is to install them all)

Figure 4-22. Post-installation options

Installing PRC-Tools

Now that Cygwin itself is installed, you have to install PRC-Tools. There are several steps to this process once again.

1. Create a temporary directory, called *C:\PRCToolsInstall*, and into it download *http://prdownloads.sourceforge.net/prc-tools/prc-tools-2.0.92-cygwin.tar.gz*.

2. Run Cygwin's *setup.exe* one more time (see Figure 4-16).

3. Instead of specifying Install from Internet, choose Install from Local Directory.

4. When prompted to choose a local packages directory, select the directory into which you just downloaded the file (see Figure 4-17).

5. When prompted for the root directory (see Figure 4-18), specify the same thing you chose when you installed Cygwin.

6. When prompted for the packages to install, choose the PRC-Tools package (see Figure 4-23). You may see one garbage item with no package name; it's OK to choose that.

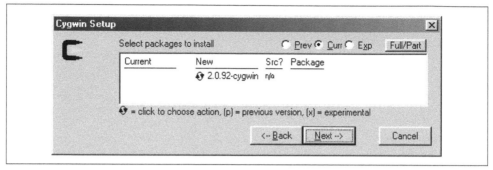

Figure 4-23. Choosing the PRC-Tools package (although the name doesn't show up)

7. Once it's installed, you'll get the choice to add an icon or menu item (see Figure 4-22). It's best to choose neither.

8. Launch Cygwin and fix the two missing symbol links by issuing the following commands:

```
cd /usr/m68k-palmos/lib
ln -s libmf.a libm.a
cd /usr/m68k-palmos/include
ln -s mathf.h math.h
```

Installing the 4.0 SDK

Now that Cygwin and PRC-Tools are installed, you need to install the 4.0 SDK. Here are those steps:

1. Download the 4.0 SDK from Palm's web site, *http://www.palmos.com/dev/tech/tools/sdk40.html*.

2. Uncompress the SDK and run the resulting Palm OS SDK 4.0 Installer.

3. When asked what type of installation, choose "Other Metrowerks CodeWarrior or PRC-Tools installation not listed" (see Figure 4-24).

4. When asked the setup type, choose GCC PRC-Tools Installation (see Figure 4-25).

5. The SDK will include the minimum files necessary to compile projects (headers, libraries, and updated tools). You'll also want to have the example files and documentation. Download and decompress them into convenient locations. You will find these example files at *http://www.palmos.com/dev/tech/tools/sdk40.html*.

6. The PRC-Tools expect to find the SDK in a mountpoint called */PalmDev*. Execute the following command from within Cygwin to establish the mountpoint:

```
mount -f "C:\PalmDev" /PalmDev
```

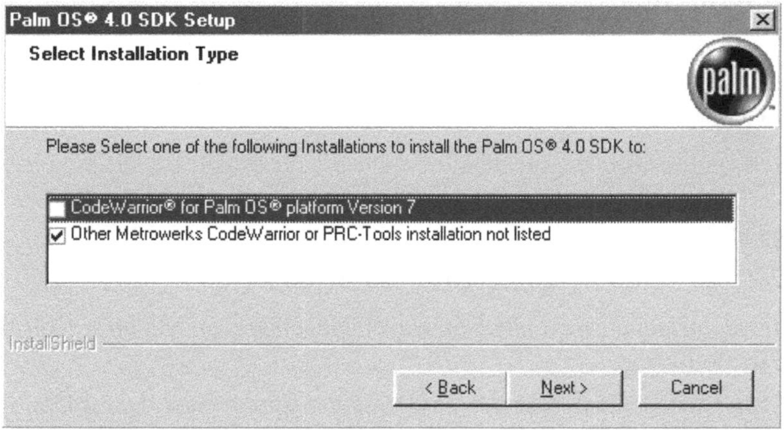

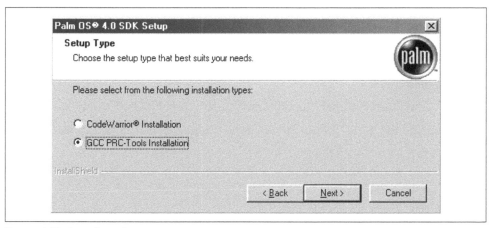

Figure 4-24. Selecting the installation type

Figure 4-25. Specifying the setup type

Installing PilRC

The last piece to install is PilRC. It is fairly easy, requiring only a couple of steps.

1. Install PilRC. The current version is 2.8. Download *pilrc_w32.zip* from *http://www.ardiri.com/index.cfm?redir=palm&cat=pilrc*.

   Uncompress it and move *pilrc-2.8* to *C:\pilrc2.8*.

2. Copy *pilrc.exe* to *C:\cygwin\usr\bin*.

The next section of the tutorial deals with installing PRC-Tools on Unix. If you are using Windows then you can skip ahead to instructions for installing a sample project, found in "Installing OReilly Sample project" on page 127.

Installing on Unix

The official distribution location for PRC-Tools is *http://prc-tools.sourceforge.net*. Our instructions are for installing PRC-Tools 2.1, pre-3, the latest version at the time this was written.

Here are the instructions for installation.

Installing PRC-Tools

The PRC-Tools is the development environment itself.

1. If you are running on an x86 box with Redhat Package Manager (RPM), download the following:

   http://prdownloads.sourceforge.net/prc-tools/prc-tools-2.0.92-1.i386.rpm

   and install it with:

   ```
   rpm -i prc-tools-2.0.92-1.i386.rpm
   ```

2. Otherwise, you'll need to do a build from the source. Download, uncompress, and build from:

   http://prdownloads.sourceforge.net/prc-tools/prc-tools-2.0.92.tar.gz

Installing the 4.0 SDK

The SDK contains the headers and libraries needed for Palm OS development.

1. Download the 4.0 SDK from *http://www.palmos.com/dev/tech/tools/sdk40.html*.

   Put it in a temporary location. The SDK is a compressed tar file.

2. Uncompress the tar file with:

   ```
   tar -zxf sdk40.tar.gz
   ```

3. Install the 4.0 SDK rpm file with:

   ```
   rpm -i palmos-sdk-4.0-1.noarch.rpm
   ```

4. This 4.0 SDK is now installed as */opt/palmdev/sdk-4.0*. If you'd like to make that the default (used if no SDK is specified), execute:

   ```
   cd /opt/palmdev
   ln -s sdk-4.0 sdk
   ```

Installing PilRC

PilRC is the resource compiler, the last piece needed for development.

1. Install PilRC. The current version is 2.8. Download *pilrc_src.tgz* from:

   http://www.ardiri.com/palm/download.cfm?file=pilrc_src.tgz

   Download it to */usr/local/src* (or some other desired location).

2. Uncompress it with:

   ```
   tar -zxf pilrc_src.tgz
   ```

3. The line endings for the files are DOS-style. This can cause problems for compilers. Fix it by changing the files to Unix-style line endings with this script:

```
cd pilrc-2.8
for fnam in *.*
do
  tr -d '\r' < $fnam > /tmp/foo
  cat /tmp/foo > $fnam
done
```

4. There's a problem with a declaration of strdup in *pilrc.c*. Comment out its declaration:

```
//char *strdup(const char *s);
```

5. Now, you're ready to build and make:

```
./configure
make pilrc
```

6. Install by copying to */usr/local/bin* (or some directory of your choice):

```
cp pilrc /usr/local/bin
```

Installing OReilly Sample project

This section of the tutorial is for both Windows and Unix users of PRC-Tools.

We know our job is to make things as simple as possible for you. As a result, we imagine that when you create a new project you would like it to be as easy as can be expected. So, presto, we have made it so. We've created a new, very simple project that has the correct structure of a Palm OS application, but that doesn't actually *do* very much. That way, it's easier to use as the basis of a new application.

Download this project from *http://www.calliopeinc.com/stationery.html*.

Cloning the Sample Project

Duplicate the *OReillyStationery* directory:

```
cp -r OReillyStationery MyProject
```

Build the project by doing a make:

```
cd MyProject
make
```

The resulting PRC can be found in *GCC/OReillyStarter.prc*.

Customizing the Output File

To change the output file, edit the *Makefile* by changing the value of the APP variable:

```
APP=MyProject
```

In addition, rename the *.def* file:

```
mv OReillyStarter.def MyProject.def
```

Now, when you make, the resulting PRC can be found in *GCC/MyProject.prc*.

A Non-Debug Build

If you'd like to build without debugging, change the CFLAGS definition in the *Makefile* from:

```
CFLAGS = -palmos4.0 $(DEBUGCFLAGS)
```

to:

```
CFLAGS = -palmos4.0 $(RELEASECFLAGS)
```

Installing a PRC on the Handheld

You should now have a working copy of CodeWarrior or PRC-Tools and a PRC file that you want to install on a handheld or look at on POSE.

Everybody (CodeWarrior and PRC-Tools users) should read this section.

Once you've got your PRC file created, you need to install it on the handheld. If you have been using a Palm device the good news is you already know how to do this. You use the same process to install this PRC file as you have for other applications.

If this is entirely new to you, then continue reading and we will show you how to install the PRC using Windows, Mac OS, and Unix.

Using Windows

Run the Palm Install Tool (part of Palm Desktop). Figure 4-26 shows the resulting dialog box. Either drag your PRC file onto the window, or click Add and choose the PRC file. At this point, the file has been copied to the install directory for the specified user and will be installed at the next sync.

 As a shortcut, you can double-click a PRC file; it'll run the Palm Install Tool, and add the PRC to the list of files to be added for the current user. Now, do a sync and the file should be installed.

Using Mac OS

Run HotSync® Manager, and choose Install Handheld Files. Figure 4-27 shows the resulting dialog box. Either drag your PRC file onto the window or click the Add to List button and choose the PRC file. At this point, the file has been copied to the install directory for the given user and will be installed at the next sync.

Now, do a sync and the file should be installed.

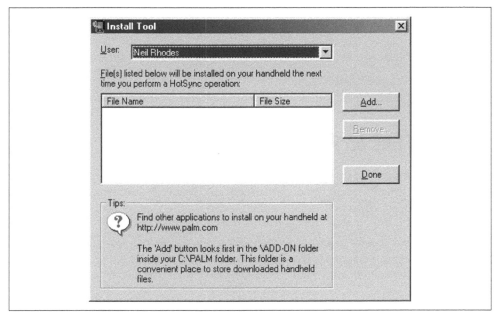

Figure 4-26. Palm Install Tool for Windows

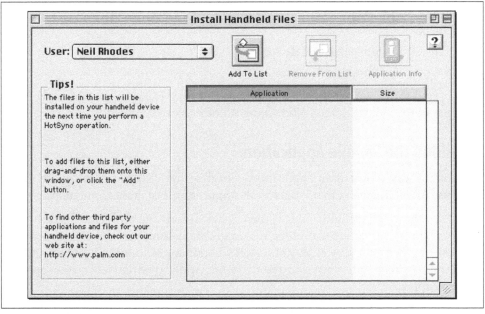

Figure 4-27. Palm Install Handheld Files dialog box for Mac OS

Using Unix

To install using Unix, use the *pilot-xfer* application (part of the Pilot-Link project). Execute the following:

```
pilot-xfer --install filename.prc
```

Then, do a sync from the handheld.

Installing PRC on POSE

We are going over the bare bones basics of POSE here; this is just enough to get you started. We'll cover POSE in much more detail in Chapter 7. Feel free to jump ahead if you want more information.

 We discuss POSE version 3.2. Later versions will almost certainly emulate additional devices. The latest version of POSE can be downloaded from *http://www.palmos.com/dev/tech/tools/emulator/*.

Get Your ROM Image

Although POSE emulates the hardware device, it still needs the OS itself, which is found on a ROM within an actual hardware device. There are two ways to obtain a ROM image:

- Transfer one from an actual device
- Download one from the Internet

We covered these two methods for obtaining an actual ROM in the earlier sections, "POSE and ROM Images" and "Retrieving ROM from a Handheld."

Installing the Sample Application

The easiest way to install an application is to drag the PRC file onto the Emulator window. An alternative is to use the Install Application/Database menu item.

Regardless of which method you use, there is a weird update problem of which to be aware. If the POSE device is running the Application launcher when you install the application, then your new application icon will not appear until you launch another program. At this point, when you return to the Application launcher your application will appear.

This occurs because the Application launcher has no way of knowing that POSE has just installed a new application onto the (emulated) handheld. Restarting the Application launcher forces it to look again at the applications that exist. At this point, it sees the new one (see Figure 4-28). The best thing to do is switch to an application other than the Application launcher before installing. If you fail to do so, the easiest way to deal with this problem is to quickly switch from the Application launcher to a different application (like Calc), and then switch back.

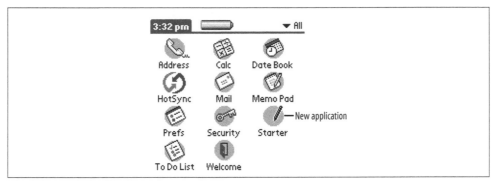

Figure 4-28. The application showing in the Application launcher

Tap on the new application in the Application launcher to run it and see the main form of the application (see Figure 4-29).

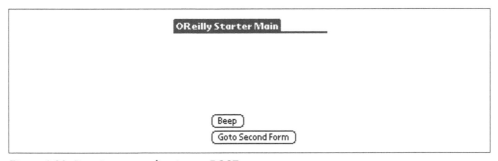

Figure 4-29. Running our application on POSE

Modifying the Sample Application

Now that you have your development environment and tools working and have successfully downloaded and run the sample application on both a handheld and POSE, it is time to modify some things. In order to get some practice making changes to the application and rebuilding, we have four different changes we'd like you to make to the sample:

- Change the application name.
- Change the location of a button.
- Register the creator ID and change to appropriate settings.
- Add a second button that beeps.

As you might have expected, the changes move from easier to more difficult.

Change the Application Name

The task at this point is to change the application name that appears in the Application launcher from Starter to Hello. Here are the steps you take:

1. In *Resources.rcp*, change the following line:

   ```
   APPLICATIONICONNAME 1000 "Starter"
   ```

   to:

   ```
   APPLICATIONICONNAME 1000 "Hello"
   ```

2. Make the application (which should cause PilRC to run and the PRC to be rebuilt).

3. Load the application on the handheld or POSE to see the changed icon name (see Figure 4-30).

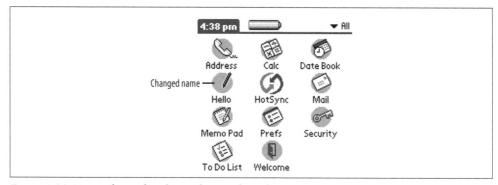

Figure 4-30. Name changed in the Application launcher

Change the Location of a Button

Now, it time to change the location of the Goto Second Form button so that it's up and to the left of where it was originally located. Here are the steps:

1. Open *Resources.rcp*, and change the following lines (we're changing the top-left coordinates of the Goto Second Form button):

   ```
   BUTTON "Goto Second Form" ID MainGotoSecondFormButton AT
     (PrevLeft PrevBottom + 5 AUTO AUTO)
   ```

   to:

   ```
   BUTTON "Goto Second Form" ID MainGotoSecondFormButton AT
     (20 20 AUTO AUTO)
   ```

2. Make the application (which should cause PilRC to run and the PRC to be rebuilt).

3. Load the application on the handheld or POSE to see the changed button location (see Figure 4-31).

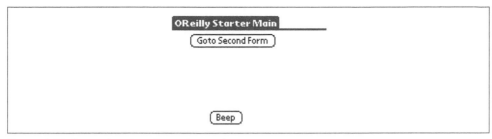

Figure 4-31. Button location changed in application

Register the Creator ID and Set It Appropriately

All Palm OS applications require a unique four-character creator ID. Before you distribute your application, you'll need to register a creator ID and change your application to use it. You register a unique creator ID with Palm at *http://www.palmos.com/dev/tech/palmos/creatorid*. There's no charge for registering and it is simple to do. All that is required is a unique four-character ID (note that all lowercase letters are reserved by Palm). There's a lookup function provided to see whether someone has already used the creator ID in which you're interested.

You should register your creator ID as soon as you begin work on any application that you'll be distributing. To encourage this virtuous behavior we have included this task within the tutorial. Before we get to those tasks, however, we want to show what it looks like to register an ID with Palm.

Figure 4-32 shows the creator ID registration form filled in with the creator ID NR01. Figure 4-33 shows the result of submitting the registration to Palm. Now, we've got that unique creator ID and no other application can register it.

It's up to us to actually change the application itself to use our new ID (and yes, we'll need a different creator ID for every application we distribute). We'll actually be changing two things:

- The creator ID of the database itself
- The name of the database (which, by convention, includes the creator ID appended to it)

We'll discuss databases, creator IDs, and database names in more detail in Chapter 10.

Changing the creator ID in CodeWarrior

Here are the steps you use to change the creator ID in CodeWarrior:

1. Open the Target Settings dialog box by choosing OReilly Starter (Debug) Settings from the Edit menu (or just click on the Target Settings icon in the project—it's the leftmost icon in the Project window).

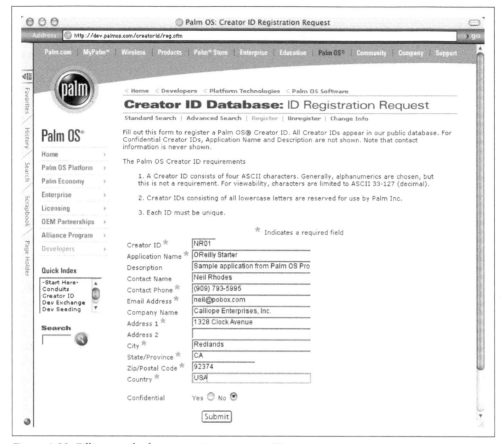

Figure 4-32. Filling out the form to register a creator ID

2. Choose the PalmRez PostLinker panel, and change the ???? (the default creator ID) in two places in the dialog box:

   - Change the creator ID from ???? to NR01
   - Change the Database Name from OReilly Starter-???? to OReilly Starter-NR01

   Then click Apply (or Save on Mac OS) and close the dialog box.

3. Now you can make, and it will rebuild your application using the new creator ID. Keep in mind, however, that there are two targets for this project:

   - A debug target
   - A release target

   We've got to change the creator ID for both of them.

4. To change the second target, (using the pop up at the top left of the project window) change OReilly Starter (debug) to OReilly Starter (release). Then, make the same changes as before in the PalmRez Post Linker panel of the Target Settings dialog box. Do another make.

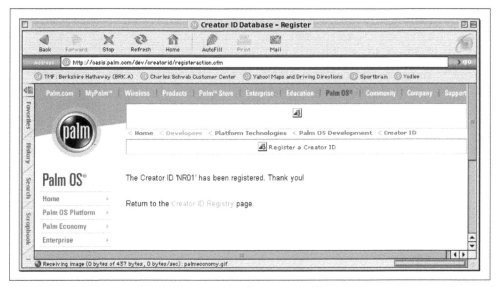

Figure 4-33. Notification that the creator ID has been registered

5. When you're done, you might want to switch the current target back to OReilly Starter (debug).

Changing the creator ID in PRC-Tools

Here are the steps you take to change the creator ID using PRC–Tools:

1. The creator ID is stored in the *.def* file. Open the *MyProject.def* file and change both occurrences of ???? to NR01:

   ```
   application { "OReillyStarter-NR01" "NR01" backup }
   ```

2. Do a make and the application will be rebuilt with the new creator ID.

Add a Second Button That Beeps

Your last task is to try adding another button to the second form. When the user taps on it, you want the device to beep.

For now, you should follow our instructions by rote without expecting explanations for things. You'll learn the reasons for this in later chapters. Here are the robotic steps you take:

1. Open *ResourceDefines.h*, and add a new constant for the new button (the new line is emphasized):

   ```
   #define SecondGotoMainFormButton   3001
   #define SecondBeepButton           3002
   ```

2. Add the button to the *.rcp* file. This will make the button appear when the second form is shown. The new lines of code you add are emphasized:

   ```
   FORM ID SecondForm AT (0 0 160 160)
   ```

```
USABLE
BEGIN
  TITLE "OReilly Starter Second"
  BUTTON "Goto Main Form" ID SecondGotoMainFormButton AT
    (40 130 AUTO AUTO)
  BUTTON "Beep" ID SecondBeepButton AT
    (PREVLEFT PREVBOTTOM+5 AUTO AUTO)
END
```

3. Now, add code to make the button actually do something. In this case, you'll make it beep. Open *SecondForm.c* and add a new case for the new button. The new code is emphasized:

```
Boolean SecondFormHandleEvent(EventPtr eventP)
{
  Boolean handled = false;
  FormPtr frmP;

  switch (eventP->eType) {
  case frmOpenEvent:
    frmP = FrmGetActiveForm( );
    SecondFormInit(frmP);
    FrmDrawForm(frmP);
    // Here's where you'd add a call to FrmSetFocus.
    handled = true;
    break;

  case ctlSelectEvent:
    switch (eventP->data.ctlSelect.controlID) {
    case SecondGotoMainFormButton:
      FrmGotoForm(MainForm);
      handled = true;
      break;
    case SecondBeepButton:
      SndPlaySystemSound(sndAlarm);
      handled = true;
      break;
    }
    break;

  case frmCloseEvent:
    SecondFormDeinit(FrmGetActiveForm( ));
    handled = false;
    break;

  default:
    break;
  }

  return handled;
}
```

4. Finally it is time to build the PRC.

5. Once it is built, install it on the handheld or on POSE (you may have to enable sound on POSE in the Preferences dialog box in order to hear anything).

6. When you open the second form, it should contain a new button. Tapping on it should cause a beep.

You should now be ready to delve into the intricacies of the Palm OS. With a working development environment, a small bit of practice working with a project, and sample application, it is time to learn about the OS in detail.

## CHAPTER 5

Structure of an Application

Before you can write a Palm application, you need to know how it interacts with the OS and how it is organized. Prior to this discussion, we cover the standard terminology and naming conventions within the Palm OS. Once you know what the words mean, we can talk about the application and the OS.

We start with a discussion of how an application is structured to run on the Palm OS. You will learn that a Palm application is an event-driven system and that its routines are structured to handle various types of events. We will describe an application's life cycle—its starting, running, and closing. To help solidify your understanding of these points, we provide a simple application, OReilly Starter, which is a prototypical Palm application. We walk you through its organization (for example, its source files, utility files, and so on) and then show you the source code in its routines. While the application doesn't do much, it contains all of the standard routines and has the correct structure for any Palm application. You can use it as the starting point for your own work.

Typically, an application launches when a user opens it; you will learn how to handle this. We will also discuss other times the OS may access an application and what you need to do about it. These instances require you to structure your application so that it can provide information or launch as necessary. Lastly, there are some tricks you might want to add that allow shortcut access from within your application (for example, a hard button). Or, you might want to be a tyrant and take over the unit completely, denying access to other applications while your application is running.

Terminology

Like every operating system, the Palm OS has it own set of necessary terminology for you to learn. Much of it may be familiar to you already from other systems on which you have worked. We suggest that you skim through the list and concentrate on the items that are new to you. New and unique terms are listed first.

Form

An application form (what many people would think of as a window) that usually covers the entire screen (modal forms cover only the bottom part of the screen, however). A form optionally contains controls, text areas, and menus. In a Palm OS application there is only one active form allowed at a time. Chapter 8 covers forms in detail.

Window

A rectangular area in which things like dialog boxes, forms, and menus are drawn by the application. The Window Manager makes sure that windows display properly relative to each other (for example, it has the ability to restore the old contents when a window is closed).

Database

A collection of persistent memory chunks. There are two kinds:

Resource

A piece of data stored in a resource database. Each resource is identified by a resource type and number. *Note that a Palm application is simply a collection of resources.* Chapter 8 covers resources in more detail.

Record

A memory chunk identified by a unique record ID located in a database. Applications typically store data in record databases.

Event

A data structure that describes things that happen in an application. These can be low-level hardware events such as a pen down, pen up, or hardware key press. They can also be higher-level events such as a character entry, a menu item selection, or a software button press.

The Palm OS is an event-driven system. Only one application is open at a time. When that application is running, it runs an event loop that retrieves events and continues to handle them until the user starts another application.

Main event loop

The main loop of execution in an application that repeatedly retrieves events, and then acts on them.

Launch code

A parameter passed to an application that specifies what the application should do when that particular launch code is executed. An application typically handles more than one launch code. This is the communication method used between the OS and a non-running application and between applications.

Menu

Menus are stored in resources grouped together into menu bars and are displayed when the user taps the menu area. See Chapter 11 for more details.

Menu bar
>A collection of menus stored in a resource. Each form can have a menu bar associated with it.

Dialog box
>A window containing controls that require the user to make a decision. In other words, the dialog box must be dismissed (usually by tapping on one of its buttons) before the application can continue.

Alert
>A simple dialog box with only an icon, text, and buttons.

Palm OS Conventions

There are also a variety of Palm coding conventions that are useful to know. There are type conventions and standard naming practices for everything from functions to managers. It is worth getting a clearer idea of what these are before wading knee-deep into your first coding project. These are the ones you should learn.

Types

Here are the main types used by the Palm OS:

UInt32
>An unsigned 32-bit integer.

Int32
>A signed 32-bit integer.

UInt16
>An unsigned 16-bit integer.

Int16
>A signed 16-bit integer.

UInt8
>An unsigned 8-bit integer.

Int8
>A signed 8-bit integer.

Boolean
>A 1-byte true or false value.

Char
>A 1-byte character that will only work on systems with 1-byte encodings.

WChar
>A 2-byte character suitable for all encodings (including for Japanese, Chinese, and so on).

Err
>A 2-byte integer used for errors. The value errNone signifies no error.

Coord
>A signed 2-byte integer used to represent a screen or window coordinate.

MemPtr
>Specifies a (4-byte) pointer to an allocated chunk in memory.

MemHandle
>A (4-byte) reference to a relocatable chunk of memory (see Chapter 6 for more details).

Function and Manager Naming Conventions

The Palm OS uses mixed-case for names, with an initial uppercase for functions and types. Constants and enumerations begin with lowercase letters. The following snippet of code shows the conventions in action (emphasis shows functions, types, and enumerations):

```
FormPtr form;
UInt32  romVersion;
FtrGet(sysFtrCreator, sysFtrNumROMVersion, &romVersion);
FrmSetEventHandler(form, MyHandler);
```

The Palm OS is divided into functional areas called managers. Each manager has its own header file (for example *Form.h*). Every routine in that manager usually begins with a manager abbreviation (for example: EvtGetEvent is part of the Event Manager, declared in *Event.h*; FrmGotoForm is part of the Form Manager, declared in *Form.h*). Table 5-1 contains example abbreviations.

Table 5-1. Standard manager abbreviations

Abbreviation	Manager
Alm	Alarm Manager
Dm	Data Manager
Evt	Event Manager
Ftr	Feature Manager
Mem	Memory Manager
Snd	Sound Manager
Str	String Manager
Sys	System Manager
Txt	Text Manager

C Library Conventions

You will not normally use standard C library routines like strlen or memcpy. While these functions are available as libraries, using them in your code bloats the size of your application. Since space is always tight, you have been provided with another way to use such routines; you'll use the ones in ROM that are small and quick. Table 5-2 shows the Palm OS-equivalents for standard C routines.

Table 5-2. Equivalents to standard C routines

Standard C routine	Palm OS routine	Additional information
strlen	StrLen	
strcpy	StrCopy	
strncpy	StrNCopy	Doesn't pad with extra null terminators.
strcat	StrCat	
strncat	StrNCat	Last parameter is the total length of the string (including null terminator) rather than the number of characters to copy. Doesn't append an extra null terminator if source string is empty.
strcmp	StrCompare	
strncmp	StrNCompare	
itoa	StrIToA	
strchr	StrChr	
strstr	StrStr	
sprintf	StrPrintF	Limited subset of sprintf, for example, no %f.
svprintf	StrVPrintF	Limited subset of svprintf, for example, no %f.
malloc	MemPtrNew	Although you'll probably use handles instead.
free	MemPtrFree	
memmove	MemMove	
memset	MemSet	Warning: the last two parameters have been reversed!
memcmp	MemCmp	

That sums up the important conventions you need to know about to create a Palm application.

The Palm OS and an Application

When the Palm OS wants to communicate with an application that may not be running, it calls the application's PilotMain routine.

The Main Routine: PilotMain

This is the main entry point into a Palm OS application; it is always a function named PilotMain. Given its responsibilities, it is worth looking at this routine in some detail. First, we'll start with the parameters, and then we'll show you the code. Following the code is a walk-through discussion of what is happening.

A quick look at PilotMain

The first parameter is the launch code, which specifies why the function is being called. Whenever your application is being opened normally, this parameter will be the constant sysAppLaunchCmdNormalLaunch. The second and third parameters are used when the application is opened at other times (see Example 5-1).

Example 5-1. Typical PilotMain (app-specific portions are emphasized)

```
UInt32 PilotMain(UInt16 launchCode, MemPtr launchParameters,
  UInt16 launchFlags)
{
#pragma unused(launchParameters)
  Err error;

  switch (launchCode) {
  case sysAppLaunchCmdNormalLaunch:
    error = RomVersionCompatible(kOurMinVersion, launchFlags);
    if (error != errNone)
      return error;
    error = AppStart();
    if (error != errNone)
      return error;

    FrmGotoForm(MainForm);
    AppEventLoop();
    AppStop();
    break;

  default:
    break;
  }

  return errNone;
}
```

If the launch code is sysAppLaunchCmdNormalLaunch, we first check to make sure that the version of the device we are running on is one that we support (you'll have to define the minimum version appropriate for your application).

 A *pragma* is a compiler-specific directive. The #pragma unused(launchParameters) is an indication to CodeWarrior that the parameter launchParameters is not used in the function. With this in place, CodeWarrior won't be constantly warning us of the unused parameter. GCC (as it should) ignores the pragma.

While we will talk about each of the routines called in our PilotMain in greater detail in just a moment, briefly, this is what they do. First, we call our own routine, AppStart, which does application-specific initialization. The call to FrmGotoForm specifies that the MainForm will initially be displayed (if we left that out, the display would be blank since no form was opened). It will queue a `frmLoadEvent` in the Event Manager's event queue (we'll talk more about form events in Chapter 8).

Now, the application's motor—our event loop, `AppEventLoop`—runs until the user does something to close the application. At that point, we handle termination in `AppStop`.

The Startup Routine: AppStart

Here is where we handle all the standard opening and initialization of our application. In a typical application, this would include opening our databases and reading user preference information. In our skeleton application (OReilly Starter), we won't do anything.

Although it's common to name this routine `AppStart`, it's only a convention, not a requirement like the name of `PilotMain`.

 Note that we call `FrmGotoForm` in our `PilotMain` rather than here. This is important because an application will eventually need to support Find. In that case, another launch code will require us to initially open a different form. Because of this, we need `FrmGotoForm` to be in a location that allows us to switch between forms depending on how the application gets opened.

Since we have a very simple application, our `AppStart` does nothing:

```
static Err AppStart(void)
{
    return 0;
}
```

Note that we have a `static` declaration here for the benefit of CodeWarrior. If we leave off the `static`, then CodeWarrior will warn us that the function doesn't have a prototype.

CodeWarrior complains about this potential error because the function might have been declared in a header file that wasn't included in this file. Furthermore, that declaration might declare the function differently (for example, different numbers or types of parameters). Specifying that the function is `static` guarantees that the function won't be called from outside this file, thus no separate function declaration is required.

In general, always add a `static` when defining functions that are only used within a single file. This is the purpose for the keyword after all.

The Closing Routine: AppStop

Normally, in `AppStop` we handle all the standard closing operations, such as closing our database, saving the current state in preferences, and so on. Because we are creating such a simple application, we don't actually have to do those things. However, like all applications, ours needs to make sure that any open forms are closed. FrmCloseAllForms will do that closing.

```
static void AppStop(void)
{
  FrmCloseAllForms( );
}
```

The Main Event Loop

In PilotMain, after the initialization there is a call to the one main event loop, AppEventLoop. In brief, this is what happens in this loop:

- We continually process events—handing them off wherever possible to the system.
- We go through the loop, getting an event with EvtGetEvent, and then dispatch that event to one of four event handlers, each of which gets a chance to handle the event.
- If any of the event handlers returns true, it has handled the event and we don't process it any further.
- EvtGetEvent then gets the next event in the queue and our loop repeats the process all over again.
- The loop doggedly continues in this fashion until we get the appStopEvent, at which time we exit the function and clean things up in AppStop.

Example 5-2 shows the code for a typical *AppEventLoop*.

Example 5-2. Typical AppEventLoop

```
void AppEventLoop(void)
{
  Err error;
  EventType event;

  do {
    EvtGetEvent(&event, evtWaitForever);

    if (! SysHandleEvent(&event))
      if (! MenuHandleEvent(0, &event, &error))
        if (! AppHandleEvent(&event))
          FrmDispatchEvent(&event);

  } while (event.eType != appStopEvent);
}
```

Handling events with EvtGetEvent

This Event Manager routine's sole job is to get the next event from the queue. It takes as a second parameter a timeout value (in ticks—SysTicksPerSecond returns the units, which is 100 on all devices as of mid-2001). `EvtGetEvent` returns when either an event has occurred, or when the timeout value has elapsed (in which case it fills in an event code of `nilEvent`).

 `EvtGetEvent` can actually return with a `nilEvent` at any time, regardless of whether the timeout value has elapsed.

We don't have anything to do until an event occurs (this application has no idle-time processing to do), so we pass the `evtWaitForever` constant, specifying that we don't want a timeout.

The Event Queue and Application Event Loop

At this point, it is worth looking in more detail at the events that are received from `EvtGetEvent`. Events can be of all different types: anything from low-level to high-level ones. In fact, one useful way to look at a Palm application is simply as an event handler—it hands all sorts of events off to various managers, which in turn may post new events back to the queue where they will get handled by other event handlers. We will discuss more sophisticated examples of this later (see "Scenarios" later in this chapter), but for now we will look at a very simple set of events to get an idea of how all this works together. Imagine the user has our application open and taps the stylus on the screen in the area of the silk-screened menu button. The first time through the event queue the `SysHandleEvent` routine handles the event, interprets it, and creates a new event that gets put back in the queue (see Figure 5-1).

When this new event comes through the loop, it will get passed through `SysHandleEvent` and on to the `MenuHandleEvent` as it is now recognizable as a menu request (see Figure 5-2). `MenuHandleEvent` will display the menu bar and drop down one of the menus. If the user now taps outside of the menu, the menus will disappear.

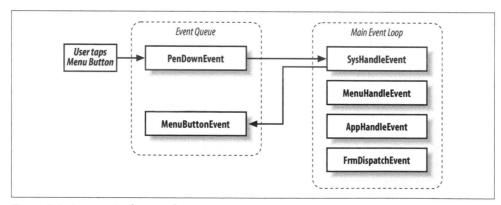

Figure 5-1. An event in the event loop

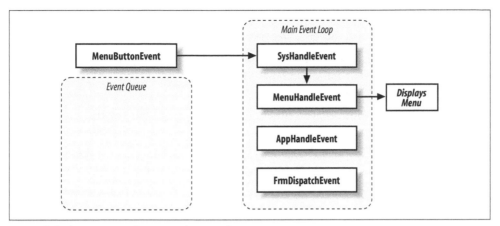

Figure 5-2. A regurgitated event in the event loop

If a menu item is selected, however, then a new event is generated and posted to the queue. This event is retrieved by the event loop where it is passed through SysHandleEvent, and then on to MenuHandleEvent, and continues until some code handles the menu item. Given the way this process works, you can see that the different managers are interested in different types of events. Keeping this in mind, let's now return to our code and look at the event loop and the four routines in it.

The Four Routines of the Main Event Loop

You have briefly seen the four routines and their order in the main event loop. Here is a more detailed look at the responsibilities of each routine.

SysHandleEvent

```
if (! SysHandleEvent(&event))
```

The first routine in the loop is always SysHandleEvent as it provides functionality common to all Palm applications. For example, it handles key events for the built-in application buttons. It does so by posting an appStopEvent to tell the current application to quit. After the application quits, the system launches the desired application.

It also handles pen events in the silk-screened area (the graffiti input area and the silk-screened buttons). For example, if the user taps on Find, SysHandleEvent will completely handle the Find, returning only when the Find is done.

SysHandleEvent likewise handles the Power key, dealing with putting the device to sleep and/or turning backlighting on or off, depending on the duration of the Power key press.

MenuHandleEvent

```
if (! MenuHandleEvent(0, &event, &error))
```

The second routine in our event loop is MenuHandleEvent. As you might have imagined, the MenuHandleEvent handles events involving menus. These events occur when a user taps on the following:

- Menu silk-screen button. The function finds the menu bar for the current form and displays it by creating a window.
- Title of a form. This acts the same way as if the user tapped on the Menu silk-screen button.
- Somewhere else while a menu is being displayed. The function closes the menu when the user taps outside of it.

As would be expected, it closes the menu and menu bar if the user taps on a menu item. At this point, it posts a menu event that will be retrieved in a later call to EvtGetEvent.

The first parameter to MenuHandleEvent specifies which menu to handle (0 means the current menu and is what you'll always pass). The last parameter is a pointer to an error return result; note, however, that virtually all applications (including ours) ignore the error result.

Unlike all other managers, the Menu Manager routines use a four-character prefix (Menu) rather than the three characters common to the others. In addition, unlike SysHandleEvent and FrmDispatchEvent, which take only the event and return a Boolean, MenuHandleEvent takes two extra parameters. (We get the feeling that whoever wrote the Menu Manager skipped some of the meetings on API design that the rest of the OS team attended.)

AppHandleEvent

```
if (! AppHandleEvent(&event))
```

The third routine, AppHandleEvent, is also a standard part of the event loop and is responsible for loading forms and associating an event handler with the form. This routine handles any events that it wants to process application-wide (as opposed to the majority of events, which are form-specific). This code is not part of the OS; you write it. However, it will be very similar from application to application. Example 5-3 shows a typical example of the routine.

Example 5-3. Typical AppHandleEvent (app-specific portions are emphasized)

```
static Boolean AppHandleEvent(EventPtr event)
{
  UInt16 formId;
  FormPtr form;

  if (event->eType == frmLoadEvent) {
```

```
        // Load the form resource.
        formId = event->data.frmLoad.formID;
        form = FrmInitForm(formId);
        ErrFatalDisplayIf(!form, "Can't initialize form");
        FrmSetActiveForm(form);

        // Set the event handler for the form.  The handler of the currently
        // active form is called by FrmHandleEvent each time it receives an event.
        switch (formId) {
        case MainForm:
          FrmSetEventHandler(form, MainFormHandleEvent);
          break;

        case SecondForm:
          FrmSetEventHandler(form, SecondFormHandleEvent);
          break;

        default:
          ErrFatalDisplay("Invalid Form Load Event");
          break;

        }
        return true;
    } else
        return false;
}
```

A frmLoadEvent is a request to load a particular form. It is our responsibility to load the requested form (the OS won't load a form automatically). We initialize the specified form ID (FrmInitForm) and then make it the one-and-only active form (FrmSetActiveForm). Finally, we set the form's event handler (FrmSetEventHandler). If you create a new form, you'll write an event handler for it, and then add a new case to the switch statement, setting the event handler.

FrmDispatchEvent

```
FrmDispatchEvent(&event);
```

This fourth and last routine in the event loop is the one that indirectly provides form-specific handling. FrmDispatchEvent calls FrmHandleEvent, which provides standard form functionality (for example, a pen-down event on a button highlights the button, a pen-up on a button posts a ctlSelectEvent event to the event queue). Cut, copy, and paste in text fields are other examples of functionality handled by FrmHandleEvent.

In order to provide form-specific handling, FrmDispatchEvent calls the form's installed event handler first before calling FrmHandleEvent. If the event handler returns true, no further processing happens. If it returns false, FrmDispatchEvent will then call FrmHandleEvent, which will provide the standard functionality. Thus, your event handler always gets the first crack at events occurring within a form. Here's pseudocode for FrmDispatchEvent to give you an idea of what it will look like:

```
Boolean FrmDispatchEvent(EventType *event)
{
  Boolean handled = result of calling Form's event handler;
  if (handled)
    return true;
  else
    return FrmHandleEvent(event);
}
```

A Simple Application—OReilly Starter

Now it's time to apply what you just learned about an application's interaction with the OS, its PilotMain routine, and the event loop to an actual application. We are using OReilly Starter, the application we first discussed in Chapter 4.

What the Application Does—Its User Interface

Our OReilly Starter application has two forms. On the first form, there are two buttons. Pressing the first one causes the Palm device to beep. Pressing the second button switches the view to the second form. The second form has a single button that returns to the previous form (see Figure 5-3). This is all there is to our simple application.

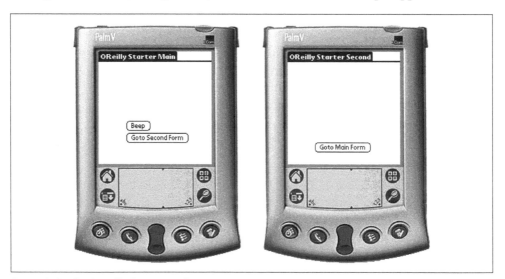

Figure 5-3. The OReilly Starter application

An Overview of the Source Files

Here are the source files that make up this application (as opposed to the tools-specific files like CodeWarrior *.mcp* files or PRC-Tools *.def* files).

Main.c

> This file contains the main entry point (PilotMain) of the application. It also includes the event loop, application startup and shutdown code, and the code to load forms as needed.

MainForm.c

> This contains the code that handles everything that occurs in the first form.

SecondForm.c

> This contains the code for the second form.

Utils.c

> This contains some utility routines that can be used throughout the application. You can include this same source file in all your applications.

Resources.rcp

> This PilRC file contains the UI elements (the forms, form objects, and the application name).

ResourceDefines.h

> This file defines constants for all the application's resources. This file is included by the *.c* files, as well as *Resources.rcp*.

MainForm.h

> This declares the event handler for the main form. This is included by both *Main.c* and *MainForm.c*.

SecondForm.h

> This declares the event handler for the second form. It is also included by both *Main.c* and *SecondForm.c*.

Constants.h

> This file contains the defined constants used throughout the application.

Utils.h

> This declares the utility functions in *Utils.c*.

The Source File of Main.c

Main.c starts with the *#include* files (see Example 5-4).

Example 5-4. First part of Main.c: #defines and #includes

```
#define DO_NOT_ALLOW_ACCESS_TO_INTERNALS_OF_STRUCTS
#include <BuildDefines.h>
#ifdef DEBUG_BUILD
#define ERROR_CHECK_LEVEL ERROR_CHECK_FULL
```

Example 5-4. First part of Main.c: #defines and #includes (continued)

```
#endif
#include <PalmOS.h>
#include "ResourceDefines.h"
#include "MainForm.h"
#include "SecondForm.h"
#include "Utils.h"
#include "Constants.h"
```

 PalmOS.h is an include file that contains most of the standard Palm OS include files. By default, it defines an ERROR_CHECK_LEVEL of ERROR_ CHECK_PARTIAL, which is suitable for a release build. It doesn't, however, provide the checking we'd like for a debug build (see Chapter 7 for more information on debug builds). Thus, if we're compiling a DEBUG_BUILD, we redefine ERROR_CHECK_LEVEL. We must *#include BuildDefines.h* first, in order to obtain the definition of ERROR_CHECK_FULL.

We define DO_NOT_ALLOW_ACCESS_TO_INTERNALS_OF_STRUCTS to help with good coding practices. This will cause the 4.0 SDK to generate a compile-time error for us if we try to access fields within OS structures directly, rather than through appropriate API calls. You should always use the APIs, rather than fool around within an OS structure directly.

Example 5-5 shows the remainder of *Main.c*.

Example 5-5. Remaining functions in Main.c

```
static Boolean AppHandleEvent(EventPtr event)
{
  UInt16 formId;
  FormPtr form;

  if (event->eType == frmLoadEvent) {
    // Load the form resource.
    formId = event->data.frmLoad.formID;
    form = FrmInitForm(formId);
    ErrFatalDisplayIf(!form, "Can't initialize form");
    FrmSetActiveForm(form);

    // Set the event handler for the form.  The handler of the currently
    // active form is called by FrmHandleEvent each time it receives an event.
    switch (formId) {
    case MainForm:
      FrmSetEventHandler(form, MainFormHandleEvent);
      break;

    case SecondForm:
      FrmSetEventHandler(form, SecondFormHandleEvent);
      break;

    default:
      ErrFatalDisplay("Invalid Form Load Event");
```

Example 5-5. Remaining functions in Main.c (continued)

```
      break;

    }
    return true;
  } else
    return false;
}

static void AppEventLoop(void)
{
  Err error;
  EventType event;

  do {
    EvtGetEvent(&event, evtWaitForever);

    if (! SysHandleEvent(&event))
      if (! MenuHandleEvent(0, &event, &error))
        if (! AppHandleEvent(&event))
          FrmDispatchEvent(&event);

  } while (event.eType != appStopEvent);
}


static Err AppStart(void)
{
   return errNone;
}


static void AppStop(void)
{
  FrmCloseAllForms( );
}

UInt32 PilotMain(UInt16 launchCode, MemPtr launchParameters,
  UInt16 launchFlags)
{
#pragma unused(launchParameters)
  Err error;

  switch (launchCode) {
  case sysAppLaunchCmdNormalLaunch:
    error = RomVersionCompatible (kOurMinVersion, launchFlags);
    if (error)
      return error;
    error = AppStart( );
    if (error)
      return error;

    FrmGotoForm(MainForm);
    AppEventLoop( );
```

Example 5-5. Remaining functions in Main.c (continued)

```
    AppStop( );
    break;

  default:
    break;
  }

  return errNone;
}
```

kOurMinVersion is defined as Version 3.0 of the Palm OS in *Constants.h*.

The Form Files of the Application

Main.c is the source file containing routines responsible for handling the main form (see Example 5-6).

Example 5-6. MainForm.c

```
/*
 Copyright (c) 2000-2001, Neil Rhodes and Julie McKeehan
         neil@pobox.com
 All rights reserved.

From the book "Palm OS Programming (2nd edition)" by O'Reilly.

Permission granted to use this file however you see fit.
*/

#define DO_NOT_ALLOW_ACCESS_TO_INTERNALS_OF_STRUCTS
#include <BuildDefines.h>
#ifdef DEBUG_BUILD
#define ERROR_CHECK_LEVEL ERROR_CHECK_FULL
#endif
#include <PalmOS.h>
#include "ResourceDefines.h"
#include "MainForm.h"


static void MainFormInit(FormPtr form)
{
#pragma unused(form)
  // Warning-- don't do any drawing in this routine.
  // Also, don't call FrmSetFocus from here (it must be called *after*
  // FrmDrawForm).
}

static void MainFormDeinit(FormPtr form)
{
#pragma unused(form)
}
```

Example 5-6. MainForm.c (continued)

```
Boolean MainFormHandleEvent(EventPtr event)
{
  Boolean handled = false;
  FormPtr form;

  switch (event->eType)
  {
  case frmOpenEvent:
    form = FrmGetActiveForm( );
    MainFormInit(form);
    FrmDrawForm(form);
    // Here's where you'd add a call to FrmSetFocus.
    handled = true;
    break;


  case ctlSelectEvent:
  switch (event->data.ctlSelect.controlID) {
    case MainBeepButton:
      SndPlaySystemSound(sndWarning);
      handled = true;
      break;

    case MainGotoSecondFormButton:
      FrmGotoForm(SecondForm);
      handled = true;
      break;
    }
    break;

  case frmCloseEvent:
    MainFormDeinit(FrmGetActiveForm( ));
    handled = false;
    break;

  default:
    break;
  }
  return handled;
}
```

The event handler for the main form handles three different kinds of events:

- frmOpenEvent
- frmCloseEvent (discussed in Chapter 8, along with the previous event)
- ctlSelectEvent (specifies that a control has been chosen)

The MainFormInit and MainFormDeinit routines are there because it is quite common to need to do some initialization when a form opens. You will often need to do some cleanup when a form closes. This is where such things should happen.

The `MainFormHandleEvent` handles the `ctlSelectEvent` by looking to see what control was chosen:

- If the beep button is chosen, it plays a sound.
- If the Goto button is chosen, it calls `FrmGotoForm`, which closes this form and opens the other one.

The EventType data structure

In order to handle events within your form's event handler, you have to become familiar with the `EventType` data structure (the data that comes back from `EvtGetEvent`). Here are the fields within that structure:

eType
> The type of the event (an enumeration: examples are `menuEvent`, `penDownEvent`, `keyDownEvent`, and so on).

penDown
> Was the stylus down when this event occurred?

tapCount
> For OS 3.5 and later, the number of successive taps. On a double-tap, you'll get two events. The first will have a `tapCount` of 1, and the second a `tapCount` of 2. Note: the value in this field is undefined prior to the 3.5 version of the OS.

screenX
> The horizontal location of the stylus (in screen coordinates).

screenY
> The vertical location of the stylus (in screen coordinates).

Each event type also has specific associated data. For example, menu events have the menu item ID, control events have the control ID, key events have the character. This data is stored in a union of structures, with a separate structure defined for each kind of event. The union of structures' name is data. Within that union, the name of the structure is the name of the event type, without the event suffix. For example, the data for a menuEvent is found in the `data.menu` structure, the data for a `ctlSelectEvent` is found in `data.ctlSelect`.

Example 5-7 shows *SecondForm.c*, which contains the code responsible for the second form.

Example 5-7. SecondForm.c

```
/*
 Copyright (c) 2000-2001, Neil Rhodes and Julie McKeehan
   neil@pobox.com
 All rights reserved.

From the book "Palm OS Programming (2nd edition)" by O'Reilly.

Permission granted to use this file however you see fit.
```

Example 5-7. SecondForm.c (continued)

```c
*/

#define DO_NOT_ALLOW_ACCESS_TO_INTERNALS_OF_STRUCTS
#include <BuildDefines.h>
#ifdef DEBUG_BUILD
#define ERROR_CHECK_LEVEL ERROR_CHECK_FULL
#endif
#include <PalmOS.h>
#include "ResourceDefines.h"
#include "SecondForm.h"


static void SecondFormInit(FormPtr form)
{
#pragma unused(form)
  // Warning-- don't do any drawing in this routine.
  // Also, don't call FrmSetFocus from here (it must be called *after*
  // FrmDrawForm).
}

static void SecondFormDeinit(FormPtr form)
{
#pragma unused(form)
}


Boolean SecondFormHandleEvent(EventPtr event)
{
  Boolean handled = false;
  FormPtr form;


  switch (event->eType) {
  case frmOpenEvent:
    form = FrmGetActiveForm();
    SecondFormInit(form);
    FrmDrawForm(form);
    // Here's where you'd add a call to FrmSetFocus.
    handled = true;
    break;


  case ctlSelectEvent:
    switch (event->data.ctlSelect.controlID) {
    case SecondGotoMainFormButton:
      FrmGotoForm(MainForm);
      handled = true;
      break;
    }
    break;

  case frmCloseEvent:
    SecondFormDeinit(FrmGetActiveForm());
```

Example 5-7. SecondForm.c (continued)

```
      handled = false;
      break;

    default:
      break;
  }

  return handled;
}
```

This code is very similar in structure to that of *MainForm.c*. The difference is what happens when a control is chosen.

The Utility and Resource Files

Here is a look at the utility and resource files that OReilly Starter uses.

Utils.c contains several utility routines in this source file, but we use only one in this application. Example 5-8 shows that sole routine.

Example 5-8. Utils.c (abridged to show only the routine we use)

```
/*
 Copyright (c) 2000-2001, Neil Rhodes and Julie McKeehan
     neil@pobox.com
 All rights reserved.

From the book "Palm OS Programming (2nd edition)" by O'Reilly.

Permission granted to use this file however you see fit.
*/

#define DO_NOT_ALLOW_ACCESS_TO_INTERNALS_OF_STRUCTS
#include <BuildDefines.h>
#ifdef DEBUG_BUILD
#define ERROR_CHECK_LEVEL ERROR_CHECK_FULL
#endif
#include <PalmOS.h>
#include "Utils.h"
#include "ResourceDefines.h"

Err RomVersionCompatible(UInt32 requiredVersion, UInt16 launchFlags)
{
  UInt32 romVersion;

  // See if we're on minimum required version of the ROM or later.
  FtrGet(sysFtrCreator, sysFtrNumROMVersion, &romVersion);
  if (romVersion < requiredVersion) {
    UInt16 safeToCallAlertFlags;

    safeToCallAlertFlags =
      sysAppLaunchFlagNewGlobals | sysAppLaunchFlagUIApp;
```

```
    if ((launchFlags & (safeToCallAlertFlags)) == safeToCallAlertFlags) {
      FrmAlert (RomIncompatibleAlert);

      // Pilot 1.0 will continuously relaunch this application unless we switch to
      // another safe one.
      if (romVersion < sysMakeROMVersion(2,0,0,sysROMStageRelease,0))
        AppLaunchWithCommand(sysFileCDefaultApp,
          sysAppLaunchCmdNormalLaunch, NULL);
    }

    return (sysErrRomIncompatible);
  }

  return errNone;
}
```

You'll normally use this routine as-is in every application you write. It works by calling the Feature Manager (which contains runtime information about the Palm device) to find out what ROM version this Palm device is running. If the version is not earlier than the requested one, the routine returns no error. Otherwise, it will display an alert and return an error. Last of all, it deals with a potentially infinite relaunch problem in the 1.0 version of the OS by explicitly launching some other application.

The *Resources.rcp* PilRC file, shown in Example 5-9, can be compiled by either the PilRC command line, when using the PRC-Tools, or by the PilRC plug in, when using the CodeWarrior environment.

Example 5-9. Resources.rcp

```
#include "ResourceDefines.h"

APPLICATIONICONNAME 1000 "Starter"

ALERT ID RomIncompatibleAlert
CONFIRMATION
BEGIN
  TITLE "System Incompatible"
  MESSAGE "System Version 3.0 or greater " \
    "is required to run this application."
  BUTTONS "OK"
END

FORM ID MainForm AT (0 0 160 160)
USABLE
BEGIN
  TITLE "OReilly Starter Main"
  BUTTON "Beep" ID MainBeepButton AT (40 100 AUTO AUTO)
  BUTTON "Goto Second Form" ID MainGotoSecondFormButton AT
    (PrevLeft PrevBottom + 5 AUTO AUTO)
END
```

Example 5-9. Resources.rcp (continued)

```
FORM ID SecondForm AT (0 0 160 160)
USABLE
BEGIN
  TITLE "OReilly Starter Second"
  BUTTON "Goto Main Form" ID SecondGotoMainFormButton AT
    (40 130 AUTO AUTO)
END
```

This defines the name of the application as it appears in the Application launcher, the alert that's shown if run on an older system, and the two forms.

Header Files

Example 5-10 shows *Constants.h*, which defines two constants: our creator ID and the minimum version for which we'll run.

Example 5-10. Constants.h

```
#ifndef CONSTANTS_H
#define CONSTANTS_H

#define kAppFileCreator         '????'

// The minimum OS version we support.
#define kOurMinVersion  sysMakeROMVersion(3,0,0,sysROMStageRelease,0)
#endif
```

The next file, *ResourceDefines.h*, is included by both the *.c* files and the *.rcp* file to define the constants used by the UI (see Example 5-11).

Example 5-11. ResourceDefines.h

```
#define RomIncompatibleAlert        1001

#define MainForm                    2000
#define MainBeepButton              2001
#define MainGotoSecondFormButton    2002

#define SecondForm                  3000
#define SecondGotoMainFormButton    3001
```

MainForm.h file defines the function that is exported from *MainForm.c* (see Example 5-12).

Example 5-12. MainForm.h

```
#ifndef MAINFORM_H
#define MAINFORM_H

Boolean MainFormHandleEvent(EventPtr event);

#endif
```

SecondForm.h file defines the function that is exported from *SecondForm.c* (see Example 5-13).

Example 5-13. SecondForm.h

```
#ifndef SECONDFORM_H
#define SECONDFORM_H

Boolean SecondFormHandleEvent(EventPtr event);


#endif
```

Utils.h exports some useful utility routines (see Example 5-14).

Example 5-14. Utils.h

```
#ifndef UTILS_H
#define UTILS_H

Err RomVersionCompatible(UInt32 requiredVersion, UInt16 launchFlags);
void *GetObjectPtr(FormPtr form, UInt16 objectID);
void *GetObjectPtrFromActiveForm(UInt16 objectID);

#endif
```

OReilly Starter Summary

In this simple application, we have all the major elements of any Palm application. In review, these are:

- A set of necessary include files
- A startup routine called AppStart, which handles all our initial setup
- A PilotMain routine that starts an AppEventLoop to handle events passed to it by the system
- An event loop that continually hands events to a series of four managing routines—SysHandleEvent, MenuHandleEvent, AppHandleEvent, and FrmDispatchEvent
- Routines to handle our form-specific functionality
- A closing routine called AppStop, which handles the proper closing of our application

Other Times Your Application Is Called

You know how an application works within the OS and now you know about the organizational structure and content of the various source files used to create an application. The last remaining piece of the puzzle is other times the OS communicates with an application. Let's turn to the details of this.

The Palm OS makes a distinction between communicating with the active application and communicating with a possibly nonactive application. In this first case, the active application is busy executing an event loop, and can be communicated with by posting events to the event queue. As shown earlier in our example, this was how our application got closed; the appStopEvent was posted to the event queue. When the active application gets that event, it quits.

Because there are other times that your application gets called by the Palm OS, there needs to be a way to communicate with it in those instances as well. First, let's look at a partial list of the circumstances under which the system might want to talk to your application:

- When the user does a Find, the system must ask each installed application to look for any records that match the Find request.
- When beamed data is received, the system must ask the appropriate application (the one that is registered to receive the data) to handle the incoming item.
- When a HotSync occurs, each application is notified after its data has been synced.
- After a reset, each application is notified that a reset has occurred.
- If the system time or date changes, each application is notified.
- If the country changes, each application is notified.

In all these cases, a communication must take place to a nonactive or closed application. The question is: how does the system do this? The answer: its PilotMain routine is called with different launch codes.

Launch Codes

Within the Palm OS, it is the launch code that specifies to the application which of the previously mentioned circumstances exists and what the application needs to do. These codes arrive at the application's PilotMain routine by way of its launchCode parameter. Here are some common launch codes:

sysAppLaunchCmdFind

This code tells the application to look up a particular text string and return information about any matching data. Called by the system when the user does a Find.

sysAppLaunchCmdGoTo

This code tells the application to open if it isn't already open and then to go to the specified piece of data. Called by the system when the user taps on a found item.

sysAppLaunchCmdNormalLaunch

As we have already seen, this code opens the application normally.

sysAppLaunchCmdSystemReset

Sent after a reset occurs.

In the 4.0 OS and prior ones, some launch codes are sent to every installed application (for example, after a sync, a reset, or a time change). When a user has many applications installed, this broadcast can be slow. In the future, they may only be sent to those applications that have registered for that particular notification. This registration is available with a Palm OS 3.5 call SysNotifyRegister.

Launch Flags

The launch flags specify important information about how the application is being executed. Here are some examples:

- They may specify whether the application's global variables are available. For performance reasons, globals are not available on many launch codes (this can make the call to PilotMain very fast, as the app's global variables don't need to be allocated or initialized). If globals aren't available, it only makes sense that you can't read from or write to any global.
- They may specify whether the application is now the active application.
- They may specify whether it had already been open as the active application.
- They may specify whether some other application is active.

Scenarios

To help clarify the relationship between the application and the times when the system calls it, let's look at examples of when this happens and the flow of code.

Normal launch

Your application gets a launch code of sysAppLaunchCmdNormalLaunch when it's opened, and launch flags of hexadecimal 0x8e, specifying the following, OR-ed together:

sysAppLaunchFlagDataRelocated
> This is a private Palm OS flag.

sysAppLaunchFlagUIApp
> The application should show a UI.

sysAppLaunchFlagNewGlobals
> The application has just been allocated global variables.

sysAppLaunchFlagNewStack
> The application has been allocated a new stack.

Find when another application is active

When the Memo Pad is the active application, and the user does a Find, the Find Manager calls the PilotMain of every installed application. When our application is called, the launch code is 1 (sysAppLaunchCmdFind), and the launch flag is 0 (no globals, no UI).

Find when your application is active

Things happen differently when we do a Find with our application already open. In this case, PilotMain is still called with the same launch code: sysAppLaunchCmdFind, but now the launch flag is different. It is 0x10 (sysAppLaunchFlagSubCall), specifying that the OReilly Starter application is already open and running. This means that global variables have been allocated and initialized, and we are running as an indirect subroutine call from the application.

Figure 5-4 shows the stack trace when the Find is done in this case. The stack trace shows that PilotMain is called (indirectly) from our AppEventLoop (which itself is called from our original PilotMain).

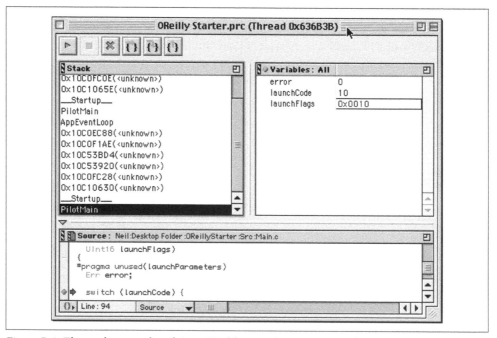

Figure 5-4. The stack trace when doing a Find from within our own application

Examples

There are other communications between the Palm OS and your application that you might want to handle in your code. Particular events, or overall access might be important for you to control. In any case, here are events some applications want to handle:

- A particular pen-down event
- The input of a graffiti character
- How to take over the hard buttons for your own use within your application
- How to take over the entire device and not allow any other applications to run

Let's take a look at the code required to handle each of these instances.

Handling a Pen-Down Event

Normally, you will not handle pen-down events directly, but instead handle higher-level events like ctlSelectEvent. However, occasionally, applications will want to be on the lookout for a penDown event. An example is the Address Book: tapping and releasing on the display of an address in the display view switches to the edit view.

The source code to the Address Book is part of the Palm OS 3.5 SDK. The RecordViewHandleEvent in *Address.c* from that example contains the following case:

```
case penDownEvent:
        handled = RecordViewHandlePen(event);
        break;
```

RecordViewHandlePen handles penDown events in the display-only view of the record (see Example 5-15).

Example 5-15. RecordViewHandlePen in the Address Book source

```
static Boolean RecordViewHandlePen (EventType * event)
{
   Boolean      handled = false;
   FormPtr      frm;
   RectangleType r;
   Int16        x, y;
   Boolean      penDown;

   // If the user taps in the RecordViewDisplay take her to the Edit View.
   frm = FrmGetActiveForm( );
   FrmGetObjectBounds(frm, FrmGetObjectIndex(frm, RecordViewDisplay), &r);
   if (RctPtInRectangle (event->screenX, event->screenY, &r))
      {
      do
         {
         PenGetPoint (&x, &y, &penDown);
         } while (penDown);

      if (RctPtInRectangle (x, y, &r))
         FrmGotoForm (EditView);

      handled = true;
      }

   return handled;
}
```

The calls to the Form Manager routines FrmGetActiveForm and FrmGetObjectBounds yield the rectangle containing the address display area. RctPtInRectangle checks to see whether the pen-tap location (event->screenX and event->screenY) are within those bounds. Note that it then enters a loop calling PenGetPoint until the user releases the stylus. If the user lets go within those same bounds, the code switches to the edit view.

Handling a Graffiti Character

To show you an example of handling a graffiti character, we turned to the Reptoids game (one of the samples in the Palm OS 3.5 SDK). While the game is running, entering a "t" character displays the amount of time spent playing on-screen.

The *Rocks.c* file has the following check in `MainViewHandleEvent`:

```
else if (event->eType == keyDownEvent)
    {
    // Time spent playing.       (Quick code at this point.)
    if (event->data.keyDown.chr == 't')
        {
        // ... Code that displays game-time is here.
        }

    return true;
    }
```

Note that the routine checks the incoming character by looking within the event: `event->data.keyDown.chr`.

Overriding Hard-Button Behavior

Some applications want to redirect the hard button presses (the Date Book key, for instance) for their own use. An obvious example would be games. Pressing a hard button generates a `keyDownEvent` and as such can be looked for by an application. Indeed, the `keyDownEvent` is sent for all of these:

- The four application buttons
- The Power button
- The scroll buttons
- The Find button
- The Calculator button
- The antenna being raised on a Palm VII

In all the instances, a special modifier bit (the `commandKeyMask`) is set in the modifiers associated with that key. This distinguishes it from a normal Graffiti character.

However, for all but the scroll buttons, the system handles the `keyDownEvent`, and doesn't allow the form's event handler to deal with it.

Now, let's see how we can use this information to modify our source code to our advantage. We will make an application where tapping on the Date Book key doesn't bring up the Date Book, but instead does something app-specific.

First off, we need to avoid calling `SysHandleEvent` when that key is pressed (see Example 5-16).

Example 5-16. AppEventLoop that doesn't call SysHandleEvent for taps on the Date Book key

```
static void AppEventLoop(void)
{
  Err error;
  EventType event;

  do {
    Boolean isDatebookKey;

    EvtGetEvent(&event, evtWaitForever);

    isDatebookKey = (event.eType == keyDownEvent)
      && (TxtCharIsHardKey(event.data.keyDown.modifiers,
         event.data.keyDown.chr))
      && (event.data.keyDown.chr == vchrHard1);

    if (isDatebookKey || ! SysHandleEvent(&event))
      if (! MenuHandleEvent(0, &event, &error))
        if (! AppHandleEvent(&event))
          FrmDispatchEvent(&event);

  } while (event.eType != appStopEvent);
}
```

Note that we figure out whether it is a hard key, and then whether it is the Date Book key (vchrHard1). If it is, we don't call SysHandleEvent, and so the normal processing for that character won't happen. However, the event will be passed to FrmDispatchEvent (after being ignored by MenuHandleEvent and AppHandleEvent), and from there to our event handler. Here's code in MainFormHandleEvent that switches to the second form if the Date Book key is pressed:

```
switch (event->eType)
  {
  case keyDownEvent:
    if (TxtCharIsHardKey(event->data.keyDown.modifiers,
         event->data.keyDown.chr)
      && (event->data.keyDown.chr == vchrHard1)) {
      FrmGotoForm(SecondForm);
      handled = true;
    }
    break;
```

Controlling the Exiting of an Application

Some turnkey applications take over the machine and don't allow any other applications to run. For example, a Palm OS device carried by delivery people might only run a delivery application; it's locked for any other purpose.

Admittedly, this is a very rare UI. A standard Palm application should always quit when the user requests another application (by pressing one of the hard buttons, for instance). Standard applications should not have an explicit UI for quit, however. Users implicitly quit an application by starting another.

How do you write an application that takes control of the Palm OS unit and won't let go? It's simple. In order to keep other applications from running, you rudely refuse to exit from your main event loop. As a result, the application never quits (except on a reset). All the OS can do is post an appStopEvent to the event queue, requesting (nay, strongly urging!) your application to quit. It's up to the application itself to actually quit, though.

In the simplest case, you might just code your event loop so that it never exits (see Example 5-17).

Example 5-17. AppEventLoop that never exits

```
static void AppEventLoop(void)
{
  Err error;
  EventType event;

  do {
    EvtGetEvent(&event, evtWaitForever);

    if (! SysHandleEvent(&event))
      if (! MenuHandleEvent(0, &event, &error))
        if (! AppHandleEvent(&event))
          FrmDispatchEvent(&event);

  } while (true);  // Don't ever quit.
}
```

This will ensure that your application, once running, will never exit. It'll silently ignore an appStopEvent that is posted to the event queue.

Another scenario is an application that won't quit unless given a specific command. Some turnkey applications provide a mechanism (perhaps a password-protected button or menu item) to quit the application and open up the unit to the rest of the Palm UI. The easiest way to implement this is to have a global variable specifying whether appStopEvents should be ignored. When the button is pressed, the application can post an appStopEvent, and set the variable. Here's how the event loop would change:

```
static  void AppEventLoop(void)
{
  Err error;
  EventType event;

  do {
    EvtGetEvent(&event, evtWaitForever);
```

```
          if (! SysHandleEvent(&event))
            if (! MenuHandleEvent(0, &event, &error))
              if (! AppHandleEvent(&event))
                FrmDispatchEvent(&event);

        } while (!(event.eType == appStopEvent && AppShouldStop()));
      }
```

AppShouldStop just returns the value of the global:

```
    Boolean gShouldStop = false;

    Boolean AppShouldStop()
    {
      return gShouldStop;
    }
```

Now, when the specific action occurs (like pressing a button or choosing a menu item), a routine MakeAppStop would be called to set the global, and post an appStopEvent to the event queue (see Example 5-18).

Example 5-18. MakeAppStop that causes the application to quit

```
void MakeAppStop()
{
  UInt32 romVersion;

  gShouldStop = true;
  FtrGet(sysFtrCreator, sysFtrNumROMVersion, &romVersion);
  if (romVersion < sysMakeROMVersion(2,0,0,sysROMStageRelease,0)) {
    AppLaunchWithCommand(sysFileCDefaultApp,
      sysAppLaunchCmdNormalLaunch, NULL);
  } else
    PostAppStopEvent(); // Launch previous app.
}
```

 Palm OS 1.0 relaunches the last application, so the code must explicitly launch an application in this case. (The default application is the one that is shown after a reset.) Any post-1.0 OS launches the previous application, so the code just posts an appStopEvent.

Here's the code that posts the appStopEvent. Note that whenever you create an event yourself, you should zero out the entire structure so that unused fields are zero:

```
    static void PostAppStopEvent()
    {
      EventType event;

      // Set all unused fields to 0.
      MemSet(&event, sizeof(event), 0);

      event.eType = appStopEvent;
      EvtAddEventToQueue(&event);
    }
```

What to Remember

In this chapter, we have given you a description of important terminology, standards, and a description of how an application interacts with the Palm OS on a device. Most importantly, you should remember the following:

- *A Palm application is an event-driven system.* The system's event queue feeds a constant flow of events to your application and it is up to you to handle them.

- Events are fed to four different routines (SysHandleEvent, MenuHandleEvent, AppHandleEvent, FrmDispatchEvent) in your event loop. Each routine has responsibilities for various events.

- A standard Palm application has a main routine, PilotMain, from which everything is called. We showed you a sample program that contains a typical PilotMain routine that you will use in your own applications.

- There are times, other than when opened by the user, when your application may be called by the system. Launch codes and the various launch flags tell your application how it was called by the system and what is expected.

From all of this information, you should now be well on your way to understanding this application architecture. In the following chapters, you will be using this information to move beyond our simple OReilly Starter application to create a full-featured application.

## CHAPTER 6

Memory Manager

Some hardware devices and operating systems have memory to burn. It is hardly an understatement to say that this is not true of the Palm OS and its devices (nor will it be true anytime soon). Memory is important because of its scarcity, so you better understand how to use it carefully and cleverly if you are going to write good Palm programs. Teaching you about Palm OS memory and how to use it is the goal of this chapter. Remembering these lessons, alas, will probably only occur when you have been burned a few times from memory shortage or limitations in your code.

Types of Memory

All Palm devices have two types of memory: read-only memory (ROM) and random access memory (RAM). This may not seem so different from other operating systems, you might be thinking to yourself. Well, there are some unique twists in the Palm OS. Let's talk about ROM first and then RAM to see how they are used differently.

Read-Only Memory (ROM)

Read-only memory (ROM) contains:

- The operating system
- The built-in applications
- Default databases

This ROM is an actual masked ROM on some devices (for example, Handspring Visor and Palm m100). On most devices, however, this memory is actually Flash RAM, which can be programmatically changed. The fact that Flash can be changed is what allows most devices to be updated with later versions of the OS. In addition, there are third-party applications that allow users to add databases or applications to the Flash. This is normally done to take advantage of unused space in Flash, and to have databases or applications that will be preserved even after a hard reset.

 At this point, there is no official support for adding databases or applications to Flash other than in the Symbol units (the Symbol SDK has a utility for creating ROM images that includes specific databases and applications).

Most devices have 2 MB ROM, although original PalmPilots had as little as 512 KB ROM. Adding items to Flash works best with units like Symbol's, which can be obtained with as much as 4 MB ROM. Such luxurious amounts leave plenty of room for adding additional data or applications.

Random-Access Memory (RAM)

The second type of memory is random-access memory (RAM). It contains:

- Add-on applications
- Preferences
- User data
- Runtime storage (dynamic memory)

This random-access memory is divided into two areas. The first is a storage area containing the add-on apps, preferences, and user data. The second, a dynamic area, is shared by the OS and the active application. It contains the system's global variables, the system's dynamic allocations, the active application's globals, its stack, and its dynamic allocations. Figure 6-1 shows the division.

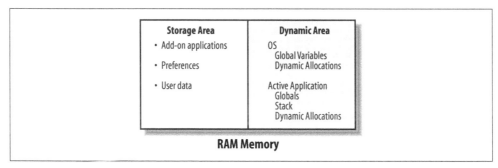

Figure 6-1. RAM usage on the handheld

You might wonder why the Palm OS stores data in memory only (certainly a nonstandard approach). If you remember from Chapter 1 that one of the Palm's essential features was speed, it should all be clear to you. Having the data directly addressable in memory helps to make Palm units fast. Desktop operating systems, which need to read data from a filesystem (usually on a hard disk), are much slower as a result of all those read and write calls to disk. Because Palm applications can read their data from memory directly, they bypass this time lag.

Maintaining state

The dynamic memory requires power in order to maintain its state. This is done through the unit's batteries. What happens when the batteries get worn out and need to be replaced? There's a super-capacitor that provides from 30 seconds to 2 minutes of power to the device. This allows enough time for the user to replace the batteries without the danger of data loss.

Don't leave things to chance, however, is another motto of the Palm. Notice when there is a low-battery alert that the OS suggests that the user do a HotSync backup *first* before replacing the batteries. If the user does so, even if there's a problem while replacing the batteries, the data will have already been backed up.

What happens if the user ignores the low-battery alert, and continues to use the device? Rather than letting the batteries get used up completely, the OS will shut the device down while there's still a reserve. At that point, the device will appear to be dead: the screen will be blank, and the device will ignore the Power button. In reality, the OS is refusing to power-on the device, choosing instead to use the reserve to keep the dynamic memory alive. There should be enough charge in the batteries to maintain the memory state for approximately one month.

 The dynamic state is affected on a reset, however. When the user does a reset, the dynamic area of RAM is cleared, preserving only the storage area. The user's data and applications aren't harmed unless the user does a hard-reset.

Writing to the RAM memory

You might be wondering what's to prevent the writing to either the dynamic memory or, worse yet, the storage memory? For example, what about a poorly written application that accidentally writes through an invalid pointer? There are several solutions that operating systems have taken to this problem. In an OS like Linux, each application has its own address space, and the user's data and applications are in files. Thus, a bad pointer write can only harm the current application. On the Palm OS, such a solution won't work because there are no separate address spaces and there's only one application running. Writing into the dynamic area might not be so bad; that can always be fixed by resetting. Writing into the storage area would be awful, however, as it would overwrite applications or data. So some solution must have been found.

The Palm OS solution to the problem is hardware write protection on the storage area of RAM. Code can read directly from any area of RAM, whether it's the storage area or the dynamic area. Writing to the dynamic area is done directly. Writing to the storage area, however, will fail due to the write protection. In order for an application to modify the storage area, it must call the OS, which will first validate the call, ensuring that the write is to a valid block of the storage heap. Once it has done so, it will turn off the hardware write protection, do the write, and then turn it back on.

There is a cost to be paid for this solution, however. Writes to the storage area are substantially slower than reads (we'd guess there are probably a couple of hundred extra instructions to prepare for the write). If you're writing 1 byte to the storage area, it's probably hundreds of times slower than writing that same byte to the dynamic area. If you write thousands of bytes at once, though, the overhead of preparation is amortized over all of the thousands of bytes.

Amount of dynamic memory available

The amount of dynamic memory depends on two things:

- The version of the OS
- The amount of RAM on the device

In the 3.0 OS and earlier, if the RAM is 512K or less, the dynamic area is 32K; if the RAM is 1 MB or less, the dynamic area is 64K, otherwise, the area is 96K. In the 3.1 to 3.3 OS, 128K is allocated to the system heap. In the 3.5 OS, the amount depends on the amount of RAM: less than 2 MB gives a 64K dynamic area, 2 MB gives a dynamic area of 128K, 4 MB or more gives a 256K dynamic area. Not all of that dynamic area is available for your application to use. Table 6-1 shows how the dynamic memory is allocated to various system components for some OS versions.

Table 6-1. Usage of the dynamic area for some configurations

	OS 3.5 with 4 MB	OS 3.0 with 2 MB	OS 2.0 with 512 KB
System globals	40 KB	6 KB	2.5 KB
TCP/IP	32 KB	32 KB	0 KB
System dynamic allocations (IrDA, Find, Window Manager, etc.)	>18 KB	18 KB	15 KB
Application stack	3. 5 KB (default)	3.25 KB (default)	2.5 KB
Remainder (application globals and dynamic allocation)	<162.5 KB	36.75 KB	12 B
Total dynamic area size	256 KB	96 KB	32 KB

 If you'd like your application to run on any device, limit your globals (including static variables in a function) plus dynamic allocations to a maximum of 12 KB. For 3.0 and above, you can relax that to 36 KB.

Note that these sizes don't include your actual executable code. When your application runs, the code executes directly from the storage area, as opposed to desktop machines, where code is loaded from a file into dynamic memory.

Dynamic Memory Allocation

Memory is allocated in chunks, which can be either *relocatable* (the Memory Manager can move them), or *nonrelocatable* (they can never move). Since there's no virtual memory, and since the amount of memory is limited, it's important to avoid fragmenting available memory.

 Fragmenting means having free memory interspersed with allocated memory so that although there may be enough free memory available to satisfy a particular memory allocation, it isn't contiguous, and therefore the memory allocation fails.

The Palm OS Memory Manager provides a mechanism for fighting fragmentation: relocatable blocks. When you allocate a relocatable block, you allow the Memory Manager to move that block as necessary to coalesce free memory blocks into contiguous space (see Figure 6-2). Of course, there may be times that you don't want the memory block to be moved. In such cases, you can lock the block. This tells the Memory Manager not to move it until it is unlocked.

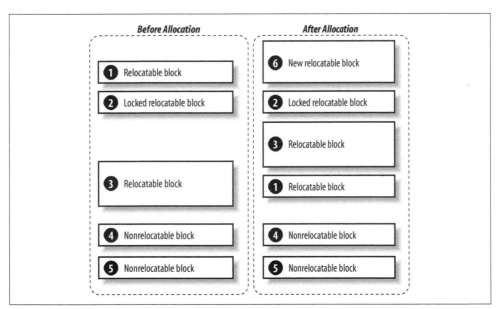

Figure 6-2. The Memory Manager can shuffle unlocked relocatable blocks as necessary

Using Memory Handles

Since the address of the memory block can move, the Memory Manager doesn't return a pointer on allocation. Instead, it returns something called a *handle*. The handle itself doesn't directly contain the address, instead, you call a Memory Manager routine to lock the handle; it returns the address of the locked chunk.

Handles have a lock count, which is incremented every time you lock a chunk and decremented every time you unlock it. When the lock count is greater than 0, the block is locked. If the lock count reaches 0, it is unlocked. This lock count allows nesting of multiple locks (up to a maximum of 14).

Memory Chunk Size Limitations

Although, as you'll see, the APIs for specifying the size of a chunk of memory (relocatable or nonrelocatable) use 32-bit unsigned integers (allowing a maximum theoretical size of 4 GB), the current implementation imposes a limit significantly less than this. No chunk can be larger than slightly less than 64 KB (the exact number is 65,505 bytes, which is 31 bytes less than 64 KB).

The implementation limit of slightly less than 64 KB is there because the protocol used by the HotSync process can't transfer a record larger than this limit. To prevent developers from creating records that can't be read by the HotSync process, the OS prevents any large chunks at all. This seems too draconian to us, especially since some applications may not need or use the HotSync process for their data. For example, HotSync Server doesn't have this 64 KB limitation on record sizes.

Chunks have a minimum size of 1 byte. Unlike the standard C library, whose *malloc* allows 0-size allocations, the Palm OS does not allow them. Chunks are always allocated with a specific heap. Chapter 8 discusses how the storage area of RAM is actually a memory heap, just as the dynamic area is a memory heap.

Dynamic Memory APIs

There are many Memory Manager functions about which you should know. (The declarations for the Memory Manager can be found in the header file *<MemoryMgr.h>*.) These functions deal with:

- Memory allocation
- Locking of relocatable memory blocks
- Block size information
- Heap information

In the following sections, we tell you what the function does and any useful information we know about its implementation.

Allocation

There is a set of APIs for allocating and freeing memory.

MemHandle MemHandleNew(UInt32 size)
> MemHandleNew returns a relocatable memory chunk of the desired size or NULL on an error. The error signifies that there is not enough memory (memErrNotEnoughSpace represents this error).

Err MemHandleFree(MemHandle h)
> This deallocates a relocatable memory chunk; it may be called even for a locked chunk. *Don't call it more than once for a given chunk, and don't call it with* NULL.

MemPtr MemPtrNew(UInt32 size)
> MemPtrNew returns a nonrelocatable memory chunk of the desired size or NULL on an error signifying memErrNotEnoughSpace.

void MemPtrFree(MemPtr p)
> This frees a chunk previously allocated with MemPtrNew. It can also be used to free a locked relocatable block. *Don't free a pointer more than once and don't call this routine with a* NULL *pointer.*

Locking memory chunks

There are APIs for locking and unlocking memory chunks.

MemPtr MemHandleLock(MemHandle h)
> This locks the relocatable memory chunk and returns a pointer to the locked block. It is an error to call this routine if the handle has already been locked the maximum number of times (14). In such a case, the user sees a Reset dialog box with the error "chunk overlocked."

Err MemHandleUnlock(MemHandle h)
> This unlocks the locked relocatable memory chunk. It is an error to call this routine if the lock count was already 0 (the chunk was already unlocked). In such a case, the user sees a Reset dialog box with the error "chunk underlocked."

Err MemPtrUnlock(MemPtr p)
> This unlocks the locked relocatable block referenced by the pointer. It's an error to call this routine if the lock count was already 0 (the chunk was already unlocked). In that case, the user sees a Reset dialog box with the error "chunk underlocked." This function can be used if you no longer have access to the handle.

Some programmers prefer to always unlock using `MemPtrUnlock` rather than `MemHandleUnlock` because it is marginally faster (`MemHandleUnlock` first finds its pointer, and then calls `MemPtrUnlock`). An example might look like this:

```
MemPtr  p = MemHandleLock(h);
// Do something with p.
MemPtrUnlock(p)
```

This small speed increase has to be weighed against the confusion it adds to the code; we find that it is much easier to read code that always pairs a `MemHandleLock` with an associated `MemHandleUnlock`:

```
MemPtr  p = MemHandleLock(h);
// Do something with p.
MemHandleUnlock(h)
```

`MemHandle MemPtrRecoverHandle(MemPtr p)`

This returns the handle associated with the passed-in locked pointer. This can be useful if you've misplaced the handle.

Memory size information

There are APIs for determining the size of a chunk, and for resizing a chunk.

`UInt32 MemHandleSize(MemHandle h)`

This returns the size allocated for the relocatable block.

`UInt32 MemPtrSize(MemPtr p)`

This returns the size allocated for the block pointed to by p.

`Err MemHandleResize(MemHandle h, UInt32 newSize)`

This resizes the specified block to the new size. If the block is locked, then a resize to a smaller size will succeed, but a resize to a larger size will probably fail (unless there happens to be free space just after the locked block).

`Err MemPtrResize(MemPtr p, UInt32 newSize)`

This attempts to resize the specified block to the new size. A resize to a smaller size will succeed, but a resize to a larger size will probably fail (unless there is contiguous free space).

Heap information

There are APIs for finding out information about cards and heaps.

`UInt16 MemNumCards(void)`

This returns the number of cards on the device (see "Cards and Local IDs" later in this chapter for more information about cards).

`UInt16 MemNumHeaps(UInt16 cardNumber)`

This returns the number of memory heaps on the specified card.

```
UInt16 MemHeapID(UInt16 cardNo, UInt16 heapIndex)
```
This returns, for a given heap number, its heap ID number. Heap IDs are assigned sequentially, starting with 0. Heap ID 0 on card number 0 is the dynamic heap.

```
Err MemHeapFreeBytes(UInt16 heapID, UInt32 *freeP, UInt32 *maxP)
```
This returns (in its pointer parameters) the amount of free space available in the heap with the given heap ID. It returns the free space in two ways: the total amount of free space, and the maximum contiguous free space.

```
UInt32 MemHeapSize(UInt16 heapID)
```
This returns the total size of the heap with the given heap ID.

```
UInt16 MemPtrHeapID(MemPtr p)
```
This returns the heap ID of the heap to which the pointer has been allocated.

Example

Looking at bare APIs can only tell you just so much about how to implement them. Since code examples can help clarify APIs, we have provided you with a couple. The first example shows you how to allocate using structures and the second one shows you how to duplicate a string into a handle.

Writing to a block using a structure

It is common to specify the contents of a block (relocatable or nonrelocatable) using a structure. The size of the block is determined by the size of the structure. Reading and writing to the block is done using the -> C operator to read from or write to specific fields given the pointer to the structure. When locking a relocatable block, the pointer returned is usually assigned to a specific pointer type, rather than the generic MemPtr type.

Example 6-1 is taken from the Mail application, one of the Palm OS 3.5 SDK examples. The file *MailSync.c* has a routine that creates a relocatable block the size of a SyncUIStateType structure, and then fills in the fields of the structure.

As you look at Example 6-1, note that there is a C/C++ issue worth discussing. First, notice that the line:

```
stateP = MemHandleLock (stateH);
```

assigns the MemPtr returned from MemHandleLock to the stateP variable (of type SyncUIStatePtr). If you were to compile this code with the C++ compiler, rather than the C compiler, an explicit cast would be required:

```
stateP = (SyncUIStatePtr) MemHandleLock (stateH);
```

In C, though, no cast is necessary when assigning a MemPtr to any other pointer.

Example 6-1. Using a structure to read/write fields in a block (emphasized lines are relevant)

```
static MemHandle SyncSaveUIState (Boolean local)
{
  FormPtr frm;
  ListPtr lst;
  FieldPtr fld;
  ControlPtr ctl;
  MemHandle stateH;
  SyncUIStatePtr  stateP;

  frm = FrmGetActiveForm ( );

  // Allocate a handle to hold the UI state.
  stateH = MemHandleNew (sizeof (SyncUIStateType));
  if (! stateH) return (NULL);
  stateP = MemHandleLock (stateH);

  // Local or remote HotSync options?
  stateP->local = local;

  // Get the sync type (all, send only, or filter or Unread).
  stateP->syncType = FrmGetControlGroupSelection (frm, SyncTypeGroup);

  // Get the "Retrieve All High Priority" checkbox setting.
  ctl = GetObjectPtr (SyncRetrieveAllCheckbox);
  stateP->retrieveHighPriority = (CtlGetValue (ctl) == true);

  // Get the "Ignore / Retrieve Messages Containing" setting.
  lst = GetObjectPtr (SyncMessageContaingList);
  stateP->messageContaing = (MailFilterType) LstGetSelection (lst);

  // Get length that retrieved messages should be truncated to.
  stateP->maxLength = TruncateLen;

  // Get the to, from, and subject filters.
  fld = GetObjectPtr (SyncToField);
  stateP->to = FldGetTextHandle (fld);
  FldSetTextHandle (fld, 0);

  fld = GetObjectPtr (SyncFromField);
  stateP->from = FldGetTextHandle (fld);
  FldSetTextHandle (fld, 0);

  fld = GetObjectPtr (SyncSubjectField);
  stateP->subject = FldGetTextHandle (fld);
  FldSetTextHandle (fld, 0);

  MemHandleUnlock (stateH);

  return (stateH);
}
```

The emphasized lines show the calls of interest. The basic approach is to allocate a handle, lock it and assign to a structure pointer, assign to fields using the structure pointer, and then unlock the handle and return it.

Strings in a block

The Palm OS 3.5 example NetSample has a file, *AppStdio.c*, containing a utility routine that duplicates a string into a newly allocated handle (see Example 6-2).

Example 6-2. Routine that duplicates the passed-in string, returning it as a MemHandle

```
static MemHandle PrvCloneStr(Char * srcStr)
{
  UInt16    len;
  MemHandle   stringH;
  Char *    stringP;

  len = StrLen(srcStr);
  if (!len) return NULL;

  stringH = MemHandleNew(len+1);
  if (stringH) {
    stringP = MemHandleLock(stringH);
    StrCopy(stringP,srcStr);
    MemPtrUnlock(stringP);
    }
  return stringH;
}
```

This shows an example of pairing a call to MemHandleLock with a corresponding call to MemPtrUnlock.

Stack Space

Prior to OS 3.0, the stack space was fixed at about 2.5 KB. For OS 3.0 and beyond, an application can provide a resource specifying a desired stack size. If no such resource is defined, the default stack size is 4 KB.

Keep in mind that stack space is used by all of the following:

- Your application code directly
- The OS, whenever you call an OS routine
- Other applications when called by the OS (e.g., during a Find, a Beam Receive, or an Alarm)

For those launch codes where the OS provides a new stack to an application (like sysAppLaunchCmdNormalLaunch), it does so by allocating a nonrelocatable memory block, and setting up the processor's stack pointer to the *last* byte of that memory block. On the processors currently used by the Palm OS, the stack grows *down* (as items are pushed on the stack, the stack pointer points to lower memory addresses).

In order to specify a stack size other than the default, you'll need a 'pref' resource, with ID 0. The resource consists of the following:

Priority
> A 2-byte integer specifying the priority of this application. It is currently unused, but you should set it to 30.

stackSize
> A 4-byte desired stack size (in bytes). The default, if you don't provide a stack size is 0xD00 (3.25 KB) for OS 3.0 to OS 3.3, and 3.5 KB for OS 3.5 and OS 4.0.

minHeapSpace
> A 4-byte minimum heap size necessary for this application to run. It is currently unused, but you should set it to 0x1000 (4 KB).

APIs

There is a single API that returns information about the stack.

Boolean SysGetStackInfo(MemPtr *topOfStack,MemPtr *bottomOfStack)
> This 3.0 or later routine returns false if the stack has been overwritten (the system allocates a sentinel value at the end of the stack; if that value is modified, the system concludes that the stack has been overwritten).

> The parameters are used to return the top of the stack (the end of it) and the bottom of the stack (where it starts). On current processors used by the Palm OS, the stack grows down, so bottomOfStack will be less than topOfStack.

 On Versions 3.0 through 3.3 of the OS, a bug in this routine causes it to always return false. It appears to be fixed in OS 3.5.

Example

We have provided a couple of examples on using stack space. We show you how to set the stack size, how to find out what the stack size is, how much of it has been used, and how much of it remains.

Setting stack size

Here's a *StackSpace.rcp* file that specifies a resource requesting a 0x1400 (5 KB) stack:

```
HEX "pref" ID 0
  0x00 0x00
  0x00 0x00 0x14 0x00
  0x00 0x00 0x10 0x00
```

Determining stack size

Here's a routine that returns the total stack space allocated to the active application:

```
UInt32 GetTotalStackSpace( )
{
  MemPtr  bottomOfStack;
  MemPtr  topOfStack;

  SysGetStackInfo(&topOfStack, &bottomOfStack);
  return (UInt32) Abs((char *) bottomOfStack - (char *) topOfStack);
}
```

Notice that we take the absolute value of the difference between the bottom and the top of stack. This way we don't have to worry about whether the stack grows up or down in memory.

Determining how much stack has been used

Here's a routine that returns the number of bytes of stack that have been used:

```
UInt32 GetStackSpaceUsed( )
{
  MemPtr  bottomOfStack;
  MemPtr  topOfStack;
  UInt16  aStackBasedVariable;

  SysGetStackInfo(&topOfStack, &bottomOfStack);
  return (UInt32)
    Abs((char *) &aStackBasedVariable - (char *) bottomOfStack);
}
```

Note that the variable aStackBasedVariable is used only to determine its address. Since it's a stack-based variable, the difference between it and the bottomOfStack is the total amount used. In fact, we could just as well have used the address of one of the two existing stack-based variables (bottomOfStack or topOfStack), but the code would have been less clear.

Determining the amount of stack remaining

Here's a routine that returns the number of bytes of stack that remain usable.

```
UInt32 GetStackSpaceRemaining( )
{
  MemPtr  bottomOfStack;
  MemPtr  topOfStack;
  UInt16  aStackBasedVariable;

  SysGetStackInfo(&topOfStack, &bottomOfStack);
  return (UInt32) Abs((char *) &aStackBasedVariable - (char *) topOfStack);
}
```

Note that the variable aStackBasedVariable is used only to determine its address. Since it's a stack-based variable, the difference between its address and the topOfStack is the total amount of space still available.

Handling Large Amounts of Data

With all the different limitations on allocating memory, including the size of the dynamic heap, and the maximum size of an allocated chunk, it is not surprising that techniques to get around these problems would be useful. Since helpful is what we aim to be, we provide a couple of ways around these limitations.

Relocatable Chunks in the Storage Area

If you need to allocate a 50K chunk of memory (for a buffer, perhaps), you won't be able to use the dynamic heap. At least not if you'd like to be able to run on all device/OS releases. What you can do, however, is allocate a chunk of memory from the storage heap instead. The Data Manager call DmNewHandle will allocate a relocatable chunk of memory in the storage heap that is not attached to any database. Like all chunks in the storage heap, it's directly addressable in memory. Thus, you can read it just as if it were in the dynamic heap. That is, after locking it, of course. To write to the chunk, you'd need to use one of the Data Manager calls DmWrite, DmSet, or DmStrCopy (see Chapter 9). Just like MemHandleNew, DmNewHandle restricts allocations to slightly less than 64 KB.

When you are through with the chunk, you can free the handle with MemHandleFree. There is a real potential for mischief in this strategy, however. If you fail to free handles allocated with DmNewHandle, they will not be automatically freed when your application quits (unlike in the dynamic heap). Fortunately, at least on a soft reset, the Data Manager scans the storage heap, freeing any handles that aren't part of a database.

 The 3.5 version of the OS has a bug that prevents chunks allocated with DmNewHandle (and not in any database) from being reclaimed on a system reset. This was fixed in the 3.5.1 ROM (for the m100), and in the 3.5.2 update (available as a download). If you're running the 3.5 OS and a reset occurs while you've got such a handle allocated, the user's storage area will lose space.

Feature Memory

The Feature Manager provides support for features, which allow you to find out what services are available in a device (from the OS, or third-party code that can also register features). Features are also used for finding the ROM version on which your application is running (see Example 6-3). Features are referenced with a 32-bit creator code, and a feature number (different creator codes can use the same feature number).

Example 6-3. Finding the ROM version using the Feature Manager

```
UInt32 GetRomVersion( )
{
    UInt32 romVersion;
```

Example 6-3. Finding the ROM version using the Feature Manager

```
    FtrGet(sysFtrCreator, sysFtrNumROMVersion, &romVersion);
    return romVersion;
}
```

The post-3.0 versions of the Palm OS have also added support for Feature Memory—a nifty little way to allocate memory that is:

- Maintained even when an application closes
- Stored in the storage heap
- Possibly larger than 64 KB (for Palm OS 3.5 and above)

You should realize, however, that few applications have a need to justify the use of feature memory. It is primarily intended for shared libraries or other types of code that need access to memory, but don't have global variables available.

Applications can take advantage of feature memory, however, as a way to allocate a chunk larger than 64 KB (for Palm OS 3.5 and above). Of course, the allocation may fail if the storage heap doesn't have enough contiguous space.

Feature memory is maintained until a system reset or until it is explicitly freed. Since the memory is in the storage heap, writing is done with DmWrite, DmSet, or DmStrCopy.

 The 3.5 version of the OS has a bug (fixed in 3.5.1 and above) that prevents feature memory from being reclaimed on a system reset. As a result, we advise you not to use feature memory on the 3.5 OS (a system reset while feature memory has been allocated will cause users to lose space from their storage area).

Allocating feature memory

You allocate feature memory using FtrPtrNew (see Example 6-4).

Example 6-4. Allocating feature memory

```
MemPtr AllocateFeatureMemory(UInt32 amountToAllocate)
{
    UInt32  creator = '????';
    UInt16  featureNumber = 5;
    MemPtr  mem;
    Err     err;

    err = FtrPtrNew(creator, featureNumber, amountToAllocate, &mem);
    if (err == 0)
        return mem;
    else
        return NULL;
}
```

Of course, a real application won't use ???? as the creator; it will use its registered creator ID instead.

Retrieving feature memory

To retrieve the feature memory associated with a particular feature, you'll use `FtrGet` (see Example 6-5).

Example 6-5. Retrieving feature memory

```
MemPtr RetrieveFeatureMemory( )
{
    UInt32  creator = '????';
    UInt16  featureNumber = 5;
    MemPtr  mem;
    Err     err;

    err = FtrGet(creator, featureNumber, (UInt32 *) &mem);
    if (err == 0)
        return mem;
    else
        return NULL;
}
```

Freeing feature memory

You free up the feature memory with `FtrPtrFree` (see Example 6-6).

Example 6-6. Freeing feature memory

```
Err FreeFeatureMemory( )
{
    UInt32  creator = '????';
    UInt16  featureNumber = 5;

    return FtrPtrFree(creator, featureNumber);
}
```

File Streaming

The file streaming API provides an API similar to C standard I/O (studio). There are routines for dealing with files, including open, close, read, write, seek, create, and delete. These files (actually implemented as multiple records in a database) can be larger than 64 KB.

Note that file streaming is slower (both reading and writing) when compared to dealing with an in-memory chunk, since they require OS calls. See Chapter 10 for more information on using file streaming.

Owner IDs

While your application is running, all memory blocks that are allocated are automatically marked with an owner ID as belonging to the application. When the application quits, the Memory Manager scans the dynamic heap, freeing any such marked blocks, while leaving any system blocks alone.

 We shouldn't need to tell you that a well-written application should clean up after itself and not rely on this behavior of the system. Given the realities of application development, however, it is a good thing for users that this system behavior exists. Otherwise, starting and then stopping an application might suck up space in the dynamic heap. Such a bug would be very aggravating.

Owner IDs are useful for debugging as well. If you run your application with 3.5 OS or later debugging ROM (see Chapter 7), the owner IDs are used to warn you if you haven't freed all the memory you've allocated when you quit the application.

Persistent Memory and Owner IDs

Sometimes, while your application is running, the system needs to allocate system memory whose contents are maintained (for example, if an application opens TCP/IP, the system allocates memory, including buffers, that remain even when the application closes). It marks a block as system memory by setting the owner ID to 0.

Although it doesn't happen often, occasionally, an application may need to allocate a memory chunk that is maintained when the application closes. The best example of this case is when Application 1 launches Application 2, passing it a pointer to parameters. This pointer must point to dynamically allocated memory. (It can't point to a global in Application 1, because those globals are freed when Application 1 exits; it can't point to the stack because Application 1's stack is destroyed when Application 1 exits). This block of memory can't be deallocated when Application 1 exits, because it must still exist when Application 2 runs. The only solution is for Application 1 to set the owner ID of the chunk to 0. That way, it'll stick around while Application 1 quits and Application 2 can reference it. (Note that the OS will free up the parameters to Application 2 when Application 2 itself quits.)

APIs

Here are a couple of APIs:

Err MemPtrSetOwner (MemPtr p, UInt16 owner)
   This sets the owner of the particular pointer to the given owner. A 0 signifies the system.

Err MemHandleSetOwner (MemHandle h, UInt16 owner)
   This sets the owner of the particular handle to the given owner. A 0 signifies the system.

Owner ID Example

It seemed useful to give you an example of an application that needed some persistent memory. Example 6-7 shows one application launching another. It is from the Date Book example (LaunchToDoWithRecord in *DateAgenda.c*) and shows launching the To Do application. The parameter block must eventually be freed; in fact, the system deallocates it when the To Do application exits.

Example 6-7. Setting a memory block to be owned by the system (emphasized code is of interest)

```
if (recordH)
    {
    toDoRecP = (ToDoDBRecordType*) MemHandleLock (recordH);
    length = StrLen (&toDoRecP->description);
    MemHandleUnlock (recordH);

    // Create the param block (system is responsible for disposal).
    gotoParamsP = MemPtrNew(sizeof(GoToParamsType));
    if (gotoParamsP)
        {
        // Fill it in
        MemPtrSetOwner (gotoParamsP, 0);
        gotoParamsP->recordNum      = inRecordNum;
        gotoParamsP->matchPos       = length;  // Put cursor at end of string.
        gotoParamsP->matchFieldNum  = descSearchFieldNum;
        gotoParamsP->searchStrLen   = 0;    // Length of match (for Date Book).
        gotoParamsP->matchCustom    = 0;    // Length of match (for To Do).

        DmOpenDatabaseInfo(inDB, &gotoParamsP->dbID, NULL, NULL,
          &gotoParamsP->dbCardNo, NULL);

        launchCmd = sysAppLaunchCmdGoTo;
        launchParamsP = gotoParamsP;
        }
    else
        {
        ErrNonFatalDisplay ("Not enough memory to go to requested record");
        }
    }
else
    {
    ErrDisplay ("Couldn't find the displayed ToDo record!!!");
    }

AppLaunchWithCommand (sysFileCToDo, launchCmd, launchParamsP);
```

Cards and Local IDs

The Palm OS contains support for multiple numbered memory cards, in which each card can hold RAM and/or ROM. Every Palm OS device contains an internal card, with number 0, containing both RAM and ROM. The Handspring devices support an external ROM card (actually Flash), with number 1.

The Memory Manager doesn't store raw addresses to refer to memory chunks, but instead stores the offset of the chunk relative to the beginning of the card. Such an offset is called a local ID. By storing items this way, the base address of the card can change without requiring any changes to the structure of the heap.

 This flexibility isn't used currently (and, in fact, probably never will be), since it's not possible to move a card to a different base address. You can imagine, however, a device with multiple card slots, where the base address of a card would depend on into which slot it was inserted. This flexibility is there and is reflected in some APIs. You'll rarely need to know about cards and local IDs. We only brought it up because we thought it was important to explain the rationale behind the APIs requiring card numbers and local IDs.

Given a card number and a local ID, you can obtain the associated address. You can also go the other way, breaking apart a pointer to a chunk to a card number and local ID.

APIs

Here is a list of APIs:

`LocalID MemHandleToLocalID(MemHandle h)`
This returns the local ID to the chunk referred to by `h`.

`LocalIDKind MemLocalIDKind(LocalID local)`
This returns the constant `memIDHandle` if the given local ID refers to a handle, and `memIDPtr` if it refers to a pointer. It doesn't need the card number because the Memory Manager (currently) always stores handles as odd addresses.

`MemPtr MemLocalIDToGlobal(LocalID local, UInt16 cardNo)`
This returns either a pointer or a handle (that is, it might return a `MemHandle`, even though it is declared to return a `MemPtr`) referred to by the given local ID and card number. You need to know whether it is a handle or pointer before using it.

`MemPtr MemLocalIDToLockedPtr(LocalID local, UInt16 cardNo)`
This returns a pointer given the local ID and card number. If the local ID refers to a handle, this routine will lock it and return the associated pointer.

`MemPtr MemLocalIDToPtr(LocalID local, UInt16 cardNo)`
This returns a pointer given the local ID and card number. If the local ID refers to a locked handle, this routine will return the associated pointer. If it refers to an unlocked handle, a system alert will be displayed.

`UInt16 MemPtrCardNo(MemPtr p)`
Given a pointer, this returns its card number.

`LocalID MemPtrToLocalID(MemPtr p)`
Given a pointer, this returns its local ID.

Using Memory Effectively

Here are some tips to help you use the Memory Manager efficiently in your code. First, we engage in the classic debate of whether to use pointers or handles. Next, we remind you to check allocations. We conclude this section with an axiom of ours: keep the heap small.

Deciding Whether to Use Pointers or Handles

It can often be unclear when it is appropriate to use pointers (nonrelocatable blocks) and when to use handles (relocatable blocks). Here are some rules:

Use a pointer when working with a block of memory that exists for only a short time.
  Relocating is only necessary when the Memory Manager needs to allocate more memory. If you've got some code that allocates a block of memory, works with it, and then deallocates it, there's no need for it to be relocatable (since there will be no allocations during the lifetime of the block).

Use a pointer for a block of memory that must remain locked for its lifetime.
  For example, to set the label of a control at runtime requires a pointer. One way to store the label would be to allocate a handle, immediately lock it, and then keep it locked for the lifetime of the control. A better approach would be to go ahead and allocate a pointer. A relocatable block that's always locked can't be relocated, so it might as well have been nonrelocatable. Not only would there be slightly more code when using handles, the relocatable block would be locked in the middle of the heap, causing fragmentation. Pointers are all allocated together, at one end of the heap, so as to avoid fragmentation.

Use a handle for blocks that will need resizing.
  Nonrelocatable blocks can't increase in size, so handles are needed in this case.

Use a handle for data that is needed only occasionally.
  While it's not needed, keep it unlocked, so that the Memory Manager can move it as necessary. During the time that it is needed (for reading and/or writing), lock it.

Check Allocations and Resizes

There's not much memory available on Palm devices (yes, we know we have already mentioned this). As a result, you should get into the habit of checking every allocation and every resize to verify the success of the operation. Example 6-8 shows the wrong way to do things. It contains some code from ReplyApply in *Mail.c* from the Mail example (part of the OS 3.5 SDK) that doesn't check; it just blindly assumes that the memory allocation will succeed.

Example 6-8. Code that will blindly plow ahead if MemPtrNew doesn't succeed

```
subject = MemPtrNew (StrLen(prefix) + StrLen (record.subject)  + 1);
StrCopy (subject, prefix);
```

Ideally, your application will fail gracefully if unable to allocate memory. Example 6-9 shows some code from the Mail application (`SyncSavePreferences` in *MailSync.c*) that returns from the current function if memory allocation fails.

Example 6-9. Example of code that fails gracefully

```
prefsP = MemPtrNew (prefsSize);
if (! prefsP) return;
```

Another choice is to check the memory allocation and force a system reset if the allocation fails. In many cases, this is all you can do, since some memory allocations are quite necessary. The user shouldn't lose any data, since the storage heap is maintained on a reset. Example 6-10 shows an example of this approach, again from the Mail application (`MessageViewSetTitle` in *Mail.c*). We'll discuss `ErrFatalDisplayIf`, which puts up a fatal system alert, in Chapter 7.

Example 6-10. Example of code that forces a reset

```
title = MemPtrNew (len + 1);
ErrFatalDisplayIf (!title, "Out of memory");
```

Our Philosophy on Using Memory Efficiently

You can't go wrong if you follow the philosophy, ask not "What can my heap do for me?" but rather ask "What can I do for my heap?"

In other words, don't concentrate on how much you are required to leave free in the dynamic heap. Instead, concentrate on how little your application can use and still run.

MemoryTestAPIs Example

We have written a small sample program to help you test memory usage. Our MemoryTestAPIs example provides menu items that call many of the Memory Manager APIs. It allows you to test what happens when certain calls are made to the Memory Manager APIs by tapping, rather than requiring you to write code. Figure 6-3 shows the menus of the application.

The Code

There is no sanity checking before calling functions in this code (it is quite intentional!). For example, it doesn't check to see whether we've allocated a handle before locking. The reason for this is so you, as a user, can call the APIs and see what the OS does with different sequences of calls.

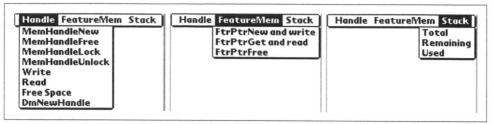

Figure 6-3. The menus of the MemoryTestAPIs application

Let's walk through the code for each of the menus in order. We'll look at the Handle menu and see what tricks we can cause when creating, freeing, locking, and unlocking handles. Next, we will mess about with pointers in FeatureMem menu. The last menu gives you information about the stack.

The code for all the Handle menu items share the following two variables:

```
static MemHandle gHandle;
static MemPtr gPointer;
```

Handle → MemHandleNew

This code calls `MemHandleNew`, allocating 1,000 bytes. If the function returns `NULL`, it displays an Alert notifying the user:

```
gHandle = MemHandleNew(1000);
if (!gHandle)
  DisplayOutOfMemoryAlert();
```

Handle → MemHandleFree

This code deallocates the handle:

```
MemHandleFree(gHandle);
```

Handle → MemHandleLock

This code calls `MemHandleLock`, saving the address of the locked block in gPointer:

```
gPointer = MemHandleLock(gHandle);
```

Handle → MemHandleUnlock

This code calls `MemHandleUnLock`:

```
MemHandleUnlock(gHandle);
```

Handle → Write

This just copies a string to gPointer:

```
StrCopy(gPointer, "Hello");
```

Handle → Read

The code displays an alert showing the string pointed to by gPointer. We wrote a utility function, DisplayStringInAlert, which displays two strings in an alert. (This code is on our web site, *http://www.calliopeinc.com/palmprog2/*, if you want to see how the function works.)

```
DisplayStringsInAlert("Read: ", gPointer);
```

Figure 6-4 shows an example.

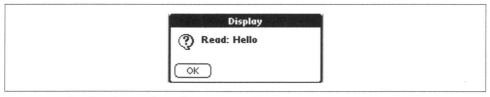

Figure 6-4. The alert shown after calling MemHandleRead

Handle → FreeSpace

This code displays an alert showing how much space is available. Figure 6-5 shows an example of the alert.

```
UInt32 freeSpace;
UInt32 maxSpace;
Char freeSpaceAsString[10];
UInt16 dynamicHeapID = 0;
Err err;

err = MemHeapFreeBytes(dynamicHeapID, &freeSpace, &maxSpace);
if (err == 0) {
    StrPrintF(freeSpaceAsString, "%ld", freeSpace);
    DisplayStringsInAlert("free space:", freeSpaceAsString);
}
```

Figure 6-5. The alert shown after calling MemHeapFreeBytes

Handle → DmNewHandle

The code allocates a handle in the storage heap (NULL signifies on card 0). It displays an alert if there isn't enough space.

```
gHandle = DmNewHandle(NULL, 10000);
if (!gHandle)
  DisplayOutOfMemoryAlert();
```

FeatureMem → FtrPtrNew and write

The code allocates feature memory (see AllocateFeatureMemory earlier in this chapter). Since the chunk is in the storage heap, and therefore write-protected, we must use DmStrCopy rather than StrCopy.

```
MemPtr p;

p = AllocateFeatureMemory(50000);
DmStrCopy(p, 0, "Hello");
```

FeatureMem → FtrPtrGet and read

This code retrieves the feature memory (see RetrieveFeatureMemory earlier in this chapter). It then displays the string pointed to by p in an alert.

```
MemPtr p;

p = RetrieveFeatureMemory();
DisplayStringsInAlert("Feature memory:", p);
```

FeatureMem → FtrPtrFree

The code frees the feature memory (see the code for FreeFeatureMemory, earlier).

```
FreeFeatureMemory();
```

Stack → Total

This code retrieves the total stack space (see GetTotalStackSpace earlier in this chapter) and displays it in an alert.

```
Char spaceAsString[10];

StrPrintF(spaceAsString, "%ld", GetTotalStackSpace());
DisplayStringsInAlert("total stack:", spaceAsString);
```

Stack → Remaining

The code retrieves the remaining stack space (see GetStackSpaceRemaining earlier in this chapter) and displays it in an alert.

```
Char spaceAsString[10];

StrPrintF(spaceAsString, "%ld", GetStackSpaceRemaining());
DisplayStringsInAlert("stack remaining:", spaceAsString);
```

Stack → Used

The code retrieves the used stack space (see GetStackSpaceUsed earlier in this chapter) and displays it in an alert.

```
Char spaceAsString[10];

StrPrintF(spaceAsString, "%ld", GetStackSpaceUsed());
DisplayStringsInAlert("stack used:", spaceAsString);
```

Testing the Application

Here are some different tests you can run with this application:

- Allocate a handle with `MemHandleNew`, and then lock it more than 14 times.
- Allocate a handle, lock it, and then unlock it more than once.
- Allocate five handles and check the memory space between each allocation (notice the amount of memory decreasing).
- Allocate with `MemHandleNew`, lock, write, read, unlock, and then free the handle. These should all work without error.

What to Remember

You learned how memory is structured in the Palm OS. Of the two kinds of memory (ROM and RAM), we spent most of the time discussing RAM. It is the memory primarily available to applications. RAM memory is used for both application data and the dynamic memory in which an application's stack and globals must run. We looked at the Memory Manager APIs and showed you some sample code to help clarify their use.

Next, we turned to the important discussions of how to work around some of the size limitations imposed on your data and how to use memory effectively given its scarcity. Last of all, we offered you some advice and a helpful sample program to let you test what happens when your pointer and handle allocations get out of control.

## CHAPTER 7

Debugging Palm Applications

There are a variety of useful debugging tools for your Palm OS application. The best by far is the Palm OS Emulator (POSE). With it you can code, build, and test your handheld application, with nothing more than a desktop computer. The strategic use of the reset buttons can be useful as well. There are also a number of hidden Graffiti shortcut characters that offer you debugging aids and shortcuts. Source-level debugging is available for both CodeWarrior and the PRC-Tools and can go a long way towards easier problem fixing.

In this chapter, we will show you how to use all of these methods to debug your applications. We will also discuss Gremlins—the useful testing creatures that bear not the slightest resemblance to the fanciful beings. Gremlins in the Palm world are little monkeys who bash about randomly on your code looking for problems. You may not like them, but you will find them very helpful for catching bugs you might otherwise miss.

 In the first edition of this book, we put this chapter much later, at the end of the section. Upon reflection, we think this was a mistake. We moved it to the front because we want you to become familiar with these tools as soon as possible, and certainly before you delve too deeply into any real coding. Read this chapter carefully and take the time to learn how to use all of these tools before you start writing your own application. Following this one bit of advice will save you hours of frustration.

There is no overall relationship between these various tools. They just represent what is available to help with problems in your code. Feel free to read topics in whatever order you like, but make sure to pay special attention to POSE; it really is an indispensable debugging aid.

POSE

POSE emulates, at the hardware level, a Palm handheld. It emulates a Motorola Dragonball processor, a display, and so on. Since the actual Palm OS handhelds also contain ROM, the emulator must deal with this by requiring ROM as well. It uses a file containing a ROM image. POSE can emulate any OS version, depending on the ROM you provide. Figure 7-1 shows POSE emulating some different devices.

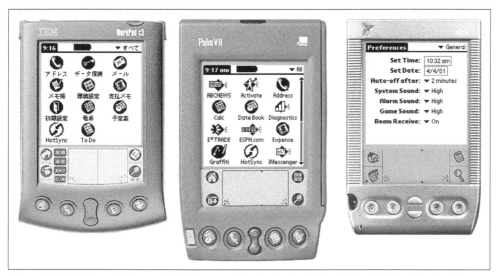

Figure 7-1. POSE emulating an IBM Japanese Workpad c3, a Palm VII, and a Handspring Visor

 POSE is based on Copilot, an application written by Greg Hewgill. Mac OS and Unix versions were created by others. A Palm tools engineer, Keith Rollin, began his job at Palm by doing a quick project to unify the disparate ports. Years later, he's still hard at work on POSE, continually adding features and adding support for new hardware devices.

POSE is supported by Palm for Windows, Mac, and Linux/Unix. Better yet, source code is provided. You are free to make changes, but if you do, please contribute them back to Palm. Your enhancements may be incorporated in the main code base, making life better for everybody.

 POSE can be downloaded from *http://www.palmos.com/dev/*. You should always check Palm's web site for the most recent version, as this tool evolves rapidly. It also comes with the Metrowerks CodeWarrior for Palm OS. In this chapter, we discuss POSE 3.2, the version current as of mid-2001.

Note that Palm requires a no-fee license in order to download ROMs. Executing this license can be somewhat time-consuming, especially outside of the U.S. So, do it now or you will be sorry.

Debug and release versions of ROMs can be downloaded from Palm's web site (*http:// www.palmos.com/dev/*). The debug versions do extra sanity-checking on calls, which can catch some problems that would cause a crash on a nondebug ROM (or problems that don't cause an error today but are still wrong). You should always do testing with debug ROMs. We certainly hope it goes without saying that you should fix any problems that the debug ROMs show.

Release ROMs can also be downloaded directly from a device by running a special transfer application on the handheld that communicates with POSE over a serial. This transfer application, along with instructions on how to use it, are part of the POSE distribution.

POSE Sessions

A session consists of:

- A choice of ROM file.
- A choice of device to emulate.
- A snapshot of the memory associated with the device. This can be saved to a file in order to resume the session from exactly where it left off.

You create a new session using the New menu item (on Windows, right-click to display the menu). In the New Session dialog box, you specify the following:

- The ROM file to use.
- The device you want to emulate (note that once you choose a ROM file, this list is truncated to those devices with which it is compatible).
- The skin (that is, the artwork to use for the device).
- The memory size.

See Figure 7-2 for a look at the New Session dialog box. Once you've created a session, you can save it as a file. By default, when you run POSE, it reopens the last session file you used.

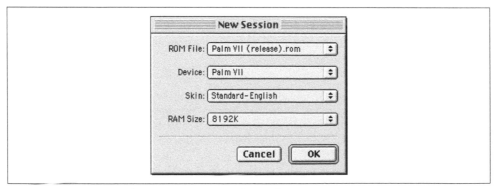

Figure 7-2. New Session dialog box customizes the emulation

If you have the Caps Lock key on when you launch POSE, it will instead present a New Session dialog box. This can be very handy if you've got a corrupted session file.

Installing Applications and PDBs on POSE

There are a couple of ways to install applications (*.prc* files) and databases (*.pdb* files). The easiest method is to drag a file and drop it onto the emulator window.

An alternative is to use the Install Application/Database menu item. The advantage this method offers is a list of shortcuts for the last few files you've installed (see Figure 7-3).

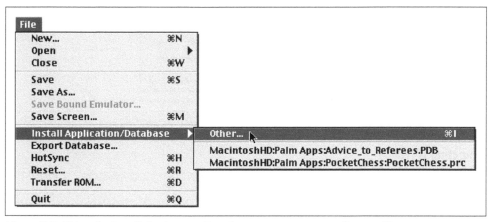

Figure 7-3. Using the Install Application/Database menu item to install a .prc file

Communications

POSE handles some communication types, like serial and TCP/IP, but doesn't support infrared (IrDA) or USB (you'll need to use an actual device to test those features). Let's look at how to handle serial first and TCP/IP second. You configure the communication emulation of POSE in the Preferences dialog box (see Figure 7-4).

Emulating serial

The emulator does a low-level emulation of the serial port found on the Dragonball, which it routes to the serial port on the desktop machine. This serial emulation is very, very good. We've used it to communicate with many serial devices, including GPS devices, the HotSync application running on the same desktop, and vending machines (yes, open up most vending machines and you'll find a serial port).

POSE can also reroute serial traffic over a TCP/IP connection, allowing your serial port data to actually be transmitted via TCP/IP to some other application.

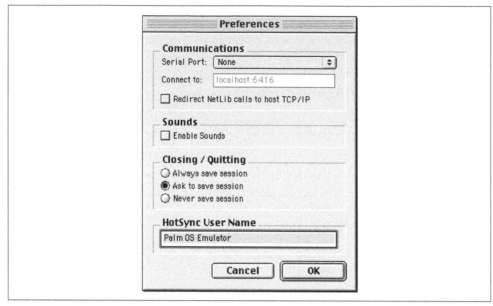

Figure 7-4. Preferences dialog box controls serial emulation and TCP/IP redirection

Emulating TCP/IP

POSE can either use the TCP/IP stack of the Palm OS, which requires a PPP/SLIP connection, or can use the desktop's TCP/IP stack.

When using the stack of the Palm OS, one possibility is to hook up a modem to the serial port, and dial up to your favorite ISP (exactly as you would from a Palm device with a modem). Another is to have a PPP server running on your desktop machine. In this case, you have the PPP server use one serial port (let's say COM1), and have POSE use another serial port (let's say COM2). Attach a null-modem cable between the two ports, and suddenly POSE will be communicating with the PPP server.

 Mochasoft has an inexpensive PPP server called Mocha PPP that works well for this purpose. See *http://www.mochasoft.dk* for details.

There is also another useful alternative. Rather than using the TCP/IP stack of the Palm OS, you can cause POSE to redirect TCP/IP services. That is, each TCP/IP call in the Palm OS (like NetLibConnect) is actually mapped to a corresponding call in the desktop OS (like connect). Since you're using the desktop's TCP/IP services, you can take advantage of the connectivity and speed of the desktop's Internet connection. A slight, but important, disadvantage is that you're no longer actually using the same code as you would be on the handheld. Since there are subtle differences in the redirected code as opposed to the original Palm OS code, you must be sure to test your network application with the actual Palm OS TCP/IP stack at some point.

Error Checking with POSE

Since POSE is emulating the instructions of a Dragonball, it can do checks at each instruction. It checks every memory reference to see whether what is being done is valid. If it isn't, it'll present an error (see Figure 7-5). POSE also has knowledge of the Palm OS and understands the layout of the Memory Manager.When an error occurs, you can reset POSE, click the Debug button to drop into your debugger, or continue to try to go on past the error.

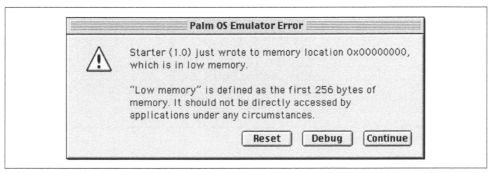

Figure 7-5. POSE error dialog box

POSE catches the following important problems (see the Debug Options dialog box in Figure 7-6 for a complete list):

- Overflowing stack space
- Reading/writing outside of a valid chunk
- Reading/writing to chunks that have been freed already
- Accessing hardware directly (for example, writing directly to the screen)
- Writing to low-memory globals
- Reading or writing directly from UI Manager data structures (rather than using approved APIs)

The checks done by POSE complement the checks done by the debug ROMs. Each checks things the other doesn't.

Some developers who get errors when running on POSE with debug ROMs don't bother fixing them; such lazy ingrates justify themselves with comments like "it works fine on a real device." Here are two important problems with such arguments:

- It assumes that the code actually does work fine on a real device and this may certainly not be true. In our experience, POSE will report errors that would occur intermittently on a device. For example, reading from a freed block will happen to work unless the Memory Manager has reused the freed block in the meantime (something it can do frequently).
- Many of the reported errors may not cause errors on a current device, but will in the future (that is, your application will no longer work on future devices).

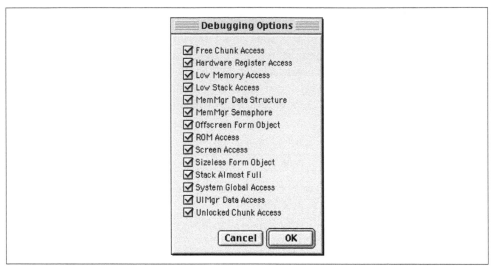

Figure 7-6. Debugging Options dialog box of POSE

Logging

The Logging Options dialog box (see Figure 7-7) controls different information that can be logged to a text file. It includes things such as events in the event queue, system calls, as well as all data sent or received over serial, TCP/IP, or Exchange Manager (beaming/sending).

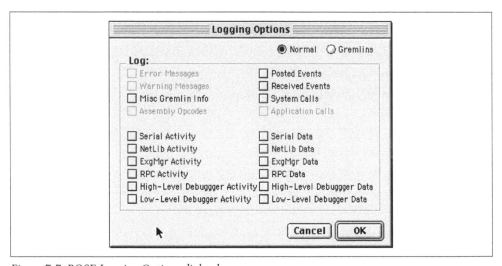

Figure 7-7. POSE Logging Options dialog box

Here's some sample output showing logged received events:

```
1.340:  <-  EvtGetPen: screenX=10, screenY=178, penDown=1.
1.349:  <-  EvtGetPen: <<<eliding identical events>>>.
1.440:  <-  EvtGetPen: screenX=10, screenY=178, penDown=0.
```

```
1.441:  <-  EvtGetSysEvent: penUpEvent      X:10   Y:178
1.445:  <-  EvtGetEvent: penUpEvent      X:10   Y:178
1.445:  <-  EvtGetSysEvent: keyDownEvent    Key:0x108 (vchrLaunch), Modifiers:
0x0008
1.450:  <-  EvtGetEvent: keyDownEvent     Key:0x108 (vchrLaunch), Modifiers: 0x0008
1.467:  <-  EvtGetEvent: appStopEvent
1.639:  <-  EvtGetEvent: frmLoadEvent    ID: 1000
1.647:  <-  EvtGetEvent: frmOpenEvent    ID: 1000
2.364:  <-  EvtGetEvent: winEnterEvent    Enter: 0x000034e4   Exit: 0x00000000   Enter
Form: "9:45 am"
3.173:  <-  EvtGetSysEvent: penDownEvent    X:19   Y:19
3.177:  <-  EvtGetEvent: penDownEvent    X:19   Y:19
3.246:  <-  EvtGetPen: screenX=19, screenY=19, penDown=1.
3.255:  <-  EvtGetPen: <<<eliding identical events>>>.
3.276:  <-  EvtGetPen: screenX=19, screenY=18, penDown=1.
3.276:  <-  EvtGetPen: screenX=19, screenY=18, penDown=0.
3.298:  <-  EvtGetEvent: appStopEvent
3.739:  <-  EvtGetEvent: frmLoadEvent    ID: 1000
3.748:  <-  EvtGetEvent: frmOpenEvent    ID: 1000
3.865:  <-  EvtGetEvent: winEnterEvent    Enter: 0x000034a4   Exit: 0x00000000   Enter
Form: "Address"
3.866:  <-  EvtGetSysEvent: penUpEvent      X:19   Y:18
3.870:  <-  EvtGetEvent: penUpEvent      X:19   Y:18
```

Sometimes, when an error occurs, you will find yourself in the situation where it's unclear what sequence of events led up to the error (especially with Gremlins). If you have logging turned on, you can look at that sequence of events. This might be just the trick to figuring out why the error is occurring.

Profiling

POSE can do very accurate profiling of your application to determine where it spends its time. This will obviously help you do intelligent optimizing. In order to profile smartly, you need to do the following:

1. Use a special profiling version of POSE (Palm OS Emulator-Profile). It runs slightly slower than the regular version because it has the ability to count every instruction.

2. Build your application with function names embedded in the code. For CodeWarrior, in the 68K Processor panel of the Target Settings dialog box, you'll need to set the MacsBug Symbols pop up to New Style. For PRC-Tools, you'll need to use the -mdebug-labels option to GCC.

3. Start your application.

4. Use Start in the Profile menu to start POSE measuring.

5. Exercise the portion of your application you want to test.

6. Use Stop in the Profile menu to stop POSE measuring.

7. Use Dump in the Profile menu to dump the profiling information.

POSE outputs the profiling information in two formats: tab-delimited text file, and Metrowerks Profiler output (*.mwp*). Here's a (very) abbreviated dump of the text file:

```
index parent  depth function name  count only cycles only msec only %  plus kids
cycles  plus kids msec
5298    5293    36  DmDatabaseInfo  1    742 0.000     0.0 10572    0.000    0.0 0.045
0.045   0.027   2
5322    5298    37  MemPtrUnlock    1    404 0.000     0.0 4944     0.000    0.0 0.024
0.024   0.027   2
5334    5322    38  MemSemaphoreRelease 1  288 0.000    0.0 2012     0.000    0.0 0.017
0.017   0.013   1
```

We're sure it must be possible to write some Excel macros to easily slice and dice the information, but we've never had to do so; we always examine the measurements using Metrowerks Profiler, which unfortunately runs only on Mac OS (see Figure 7-8). An alternative is to use KProf, a Linux application that displays profiling information, and that supports POSE profiling output (download from *http://kprof.sourceforge.net*).

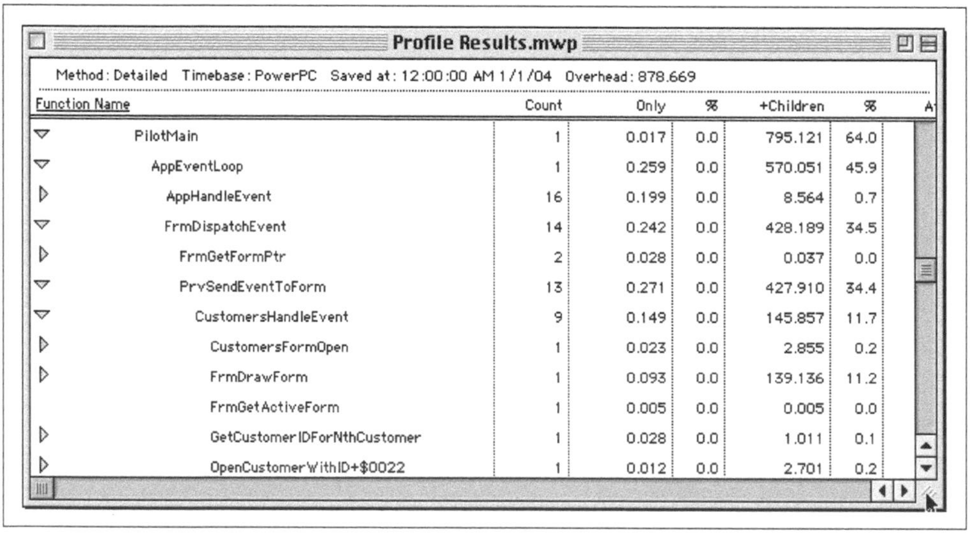

Figure 7-8. Metrowerks Profiler

Remote Scripting

POSE listens on a TCP/IP socket (port number 6415) for commands to control its behavior. It can control high-level things (such as creating or saving a session) as well as Palm OS–level things (such as posting events or calling Palm OS system calls).

POSE comes with some PERL scripts that use these remote control facilities. This example automates skipping past the startup application (including pen calibration):

```
#######################################################################
#
# File:      SkipStartup.pl
#
# Purpose:   Skip the Palm V startup application.
#
# Description:  Run this script to skip past the application that
```

```
#          automatically starts when cold-booting a Palm V
#          (or Palm IIIx).  It generates the appropriate
#          pen events to "tap past" the initial forms.
#
#####################################################################

use EmRPC;       # EmRPC::OpenConnection, CloseConnection
use EmFunctions;
use EmUtils;     # TapPenSync, TapButtonSync


EmRPC::OpenConnection(6415, "localhost");

  TapPenSync (100, 100);        # Tap past first setup screen.
  TapPenSync (100, 100);        # Tap past second setup screen.

  TapPenSync (10, 10);          # First tap in pen calibration screen.
  TapPenSync (160-10, 160-10);  # Second tap in pen calibration screen.
  TapPenSync (80, 60);          # Confirmation tap in pen calibration screen.

  TapButtonSync ("Next");       # Tap Next button.
  TapButtonSync ("Done");       # Tap Done button.

EmRPC::CloseConnection( );
```

One use of this facility is for regression testing. If you find a bug in your application, you can write a script that reproduces the error, and later run that script to verify the bug is fixed and doesn't reappear.

 The Gremlins feature of POSE (automated mindless testing) is so important that we don't cover it here, but instead have an entire section on it later in this chapter.

Major Advantages of POSE

In our programming, we use POSE almost exclusively. Every once in a while, we download to an actual device for testing, but all the following reasons should make it clear why this is a less attractive alternative:

POSE doesn't need batteries
We don't have to buy AAA batteries nearly as often.

POSE doesn't need cables to download an application
It can download directly from your desktop machine.

POSE can use the keyboard
You can use the keyboard as an alternative to Graffiti.

POSE on a laptop is a self-contained environment
We've done development and testing at the beach, in the car, poolside, and in many other places where it would have been inconvenient to also have had a Palm OS device and associated cabling.

POSE detects bad programming practices
> Though we personally don't need to worry about this, since there are never bugs in *our* code, POSE is great for finding all sorts of violations. It lets you know if you are trying to access low memory, system globals, screen memory, hardware registers, unallocated memory, and so on.

Screenshots are a snap
> It's easy to take screenshots (for product manuals or books!).

You can do source-level debugging of serial and TCP/IP applications
> On an actual device, the source-level debugger communicates to the device over the port that would otherwise be doing serial or TCP/IP. Therefore, you can't do source-level debugging. With POSE, you can.

You can use POSE to demonstrate a Palm OS application
> With an LCD projector, hundreds of people can see your application being demonstrated. If you don't know that this is an advantage, try displaying a Palm application running on an actual handheld to even two people.

Minor Disadvantages of POSE

Though we hate to admit it, POSE is bad for certain things:

The speed isn't the same as on an actual device
> POSE can be faster or much slower than an actual device, depending on the particulars of the desktop machine running it. (This makes optimizing difficult.)

This isn't the device on which your final application will run
> As a result, you still need to test with the nondebug version of the ROM. Even after testing with a nondebug ROM under POSE, you still want to test on an actual handheld device. (Don't be tempted to ignore this step. We have seen many release stopping problems that would have been caught in time if the developer had tested on the actual device sooner.)

Graffiti is harder to use
> It's much harder to use Graffiti with a mouse (or touchpad) than it is with a stylus.

POSE doesn't contain support for infrared
> This means all infrared functionality must be tested with actual handheld devices.

Once you have used POSE for a while, we think you will find it hard to imagine how you could have done handheld development without it. It is a very useful development and debugging tool.

Graffiti Debugging Shortcuts

There are a number of hidden debugging aids that you can access using the Graffiti shortcut mechanism.

These debugging mechanisms can drain your battery quickly or wreak havoc with your data. Use them judiciously; no matter what, turn them off as soon as you are through with them.

The Graffiti debugging shortcuts are accessed by writing the Graffiti shortcut character (a cursive lowercase L) followed by two taps (the two taps generate a dot, or period), followed by a specific character or number. It's common to open the Find dialog box before writing them (see Figure 7-9). (Find has a text field that's available in all applications, and it's nice to have the feedback of seeing the characters as you write them.)

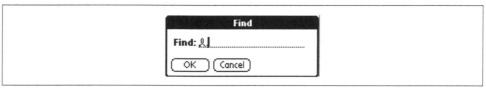

Figure 7-9. The Find dialog box with a shortcut

Here is a complete list of these shortcuts:

.1

Enters debugger mode. The device opens the serial port and listens for a low-level debugger to connect to it (e.g., the Palm Debugger application). Do a soft reset to exit this mode.

.2

Enters console mode. The device opens the serial port and listens for a high-level debugger like CodeWarrior to connect to it. Do a soft reset to exit this mode.

.3

Turns off the power auto-off feature. The device does not power off after idle time (although the Power key still works). Do a soft reset to exit this mode.

.4

Displays the user's name and HotSync numeric ID.

.5

Erases the user's name and HotSync numeric ID. On the next HotSync, this device appears to be a never-before-synced device. Syncing to an existing user recognizes all the records on the device as new; thus, they are all duplicated for the existing user on the desktop and handheld.

.6

Displays the ROM build date and time.

.7

Switches between various battery profiles (to adjust when the battery warning alerts appear).

✗ .8

Toggles the backlight mode on certain devices (like the Palm V, or Palm IIIx). The white pixels are backlit instead of the black pixels.

✗ .t

Toggles loopback mode on and off for the Exchange Manager. This allows loopback mode testing even for applications that haven't set the localMode field to true in the ExgSocketType structure (like the built-in applications, for instance). See Chapter 12 for information on initializing the ExgSocketType structure.

✗ .s

Toggles between serial and IR modes on the device. In serial mode, information that would normally be sent via infrared is sent via the serial port. This works on devices with a built-in IR port, but may or may not work on an OS 3.0 upgraded unit that has an IR port on the memory card.

Source-Level Debugging

The source-level debugging is different between CodeWarrior and PRC-Tools. We'll look at each in turn.

Source-Level Debugging with CodeWarrior

CodeWarrior can do source-level debugging either with a handheld (attached via serial or USB) or with POSE.

You first need to enable source-level debugging with Enable Debugger from the Project menu. This is a toggle menu item; if it says Disable Debugger, then debugging is enabled.

Choosing a target

You need to tell CodeWarrior whether you are using POSE or the handheld; then it needs to acquire its target.

To use POSE, select Palm OS Emulator from the Target pop-up menu in the Palm Connection Settings panel of the Preferences dialog box (see Figure 7-10).

In order to debug, POSE has to be running. When you choose Debug from the Project menu, CodeWarrior automatically downloads the PRC file to the Emulator and (by default) stops at the first line of the program.

 If the "Always launch emulator" option is set, CodeWarrior will automatically launch POSE when you start CodeWarrior.

To use the handheld, specify the target as Palm OS Device in Preferences (see Figure 7-11). When you choose Debug from the Project menu, CodeWarrior prompts you to enter console mode (see Figure 7-12). Use Shortcut, tap, tap, 2 on the handheld and click OK in the CodeWarrior dialog box. CodeWarrior then automatically downloads the PRC file to the device and stops at the program's first line of the program.

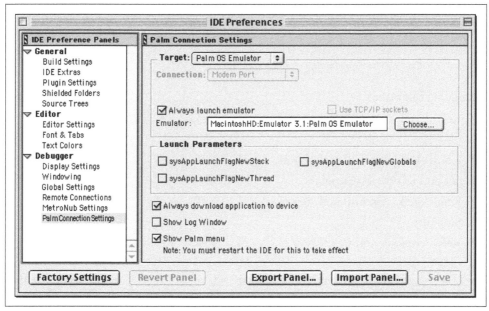

Figure 7-10. Selecting options for debugging using POSE

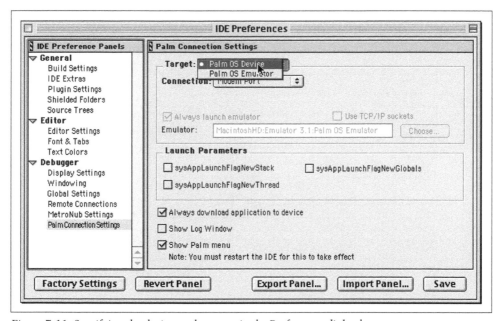

Figure 7-11. Specifying the device as the target in the Preferences dialog box

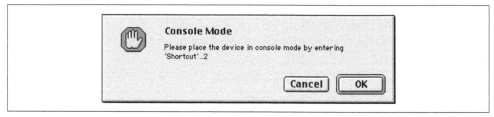

Figure 7-12. CodeWarrior prompting to enter console mode

Debugging commands

Figure 7-13 shows CodeWarrior source-level debugging in action. With it you can do all of the following:

- Control execution of the program
- Set and remove breakpoints
- Single-step (step into and step over)
- Step out
- View variables and memory

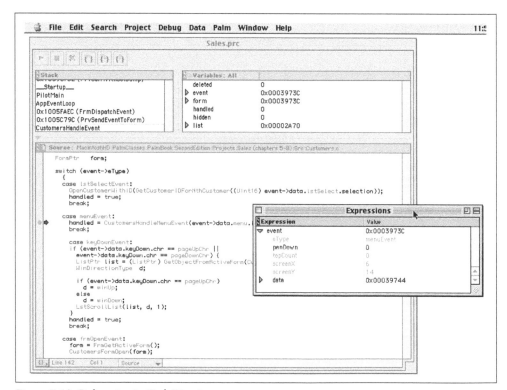

Figure 7-13. Debugging in CodeWarrior

Console window

While you are debugging, a Console window is available to you. From the Palm menu, choose the Open Debug Console menu item to open this window. In this command line–oriented window, you can issue commands to the device (or emulator) in order to obtain information about memory and databases and to export databases.

Common debugger commands are:

help
>   Displays a list of all commands.

help *command*
>   Displays help for the specified command.

dir 0
>   Lists all the databases on card 0. This is useful to see whether your application's database or databases exist.

ht *heapNumber*
>   Displays a summary of the given heap. A heap number of 0 specifies the dynamic heap. Here's example output (note that it shows the amount of free space available):

```
Displaying Heap ID: 0000, mapped to 00001B00, first free: 00003890
-----------------------------------------------------------------------
Heap Summary:
  flags:             2000
  size:              03E500
  numHandles:        #200
  Free Chunks:       #2     (0373AA bytes)
  Movable Chunks:    #25    (001A58 bytes)
  Non-Movable Chunks: #49   (0053CA bytes)
  Owner  0:          005968 bytes
  Owner  1:          0004DA bytes
  Owner  2:          000FE0 bytes
```

hd *heapNumber*
>   Displays not just a summary, but all the chunks in a heap. A heap number of 0 specifies the dynamic heap. This allows you to see which chunks are where, which are locked, which are unlocked, and so on. It's not necessary to see the heap in such detail very often, however.

Source-Level Debugging with PRC-Tools

The PRC-Tools can debug an application running on the handheld or in POSE; however, to debug on the handheld, you need to run a special application, GDBPanel.

1. Compile and link your application with the -g flag.
2. Load your application on either POSE or the handheld.
3. (This step isn't needed for POSE.) Install and run GDBPanel on the handheld.

4. Run GDB. Pass your linked file as a command-line argument—*not* the PRC (if your application is *foo*, pass *foo* as the parameter, not *foo.prc*):

```
m68k-palmos-gdb your_linked_app
```

5. Within GDB, specify the target with which to connect. Here are your choices. For POSE on the local machine:

```
target palmos
```

To specify POSE on a different machine:

```
target palmos hostnameOrIPAddress:2000
```

To specify a device on COM1: (Windows):

```
target palmos COM1:
```

To specify a device on */dev/ttyS0* (Unix/Linux):

```
target palmos /dev/ttyS0
```

6. Within POSE, start your application. GDB will stop at the first line.

Here are the most important commands that GDB supports:

print *expressionToPrint1, …, expressionToPrintN*

Use the print command to look at the values of variables. Here's an example:

```
print *myStructPtr, theString[5], myOtherStruct.x
```

backtrace

Prints a stack crawl, showing each function in the stack, including parameter names and values.

step

Single steps, stepping into functions.

next

Single steps, stepping over functions.

cont

Continues running the program until it reaches a breakpoint, causes an error, or exits.

break *funcNameOrLineNumber*

Sets a breakpoint. You can break at a function:

```
break MyFunction
```

Or you can set a breakpoint at a specific line number in a file:

```
break MyFile.c:16
```

quit

Quits the program. If the program is still running, you are prompted for GDB to automatically quit it (by resetting POSE).

help

There are, of course, many other functions. Use help to find out more about them all.

GDB is a text-oriented debugger, where commands and responses to commands are interleaved. Here's an example of GDB running (emphasized lines contain user input):

```
(gdb) cont
Continuing.

Breakpoint 2, MainFormHandleEvent (eventP=0x185f4) at MainForm.c:38
38          Boolean handled = false;
(gdb) list
33      }
34
35
36      Boolean MainFormHandleEvent(EventPtr eventP)
37      {
38        Boolean handled = false;
39        FormPtr frmP;
40
41        switch (eventP->eType)
42        {
(gdb) print eventP->eType
$3 = frmTitleSelectEvent
```

Theoretically, the free text editor GNU Emacs can be used as an Integrated Development Environment (IDE) that can control the debugging process. As you debug, Emacs makes sure that the source file with the current line is always displayed, and it provides some menu commands that can be used instead of typing into GDB.

Gremlins

There are two approaches to testing software, which can often be used in a complementary fashion:

Functionality testing

Careful systematic testing on a feature-by-feature basis, making sure everything works as advertised

Bashing on it

An almost random use of the software to make sure it doesn't break when stressed

Gremlins does the second sort of testing. Imagine, if you will, a very inquisitive monkey given a Palm OS device with your application on it. The monkey grabs the stylus and starts tapping away. Let's look at some characteristics of the monkey:

- It's especially attracted to buttons, pop-ups, and other active items on the screen. It taps in nonactive areas on the screen but not very often; it likes active areas.

- It's a literate monkey that knows Graffiti. It inputs Graffiti characters—sometimes garbage runs of characters but occasionally fragments of Shakespeare.

- It's hyperactive. On one of our machines, it can do about 100 events a second.

- It's well behaved. If told to debug a certain application, it won't switch out of that application.

You start a Gremlin from the Gremlins dialog box of POSE by selecting New from the Gremlins menu. In this dialog box you specify which Gremlin you want to use and on what application (see Figure 7-14). You get to choose from 1,000 of them, each of which acts slightly differently in terms of the events it generates (the number is a seed to a pseudorandom number generator). Looking at Figure 7-14, you see that we've specified our own Sales application to test. You can also specify more than one application in order to check for problems between applications, or for problems in launching or quiting your application.

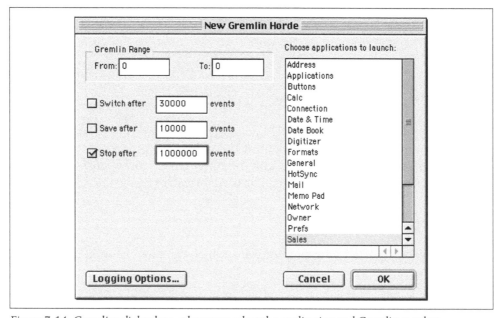

Figure 7-14. Gremlins dialog box, where you select the application and Gremlin number

Gremlins goes to work by generating events and causing your application to respond to them. A Gremlin generates pen-downs (mostly on active areas), inputs keys, and does everything a user could do. You'll find, however, that it will end up exercising parts of your program you'd never tested: fields with more characters than you'd anticipated or more records than you'd planned for (to the extent that the entire storage heap will probably be filled). Here are the various things you can specify for Gremlins:

- You can choose a range of Gremlin numbers (each does the same thing every time you run it). We'll talk more about specifying a range (rather than just the same start and end number) later in this chapter.

- You can choose one or more applications (from among those installed) and the Gremlin will run only those applications.

- You can specify the number of events to run (it's not uncommon to have a bug that shows up only after hundreds of thousands of events).

Figure 7-15 shows the dialog box that occurs during the Gremlins run.

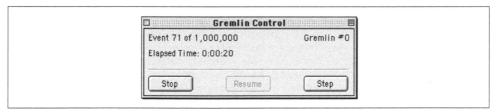

Figure 7-15. Dialog box shown during a Gremlins run

If you encounter an error while running Gremlins (as is often the case), the dialog box shown in Figure 7-16 tells you about the problem. You can click the Debug button to go directly to the debugger.

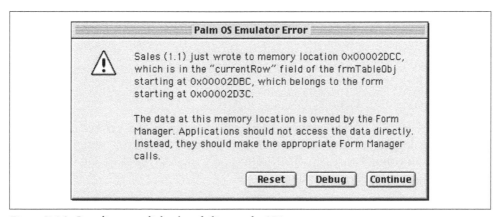

Figure 7-16. Gremlin error dialog box failing on the 971st event

If you choose to log information (see Figure 7-14 for the Logging Options button), POSE creates a file (named *Log #n.txt*, where *n* increments on every run). This is useful if you want to know how far Gremlins got before an error occurred, or to find out events that happened before the error. Here's an example output:

```
Gremlin #2 started, 10 steps.
>>> EvtEnqueueKey: ascii = 0x007C, keycode = 0x0000, modifiers = 0x0000.
<<< 0: keyDownEvent     Key:'|' 0x7c,  Modifiers: 0x0000
>>> EvtEnqueuePenPoint: pen->x=99, pen->y=150.
<<< 1: penDownEvent     X:97    Y:136
<<< 1: ctlEnterEvent    ID: 10307
>>> EvtEnqueuePenPoint: pen->x=91, pen->y=157.
<<< 2: EvtGetPen: screenX=89, screenY=143, penDown=1.
>>> EvtEnqueuePenPoint: pen->x=156, pen->y=87.
<<< 3: EvtGetPen: screenX=154, screenY=73, penDown=1.
>>> EvtEnqueuePenPoint: pen->x=-1, pen->y=-1.
<<< 4: EvtGetPen: screenX=154, screenY=73, penDown=0.
```

```
<<< 4: ctlExitEvent
<<< 4: penUpEvent        X:154   Y:73
>>> KeyHandleInterrupt: periodic=0, status=0x00000020.
>>> EvtEnqueueKey: ascii = 0x0069, keycode = 0x0000, modifiers = 0x0000.
<<< 6: keyDownEvent    Key:'i' 0x69,  Modifiers: 0x0000
>>> EvtEnqueueKey: ascii = 0x0079, keycode = 0x0000, modifiers = 0x0000.
<<< 7: keyDownEvent    Key:'y' 0x79,  Modifiers: 0x0000
>>> EvtEnqueueKey: ascii = 0x0044, keycode = 0x0000, modifiers = 0x0000.
<<< 8: keyDownEvent    Key:'D' 0x44,  Modifiers: 0x0000
>>> EvtEnqueueKey: ascii = 0x0065, keycode = 0x0000, modifiers = 0x0000.
<<< 9: keyDownEvent    Key:'e' 0x65,  Modifiers: 0x0000
>>> EvtEnqueueKey: ascii = 0x0020, keycode = 0x0000, modifiers = 0x0000.
<<< 10: keyDownEvent    Key:' ' 0x20,  Modifiers: 0x0000
Gremlin #2 stopped at 11 of 10 after 378 msecs.
```

If you request "Log system calls," the system calls that are executed are output. Here's a portion of output where logging was requested (some of the lines were removed for brevity):

```
96.790 (974):    <- EvtGetEvent: penUpEvent      X:17   Y:158
96.790 (974):    --- System Call 0xA0A9: SysHandleEvent.
96.790 (974):    --- System Call 0xA3AE: TsmHandleEvent.
96.790 (974):    --- System Call 0xA2AB: .
96.790 (974):    --- System Call 0xA1BF: MenuHandleEvent.
96.790 (974):    --- System Call 0xA1A0: FrmDispatchEvent.
96.790 (974):    --- System Call 0xA327: FrmValidatePtr.
96.790 (974):    --- System Call 0xA016: MemPtrSize.
96.791 (974):    --- System Call 0xA016: MemPtrSize.
```

Logs are verbose; it's not uncommon to have an average of 10K per event when certain types of logging are enabled. Rather than letting the log grow without bounds, POSE reuses log files that reach 1024K. Thus, only the last 1024K of log information is saved—a nice refinement, we think.

Gremlin ranges

If you fire up your machine to do a Gremlins run overnight using just one Gremlin number, when you come back in the morning, it'll either still be running, or you'll have an error. But what that means is for the investment of an evening, you've found at most one error. The more efficient programmers among you will obviously want to know how you can you come back in the morning and get multiple errors.

One way would be to have multiple machines, each running your application starting at a different Gremlin number. An alternative is to use Gremlin ranges. With these, POSE itself will multitask by trying different Gremlin numbers. The numbers on the lines show the order in which the Gremlins are run.

When you use Gremlin ranges, POSE saves a snapshot of the beginning session. It then runs the first Gremlin number in the given range for a certain number of events (specified by the "Switch after" number). If an error occurs before getting to that number, it logs the error, and moves on to the next number. If it gets to that number without hitting an error, it saves its state (in a snapshot), and then moves on to the next Gremlin number. Basically, it runs each Gremlin number round-robin, giving them each a certain number of events before moving on to the next.

When you come back in the morning you can have a whole lot of errors; as many errors as you've specified in the range. Figure 7-17 shows a Gremlin range running three Gremlin numbers.

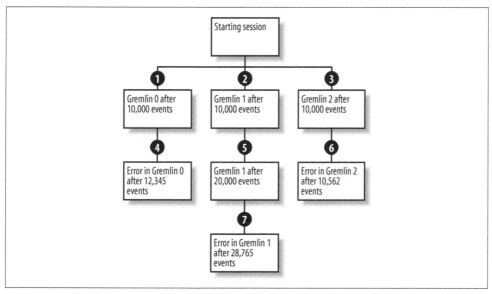

Figure 7-17. Running Gremlin Range from 0 to 2 switching after every 10,000 events. The numbers on the lines show the Gremlin run order.

Saved Gremlin state

You can cause the Gremlin to save its state after a given number of events. This saved state (actually just a session) file can be reopened in POSE. This feature is useful as a way to reproduce a problem without rerunning all the events from the beginning. For example, we had an error just prior to 1,200,000 events. When the error occurred, we really wanted to have it stopped a few events earlier. By using the saved state from 1,100,000 events, we only had to run slightly less than 100,000 events to reproduce the error, rather than the entire 1,200,000 events.

Unfortunately, this saved state can't be used to do source-level debugging with CodeWarrior or GDB (PRC-Tools). However, it can be used with the low-level Palm-Debugger (discussed later this chapter). This can be done because PalmDebugger can attach to a running application as-is.

Because this saved state can't be used with source-level debugging, its utility is somewhat limited.

Gremlins and Gadgets

Gremlins generate pen taps almost exclusively on active areas of the screen: buttons, fields, lists, places where there are form objects. This means that areas of the screen where there are no form objects are almost completely ignored. You can take advantage of this behavior in your application if you wish. A good testing technique can be to place an empty gadget in an area of your screen where tapping does something; this way, you will grab the Gremlin's attention, and it will do some tapping there.

Using Gremlins Repeatedly

One very nice thing about Gremlins is that even though each Gremlin (of the 1,000 different ones) has its own sequence of events that it generates, a specific Gremlin always generates the *same* sequence of events (at least for a particular application). Start with a fresh POSE with your application newly added on it. Then, if you run Gremlin 5 and your application crashes after event 3,006, you can reproduce the problem. Start with the same configuration and Gremlin 5 and the crash will happen again at 3,006. We're sure you'll appreciate the ability to reproduce the bug easily.

Optimizing Gremlin Debugging

We believe that any nontrivial application that hasn't been tested with Gremlins won't pass a Gremlins run. It's very effective at finding bugs. If you run your application with Gremlins, you commonly find an error fairly quickly (within 5,000–10,000 events). Then, after you fix that error, you'll run for about 50,000 events. Each time you fix an error, the number of events between errors keeps increasing.

Here are some steps you can take to make sure your Gremlin running is efficient:

- Make sure you start your Gremlins run in a known configuration.
- Have a known amount of memory available (best done by starting with a fresh session file with POSE by deleting the old session file).
- Fill up most of the memory (by adding applications or databases); that way, Gremlins will be able to test what happens when your allocations to the storage heap fail.
- Save this session file, this is your known starting state.
- Let Gremlins launch your application (so that from the beginning your application is receiving events from Gremlins).
- Test your application with Gremlins set to generate one million events (start it before you go home at night). That's enough to catch almost anything (although we had one bug that didn't show itself until after 1,200,000 events).
- You certainly don't need to try each of the 1,000 different Gremlins. Start with just numbers 0 and 1. As you pass those, start using Gremlin Ranges to test more of the different Gremlin sequences.

- Run Gremlins while your source-level debugger is active (unless you are using Gremlin ranges). That way, if and when your application crashes, you can drop into the debugger and see what's going on. If you can't tell what's going on at the error, Gremlins does provide the ability to step event by event. The log shows the event number at which the error occurs. You can rerun Gremlins (starting with your starting configuration you saved) until 5 or 10 events before the error. Then you can step event by event until the error occurs. This may give you a better context in which to figure out what's going on.

Error Manager

The Error Manager (declarations in *<ErrorMgr.h>*) defines some useful routines for dealing with errors. Its main approach to this is to display a fatal alert (see Figure 7-18) showing an error description, file and line number, and a Reset button.

Figure 7-18. A fatal system alert

There are two severity levels in your source code: fatal and nonfatal, and three build-time error check levels: ERROR_CHECK_FULL, ERROR_CHECK_PARTIAL, and ERROR_CHECK_NONE. These control whether the error calls cause the fatal alert to be displayed, or whether the error calls do nothing.

Here are the available calls:

ErrFatalDisplay(msg)
   Displays the given msg in a fatal alert if the error check level is ERROR_CHECK_FULL or ERROR_CHECK_PARTIAL. It does nothing if the error check level is ERROR_CHECK_NONE.

ErrNonFatalDisplay(msg)
   Displays the given msg in a fatal alert if the error check level is ERROR_CHECK_FULL. It does nothing if the error check level is ERROR_CHECK_PARTIAL or ERROR_CHECK_NONE.

ErrFatalDisplayIf(condition, msg)
   If condition is true, it acts like ErrFatalDisplay. If condition is false, it does nothing.

ErrNonFatalDisplayIf(condition, msg)
   If condition is true, it acts like ErrNonFatalDisplay. If condition is false, it does nothing.

Here's an example of `ErrFatalDisplayIf`, which causes a fatal alert if the record can't be retrieved:

```
h = DmGetRecord(db, index);
ErrFatalDisplayIf(h == NULL,"can't get record");
```

You should use `ErrNonFatalDisplayIf` for more strenuous checking.

Originally, Palm planned to build ROMs with `ERROR_CHECK_NONE` so that these fatal system alerts wouldn't be presented to the user (instead, an error would be returned to the caller). These alerts were caused by logic errors in applications, however, and so for safety's sake the plan changed. Palm decided it would be better to stop a faulty application dead in its tracks rather than let it continue (and thereby hang its hopes on the application looking at the returned error code). Therefore, release ROMs are built with an error check level of `ERROR_CHECK_PARTIAL` (calls to `ErrFatalDisplay` cause a fatal alert) and debug ROMs are built with an error check level of `ERROR_CHECK_FULL` (both `ErrFatalDisplay` and `ErrNonFatalDisplay` cause fatal alerts).

Palm OS Sources

A useful resource provided by Palm is an abridged version of the Palm OS source code. This is available from Palm and contains code to almost the entire OS. The lowest-level kernel and communications code are omitted.

In order to obtain the sources, you do need to execute a fairly involved license agreement (in part, specifying that you'll only use the source code for debugging your Palm OS application). There is no fee involved, although obtaining, executing, and returning the license to Palm takes a bit of time. If you want to be a serious Palm OS application programmer, however, you should obtain the OS source.

The OS sources can help in the following ways:

They are useful to figure out why a fatal alert is occurring.
Before source code was available, a common programmer question was "My program crashes with error blah-blah, File *MemMgr.c*, Line 1234; what's wrong?" A Palm engineer would then open up the *MemMgr.c* file from the Palm OS source code, go to line 1234, and look at the call to the error manager there. The engineer would then report back to the programmer the circumstances under which the error manager was called. Now, you can handle the debugging problem without waiting around for help from someone at Palm.

It's easier to deal with imperfect documentation.
Although the Palm OS documentation is good (and getting better all the time!), cases occur where the documentation is confusing, missing, misleading, or wrong. Having the ability to go directly to the source code allows you to verify the information directly from the horse's mouth. This makes life easier for everyone.

They provide ideas on how to optimize your code.

By looking at the (current) implementation of APIs, you can get an idea of why particular API calls take the time they do. This can help you figure out alternative ways to make tasks faster.

You can learn more about the OS.

Reading the Palm OS source will teach you more about what the Palm OS does, and how it does it.

Given these useful points, there is one proviso to remember: don't code based on what the source code does, but rather on what is documented in the APIs. Use the source code for good (understanding the docs) and not evil (calling undocumented routines).

Low-Level Debugging with PalmDebugger

The PalmDebugger is an 68K assembly-level command-line debugger. It runs under Mac OS and Windows, and can debug with POSE directly, or with devices via serial or (on Windows only) USB. Figure 7-19 shows it in action.

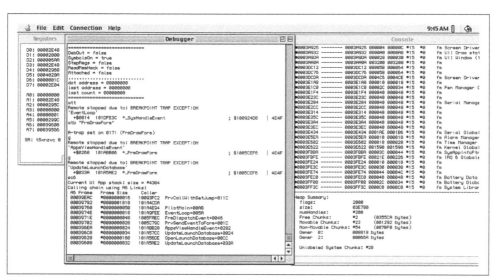

Figure 7-19. PalmDebugger in action

There are some things you can do with a low-level debugger that you can't do with a source-level debugger like CodeWarrior. The most important is you can set breakpoints on operating system routines instead of just on your own code. For example, you can cause a break every time `FrmDrawForm` is called. To get started with PalmDebugger, choose a connection type: port or POSE, and then initiate the communication.

POSE

PalmDebugger initiates communication with POSE; enter the `att` command in the Debugger window.

port
> Communication with the device must start with the device: enter Shortcut, tap, tap, 1 from the device, which will cause a break into PalmDebugger.

Once you have established a communication you can issue commands. Some of the most useful are:

sc6 *(Stack-Crawl A6)*
> Displays a stack trace, showing the call chain.

atb "OSRoutine" *(A-Trap Break)*
> Sets a break on the given OS routine (e.g., from atb "FrmDrawForm"). Anytime the routine is called (from anywhere, including within the OS itself), execution will stop and the debugger will be entered.

atc *(A-Trap Clear)*
> Clears all A-Trap Breaks.

il *(Instruction List)*
> Displays the instructions from the current program counter. The command "il :" will display starting at the beginning of the routine containing the program counter.

s *(Step)*
> Steps a single instruction, stepping into subroutines.

t *(trace)*
> Steps a single instruction, stepping over subroutines.

help
> Displays help about commands.

 On the Mac OS, when you enter a command into the Debugger window, you must end the line with Command+Return, or the Enter key on the numeric keypad. Ending a line with a normal return will just start a new line, and won't actually execute anything.

Device Reset

There are a few neat debugging aids you can perform directly on the handheld:

Soft reset
> Press the Reset button with a blunt, thin instrument (e.g., an unfolded paper clip, or the tool embedded inside many a stylus). This resets the dynamic heap but not the storage heaps, so no data is lost. Each installed application receives the sysAppLaunchCmdSystemReset launch code. This reset also removes any orphaned chunks in the storage heap (chunks that are not members of any database).

Hard reset
> Press and release the Reset button while holding down the Power key. You are provided with the option to erase everything in RAM, including all your data.

Debug reset

Press (and release) the Reset button while pushing the Down-arrow key. This puts the Palm device into debug mode, where it waits for a low-level debugger (like PalmDebugger) to connect. You see a flashing box in the upper left.

No-notify reset

Pressing (and release) the Reset button while holding down the Up-arrow key. The OS boots without sending reset launch codes to each application. This is essential if you have a bug in your `PilotMain` (like trying to access globals without checking the launch code).

 It's not uncommon to accidentally access globals when you shouldn't in your `PilotMain` (the typical culprit is the failure to check the launch code). You can get into a vicious cycle in such cases. After a reset, your application is sent the `sysAppLaunchCmdSystemReset` launch code, at which point you access globals, at which point you crash and cause a reset, and so on, and so on, and so on.

The solution is to use the no-notify reset, which allows the device to successfully boot. Then you can delete your application, fix the `PilotMain`, and download a new version. Of course, a hard reset would also solve the problem, but the cure would be worse than the disease.

Using Simulator on Mac OS

CodeWarrior running on the Mac OS has a feature not found on the Windows version: the Simulator. The Simulator consists of some Mac OS libraries that contain a subset of the Palm OS. When you create a Simulator version of your application, you actually build a Mac OS application that simulates a Palm OS application. It does not simulate the entire Palm OS, only your application. No other applications are present. Figure 7-20 shows a Simulator application running.

Back in the dark ages, before POSE was available, the Simulator was an almost indispensable tool. Like POSE, the Simulator doesn't require a Palm device to be connected. It also allows debugging applications that use serial communications (tough to do if you're debugging with the device itself and have the one-and-only serial port connected to the debugger).

Now that POSE is available, however, the Simulator is much less useful. In fact, we don't use it anymore. We can think of only one advantage that the Simulator has compared to POSE: it is faster. On a reasonably fast Mac OS machine, POSE is quick enough, so the speed isn't much of an issue.

Release/Debug Targets

It's common to create two different builds: one for debugging and one for actual production (release) code. The differences between the two are as follows:

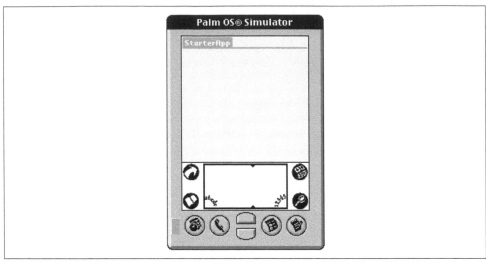

Figure 7-20. A simple Palm OS application running as a Simulator application on Mac OS

Optimization level

For ease of debugging, you usually turn off optimization. If you don't, funny things can occur. For example, if you have two stack variables that are actually located at the same position in memory, then changing one makes the other appear to change in the debugger. For your release version, however, you want to turn on optimization.

Embedded routine names

Embedded routine names are important for debugging so that you can do profiling. They unnecessarily bulk up to your shipping application—so pitch them. As an example, one C++ application we wrote went from 110K to 99K just by turning off embedded routine names.

Fatal error display

On a debug build, both `ErrFatalDisplay` and `ErrNonFatalDisplay` macros are expanded to calls to display fatal errors. On a release build, the `ErrNonFatalDisplay` macros do nothing, although the `ErrFatalDisplay` macros still display fatal errors.

`DEBUG_BUILD` *symbol is set*

You can conditionally compile in debug code by enclosing it in:

```
#ifdef DEBUG_BUILD
...
#endif
```

Of course, don't do all your testing with the debug version, and then build a release version and ship that without testing. You need to test with the release version, especially since optimizations can often cause problems.

Releasing and debugging builds in CodeWarrior

Latent bugs in your source are often exposed due to the optimizer (and occasionally, the optimizer itself has bugs).

In CodeWarrior, the changes are made to the Target Settings dialog box. Figure 7-21 shows the C/C++ Language, 68K Processor, and Global Optimizations panels where the changes are made.

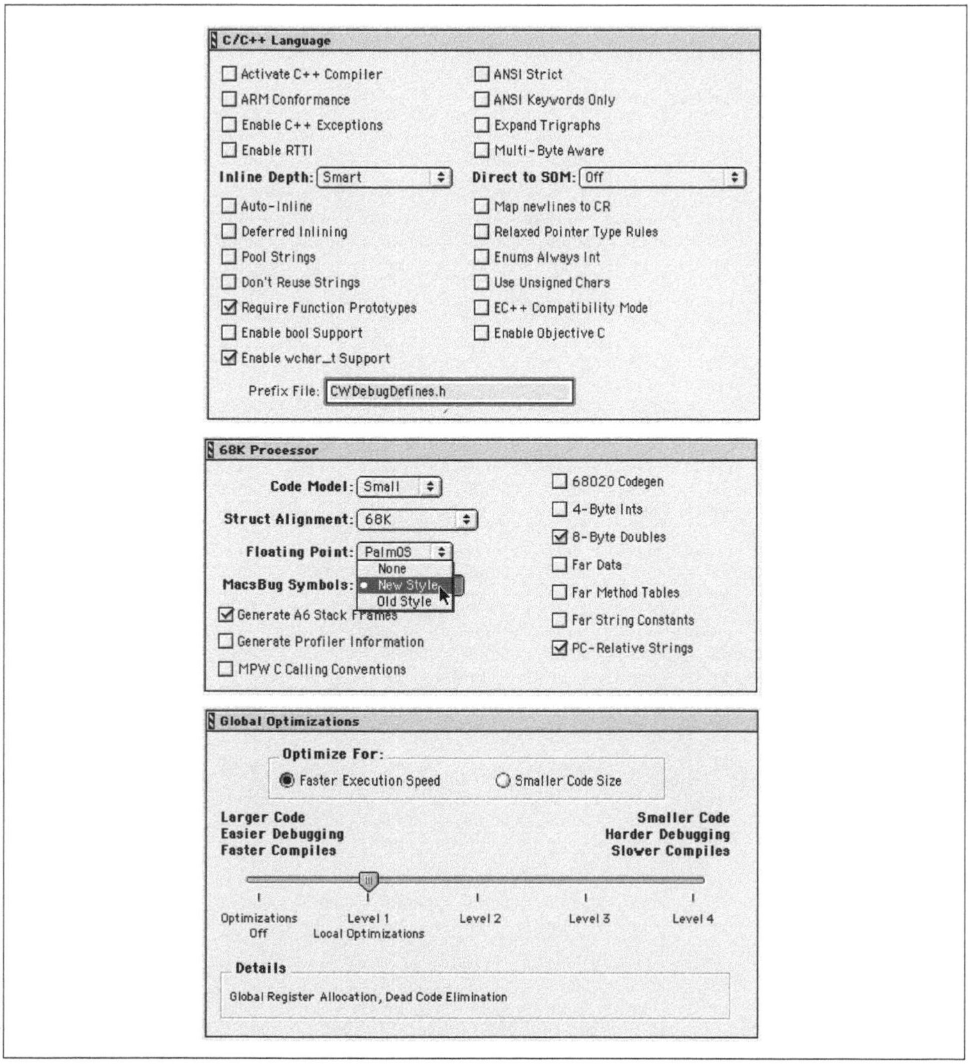

Figure 7-21. The panels from the Target Settings dialog box for the debug version of an application

The OReilly Starter project comes preconfigured with two different targets, whose settings are configured appropriately.

Releasing and debugging builds in PRC-Tools

In PRC-Tools, the change is to the makefile. A make variable is defined for the debug options, and another for the release options:

```
DEBUGCFLAGS= -g -DDEBUG_BUILD
RELEASECFLAGS= -O2
```

If you want a debug build, you set:

```
CFLAGS = $(COMMONCFLAGS) $(DEBUGCFLAGS)
```

If you want a release build, you set:

```
CFLAGS = $(COMMONCFLAGS) $(RELEASECFLAGS)
```

## CHAPTER 8

Resources and Forms

This chapter describes the forms you create in a Palm OS application. We also explain how the resources associated with these forms are created and used. We explain each type of form, describe important APIs, and then give you some programming tips where applicable. After looking at each type of form, we show you sample code in which the forms are implemented. Many of these forms are in our Sales application. Some, however, are more easily understood in smaller pieces of sample code and so we show them to you in this way.

A form without any objects would be no more interesting than a blank window. In order to make a form useful it needs to be populated with form objects, which are the subject of the following chapter. In this chapter, you learn the details of implementing forms in an application. In the next chapter, you learn any remaining form details and how to implement the objects in those forms. If it were not already obvious, these two chapters are closely related and should be read together.

Resources

A resource is a relocatable block marked with a 4-byte type (usually represented as four characters, like code or tSTR) and a 2-byte ID. Resources are stored in a resource database (on the desktop, these files end in the extension *.prc*).

A Palm OS application is stored in the form of resources; in other words, an application is a resource database. One of the resources in this database contains code, another resource contains the application's name, another the application's icon, and the rest contain the forms, alerts, menus, strings, and other elements of the application. The Palm OS uses these resources directly from the storage heap (after locking them) via the Resource Manager.

The two most common tools to create Palm OS application resources are:

- Palm's Constructor, a graphical resource editor
- PilRC, which compiles text descriptions of resources—available to use with the PRC-Tools tool chain or as a plug-in to CodeWarrior

We use PilRC in our examples because it's cross-platform (works with both PRC-Tools and CodeWarrior), and it's easy to show the textual resource declarations in this book (as opposed to many screen dumps from Constructor).

Creating Resources in PilRC

PilRC is a resource compiler that takes textual descriptions (stored in an *.rcp* file) of your resources and compiles them into the binary format required by a *.prc* file. Unlike Constructor, PilRC doesn't allow you to visually create your resources; instead, you type in text to designate their characteristics.

There is an open source Java-based graphical editor for *.prc* files: PilRCEdit (*http://www.wn.com.au/rnielsen/pilrcedit/* or *http://www.sourceforge.net/projects/pilrcedit/*). It provides a pixel-perfect display of what a *.rcp* file will look like on the Palm with up to 4x zoom (see Figure 8-1). The PilRC manual is found in Appendix C.

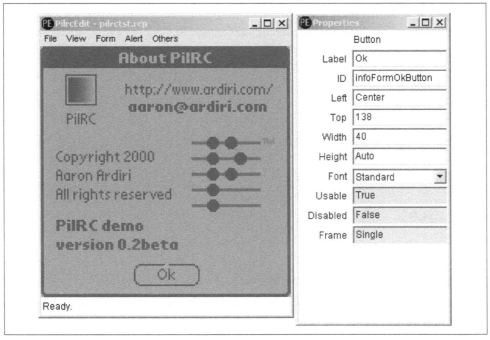

Figure 8-1. PilRCEdit displaying a preview of a form from a .rcp file

The pretty points of PilRC

PilRC does do some of the grunt work of creating resources for you. For example, you don't need to specify a number for every item's top and left coordinates and every item's width and height. PilRC has a mechanism for automatically calculating the width or height of an item based on the text width or height. This works especially well for things like buttons, push buttons, and checkboxes.

It also allows you to specify center justification of items. Beyond this, you can even justify the coordinates of one item based on those of another; you use the size or location of the previous item. These mechanisms make it possible to specify the relationships between items on a form, so that changes affect not just one, but related groups of items. Thus, you can move an item or resize it and have that change affect succeeding items on the form as well.

PilRC example

Here's a PilRC example. It is a simple form that contains:

- A label
- Three checkboxes whose left edges line up under the right edge of the label
- Three buttons at the bottom of the form, each with 4 pixels of space between the borders of the buttons

Figure 8-2 shows you the graphical description of this form. Example 8-1 is the textual description upon which it is based.

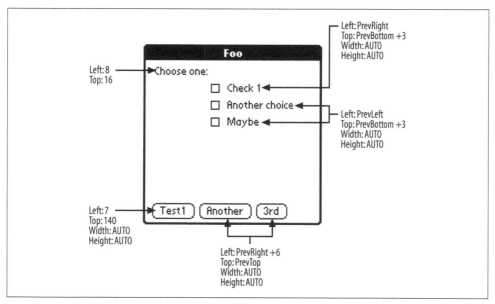

Figure 8-2. Aligning objects in a PilRC resource

Example 8-1. PilRC source for the form from Figure 8-2

```
FORM ID 1 AT (2 2 156 156)
USABLE
MODAL
```

Example 8-1. PilRC source for the form from Figure 8-2 (continued)

```
BEGIN
   TITLE "Foo"
   LABEL "Choose one:" 2001  AT (8 16)

   CHECKBOX "Check 1" ID 2002 AT (PrevRight PrevBottom+3 AUTO AUTO) GROUP 1
   CHECKBOX "Another choice" ID 2003 AT (PrevLeft PrevBottom+3 AUTO AUTO)
      GROUP 1
   CHECKBOX "Maybe" ID 2004 AT (PrevLeft PrevBottom+3 AUTO AUTO) GROUP 1

   BUTTON "Test1" ID 2006 AT (7 140 AUTO AUTO)
   BUTTON "Another" ID 2007 AT (PrevRight+6 PrevTop AUTO AUTO)
   BUTTON "3rd" ID 2008 AT (PrevRight+6 PrevTop AUTO AUTO)
END
```

Although this example uses raw resource IDs (2001, 2002, and so on), you shouldn't normally embed resource IDs directly into your *.rcp* files. The right way to do this with PilRC is to use constants defined in a *.h* file.

Aligning form objects with PilRC

In our form, note that the checkboxes and buttons all have AUTO width and height. The widths are computed with information based on the width of the text and the height is set to the font height plus one.

You can look at the PilRC resources for our form (in Example 8-1) and the annotations in Figure 8-2 to see an example of aligning objects this way. The left of the first checkbox is set to the right of the previous object (the label). The remaining checkboxes are set to the left of the previous objects. The tops of the checkboxes are set to 3 pixels below the bottom of the previous objects: thus the label and checkboxes are on successive lines.

The buttons are handled in a similar manner. The first button is set 7 pixels from the left of the form: the remainder is 6 pixels to the right of the preceding button (with the 1-pixel frame around each of them—this leaves 4 pixels of whitespace between the buttons). The tops of the last two buttons are aligned with the previous objects: thus, all three buttons are horizontally aligned.

Using constants for your resources

If you create a header file that defines symbolic constants, you can include that header file both in your C code and in your PilRC *.rcp* definition file. PilRC allows you to include a file using #include and understands C-style #define statements. You are simply sharing your #defines between your C code and your resource definitions.

 PilRC does have an -H flag that automatically creates resource IDs for symbolic constants you provide, although this flag isn't supported by the plug-in to CodeWarrior.

Here's a header file we've created, *ResDefs.h*, with constant definitions:

```
#define MainForm        8000
#define MainDoneButton  8002
#define MainNameField   8001
```

We include that in our *.c* file and then include it in our *resources.rcp* file:

```
#include "ResDefs.h"

FORM ID MainForm AT (0 0 160 160)
BEGIN
   TITLE "Form title"
   LABEL "Name:" AUTOID AT (11 35) FONT 1
   FIELD ID MainNameField AT (PrevRight PrevTop 50 AUTO) UNDERLINED
       MULTIPLELINES MAXCHARS 80
   BUTTON "Done" ID MainDoneButton AT (CENTER 143 AUTO AUTO)
END
```

Note that the label doesn't have an explicit ID, but uses AUTOID. An ID of AUTOID causes PilRC to create a unique ID for you automatically. This is handy for items on a form that you don't need to refer to programmatically from your code—as is often the case with labels.

Reading Resources

Occasionally, you may need to use the Resource Manager to obtain a resource from your application's resource database directly. Here's what you do:

1. Get a handle to the resource.

2. Lock it.

3. Mess with it, doing whatever you need to do.

4. Unlock it.

5. Release it.

You retrieve a resource with a call to DmGetResource. This function gives you a handle to that resource as an unlocked relocatable block. To find the particular resource you want, specify the resource type and ID when you make the call. DmGetResource searches through the application's resources and the system's resources. When it finds the matching resource, it returns its handle. You lock the handle with a call to MemHandleLock. When you are finished with the resource, you call DmReleaseResource to release it.

Here's some sample code that retrieves a string resource, uses it, and then releases it:

```
void GetStringResource()
{
  MemHandle  h;
  Char       *s;

  h = DmGetResource('tSTR', 1099);
  s = (Char *) MemHandleLock(h);
```

```
    // Use the string s.
    MemHandleUnlock(h);
    DmReleaseResource(h);
}
```

Actually, `DmGetResource` searches through the entire list of open resource databases, including the system resource database stored in ROM. Use `DmGet1Resource` to search through only the topmost open resource database; this is normally your application.

Writing Resources

Although it is possible to write to resources (see "Modifying a Record" in Chapter 10), it is uncommon; most resources are used only for reading.

Form Characteristics

There are three types of forms commonly found in your application:

- Alerts
- Dialog boxes
- Modeless forms

You should think of a form as a container for the visual elements (form objects) of your application. Unlike desktop operating systems in which overlapping windows can each be active and brought to the front by tapping, on the Palm OS, there is only one active form (the frontmost one). Any other forms are inactive; their objects don't respond to stylus taps.

Within the Palm OS there are two types of forms: modal and modeless. Table 8-1 shows you the characteristics of both types.

Table 8-1. Characteristics of modal and modeless forms

Modeless	Modal
Fills the screen (160 × 160 pixels)	Horizontally fills the screen
	Justified to the bottom of the screen
No frame	2-pixel frame
Title left-justified	Title centered

Each form has these characteristics:

Form attributes
> These are attributes defined for the form. They control the form's behavior and appearance. They are normally specified in the resource, although some of the attributes can be changed at runtime.

Title

> This null-terminated string is the title of the form. For modal forms, the title is centered; for modeless ones, the title is at the top-left of the form. Modeless forms need not have titles, though they should so that the user knows which application is running.

Modal

> This bit specifies whether the forms should be drawn as modal forms (with framing and the title centered). The frame of a modal form is drawn outside the bounds of the form. Thus, a modal form taking up the bottom half of the screen would have bounds (left: 2, top: 82, width: 156, height: 76).

Save behind

> This bit specifies whether the bits underneath the form should be saved just before the form is first drawn in order to be restored when the form closes. If this bit is not set (or if there isn't enough memory to save the bits underneath), a frmUpdateEvent is sent to the underlying form when this form is closed. See "frmUpdateEvent" later for further details.

> Prior to OS 3.5, set this bit for modal dialog boxes in order for the area underneath the dialog box to be erased before the form is drawn.

Help ID

> If this number is nonzero, it specifies the ID number of a string resource containing help text. For a modal form with a nonzero help ID, the Form Manager will draw the "i" button at the top-right of the form and will handle taps on the button by displaying a "tips" form with the contents of the help string resource. The Form Manager ignores the help ID for a modeless form.

Menu ID

> If this number is nonzero, it specifies the ID number of a menu bar for this form. A zero for this ID specifies no menu bar.

Default button ID

> If a modal form is being displayed and the user taps on the Launcher icon (or taps on one of the hard buttons to switch applications), the modal form is dismissed, simulating a press on the default button ID. You'll usually set this to a "safe" value (e.g., if the dialog box is confirming a delete, the "safe" choice is to cancel the delete).

Form Events

There are five form-level events sent by the Form Manager to an application:

frmLoadEvent

> This specifies that a form needs to be loaded. While there is no default handling for this event, this is certainly the event for which your application-wide event handler is looking (see Chapter 5). In response to this event, the event handler must do the following:

- Initialize the form
- Make it the active form
- Install an event handler for it

frmOpenEvent

This specifies that a form is being opened. There is no default handling for this event. Your form-specific event handler needs to draw the form (after initializing any form objects that it desires).

 Do not do any drawing to the screen before calling FrmDrawForm (the 3.5 or later debug ROMs will cause an error if you try). You may do initialization of form objects, which will then draw with their new values when the form itself draws. Since the bits underneath for the form are saved on the first FrmDrawForm (see "Save behind" earlier), you don't want to do any drawing before that, or the wrong bits will be saved.

frmCloseEvent

This is sent when a form is being closed. The default handling for this event is to erase the form (restoring the bits underneath, if Save Behind is set), and delete it from memory. You'll often want to look for this event so as to undo the effects of any initialization you did on the frmOpenEvent (e.g., deallocate allocated memory). You'll still want to return false from your event handler, however, so that the default handling will take place.

frmUpdateEvent

This is sent when a form needs to be redrawn. There's no indication concerning what part of the form needs to be redrawn, although the current clipping will be restricted to the area needing updating. The default handling for this event is to redraw the form. If you're doing extra drawing on top of the form, you'll need to handle this event by drawing the form, and then doing your additional drawing.

This event is not sent very often, because a form on top of another form usually has the Save Behind bit set. This event is sent if:

- The Save Behind bit is not set.
- Or, there was not enough memory to save the bits behind.
- Or, the 3.5 (or later) debug ROM is used. Since the update event is rarely sent, it's easy for developers to fail to notice that they aren't handling the frmUpdateEvent when they should be (or are handling it wrong). The 3.5 debug ROM forces this event to be sent (rather than saving the bits behind) in order to force what would be a rare occurrence (a frmUpdateEvent) to happen every time.

frmSaveEvent

This signifies that the contents of a form should be saved to the application's database. It is sent by FrmSaveAllForms, which sends this event to all open forms. The OS itself never calls FrmSaveAllForms; it is there for an application developer to call, commonly in response to the sysAppLaunchCmdSaveData launch code, which is sent to the running application before a Find.

If you support Find, and have data in a form that needs to be saved to the database before a Find, then you'll send FrmSaveAllForms in response to sysAppLaunchCmdSaveData. This will send the frmSaveEvent to your form's event handler, which will need to save the current on-screen contents to your database.

Form-Level APIs

These are the APIs in the Form Manager having to do with the form as a whole (rather than form objects, which we'll cover later). As always, we don't cover every API, but only those that you will most commonly need in your application development.

FormType * FrmInitForm(UInt16 formID)
> This reads the form resource with the specified form ID and creates an in-memory representation of that form. You call this from your application-wide event handler in response to a frmLoadEvent.

void FrmSetActiveForm(FormType *form)
> This makes the passed-in form the one-and-only active form. You call this in response to a frmLoadEvent.

void FrmDrawForm(FormType *form)
> This draws the specified form. As of the 3.5 OS, for modal forms, it will erase what is underneath before drawing. Prior to that, only forms with the "save behind" bit attribute set were erased before drawing.

 Of course, it logically follows that you shouldn't do any drawing yourself onto the screen before calling FrmDrawForm; if you do, it will be erased.

FormType *FrmGetFormPtr(UInt16 formID)
> This returns the on-screen form whose form ID matches that of the passed-in value. If there is no matching form, it returns NULL.

FormType *FrmGetActiveForm( )
> This returns the form that is active. Note that it will not always be your form. For example, when the OS needs to redraw the screen, it sends each form, whether active or not, a frmUpdateEvent. However, in those cases, the OS will temporarily set the active form to the form whose event handler is called.

void FrmGotoForm(UInt16 formID)
> This posts a frmCloseEvent for the active form, and a frmLoadEvent and frmOpenEvent for the specified form ID. Since it just posts events, it's not until the application goes back through the event loop that the frmCloseEvent is retrieved. This will then close the current form.

```
void FrmPopupForm(UInt16 formID)
```
This is like `FrmGotoForm`, but it doesn't close the active form. Thus, the current form will remain open, as will the new one. This requires more memory than using `FrmGotoForm`, which closes the active form first. Use `FrmReturnToForm` to return from a form popped-up with `FrmPopupForm`. We don't often use this call, but it's one way to display a modal form on top of a modeless form. We recommend `FrmDoDialog` instead (see the later section, "Modal Dialog Boxes").

```
void FrmReturnToForm(UInt16 formID)
```
This closes the active form (immediately, not via a posted event), and makes the specified form active. If the form ID is 0, it makes the topmost form active. This is used in conjunction with `FrmPopupForm`.

```
void FrmSaveAllForms()
```
This calls each form's event handler with a `frmSaveEvent`. The OS never calls `FrmSaveAllForms`; it is there for an application developer to call, commonly in response to the `sysAppLaunchCmdSaveData` launch code, which is sent to the running application before a Find.

```
void FrmDeleteForm(const FormType *form)
```
This disposes the specified form and it is called by default for a `frmCloseEvent`. You explicitly call it after showing a dialog box you've displayed with `FrmDoDialog`.

```
void FrmCopyTitle(FormType *form, const Char *newTitle)
```
This changes the title of the form. Note that this routine copies the given form into the space allocated in the form resource. It is essential, therefore, to make the title long enough in your resource (fill it with blank characters), so that you don't overwrite data beyond the allocated title.

Modeless Forms

You'll normally call `FrmGotoForm` to display a modeless form. It will then post:

- A `frmCloseEvent` for the active form (if any; as your program begins, there is no active form)
- A `frmLoadEvent` and a `frmOpenEvent` for the specified form

Your application-wide event handler, often named `AppHandleEvent`, handles the `frmLoadEvent` by calling `FrmInitForm`, `FrmSetActiveForm`, and `FrmSetEventHandler` to set the event handler for the form. In your form-specific event handler, you handle the `frmOpenEvent` by calling `FrmDrawForm` to draw the form.

Every modeless form in your application will require a form-specific event handler, and a case statement in your application-wide event handler, `AppHandleEvent`. You call `FrmSetEventHandler` to associate that form-specific event handler with the form. In order to display the form, you'll call `FrmGotoForm` to specify that form's form ID.

Alerts

An alert is a very constrained modal dialog box (see Figure 8-3). It is a modal dialog box with an icon, a message, and one or more buttons at the bottom that dismiss the dialog box.

Figure 8-3. An alert showing an information icon, a message, and a button

As we discussed in Chapter 3, there are four different types of alerts (notification, warning, question, and error). The user can distinguish the alert type from the icon shown.

UI guidelines recommend that modal dialog boxes have an Info button at the top-right that provides help for the dialog box. To do so, create a string resource with your help text and specify the string resource ID as the help ID in the alert resource.

Customizing an Alert

You can customize the message in an alert. You do this with runtime parameters that allow you to create as many as three textual substitutions in the message. In the resource, you specify a placeholder for the runtime text with ^1, ^2, or ^3. Instead of calling FrmAlert, you call FrmCustomAlert. The first string replaces any occurrence of ^1, the second replaces any occurrence of ^2, and the third replaces occurrences of ^3.

When you call FrmCustomAlert, you can pass NULL as the text pointer only if there is no corresponding placeholder in the alert resource. If there is a corresponding place-holder, then passing NULL will cause a crash. Pass a string with one space in it (" ") instead.

That is, if your alert message is "My Message ^1 (^2)", you can call:

```
FrmCustomAlert(MyAlertID, "string", " ", NULL)
```

but not:

```
FrmCustomAlert(MyAlertID, "string", NULL, NULL)
```

Make sure that any alerts you display with FrmAlert don't have ^1, ^2, or ^3 in them since FrmAlert(alertID) is equivalent to FrmCustomAlert(alertID, NULL, NULL, NULL). The Form Manager will try to replace any occurrences of ^1, ^2, or ^3 with NULL and this will certainly cause a crash.

Some versions of the OS prior to Version 3.1 have a bug in FrmCustomAlert that causes an error when replacing a placeholder with an empty string (" "). A fix for this is to pass a string with a single space (" ") instead.

Alert APIs

Here is a list of alert APIs:

UInt16 FrmAlert(UInt16 alertResourceID)
This displays the alert with the given resource ID. It returns when the user presses one of the buttons or switches to another application (for example by tapping on the Application launcher icon). The return result is the button number of the pressed button (where the first button is number 0). If the user switches to another application, it returns the default button ID.

UInt16 FrmCustomAlert(UInt16 alertResourceID, const Char *s1, const Char *s2, const Char *s3)
This is like FrmAlert, but it replaces any occurrences of ^1 in the message with s1, ^2 with s2, and ^3 with s3.

Alert Example

Here's a resource description of an alert with two buttons and help text:

```
ALERT ID MyAlert
CONFIRMATION
DEFAULTBUTTON 1
HELPID 1000
BEGIN
    TITLE "My Alert Title (^1)"
    MESSAGE "My Message (^1) (^2) (^1)"
    BUTTONS "OK" "Cancel"
END

STRING ID 1000 "This describes how to use the alert."
```

If you display the alert with FrmCustomAlert, it appears as shown in Figure 8-4. Note that FrmCustomAlert doesn't replace strings in the title.

Figure 8-4. An alert displayed with FrmCustomAlert.

```
if (FrmCustomAlert(MyAlert, "foo", "bar", NULL) == 0) {
   // User pressed OK.
} else {
   // User pressed Cancel.
}
```

Tips on Creating Alerts

Here are a few tips that will help you avoid common mistakes made in alerts:

Button capitalization
> Buttons in an alert should be capitalized. Thus, a button should be titled "Cancel" and not "cancel."

OK buttons
> An "OK" button should be exactly that. Don't use "Ok," "Okay," "ok," or "Okey-dokey." OK?

Using ^1, ^2, ^3
> The ^1, ^2, ^3 placeholders aren't replaced in the alert title or in buttons, but only in the alert message.

Modal Dialog Boxes

A modal dialog box is different from a modeless form in the following ways:

Appearance
> A modal dialog box has a full-width title bar with the title centered and with buttons from left-to-right along the bottom. Most modal dialog boxes should have an Info button that provides additional help.

Behavior
> The Find button doesn't work while a modal dialog box is being displayed.

Dialog Box APIs

Here is a list of dialog box APIs:

`UInt16 FrmDoDialog(FormType *formP)`
> This routine displays the given form and doesn't return until the user presses one of the buttons or switches to another application (for example by tapping on the Application launcher icon). The return result is the ID of the pressed button. If the user switches to another application, it returns the default button ID.
>
> If the form has an event handler, `FrmDoDialog` will call the event handler for each event.

Flexible Modal Dialog Boxes

The easiest way to display a modal dialog box is to use FrmAlert or FrmCustomAlert. The fixed structure of alerts (icon, text, and buttons) may not always match what you need, however. For example, you may need a checkbox or other control in your dialog box (see Figure 8-5).

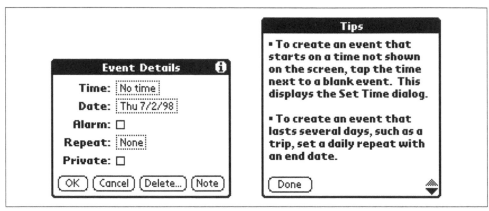

Figure 8-5. Modal dialog box (on left) with "i" button bringing up help (on right)

If you need this type of flexible modal dialog box, then you should use a form resource (setting the modal and "save behind" attributes of the form), and then display the dialog box using code like in Example 8-2 (you'll commonly have one such routine for every one of your modal dialog boxes).

Example 8-2. Display a specific form modally; emphasized code is where you would customize

```
// returns object ID of hit button
static UInt16 DisplayMyFormModally(void)
{
    FormPtr frm = FrmInitForm(MyForm);
    UInt16    hitButton;

    // Set an event handler, if you wish, with FrmSetEventHandler.
    // Initialize any form objects in the form.

    hitButton = FrmDoDialog(frm);

    // Read any values from the form objects here
    // before the form is deleted.

    FrmDeleteForm(frm);
    return hitButton;
}
```

When you present a modal form you initialize the form explicitly with FrmInitForm before calling FrmDoDialog. You will not add another case to the switch statement in AppHandleEvent.

FrmDoDialog returns the button ID of the tapped button, or the default button ID if the user switches to a different application.

For example, if you've got a form with an icon, a label, and two buttons where the first button has a button ID of 1001 and the second button has a button ID of 1002, FrmDoDialog will return either 1001 or 1002, depending on whether the first or second button is pressed.

If you need to initialize any form objects, or read their values after the dialog box has been dismissed, you'll need to add code to do that. If you need some dynamic behavior in the dialog box (for example, if clicking a checkbox causes some other behavior on the dialog box), then you'll need an event handler for the dialog box. Examples of doing both of these are shown in the "Edit Customer" section in Chapter 9.

A Tip for Modal Forms

When you call FrmDoDialog with a modal form, an associated event handler won't get a frmOpenEvent and it doesn't have to call FrmDrawForm. Since the event handler won't be notified that the form is opening, any form initialization must be done before you call FrmDoDialog.

Modal Form Sizes

You don't want your modal form to take up the entire screen real estate; center it horizontally at the bottom of the screen, and make sure that the borders of the form can be seen. You'll need to inset the bounds of your form by 2 pixels in each direction.

In order to do the insetting, we normally define the form's height in a *.h* file:

```
#define kMyModalFormHeight    100
```

Then, in the *.rcp* file, specify the bounds of the form with respect to that form height:

```
FORM ID MyModalForm AT (2 158 - kMyModalFormHeight 156 kMyModalFormHeight)
MODAL
SAVEBEHIND
BEGIN
  ...
END
```

Help for Modal Forms

The Palm User Interface Guidelines specify that modal dialog boxes should provide online help through the "i" button at the top right of the form (see Figure 8-5). You provide this help text as a string resource that contains the appropriate help message. In your form (or alert) resource, you then set the help ID to the string resource ID. The Palm OS will take care of displaying the "i" button (only if the help ID isn't 0), and the help text if the button is tapped.

Forms in the Sales Application

Now that we have given you specific information about resources and forms, it is time to add a few forms to the Sales application. We'll show you the resource definitions of some of the forms, alerts, and help text. We won't show you all the code, however, as it would get exceedingly repetitious and not teach you anything new. Most specifically, we won't show the code to bring up every alert. Furthermore, we won't cover forms with any important form objects in them; they are covered in the next chapter.

Here are the forms we are now going to add to the Sales application:

Alerts
We implement several alerts and a custom alert.

The Delete Customer form
We implement some buttons and checkboxes, and have a help string that the user can see by tapping the Info button of the dialog box.

In each implementation we show you any definitions or resources (shown in text in PilRC format), and the necessary code.

Eventually we also need to make sure our application navigates between our various forms and dialog boxes correctly. This is taken care of in our AppHandleEvent function, which we cover in the next chapter (after implementing all of our forms).

Alerts

Here are the defines for the alert IDs, the buttons in the Delete Item alert, and the Product Exists alert (these are the alerts that have more than one button):

```
#define RomIncompatibleAlert                    1001

#define DeleteItemAlert                         1201
#define DeleteItemOK                            0
#define DeleteItemCancel                        1

#define NoItemSelectedAlert                     1000

#define AboutBoxAlert                           1100

#define ProductExistsAlert                      1200
#define ProductExistsAdd                        0
#define ProductExistsCancel                     1
```

Defining the alerts

Here are the alerts themselves, starting with an alert from the Product Details form. This first alert is displayed when the user taps the Details button without having selected an item first (see Figure 8-6).

Here is the resource for the alert:

```
ALERT ID NoItemSelectedAlert
INFORMATION
BEGIN
  TITLE "Select Item"
  MESSAGE "You must have an item  selected to perform this command.  " \
    "To  select an item, tap on the product name of the item."
  BUTTONS "OK"
END
```

Figure 8-6. Select Item alert

The alert in Figure 8-7 shows that the selection is a duplication of a previously existing item in the order.

Figure 8-7. Product Exists alert

Here is the resource for the alert:

```
ALERT ID ProductExistsAlert
CONFIRMATION
BEGIN
  TITLE "Product Exists"
  MESSAGE "You've already got an item with the product ^1.  " \
    "Delete this item and add to the existing one?"
  BUTTONS "Add to Existing" "Cancel"
END
```

We check to make sure that the OS version is compatible as we only work on 3.0 or higher OS. Figure 8-8 shows the form that is displayed with an incompatible version.

Here is the resource:

```
ALERT ID RomIncompatibleAlert
ERROR
```

```
BEGIN
  TITLE "System Incompatible"
  MESSAGE "System Version 3.0 or greater is required to run this " \
    "application."
  BUTTONS "OK"
END
```

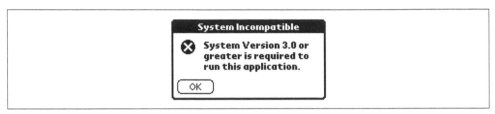

Figure 8-8. Incompatible ROM alert

This is our delete confirmation alert (see Figure 8-9). Notice that it is drawn so that the user can see what item is being deleted (in the Item dialog box behind the alert).

Figure 8-9. Delete Item confirmation alert

Here is the resource for the alert:

```
ALERT ID DeleteItemAlert
CONFIRMATION
BEGIN
  TITLE "Delete Item"
  MESSAGE "Delete selected order item?"
  BUTTONS "OK" "Cancel"
END
```

Our Application Info dialog box is shown in Figure 8-10.

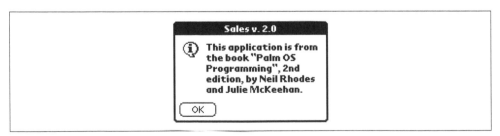

Figure 8-10. Application Info dialog box

Here is the resource:

```
ALERT ID AboutBoxAlert
INFORMATION
BEGIN
  TITLE "Sales v. 2.0"
  MESSAGE "This application is from the book \"Palm OS Programming\", " \
    "2nd edition, by Neil Rhodes and Julie McKeehan."
  BUTTONS "OK"
END
```

Calling FrmAlert in our application

We won't show every call to FrmAlert (the call that displays each of these alerts).
Here, however, is a piece of code from OrderHandleMenuEvent, which shows two calls
to FrmAlert. The code is called when the user chooses to delete an item. If nothing is
selected, we put up an alert to notify the user of that. If an item is selected, we put up
an alert asking if they really want to delete it:

```
case RecordDeleteItem:
  if (!gRowSelected)
    FrmAlert(NoItemSelectedAlert);
  else {
    UInt16 itemNumToDelete = gCurrentSelectedItemIndex;
    MenuEraseStatus(0); // Because we'll turn off insertion point when
                        //   deselecting, command bar will then restore it!
    if (OrderDeselectRowAndDeleteIfEmpty()) {
      // It was an empty row anyway, don't bother them.
    } else if (FrmAlert(DeleteItemAlert) == DeleteItemOK) {
        DeleteNthItem(itemNumToDelete);
        gCurrentOrderChanged = true;
      LoadFields(true);
    }
  }
```

Calling FrmCustomAlert

Here's a piece of code showing a call to FrmCustomAlert. It is used when the user
selects a product from the pop up that matches that of an existing product. It's part
of OrderHandleEvent, handling the popSelectEvent:

```
if (ProductIDExistsInOrder(productID, &itemIndex)) {
  GetProductNameFromProductID(productID,
    productName);
  if (FrmCustomAlert(ProductExistsAlert, productName, NULL, NULL)
    != ProductExistsCancel) {
```

Delete Customer

Our Delete Customer dialog box has a checkbox in it, so we can't use an alert. We
use a modal dialog box instead. Here are the declarations for the form, form objects
(buttons, checkboxes), and help string:

```
#define DeleteCustomerForm                1400
#define DeleteCustomerOKButton            1404
#define DeleteCustomerCancelButton        1405
#define DeleteCustomerSaveBackupCheckbox  1403
#define DeleteCustomerHelpString          1400
```

Figure 8-11 shows what the form looks like. The Delete Customer dialog box resource is shown in Example 8-3.

Figure 8-11. Delete Customer dialog box

Example 8-3. Delete Customer resource definition

```
STRING ID DeleteCustomerHelpString "The Save Backup Copy option will " \
  "store deleted records in an archive file on your desktop computer at " \
  "the next HotSync. Some records will be hidden but not deleted until then."
FORM ID DeleteCustomerForm
  AT (2 158 - kDeleteCustomerFormHeight  156 kDeleteCustomerFormHeight)
MODAL
SAVEBEHIND
HELPID DeleteCustomerHelpString
BEGIN
  TITLE "Delete Customer"
  FORMBITMAP AT (13 19) BITMAP 10005
  LABEL "Delete selected\ncustomer?" ID 1402 AT (42 20) FONT 1
  CHECKBOX "Save backup copy on PC?" ID DeleteCustomerSaveBackupCheckbox
    AT (12 53 140 12) LEFTANCHOR  FONT 1 GROUP 0 CHECKED
  BUTTON "OK" ID DeleteCustomerOKButton AT (kDefaultButtonInModalLeft
    BOTTOM@(kDeleteCustomerFormHeight - kDefaultButtonInModalBottomMargin)
    36 kDefaultButtonHeight)
    LEFTANCHOR FRAME
    FONT 0
  BUTTON "Cancel" ID DeleteCustomerCancelButton
    AT (PREVRIGHT + kInterButtonWidth PREVTOP 36 kDefaultButtonHeight)
    LEFTANCHOR FRAME FONT 0
END
```

The bitmap (10005) is a resource in the system ROM; the Palm OS header files define ConfirmationAlertBitmap as its resource ID.

Example 8-4 shows the code that displays the dialog box. Note that we set the value of the checkbox before calling FrmDoDialog (we'll talk about how to do that next chapter). We take a look at it again to see if the user has changed the value after FrmDoDialog returns but before we delete the form.

Example 8-4. Displaying the Delete Customer dialog box

```
Boolean AskDeleteCustomer(void)
{
  FormPtr form = FrmInitForm(DeleteCustomerForm);
  UInt16  hitButton;
  UInt16  ctlIndex;

  // Set the "save backup" checkbox to its previous setting.
  ctlIndex = FrmGetObjectIndex(form, DeleteCustomerSaveBackupCheckbox);
  FrmSetControlValue(form, ctlIndex, gSaveBackup);

  hitButton = FrmDoDialog(form);
  if (hitButton == DeleteCustomerOKButton)
    gSaveBackup = (Boolean) FrmGetControlValue(form, ctlIndex);
  FrmDeleteForm(form);
  return (Boolean) (hitButton == DeleteCustomerOKButton);
}
```

For now, these are all of the forms we are going to add to the Sales application. The remainder of the forms will be added in the following chapter after we discuss the form objects that populate them.

CHAPTER 9

Form Objects

This chapter describes Palm OS form objects. We show you how to use these objects by explaining their characteristics and any important events or APIs. We also give you some programming tips that will help you avoid the common problems with these objects.

We show you each type of form object generally moving from most simple to most difficult. We also give you sample code for each object. Many of these objects are in forms in our Sales application. Some, however, are more easily understood in smaller pieces of sample code. This is particularly true for the table form object for which we give you a standalone example.

Form Object Characteristics

The elements that populate a form are called form objects. Before getting into the details of specific form objects, however, there are some important things to know about how forms deal with all form objects.

The form contains an array of form objects. Each form object has the following:

Data

For example, a checkbox contains a Boolean with the current checkbox value. A label contains the text and the font used for the label. A scrollbar contains the current scroll value, along with minimum and maximum values.

Index

The index is the (0-based) index of the form object within the form. Most (but, to keep you on your toes, not quite all) Form Manager routines require a form object index to specify a particular form object.

ID

The form object ID is a number that you specify for the form object in the form resource. These ID numbers are commonly unique across all forms (for example, the form object IDs for a form with ID 1000 would commonly have IDs 1001, 1002, 1003, and so on), but there's nothing preventing form objects in different forms from sharing a common ID. You'll need to convert an ID into an index number before calling most Form Manager routines.

Usable bit

A form object that is not usable is not drawn, and taps on it are ignored. A better name for this bit would probably have been visible.

What We Talk About Next

First, we will show you important form object events. Next, we cover APIs. Finally, we move to a description and code for each type of form object. Here is the order in which we cover them:

- Labels
- Bitmaps
- Graffiti Shift Indicators
- Lists
- Controls (buttons, checkboxes, push buttons, repeating buttons, pop-up triggers, selector triggers, graphical controls, and sliders)
- Gadgets
- Fields
- Scrollbars
- Tables

Form Object Events

Many of the form objects post specific kinds of events when they are tapped on or used. To use a particular type of form object, you'll need to know what kinds of events that form object produces. Most of the form objects have similar structures:

- When the stylus is pressed on the object, it sends an enter event. In response to the enter event, the object responds appropriately while the stylus is pressed down. For example, a button highlights while the pen is within the button and unhighlights while it is outside the button, a scrollbar sends sclRepeatEvents while the user has a scroll arrow tapped, a list highlights the row the stylus is on and scrolls if necessary when the pen reaches the top or bottom of the list.
- When the stylus is released on the object, it sends a select event. If the stylus is released outside the object, it sends an exit event.

In all these events, the ID of the tapped form object is provided as part of the event, as well as a pointer to the form object itself. The ID allows you to distinguish between different instances, which generate the same types of events. For example, two buttons would both generate a `ctlSelectEvent` when tapped; you'd use the ID to distinguish between them.

Events Generated by a Successful Tap

Most often, you want to know only when an object has been successfully tapped; that is, the user lifts the stylus while still within the boundaries of the object. Table 9-1 contains the events that you will use most often.

Table 9-1. Events generated by taps

Event	Objects that generate that event
`ctlSelectEvent`	Controls
`frmTitleSelectEvent`	Titlebar of a form
`lstSelectEvent`	Lists
`popSelectEvent`	Pop-up triggers
`tblSelectEvent`	Tables
`ctlRepeatEvent`	Repeating buttons, sliders (while the slider thumb is being moved)
`sclRepeatEvent`	Scrollbars

Events Generated by Maintaining a Press

Sometimes, you'll need to be notified of a repetitive action while a form object is being pressed. The events are shown in Table 9-2.

Table 9-2. Events generated by maintaining a press

Event	Objects that generate that event
`ctlRepeatEvent`	Repeating buttons
`sclRepeatEvent`	Scrollbars

Events Generated by the Start of a Tap

Occasionally, you'll want to know when the user starts to tap on a form object. For example, when the user starts to tap on a pop-up trigger you may want to dynamically fill in the contents of the pop-up list before it is displayed. You'd do that in the `ctlEnterEvent`, while looking for the appropriate control ID. The events sent when the user starts to tap on a form object are shown in Table 9-3.

Table 9-3. Events generated by the start of a tap

Event	Objects that generate that event
ctlEnterEvent	Controls
fldEnterEvent	Fields
frmTitleEnterEvent	Titlebar of a form
lstEnterEvent	List
sclEnterEvent	Scrollbars
tblEnterEvent	Tables

Events Generated by the End of an Unsuccessful Tap

Sometimes you'll want to know when a form object has been unsuccessfully tapped (the user tapped the object, but swished the stylus outside of the boundaries before lifting it). For example, if you allocate some memory in the enter event, you'd deallocate the memory in both the select event, and in the corresponding exit event (covering all your bases, so to speak). The events are shown in Table 9-4.

Table 9-4. Events generated by the end of an unsuccessful tap

Event	Objects that generate that event
ctlExitEvent	Controls
lstExitEvent	Lists
tblExitEvent	Tables

Note that although there is a frmTitleSelectEvent, there is no corresponding frmTitleExitEvent. We know of no reason why this is so; it is just one of the many imponderable mysteries of the Palm OS.

Form Object APIs

These are the most important form object APIs.

Converting Between IDs and Indexes

Most Form Manager routines require a form object index, but what you've specified in the form resource is a form object ID. As a result, you'll find yourself converting from IDs to indexes very often.

UInt16 FrmGetObjectIndex(const FormType *form, UInt16 formObjectID)
　　FrmGetObjectIndex searches through the objects in the form, returning the index of the one that matches the given object ID. You will be using this routine all the time.

```
UInt16 FrmGetObjectID(const FormType *form, UInt16 formObjectIndex)
```
FrmGetObjectID returns the ID of the form object at the specified index. It is not commonly needed.

We don't know why the Palm OS architects thought it necessary to have both form object IDs and form object indexes (it seems as though using indexes would have been simpler).

 Unfortunately, you'll find it very easy to accidentally pass an ID to a routine expecting an index. Since the data types (UInt16) are exactly the same, the compiler can't catch this type of error. Instead, you'll get a runtime error when the object at that index can't be found (since you'll be passing a number like 1000 to specify a 0-based index).

Hiding and Showing Objects

The initial state of the usable bit for each form object is specified in the form resource. Sometimes, you may want to dynamically hide or show a specific form object. You can do this with FrmHideObject or FrmShowObject.

```
void FrmHideObject(FormType *formP, UInt16 objIndex)
```
This function hides the given object.

```
void FrmShowObject(FormType *formP, UInt16 objIndex)
```
This function shows the given object.

Form Object Pointers

Whenever you need to do something with an object, you will need to get it from the form. You do this with a pointer and the function, FrmGetObjectPtr. The return result of FrmGetObjectPtr depends on the type of form object.

```
void *FrmGetObjectPtr (const FormType *formP, UInt16 objIndex)
```
This returns the form object pointer for the given index from the given form.

FrmGetObjectPtr returns one of the following depending on the type of the form object kept at that index:

- FieldPtr
- ControlPtr
- GraphicControlPtr
- SliderControlPtr
- ListPtr
- TablePtr
- ScrollBarPtr

If you're using C, you can assign the result of FrmGetObjectPtr directly to a variable of the correct type:

```
ListPtr list;
list = FrmGetObjectPtr(myForm, myListIndex);
```

However, C++ type-checking is stricter, requiring an explicit cast when converting a void * to another pointer type. Thus, we always add an explicit cast, which works with both C or C++:

```
ListPtr list;
list = (ListPtr) FrmGetObjectPtr(myForm, myListIndex);
```

 If you are using only C++ and don't need C compatibility, a better cast is:

```
        list = static_cast<ListType *>( FrmGetObjectPtr( ...));
```

There are utility routines to find the bounds or location of an object, or to change its bounds or location.

void FrmGetObjectPosition(const FormType *formP,
UInt16 objIndex, Coord *x, Coord *y)
> This returns the top-left position (in form coordinates) of the object at the given index.

void FrmSetObjectPosition(FormType *formP, UInt16 objIndex, Coord x, Coord y)
> This moves the object so that its top-left position is at the given (form) coordinates. Note that this doesn't erase the object at its old position or redraw it at its new position. Therefore, you'll normally want to call FrmHideObject before and FrmShowObject after.

void FrmGetObjectBounds(const FormType *formP, UInt16 objIndex,
RectangleType *rP)
> This returns the bounds (in form coordinates) of the object at the given index.

void FrmSetObjectBounds(FormType *formP, UInt16 objIndex,
const RectangleType *bounds)
> This changes the bounds of the object. Note that it doesn't erase the object at its old position or redraw it at its new position.

Error Checking

FormObjectKind FrmGetObjectType(const FormType *formP, UInt16 objIndex)
> This returns the type of the object at the given index (one of frmFieldObj, frmControlObj, frmListObj, frmTableObj, frmBitmapObj, frmLineObj, frmFrameObj, frmRectangleObj, frmLabelObj, frmTitleObj, frmPopupObj, frmGraffitiStateObj, frmGadgetObj, or frmScrollBarObj).

You can use `FrmGetObjectType` with `FrmGetObjectPtr` to ensure that the type of the form object you retrieve is the type you expect. Here's an example that retrieves a `FieldPtr`, using additional error checking to verify the type:

```
FieldPtr GetFieldPtr(FormPtr frm,UInt16 objectIndex)
{
    if (FrmGetObjectType(frm, objectIndex) != frmFieldObj) {
      ErrFatalDisplay("Form object isn't a field");
      return NULL;
    } else
    return (FieldPtr) FrmGetObjectPtr(frm, objectIndex);
}
```

In a finished application, of course, your code shouldn't be accessing form objects of the wrong type. During the development process, however, it is frightfully easy to accidentally pass the wrong index to `FrmGetObjectPtr`. Thus, using a safety checking routine like `GetFieldPtr` can be helpful in catching programming errors that are common in early development.

Types of Form Objects

Now we will discuss each individual type of form object in detail.

Labels

Label objects can be a little bit tricky if you are going to change the label at runtime. They are a snap if the label values don't switch. Here is the most important label function:

```
void FrmCopyLabel(FormType *formP, UInt16 labelID, const Char *newLabel)
```

`FrmCopyLabel` copies the contents of the new label to the label with the given ID. Unlike almost all the other Form Manager APIs, `FrmCopyLabel` takes an ID as a parameter, rather than an index.

Note the name of this function includes `Copy`. This means that the new label will overwrite the contents of the old label. You will have trouble if the length of the new label is longer than the length specified in the resource. Longer strings will definitely cause errors, since `FrmCopyLabel` will blindly write beyond the space allocated for the label. Thus, this function makes sure you've allocated enough space in your resource.

Unfortunately, prior to OS 3.5, `FrmCopyLabel` would redraw the new label, but would not erase the old one. You can have problems with this in cases where the new text is narrower than the old text; remnants of the old text are left behind like so much screen litter. One way to avoid this problem is to hide the label before doing the copy, and then show it afterward. Here is an example of that:

```
void SetLabelInForm(FormType *form, UInt16 labelID, const char *newText)
{
  UInt16 labelObjectIndex = FrmGetObjectIndex(form, labelID);
```

```
    FrmHideObject(form, labelObjectIndex);
    FrmCopyLabel(form, labelID, newText);
    FrmShowObject(form, labelObjectIndex);
}
```

In general, because of these problems, labels aren't well suited for text that needs to change at runtime. In most cases, if you've got some text on the screen that needs to change, you are better off not using a label. A preferable choice, in such instances, is a field that has the editable and underline attributes turned off.

 To change the label of a control (like a checkbox, for instance), do not use `FrmCopyLabel`; instead, use the Control Manager routine `CtlSetLabel`.

Example

Here's a PilRC example of a form with a label:

```
FORM ID SecondForm AT (0 0 160 160)
USABLE
BEGIN
  TITLE "FormTitle"
  LABEL "My Label" AUTOID AT (20 30)
END
```

Figure 9-1 shows the resulting form and object.

FormTitle _____

My Label

Figure 9-1. Example of a label

Bitmaps

Bitmap objects are used to display bitmaps from a separate bitmap resource. The Palm OS defines *bitmap families* as sets of related bitmaps, each the same size, containing bitmaps of various bit-depths (number of bits per pixel). To draw a bitmap family, Palm OS searches for the highest bit-depth bitmap in the family, less than or equal to the current screen depth so it shows the highest-quality bitmap from the family.

Here's a PilRC example of a form with a bitmap:

```
FORM ID SecondForm AT (0 0 160 160)
USABLE
BEGIN
  TITLE "FormWithBitmap"
  FORMBITMAP AT (30 50) BITMAP TheFormBitmapID
END

BITMAPFAMILY ID TheFormBitmapID "bmp1bpp.bmp"
  "bmp2bpp.bmp" "bmp4bpp.bmp" "bmp8bpp.bmp" "bmp16bpp.bmp"
```

The bitmap family contains five bitmaps, one each for the depths 1, 2, 4, 8, and 16. Each of the bitmaps *must* have the same bounds; the OS relies on the fact that the bitmap family bounds can be obtained from the first bitmap in the family.

Application icons

Bitmap families are also used for the icons displayed for the application in the Application launcher. Your application should have two families:

- A large one (22 pixels wide by 22 pixels high)
- A small one (15 pixels wide by 9 pixels high)

Although the large size is officially 22×22, you can actually specify a larger icon: the icon will be centered horizontally, and top-justified. You can use 32 pixels wide by 22 pixels high (but do try to avoid the temptation to use the extra bitmap width). Another common choice is 32×32 (don't use the bottom 10 rows; they're used by the Application launcher for the application name).

Here is a PilRC example that defines icons for 1, 2, 4, and 8 bit depths for the two required families:

```
ICONFAMILY "Sales1.bmp" "Sales2.bmp" "Sales4.bmp" "Sales8.bmp" TRANSPARENTINDEX 0

SMALLICONFAMILY "Sales1s.bmp" "Sales2s.bmp" "Sales4s.bmp" "Sales8s.bmp"
   TRANSPARENTINDEX 0
```

We set a transparent index. Pixels of that index aren't drawn; any background can be seen underneath those pixels.

 The *.bmp* format is a Windows bitmap format. Just about all image editing programs (on any platform) can save in this format. The Palm OS does not use Windows bitmap format; PilRC converts fromt he Windows *.bmp* format into the Palm OS bitmap format.

Graffiti Shift Indicator

A Graffiti Shift Indicator (GSI) is very simple: there's no code involved. All you do is specify its location: the OS will then use the location you've designated to display the state of Graffiti. The GSI should be located at 8 pixels from the right and 10 pixels from the bottom. For a modeless form, that yields:

```
GRAFFITISTATEINDICATOR AT (152 150)
```

For a modal form, you'll need to account for the 2-pixel inset, and the potentially different height. Define the following in a *.h* file:

```
#define kGSIFromBottom 10
#define kGSIInModalLeft 148
```

Then, in your *.rcp* file, you can specify your Graffiti Shift Indicator with:

```
GRAFFITISTATEINDICATOR AT (kGSIInModalLeft kMyFormHeight - kGSIFromBottom)
```

Lists

A list can be used "as is" without any programmatic customization. In the resource, you can specify the text of each list row and the number of rows that can be displayed at one time (the number of visible items). The list will automatically provide scroll arrows if the number of items is greater than the number that can be shown.

Lists are used both alone and with pop-up triggers. If you are using a standalone list, you'll receive a lstSelectEvent when the user taps on a list item. The List Manager highlights the selected item.

Here are some of the common routines you'll use with lists:

void LstSetSelection(ListType *listP, Int16 itemNum)
: This sets which item is selected (itemNum is a zero-based item number). Specifying noListSelection causes no items in the list to be selected. By default, a list opens with the first item selected.

Int16 LstGetSelection(const ListType *listP)
: This returns which item is selected (0-based). A result of noListSelection means that no item is selected.

Int16 LstGetNumberOfItems(const ListType *listP)
: This returns the total number of items in the list.

Int16 LstGetVisibleItems(const ListType *listP)
: This returns the total number of visible items (that is, the number of visible rows, which may be less than the total number of items).

Char *LstGetSelectionText(const ListType *listP, Int16 itemNum)
: This routine returns the text for the item with the given number (it really should have been called LstGetItemText).

Boolean LstScrollList(ListType *listP,
WinDirectionType direction, Int16 itemCount)
: This scrolls the list in the given direction (either winUp or winDown) through the specified number of items.

void LstSetTopItem(ListType *listP, Int16 itemNum)
: This scrolls the list, if necessary, so that the specified item is the top-most one.

void LstMakeItemVisible(ListType *listP, Int16 itemNum)
: This scrolls the list, if necessary, so that the specified item is visible.

LstSetListChoices(ListType *listP, Char **itemsText, Int16 numItems)
: This specifies the number of items in the list and their strings (replacing any strings specified in the resource).

void LstSetDrawFunction(ListType *listP, ListDrawDataFuncPtr func)
: This specifies a custom drawing routine that will be called to draw each row of the list.

A sample that displays a specific list item

Here's some sample code that selects the 11th item in a list (the first item is at 0) and scrolls the list, if necessary, so that item is visible:

```
void SelectAndMakeVisible(FormPtr form)
{
  ListPtr list;

  list = (ListPtr) FrmGetObjectPtr(form,
    FrmGetObjectIndex(form, MainMyList));

  LstSetSelection(list, 10);
  LstMakeItemVisible(list, 10);
}
```

Custom versus noncustom lists

If you want to specify the contents of the list at runtime, there are two ways to do it:

- Use `LstSetListChoices` to pass an array of strings that will become the new items. The List Manager retains the strings and draws each string as necessary.
- Use `LstSetDrawFunction` to provide a callback function that is responsible for drawing the contents of each row.

You'll find that the second way is almost always easier than the first. Let's look at a sample written twice, using the first approach and again using the second.

The sample draws a list composed of items in a string list resource. A string list resource contains a prefix string, followed by a list of different strings. Here's the PilRC definition of our string list (called a string table by PilRC):

```
STRINGTABLE MyStringTable "" "First" "Second" "Third" "Fourth" "Fifth"
  "Sixth"
```

There's no particular significance to retrieving the items from a string list resource; we just needed some example that required obtaining some strings at runtime.

There's a system utility routine, `SysStringByIndex`, that, given an index number, returns the string at that index prepended with the prefix string. We'll use that to obtain the strings from the string list.

Creating a runtime list with LstSetListChoices

Using the first approach, we need to create an array with each element pointing to a string. We'll store that array as a global (so that we can deallocate it later):

```
static Char **gStringsPtrArray = NULL;
```

We define some useful constants:

```
#define MyStringTable           1000
#define kNumStringsInTable       6
#define kMaxTableStringLength    20
```

When the form containing the list is opened, we'll initialize the array, and then call LstSetListChoices to provide the array to the List Manager (see Example 9-1).

Example 9-1. Initializing a list with an array of strings

```
void SecondFormInit(FormPtr frmP)
{
  ListPtr list;

  list = (ListPtr) FrmGetObjectPtr(frmP,
    FrmGetObjectIndex(frmP, SecondMyList));

  if (SetupStrings() == errNone) {
    LstSetListChoices(list, gStringsPtrArray, kNumStringsInTable);
  }
}
```

SetupStrings is responsible for actually creating the array (see Example 9-2).

Example 9-2. Creating an array of strings from a string list resource

```
Err SetupStrings()
{
  UInt16  i;

  gStringsPtrArray = (Char **)
    MemPtrNew(sizeof(Char *) * kNumStringsInTable);
  if (!gStringsPtrArray)
    return memErrNotEnoughSpace;

  for (i = 0; i < kNumStringsInTable; i++)
    gStringsPtrArray[i] = NULL;

  for (i = 0; i < kNumStringsInTable; i++) {
    Char s[kMaxTableStringLength + 1];

    SysStringByIndex(MyStringTable, i, s, sizeof(s));
    gStringsPtrArray[i] = (Char *) MemPtrNew(StrLen(s) + 1);
    if (!gStringsPtrArray[i]) {
      FreeStrings();
      return memErrNotEnoughSpace;
    } else
      StrCopy(gStringsPtrArray[i], s);
  }
  return errNone;
}
```

SetupStrings creates an array of character pointers, each of which points to a separately allocated string. If any of the allocations fail, it calls FreeStrings (see Example 9-3) to deallocate all memory allocated so far.

Example 9-3. FreeStrings frees memory used by the strings and the array itself

```
void FreeStrings()
{
  UInt16  i;

  if (gStringsPtrArray) {
    for (i = 0; i < kNumStringsInTable; i++) {
      if (gStringsPtrArray[i])
        MemPtrFree(gStringsPtrArray[i]);
    }
    MemPtrFree(gStringsPtrArray);
  }
}
```

When the form closes, we must deallocate the memory:

```
void SecondFormDeinit(FormPtr frmP)
{
#pragma unused(frmP)
  FreeStrings();
}
```

Creating a runtime list with LstSetDrawFunction

Here's the alternative way of customizing the list at runtime. Our initialization routine must initialize the number of rows in the list and must install a callback routine:

```
void SecondFormInit(FormPtr frmP)
{
  ListPtr list;

  list = (ListPtr) FrmGetObjectPtr(frmP,
    FrmGetObjectIndex(frmP, SecondMyList));

  LstSetDrawFunction(list, DrawOneString);
  LstSetListChoices(list, NULL, kNumStringsInTable);
}
```

DrawOneString gets the appropriate string from the list and draws it. As well as just drawing the text itself, we could have done additional drawing (lines, bitmaps, and so on) in the callback routine.

```
void DrawOneString(Int16 itemNum, RectangleType *bounds,
  Char **itemsText)
{
#pragma unused(itemsText)
  Char s[kMaxTableStringLength + 1];

  SysStringByIndex(MyStringTable, (UInt16) itemNum, s, sizeof(s));
  WinDrawChars(s, StrLen(s), bounds->topLeft.x, bounds->topLeft.y);
}
```

There is no cleanup necessary when the form is completed.

There are a number of reasons to prefer the second approach to the first one. The first approach has more code and it also uses more memory (because of the allocated array, and the allocated strings). The second approach has more flexibility—we could have drawn text in different fonts or styles in the drawing routine, or done additional drawing on a row-by-row basis. The last advantage is that if there are many items in the list, the first approach will take longer, as the strings for each list item will need to be obtained before the list is drawn; the second approach is pay-as-you-go: each string is obtained only as it needs to be drawn.

Controls

The control form objects are buttons, checkboxes, push buttons, selector triggers, repeating buttons, pop-up triggers, graphical controls, and sliders. All controls have the attributes shown in Table 9-5.

Table 9-5. Control attributes

Part	Function
Label	The text displayed in the control
Value	The current state of the control (for checkboxes and push buttons, 1 means on, 0 means off)
Font	The font used for the label

Control APIs

Here are the most useful APIs when using controls:

void CtlSetValue(ControlType *controlP, Int16 newValue)
　　This sets the value of the control (used for checkboxes, push buttons, and sliders).

Int16 CtlGetValue(const ControlType *controlP)
　　This returns the value of the control. For checkboxes and push buttons, a value of 1 means the control is on, and a 0 means it is off. For a slider, it is the value of the slider. For other controls, the value is not very useful.

FrmSetControlValue(const FormType *formP, UInt16 controlID, Int16 newValue)
　　Like CtlSetValue, this sets the value of the control (useful for checkboxes, push buttons, and sliders). FrmSetControlValue is a shortcut, since it requires only a control ID rather than a ControlPtr.

Int16 FrmGetControlValue(const FormType *formP, UInt16 controlID)
　　Like CtlGetValue, this returns the value of the control. FrmGetControlValue is often a shortcut, since it requires only a control ID rather than a ControlPtr.

UInt16 FrmGetControlGroupSelection(const FormType *formP, UInt8 groupNum)
　　This returns the index of the control that is on in the given group. It can be useful when you need to find which of a group of push buttons is on.

```
void FrmSetControlGroupSelection(const FormType *formP,
UInt8 groupNum, UInt16 controlID)
```
This sets which control is on in a given group. It will also turn off the previous selection within the group.

`const Char *CtlGetLabel(const ControlType *controlP)`

This returns the label of the control.

`void CtlSetLabel(ControlType *controlP, const Char *newLabel)`

This sets the label of the control. Note that since this copies the pointer (rather than the entire label), the text of the passed-in label must be maintained for the life of the control.

`void CtlHitControl(const ControlType *controlP)`

This simulates hitting the control. This can be useful, for example, when you need to have a menu event that does the same thing as a button. Simply have the menu event force a call to `CtlHitControl`.

Using graphical labels rather than text labels for controls

The 3.5 OS added graphical controls that display bitmaps rather than text. A graphical control has two bitmaps (actually bitmap families): one represents the selected state, and one represents the unselected state. These graphical controls affect the appearance of the control. Graphics, as opposed to text, can be used for buttons, push buttons, pop-up triggers, selector triggers, and repeating buttons.

Here's a specification of a graphical push button in PilRC:

```
BUTTON  "" ID 1001  AT (20 30 AUTO AUTO) GRAPHICAL NOFRAME
    BITMAPID 1001 SELECTEDBITMAPID 1002
```

Buttons

A `ctlSelectEvent` is sent.

You won't often need to call the Control Manager for buttons.

Push buttons

A `ctlSelectEvent` is sent.

To allow for exclusive choices, push buttons have a group. Only one push button in a group can be on at a time (this is enforced by the Control Manager). The exception to this is group 0, which can have multiple push buttons on at a time.

Checkboxes

A `ctlSelectEvent` is sent.

For no good reason, checkboxes, like push buttons, can be organized into groups. Since the UI of checkboxes indicates that they should be independent of one another, their group should always be zero.

Here's an example that shows turning a checkbox on:

```
FrmSetControlValue(form, MyCheckboxID, 1);
```

Selector triggers

A ctlSelectEvent is sent.

The selector trigger displays text in a dotted rectangle and will notify you when the user taps on it. It has no default behavior that occurs on such a tap, however. It's up to you to put up a dialog box to obtain the user's input and then to change the label of the selector trigger to reflect that input.

Here's an example from the Date Book; it is the date selector trigger in the Details dialog box (note that the event handler has already determined that a ctlSelectEvent occurred):

```
case DetailsDateSelector:
  DetailsSelectDate (details);
  handled = true;
  break;
```

The DetailsSelectDate routine puts up a dialog box (using SelectDay) and then updates the label of the control appropriately (see Example 9-4).

Example 9-4. Displays a Details dialog box; shows using CtlSetLabel

```
void DetailsSelectDate (DetailsPtr details)
{
  Int16 month, day, year;
  Char* label;
  Char* title;
  ControlPtr ctl;

  year = details->when.date.year + firstYear;
  month = details->when.date.month;
  day = details->when.date.day;

  title = MemHandleLock(DmGetResource (strRsc, startDateTitleStrID));

  if (SelectDay (selectDayByDay, &month, &day, &year, title))
    {
    // Set the label of the date selector.
    ctl = GetObjectPtr (DetailsDateSelector);
    label = (Char *)CtlGetLabel (ctl);  // OK to cast; we call CtlSetLabel
    DateToDOWDMFormat (month, day, year, ShortDateFormat, label);
    CtlSetLabel (ctl, label);
    ...
    }
  MemPtrUnlock (title);
}
```

Repeating buttons

A `ctlRepeatEvent` (*not* a `ctlSelectEvent`) is sent.

For repeating buttons, your event handler must return false, otherwise the control will stop repeating.

Example 9-5 is from the Date Book, part of `DayViewHandleEvent`, the event handler for the day view.

Example 9-5. Handling ctlRepeatEvents in the Details dialog box of the Date Book

```
// Handle the scrolling controls.
else if (event->eType == ctlRepeatEvent)
  {
  switch (event->data.ctlRepeat.controlID)
    {
    case DayPrevWeekButton:
      DateAdjust (&Date, -daysInWeek);
      DayViewDrawDate (Date);
      break;

    case DayNextWeekButton:
      DateAdjust (&Date, daysInWeek);
      DayViewDrawDate (Date);
      break;

    case DayUpButton:
      DayViewScroll (winUp, false);
      break;

    case DayDownButton:
      DayViewScroll (winDown, false);
      break;
    }
  }
```

Note that `handled` is not set to `true`, so it remains false.

Pop-up trigger objects

A `popSelectEvent` is sent.

Pop-up triggers need associated lists. A list's bounds should be set so that its left bounds are the bounds of the trigger and its width is at least as wide as the trigger. In addition, the usable attribute must be set to false so that it won't appear until the pop-up trigger is pressed.

When the pop-up trigger is pressed, the list is displayed. When a list item is chosen, the pop-up label is set to the chosen item. These actions occur automatically; no code needs to be written. When a new item is chosen from the pop up, a popSelectEvent is sent. Some associated data is sent with the event such as the list ID, the list pointer, a pointer to the trigger control, and the indexes of the previously selected item and newly selected items.

Example 9-6 shows an example resource.

Example 9-6. An example resource for a pop-up trigger including the list

```
#define MainForm        1100
#define MainTriggerID   1102
#define MainListID      1103

...

FORM ID 1100 AT (0 0 160 160)
BEGIN
    POPUPTRIGGER "States" ID MainTriggerID AT (55 30 44 12)
        LEFTANCHOR NOFRAME FONT 0
    POPUPLIST ID MainTriggerID MainListID
    LIST "California" "Kansas" "New Mexico" "Pennsylvania" "Rhode Island"
        "Wyoming" ID MainListID AT (64 29 63 33) NONUSABLE DISABLED FONT 0
END
```

Here's an example of handling a popSelectEvent in an event handler (from the 3.5 Palm OS To Do example):

```
    else if (event->eType == popSelectEvent)
      {
      if (event->data.popSelect.listID == DetailsDueDateList)
        {
        DetermineDueDate (event->data.popSelect.selection, &dueDate);
        DetailsSetDateTrigger (dueDate);
        handled = true;
        }
      }
```

If you are using a custom drawing routine for your list, you'll need to set the label of the control yourself (using CtlSetLabel) and return true. If you return false, the default code will attempt to read from the nonexistent array of strings.

Sliders

The 3.5 OS was the first to include sliders, a graphical control to choose a numeric value in between some minimum and maximum. Sliders can be customized with two bitmaps: one representing the background and the other representing the thumb (the part that moves). Table 9-6 shows the events that are generated while a slider is being manipulated.

Table 9-6. Events generated when a slider is manipulated

Event	When it occurs
ctlEnterEvent	When the pen taps on the slider's background.
ctlEnterEvent	When the pen goes down on the slider's thumb.
ctlSelectEvent	When the pen is lifted from the slider. The slider's ID number and the coordinates of the new thumb location are sent with the ctlSelectEvent.

Here's a specification of a slider in PilRC using the default background and thumb:

```
SLIDER ID 1001  AT (20 30 114 15) MINVALUE 0 MAXVALUE 10 PAGESIZE 10
```

And here's one that specifies a custom background and thumb:

```
SLIDER ID 1001  AT (20 30 114 15) MINVALUE 0 MAXVALUE 10 PAGESIZE 10
  THUMBID 1001 BACKGROUNDID 1002
```

Gadgets

Once you have rifled through the other objects and haven't found anything suitable for the task you have in mind, you are usually left with one choice: a gadget. This form object is the one you use when nothing else will do.

A gadget is a custom form object with on-screen bounds that can have data programmatically associated with it. (You can't set data for a gadget from a resource.) It also has an object ID.

All the Form Manager knows about a gadget is its bounds, its object ID, and its data pointer. Everything else you need to handle yourself.

The 3.5 OS also added the concept of an *extended gadget*; this allows you to set a gadget handler for a gadget. This gadget handler is responsible for drawing, freeing data, erasing, and handling taps. The gadget handler provides an easy way to encapsulate all the code involved with a gadget.

Gadget APIs

Here are some useful gadget APIs:

void FrmSetGadgetData(FormType *formP, UInt16 objIndex, const void *data)
> This sets the data for the gadget at the given index. The Form Manager does nothing with the data you pass other than save the pointer for later retrieval.

void *FrmGetGadgetData(const FormType *formP, UInt16 objIndex)
> This retrieves the data for the gadget at the given index.

void FrmSetGadgetHandler(FormType *formP, UInt16 objIndex, FormGadgetHandlerType *attrP)
> This 3.5 OS and later routine sets the gadget handler for the gadget at the given index.

Gadget responsibilities

The two biggest tasks that the gadget needs to handle are:

- All the drawings in the gadget on the screen
- All the taps on the gadget

There are two times when the gadget needs to be drawn—when the form first gets opened and whenever your event handler receives a frmUpdateEvent (these are the same times you need to call FrmDrawForm). For an extended gadget, the gadget handler is automatically called whenever the gadget needs to be redrawn. For a simple gadget, you must determine when to draw the gadget yourself.

If you'll be saving data associated with the gadget, use the FrmSetGadgetData function. You also need to initialize the data when your form is opened.

The Advantages of Gadgets

Although you could draw and respond to taps without a gadget, it has three advantages over a totally custom-coded structure:

- The gadget maintains a pointer that allows you to store gadget-specific data.
- The gadget maintains a rectangular bounds specified in the resource.
- Gremlins, the automatic random tester, recognizes gadgets and taps on them. This is an enormous advantage because Gremlins relentlessly tap on them during testing cycles. While it is true that it will tap on areas that lie outside the bounds of any form object, it is a rare event. Gremlins are especially attracted to form objects; they like to spend time tapping in them. If you didn't use gadgets, your code would rarely receive taps during this type of testing.

A simple gadget

Let's look at an example gadget that stores the integer 0 or 1 and displays either a vertical or horizontal line. Figure 9-2 contains a view of the main form that displays our gadget.

Figure 9-2. A simple gadget

Tapping on the gadget flips the integer and the line. Here's the resource declaration of the gadget:

```
FORM ID MainForm AT (0 0 160 160)
USABLE
BEGIN
  TITLE "OReilly Starter Main"
  GADGET ID MainGadget AT (60 60 30 20)
END
```

Here's the form's initialization routine that initializes the data in the gadget:

```
void MainFormInit(FormPtr form)
{
  MemHandle h = MemHandleNew(sizeof(UInt8));

  if (h) {
    * (UInt8 *) MemHandleLock(h) = 1;
    MemHandleUnlock(h);
    FrmSetGadgetData(form, FrmGetObjectIndex(form, MainGadget), h);
  }
}
```

When the form is closed, the gadget's data handle must be deallocated:

```
void MainFormDeinit(FormPtr form)
{
  MemHandle h;

  h = (MemHandle) FrmGetGadgetData(form,
    FrmGetObjectIndex(form, MainGadget));
  if (h)
    MemHandleFree(h);
}
```

Example 9-7 shows the routine that draws the horizontal or vertical line.

Example 9-7. Gadget drawing routine

```
// Draws  | or - depending on the data in the gadget.
static
void GadgetDrawWithData(RectangleType *bounds, MemHandle data)
{
  Coord          fromx, fromy, tox, toy;

  if (data) {
    UInt8        *dataP = (UInt8 *) MemHandleLock(data);

    switch (*dataP) {
    case 0:
      fromx = bounds->topLeft.x + bounds->extent.x / 2;
      fromy = bounds->topLeft.y;
      tox = fromx;
      toy = fromy + bounds->extent.y - 1;
      break;
    case 1:
      fromx = bounds->topLeft.x;
```

Example 9-7. Gadget drawing routine (continued)

```
        fromy = bounds->topLeft.y + bounds->extent.y / 2;
        tox = fromx + bounds->extent.x - 1;
        toy = fromy;
        break;
    default:
        fromx = tox = bounds->topLeft.x;
        fromy = toy = bounds->topLeft.y;
        break;
    }
    MemHandleUnlock(data);
    WinEraseRectangle(bounds, 0);
    WinDrawLine(fromx, fromy, tox, toy);
    }
}
```

Here is a wrapper function that draws a gadget given its gadget ID:

```
    void GadgetDraw(FormPtr form, UInt16 gadgetID)
    {
        RectangleType  bounds;
        UInt16         gadgetIndex = FrmGetObjectIndex(form, gadgetID);
        MemHandle      data;

        data = (MemHandle) FrmGetGadgetData(form, gadgetIndex);
        FrmGetObjectBounds(form, gadgetIndex, &bounds);
        GadgetDrawWithData(&bounds, data);
    }
```

When our application event handler is sent a `frmOpenEvent` or `frmUpdateEvent`, the gadget must be drawn. We add code to our event handler to do so (see Example 9-8).

Example 9-8. Part of event handler with gadget-drawing calls emphasized

```
case frmOpenEvent:
  form = FrmGetActiveForm( );
  MainFormInit(form);
  FrmDrawForm(form);
  GadgetDraw(form, MainGadget);
  handled = true;
  break;

case frmUpdateEvent:
  form = FrmGetActiveForm( );
  FrmDrawForm(form);
  GadgetDraw(form, MainGadget);
  handled = true;
  break;
```

Every time the user taps down on the form, the form's event handler needs to check to see whether the tap is on the gadget. It does so by comparing the tap point with the gadget's bounds. Example 9-9 is the code from the event handler.

Example 9-9. Part of event handler handling pen down events

```
case penDownEvent:
  {
   FormPtr        form = FrmGetActiveForm( );
   UInt16         gadgetIndex = FrmGetObjectIndex(form, MainGadget);
   RectangleType  bounds;

   FrmGetObjectBounds(form, gadgetIndex, &bounds);
   if (RctPtInRectangle (event->screenX, event->screenY, &bounds)) {
     GadgetTap(form, MainGadget, event);
     handled = true;
   }
  }
  break;
```

We also have a GadgetTap function that handles a tap and acts much like a button—highlighting and unhighlighting as the stylus moves in and out of the gadget (see Example 9-10).

Example 9-10. Routine that handles taps on a gadget

```
// It'll work like a button: invert when you tap in it.
// Stay inverted while you stay in the button. Leave the button, uninvert,
// let go outside, nothing happens; let go inside, data changes/redraws.
void GadgetTap(FormPtr form, UInt16 gadgetID, EventPtr event)
{
#pragma unused(event)
   UInt16         gadgetIndex = FrmGetObjectIndex(form, gadgetID);
   MemHandle      data = (MemHandle) FrmGetGadgetData(form, gadgetIndex);
   Int16          x, y;
   Boolean        penDown;
   RectangleType  bounds;
   Boolean        wasInBounds = true;

   if (data) {
      FrmGetObjectBounds(form, gadgetIndex, &bounds);
      WinInvertRectangle(&bounds, 0);
      do {
         Boolean  nowInBounds;

         PenGetPoint (&x, &y, &penDown);
         nowInBounds = RctPtInRectangle(x, y, &bounds);
         if (nowInBounds != wasInBounds) {
            WinInvertRectangle(&bounds, 0);
            wasInBounds = nowInBounds;
         }
      } while (penDown);
      if (wasInBounds) {
         UInt8    *dataPtr = (UInt8 *) MemHandleLock(data);
         *dataPtr = (UInt8) !(*dataPtr);
         MemHandleUnlock(data);

         // GadgetDraw will erase--we don't need to invert.
         GadgetDrawWithData(&bounds, data);
```

Example 9-10. Routine that handles taps on a gadget (continued)

```
    } // Else gadget is already uninverted.
  }
}
```

This is all the code for our simple gadget. There are other things that we would have to do, however, if we wanted to have multiple gadgets on a single form. We'd need to do the following:

- Modify the form open and close routines to allocate and deallocate handles for each gadget in the form.
- Modify the event handler to check for taps in the bounds of each gadget, rather than just the one.
- Draw each gadget on an open or update event.

A sample using extended gadgets

Now we are going to look at the same example, but we will use an extended gadget (3.5 OS or later) instead of a simple gadget. Important differences are emphasized.

Here's the resource declaration:

```
FORM ID MainForm AT (0 0 160 160)
USABLE
BEGIN
  TITLE "OReilly Starter Main"
  GADGET MainExtendedGadget AT (125 60 30 20)
END
```

The initialization is similar, but we must initialize the gadget handler along with the data (see Example 9-11).

Example 9-11. Initialization of extended gadget

```
void MainFormInit(FormPtr form)
{
  MemHandle h = MemHandleNew(sizeof(UInt8));

  if (h) {
    UInt16 gadgetIndex = FrmGetObjectIndex(form, MainExtendedGadget);
    * (UInt8 *) MemHandleLock(h) = 1;
    MemHandleUnlock(h);
    FrmSetGadgetData(form, gadgetIndex, h);
    FrmSetGadgetHandler(form, gadgetIndex, GadgetHandler);
  }
}
```

The gadget handler itself (see Example 9-12) relies on the previously written routines GadgetTap and GadgetDrawWithData.

Example 9-12. The gadget handler handling all events relevant to the gadget

```
Boolean GadgetHandler(FormGadgetType *gadgetP, UInt16 cmd, void *paramP)
{
  Boolean   handled = false;
  EventPtr  event;

  switch (cmd) {
  case formGadgetDrawCmd:
    GadgetDrawWithData(&gadgetP->rect, (MemHandle) gadgetP->data);
    gadgetP->attr.visible = true;// Required by Form Manager.
    handled = true;
    break;

  case formGadgetHandleEventCmd:
    event = (EventType *) paramP;
    if (event->eType == frmGadgetEnterEvent)
      GadgetTap(FrmGetActiveForm(), gadgetP->id, event);
    handled = true;
    break;

  case formGadgetDeleteCmd:
    if (gadgetP->data)
      MemHandleFree((MemHandle) gadgetP->data);
    handled = true;
    break;
  }
  return handled;
}
```

After drawing, the gadget handler must set the `visible` attribute to true. This is needed so that `FrmHideObject` will know to erase the object. If it isn't set, `FrmHideObject` returns immediately.

We no longer need any special code in the form's event handler, or in its deinitialization routine.

Comparing the extended gadget to the simple gadget, we note that the extended gadget is simpler to reuse. Now, if we want multiple gadgets on the same form, all we need to do is create them in our resource, and then initialize them; the gadget handler deals with the rest. There's no need to modify the event handler at all.

Gadget tip

If you are creating an application that will run on 3.5 OS or greater, by all means use extended gadgets; they're easier to reuse. However, if your application must run on prior OS versions as well, stick with the original gadget; it'll work on all OS versions.

Fields

Editable text objects, known as fields, require attention to many details. Among the most important details are the need to use handles instead of pointers, correctly reading from and writing to fields, and correctly setting the focus of a field. Let's look at each of these details in turn.

Setting text in a field

Accessing an editable field needs to be done in a particular way. Here are the important points:

- You must use a handle instead of a pointer because the ability to resize the text requires the use of a handle.
- You must make sure to get the field's current handle and expressly free it in your code. Example 9-13 shows you how to do this.

Example 9-13. Setting a field to edit a given handle

```
void SetFieldTextFromHandle(FieldPtr field, MemHandle newHandle,
  Boolean redraw)
{
  MemHandle   oldHandle;

  // Get the field and the field's current text handle.
  oldHandle = FldGetTextHandle(field);

  // Set the field's text to the new text.
  FldSetTextHandle(field, newHandle);
  if (redraw)
    FldDrawField(field);

  // Free the handle AFTER we call FldSetTextHandle().
  if (oldHandle)
    MemHandleFree(oldHandle);
}
```

This bit of code is responsible for getting the field handle with FldGetTextHandle and disposing of it with MemHandleFree at the end of the routine.

Last, we redraw the field (if requested) with FldDrawField. If we had not done so, the changed text wouldn't be displayed. The redraw parameter is there because no drawing is allowed before the form has been drawn. Thus, calls to SetFieldTextFromHandle from a form's initialization routine pass false for redraw.

Were we not to dispose of the old handles of editable text fields in the application, we would get slowly growing memory leaks all over the running application. Imagine that every time an editable field were modified programmatically its old handle were kept in memory, along with its new handle. It wouldn't take long for our running application to choke the dynamic heap with its vampire-like hunger for memory. Furthermore, debugging such a problem would require real diligence as the cause of the problem would not be readily obvious.

Note that when a form closes, each field within it frees its handle. If you don't want that behavior for a particular field, call FldSetTextHandle(fld, NULL) before the field is closed. When the user starts writing in that field, the Field Manager will automatically allocate a handle for it if it doesn't have one already.

Field utility routines

Here are some utility routines that you will find useful in creating fields. The first one sets a field's text to that of a string, allocates a handle, and copies the string for you (see Example 9-14).

Example 9-14. Setting a field's text to a given string

```
Err SetFieldTextFromStr(FieldPtr field, Char *s, Boolean redraw)
{
   MemHandle      h;

   h = FldGetTextHandle(field);
   if (h) {
     Err  err;

     FldSetTextHandle(field, NULL);
     err = MemHandleResize(h, StrLen(s) + 1);
     if (err != errNone) {
       FldSetTextHandle(field, h);  // Restore handle.
       return err;
     }
   } else {
     h = MemHandleNew(StrLen(s) + 1);
     if (!h)
       return memErrNotEnoughSpace;
   }
   // At this point, we have a handle of the correct size.

   // Copy the string to the locked handle.
   StrCopy((Char *) MemHandleLock(h), s);
   // Unlock the string handle.
   MemHandleUnlock(h);

   FldSetTextHandle(field, h);
   if (redraw)
     FldDrawField(field);
   return errNone;
}
```

The second utility routine clears the text from a field:

```
   void ClearFieldText(FieldPtr field, Boolean redraw)
   {
     SetFieldTextFromHandle(field, NULL, redraw);
   }
```

Modifying text in a field

One way to make changes to text is to use FldDelete, FldSetSelection, and FldInsert. These routines do the following:

FldDelete
> This deletes a specified range of text.

FldInsert
> This inserts text at the current selection.

FldSetSelection
> This sets the selection.

By making judicious calls to these routines, you can change the existing text into whatever new text you desire. The routines are easy to use. They have a flaw, however, that may make them inappropriate to use in some cases: FldDelete and FldInsert redraw the field. If you're making multiple calls to these routines for a single field (let's say, for example, you were replacing every other character with an "X"), you'd see the field redraw after every call. Users might find this distracting. Be careful with fldChanged-Events as well. Each of these routines posts a fldChangedEvent to the event queue; if you make multiple calls before returning to your event loop, the event queue can overflow.

An alternative approach involves directly modifying the text in the handle. However, you must not change the text in a handle while it is being used by a field; doing so confuses the field and its internal information is not updated correctly. Among other things, line breaks won't work correctly.

To properly change the text, first remove it from the field, modify it, and then put it back. Example 9-15 shows how to do that.

Example 9-15. Editing the text of a field programmatically

```
void ConvertToLowercase(FieldPtr field)
{
  MemHandle  h;

  // Get the field's current text handle.
  h = FldGetTextHandle(field);
  if (h) {
    Char *s;

    FldSetTextHandle(field, NULL);

    s = (Char *) MemHandleLock(h);
    StrToLower(s, s);
    MemHandleUnlock(h);

    SetFieldTextFromHandle(field, h, true);
  }
}
```

This example simply converts any uppercase characters in the field to lowercase.

Getting text from a field

To read the text from a field, you can use FldGetTextHandle. It is often more convenient, however, to obtain a pointer instead by using FldGetTextPtr. It returns a locked pointer to the text. Note that this text pointer can become invalid if the user subsequently edits the text. This happens when there isn't enough room left for new text—the Field Manager unlocks the handle, resizes it, and then relocks it.

If the field is empty, it won't have any text associated with it. In such cases, FldGetTextPtr returns NULL. Make sure you check for this case.

Setting the focus of a field

When a form containing editable text fields is displayed, one of the text fields should contain the focus; this means it displays an insertion point and receives any Graffiti input. You must choose the field that has the initial focus by setting it in your code. The user can change the focus by tapping on a field. The Form Manager handles changing the focus in this case.

You must also handle the vchrPrevField and vchrNextField characters; these allow the user to move from field to field using Graffiti (the Graffiti strokes for these characters are ʌ and ʏ).

To move the focus, use FrmSetFocus. Here's an example that sets the focus to the MyFormMyTextField field:

```
FormPtr frm = FrmGetActiveForm( );

FrmSetFocus(frm, FrmGetObjectIndex(frm, MyFormMyTextField));
```

 On a pre-3.5 OS, FrmSetFocus must be called after the first call to FrmDrawForm. Otherwise, the flashing insertion point won't be displayed. In the 3.5 OS and later, you can safely call FrmSetFocus in your form's initialization routine, before the first call to FrmDrawForm.

Field gotchas

As might be expected, if you have a complicated field, there are a number of things to watch out for in your code:

Preventing deallocation of a handle
    When a form containing a field is closed, the field frees its handle (with FldFreeMemory). In some cases, this is fine (for instance, if the field automatically allocated the handle because the user started writing into an empty field). In other cases, it is not. For example, when you've used FldSetTextHandle so that a

field will edit your handle, you may not want the handle deallocated—you may want to deallocate it yourself or retain it.

To prevent the field from deallocating your handle, call `FldSetTextHandle(fld, NULL)` to set the field's text handle to `NULL`. Do this when your form receives a `frmCloseEvent`.

FldSetTextPtr considered harmful
> `FldSetTextPtr` can only be used on read-only fields. In addition, if your field is multiple line, you must call `FldRecalculateField` after calling `FldSetTextPtr`, or the field will never draw. In general, we never use this routine; instead we always use the utility routine `SetFieldTextFromStr`, which was discussed earlier.

Preventing memory leaks
> When you call `FldSetTextHandle`, any existing handle in the field is not automatically deallocated. To prevent memory leaks, you'll normally want to do the following:
>
> 1. Get the old handle with `FldGetTextHandle`.
> 2. Set the new handle with `FldSetTextHandle`.
> 3. Deallocate the old handle.

Don't use FldSetTextPtr and FldSetTextHandle together
> `FldSetTextPtr` should be used only for noneditable fields for which you'll never call `FldSetTextHandle`. The two routines are poor playmates as they don't get along.

Remove the handle when editing a field
> If you're going to modify the text within a field's handle, first remove the handle from the field with `FldSetTextHandle(fld, NULL)`, modify the text, and then set the handle back again.

Compacting string handles
> The length of the handle in a field may be longer than the length of the string itself, since a field expands a handle in chunks. When a handle has been edited with a field, call `FldCompactText` to shrink the handle to the length of the string (actually, one byte longer than the length of the string for the trailing null byte).

Scrollbars

A scrollbar doesn't know anything about scrolling or about any other form objects. It is just a form object that stores a current number, along with a minimum and maximum. The UI effect is the result of the scrollbar's allowing the user to modify that number graphically within the constraints of the minimum and maximum.

Scrollbars were introduced in Palm OS 2.0 and therefore aren't available in the 1.0 OS. If you intend to run on 1.0 systems, your code will need to scroll using buttons.

The events generated while a scrollbar is being manipulated are shown in Table 9-7.

Table 9-7. Events generated while a scrollbar is being manipulated

Event	When it occurs
sclRepeatEvent	While the user holds the stylus down
sclExitEvent	When the user releases the stylus

Scrollbar coding requirements

There are a few things that you need to handle in your code:

- You must respond to a change in the scrollbar's current value by scrolling the objects over which the scrollbar is supposed to be moving.

  Here is how you do that: your event handler receives a sclRepeatEvent while the user holds the stylus down and a sclExitEvent when the user releases the stylus. Your code is on the lookout for one or the other event, depending on whether your application wants to scroll immediately (as the user is scrolling with the scrollbar) or postpone the scrolling until the user has gotten to the final scroll position with the scrollbar.

- Make sure your event handler returns false in the case of a sclRepeatEvent. Otherwise, scrolling will abruptly stop (the scrollbar uses the sclRepeatEvent to continue scrolling, so you shouldn't stop the event processing).

- You must change the scrollbar if the current scroll position changes through other appropriate user actions; for example, if the user pushes the hardware scroll buttons or drag-scrolls through text.

- You must change the scrollbar if the scroll maximum value changes, for example, when typing changes the total number of lines (a field sends a fldChangedEvent at this point if its resource attribute hasScrollbar is set).

Updating the scrollbar based on the insertion point

Let's look at the code for a sample application that has a field connected to a scrollbar. We need a routine (see Example 9-16) that will update the scrollbar based on the current insertion point, field height, and number of text lines (FldGetScrollValues is designed to return these values).

Example 9-16. UpdateScrollbar updates the value of the scrollbar

```
void UpdateScrollbar(FormPtr form, UInt16 fieldID, UInt16 scrollbarID)
{
    ScrollBarPtr    scroll;
```

Example 9-16. UpdateScrollbar updates the value of the scrollbar

```
FieldPtr        field;
UInt16          currentPosition;
UInt16          textHeight;
UInt16          fieldHeight;
UInt16          maxValue;

field = (FieldPtr) FrmGetObjectPtr(form,
   FrmGetObjectIndex(form, fieldID));
FldGetScrollValues(field, &currentPosition, &textHeight, &fieldHeight);

// If the field is 3 lines and the text height is 4 lines,
// then we can scroll so the first line is at the top
// (scroll position 0) or so the second line is at the top
// (scroll postion 1). These two values are enough to see
// the entire text.
if (textHeight > fieldHeight)
   maxValue = textHeight - fieldHeight;
else if (currentPosition)
   maxValue = currentPosition;
else
   maxValue = 0;

scroll = (ScrollBarPtr)
   FrmGetObjectPtr(form, FrmGetObjectIndex(form, scrollbarID));

// On a page scroll, want to overlap by one line (to provide context).
SclSetScrollBar(scroll, (Int16) currentPosition, 0,
   (Int16) maxValue, (Int16) fieldHeight - 1);
}
```

We update the scrollbar when the form is initially opened:

```
void MainFormInit(FormPtr form)
{
   UpdateScrollbar(form, MainField, MainScrollbar);
}
```

Updating the scrollbar when the number of lines changes

We also have to update the scrollbar whenever the number of lines in the field changes. Since we set the hasScrollbar attribute of the field in the resource, when the lines change, the fldChangedEvent passes to our event handler (in fact, this is the only reason for the existence of hasScrollbar). Here's the code we put in the event handler:

```
case fldChangedEvent:
   UpdateScrollbar(FrmGetActiveForm( ), MainField, MainScrollbar);
   handled = true;
   break;
```

At this point, the scrollbar updates automatically as the text changes.

Updating the display when the scrollbar moves

Next, we've got to handle changes made via the scrollbar. Of the two choices open to us, we want to scroll immediately, so we handle the sclRepeatEvent:

```
case sclRepeatEvent:
  ScrollLines(FrmGetActiveForm( ), MainField, MainScrollbar,
    event->data.sclRepeat.newValue - event->data.sclRepeat.value, false);
  break;
```

ScrollLines (see Example 9-17) is responsible for scrolling the text field (using FldScrollField). Things can get tricky, however, if there are empty lines at the end of the field. When the user scrolls up, the number of lines is reduced. Thus, we have to make sure the scrollbar gets updated to reflect this change (note that winUp and winDown are constant enumerations defined in the Palm OS include files).

Example 9-17. ScrollLines will scroll forward or backward, updating the field and the scrollbar

```
void ScrollLines(FormPtr form, UInt16 fieldID, UInt16 scrollbarID,
  Int16 numLinesToScroll, Boolean redraw)
{
  FormPtr      frm = FrmGetActiveForm( );
  FieldPtr     field;

  field = (FieldPtr) FrmGetObjectPtr(frm, FrmGetObjectIndex(frm, fieldID));
  if (numLinesToScroll < 0)
    FldScrollField(field, (UInt16) -numLinesToScroll, winUp);
  else
    FldScrollField(field, (UInt16) numLinesToScroll, winDown);

  // If there are blank lines at the end and we scroll up, FldScrollField
  // makes the blank lines disappear. Therefore, we've got to update
  // the scrollbar.
  if ((FldGetNumberOfBlankLines(field) && numLinesToScroll < 0) ||
    redraw)
    UpdateScrollbar(form, fieldID, scrollbarID);
}
```

Updating the display when the scroll buttons are used

Next on the list of things to do is handling the hardware scroll buttons. When the user taps either of the scroll buttons, we receive a keyDownEvent. Example 9-18 shows the code in our event handler that takes care of these buttons.

Example 9-18. Portion of event handler handling page down and page up characters

```
case keyDownEvent: {
  WChar c = event->data.keyDown.chr;

  // Check for virtual char. On 2-byte system (like Japanese), we could have
  // a real character that maps to vchrPageUp or vchrPageDown.
  if (TxtGlueCharIsVirtual(event->data.keyDown.modifiers, c)) {
    if (c == vchrPageUp) {
      PageScroll(FrmGetActiveForm( ), MainField, MainScrollbar, winUp);
```

```
        handled = true;
    } else if (c == vchrPageDown) {
        PageScroll(FrmGetActiveForm( ), MainField, MainScrollbar, winDown);
        handled = true;
    }
  }
}
break;;
```

Scrolling a full page

Finally, Example 9-19 shows our page-scrolling function. Of course, we don't want to scroll if we've already scrolled as far as we can. FldScrollable tells us if we can scroll in a particular direction. We use ScrollLines to do the actual scrolling and rely on it to update the scrollbar.

Example 9-19. PageScroll scrolls a full page forward or backward

```
void PageScroll(FormPtr form, UInt16 fieldID, UInt16 scrollbarID,
  WinDirectionType direction)
{
    FieldPtr        field;

    field = (FieldPtr) FrmGetObjectPtr(form,
      FrmGetObjectIndex(form, fieldID));
    if (FldScrollable(field, direction)) {
        Int16 linesToScroll = (Int16) FldGetVisibleLines(field) - 1;

        if (direction == winUp)
            linesToScroll = -linesToScroll;
        ScrollLines(form, fieldID, scrollbarID, linesToScroll, true);
    }
}
```

Tables

Tables are useful forms if you need to display and edit multiple columns of data. (Use a list to display a single column; see the section "Lists," earlier in this chapter.) Figure 9-3 contains three examples of tables from the built-in applications. As you can see, tables can contain a number of different types of data—everything from text, to dates, to numbers. (Notice that the first item in the To Do list has a note icon associated with it.)

While the List Manager automatically supports scrolling, the Table Manager does not. You have to add that support if you need it.

The height and width of table columns and rows are independently adjustable (in fact, editing a text field automatically makes a row change size).

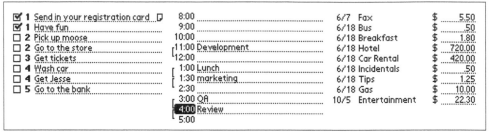

Figure 9-3. Sample tables from the built-in applications

The Palm OS Table Manager offers greater built-in support for displaying data than for editing it. The following sections list the data types and whether the Table Manager supports them for display purposes only or for editing as well.

Display-only data types

The following are display-only data types:

- Numbers
- Dates
- Labels (noneditable text)

Edit and display data types

The following are edit and display data types:

- Text (including an optional note icon; see Figure 9-3)
- Pop-up triggers
- Checkboxes

Other types of controls or form objects are not supported within tables (for example, push buttons, selector triggers, bitmaps, and so on).

Unlike other controls, tables require some programming in order to work. The table stores data for each cell in two parts—an integer and a pointer. The data is used differently, depending on the type of the column. Because of this, you must specify a data type for each column. Here are the possible specifications you can make.

 The source code for the 1.0 OS Table Manager can be found in Palm's Knowledge Base article #1152 (*http://oasis.palm.com/dev/kb/samples/1152.cfm*).

Display-only data types

These are the actual names of data types supported by the Table Manager. These display-only types cannot be edited.

dateTableItem

This displays a date (in month/day format). The data for a cell should be an integer that can be cast to a DateType. If the value is –1, a hyphen (–) is displayed; otherwise, the actual date is shown. If the displayed date is earlier than the handheld's current date, an exclamation point (!) is appended to it. Tapping on a date highlights the cell.

labelTableItem

This displays the text stored in the pointer portion of the cell with an appended colon (:). Tapping on a label highlights the cell.

numericTableItem

This displays the number stored in the integer portion of the cell. Tapping on a numeric cell highlights the cell.

Editable data types

These are the types of data that the user can change or edit as necessary:

checkboxTableItem

This displays a checkbox with no associated label. The data for a particular cell should be an integer with a value of either 0 or 1. Clicking on the checkbox toggles the value. Tapping on a checkbox doesn't highlight the row.

popupTriggerTableItem

This displays an item from a pop-up list (with a down arrow before it and a colon after it). The list pointer is stored in the pointer data of the cell; the item from the list is stored in the integer data of the cell. Tapping on a pop-up trigger displays the pop up, allowing the user to change the value in the integer.

textTableItem

This displays a text cell that can be edited. The column that contains these cells needs a load routine that provides a handle. This handle has an offset and length that are used when editing the text cell. An optional save routine is called after editing.

textWithNoteTableItem

This is similar to textTableItem, but it also displays a note icon at the right-hand side of the cell. Tapping on the note icon highlights the cell.

narrowTextTableItem

This is like textTableItem, but it reserves space at the right-hand side of the cell. The number of pixel spaces reserved is stored in the integer data of the cell. This is often used for text fields that have 0 or more icons and need to reserve space for them.

customTableItem

This is used for a custom cell. A callback routine needs to be installed for the column; it will be called to draw the contents of each cell at display time. The callback routine can use the integer and pointer data in the cell for whatever it likes. Tapping on a custom table cell highlights the cell.

 Although *Table.h* defines a `timeTableItem` type, this type doesn't actually work.

Initializing tables

There are some difficulties with initializing tables. When you initialize a table, you should first set the types of each column. You can further mark each row and column as usable or unusable. By default, rows start out usable while columns start out unusable. At a minimum, therefore, you'll need to make your columns usable as you initialize your table. By dynamically switching a column (or row) from unusable to usable (or usable to unusable), you can make it appear (or disappear).

If you make changes to the data in a cell, you need to mark that row invalid so that it will be redisplayed when the table is redrawn. For some mysterious reason, by default, rows are usable, but columns are not. If you don't explicitly mark your columns as usable, they won't appear.

You can set a 2-byte ID and a 4-byte data value, which are associated with each row. If you're displaying records from a database, it's common to set the row ID to the record number.

The following sections describe a table sample in a simple application that shows you how to use all the table data types available in the Table Manager. Figure 9-4 shows the running application. You can see that it contains one table with seven columns and seven rows (actually, there are eight, but one isn't shown). Note that the columns go from the easiest data types to code to the hardest (number, checkbox, label, date, pop-up trigger, various text data types, and custom). The text in each row is from a record in a database associated with the table sample.

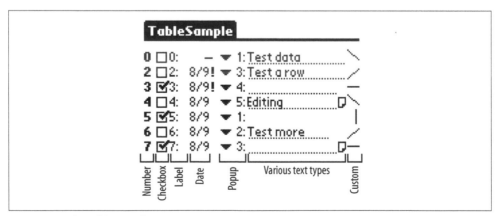

Figure 9-4. The table sample

Resource

Here's the declaration of the resource that defines the number of rows, and the number and width of each column:

```
FORM ID MainForm AT (0 0 160 160)
BEGIN
    TITLE "TableSample"
    TABLE ID MemoPadMainTableTable AT (0 21 160 120) ROWS 8 COLUMNS 7
        COLUMNWIDTHS 6 12 6 25 23 73 13
    LIST "1" "2" "3" "4" "5" ID MemoPadMainListList AT (131 22 20 55)
        NONUSABLE DISABLED FONT 0
END
```

Initialization of the records in the database

When the application opens, the database is opened. If the database doesn't exist, it is created and initialized with a number of records, each of which is initialized to an empty string (one null-byte for the null-terminator). Example 9-20 shows the code.

Example 9-20. Opens the database, creating it if necessary

```
Err AppStart(void)
{
  Err err = 0;

  gDB = DmOpenDatabaseByTypeCreator('DATA', kCreator, dmModeReadWrite);
  if (!gDB) {
    err = DmGetLastErr();
    if (err == dmErrCantFind) {
      err = DmCreateDatabase(0, "TestTable-PBK3", kCreator, 'DATA', false);
      if (err == 0) {
        gDB = DmOpenDatabaseByTypeCreator('DATA', kCreator, dmModeReadWrite);
        if (gDB) {
          UInt16 i;

          // Create initial records.
          for (i = 0;i < kNumRows && err == 0; i++) {
            UInt16 index = dmMaxRecordIndex;
            MemHandle h = DmNewRecord(gDB, &index, 1);
            if (!h)
              err = DmGetLastErr();
            else {
              MemPtr p = MemHandleLock(h);
              Char  null = 0;

              err = DmWrite(p, 0, &null, sizeof(null));
              MemHandleUnlock(h);
              DmReleaseRecord(gDB, index, true);
            }
          }
        }
      }
    }
  }
}
```

Example 9-20. Opens the database, creating it if necessary (continued)

```
  return err;
}
```

When the application closes, the database is closed:

```
    static void AppStop(void)
    {
      FrmCloseAllForms();
      DmCloseDatabase(gDB);
    }
```

Initialization of the simple table sample

Initializing this table requires initializing the style and data for each cell in the table. Example 9-21 shows you the entire initialization method. First, look at the entire block of code; then we'll discuss it, bit by bit.

Example 9-21. Initialization of the table

```
void MainFormInit(FormPtr form)
{
  TablePtr           table;
  Int16              numRows;
  Int16              row;
  Int16              col;
  static char *      labels[kNumRows] =
                       {"0", "1", "2", "3", "4", "5", "6", "7"};
  DateType           dates[kNumRows];
  ListPtr            list;
  TableItemStyleType style;
  MemHandle          h;

  // We'll have a missing date, and then some before
  // and after the current date.
  * ((UInt16 *) &dates[0]) = (UInt16) noTime;
  for (row = 1; row < kNumRows; row++) {
    dates[row].year = 1997 + row - firstYear; // Palm 1st year starts at 1904.
    dates[row].month = 8;
    dates[row].day = 9;
  }

  table = (TablePtr) FrmGetObjectPtr(form,
    FrmGetObjectIndex(form, MainTableTable));
  list = (ListPtr) FrmGetObjectPtr(form,
    FrmGetObjectIndex(form, MainListList));

  numRows = TblGetNumberOfRows(table);
  for (row = 0; row < numRows; row++) {

    TblSetItemStyle(table, row, 0, numericTableItem);
    TblSetItemInt(table, row, 0, row);

    TblSetItemStyle(table, row, 1, checkboxTableItem);
```

Example 9-21. Initialization of the table (continued)

```
    TblSetItemInt(table, row, 1, row % 2);

    TblSetItemStyle(table, row, 2, labelTableItem);
    TblSetItemPtr(table, row, 2, labels[row]);

    TblSetItemStyle(table, row, 3, dateTableItem);
    TblSetItemInt(table, row, 3, (Int16) DateToInt(dates[row]));

    TblSetItemStyle(table, row, 4, popupTriggerTableItem);
    TblSetItemInt(table, row, 4, row % 5);
    TblSetItemPtr(table, row, 4, list);

    switch (row % 3) {
    case 0:
      style = narrowTextTableItem;
      TblSetItemInt(table, row, 5, row * 2);
      break;
    case 1:
      style = textWithNoteTableItem;
      break;
    case 2:
      style = textTableItem;
      break;
    }
    TblSetItemStyle(table, row, 5, style);
    h = DmGetRecord(gDB, (UInt16) row);
    if (h) {
      TblSetRowData(table, row, (UInt32) h);
      TblSetRowID(table, row, (UInt16) row);
    }

    TblSetItemStyle(table, row, 6, customTableItem);
    TblSetItemInt(table, row, 6, row % 4);
  }
  TblSetRowUsable(table, 1, false); // Just to see what happens.

  for (col = 0; col < kNumColumns; col++)
    TblSetColumnUsable(table, col, true);

  TblSetLoadDataProcedure(table, 5, CustomLoadItem);
  TblSetSaveDataProcedure(table, 5, CustomSaveItem);

  TblSetCustomDrawProcedure(table, 6, CustomDrawItem);
}
```

Let's look at the columns in order (remember their position and complexity match)
from easiest to most difficult.

Column 0: handling numbers

The code starts with a numeric column that is quite an easy data type to handle. We use the row number as the number to display. Here's the code that executes for each row. As you can see, there is not a lot to it:

```
TblSetItemStyle(table, row, 0, numericTableItem);
TblSetItemInt(table, row, 0, row);
```

Column 1: a checkbox

This second column displays a simple checkbox. We set the initial value of the checkbox to be off for even row numbers and on for odd row numbers:

```
TblSetItemStyle(table, row, 1, checkboxTableItem);
TblSetItemInt(table, row, 1, row % 2);
```

Column 2: a label

This column displays a label that contains a piece of noneditable text. We set the text to successive values from a text array. The Table Manager appends a colon to the label:

```
static char *labels[kNumRows] = {"0", "1", "2", "3", "4", "5", "6", "7"};
// For each row:
    TblSetItemStyle(table, row, 2, labelTableItem);
    TblSetItemPtr(table, row, 2, labels[row]);
```

Column 3: a date

In the date column, we create an array of dates that are used to initialize each cell. Note that the first date is missing, which is why the "–" is displayed instead of a date. The remaining dates range over successive years; some dates are before the current time and others are after it:

```
DateType            dates[kNumRows];

// We'll have a missing date, and then some before
// and after the current date.
* ((UInt16 *) &dates[0]) = (UInt16) noTime;
for (row = 1; row < kNumRows; row++) {
  dates[row].year = 1997 + row - firstYear; // Palm first year starts at 1904.
  dates[row].month = 8;
  dates[row].day = 9;
}
// For each row:
  TblSetItemStyle(table, row, 3, dateTableItem);
  TblSetItemInt(table, row, 3, (Int16) DateToInt(dates[row]));
```

Column 4: a pop-up trigger

As with any pop-up trigger, we have to create a list in our resource. We've created one that has the values 1, 2, 3, 4, and 5. For each cell in the column, we set the pointer value to the list itself, then set the data value as the item number in the list:

```
ListPtr            list;
list = (ListPtr) FrmGetObjectPtr(form,
    FrmGetObjectIndex(form, MainListList));
// For each row:
  TblSetItemStyle(table, row, 4, popupTriggerTableItem);
  TblSetItemInt(table, row, 4, row % 5);
  TblSetItemPtr(table, row, 4, list);
```

Column 5: handling text

Now let's look at the text columns. Notice that we use all three of the available text column types. We change which one we use depending on the row:

```
switch (row % 3) {
case 0:
  style = narrowTextTableItem;
  TblSetItemInt(table, row, 5, row * 2);
  break;
case 1:
  style = textWithNoteTableItem;
  break;
case 2:
  style = textTableItem;
  break;
}
TblSetItemStyle(table, row, 5, style);
```

With the narrow text table item, we set the integer data as a pixel reserve on the right-hand side. We give each row a different pixel reserve so that we can see the effect:

```
TblSetItemInt(table, row, 5, row * 2);
```

Each of the text items requires a custom load procedure to provide the needed handle for the cell:

```
TblSetLoadDataProcedure(table, 5, CustomLoadItem);
```

We customize the saving, as well (because we will need to set the dirty bit of the record if the text was edited):

```
TblSetSaveDataProcedure(tableP, 5, CustomSaveItem);
```

For each row, we'll save a handle to a record from our database, and the record number for that record:

```
MemHandle          h;

h = DmGetRecord(gDB, (UInt16) row);
if (h) {
  TblSetRowData(table, row, (UInt32) h);
  TblSetRowID(table, row, (UInt16) row);
}
```

We'll look at the custom load and save routines that we just specified after we discuss the last column.

Column 6: handling custom content

The final column is a custom column that displays a line at one of four angles. The angle is determined by the integer data in the cell. We initialize the integer data to a value between 0 and 3, depending on the row:

```
TblSetItemStyle(table, row, 6, customTableItem);
TblSetItemInt(table, row, 6, row % 4);
```

We set a custom draw procedure for that column:

```
TblSetCustomDrawProcedure(table, 6, CustomDrawItem);
```

Displaying the columns

In order to make the columns display, we have to mark them as usable:

```
for (col = 0; col < kNumColumns; col++)
  TblSetColumnUsable(table, col, true);
```

Just as an exercise, we mark row 1 as unusable (now it won't appear in the table):

```
TblSetRowUsable(tableP, 1, false);   // Just to see what happens.
```

Custom load routines

The custom load routines that we used with the text columns need to return three things:

- A handle
- An offset within it
- A length within it

The Table Manager calls on the Field Manager to display and edit the range within the handle. It's our job to provide one handle for every text cell. The Table Manager will call our load routine when it needs to draw a text cell (in which case editable will be false), and when it needs to edit a text cell (in which case editable will be true). Example 9-22 shows our custom load routine.

Example 9-22. The routine that loads text for a given cell

```
Err CustomLoadItem(void *tbl, Int16 row, Int16 column,
  Boolean editable, MemHandle * dataH, Int16 *dataOffset,
  Int16 *dataSize, FieldPtr fld)
{
#pragma unused(column, editable)
  TablePtr table = (TablePtr) tbl;
  Char   *s;

  if ((row % 4) == 1) {
    FieldAttrType attrs;
```

Example 9-22. The routine that loads text for a given cell (continued)

```
    FldGetAttributes(fld, &attrs);
    attrs.editable = false;
    attrs.underlined = noUnderline;
    FldSetAttributes(fld, &attrs);
  }
  *dataH = (MemHandle) TblGetRowData(table, row);
  *dataOffset = 0;
  if (*dataH) {
    s = (Char *) MemHandleLock(*dataH);
    *dataSize = StrLen(s) + 1;
    MemHandleUnlock(*dataH);
  }

  return errNone;
}
```

Just for fun, we set every fourth text row to be uneditable (by adjusting the attributes of the field itself). After doing that, we get the handle (that was previously stored in the row), and figure out the length of the text. We set our offset to 0 and the data size to the length of the text (plus 1 for the null byte).

Custom save routine

This save routine (see Example 9-23) needs to set the dirty bit of the record to true if the text for that record has been edited.

Example 9-23. Routine that is called when the user finishes editing a text cell

```
Boolean CustomSaveItem(void *table, Int16 row, Int16 column)
{
#pragma unused(column)
  FieldPtr field = TblGetCurrentField(table);

  // If the field has been edited, set the dirty bit for that record.
  if (field && FldDirty(field)) {
    UInt16 attr;
    UInt16 recordNumber = (UInt16) TblGetRowID(table, row);
    if (DmRecordInfo(gDB, recordNumber, &attr, NULL, NULL) == 0) {
      attr |= dmRecAttrDirty;
      DmSetRecordInfo(gDB, recordNumber, &attr, NULL);
    }
  }
  return false; // The table should not be redrawn.
}
```

Releasing the records

Our initialization routine for the form did a DmGetRecord on each record so that the records could be edited in the table. Eventually, we need to release those records; we'll do so in the deinitialization routine for the form (see Example 9-24).

Example 9-24. Releases each of the records

```
void MainFormDeinit(void)
{
  Int16 row;
  FormPtr form = FrmGetActiveForm( );
  TablePtr table;
  Int16 numRows;

  table = (TablePtr) FrmGetObjectPtr(form,
    FrmGetObjectIndex(form, MainTableTable));
  numRows = TblGetNumberOfRows(table);
  for (row = 0; row < numRows; row++) {
    UInt16 recordNumber = (UInt16) TblGetRowID(table, row);

    DmReleaseRecord(gDB, recordNumber, false);
  }
}
```

We pass false as the third parameter to DmReleaseRecord so that it won't set the dirty
bit. Remember we've already set the dirty bit for those records that need it within
our custom save routine.

Custom draw routine

We need a drawing routine that creates our rotating line (see Example 9-25).

Example 9-25. Custom routine to draw a cell

```
// Draws either \, |, /, or -
static void CustomDrawItem(void *tbl, Int16 row, Int16 column,
  RectanglePtr bounds)
{
  TablePtr  table = (TablePtr) tbl;
  Coord     fromx, fromy, tox, toy;

  switch (TblGetItemInt(table, row, column)) {
  case 0:
    fromx = bounds->topLeft.x;
    fromy = bounds->topLeft.y;
    tox = fromx + bounds->extent.x - 1;
    toy = fromy + bounds->extent.y - 1;
    break;
  case 1:
    fromx = bounds->topLeft.x + bounds->extent.x / 2;
    fromy = bounds->topLeft.y;
    tox = fromx;
    toy = fromy + bounds->extent.y - 1;
    break;
  case 2:
    fromx = bounds->topLeft.x + bounds->extent.x - 1;
    fromy = bounds->topLeft.y;
    tox = bounds->topLeft.x;
    toy = fromy + bounds->extent.y - 1;
    break;
```

Example 9-25. Custom routine to draw a cell (continued)

```
  case 3:
    fromx = bounds->topLeft.x;
    fromy = bounds->topLeft.y + bounds->extent.y / 2;
    tox = fromx + bounds->extent.x - 1;
    toy = fromy;
    break;
  default:
    fromx = tox = bounds->topLeft.x;
    fromy = toy = bounds->topLeft.y;
    break;
  }
  WinDrawLine(fromx, fromy, tox, toy);
}
```

Handling a table event

If we tap on a cell in the custom column, we want the angle of the line to change. We do that by changing the integer value. The tblSelectEvent is posted to the event queue when a custom cell is successfully tapped (that is, the user taps on and releases the same cell).

> While you might assume that the tblSelectEvent is where you change the value and redraw, this isn't the case. The Table Manager highlights the selected cell, and we overwrite the highlighting when we redraw. If we switch to a new cell, the Table Manager tries to unhighlight by inverting. As these are certainly not the results we want, we need to handle the call in another place.

We're going to handle the redraw in tblEnterEvent, looking to see whether the tapped cell is in our column (see Example 9-26).

Example 9-26. Event handler that looks for a tblEnterEvent in a specific column

```
Boolean MainFormHandleEvent(EventPtr event)
{
  Boolean    handled = false;
  FormPtr    form;

  switch (event->eType)
  {
      case frmOpenEvent:
      form = FrmGetActiveForm();
      MainFormInit(form);
      FrmDrawForm(form);
      handled = true;
      break;

    case frmCloseEvent:
      MainFormDeinit();
      break;
```

```
  case tblSelectEvent:
    // Handle successful tap on a cell.
    // For a checkbox or pop up, tblExitEvent will be called instead of
    // tblSelectEvent if the user cancels the control.
    break;

  case tblEnterEvent:
    {
      Int16  row = event->data.tblEnter.row;
      Int16  column = event->data.tblEnter.column;

      if (column == 6) {
        TablePtr table = event->data.tblEnter.pTable;
        int    oldValue = TblGetItemInt(table, row, column);

        TblSetItemInt(table, row, column, (oldValue + 1) % 4);
        TblMarkRowInvalid(table, row);
        TblRedrawTable(table);
        handled = true;
      }
    }
    break;
  }
  return handled;
}
```

This is all that is worth mentioning in the simple example of a table. It should be enough to guide you in the implementation of these data types in your own tables.

Our philosophy on tables is that they should only be used when you have multi-columnar data that needs live editing, and that closely matches the UI the Table Manager provides. In the first edition of this book, our Sales application used a table for the Order form. It turned out that we had lots of code working around the table, trying to get it to do what we wanted, rather than what it wanted.

Read-only multicolumnar data can always be implemented with a list: in your custom drawing routine, make multiple calls to WinDrawChars to draw each column at an appropriate horizontal offset.

Sales Application Forms and Form Objects

Now that we have all the specific information about form objects, it is time to add many of them and the rest of the forms to the Sales application. We'll show you the resource definitions of all the forms and form objects and then look at the code.

We cover the forms and the code for them in order of increasing complexity. The following list shows you our order and which types of forms and form objects are implemented in each form.

Edit Customer form

The new addition is fields, as well as some buttons and checkboxes.

Item Details form

The new items are a label, a pop-up trigger that has a list associated with it, and a Graffiti Shift Indicator. There are also buttons and fields.

Customers form

The only object in the form is a list.

Order form

This form contains a series of pop-up triggers and fields that are associated with them.

In each implementation we show you any definitions, resources (shown in text in PilRC format), and necessary code.

After dealing with these various forms and form objects we also need to make sure our application navigates between our various forms and dialog boxes correctly. This is taken care of in our `ApplicationHandleEvent` function, which we cover last.

Edit Customer

We have a bunch of resources for the Edit Customer form. Here are the #defines:

```
#define CustomerForm              1300
#define CustomerOKButton          1303
#define CustomerCancelButton      1304
#define CustomerDeleteButton      1305
#define CustomerPrivateCheckbox   1310
#define CustomerNameField         1302
#define CustomerAddressField      1307
#define CustomerCityField         1309
#define CustomerPhoneField        1313
```

Figure 9-5 shows what the Customer Information form looks like.

Figure 9-5. Customer Information dialog box

Creating the Customer Information form

Now, we get down to business and create the form. Example 9-27 shows the resource for it.

Example 9-27. The Customer Information dialog box resource

```
FORM ID CustomerForm AT (2 158 - kCustomerFormHeight 156 kCustomerFormHeight)
MODAL
SAVEBEHIND
HELPID CustomerHelpString
MENUID DialogWithInputFieldMenuBar
BEGIN
  TITLE "Customer Information"
  BUTTON "OK" ID CustomerOKButton AT
    (kDefaultButtonInModalLeft
    BOTTOM@(kCustomerFormHeight - kDefaultButtonInModalBottomMargin)
     36 kDefaultButtonHeight) LEFTANCHOR FRAME
    FONT 0
  BUTTON "Cancel" ID CustomerCancelButton
    AT (PREVRIGHT + kInterButtonWidth PREVTOP 36 kDefaultButtonHeight)
    LEFTANCHOR FRAME FONT 0
  BUTTON "Delete" ID CustomerDeleteButton
    AT (PREVRIGHT + kInterButtonWidth PREVTOP 36 kDefaultButtonHeight)
    LEFTANCHOR FRAME FONT 0
  LABEL "Name:" AUTOID AT (RIGHT@51 19) FONT 1
  LABEL "Address:" AUTOID AT (RIGHT@PREVRIGHT PREVBOTTOM+4) FONT 1
  LABEL "City:" AUTOID AT (RIGHT@PREVRIGHT PREVBOTTOM+4) FONT 1
  LABEL "Phone:" AUTOID AT (RIGHT@PREVRIGHT PREVBOTTOM+4) FONT 1
  LABEL "Private:" AUTOID AT (RIGHT@PREVRIGHT PREVBOTTOM+4) FONT 1
  FIELD ID CustomerNameField AT (54 19 97 13) LEFTALIGN FONT 0 UNDERLINED
    MULTIPLELINES MAXCHARS 80 AUTOSHIFT
  FIELD ID CustomerAddressField AT (54 PREVBOTTOM+3 97 13) LEFTALIGN FONT 0
    UNDERLINED MULTIPLELINES MAXCHARS 80 AUTOSHIFT
  FIELD ID CustomerCityField AT (54 PREVBOTTOM+3 97 13) LEFTALIGN FONT 0
    UNDERLINED MULTIPLELINES MAXCHARS 80 AUTOSHIFT
  FIELD ID CustomerPhoneField AT (54 PREVBOTTOM+3 97 13) LEFTALIGN FONT 0
    UNDERLINED  MULTIPLELINES MAXCHARS 80
  CHECKBOX "" ID CustomerPrivateCheckbox AT (54 PREVBOTTOM + 3 19 12)
    LEFTANCHOR FONT  0 GROUP 0
  GRAFFITISTATEINDICATOR
    AT (kGSIInModalLeft kCustomerFormHeight - kGSIFromBottomInModal)
END
```

Event handler for the form

Here's the event handler for the form. It's responsible for bringing up the Delete Customer dialog box if the user taps on the Delete button. If the user cancels that dialog box, we return true so that FrmDoDialog won't see the button hit (and therefore will continue displaying the dialog box):

```
static Boolean CustomerHandleEvent(EventPtr event)
{
  if (event->eType == ctlSelectEvent &&
      event->data.ctlSelect.controlID == CustomerDeleteButton) {
    if (!AskDeleteCustomer())
      return true;  // Don't bail out if they cancel the Delete dialog box.
  }
  return false;
}
```

Initialization code

Last, but not least, Example 9-28 shows the code that initializes the fields of the form, displays the dialog box, and then handles any changes made to the form. Emphasized code shows the portions that have to do with forms and form objects (rather than the Data Manager).

Example 9-28. Code to display the Customer Information dialog box

```
// isNew is true if this is a brand-new customer.
void EditCustomerWithSelection(UInt16 recordNumber, Boolean isNew,
  Boolean *deleted, EventPtr event)
{
  FormPtr    form;
  UInt16     hitButton;
  Boolean    dirty = false;
  Boolean    isEmpty = false;
  ControlPtr privateCheckbox;
  UInt16     attributes;
  Boolean    isSecret;
  FieldPtr   nameField;
  FieldPtr   addressField;
  FieldPtr   cityField;
  FieldPtr   phoneField;
  Customer   theCustomer;
  UInt16     offset = OffsetOf(PackedCustomer, name);
  MemHandle  customerHandle = DmGetRecord(gCustomerDB, recordNumber);

  *deleted = false;
  DmRecordInfo(gCustomerDB, recordNumber, &attributes, NULL, NULL);
  isSecret = (Boolean) ((attributes & dmRecAttrSecret) == dmRecAttrSecret);

  form = FrmInitForm(CustomerForm);
  FrmSetEventHandler(form, CustomerHandleEvent);

  UnpackCustomer(&theCustomer,
    (PackedCustomer *) MemHandleLock(customerHandle));

  nameField = (FieldPtr) GetObjectFromForm(form, CustomerNameField);
  addressField = (FieldPtr) GetObjectFromForm(form, CustomerAddressField);
  cityField = (FieldPtr) GetObjectFromForm(form, CustomerCityField);
  phoneField = (FieldPtr) GetObjectFromForm(form, CustomerPhoneField);

  SetFieldTextFromStr(nameField,    theCustomer.name, false);
  SetFieldTextFromStr(addressField, theCustomer.address, false);
  SetFieldTextFromStr(cityField,    theCustomer.city, false);
  SetFieldTextFromStr(phoneField,   theCustomer.phone, false);

  FrmDrawForm(form); // Must do now, because pre-3.5, focus needed to be set
                     // *after* a call to FrmDrawForm.
  // Select one of the fields.
  if (event && event->data.frmGoto.matchFieldNum) {
    FieldPtr selectedField =
      (FieldPtr) GetObjectFromForm(form, event->data.frmGoto.matchFieldNum);
```

```
      FldSetScrollPosition(selectedField, event->data.frmGoto.matchPos);
      FrmSetFocus(form,
        FrmGetObjectIndex(form, event->data.frmGoto.matchFieldNum));
      FldSetSelection(selectedField, event->data.frmGoto.matchPos,
        event->data.frmGoto.matchPos + event->data.frmGoto.matchLen);
    } else {
      FrmSetFocus(form, FrmGetObjectIndex(form, CustomerNameField));
      FldSetSelection(nameField, 0, FldGetTextLength(nameField));
    }
    // Unlock the customer.
    MemHandleUnlock(customerHandle);

    privateCheckbox =
      (ControlPtr) GetObjectFromForm(form, CustomerPrivateCheckbox);
    CtlSetValue(privateCheckbox, isSecret);

    hitButton = FrmDoDialog(form);

    if (hitButton == CustomerOKButton) {
      dirty = FldDirty(nameField) || FldDirty(addressField) ||
        FldDirty(cityField) || FldDirty(phoneField);
      if (dirty) {
        theCustomer.name = FldGetTextPtr(nameField);
        if (!theCustomer.name)
          theCustomer.name = "";
        theCustomer.address = FldGetTextPtr(addressField);
        if (!theCustomer.address)
          theCustomer.address = "";
        theCustomer.city = FldGetTextPtr(cityField);
        if (!theCustomer.city)
          theCustomer.city = "";
        theCustomer.phone = FldGetTextPtr(phoneField);
        if (!theCustomer.phone)
          theCustomer.phone = "";
      }
      isEmpty = StrCompare(theCustomer.name, "") == 0 &&
        StrCompare(theCustomer.address, "") == 0 &&
        StrCompare(theCustomer.city, "") == 0 &&
        StrCompare(theCustomer.phone, "") == 0;
      if (dirty)
        PackCustomer(&theCustomer, customerHandle);
      if (CtlGetValue(privateCheckbox) != isSecret) {
        dirty = true;
        if (CtlGetValue(privateCheckbox)) {
          attributes |= dmRecAttrSecret;
          // Tell user how to hide or mask private records.
          if (gPrivateRecordStatus == showPrivateRecords)
            FrmAlert(privateRecordInfoAlert);
        } else
          attributes &= (UInt8) ~dmRecAttrSecret;
        DmSetRecordInfo(gCustomerDB, recordNumber, &attributes, NULL);
```

```
    }
  }
  FrmDeleteForm(form);

  DmReleaseRecord(gCustomerDB, recordNumber, dirty);
  if (hitButton == CustomerDeleteButton) {
    *deleted = true;
    if (isNew && !gSaveBackup)
      DmRemoveRecord(gCustomerDB, recordNumber);
    else {
      if (gSaveBackup)  // Need to archive it on PC.
        DmArchiveRecord(gCustomerDB, recordNumber);
      else
        DmDeleteRecord(gCustomerDB, recordNumber);
      // Deleted records are stored at the end of the database.
      DmMoveRecord(gCustomerDB, recordNumber, DmNumRecords(gCustomerDB));
    }
  }
  else if (hitButton == CustomerOKButton && isNew && isEmpty) {
    *deleted = true;
    DmRemoveRecord(gCustomerDB, recordNumber);
  }
  else if (hitButton == CustomerCancelButton && isNew) {
    *deleted = true;
    DmRemoveRecord(gCustomerDB, recordNumber);
  }
}
```

In the code, we set CustomerHandleEvent as the event handler and we initialize each of the text fields before calling FrmDoDialog. After the call to FrmDoDialog, the text from the text fields is copied if the OK button was pressed and any of the fields have been changed.

Utility routines

Throughout our application, we use a couple of utility routines that retrieve a form object from a form. This first routine retrieves from a passed-in form:

```
void *GetObjectFromForm(FormPtr form, UInt16 objectID)
{
  return FrmGetObjectPtr(form,
    FrmGetObjectIndex(form, objectID));
}
```

The second retrieves from the active form:

```
void *GetObjectFromActiveForm(UInt16 objectID)
{
  return GetObjectFromForm(FrmGetActiveForm( ), objectID);
}
```

Item Details

This modal dialog box allows for editing the quantity and product of an item (see Figure 9-6).

Figure 9-6. Item details dialog box

Example 9-29 shows the resource definition for the dialog box.

Example 9-29. Item details dialog box resource

```
FORM ID ItemForm AT (2 158 - kItemFormHeight 156 kItemFormHeight)
MODAL
SAVEBEHIND
HELPID ItemHelpString
MENUID DialogWithInputFieldMenuBar
BEGIN
  TITLE "Item"
  LABEL "Quantity:" AUTOID AT (RIGHT@60 53) FONT 1
  FIELD ID ItemQuantityField AT (PREVRIGHT+2 PREVTOP 50 12) LEFTALIGN FONT 0
    UNDERLINED NUMERIC MULTIPLELINES MAXCHARS 20
  LABEL "Product:" ID 1201 AT (RIGHT@60 27) FONT 1
  POPUPTRIGGER "" ID ItemProductPopTrigger AT (PREVRIGHT+2 PREVTOP 32 12)
    LEFTANCHOR FONT 0
  POPUPLIST ID ItemProductPopTrigger ItemProductsList
  LIST "" ID ItemProductsList AT (PREVLEFT PREVTOP 94 11) NONUSABLE FONT 0
  BUTTON "OK" ID ItemOKButton
    AT (kDefaultButtonInModalLeft
    BOTTOM@(kItemFormHeight-kDefaultButtonInModalBottomMargin)
    36 kDefaultButtonHeight) LEFTANCHOR FRAME FONT 0
  BUTTON "Delete" ID ItemDeleteButton
    AT (PREVRIGHT + kInterButtonWidth PREVTOP 36 kDefaultButtonHeight)
    LEFTANCHOR FRAME FONT 0
  BUTTON "Cancel" ID ItemCancelButton
    AT (PREVRIGHT + kInterButtonWidth PREVTOP 36 kDefaultButtonHeight)
    LEFTANCHOR FRAME FONT 0
  GRAFFITISTATEINDICATOR
    AT (kGSIInModalLeft kItemFormHeight - kGSIFromBottomInModal)
END
```

Item details display code

Example 9-30 shows code that displays the dialog box.

Example 9-30. Code that displays the Item details dialog box

```
// Returns true if modified.
Boolean EditItem(Item *item, Boolean *deleted)
{
  FormPtr frm = FrmInitForm(ItemForm);
  UInt16  hitButton;

  gItem = item;
  FrmSetEventHandler(frm, ItemHandleEvent);
  ItemFormOpen( );

  hitButton = FrmDoDialog(frm);
  FrmDeleteForm(frm);
  if (hitButton == ItemCancelButton)
    return false;
  else {
    *deleted = (Boolean) (hitButton == ItemDeleteButton);
    return true;
  }
}
```

The Item dialog box uses the following globals:

```
    static Item         *gItem;
    static UInt32        gEditedProductID;
    static Char          gProductName[kMaxProductNameLength];
```

Here is what each global does:

gItem

> Points to the item being edited

gEditedProductID

> Contains the current ID (as edited)

gProductName

> Holds the product name that will be displayed as the label of the pop-up trigger

The interesting part of this dialog box is the pop-up trigger that contains both product categories and products.

When the Item details form opens, the ItemFormOpen routine gets called (see Example 9-31).

Example 9-31. Initialization code for Item details dialog box

```
void ItemFormOpen(void)
{
  ListPtr list;
  FormPtr form = FrmGetFormPtr(ItemForm);
  ControlPtr  control;
  FieldPtr field = (FieldPtr) GetObjectFromForm(form, ItemQuantityField);
  char  quantityString[kMaxNumericStringLength];
```

```
  // Initialize quantity.
  StrIToA(quantityString, (Int32) gItem->quantity);
  SetFieldTextFromStr(field, quantityString, false);

  // Select entire quantity (so it doesn't have to be selected before
  // writing a new quantity).
  FrmSetFocus(form, FrmGetObjectIndex(form, ItemQuantityField));
  FldSetSelection(field, 0, (UInt16) StrLen(quantityString));

  list = (ListPtr) GetObjectFromForm(form, ItemProductsList);
  LstSetDrawFunction(list, DrawOneProductInList);

  gEditedProductID = gItem->productID;
  control = (ControlPtr) GetObjectFromForm(form, ItemProductPopTrigger);
  if (gItem->productID) {
    Product p;
    MemHandle h;

    h = GetProductFromProductID(gItem->productID, &p, NULL);
    ErrNonFatalDisplayIf(!h, "can't get product for existing item");

    ErrNonFatalDisplayIf(StrLen(p.name) >= kMaxProductNameLength,
      "product name too long");
    StrCopy(gProductName, p.name);
    CtlSetLabel(control, gProductName);
    MemHandleUnlock(h);
  } else
    CtlSetLabel(control, kUnknownProductName);
}
```

Let's look at what happens here. First, we set the quantity field. Next, we set a custom draw function for the list. Finally, we use `CtlSetLabel` to set the label of the trigger to the product name. Note that we store the product name in a global variable because we can't use the name directly from within the record (unless we were willing to keep the record locked). The string we pass to `CtlSetLabel` must remain valid until we close the form or change the label.

Event handler code

Our event handler (see Example 9-32) captures a tap on the pop-up trigger (by looking for `ctlEnterEvent`) and also selecting an item from the pop up (with `popSelectEvent`).

Example 9-32. Event handler for Item details dialog box

```
Boolean ItemHandleEvent(EventPtr event)
{
  Boolean   handled = false;
  FieldPtr  fld;
```

Example 9-32. Event handler for Item details dialog box (continued)

```
  switch (event->eType) {
    case ctlSelectEvent:
      switch (event->data.ctlSelect.controlID) {
      case ItemOKButton:
        {
          char  *textPtr;
          UInt32  quantity;

          fld = (FieldPtr) GetObjectFromActiveForm(ItemQuantityField);
          textPtr = FldGetTextPtr(fld);
          ErrNonFatalDisplayIf(!textPtr, "No quantity text");
          quantity = (UInt32) StrAToI(textPtr);
          gItem->quantity = quantity;
          gItem->productID = gEditedProductID;
        }
        break;

      case ItemCancelButton:
        break;

      case ItemDeleteButton:
        if (FrmAlert(DeleteItemAlert) != DeleteItemOK)
          handled = true; // Don't allow further processing.
        break;
      }
      break;

    case ctlEnterEvent:
      if (event->data.ctlEnter.controlID == ItemProductPopTrigger)
        HandleProductPopupEnter(ItemProductPopTrigger, ItemProductsList,
          gEditedProductID);
      // handled = false;
      break;

    case popSelectEvent:
      if (event->data.ctlEnter.controlID == ItemProductPopTrigger){
        if (HandleProductPopupSelect(event, &gEditedProductID,
          gProductName))
          CtlSetLabel(event->data.popSelect.controlP, gProductName);
        handled = true;
        break;
      }
      break;
    }
    return handled;
}
```

Handling the pop-up trigger and list

HandleProductPopupEnter (see Example 9-33) initializes the list so that the correct item in the list is highlighted. In addition, it moves the location of the list so that it matches the location of the pop-up trigger.

Example 9-33. Code to handle tapping on a product pop up

```
void HandleProductPopupEnter(UInt16 controlID, UInt16 listID,
  UInt32 productID)
{
  FormPtr form = FrmGetActiveForm( );
  UInt16 listIndex = FrmGetObjectIndex(form, listID);
  ListPtr list = (ListPtr) FrmGetObjectPtr(form, listIndex);

  if (productID == 0) {
    SelectACategory(list, gCurrentCategory);
    LstSetSelection(list, (Int16) gCurrentCategory);
  } else {
    MemHandle h;
    Product   p;
    UInt16    attr;
    UInt16    index;
    Coord     dontCare;
    Coord     x;
    Coord     y;

    h = GetProductFromProductID(productID, &p, &index);
    ErrNonFatalDisplayIf(!h, "can't get product for existing item");
    DmRecordInfo(gProductDB, index, &attr, NULL, NULL);
    MemHandleUnlock(h);

    SelectACategory(list, attr & dmRecAttrCategoryMask);
    LstSetSelection(list,
      (Int16) (DmPositionInCategory(gProductDB, index, gCurrentCategory) +
      gNumCategories + 1));

    // Make list top match trigger top.
    FrmGetObjectPosition(form, listIndex, &x, &dontCare);
    FrmGetObjectPosition(form, FrmGetObjectIndex(form, controlID),
      &dontCare, &y);
    FrmSetObjectPosition(form, listIndex, x, y);
  }
}
```

Here's SelectACategory, which sets the current category, initializes the list with the correct number of items, and sets the list height (the number of items are shown concurrently):

```
void SelectACategory(ListPtr list, UInt16 newCategory)
{
  UInt16    numItems;

  gCurrentCategory = newCategory;
  numItems = DmNumRecordsInCategory(gProductDB, gCurrentCategory) +
    (gNumCategories + 1);
  LstSetHeight(list, (Int16) numItems);
  LstSetListChoices(list, NULL, (Int16) numItems);
}
```

When the user taps on the trigger, the list is shown. We've used DrawOneProductInList (see Example 9-34) to draw the list. It draws the categories at the top (with the current category in bold), a separator line, and then the products for that category.

Example 9-34. Routine that draws products in the product list

```
void DrawOneProductInList(Int16 itemNumber, RectanglePtr bounds,
  Char **text)
{
#pragma unused(text)
  void *p = NULL;
  FontID  curFont;
  Boolean setFont = false;
  const char  *toDraw = "";
  Int16   seekAmount = itemNumber;
  UInt16  index = 0;

  if (itemNumber == gCurrentCategory) {
    curFont = FntSetFont(boldFont);
    setFont = true;
  }
  if (itemNumber == gNumCategories)
    toDraw = "---";
  else if (itemNumber < gNumCategories) {
    CategoriesStruct *c = (CategoriesStruct *) GetLockedAppInfo(gProductDB);

    if (c) {
      toDraw = c->names[itemNumber];
      p = c;
    }
  } else {
    MemHandle h;
    DmSeekRecordInCategory(gProductDB, &index,
      seekAmount - (gNumCategories + 1), dmSeekForward, gCurrentCategory);
    h = DmQueryRecord(gProductDB, index);
    if (h) {
      PackedProduct *packedProduct = (PackedProduct *) MemHandleLock(h);
      Product s;
      UnpackProduct(&s, packedProduct);
      toDraw = s.name;
      p = packedProduct;
    }
  }
  DrawCharsToFitWidth(toDraw, bounds);
  if (p)
    MemPtrUnlock(p);
  if (setFont)
    FntSetFont(curFont);
}
```

When the user selects an item from the pop up, a popSelectEvent is generated. Our event handler calls HandleProductPopupSelect (see Example 9-35), which actually handles the selection. If a product is selected, the product name is updated (and the new product ID is returned). If a new category is selected, the list is updated with a new category, and `CtlHitControl` is called to simulate tapping again on the trigger. This makes the list reappear without work on the user's part.

Example 9-35. Routine that handles a popSelectEvent on the product pop up

```c
// Returns false if no product selected, true if one is selected
// (in which case productID and name are set).
Boolean HandleProductPopupSelect(EventPtr event, UInt32 *newProductID,
  Char *productName)
{
  ListPtr    list = event->data.popSelect.listP;
  ControlPtr control = event->data.popSelect.controlP;

  ErrNonFatalDisplayIf(event->eType != popSelectEvent,
    "wrong kind of event");
  if (event->data.popSelect.selection < (gNumCategories + 1)) {
    if (event->data.popSelect.selection < gNumCategories)
      SelectACategory(list, (UInt16) event->data.popSelect.selection);
    LstSetSelection(list, (Int16) gCurrentCategory);
    CtlHitControl(control);
    return false;
  } else {
    UInt16       index = 0;
    MemHandle    h;
    PackedProduct *packedProduct;
    Product      s;

    DmSeekRecordInCategory(gProductDB, &index,
      event->data.popSelect.selection - (gNumCategories + 1),
      dmSeekForward, gCurrentCategory);
    ErrNonFatalDisplayIf(DmGetLastErr(), "Can't seek to product");
    h = DmQueryRecord(gProductDB, index);

    ErrNonFatalDisplayIf(!h, "Can't get record");
    packedProduct = (PackedProduct *) MemHandleLock(h);
    UnpackProduct(&s, packedProduct);
    ErrNonFatalDisplayIf(StrLen(s.name) >= kMaxProductNameLength,
      "product name too long");
    StrNCopy(productName, s.name, kMaxProductNameLength);
    productName[kMaxProductNameLength-1] = '\0';  // Just in case too long.
    MemHandleUnlock(h);
    *newProductID = s.productID;
    return true;
  }
}
```

Customers Form

The Customers form contains only one form object: the list. Here are the resource definitions of the form, the list, and a menu:

```c
#define CustomersForm                 1000
#define CustomersCustomersList        1002
#define CustomersNoSendMenuBar        1100
```

Figure 9-7 shows what the form looks like. Notice that one of the customers has been masked and the locked icon appears next to it.

Figure 9-7. Customers form

Here is the resource definition for the Customers form:

```
FORM ID CustomersForm AT (0 0 160 160)
MENUID CustomersNoSendMenuBar
BEGIN
  TITLE "Sales"
  LIST "" ID CustomersCustomersList AT (0 15 160 132) DISABLED FONT 0
END
```

Initialization routines

Our initialization routine (which we call on a frmOpenEvent) sets the draw function callback for the list and sets the number (by calling InitNumberCustomers):

```
void CustomersFormOpen(FormPtr form)
{
  ListPtr list = (ListPtr) GetObjectFromForm(form, CustomersCustomersList);

  InitNumberCustomers();
  LstSetDrawFunction(list, DrawOneCustomerInListWithFont);
  LstSetSelection(list, noListSelection);

  // Code deleted to change the menu bar on 4.0 and later devices.
}
```

InitNumberCustomers calls LstSetListChoices to set the number of elements in the list. It is called when the form is opened and when the number of customers changes (this happens if a customer is added):

```
void InitNumberCustomers(void)
{
  ListPtr list = (ListPtr) GetObjectFromActiveForm(CustomersCustomersList);
    // If we use DmNumRecords, we'll count the deleted records too.
  UInt16  numCustomers =
    DmNumRecordsInCategory(gCustomerDB, dmAllCategories);

  LstSetListChoices(list, NULL, (Int16) numCustomers);
}
```

Event handler

Our event handler handles an open event by calling `CustomersFormOpen`, then draws the form:

```
case frmOpenEvent:
  CustomersFormOpen( );
  FrmDrawForm(FrmGetActiveForm( ));
  handled = true;
  break;
```

A `lstSelectEvent` is sent when the user taps (and releases) on a list entry. Our event handler calls `OpenNthCustomer` to open the Order form for that customer:

```
case lstSelectEvent:
  listIndex = (UInt16) event->data.lstSelect.selection;

  LstSetSelection(event->data.lstSelect.pList, noListSelection);
  // Code deleted that puts up Security dialog box if record is masked.
  OpenCustomerWithID(GetCustomerIDForNthCustomer(listIndex));
  handled = true;
  break;
```

`OpenNthCustomer` calls `FrmGotoForm` to switch to a different form:

```
void OpenCustomerWithID(Int32 customerID)
{
  if ((gCurrentOrder =  GetOrCreateOrderForCustomer(
    customerID, &gCurrentOrderIndex)) != NULL)
    FrmGotoForm(OrderForm);
}
```

The event handler has to handle the Page up and Page down scroll keys (see Example 9-36). It calls the list to do the actual scrolling (note that our routine scrolls by one row at a time, instead of by an entire page).

Example 9-36. Portion of event handler that deals with Page up and Page down keys

```
case keyDownEvent:
  if (TxtGlueCharIsVirtual(event->data.keyDown.modifiers,
    event->data.keyDown.chr) &&
    event->data.keyDown.chr == vchrPageUp ||
    event->data.keyDown.chr == vchrPageDown) {
    ListPtr list = (ListPtr) GetObjectFromActiveForm(CustomersCustomersList);
    WinDirectionType  d;

    if (event->data.keyDown.chr == vchrPageUp)
      d = winUp;
    else
      d = winDown;
    LstScrollList(list, d, 1);
  }
  handled = true;
  break;
```

When a new customer is created, code in `CustomerHandleMenuEvent` calls `EditCustomer` to put up a modal dialog box for the user to enter the new customer data. When the modal dialog box is dismissed, the Form Manager automatically restores the contents of the Customers form. The Customers form also needs to be redrawn, as a new customer has been added to the list. `CustomerHandleMenuEvent` calls `RedrawCustomersAfterChange`, which sends our event handler a `frmUpdateEvent`:

```
EditCustomer(recordNumber, true, &deleted);
RedrawCustomersAfterChange();
```

Here's `RedrawCustomersAfterChange`, which redraws the list after a customer is added:

```
void RedrawCustomersAfterChange(void)
{
  ListPtr list = (ListPtr) GetObjectFromActiveForm(CustomersCustomersList);

  LstEraseList(list); // Erase list *before* updating num items.
  InitNumberCustomers();
  LstDrawList(list);  // Draw list *after* updating num items.
}
```

Order Form

In the first edition of this book, we used a table to display the items. For the second edition, we've rewritten this form. Instead of a table, we now use a set of pop-up triggers along with a set of fields that may be hidden or displayed depending on how many items are visible. We no longer use a table because of the difficulties that arise in using the Table Manager for anything other than those things that are explicitly supported (for example, tables don't support editing numbers).

Example 9-37 shows the declarations of our constants for our form and form objects.

Example 9-37. Constant declarations for the Order form

```
#define OrderForm                     1100
#define OrderNewButton                1102
#define OrderDetailsButton            1103
#define OrderDoneButton               1104
#define OrderProductsList             1106
#define OrderScrollbarScrollBar       1105
#define OrderItemsTable               1101
#define OrderItemFirstField           1111
#define OrderItem1Field               OrderItemFirstField
#define OrderItem2Field               1112
#define OrderItem3Field               1113
#define OrderItem4Field               1114
#define OrderItem5Field               1115
#define OrderItem6Field               1116
#define OrderItem7Field               1117
#define OrderItemLastField            OrderItem7Field

#define kFirstFieldTop                20
```

Example 9-37. Constant declarations for the Order form (continued)

```
#define OrderItemFirstPopup                    1121
#define OrderItem1Popup                        OrderItemFirstPopup
#define OrderItem2Popup                        1122
#define OrderItem3Popup                        1123
#define OrderItem4Popup                        1124
#define OrderItem5Popup                        1125
#define OrderItem6Popup                        1126
#define OrderItem7Popup                        1127
#define OrderItemLastPopup                     OrderItem7Popup
```

Figure 9-8 shows you what the new version of the form looks like.

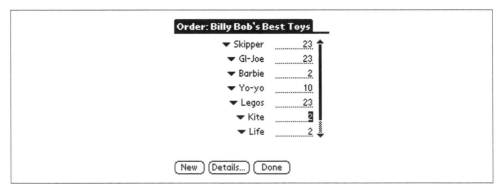

Figure 9-8. Order form

Example 9-38 shows the resource for the form.

Example 9-38. Order form resource

```
FORM ID OrderForm AT (0 0 160 160)
MENUID OrderMenuBar
BEGIN
  TITLE "Order"
  POPUPTRIGGER "" ID OrderItem1Popup AT (5 kFirstFieldTop 90 AUTO) RIGHTANCHOR
    FONT 0
  POPUPLIST ID OrderItem1Popup OrderProductsList
  POPUPTRIGGER "" ID OrderItem2Popup
    AT (PREVLEFT PREVBOTTOM+3 PREVWIDTH PREVHEIGHT) RIGHTANCHOR FONT 0
  POPUPLIST ID OrderItem2Popup OrderProductsList
  POPUPTRIGGER "" ID OrderItem3Popup
    AT (PREVLEFT PREVBOTTOM+3 PREVWIDTH PREVHEIGHT) RIGHTANCHOR FONT 0
  POPUPLIST ID OrderItem3Popup OrderProductsList
  POPUPTRIGGER "" ID OrderItem4Popup
    AT (PREVLEFT PREVBOTTOM+3 PREVWIDTH PREVHEIGHT) RIGHTANCHOR FONT 0
  POPUPLIST ID OrderItem4Popup OrderProductsList
  POPUPTRIGGER "" ID OrderItem5Popup
    AT (PREVLEFT PREVBOTTOM+3 PREVWIDTH PREVHEIGHT) RIGHTANCHOR FONT 0
  POPUPLIST ID OrderItem5Popup OrderProductsList
  POPUPTRIGGER "" ID OrderItem6Popup
```

Example 9-38. Order form resource (continued)

```
    AT (PREVLEFT PREVBOTTOM+3 PREVWIDTH PREVHEIGHT) RIGHTANCHOR FONT 0
  POPUPLIST ID OrderItem6Popup OrderProductsList
  POPUPTRIGGER "" ID OrderItem7Popup
    AT (PREVLEFT PREVBOTTOM+3 PREVWIDTH PREVHEIGHT) RIGHTANCHOR FONT 0
  LIST "" ID OrderProductsList
    AT (PREVRIGHT-67 25 67 99) NONUSABLE DISABLED FONT 0
  POPUPLIST ID OrderItem7Popup OrderProductsList

  FIELD ID OrderItem1Field AT (103 kFirstFieldTop 40 13)
    RIGHTALIGN NUMERIC FONT 0 UNDERLINED SINGLELINE MAXCHARS 20
  FIELD ID OrderItem2Field AT (PREVLEFT PREVBOTTOM+2 PREVWIDTH PREVHEIGHT)
    RIGHTALIGN NUMERIC FONT 0 UNDERLINED SINGLELINE MAXCHARS 20
  FIELD ID OrderItem3Field AT (PREVLEFT PREVBOTTOM+2 PREVWIDTH PREVHEIGHT)
    RIGHTALIGN NUMERIC FONT 0 UNDERLINED SINGLELINE MAXCHARS 20
  FIELD ID OrderItem4Field AT (PREVLEFT PREVBOTTOM+2 PREVWIDTH PREVHEIGHT)
    RIGHTALIGN NUMERIC FONT 0 UNDERLINED SINGLELINE MAXCHARS 20
  FIELD ID OrderItem5Field AT (PREVLEFT PREVBOTTOM+2 PREVWIDTH PREVHEIGHT)
    RIGHTALIGN NUMERIC FONT 0 UNDERLINED SINGLELINE MAXCHARS 20
  FIELD ID OrderItem6Field AT (PREVLEFT PREVBOTTOM+2 PREVWIDTH PREVHEIGHT)
    RIGHTALIGN NUMERIC FONT 0 UNDERLINED SINGLELINE MAXCHARS 20
  FIELD ID OrderItem7Field AT (PREVLEFT PREVBOTTOM+2 PREVWIDTH PREVHEIGHT)
    RIGHTALIGN NUMERIC FONT 0 UNDERLINED SINGLELINE MAXCHARS 20
  SCROLLBAR ID OrderScrollbarScrollBar
    AT (PREVRIGHT+4 kFirstFieldTop 7 PREVBOTTOM- kFirstFieldTop)
    VALUE 0 MIN 0 MAX 0 PAGESIZE 0

  BUTTON "New" ID OrderNewButton
    AT (kDefaultButtonLeft BOTTOM@kDefaultButtonBottom
    AUTO kDefaultButtonHeight)
    LEFTANCHOR FRAME FONT 0
  BUTTON "Details..." ID OrderDetailsButton
    AT (PREVRIGHT + kInterButtonWidth PREVTOP 40 kDefaultButtonHeight)
    LEFTANCHOR FRAME FONT 0
  BUTTON "Done" ID OrderDoneButton
    AT (PREVRIGHT + kInterButtonWidth PREVTOP 36 kDefaultButtonHeight)
    LEFTANCHOR FRAME FONT 0
  GRAFFITISTATEINDICATOR AT (kGSILeft kGSITop)
END
```

Initialization routine

When the order form opens, we initialize it with OrderFormOpen (see Example 9-39).

Example 9-39. Initialization routine for Order form

```
void OrderFormOpen(FormPtr form)
{
  UInt16    i;

  gNumRows = OrderItemLastField - OrderItemFirstField + 1;

  gFields = (FieldPtr *) MemPtrNew(sizeof(FieldPtr) * gNumRows);
```

Example 9-39. Initialization routine for Order form (continued)

```
  ErrFatalDisplayIf(!gFields, "can't allocate memory");
  for (i = 0; i < gNumRows; i++)
    gFields[i] = (FieldPtr) GetObjectFromForm(form, OrderItemFirstField + i);
  gRowSelected = false;
  gCurrentOrderChanged = false;
  gTopVisibleItem = 0;
  LoadFields(false);
  LstSetDrawFunction((ListPtr) GetObjectFromForm(form, OrderProductsList),
    DrawOneProductInList);

  OrderSetTitle( );
}
```

We allocate an array of `FieldPtr`, which we initialize to point to each field (this
allows us to get to a particular field for a row easily). We set the draw function for
the one list that is shared among all the pop-up triggers. We also set the title of the
form to reflect the customer name with `OrderSetTitle`.

Global variables

We also have some global variables for this form that are used throughout the code:

```
Char      gProductNames[OrderItemLastPopup - OrderItemFirstPopup + 1]
                        [kMaxProductNameLength]; // Prod names for triggers.
UInt16    gTopVisibleItem;             // Which item is in the first row.
Boolean   gRowSelected = false;        // True if something is selected.
UInt16    gCurrentSelectedItemIndex;   // Which item is selected (meaningful
                                       // only if gRowSelected is true).
```

Setting pop-up triggers and fields

`LoadFields` (see Example 9-40) sets the labels of the pop-up triggers and sets the
fields. It also hides and shows rows as necessary, sets the scrollbar, and sets the focus
to the selected field.

Example 9-40. LoadFields prepares display of rows

```
void LoadFields(Boolean redraw)
{
  FormPtr   form = FrmGetActiveForm( );
  UInt16    row;
  UInt16    lastPossibleTopItem = GetLastPossibleTopItem( );
  Boolean   hadFocus = false;
  UInt16    focusedItem;

  // If we have a currently selected item, make sure that it is visible.
  if (gRowSelected)
    if (gCurrentSelectedItemIndex < gTopVisibleItem ||
      gCurrentSelectedItemIndex >= gTopVisibleItem + gNumRows) {

      hadFocus = true;
      focusedItem = RowNumberToItemNumber(gCurrentSelectedItemIndex);
```

Example 9-40. LoadFields prepares display of rows (continued)

```
      DeselectRow(true);
      gTopVisibleItem = gCurrentSelectedItemIndex;
  }

  // Scroll up as necessary to display an entire page of info.
  if (gTopVisibleItem > lastPossibleTopItem)
    gTopVisibleItem = lastPossibleTopItem;

  gNumVisibleRows = gCurrentOrder->numItems - gTopVisibleItem;
  if (gNumVisibleRows > gNumRows)
    gNumVisibleRows = gNumRows;
  for (row = 0; row < gNumVisibleRows; row++) {
      ShowHideRow(form, row, true);
      InitRow(row, row + gTopVisibleItem, redraw);
  }
  for (row = gNumVisibleRows; row < gNumRows; row++)
      ShowHideRow(form, row, false);
  SclSetScrollBar(
    (ScrollBarPtr) GetObjectFromForm(form, OrderScrollbarScrollBar),
    (Int16) gTopVisibleItem, 0, (Int16) lastPossibleTopItem,
    (Int16) gNumRows - 1);

  if (hadFocus)
    SelectItem(focusedItem);
}
```

Hiding and showing objects

ShowHideRow either shows or hides the two objects in a row (the pop-up trigger and the field):

```
    void ShowHideRow(FormPtr form, UInt16 row, Boolean show)
    {
      ShowHideIndex(form, FrmGetObjectIndex(form, row + OrderItemFirstField),
        show);
      ShowHideIndex(form, FrmGetObjectIndex(form, row + OrderItemFirstPopup),
        show);
    }
```

It calls a utility routine ShowHideIndex, which shows or hides a particular form object:

```
    void ShowHideIndex(FormPtr form, UInt16 objIndex, Boolean show)
    {
      if (show)
        FrmShowObject(form, objIndex);
      else
        FrmHideObject(form, objIndex);
    }
```

Initializing the data

LoadFields also calls InitRow (see Example 9-41), which initializes the data for a specific row.

Example 9-41. InitRow initializes the form objects for a specific row

```
void InitRow(UInt16 row, UInt16 itemIndex, Boolean redraw)
{
  Char    buffer[kMaxNumericStringLength + 1];
  ControlPtr  popup;
  UInt32      productID;

  StrIToA(buffer, (Int32) gCurrentOrder->items[itemIndex].quantity);
  SetFieldTextFromStr(GetFieldForRow(row), buffer, redraw);

  popup = GetPopupForRow(row);
  productID = gCurrentOrder->items[itemIndex].productID;
  if (productID)
    GetProductNameFromProductID(productID, gProductNames[row]);
  else
    StrCopy(gProductNames[row], kUnknownProductName);
  CtlSetLabel(popup, gProductNames[row]);
}
```

It must copy the product name into the global array of product names so that the string will remain around for the life of the control.

Handling keystrokes

We handle two unusual keystrokes:

Carriage return

> This stops editing a row (just as in the Expense application).

A number

> If no row is selected, a new row is created with that number as the first character in the field.

Example 9-42 shows our routine that does these things.

Example 9-42. Handling keystrokes in the Order form

```
Boolean OrderHandleKey(EventPtr event)
{
  UInt16  c = event->data.keyDown.chr;
  Boolean handled = false;

  if (TxtGlueCharIsVirtual(event->data.keyDown.modifiers,
    event->data.keyDown.chr)) {
    // Bottom-to-top screen gesture can cause this, depending on
    // configuration in Prefs/Buttons/Pen.
    if (c == vchrSendData)
      handled = OrderHandleMenuEvent(RecordBeamCustomer);
    else if (c == vchrPageUp || c == vchrPageDown) {
      Int16 numRowsToScroll = (Int16) gNumRows;

      OrderDeselectRowAndDeleteIfEmpty();
      if (c == vchrPageUp)
```

Example 9-42. Handling keystrokes in the Order form (continued)

```
          numRowsToScroll = -numRowsToScroll;
        OrderScrollRows(numRowsToScroll);
        handled = true;
      }
  } else if (c == linefeedChr) {
    // The return character takes us out of edit mode.
    OrderDeselectRowAndDeleteIfEmpty( );
    handled = true;
  } else if (!gRowSelected && TxtGlueCharIsAlNum(c) &&
    !TxtGlueCharIsAlpha(c)) {
    // We can't use TxtGlueCharIsNum(c) in 4.0 SDK
    // because the macro is broken.
    UInt16  itemNumber;

    if (AddNewItem(&itemNumber)) {
      SelectItem(itemNumber);
      // handled = false; // Pass it through to the field.
    }
  }
  return handled;
}
```

Handling events

Just as in the Item details form, we must handle the `ctlEnterEvent` when the user taps on a pop-up trigger, and the `popSelectEvent` when the user selects an item. See Example 9-43 in which the emphasized code is relevant to the UI of form objects.

Example 9-43. Portion of the Order form's event handler

```
case ctlEnterEvent:
  if (event->data.ctlSelect.controlID >= OrderItemFirstPopup &&
    event->data.ctlSelect.controlID <= OrderItemLastPopup) {
    UInt16 row = event->data.ctlSelect.controlID - OrderItemFirstPopup;
    if (! (gRowSelected &&
      RowNumberToItemNumber(row) == gCurrentSelectedItemIndex)) {
      OrderDeselectRowAndDeleteIfEmpty( );
      SelectItem(RowNumberToItemNumber(row));
    }
    HandleProductPopupEnter(event->data.ctlSelect.controlID,
      OrderProductsList,
      gCurrentOrder->items[gCurrentSelectedItemIndex].productID);
    //handled = false;  // Still want the pop up to occur.
  }
  break;

case popSelectEvent:
  if (event->data.popSelect.controlID >= OrderItemFirstPopup &&
    event->data.popSelect.controlID <= OrderItemLastPopup) {
    UInt32  productID;
    UInt16    row;
    Char    newProductName[kMaxProductNameLength];
```

Example 9-43. Portion of the Order form's event handler

```
  row = event->data.popSelect.controlID - OrderItemFirstPopup;
  if (HandleProductPopupSelect(event, &productID, newProductName)) {
    UInt16  oldItemIndex = RowNumberToItemNumber(row);
    UInt16  itemIndex = oldItemIndex;

    SaveCurrentField();
    if (ProductIDExistsInOrder(productID, &itemIndex)) {
      GetProductNameFromProductID(productID,
        productName);
      if (FrmCustomAlert(ProductExistsAlert, productName, NULL, NULL)
        != ProductExistsCancel) {
        UInt32  newItemTotal;
        DeselectRow(true);

        newItemTotal = gCurrentOrder->items[itemIndex].quantity +
          gCurrentOrder->items[oldItemIndex].quantity;
        DmWrite(gCurrentOrder, OffsetOf(Order, items[itemIndex].quantity),
          &newItemTotal, sizeof(newItemTotal));
        DeleteNthItem(oldItemIndex);
        LoadFields(true); // Remove deleted row from screen.
        if (oldItemIndex < itemIndex)
          itemIndex--;   // Because we've removed an item before this one.
        SelectItem(itemIndex);
      }
    } else {
      DmWrite(gCurrentOrder,
        OffsetOf(Order,
        items[gCurrentSelectedItemIndex].productID),
        &productID,
        sizeof(productID));
      StrCopy(gProductNames[row], newProductName);
      CtlSetLabel(event->data.popSelect.controlP, gProductNames[row]);
    }
    gCurrentOrderChanged = true;
  }
  handled = true;
}
break;
```

Scrolling

SelectItem (see Example 9-44) scrolls the given item into view (if necessary), sets the focus to the field in the row, and highlights all the text in the field (so the user can start writing to change the text).

Example 9-44. SelectItem will select (and highlight) a given item

```
void SelectItem(UInt16 itemNumber)
{
  FormPtr form;
  UInt16  fieldIndex;
```

Example 9-44. SelectItem will select (and highlight) a given item (continued)

```
  FieldPtr  field;

  ErrFatalDisplayIf(gRowSelected, "row already selected");
  gRowSelected = true;
  gCurrentSelectedItemIndex = itemNumber;
  if (itemNumber < gTopVisibleItem ||
    itemNumber >= gTopVisibleItem + gNumVisibleRows) {
    UInt16    lastPossibleTopItem = GetLastPossibleTopItem();

    gTopVisibleItem = itemNumber;
    if (gTopVisibleItem < lastPossibleTopItem)
      gTopVisibleItem = lastPossibleTopItem;
    LoadFields(true);
  }
  form = FrmGetActiveForm();
  fieldIndex = FrmGetObjectIndex(form,
    RowNumberToFieldID(ItemNumberToRowNumber(itemNumber)));
  FrmSetFocus(form, fieldIndex);
  field = GetCurrentField();
    // Select all the text for easy typing.
  FldSetSelection(field, 0, FldGetTextLength(field));
}
```

Deselecting a row

A routine exists for deselecting a row:

```
    void DeselectRow(Boolean removeFocus)
    {
     if (removeFocus)
        FrmSetFocus(FrmGetActiveForm(), noFocus);
      gRowSelected = false;
    }
```

When the user leaves a row, but hasn't specified an item, we delete the item (similar to the Expense application). This is a routine with the very long name OrderDeselectRowAndDeleteIfEmptyHelper (see Example 9-45).

Example 9-45. Routine deselects a row (and may delete it)

```
Boolean OrderDeselectRowAndDeleteIfEmptyHelper(Boolean removeFocus)
{
  Boolean    empty;

  if (!gRowSelected)
    return false;

  SaveCurrentField();

  // If the item ID is 0, delete the item.
  empty = (Boolean)
    (gCurrentOrder->items[gCurrentSelectedItemIndex].productID == 0);
```

Example 9-45. Routine deselects a row (and may delete it) (continued)

```
  if (empty) {
    gCurrentOrderChanged = true;
    DeleteNthItem(gCurrentSelectedItemIndex);

    LoadFields(true);
  }
  DeselectRow(removeFocus);

  return empty;
}
```

Two utility routines act as wrappers for this function:

```
    static Boolean OrderDeselectRowAndDeleteIfEmpty(void)
    {
      return OrderDeselectRowAndDeleteIfEmptyHelper(true);
    }

    static Boolean OrderDeselectRowAndDeleteIfEmptyButDontRemoveFocus(void)
    {
      return OrderDeselectRowAndDeleteIfEmptyHelper(false);
    }
```

This is the code for most of the Order form (there are some minor routines that aren't covered); if you want to see the code in its entirety look in Appendix B, which contains all the source code for the Sales application.

Switching Forms

The `AppHandleEvent` (see Example 9-46) needs to load forms when a `frmLoadEvent` occurs (this is not necessary for forms shown with `FrmDoDialog`).

Example 9-46. AppHandleEvent for the Sales application

```
Boolean AppHandleEvent(EventPtr event)
{
  FormPtr frm;
  UInt16    formId;
  Boolean handled = false;

  switch (event->eType) {
  case frmLoadEvent:
    // Load the form resource specified in the event, then activate the form.
    formId = event->data.frmLoad.formID;
    frm = FrmInitForm(formId);
    FrmSetActiveForm(frm);

    // Set the event handler for the form.  The handler of the currently
    // active form is called by FrmDispatchEvent each time it receives
    // an event.
```

Example 9-46. AppHandleEvent for the Sales application (continued)

```
    switch (formId)
    {
    case OrderForm:
      FrmSetEventHandler(frm, OrderHandleEvent);
      break;

    case CustomersForm:
      FrmSetEventHandler(frm, CustomersHandleEvent);
      break;

    }
    handled = true;
    break;

  case menuEvent:
    if (event->data.menu.itemID == OptionsAboutSales) {
      FrmAlert(AboutBoxAlert);
      handled = true;
    }
    break;
  }
  return handled;
}
```

That is all there is of interest to the forms and form objects in the Sales application. This material took a great deal of space to discuss because of the large number of objects we needed to show you, and not necessarily because of the complexity of the subject material. This is all good news, however, as a rich set of forms and form objects means greater flexibility in the types of applications you can create for Palm OS devices.

You should now have a fairly good idea of how to implement the forms and form objects available within the Palm OS. From the general discussion on each object to the implementations in the samples, you now have enough information to add these objects to your own code. Now it is time to look at how you add data to an application.

Databases

Now we are going to talk about how data is organized. In Chapter 6, we told you that data, rather unusually, resides in RAM memory in the Palm OS. This memory is in turn divided into two sections: the dynamic and storage heaps. Permanent data resides in the storage heap and is accessed via the Data Manager (the dynamic heap that we talked about in Chapter 6 is managed strictly by the Memory Manager).

We will give you an overview of how data and databases are organized in the Palm OS. We will cover everything you need to know, from types of databases to creating databases, modifying them, creating individual data records; adding, modifying, and deleting them from a database; and different ways of handling sorting. We will also cover other essential topics such as how to deal with secret records and working around the 64K size limitation. Finally, we will take all this information and apply it to the creation of the databases and records in our Sales sample application. We will show you the source code for the routines that handle all of these database and record tasks.

Overview of Databases and Records

To begin with, don't get your hopes up when you hear the word *database*. The Data Manager doesn't support anything like a desktop database: no fields, no indexing, no select statements. At its heart, a Palm database is just an array of memory chunks.

Once you get past its unusual location, the organization of data and databases on the Palm OS is fairly simple. It's organized into two components: databases and records. The relationship between the two is straightforward. A database is a related collection of records. Records are relocatable blocks of memory (handles) and an individual record can't exceed 64 KB in size. A database on the Palm OS consists of an array of record handles. This simplicity is one reason for the very fast performance of the Data Manager.

There are two different types of databases:

Record databases
> These are normally used to store application data and are synced by conduits. They are also called PDBs.

Resource databases
> These are normally applications, overlays (localized resources), and shared libraries and don't normally change at runtime. They are also called PRCs.

Let's look at record databases first. After that, we will turn to resource databases.

Record Databases

A database, as a collection of records, maintains certain key information about each record. This information includes:

- The location of the record.
- A 3-byte unique ID. This ID is unique only within a given database. It is assigned automatically by the Data Manager when the record is created.
- A 1-byte attribute. This attribute contains a 4-bit category, a deleted bit, a dirty bit, a busy bit, and a secret (or private) bit.

In the Palm 3.0 OS and later, there is one large storage heap; in previous versions, there were many small heaps. Because a database resides in a storage heap, its records might not be in the same heap (see Figure 10-1).

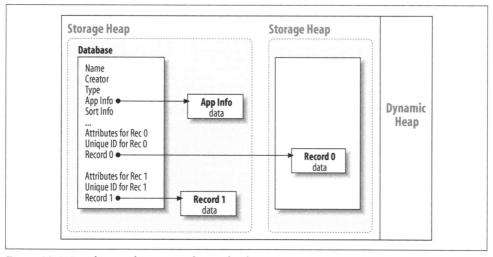

Figure 10-1. Database with two records in a database in persistent memory

Databases also contain the following other types of information:

An application info block
This usually contains category names as well as other database-wide information.

A sort info block
This is where you could store a list of record numbers in a variant order. For example, address book entries might be sorted by company rather than by a person's name. Most applications don't use a sort info block.

Name, type, and creator
Databases are created with a name (which must be unique), a four-character type, and a four-character creator. When a user deletes an application, the Palm OS automatically deletes all databases that share the same creator. The preferences record is removed at the same time. So that this cleanup can happen correctly, it's important that your databases use the creator of their application.

Resource Databases

A resource database is similar to a record database, but the information about each record is different. Naming is also different: records in resource databases are normally called resources. Each resource (record) no longer has a unique ID and attributes. Instead, it has:

- A 4-byte type (usually referred to with a four-character constant)
- A 2-byte ID number

To retrieve a resource from a resource database, you specify the type and ID—the Data Manager iterates through the database, quickly finding the desired resource.

As we said earlier, an application is a resource database. Here are a few of the resources you might find in an application:

code 0
Contains a compressed representation of the application's global variables

code 1
The application's code

tFRM 1000
Contains the data for the form and form objects with ID 1000

Talt 1000
Contains the data for the alert with ID 1000

tAIN 1000
The name of the application (as seen in the Launcher)

Write-Protected Memory

In order to maintain the integrity of the storage heap, its hardware is write protected. This ensures that a rogue application referencing a stray pointer can't accidentally destroy important data or applications. Therefore, changes to the databases can be made only through the Data Manager APIs. These APIs check that writes are made only within an allocated chunk of memory—writes to random areas or past the end of an allocated chunk are not allowed.

Palm 3.0 OS Heap Changes

In pre-3.0 versions of the OS, a database heap was limited to 64 KB. The persistent area of memory was therefore divided into many different database heaps. In this pre-3.0 world, it was much harder to manage memory, since each allocated record had to fit within one heap. The 3.0 OS does not have that 64 KB limit on database heaps. Instead, the persistent memory area contains just one large database heap.

 The multiple database heaps lead to a problem: although there is free memory available, there might not be enough available for a record. The situation occurs when you have, for example, 10 database heaps 64 KB in size, and each is half full. Although there is 320 KB memory available, a record of size 40 KB can't be allocated (because no single heap can hold it). The original 1.0 OS exacerbated this problem with an ill-chosen strategy for database allocations: records were allocated by attempting to keep heaps equally full. This made large record allocations more and more difficult as previous allocations were made.

The 2.0 OS switched to a first-fit strategy (a record is allocated in the first heap in which it will fit). A change to the 2.0 OS (found in the System Update 2.0.4) modified the strategy (if there isn't room in an existing heap for a chunk, chunks from the most empty heap are moved out of that heap until there is enough space). It isn't until 3.0, however, that a full fix (one large heap) is in place.

Where Databases Are Stored

The Palm OS Data Manager supports multiple cards. Cards are numbered, starting with the internal card, which is 0. When you create a database, you specify the card on which it is created.

The Handspring devices are the only ones (as of mid-2001) that use this support of the Data Manager. A Springboard flash module appears as a read-only card number 1 (a utility program will copy databases and/or applications to or from the card).

Although other manufacturers support expansion cards—CompactFlash (CF), Memory Stick, and Secure Digital—they are not accessible via the Data Manager. Instead, the data on those expansion cards appears as a filesystem, and is manipulated using the new 4.0 OS Virtual Filesystem (VFS) Manager. We won't be covering the VFS Manager in this book.

How Records Are Stored Versus How They Are Referenced

While your application is running, you reference database records using handles. Database records are not stored like this, however. Within the database heap, they are stored as local IDs. A local ID is an offset from the beginning of the card on which it is located. Because items are stored this way, the base address of the card can change without requiring any changes in the database heap.

A future (hypothetical) Palm OS device with multiple card slots would have separate base addresses for each slot. Thus, the memory address for a chunk on a memory card would depend on what slot it was in (and thus what its base address was).

This is relevant to your job as an application writer when you get to the application info block in the database. Application info (and sort info) blocks are stored as local IDs. You need to convert a handle to a local ID (using a Memory Manager function) and store the local ID. When retrieving the local ID, you must convert it back to a handle before using it.

Opening, Creating, and Closing Databases

You handle these operations in a straightforward manner in Palm applications.

Opening a Database

You can specify a database to open using one of the following:

- Type and creator
- Name and card number

The type and creator is usually more convenient, but you can run into a problem if more than one database exists with the same type and creator. This might happen, for instance, in a book-reading program, where every downloaded book is a database with the same type and creator, but with a different name. If more than one database exists, one of them (no guarantee which one) will be opened.

An open database is referenced by a `DmOpenRef`, which is a pointer to information about the database. If an open fails, it returns `NULL`. Many Data Managers return an error code explicitly. For those that don't, call `DmGetLastErr` to determine the last error.

Opening by type and creator

You usually open your database using the type and creator. Example 10-1 shows opening the Memo Pad database (which has a type of `DATA` and a creator ID of `memo`) for read-write access.

Example 10-1. Opening the Memo Pad database by type and creator

```
Err OpenMemopadByTypeCreator(DmOpenRef *refPtr)
{
  Err      err = errNone;
  UInt16   mode = dmModeReadWrite;
  DmOpenRef ref;

  ref = DmOpenDatabaseByTypeCreator('DATA', 'memo', mode);
  if (ref == NULL)
    err = DmGetLastErr( );
  *refPtr = ref;
  return err;
}
```

In your application, you'll usually use a mode of dmModeReadWrite, since you may be modifying records in the database. If you know that you aren't making any modifications, then use a dmModeReadOnly mode.

> You may be surprised at the use of multicharacter constants like 'DATA'. These multicharacter constants evaluate to a 32-bit number (four 8-bit characters). Most C programmers (other than Mac OS programmers) have never seen the use of these multicharacter constants. They're used in the Palm OS APIs as succinct, readable constants.

If your application supports private records, then you should honor the user's preference of whether to show private records by applying dmModeShowSecret to the mode, as necessary. Example 10-2 shows code that applies the dmModeShowSecret appropriately.

Example 10-2. Opening the Memo Pad while taking into account the user's privacy request

```
Err OpenMemopadByTypeCreatorBetter(DmOpenRef *refPtr)
{
  Err      err = errNone;
  UInt16   mode = dmModeReadWrite;
  DmOpenRef ref;

  if (PrefGetPreference(prefShowPrivateRecords) != hidePrivateRecords)
    mode |= dmModeShowSecret;
  ref = DmOpenDatabaseByTypeCreator('DATA', 'memo', mode);
  if (ref == NULL)
    err = DmGetLastErr( );
  *refPtr = ref;
  return err;
}
```

Opening by name

It's also possible to open a database by name and card number. It's a two-step process however. The fact that it requires two steps, and that the card number is needed, explains why most applications open by type and creator.

Example 10-3 shows opening the Memo Pad database (whose name is MemoDB) on card number 0.

Example 10-3. Opening a database by name

```
Err OpenMemopadByName(DmOpenRef *refPtr)
{
  Err        err = errNone;
  UInt16     mode = dmModeReadWrite;
  DmOpenRef ref = NULL;
  LocalID    dbID;
  UInt16     cardNumber = 0;

  dbID = DmFindDatabase(cardNumber, "MemoDB");
  if (dbID == NULL)
    err = DmGetLastErr();
  else {
    ref = DmOpenDatabase(cardNumber, dbID, mode);
    if (ref == NULL)
      err = DmGetLastErr();
  }
  *refPtr = ref;
  return err;
}
```

Closing a Database

When you are finished with a database, call `DmCloseDatabase`:

```
err = DmCloseDatabase(myDB);
```

Don't leave databases open unnecessarily because each open database takes approximately 75 bytes of room in the dynamic heap. A good rule of thumb might be that if the user isn't in a form that has access to the data in that database, it shouldn't be open.

Note that when you close a database, you need to make sure all your records are left as you found them: unlocked and not busy. If you fail to do so, then a debug ROM will warn you (as shown in Figure 10-2).

Creating a Database

To create a database, you normally use `DmCreateDatabase`:

```
Err DmCreateDatabase(UInt16 cardNo, const Char *nameP,
                     UInt32 creator, UInt32 type, Boolean resDB)
```

The creator is the unique creator you've registered at the Palm developer web site (*http://www.palmos.com/dev*). You use the type to distinguish between multiple databases with different types of information in them (use any four characters you want, but realize that Palm defines the format of all lowercase types, like app1). The nameP is

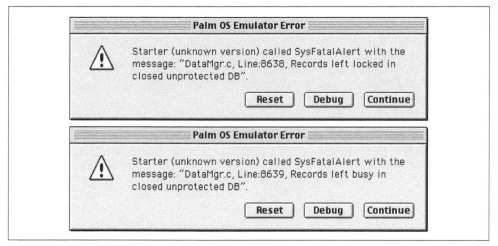

Figure 10-2. A debug ROM warns if records are left locked or busy when a database is closed

the name of the database, and it *must be unique*. The last parameter, resDB is true
when you are creating a resource database, and false otherwise.

 While creating databases on card 0 is fine, other code in the application shouldn't rely on the value of the card being 0. By not hardcod-
ing this value, the application will work with multiple card devices.

In order to guarantee that your database name is unique, you need to include your
creator ID as part of your database name. Developer Support recommends that you
name your database with two parts, the database name followed by a hyphen (–) and
your creator code. An application with a creator ID of "Neil" that created two databases might name them as follows:

```
Database1-Neil
Database2-Neil
```

Create your database in your AppStart routine

You normally create your database from within your AppStart routine. This is in
cases for which the database does not yet exist. Example 10-4 shows a routine to do
that.

Example 10-4. A routine that opens a database, creating it if necessary

```
Err OpenDB(DmOpenRef *refPtr, UInt16 mode)
{
  Err err;
  DmOpenRef ref = 0;

  // Find the MyData database.  If it doesn't exist, create it.
  ref = DmOpenDatabaseByTypeCreator('DATA', 'SLE2', mode);
```

```
  if (!ref) {
    err = DmGetLastErr( );
    if (err == dmErrCantFind) {
      err = DmCreateDatabase(0, "MyData-SLE2", 'SLE2',
        'DATA', false);
      if (err)
        return err;

      ref = DmOpenDatabaseByTypeCreator('DATA', 'SLE2', mode);
      if (!ref)
        err = DmGetLastErr( );
    }
  }
  *refPtr = ref;
  return err;
}
```

The order of the type and creator parameters is swapped between DmOpenDatabaseByTypeCreator and DmCreateDatabase. Beware of copying and pasting.

Creating a database from an image

If your application has a database that should be initialized with a predefined set of records, it may make sense to "freeze-dry" a database as a resource in your application. Thus, when you build your application, add an existing database image to it. Then, when your application's AppStart routine is called, if the database doesn't exist, you can create it and initialize it from this freeze-dried image. A database image is just the bytes from a Palm database (*.pdb*) file.

You could just provide your user with a *.pdb* file to download. The advantage is that your application is smaller; the disadvantage is that the user might not download the file. In this case, you'd still need to check for the existence of your databases.

Example 10-5 shows how to create a database from an image stored in a resource.

Example 10-5. Creating a database from an image stored in a resource

```
Err CreateFromImage( )
{
  Err       err;
  MemHandle imageHandle = DmGetResource('DBIM', 1000);

  if (!imageHandle)
    return DmGetLastErr( );
  err = DmCreateDatabaseFromImage(MemHandleLock(imageHandle));
  MemHandleUnlock(imageHandle);
  DmReleaseResource(imageHandle);

  return err;
}
```

This code assumes that there's a resource of type DBIM with ID 1000 in your application's resource database that contains an appropriate image. You can create an image on the Palm OS Emulator (writing Palm code to do so), and then use the Export Database menu item to export it to the desktop as a *.pdb* file.

In PilRC, you'd use the following line to create the DBIM resource from a *.pdb* file named "Foo.pdb":

```
DATA "DBIM" ID 1000 "Foo.pdb"
```

A more flexible way to create a database from a database image is to use the Exchange Manager routine ExgDBRead. This routine (which really should be part of the Data Manager), also creates a database from the bytes of a *.pdb* file. The difference is that DmCreateDatabaseFromImage requires a pointer to the memory containing the bytes, whereas ExgDBRead repeatedly calls a routine you provide that successively provides the bytes of the *.pdb*.

There's also an inverse function, ExgDBWrite, that takes a database on the handheld, and generates from it the bytes of a *.pdb* or *.prc* file.

Creating the Application Info Block in a Database

The application info block is a block of memory that is associated with your database as a whole. You can use it for database-wide information. For example, you might have a Checkbook application with a database of checks and want to keep the total value of all the checks. Or you might allow the user to choose from more than one sort order and need to keep track of the current sort order. Or you might need to keep track of category names. In each of these cases, the application info block is an appropriate place to keep this information. Example 10-6 shows how to allocate and initialize the application info block (normally used when you create your database).

Example 10-6. Creating an AppInfo block whose contents are specified by a structure

```
typedef struct {
  AppInfoType appInfo;
  UInt16   field1;
  // Other fields here.
} MyAppInfoType;


Err CreateAppInfoBlockForDB(DmOpenRef db)
{
  UInt16        cardNo;
  LocalID       dbID;
  LocalID       appInfoID;
  MyAppInfoType *appInfoP;
  Err           err;
  MemHandle     h;

  err = DmOpenDatabaseInfo(db, &dbID, NULL, NULL, &cardNo, NULL);
```

```
   if (err != errNone)
     return err;

   h = DmNewHandle(db, sizeof(MyAppInfoType));
   if (!h)
     return dmErrMemError;

   appInfoID = MemHandleToLocalID(h);
   err = DmSetDatabaseInfo(cardNo, dbID, NULL, NULL, NULL,
     NULL, NULL, NULL, NULL, &appInfoID, NULL, NULL, NULL);

   if (err == errNone) {
     appInfoP = (MyAppInfoType *) MemHandleLock(h);
     err = DmSet(appInfoP, 0, sizeof(MyAppInfoType), 0); // clear all fields

     // Use DmWrite here to write to the fields of appInfoP
     // and/or call CategoryInitialize to initialize appInfo
     // CategoryInitialize(&appInfoP->appInfo, 1000);

     MemPtrUnlock(appInfoP);
   } else
     MemHandleFree(h);
   return err;
}
```

Note that you can't use `MemHandleNew` to allocate the block because you want the block to be in the same heap as the database and not in the dynamic heap. Therefore, use `DmNewHandle`. Also, you can't directly store the handle in the database. Instead, you must convert it to a local ID.

 Remember that a local ID is an offset from the beginning of the card. This is necessary for the future in case multiple slots are supported. In such a case, the memory addresses would be dependent on the slot in which the card was placed.

If you use the Category Manager to manage your database, you need to make sure the first field in your application info block is of type `AppInfoType` (this stores the mapping from category number to category name). To initialize this field, call `CategoryInitialize`:

```
   CategoryInitialize(&appInfoP->appInfo, 1000);
```

The second parameter is the resource ID of a list of initial category names. You need to add one of these to your resource file (it's common to initialize it with Unfiled, Business, and Personal):

```
   CATEGORIES ID 1000 "Unfiled" "Business" "Personal"
```

Iterating Through Databases

The Data Manager provides a mechanism for iterating through databases of a specific type, or creator, or both. Here's the declaration of the routine to do so:

```
Err DmGetNextDatabaseByTypeCreator(Boolean newSearch,
  DmSearchStatePtr stateInfoP, UInt32 type, UInt32 creator,
  Boolean onlyLatestVers, UInt16* cardNoP, LocalID* dbIDP)
```

The first time you call this routine, you pass in `true` for the `newSearch` parameter, and a pointer to a `DmSearchStateType` variable as the `stateInfoP` parameter. On subsequent calls, pass `false` for the `newSearch` parameter, and continue passing a pointer to the same `DmSearchStateType` variable (that's where the routine stores its state information as it performs its iteration). On return, the routine will provide the card number and local ID of the found database (or will return the error `dmErrCantFind` if there are no more databases).

By passing in 0 as the type or creator, you can force a wildcard search. For example, passing 0 as the creator causes `DmGetNextDatabaseByTypeCreator` to return all databases that match the given type, regardless of the creator. Passing 0 for both the creator and type causes it to return all databases.

Example 10-7 uses `DmGetNextDatabaseByTypeCreator` to iterate through all the applications on the handheld and return the total number.

Example 10-7. Iterating over the databases to return the total number of applications

```
UInt16 GetNumApps()
{
  Boolean newSearch = true;
  UInt16  total = 0;
  UInt16  card;
  LocalID dbID;
  Err     err;
  UInt32  wildcardCreator = 0;
  DmSearchStateType stateInfo;
  Boolean onlyLatestVers = true;

  do {
    err = DmGetNextDatabaseByTypeCreator(newSearch,
      &stateInfo, 'appl', wildcardCreator,
      onlyLatestVers, &card, &dbID);
    newSearch = false;
    if (err == 0)
      total++;
  } while (err == 0);
  return total;
}
```

Working with Records

Now that you know how to set up databases, you need to populate them with records.

Each application defines the structure of the records in its database. For example, the Memo Pad stores null-terminated C strings as the contents of its records. Thus, if the user creates two memos—a short one and a long one—there will be two records, one short and one long.

We'll look first at how to read an existing record, then how to modify one. Next, we'll look at creating records, and then sorting and searching for records.

Reading from a Record

Reading from a record is very simple. Although records are write protected, they are still in RAM; thus, you can just get a record from a database, lock it, and then read from it. You obtain a record using DmQueryRecord:

```
MemHandle DmQueryRecord(DmOpenRef dbP, UInt16 index)
```

It requires an open database, along with a record number (also called record index): record numbers always start at 0. This routine is very simple and fast; it goes to the specified array entry in the database and returns the handle of that record.

Example 10-8 shows using DmQueryRecord to retrieve the first memo from the Memo Pad database, which it then displays in an alert (the definition for the alert isn't shown here).

Example 10-8. Retrieving the first memo from the memo database and displaying it

```
Err DisplayFirstMemo(DmOpenRef memoDB)
{
  Err err = 0;
  MemHandle myRecord = DmQueryRecord(memoDB, 0);

  if (!myRecord)
    err = DmGetLastErr( );
  else {
    Char *s = (Char *) MemHandleLock(myRecord);
    FrmCustomAlert(MyAlert, s, NULL, NULL);
    MemHandleUnlock(myRecord);
  }
  return err;
}
```

The DmQueryRecord call returns a record that is read-only; it doesn't mark the record as busy and, therefore, you shouldn't write to the record. Although Palm OS 4.0 and earlier allow writing to a record whose busy bit isn't set, future OS versions might not allow it.

Some applications will have more complicated record formats defined by a C structure. Here is such an example; it is in the To Do application whose data is specified by the following structure:

```
typedef struct {
  DateType dueDate;
  UInt8 priority;
  char descriptionAndNote[1];
} ToDoDBRecord;
```

The To Do application stores a due date, a priority, and then two null-terminated strings (description and note) back-to-back. Since C has no way to specify variable-length arrays, the structure is defined as a 1-byte character array. Its actual length will be determined by the size of the record. There's no way to specify the note directly in the structure; instead, it has to be accessed manually by skipping past the null-terminated description.

Example 10-9 shows a function that retrieves the first To Do record and displays the description and the note.

Example 10-9. Retrieving the first To Do record and displaying information from it

```
Err DisplayFirstNote(DmOpenRef noteDB)
{
  Err err = 0;
  MemHandle myRecord = DmQueryRecord(noteDB, 0);

  if (!myRecord)
    err = DmGetLastErr( );
  else {
    ToDoDBRecord *rec = (ToDoDBRecord *) MemHandleLock(myRecord);
    Char   *note;

    FrmCustomAlert(MyAlert, rec->descriptionAndNote, NULL, NULL);
    note = rec->descriptionAndNote + StrLen(rec->descriptionAndNote) + 1;
    FrmCustomAlert(MyAlert, note, NULL, NULL);
    MemHandleUnlock(myRecord);
  }
  return err;
}
```

It is common to assign the return result of MemHandleLock on a record to a structure pointer:

```
ToDoDBRecord *rec = (ToDoDBRecord *) MemHandleLock(myRecord);
```

The structure pointer is then used to read from the record.

Modifying a Record

In order to modify a record, you must use DmGetRecord, which marks the record as busy. You call DmReleaseRecord when you're finished with it. Because you can't just write to the pointer (the storage area is write protected), you must use either DmSet (to set a range to a particular character value), DmWrite (which copies a range of bytes), or DmStrCopy (which copies a string).

```
Err DmSet(void *recordP, UInt32 offset, UInt32 bytes, UInt8 value)
Err DmWrite(void *recordP, UInt32 offset, const void *srcP, UInt32 bytes)
Err DmStrCopy(void *recordP, UInt32 offset, const Char *srcP)
```

Each of these routines takes a locked record as the first parameter. The second is the offset within the record at which to start writing. The routines start by checking that the passed-in pointer is in fact a pointer to a locked record. Then, they sum the starting offset with the desired amount of data to write. If that exceeds the current size of the record, they generate an error. Otherwise, they turn off hardware protection, do a memory-to-memory copy, and then turn the hardware protection back on. The checks ensure that writes occur only within a record and not outside a record (which could overwrite the integrity of the storage heap).

 The Data Manager generates fatal errors if you make calls that are nonsensical (for example, if you write outside the bounds of a record or use a resource function on a record database). The Data Manager philosophy is that any application that makes nonsensical calls should be protected from itself: if an application is not smart enough to pass the right parameters, it isn't smart enough to check return results. While such an application would probably fail sooner or later anyway, the Data Manager ensures that it is sooner.

Often, a record has a structure associated with it. You usually read and write the entire structure as shown in Example 10-10.

Example 10-10. Modifying an entire record with one call to DmWrite

```
typedef struct {
  UInt16 field1;
  Char   field2;
} StructType;

Err ModifyEntireRecord(DmOpenRef db, UInt16 recordNumber)
{
  MemHandle  myRecord;
  StructType *s;
  StructType theStructure;
  Err        err;

  myRecord = DmGetRecord(db, recordNumber);
  if (!myRecord)
    err = DmGetLastErr();
  else {
    s = (StructType *) MemHandleLock(myRecord);
    theStructure = *s;  // Read current contents.
    theStructure.field1 = 100; // Modify desired field.
    err = DmWrite(s, 0, &theStructure, sizeof(theStructure));
```

```
    MemHandleUnlock(myRecord);
    DmReleaseRecord(db, recordNumber, true);
  }
  return err;
}
```

Another alternative is to write specific fields in the structure. A very handy thing to use in this case is the Palm OS SDK OffsetOf macro (OffsetOf returns the offset of a field within a structure). Example 10-11 shows modifying a single field.

Example 10-11. Modifying one field in a record with a call to DmWrite

```
Err ModifySingleField(DmOpenRef db, UInt16 recordNumber)
{
  MemHandle  myRecord;
  StructType *s;
  Char       newValue;
  Err        err;

  myRecord = DmGetRecord(db, recordNumber);
  if (!myRecord)
    err = DmGetLastErr();
  else {
    s = (StructType *) MemHandleLock(myRecord);
    newValue = 'Y';
    err = DmWrite(s, OffsetOf(StructType, field2), &newValue,
      sizeof(newValue));
    MemHandleUnlock(myRecord);
    DmReleaseRecord(db, recordNumber, true);
  }
  return err;
}
```

The second approach has the advantage of writing less data; it only writes what needs to change.

> The standard C library includes have an offsetof macro that works just like the Palm OS SDK macro OffsetOf. The SDK provides the macro so that you don't have to worry about including standard C library includes just to get a single macro.

DmReleaseRecord is the routine that unmarks the busy bit and, optionally, sets the dirty bit. It needs to be called after you've finished with an existing record that you obtained with DmGetRecord, or when you've finished with a new record obtained with DmNewRecord. The third parameter to DmReleaseRecord tells whether the record was actually modified or not. Passing the value true causes the record to be marked as modified. If you modify a record but don't tell DmReleaseRecord that you changed it, during a sync, the database's conduit may not realize the record has been changed.

Creating a New Record

You create a new record with `DmNewRecord`:

```
MemHandle DmNewRecord(DmOpenRef dbP, UInt16 *indexNumber, UInt32 recordSize)
```

The `recordSize` is the initial record size; you can change it later with `DmResizeRecord` (or, just `MemHandleResize` if you are making the record smaller). Make sure you specify a positive record size; zero-size records are not valid.

You'll notice that you need to specify the index number of the record as the second parameter. You initialize it with the desired record index; when `DmNewRecord` returns, it contains the actual record index.

Record indexes are zero-based; they range from 0 to one less than the number of records. If your desired record index is in this range, the new record will be created with your desired record index. All the records with that index and above are shifted up (their record indexes are increased by one). If your desired record index is ≥ the number of records, your new record will be created after the last record, and the actual record index will be returned.

Adding at the beginning of the database

To add to the beginning of the database, use 0 as a desired record index:

```
UInt16 recordIndex = 0;
myRecordHandle = DmNewRecord(db, &recordIndex, recordSize)
```

Adding at the end of the database

To add to the end of the database, use the constant `dmMaxRecordIndex` as your desired record index:

```
UInt16 recordIndex = dmMaxRecordIndex;
myRecordHandle = DmNewRecord(db, &recordIndex, recordSize)
// Now recordIndex contains the actual index.
```

Note that `dmMaxRecordIndex` is just a very large number: `0xffff`. It saves having to make two Data Manager calls: one to find the number of records and another to create the new record.

Deleting a Record

Deleting a record is slightly complicated because of the interaction with conduits and the data on the desktop. There are three possibilities that you have to take into account in your code.

Deleting a brand new record

The simplest record deletion method is to completely remove the record from the database (using `DmRemoveRecord`). This is used when the user creates a record but then

---

immediately decides to delete it. Since there's no corresponding record on the desktop, there's no information that needs to be maintained in the database. No synchronization will need to occur.

Deleting a record that exists also on the desktop

When a preexisting record is deleted, it also needs to be deleted on the desktop during the next sync. To handle this deletion from the desktop, the unique ID and attributes are still maintained in the database (but the record's memory chunk is freed). The deleted attribute of the record is set. The conduit looks for this bit setting and then deletes such records from the desktop and from the handheld on the next sync. DmDeleteRecord does this kind of deletion, leaving the record's unique ID and attributes in the database.

Deleting a record that the user wants archived

The final possibility is that the user requests that a deleted record be archived on the desktop. Figure 10-3 shows the dialog box that pops up after the user asks to delete a record. In this case, the memory chunk can't be freed (because the data must be copied to the desktop to be archived). The deleted bit is set and the memory chunk is maintained. It is treated on the handheld as if it were deleted. Once a sync occurs, the conduit copies the record to the desktop and then deletes it from the handheld database. DmArchiveRecord does this archiving.

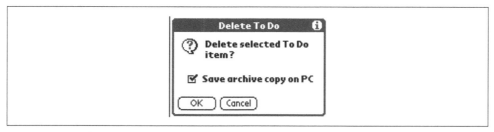

Figure 10-3. Dialog box allowing the user to archive a record on the desktop

Where to put archived and deleted records

For a sorted database, newly archived and deleted records should be moved to the end of the database. The sorting routines and DmFindSortPosition (discussed later this chapter) rely on archived and deleted records being at the end of the database. Example 10-12 shows the logic you'll probably want to use when the user deletes a record.

Example 10-12. Deleting a record per the user's request

```
Err UserDeletedRecord(DmOpenRef db, UInt16 recordNumber,
  Boolean wantsArchive, Boolean isSorted)
{
```

Example 10-12. Deleting a record per the user's request (continued)

```
  Err err;

  if (wantsArchive) //Need to archive it on PC.
    err = DmArchiveRecord(db, recordNumber);
  else
    err = DmDeleteRecord(db, recordNumber); // Leave the unique ID and attrs.
  // In sorted db, deleted records are stored at the end of the database.
  if (err == 0 && isSorted)
    err = DmMoveRecord (db, recordNumber, DmNumRecords(db));
  return err;
}
```

If the user doesn't explicitly request that a record be deleted, but implicitly requests it by deleting necessary data (e.g., ending up with an empty memo in the Memo Pad), you don't need to archive the record. Example 10-13 shows the code you use.

Example 10-13. Deleting an empty record

```
Err EmptyDeletedRecord(DmOpenRef db, UInt16 recordNumber,
  Boolean isSorted)
{
  Err err;

  err = DmDeleteRecord(db, recordNumber); // Leave the unique ID and attrs.
  // In sorted db, deleted records are stored at the end of the database.
  if (err == 0 && isSorted)
    err = DmMoveRecord (db, recordNumber, DmNumRecords(db));
  return err;
}
```

Handling Secret Records

In order for Palm OS users to feel comfortable maintaining sensitive information on their devices, the Palm OS supports *secret* (also called *private*) records. In the Security application, users can specify whether to show or hide private records. They can also specify passwords that are required before private records are shown.

Each record has a bit associated with it (in the record attributes) that indicates whether it is secret. As part of the mode you use when opening a database, you can request that secret records be skipped. "Opening a Database," earlier in this chapter, shows the code you need. Once you make that request, some of the database operations on that open database completely ignore secret records. The routines that take index numbers (like `DmGetRecord` or `DmQueryRecord`) don't ignore secret records, however, nor does `DmNumRecords`. `DmNumRecordsInCategory` and `DmSeekRecordInCategory` (only Data Manager routines that include the word `Category`) do ignore secret records, though. You can use these to find a correct index number.

The user sets the secret bit of a record in a Details dialog box for that record. Here is some code that retrieves the private setting:

```
Boolean IsPrivate(DmOpenRef db, UInt16 recordNumber)
{
  UInt16 attributes;

  DmRecordInfo(db, recordNumber, &attributes, NULL, NULL);
  return (Boolean) ((attributes & dmRecAttrSecret) == dmRecAttrSecret);
}
```

Example 10-14 shows a function that sets (or clears) the private bit.

Example 10-14. A function that sets or clears the private bit of a given record

```
Err SetPrivate(DmOpenRef db, UInt16 recordNumber, Boolean private)
{
  UInt16 attributes;
  Err    err;

  err = DmRecordInfo(db, recordNumber, &attributes, NULL, NULL);
  if (err)
    return err;
  if (private)
    attributes |= dmRecAttrSecret;
  else
    attributes &= ~dmRecAttrSecret;
  return DmSetRecordInfo(db, recordNumber, &attributes, NULL);
}
```

There is a UI requirement worth discussing here. Notice that we must put up an alert (see Figure 10-4) if the user marks a record as private while "Show all records" is enabled. As we are still showing private records, this might be confusing for a new user, who sees this private checkbox, marks something as private, and expects something to happen as a result.

Figure 10-4. Alert shown when user marks a record as private

Determining the Number of Records

You can determine the number of records with DmNumRecords:

```
UInt16 DmNumRecords(DmOpenRef db);
```

However, this counts all records, including private ones (regardless of the open mode) and deleted ones. In order to correctly handle those with different states, you'll need to use:

```
UInt16 DmNumRecordsInCategory(DmOpenRef db, UInt16 category);
```

Only category routines skip deleted records, and only category routines skip private records (if the open mode doesn't include dmModeShowSecret).

Iterating Through the Records in a Database

Whether you want only the items in a particular category or all the records, you still need to use category calls. These calls skip over deleted or archived (but still present) and private records (if the database is not opened with dmModeShowSecret).

DmQueryNextInCategory takes a database and a starting record number, and a category (or dmAllCategories). It starts from the given record number, searching linearly for a record that:

- Isn't deleted or archived (the delete bit is not set).
- Isn't private (if the database wasn't opened with dmModeShowSecret). If the database was opened with dmModeShowSecret, it ignores the private bit.
- Matches the given category (unless the category passed in was dmAllCategories, in which case, it ignores the category).

It returns the handle to the found record (or NULL if no record could be found), along with the found record number.

Example 10-15 shows code that uses DmQueryNextInCategory to visit every record.

Example 10-15. A routine that iterates through each nondeleted record

```
void VisitAllNonDeletedRecords(DmOpenRef db)
{
  UInt16 theCategory = dmAllCategories;     // Could be a specific category.
  UInt16 totalItems = DmNumRecordsInCategory(db, theCategory);
  UInt16 i;
  UInt16 recordNum = 0;

  for (i = 0; i < totalItems; i++, recordNum++) {
    MemHandle recordH = DmQueryNextInCategory (db, &recordNum,
      theCategory);

    Char *s = MemHandleLock(recordH);
      // At this point, recordNum contains the desired record number.
      // You could use DmGetRecord to get write-access and then
      // DmReleaseRecord when finished.

      // Do something with recordH.
    MemHandleUnlock(recordH);
  }
}
```

Finding a Record

If your records are sorted based on the value of a field (or fields) within the record, you can do a binary search to find a particular record. If your records aren't sorted (or you are looking for a record based on the value of an unsorted field), you need to iterate through all the records, testing each record to see whether it is the one you want. If you are looking for a unique ID, there's a call to find a record.

Finding a record given a unique ID

If you have the unique ID, you get the record number using `DmFindRecordByID`:

```
UInt16    recordNumber;
err = DmFindRecordByID(gDB, uniqueID, &recordNumber);
```

Note that this search starts at the first record and keeps looking until it finds the one with a matching unique ID.

Sorted Databases

Having a sorted database is common for a couple of reasons:

- The user can view the records in sorted order.
- Searching for a record based on the sort key can be fast (using binary search).

Comparison function

The Data Manager routines dealing with sorted databases require that you provide a comparison routine that compares two records and determines the ordering between the two. Here are the possible orderings:

- The first is greater than the second.
- The second is greater than the first.
- They are equal.

The comparison routine takes six parameters:

- Record 1
- Record 2
- An "other" integer for your own use
- The attributes and unique ID for record 1
- The attributes and unique ID for record 2
- The application info block

The extra parameters (beyond just the records) are there to allow sorting based on further information. This is information found outside the record and includes such things as attributes (its category, for instance), a unique ID, and a specified sort order. The "other" integer parameter is necessary whenever you call a routine that requires a comparison routine; it is then passed on to your comparison routine. This parameter could be used to pass a sort order to your sorting routine. Note that the application info block is rarely used as part of a comparison routine—although, it could perhaps be used to sort by alphabetized categories (first Business, then Personal, then Unfiled). Since the category names are stored in the application info block, it's needed by a comparison routine that wants to take into account category names.

The function in Example 10-16 compares first by lastName, then by firstName field. The attributes, unique ID, AppInfo block, and extra integer parameter aren't used.

Example 10-16. A comparison function that compares by last, then first name

```
Int16 CompareByLastThenFirst(void *r1, void *r2,
   Int16 unusedInt16, SortRecordInfoPtr unused1, SortRecordInfoPtr unused2,
   MemHandle appInfoH)
{
#pragma unused(unusedInt16, unused1, unused2, appInfoH)
  MyRecordType *rec1 = (MyRecordType *) r1;
  MyRecordType *rec2 = (MyRecordType *) r2;
  Int16    result;

  result = StrCompare(rec1->lastName, rec2->lastName);
  if (result == 0)
     result = StrCompare(rec1->firstName, rec2->firstName);
  return result;
}
```

The Data Manager assumes that sorted databases will always sort deleted (and archived) records at the end of the database. In fact, it won't even bother calling your comparison routine for deleted records; it assumes they always sort after any nondeleted records.

Adding in sort order

DmFindSortPosition returns the location at which to insert a new record:

```
UInt16    DmFindSortPosition(DmOpenRef dbP, void *newRecord,
          SortRecordInfoPtr newRecordInfo, DmComparF *compar, Int16 other)
```

The DmFindSortPosition finds a record (or finds where a record would be placed if it were in the database). It takes five parameters:

- The reference to the database
- The record for which to search (filled in with the fields the comparison routine will look for)
- The attributes and the unique ID for the record (if your comparison routine needs them, because the record you're passing in isn't necessarily part of the database and doesn't really have attributes or a unique ID)
- The comparison function
- The additional integer parameter to be passed to the comparison routine

DmFindSortPosition returns a number in the range 0..numberOfNonDeletedRecords. A return result of 0 signifies that the passed-in record is less than any existing records. A return result equal to the number of nondeleted records signifies that the passed-in record is ≥ the last nondeleted record. A return result, i, in the range 1.. numberOfNonDeletedRecords-1 signifies that *record i −1 ≤ passed-in record < record i.*

One use of DmFindSortPosition is to determine where to insert a new record. Example 10-17 creates a new record and inserts it at the appropriate location within an existing database.

Example 10-17. Routine that inserts a record into a sorted database

```
Err AddNewRecordInSortedOrder(DmOpenRef db)
{
  UInt16        recordIndex;
  MyRecordType  newRecord;
  MemHandle     myRecordHandle;
  MyRecordType  *newRecordPtr;
  Err           err;

  StrCopy(newRecord.firstName, "Neil");
  StrCopy(newRecord.lastName, "Rhodes");
  recordIndex = DmFindSortPosition(db, &newRecord, 0,
    CompareByLastThenFirst, 0);
  myRecordHandle = DmNewRecord(db, &recordIndex, sizeof(newRecord));
  newRecordPtr = MemHandleLock(myRecordHandle);
  err = DmWrite(newRecordPtr, 0, &newRecord, sizeof(newRecord));
  MemHandleUnlock(myRecordHandle);
  return err;
}
```

Finding a record given a key

If you have records sorted by some criterion, you can do a binary search to find a specific record. Another use of DmFindSortPosition is to find an existing record, if present. The only pitfall is DmFindSortPosition doesn't tell you whether it has found a matching record or not. Example 10-18 shows a routine that handles that shortcoming.

Example 10-18. Wrapper around DmFindSortPosition that tells whether a record already exists

```
// Returns true if record is in database (recordNumber contains location).
// Returns false if record is not there (recordNumber contains insertion pos.).
Boolean FindInSortedDatabase(DmOpenRef db, DmComparF *comparFunc,
  void *findRec, UInt16 *recordNumber)
{
  Boolean    foundIt = false;

  *recordNumber = DmFindSortPosition(db, findRec, NULL,
    comparFunc, 0);

  if (*recordNumber > 0) {
    MemHandle  h;
    void       *potentialMatchRec;
```

Example 10-18. Wrapper around DmFindSortPosition that tells whether a record already exists

```
      // Matching record would be at *recordNumber - 1.
      h = DmQueryRecord(db, *recordNumber - 1);
      potentialMatchRec = MemHandleLock(h);
      if ((*comparFunc)(findRec, potentialMatchRec, 0, NULL, NULL, NULL) == 0){
        foundIt = true;
        (*recordNumber)--;
      }
      MemHandleUnlock(h);
  }
  return foundIt;
}
```

You can call `FindInSortedDatabase` to find an existing record. If it returns `false`, the record isn't there (and `recordNumber` contains an appropriate location at which to insert the record with `DmNewRecord`). If it returns `true`, the record is there (and `recordNumber` has its location, which can be used with `DmQueryRecord` or `DmGetRecord`).

Sorting the records in a database

Just as finding an item in a sorted database requires a comparison routine, sorting a database requires a similar routine. There are two different sort routines you can use:

- `DmInsertionSort`
- `DmQuickSort`

The first, `DmInsertionSort`, uses an insertion sort. This is similar to the way most people sort a hand of cards, placing each card in its proper location one by one. The insertion sort works very quickly on an almost-sorted database. For example, if you change one record in a sorted database it may now be out of place while all the other records are still in sorted order. Use the insertion sort to put it back in order.

The second routine, `DmQuickSort`, uses a quick sort that successively partitions the records. If you don't know anything about the sort state of the database, use the quick sort. Changing the sort order (for instance, by name instead of by creation date) causes all records to be out of order. This is an excellent time to use the quick sort.

Insertion sort
```
      err = DmInsertionSort(db, CompareByFirstThenLast, 0);
```
Quick sort
```
      err = DmQuickSort(db, CompareByFirstThenLast, 0);
```

Both sorting routines put deleted and archived records at the end of the database (deleted records aren't passed to the comparison routine, since there's no record data). Keeping deleted and archived records at the end of the database isn't required for all databases, but it is a widely followed convention used by the sorting routines and by `DmFindSortPosition`.

One other difference between the two sorting routines is that DmInsertionSort is a stable sort, while DmQuickSort is not. That is, two records that compare the same will remain in the same relative order after DmInsertionSort, but might switch positions after DmQuickSort.

Sorting after a sync

If you have a conduit, you'll need to resort the records of your database after a sync. When a conduit adds (or modifies) records, they're always added at the end of the database, which can cause the database to become unsorted. Therefore, after a sync, your application should resort its database. The Memo Pad source code does an insertion sort after a sync (see Example 10-19).

Example 10-19. Memo Pad sorting after a sync

```
void MemoSort (DmOpenRef dbP)
{
  Int16 sortOrder;

  sortOrder = MemoGetSortOrder (dbP);
  if (sortOrder == soAlphabetic)
    DmInsertionSort (dbP, (DmComparF *) &MemoCompareRecords,
    (Int16) sortOrder);
}

void SyncNotification (void)
{
  DmOpenRef dbP;
  Err err;

  // Find the application's data file.
  err = MemoGetDatabase(&dbP, dmModeReadWrite);
  if (err)
    return;

  // Resort the database.
  MemoSort (dbP);

  DmCloseDatabase (dbP);
}

UInt32  PilotMain (UInt16 cmd, MemPtr cmdPBP, UInt16 launchFlags)
{
  ...
  else if (cmd == sysAppLaunchCmdSyncNotify)
    {
    SyncNotification ();
    }
  ...
}
```

The PilotMain is called after the sync. It calls SyncNotification, which opens the database, and then calls MemoSort, which sorts using DmInsertionSort.

Modifying a record in a sorted database

If you modify a record in a database that could change its sort order (for example, you change a memo in the Memo Pad, or the name in the Address Book), you'll need to resort the database. There are two different approaches:

- Resort the entire database.
- Remove the record from the database, and reinsert it in its new location.

Using the first approach, that of resorting, is very simple; it's just a call to DmInsertionSort. However, it's time-consuming. The second approach is quicker (logarithmic time), but requires more code. We don't actually want to remove the record from the database because that would free the record's contents. We could duplicate the record's contents, but that would require extra storage space, as well as the time we spend copying.

The Data Manager routine DmDetachRecord will *detach* a record from a database: it removes the record's entry from the database, but maintains the relocatable block containing the data. Similarly, one can *attach* an existing handle to a database with DmAttachRecord (unlike DmNewRecord, which actually creates a new handle). These routines can be used to move a record from one database to another (detach a record from the first and attach it to the second). We figured we might as well use them to detach a record from a database, and then reattach it at a different index on the same database. This is just what we need to resort the database.

Example 10-20 resorts a database with one out-of-place record.

Example 10-20. Resorting a record to its correct location

```
Err ResortOutOfPlaceRecord(DmOpenRef db, DmComparF *comparFunc,
  UInt16 outOfPlaceRecordNum)
{
  Err       err;
  MemHandle h;
  UInt16    attributes;
  UInt32    uniqueID;
  UInt16    newRecordNum;
  void      *p;

  err = DmRecordInfo(db, outOfPlaceRecordNum, &attributes, &uniqueID, NULL);
  if (err)
    return err;
  err = DmDetachRecord(db, outOfPlaceRecordNum, &h);
  if (err)
    return err;
  p = MemHandleLock(h);
  newRecordNum = DmFindSortPosition(db, p, NULL, comparFunc, 0);
  MemHandleUnlock(h);
  err = DmAttachRecord(db, &newRecordNum, h, NULL);
  if (err)
    return err;
  err = DmSetRecordInfo(db, newRecordNum, &attributes, &uniqueID);
```

Example 10-20. Resorting a record to its correct location (continued)

```
    return err;
}
```

Note that the routine must save the attributes and unique ID in order to restore them after reattaching the record.

You can't simplify this function to call DmFindSortPosition without calling DmDetachRecord first (with the modified record still in the database). DmFindSortPosition does a binary search and relies on the fact that all the records are in sorted order. It can return incorrect results if one or more of the records are not in order.

Dealing with Large Records

The maximum amount of data a record can hold is slightly less than 64 KB. If you have larger amounts of data to deal with, there are a couple of ways to tackle the problem. For example, let's say you'd like to store a JPEG image in each record, where the image can easily exceed 64 KB. To handle this problem you can either use file streaming or throw multiple chunks of the data into a different database.

File streaming

If you're using Palm OS 3.0 or greater, you can use the File Streaming Manager. The File Streaming Manager provides a file-based API (currently implemented as separate chunks within a database heap). You create a uniquely named file and a small record that stores only that filename. Use FileOpen to create a file:

```
UInt16    cardNo = 0;
Char      *uniqueFileName = "MyFile-CRTR";
FileHand  fileHandle;
Err       err;

fileHandle = FileOpen(cardNo, uniqueFileName, 'TYPE', 'CRTR',
    fileModeReadWrite, &err);
```

Store the unique filename as the contents of each record. Read and write with FileRead and FileWrite. When you are done reading and writing, close the file with FileClose. When you delete the record, you can delete the file with FileDelete.

One of the major disadvantages of file streams is that your conduit has no access to these files.

Multiple chunks in a separate database

If you can't use the File Streaming Manager, another solution open to you is to allocate multiple chunks in a separate database yourself. A record stores the unique IDs of each of the chunks in the separate chunk database. Here's a rough idea of how you might support a record of 500 KB (we'll have 10 records of 50 KB each). We assume we've got two open databases: db, where our "large" records are, and chunkDB, which contains our chunks. Example 10-21 shows code that allocates a new pseudo-500 KB record.

Example 10-21. Allocating one big pseudorecord as separate chunks

```
Err AllocateBigRecord(DmOpenRef db, DmOpenRef chunkDB)
{
#define kNumChunks 10
#define kChunkSize (50 * 1024L)
  typedef struct {
     UInt32 uniqueIDs[kNumChunks];
  } MyRecordType;
  MyRecordType  newRecord;
  MyRecordType  *newRecordPtr = 0;
  MemHandle     h;
  int           i;
  Err           err;

  MemSet(&newRecord, sizeof(newRecord), 0);
  for (i = 0; i < kNumChunks; i++) {
    UInt16   chunkRecordNumber = dmMaxRecordIndex;
    h = DmNewRecord(chunkDB, &chunkRecordNumber, kChunkSize);
    if (!h) {
      err = DmGetLastErr();
      break;
    }
    if ((err = DmRecordInfo(chunkDB, chunkRecordNumber, NULL,
        &newRecord.uniqueIDs[i], NULL)) != 0)
      break;
    DmReleaseRecord(chunkDB, chunkRecordNumber, true);
  }
  if (i >= kNumChunks) {
    // We were able to allocate all the chunks.
    UInt16 recordNumber = 0;
    h = DmNewRecord(db, &recordNumber, sizeof(MyRecordType));
    if (h) {
      newRecordPtr = MemHandleLock(h);
      DmWrite(newRecordPtr, 0, &newRecord, sizeof(newRecord));
      MemHandleUnlock(h);
      DmReleaseRecord(db, recordNumber, true);
    } else
      err = DmGetLastErr();
  }
  if (!err) {
    // Unable to allocate all chunks and record.
    // Delete all the chunks we allocated.
    for (i = 0; i < kNumChunks && newRecord.uniqueIDs[i] != 0; i++) {
      UInt16   recordNumToDelete;

      DmFindRecordByID(chunkDB, newRecord.uniqueIDs[i], &recordNumToDelete);
      DmRemoveRecord(chunkDB, recordNumToDelete);
    }
```

Example 10-21. Allocating one big pseudorecord as separate chunks (continued)

```
  }
  return err;
}
```

Note that if anything goes wrong in the process of creating these records, then we make sure to delete everything that has been allocated so far.

Now that you've allocated the record (and the chunks to which it points), it's fairly straightforward to edit any of the 500 KB of data. You use the unique ID to go into the appropriate chunk (reading it from the chunk database after finding the index with DmFindRecordByID).

Editing a Record in Place

The Field Manager can be set to edit a string field in place. The string need not take up the entire record; you specify the starting offset of the string and the current string length. The Field Manager resizes the handle as necessary while the string is edited.

This mechanism is a great way to handle editing a single string in a record. This doesn't work for multiples, however; you can't have multiple fields simultaneously editing multiple strings in a record. For example, if you have a record containing both last name and first name, you can't create two fields in a single form to edit both the last name and first name in place. (This makes sense because each of the fields may want to resize the single handle, and they don't have any way to coordinate with one another.)

The following sections show you the code that will do this edit job.

Initialize the field with the handle

Example 10-22 shows how to initialize the field with the handle.

Example 10-22. Initializing a field to edit a string within a record

```
void EditRecordInField(DmOpenRef db)
{
  FieldPtr    field;
  typedef struct {
      UInt16 field;
      // Other fields.
      Char textField[1]; // May actually be longer, null-terminated.
  } MyRecType;
  MemHandle   theRecordHandle;
  MemHandle   oldTextHandle = FldGetTextHandle(field);
  UInt16      theTextLength;
  UInt16      textOffset = OffsetOf(MyRecType, textField);

  if (oldTextHandle) {
      // Must dispose of the old handle or we'll leak memory.
      MemHandleFree(oldTextHandle);
```

Example 10-22. Initializing a field to edit a string within a record (continued)

```
   }
   theRecordHandle = DmGetRecord(db, recordNumber);
   theTextLength = (UInt16) MemHandleSize(theRecordHandle) - textOffset;
   FldSetText(field, theRecordHandle, textOffset, theTextLength);
}
```

As you remember from Chapter 8, the Field Manager won't deallocate a handle when you provide it a new one. Thus, in order to avoid a memory leak, our code must call MemHandleFree to free any existing handle that the field may have.

Cleanup once the editing is finished

When the editing is complete (this usually occurs when the form is closing), three things need to be taken care of:

1. Compact the text. When a field is edited, the text handle is resized in chunks rather than 1 byte at a time (otherwise, every single character a user enters would cause a memory allocation). Compacting the text resizes the text block to remove the extra space at the end of the block. Remember: memory is a scarce resource on the Palm OS, so do what you can to conserve it.

2. Reset the text handle. When a field is freed, it frees its text handle. We don't want the record in the database to be freed, so we set the field's handle to 0.

3. Release the record back to the database.

Here's the code:

```
   Boolean dirty = FldDirty(field);
   if (dirty)
      FldCompactText(field);
   FldSetTextHandle(field, NULL);
   DmReleaseRecord(db, recordNumber, dirty);
```

Examining Databases in the Sales Sample

Now that you understand how databases and records function within the storage heap space, let's look at how we use them in our Sales application.

Defining the Sales Databases

The Sales application has three different databases. The first holds customers, the second holds orders (one record for each order), and the third holds items. Here are the constant definitions for the names and types:

```
   #define kCustomerDBType  'Cust'
   #define kCustomerDBName  "Customers-SLES"
   #define kOrderDBType     'Ordr'
   #define kOrderDBName      "Orders-SLES"
```

```
#define kProductDBType  'Prod'
#define kProductDBName  "Products-SLES"
```

Reading and Writing the Customer

The customer is stored as the customer ID followed by four null-terminated strings back to back (it's "packed," so to speak). An alternative would have been to have four strings, each with a predefined maximum length. That would leave wasted space at the end of each string—a no-no on a device for which memory space is limited. Here's a structure we use for the customer record (there's no way to represent the four strings, so we just specify the first one):

```
typedef struct {
  Int32 customerID;
  char  name[1];  // Aactually may be longer than 1.
} PackedCustomer;
```

When we're working with a customer and need to access each of the fields, we use a different structure:

```
typedef struct {
  Int32   customerID;
  const char *name;
  const char *address;
  const char *city;
  const char *phone;
} Customer;
```

Example 10-23 is a routine that takes a locked PackedCustomer and fills out a customer ID—it unpacks the customer ID. Note that each field points into the PackedCustomer (to avoid allocating additional memory). The customer is valid only while the PackedCustomer remains locked (otherwise, the pointers are not valid).

Example 10-23. Unpacking back-to-back embedded strings

```
// packedCustomer must remain locked while customer is in use.
void UnpackCustomer(Customer *customer,
  const PackedCustomer *packedCustomer)
{
  const char *s = packedCustomer->name;
  customer->customerID = packedCustomer->customerID;
  customer->name = s;
  s += StrLen(s) + 1;
  customer->address = s;
  s += StrLen(s) + 1;
  customer->city = s;
  s += StrLen(s) + 1;
  customer->phone = s;
  s += StrLen(s) + 1;
}
```

We have an inverse routine that packs a customer (see Example 10-24). It takes a customer structure and packs it into a relocatable block (resizing the block as necessary).

Example 10-24. Packing a customer (back-to-back null-terminated strings)

```
void PackCustomer(Customer *customer, MemHandle customerDBEntry)
{
  // Figure out necessary size.
  UInt16    length = 0;
  Char    *s;
  UInt16    offset = 0;

  length = (UInt16) (sizeof(customer->customerID) + StrLen(customer->name) +
    StrLen(customer->address) + StrLen(customer->city) +
    StrLen(customer->phone) + 4); // 4 for string terminators.

  // Resize the MemHandle.
  if (MemHandleResize(customerDBEntry, length) == 0) {
    // Copy the fields.
    s = (Char *) MemHandleLock(customerDBEntry);
    offset = 0;
    DmWrite(s, offset, &customer->customerID,
      sizeof(customer->customerID));
    offset += (UInt16) StrLen(customer->customerID) + 1; /*1 for the Null terminator*/
    DmStrCopy(s, offset, customer->name);
    offset += (UInt16) StrLen(customer->name) + 1;
    DmStrCopy(s, offset, customer->address);
    offset += (UInt16) StrLen(customer->address) + 1;
    DmStrCopy(s, offset, customer->city);
    offset += (UInt16) StrLen(customer->city) + 1;
    DmStrCopy(s, offset, customer->phone);
    MemHandleUnlock(customerDBEntry);
  }
}
```

Reading and Writing Products

Similarly, we have structures for packed and unpacked products:

```
typedef struct {
  UInt32  productID;
  UInt32  price;  // In cents.
  const char  *name;
} Product;

typedef struct {
  UInt32  productID;
  UInt32  price;  // In cents.
  char  name[1];  // Actually may be longer than 1.
} PackedProduct;
```

Since the structure for packed and unpacked products is so similar, we could write our code not to distinguish between the two. However, in the future, we may want to represent the data in records differently from the data in memory. By separating the two now, we prepare for possible changes in the future.

The productID is unique within the database. We keep the price in cents so we don't have to deal with floating-point numbers.

Products are grouped in categories. The category (from 0 to 14) of the product record is set to its appropriate category when the product is created. The category names are stored in a category structure in the AppInfo block of the product's database:

```
typedef char  CategoryName[16];

typedef struct {
  UInt16       numCategories;
  CategoryName  names[1];
} CategoriesStruct;
```

We have routines that pack and unpack a product (see Example 10-25).

Example 10-25. Packing and unpacking products

```
void PackProduct(Product *product, MemHandle productDBEntry)
{
  // Figure out necessary size.
  UInt16    length = 0;
  Char      *s;
  UInt16    offset = 0;
  length = (UInt16) (sizeof(product->productID) + sizeof(product->price) +
    StrLen(product->name) + 1);

  // Resize the MemHandle.
  if (MemHandleResize(productDBEntry, length) == errNone) {
    // Copy the fields.
    s = (Char *) MemHandleLock(productDBEntry);
    DmWrite(s, OffsetOf(PackedProduct, productID), &product->productID,
      sizeof(product->productID));
    DmWrite(s, OffsetOf(PackedProduct, price), &product->price,
      sizeof(product->price));
    DmStrCopy(s, OffsetOf(PackedProduct, name), product->name);
    MemHandleUnlock(productDBEntry);
  }
}

// packedProduct must remain locked while product is in use.
void UnpackProduct(Product *product,
  const PackedProduct *packedProduct)
{
  product->productID = packedProduct->productID;
  product->price = packedProduct->price;
  product->name = packedProduct->name;
}
```

Working with Orders

Orders have a variable number of items:

```
typedef struct {
  UInt32  productID;
  UInt32  quantity;
} Item;
```

```
typedef struct {
  Int32 customerID;
  UInt16 numItems;
  Item  items[1]; // This array will actually be numItems long.
} Order;
```

There is zero or one order per customer. An order is matched to its customer via the customerID.

We have variables for the open databases:

```
DmOpenRef   gCustomerDB;
DmOpenRef   gOrderDB;
DmOpenRef   gProductDB;
```

Creating or Opening the Databases

Example 10-26 shows our AppStart, which opens each of the three databases. Brand new databases get initialized with some predefined data.

Example 10-26. AppStart for the Sales sample

```
Err AppStart(void)
{
  SalesPreferenceType prefs;
  UInt16              prefsSize;
  UInt16              mode = dmModeReadWrite;
  Err                 err = errNone;
  CategoriesStruct    *c;
  Boolean             created;

  // Read the preferences / saved-state information.  There is only one
  // version of the preferences, so don't worry about multiple versions.

  prefsSize = sizeof(SalesPreferenceType);
  if (PrefGetAppPreferences(kSalesCreator, kSalesPrefID, &prefs,
    &prefsSize, true) == noPreferenceFound) {
    ExgRegisterData(kSalesCreator, exgRegExtensionID, "cst");
  } else {
    gSaveBackup = prefs.saveBackup;
  }

  // Determime if secret records should be shown.
  gHideSecretRecords =
    (Boolean) PrefGetPreference(prefHidePrivateRecordsV33);
  if (!gHideSecretRecords)
    mode |= dmModeShowSecret;

  // Find the Customer database.  If it doesn't exist, create it.
  OpenOrCreateDB(&gCustomerDB, kCustomerDBType, kSalesCreator, mode,
    0, kCustomerDBName, &created);
  if (created)
    InitializeCustomers();

  // Find the Order database.  If it doesn't exist, create it.
```

Example 10-26. AppStart for the Sales sample (continued)

```
OpenOrCreateDB(&gOrderDB, kOrderDBType, kSalesCreator, mode,
  0, kOrderDBName, &created);
if (created)
  InitializeOrders();

// Find the Product database.  If it doesn't exist, create it.
OpenOrCreateDB(&gProductDB, kProductDBType, kSalesCreator, mode,
  0, kProductDBName, &created);
if (created)
  InitializeProducts();

c = (CategoriesStruct *) GetLockedAppInfo();
gNumCategories = c->numCategories;
MemPtrUnlock(c);

return err;
}
```

Example 10-27 shows a utility routine to open (and create, if necessary) each database.

Example 10-27. Utility routine that opens a database, first creating it if it doesn't exist

```
// Open a database. If it doesn't exist, create it.
Err OpenOrCreateDB(DmOpenRef *dbP, UInt32 type, UInt32 creator,
  UInt16 mode, UInt16 cardNo, char *name, Boolean *created)
{
  Err err = errNone;

  *created = false;
  *dbP = DmOpenDatabaseByTypeCreator(type, creator, mode);
  if (! *dbP)
  {
    err = DmGetLastErr();
    if (err == dmErrCantFind)
      err = DmCreateDatabase(cardNo, name, creator, type, false);
    if (err != errNone)
      return err;
    *created = true;

    *dbP = DmOpenDatabaseByTypeCreator(type, creator, mode);
    if (! *dbP)
      return DmGetLastErr();
  }
  return err;
}
```

It uses another utility routine to read the categories from the application info block for the product database (see Example 10-28).

Example 10-28. Retrieving the AppInfo chunk

```
void *GetLockedAppInfo(DmOpenRef db)
{
```

Example 10-28. Retrieving the AppInfo chunk (continued)

```
  UInt16  cardNo;
  LocalID dbID;
  LocalID appInfoID;
  Err     err;

  if ((err = DmOpenDatabaseInfo(db, &dbID, NULL, NULL,
    &cardNo, NULL)) != errNone)
    return NULL;
  if ((err = DmDatabaseInfo(cardNo, dbID, NULL, NULL, NULL, NULL, NULL,
    NULL, NULL, &appInfoID, NULL, NULL, NULL)) != errNone)
    return NULL;
  return MemLocalIDToLockedPtr(appInfoID, cardNo);
}
```

Closing the Sales Databases

When the application closes, it has to close the databases (see Example 10-29).

Example 10-29. AppStop writes preferences, closes forms, and closes databases

```
void AppStop(void)
{
  SalesPreferenceType prefs;

  // Write the preferences / saved-state information.
  prefs.saveBackup = gSaveBackup;
  PrefSetAppPreferences(kSalesCreator, kSalesPrefID, kSalesVersion, &prefs,
    sizeof(SalesPreferenceType), true);

  // Close all open forms. This will force any unsaved data to
  // be written to the database.
  FrmCloseAllForms();

  // Close the databases.
  DmCloseDatabase(gCustomerDB);
  DmCloseDatabase(gOrderDB);
  DmCloseDatabase(gProductDB);
}
```

Initializing the Sales Databases

We have routines to initialize each of the databases. At some point, these routines could be removed (instead, our conduit would initialize the database during a sync). For now, though, this gives the first-time user of our application more than just a blank slate.

Initializing the customer database

Example 10-30 shows the initialization routine for Customers.

Example 10-30. Initializing a brand new Customers database

```
void InitializeCustomers(void)
{
  Customer  c1 = {1, "Joe's toys-1", "123 Main St." ,"Anytown",
   "(123) 456-7890"};
  Customer  c2 = {2, "Bucket of Toys-2", "" ,"", ""};
  Customer  c3 = {3, "Toys we be-3", "" ,"", ""};
  Customer  c4 = {4, "a", "" ,"", ""};
  Customer  c5 = {5, "b", "" ,"", ""};
  Customer  c6 = {6, "c", "" ,"", ""};
  Customer  c7 = {7, "d", "" ,"", ""};
  Customer  *customers[7];
  UInt16  numCustomers = sizeof(customers) / sizeof(customers[0]);
  UInt16  i;

  customers[0] = &c1;
  customers[1] = &c2;
  customers[2] = &c3;
  customers[3] = &c4;
  customers[4] = &c5;
  customers[5] = &c6;
  customers[6] = &c7;
  for (i = 0; i < numCustomers; i++) {
    UInt16  index = dmMaxRecordIndex;
    MemHandle h = DmNewRecord(gCustomerDB, &index, 1);
    if (h) {
      PackCustomer(customers[i], h);
      DmReleaseRecord(gCustomerDB, index, true);
    }
  }
}
```

Initializing the product database

We have a similar routine to initialize Products (see Example 10-31).

Example 10-31. Initializing a brand new Products database

```
void InitializeProducts(void)
{
#define kMaxPerCategory 4
#define kNumCategories 3
  Product prod1 = {125, 253, "GI-Joe"};
  Product prod2 = {135, 1122, "Barbie"};
  Product prod3 = {145, 752, "Ken"};
  Product prod4 = {9,   852, "Skipper"};
  Product prod5 = {126, 253, "Kite"};
  Product prod6 = {127, 350, "Silly-Putty"};
  Product prod7 = {138, 650, "Yo-yo"};
  Product prod8 = {199, 950, "Legos"};
  Product prod9 = {120, 999, "Monopoly"};
  Product prod10= {129, 888, "Yahtzee"};
  Product prod11= {10, 899, "Life"};
  Product prod12= {20, 1199, "Battleship"};
```

Example 10-31. Initializing a brand new Products database (continued)

```
Product *products[kNumCategories][kMaxPerCategory];
UInt16  i;
UInt16  j;
MemHandle h;

products[0][0] = &prod1;
products[0][1] = &prod2;
products[0][2] = &prod3;
products[0][3] = &prod4;
products[1][0] = &prod5;
products[1][1] = &prod6;
products[1][2] = &prod7;
products[1][3] = &prod8;
products[2][0] = &prod9;
products[2][1] = &prod10;
products[2][2] = &prod11;
products[2][3] = &prod12;
for (i = 0; i < kNumCategories; i++) {
  for (j = 0; j < kMaxPerCategory && products[i][j]->name; j++) {
    UInt16      index;
    PackedProduct findRecord;
    MemHandle     h;

    findRecord.productID = products[i][j]->productID;
    index = DmFindSortPosition(gProductDB, &findRecord, 0,
      (DmComparF* ) CompareIDFunc, 0);
    h = DmNewRecord(gProductDB, &index, 1);
    if (h) {
      UInt16  attr;
      // Set the category of the new record to the category in which it
      // belongs.
      DmRecordInfo(gProductDB, index, &attr, NULL, NULL);
      attr &= (UInt16) ~dmRecAttrCategoryMask;
      attr |= (UInt16) i;      // Category is kept in low bits of attr.

      DmSetRecordInfo(gProductDB, index, &attr, NULL);
      PackProduct(products[i][j], h);
      DmReleaseRecord(gProductDB, index, true);
    }
  }
}

h = DmNewHandle(gProductDB,
  OffsetOf(CategoriesStruct, names[kNumCategories]));
if (h) {
  char  *categories[] = {"Dolls", "Toys", "Games"};
  CategoriesStruct  *c = (CategoriesStruct *) MemHandleLock(h);
  LocalID       dbID;
  LocalID       appInfoID;
  UInt16        cardNo;
  UInt16        num = kNumCategories;
  Err        err;
```

Example 10-31. Initializing a brand new Products database (continued)

```
    DmWrite(c, OffsetOf(CategoriesStruct, numCategories), &num,
      sizeof(num));
    for (i = 0; i < kNumCategories; i++)
      DmStrCopy(c,
        OffsetOf(CategoriesStruct, names[i]), categories[i]);
        MemHandleUnlock(h);
    appInfoID = MemHandleToLocalID( h);
    err = DmOpenDatabaseInfo(gProductDB, &dbID, NULL, NULL,
      &cardNo, NULL);
    if (err == errNone) {
      err = DmSetDatabaseInfo(cardNo, dbID, NULL, NULL, NULL, NULL,
        NULL, NULL, NULL, &appInfoID, NULL, NULL, NULL);
      ErrNonFatalDisplayIf(err, "DmSetDatabaseInfo failed");
    }
  }
}
```

The code inserts the products sorted by product ID (an alternative would be to create the products in unsorted order and then sort them afterward). Note also that the attributes of each record are modified to set the category of the product.

Comparison routine for sorting

Example 10-32 shows the comparison routine used for sorting products, companies, and orders.

Example 10-32. Comparison routine compares IDs at the beginning of a record

```
Int16 CompareIDFunc(Int32 *p1, Int32 *p2, Int16 i,
  SortRecordInfoPtr s1, SortRecordInfoPtr s2, MemHandle appInfoH)
{
#pragma unused(i, s1, s2, appInfoH)
  // Can't just return *p1 - *p2 because that's a Int32 that may overflow
  // our return type of Int16.  Therefore, we do the comparison ourselves
  // and check.
  if (*p1 < *p2)
    return -1;
  else if (*p1 > *p2)
    return 1;
  else
    return 0;
}
```

Initializing the Orders database

Finally, Orders must be initialized (see Example 10-33).

Example 10-33. Initializing a brand new Orders database

```
void InitializeOrders(void)
{
  Item item1 = {125, 253};
  Item item2 = {126, 999};
```

Example 10-33. Initializing a brand new Orders database (continued)

```
Item item3 =  {127, 888};
Item item4 =  {138, 777};
Item item5 =  {125, 6};
Item item6 =  {120, 5};
Item item7 =  {129, 5};
Item item8 =  {10,  3};
Item item9 =  {20,  45};
Item item10 = {125, 66};
Item item11 = {125, 75};
Item item12 = {125, 23};
Item item13 = {125, 55};
Item item14 = {125, 888};
Item item15 = {125, 456};
Item items[15];
MemHandle h;
Order   *order;
UInt16  recordNum;
UInt16  numItems = sizeof(items) / sizeof(items[0]);

items[0]  =  item1;
items[1]  =  item2;
items[2]  =  item3;
items[3]  =  item4;
items[4]  =  item5;
items[5]  =  item6;
items[6]  =  item7;
items[7]  =  item8;
items[8]  =  item9;
items[9]  =  item10;
items[10] =  item11;
items[11] =  item12;
items[12] =  item13;
items[13] =  item14;
items[14] =  item15;

order= GetOrCreateOrderForCustomer(1, &recordNum);

// Write numItems.
DmWrite(order, OffsetOf(Order, numItems), &numItems, sizeof(numItems));

// Resize to hold more items.
h = MemPtrRecoverHandle(order);
MemHandleUnlock(h);
MemHandleResize(h, OffsetOf(Order, items) + sizeof(Item) * numItems);
order = (Order *) MemHandleLock(h);

// Write new items.
DmWrite(order, OffsetOf(Order, items), items, sizeof(items));

// Done with it.
MemHandleUnlock(h);
DmReleaseRecord(gOrderDB, recordNum, true);
}
```

`OrderRecordNumber` returns the record number of a customer's order or the location at which the order should be inserted, if no such order exists (see Example 10-34).

Example 10-34. Returns a record number for Order

```
// Returns record number for order, if it exists, or where it
// should be inserted.
UInt16 OrderRecordNumber(Int32 customerID, Boolean *orderExists)
{
  Order    findRecord;
  UInt16   recordNumber;

  *orderExists = false;
  findRecord.customerID = customerID;
  recordNumber = DmFindSortPosition(gOrderDB, &findRecord, 0,
    (DmComparF *) CompareIDFunc, 0);

  if (recordNumber > 0) {
    Order *order;
    MemHandle theOrderHandle;
    Boolean foundIt;

    theOrderHandle = DmQueryRecord(gOrderDB, recordNumber - 1);
    ErrNonFatalDisplayIf(!theOrderHandle, "DMGetRecord failed!");

    order = (Order *) MemHandleLock(theOrderHandle);
    foundIt = (Boolean) (order->customerID == customerID);
    MemHandleUnlock(theOrderHandle);
    if (foundIt) {
      *orderExists = true;
      return recordNumber - 1;
    }
  }
  return recordNumber;
}
```

The Customers Form

Let's now look at how the customers are displayed in the Customers form. Customers are displayed in a list that has a drawing callback function that displays the customer for a particular row (see Example 10-35). The customers that already have an order are shown in bold to distinguish them from the others. The text pointer is unused, since we don't store our customer names in the list, but obtain them from the database.

Example 10-35. Draws a customer in a list (bold if there is no associated order)

```
void DrawOneCustomerInListWithFont(Int16 itemNumber, RectanglePtr bounds, Char **text)
{
#pragma unused(text)
  MemHandle h;
  UInt16   index = 0;

  // Must do seek to skip over secret records.
```

Example 10-35. Draws a customer in a list (bold if there is no associated order) (continued)

```
DmSeekRecordInCategory(gCustomerDB, &index,  (UInt16) itemNumber,
  dmSeekForward, dmAllCategories);
h = DmQueryRecord(gCustomerDB, index);
if (h) {
  FontID  curFont;
  Boolean setFont = false;
  PackedCustomer  *packedCustomer = (PackedCustomer *) MemHandleLock(h);

  if (!OrderExistsForCustomer(packedCustomer->customerID)) {
    setFont = true;
    curFont = FntSetFont(boldFont);
  }
  DrawCharsToFitWidth(packedCustomer->name, bounds);
  MemHandleUnlock(h);

  if (setFont)
    FntSetFont(curFont);
}
}
```

The routine uses two other routines: one that finds the customer ID for a specific row number and one that tells whether an order exists. Example 10-36 shows the routine that returns a unique ID.

Example 10-36. Returns the customer ID number of the Nth displayed customer

```
Int32 GetCustomerIDForNthCustomer(UInt16 itemNumber)
{
  Int32           customerID;
  UInt16          index = 0;
  MemHandle       h;
  PackedCustomer *packedCustomer;

  // Must do seek to skip over secret records.
  DmSeekRecordInCategory(gCustomerDB, &index, itemNumber, dmSeekForward,
    dmAllCategories);
  h = DmQueryRecord(gCustomerDB, index);
  ErrNonFatalDisplayIf(!h,
    "can't get customer in GetCustomerIDForNthCustomer");
  packedCustomer = (PackedCustomer *) MemHandleLock(h);
  customerID = packedCustomer->customerID;
  MemHandleUnlock(h);

  return customerID;
}
```

Note the use of `DmSeekRecordInCategory`, which skips over any secret records. Here's the code that calls `OrderRecordNumber` to figure out whether an order exists (so that the customer name can be bolded or not):

```
Boolean OrderExistsForCustomer(Int32 customerID)
{
  Boolean orderExists;
```

```
        OrderRecordNumber(customerID, &orderExists);
        return orderExists;
    }
```

Editing Customers

Example 10-37 shows the EditCustomerWithSelection routine that handles editing
customers, deleting customers, and setting/clearing the private record attribute
through the Customer Information dialog box. The gotoData parameter is used to
preselect some text in a field (used for displaying the results of a Find).

Example 10-37. Edits customer (as specified by the reorder number)

```
// isNew is true if this is a brand-new customer.
void EditCustomerWithSelection(UInt16 recordNumber, Boolean isNew,
  Boolean *deleted, Boolean *hidden, EventPtr event)
{
  FormPtr    frm;
  UInt16     hitButton;
  Boolean    dirty = false;
  ControlPtr privateCheckbox;
  UInt16     attributes;
  Boolean    isSecret;
  FieldPtr   nameField;
  FieldPtr   addressField;
  FieldPtr   cityField;
  FieldPtr   phoneField;
  Customer   theCustomer;
  UInt16     offset = OffsetOf(PackedCustomer, name);
  MemHandle  customerHandle = DmGetRecord(gCustomerDB, recordNumber);

  *hidden = *deleted = false;
  DmRecordInfo(gCustomerDB, recordNumber, &attributes, NULL, NULL);
  isSecret = (Boolean) ((attributes & dmRecAttrSecret) == dmRecAttrSecret);

  frm = FrmInitForm(CustomerForm);

  UnpackCustomer(&theCustomer, (PackedCustomer *) MemHandleLock(customerHandle));

  nameField = (FieldPtr) FrmGetObjectPtr(frm, FrmGetObjectIndex(frm, CustomerNameField));
  addressField = (FieldPtr) FrmGetObjectPtr(frm, FrmGetObjectIndex(frm,
CustomerAddressField));
  cityField = (FieldPtr) FrmGetObjectPtr(frm, FrmGetObjectIndex(frm, CustomerCityField));
  phoneField = (FieldPtr) FrmGetObjectPtr(frm, FrmGetObjectIndex(frm,
CustomerPhoneField));

  // Code deleted that initializes the fields.

  // Unlock the customer.
  MemHandleUnlock(customerHandle);

  privateCheckbox = (ControlPtr) FrmGetObjectPtr(frm, FrmGetObjectIndex(frm,
CustomerPrivateCheckbox));
```

```
    CtlSetValue(privateCheckbox, isSecret);

  hitButton = FrmDoDialog(frm);

  if (hitButton == CustomerOKButton) {
    dirty = FldDirty(nameField) || FldDirty(addressField) ||
      FldDirty(cityField) || FldDirty(phoneField);
    if (dirty) {
        // Code deleted that reads the fields into theCustomer.
    }
    PackCustomer(&theCustomer, customerHandle);
    if (CtlGetValue(privateCheckbox) != isSecret) {
      dirty = true;
      if (CtlGetValue(privateCheckbox)) {
        attributes |= dmRecAttrSecret;
        // Tell user how to hide private records.
        if (gHideSecretRecords)
          *hidden = true;
        else
          FrmAlert(privateRecordInfoAlert);
      } else
        attributes &= (UInt8) ~dmRecAttrSecret;
      DmSetRecordInfo(gCustomerDB, recordNumber, &attributes, NULL);
    }
  }
  FrmDeleteForm(frm);

  DmReleaseRecord(gCustomerDB, recordNumber, dirty);
  if (hitButton == CustomerDeleteButton) {
    *deleted = true;
    if (isNew && !gSaveBackup)
      DmRemoveRecord(gCustomerDB, recordNumber);
    else {
      if (gSaveBackup)  // Need to archive it on PC.
        DmArchiveRecord(gCustomerDB, recordNumber);
      else
        DmDeleteRecord(gCustomerDB, recordNumber);
      // Deleted records are stored at the end of the database.
      DmMoveRecord(gCustomerDB, recordNumber, DmNumRecords(gCustomerDB));
    }
  }
  else if (hitButton == CustomerOKButton && isNew &&
    !(StrLen(theCustomer.name) || StrLen(theCustomer.address) ||
    StrLen(theCustomer.city) || StrLen(theCustomer.phone))) {
    *deleted = true;
    // Delete Customer if it is new and empty.
    DmRemoveRecord(gCustomerDB, recordNumber);
  }
  else if (hitButton == CustomerCancelButton && isNew) {
    *deleted = true;
    DmRemoveRecord(gCustomerDB, recordNumber);
  }
}
```

The Order Form

Now look at how we handle the Order form, which is what the customers use to add, delete, or modify the quantity of an item.

Editing an item

Here's a snippet of code from `OrderSaveAmount` that modifies the quantity if it has been edited:

```
Char  *textP = FldGetTextPtr(fld);
UInt32 newQuantity = 0;

if (textP)
  newQuantity = (UInt32) StrAToI(textP);
DmWrite(gCurrentOrder,
  OffsetOf(Order, items[gCurrentSelectedItemIndex].quantity),
  &newQuantity, sizeof(newQuantity));
gCurrentOrderChanged = true;
```

Note that `DmWrite` is used to modify `gCurrentOrder`, since `gCurrentOrder` is a record in the order database and can't be written to directly.

Deleting an item

We need to delete an item in certain circumstances (if the user explicitly chooses to delete an item, or sets the quantity to 0, and then stops editing that item). Example 10-38 shows how (note that it uses `DmWrite` to move succeeding items forward and uses `MemPtrResize` to make the record smaller).

Example 10-38. Deletes specified item from the current order

```
// gCurrentOrder changes after this routine. gCurrentItem is no longer valid.
void DeleteNthItem(UInt16 itemNumber)
{
  UInt16    newNumItems;

  ErrNonFatalDisplayIf(itemNumber >= gCurrentOrder->numItems,
    "bad itemNumber");

  // Move items from itemNumber+1..numItems down 1 to
  // itemNumber .. numItems - 1.
  if (itemNumber < gCurrentOrder->numItems - 1)
    DmWrite(gCurrentOrder,
      OffsetOf(Order, items[itemNumber]),
      &gCurrentOrder->items[itemNumber+1],
      (gCurrentOrder->numItems - itemNumber - 1) * sizeof(Item));

  // Decrement numItems.
  newNumItems = gCurrentOrder->numItems - 1;
  DmWrite(gCurrentOrder,
    OffsetOf(Order, numItems), &newNumItems, sizeof(newNumItems));

  // Resize the pointer smaller. We could use MemPtrRecoverHandle,
```

Example 10-38. Deletes specified item from the current order (continued)

```
  // MemHandleUnlock, MemHandleResize, MemHandleLock.
  // However, MemPtrResize will always work
  // as long as you are making a chunk smaller.  Thanks, Bob!
  MemPtrResize(gCurrentOrder,
    OffsetOf(Order, items[gCurrentOrder->numItems]));
}
```

Adding a new item

Similarly, we must have a routine to add a new item (see Example 10-39).

Example 10-39. Adds an item to the current order

```
Boolean AddNewItem(UInt16 *itemNumber)
{
  MemHandle theOrderHandle;
  UInt16  numItems;
  Item  newItem = {0, 0};
  MemHandle oldHandle;

  ErrFatalDisplayIf(!gCurrentOrder, "no current order");
  theOrderHandle = MemPtrRecoverHandle(gCurrentOrder);
  MemHandleUnlock(theOrderHandle);

  oldHandle = theOrderHandle;
  theOrderHandle = DmResizeRecord(gOrderDB, gCurrentOrderIndex,
    MemHandleSize(theOrderHandle) + sizeof(Item));
  if (!theOrderHandle) {
    gCurrentOrder = (Order *) MemHandleLock(oldHandle);
    FrmAlert(DeviceIsFullAlert);
    return false;
  }
  gCurrentOrder = (Order *) MemHandleLock(theOrderHandle);
  numItems = gCurrentOrder->numItems + 1;
  DmWrite(gCurrentOrder, OffsetOf(Order, numItems), &numItems,
    sizeof(numItems));
  *itemNumber = gCurrentOrder->numItems - 1;
  DmWrite(gCurrentOrder, OffsetOf(Order, items[*itemNumber]), &newItem,
    sizeof(newItem));
  gCurrentOrderChanged = true;
  return true;
}
```

Note that if we can't resize the handle, we display the system alert telling the user that the device is full.

Finishing an Order record

When the Order form is closed, the records in the Order database must be updated. If there are no items, the entire order is deleted (see Example 10-40).

Example 10-40. Closing the Order form

```
void OrderFormClose(void)
{
  UInt16    numItems;
  MemHandle theOrderHandle;

  OrderDeselectRowAndDeleteIfEmpty(true);
  numItems = gCurrentOrder->numItems;
  // Unlock the order.
  theOrderHandle = MemPtrRecoverHandle(gCurrentOrder);
  MemHandleUnlock(theOrderHandle);

  // Delete Order if it is empty; release it back to the database otherwise.
  if (numItems == 0)
    DmRemoveRecord(gOrderDB, gCurrentOrderIndex);
  else
    DmReleaseRecord(gOrderDB, gCurrentOrderIndex, gCurrentOrderChanged);

  MemPtrFree(gFields);
}
```

The Item Form

Once the form is initialized, the user interacts with it until a button is tapped. The event handler for the form handles the button tap (see Example 10-41).

Example 10-41. Handling events while displaying the Item dialog box

```
Boolean ItemHandleEvent(EventPtr event)
{
  Boolean   handled = false;
  FieldPtr  fld;

  switch (event->eType) {
    case ctlSelectEvent:
      switch (event->data.ctlSelect.controlID) {
      case ItemOKButton:
        {
          char   *textPtr;
          UInt32  quantity;

          fld = (FieldPtr) GetObjectFromActiveForm(ItemQuantityField);
          textPtr = FldGetTextPtr(fld);
          ErrNonFatalDisplayIf(!textPtr, "No quantity text");
          quantity = (UInt32) StrAToI(textPtr);
          DmWrite(gCurrentOrder,
            OffsetOf(Order, items[gCurrentItemNumber].quantity),
            &quantity, sizeof(quantity));

          if (gHaveProductIndex) {
            MemHandle     h;
            PackedProduct *p;
```

```
            h = DmQueryRecord(gProductDB, gCurrentProductIndex);
            ErrNonFatalDisplayIf(!h, "Can't find the record");
            p = (PackedProduct *) MemHandleLock(h);
            DmWrite(gCurrentOrder,
              OffsetOf(Order, items[gCurrentItemNumber].productID),
              &p->productID, sizeof(p->productID));
            MemHandleUnlock(h);
          }
      }
      break;

    case ItemCancelButton:
      break;

    case ItemDeleteButton:
      if (FrmAlert(DeleteItemAlert) == DeleteItemOK)
          DeleteNthItem(gCurrentItemNumber);
      else
        handled = true;
      break;
      }
      break;

    case popSelectEvent:
      if (event->data.popSelect.listID == ItemProductsList){
      HandleClickInProductPopup(event);
      handled = true;
      }
      break;
    }
  return handled;
}
```

If the user taps OK, the code updates the quantity and product ID of the current item (if the user has edited it). If the user taps Delete, the code calls `DeleteNthItem` (which we've already seen). On a Cancel, the code doesn't modify the current order.

Summary

In this chapter, you learned how data is organized on the Palm OS and its devices. We showed you how to work with databases (creating, opening, and closing them). You learned how to deal with individual data records and how they interact with the databases in which they are stored. We described how to deal with records that are larger than 64K in size and how to handle secret records. We dealt with handling the sorting of databases, what methods to use in which circumstances, and how to handle a database with only one modified record.

You should now be able to create your own databases and records based on the Sales application source code.

<table>
<tr><td>
In this chapter:
- Menu User Interface
- Menu Resources
- Application Code for Menus
- Adding Menus to the Sample Application
- Summary
</td></tr>
</table>

CHAPTER 11

Menus

In this chapter, we explain how to create menus. Along with a discussion of the menu source code, we highlight potential problems and show workarounds. First things first, however: before you can code an application's menus, you need to know how to design them. That is a UI issue.

Menu User Interface

Palm application menus should look the same from application to application; they should share a consistent organization and set of menu items. Indeed, some menus, such as the Edit menu, should be identically organized regardless of the application.

Figure 11-1 shows a sample menu bar containing two menus: Customer and Options. The open Customer menu contains two menu items: New Customer and Beam all Customers.

Figure 11-1. Application menu bar, menus, and menu items

Note that menu items commonly have shortcuts associated with them. These are Graffiti letters that are unique to each menu item. By doing the stroke-and-letter shortcut, the user can perform the operation without first selecting the menu item.

For example, **/ N** brings up a New Customer form. As a rule, you should add these shortcuts to menu items wherever necessary and always with standard menu items. Make sure that the most frequent operations have shortcuts, and don't put a shortcut on an infrequent action (such as the About box).

Arranging Menus

Menus can also be arranged with separator bars in them to group similar items together (see Figure 11-2). Note that menus and menu items are never dimmed (grayed out). We discuss how to handle menu items that aren't applicable in certain situations in "Handling Unusable Menu Items" later in this chapter.

Standard Menu Items

There are some standards menu items your application should have.

Edit menu

A form with editable text fields should have an Edit menu containing the standard Undo, Cut, Copy, Paste, Select All, Keyboard, and Graffiti Help (see Figure 11-2).

Figure 11-2. The Order form of the Sales application with the Edit menu open

 Password dialog boxes shouldn't support Cut, Copy, or Paste.

About application

You should have an About *MyApplication* menu item; it is usually found in an Options menu. This item should bring up an alert or dialog box containing information about your application (the creator, version number, name, email address, web site, and technical support information). This dialog box is often called an About box.

Applications Can Have Multiple Sets of Menus

A set of menus is always associated with a particular form or window in the application. Thus, if you look at the Order form of our Sales application in Figure 11-2, you see that it has its own new set of menus.

You should also note that different forms in an application may share a similar set of menus and menu items. For example, the Order form and the Customer Details form both have Edit menus (see Figure 11-3).

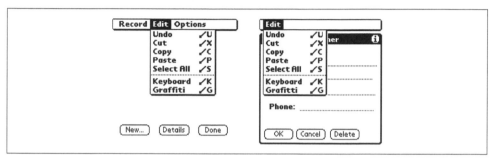

Figure 11-3. The Edit menu in two different forms

Applications Can Have Dynamic Menus

As of Palm OS 3.5, applications can also have menus that change at runtime. You can add, hide, or unhide menu items as the menu resource is being loaded. This allows you to customize the menus based on runtime information (for example, a certain menu item might only be available if an application is running on specific hardware).

That's about all of the important UI issues that you encounter in dealing with menus. Now, let's look at how to create menus.

Common Menu Shortcuts

Table 11-1 contains common menus and the standard shortcut letters used with them. Keep the same letters so that users can expect the same behavior from different applications. Items with asterisks are less common.

Table 11-1. Standard shortcut letters

Record		Edit		Options	
New <*Item*>	N	Undo	U	*Font	F
Delete <*Item*>	D	Cut	X	Preferences	R
*Attach <*Item*>	A	Copy	C	*Display Options	Y
Beam <*Item*>	B	Paste	P	*HotSync Options	H
*Purge	E	Select All	S		

Table 11-1. Standard shortcut letters (continued)

Record	Edit		Options
	Keyboard	K	
	Graffiti Help	G	

Accessing the Command toolbar with a menu shortcut

Entering the Graffiti command keystroke has different effects in OS 3.5 and later. Earlier versions of the OS displayed a command line briefly at the bottom of the screen. In the 3.5 OS, a command toolbar is displayed instead. (See Figure 11-4 for the differences between the command line and the command toolbar.) In either case, the user has the ability to enter the shortcut letter once the command line or toolbar is displayed. Both disappear within a few seconds if the user takes no action.

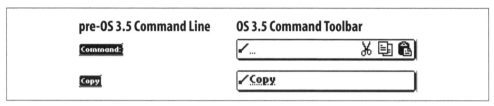

Figure 11-4. The command status as compared to the command toolbar

With the command toolbar, the user has the added capability of tapping on the icons (which are context sensitive) as an alternative to entering the shortcut letter. The context is based on the user's task. For example, if a field is being edited when the command stroke is used, then the icons on the toolbar should include Paste. If text in a field is selected, the icons should include Cut and Copy as well. If a form is being displayed, then the icons should offer beaming and other appropriate choices. While you can add your own custom icons to the toolbar, no more than four can easily be displayed at one time.

The most common icons are available as system bitmaps. Table 11-2 shows these bitmaps and the actions associated with them.

Table 11-2. Command toolbar icons and system bitmap names

Icon	Action/bitmap	Icon	Action/bitmap
🗑	Delete Record Bitmap: `BarDeleteBitmap`	✂	Cut selection Bitmap: `BarCutBitmap`
📶	Beam record Bitmap: `BarBeamBitmap`	🗐	Copy selection Bitmap: `BarCopyBitmap`
🔒	Show Security dialog box Bitmap: `BarSecureBitmap`	📋	Paste clipboard contents Bitmap: `BarPasteBitmap`
ⓘ	Show Info dialog box Bltmap: `BarInfoBitmap`	↶	Undo last action Bitmap: `BarUndoBitmap`

Menu Resources

The *.prc* file contains a resource for each menu bar in your application. Each menu bar is in turn composed of a number of menus, each of which contains menu items. Each menu item has an associated item ID and, optionally, a shortcut key.

When you design your menu bars, you need to make sure that no two menu items in menus displayed at the same time have the same shortcut key—each shortcut must be unique.

Here's a simple menu bar resource (with ID 1000) with two menus, each with two items (the item IDs are 1001, 1002, 1101, and 1102):

```
MENU 1000
BEGIN
    PULLDOWN "Menu1"
    BEGIN
        MENUITEM "Item1"    1001    "I"
        MENUITEM "Item2"    1002
    END
    PULLDOWN "Menu2"
    BEGIN
        MENUITEM "Item3"    1101
        MENUITEM "Item4"    1102
    END
END
```

To define the shortcut keys of menu items in PilRC, simply supply the character surrounded by double quotes. In our simple example, the first menu item has a shortcut key of "I."

The PilRC CodeWarrior plug-in requires that each of the item IDs in a menu be consecutive (for example, 1101, 1102, 1103). The command-line version of PilRC imposes no such restriction. However, for compatibility with both versions, we recommend that you always make your menu item IDs sequential within a menu.

Associating Menu Bars with Forms

When you create a form, you specify the ID of a menu bar to go along with it. A form whose menu bar ID is 0 has no associated menu bar. The Palm OS automatically uses the menu bar of a form while the form is active. More than one form can use the same menu bar.

Here's an example of specifying a menu bar ID for a particular form in PilRC:

```
FORM ID 1000 at (0, 0, 160, 160)
MENUID 1000
BEGIN
 ... form objects here
END
```

Application Code for Menus

There's not a lot of code that needs to be added to support menus. Furthermore, what you do add is straightforward and in some cases standard from application to application. The two routines responsibile for handling menus are:

- MenuHandleEvent
- MyFormHandleEvent

There is also some cookbook code to add that handles the Edit menu; we need to handle the About menu, as well.

MenuHandleEvent

This routine is responsible for handling menu-specific events. Chapter 5 contains a description of MenuHandleEvent and its role within your main event loop. Here is an example found in a main event loop:

```
do {
    EvtGetEvent(&event, evtWaitForever);
    if (! SysHandleEvent(&event))
        if (! MenuHandleEvent(0, &event, &error))
            if (! ApplicationHandleEvent(&event))
                FrmDispatchEvent(&event);
} while (event.eType != appStopEvent);
```

MyFormHandleEvent

Your form's event handler receives an event of type menuEvent if a menu item is chosen. It will commonly have an embedded switch statement to handle each menu item in the form. Here is one such event handler:

```
static Boolean MyFormHandleEvent(EventPtr event)
{
    Boolean      handled = false;

    switch (event->eType)
        {
        /* other event types */
        case menuEvent:
            switch (event->data.menu.itemID) {
            case MenuItem1:
              // Code to handle MenuItem1.
              handled = true;
              break;

             case MenuItem2:
               // Code to handle MenuItem2.
               handled = true;
               break;
```

```
          }
          break;
      }
    return handled;
  }
```

Handling Items in the Edit Menu

The good news about the Edit menu is that the OS already has code to handle the items in the Edit menu. The bad news is there's a case in which it doesn't work right. The Palm OS automatically handles menu items 10000–10007 (Undo through Graffiti Help). So all you have to do is create your Edit menu using those constants and the system will handle them. Example 11-1 shows an example of a menu bar.

Example 11-1. Using the system Edit menu constants

```
MENU ID TestMenuBar
BEGIN
  PULLDOWN "Edit"
  BEGIN
    MENUITEM "Undo" ID 10000 "U"
    MENUITEM "Cut" ID 10001 "X"
    MENUITEM "Copy" ID 10002 "C"
    MENUITEM "Paste" ID 10003 "P"
    MENUITEM "Select All" ID 10004 "S"
    MENUITEM "-" ID 10005
    MENUITEM "Keyboard" ID 10006 "K"
    MENUITEM "Grafitti Help" ID 10007 "G"
  END
END
```

Handling Cut and Paste correctly

The OS code that handles Cut and Paste hasn't always dealt correctly with the case of a read-only field. It will blindly try to cut or paste even in these cases (these problems are fixed in OS 3.5). If you've got a form that has a read-only field, and has an Edit menu, you'll need to work around this problem. The easiest way to do this is to modify AppHandleEvent (that routine can solve this problem for all events, since it sees all events before the form event handlers do). First, you need a utility routine to find the current field (see Example 11-2).

Example 11-2. Routine returns field with the focus

```
// Returns field that has the focus, if any, including in any embedded tables.
FieldPtr GetFocusedField(void)
{
  FormPtr frm;
  UInt16 focus;
  FormObjectKind objType;

  frm = FrmGetActiveForm ();
  focus = FrmGetFocus (frm);
```

Example 11-2. Routine returns field with the focus (continued)

```
  if (focus == noFocus)
    return NULL;

  objType = FrmGetObjectType (frm, focus);

  if (objType == frmFieldObj)
    return (FrmGetObjectPtr (frm, focus));

  else if (objType == frmTableObj)
    return (TblGetCurrentField (FrmGetObjectPtr (frm, focus)));

  return NULL;
}
```

 The 4.0 OS introduced `FrmGetActiveField`, a routine that does exactly what our utility routine `GetFocusedField` does.

Example 11-3 shows the modification to `AppHandleEvent` that will be on the lookout for a Cut or Paste within a noneditable field (important code is emphasized). If it finds such an occurrence, it returns true, causing no further processing for the event.

Example 11-3. Event handler dealing with trying to cut or paste from a noneditable field

```
Boolean AppHandleEvent(EventPtr event)
{
  UInt16 formId;
  FormPtr form;
  Boolean handled = false;

  switch (event->eType) {
  case frmLoadEvent:
    // Code to load the forms.
    handled = true;
    break;

  case menuEvent:
    {
      UInt16 itemID = event->data.menu.itemID;

      if (itemID == sysEditMenuCutCmd || itemID == sysEditMenuPasteCmd) {
        FieldPtr field = GetFocusedField();

        if (field) {
          FieldAttrType attr;

          FldGetAttributes(field, &attr);
          if (!attr.editable)
            handled = true;    // So that the cut or paste won't happen.
        }
      }
```

```
        handled = true;
        break;
      }
  }
  return handled;
}
```

The About Menu

The Palm OS provides a routine, AbtShowAbout, that allows the display of an application name and icon (see Figure 11-5). As you can see, it isn't appropriate for anything but the built-in applications.*

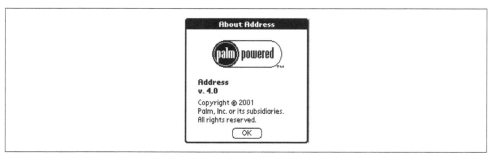

Figure 11-5. AbtShowAbout shows a Palm-specific About box

It is more useful to handle the About menu item by creating a simple alert and displaying it with FrmAlert (see Figure 11-6):

```
case OptionsAbout:
    FrmAlert(AboutBoxAlert);
    break;
```

This is fine if all you want is some text. If you have pictures, however, create a modal form and display it with FrmDoDialog. "Modal Dialog Boxes" in Chapter 8 describes how to do that.

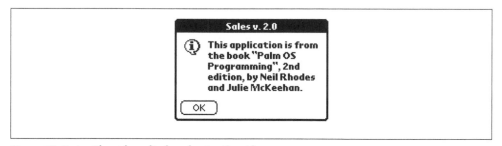

Figure 11-6. An About box displayed using FrmAlert

---

* This could change in future releases of the OS.

Menu Erase Status

There is a problem with menus and refreshing the display of the Palm screen that you should take into account in your applications. Before describing the fix to the problem, let us explain what the user does and when the problem occurs.

When the user chooses a menu item using a Graffiti shortcut key, the Menu Manager displays the status of this task in the bottom of the display. First, the Menu Manager displays a taskbar (see Figure 11-7) to indicate that a stroke has been noticed. (Prior to OS 3.5, the menu status is in the lower left and shows the word Command.) If the user then writes a valid shortcut key, the Menu Manager displays the menu item name (see Figure 11-8) and dispatches the menu event for the application to handle.

Figure 11-7. Menu status after entering a shortcut character

Figure 11-8. Menu status after entering a shortcut character and then a menu shortcut key

This shortcut key status is shown on the screen for a couple of seconds: just enough time for the user to read it and get feedback that the Palm device has noticed the stroke. After this, the status update goes away automatically.

This is all well and good, but there is one case in which you need to clear the status yourself because a problem occurs. The Palm OS notes when the user chooses a menu item using a shortcut key and saves the screen bits underneath the status area.

Once the timer goes off, the bits are restored. If you have happened to change the screen contents in that area in the meantime, the bits that are restored are stale. Figure 11-9 shows the problem.

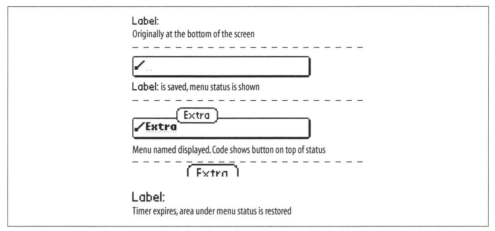

Figure 11-9. Menu code changing contents of bottom of screen without calling MenuEraseStatus

A common case where your menu code would change the screen contents is in displaying an alert or another form. Nicely enough, the Palm OS catches this case automatically and erases the status for you. You will have trouble, however, when you change the contents of the current form. Here's some sample code that shows the problem in Figure 11-9 (the code shows a previously hidden form object):

```
switch (eventP->data.menu.itemID) {
  case MainShowItem:
    {
      UInt16 index;
      FormPtr form;

      form = FrmGetActiveForm();
      index = FrmGetObjectIndex(form, MainExtraButton);
      FrmShowObject(form, index);
    }
    handled = true;
    break;
}
break;
```

You need to deal with this problem by doing your own erasing. The call to clear the status is MenuEraseStatus. The fix to the code that exhibits the problem is simply a call to MenuEraseStatus before modifying the screen:

```
switch (eventP->data.menu.itemID) {
  case MainShowItem:
    {
      UInt16 index;
      FormPtr form;
```

```
        form = FrmGetActiveForm( );
        index = FrmGetObjectIndex(form, MainExtraButton);
        MenuEraseStatus(NULL);
        FrmShowObject(form, index);
    }
    handled = true;
    break;
}
break;
```

You have to be careful with this fix, however, as it is a double-edged sword. You don't want to call MenuEraseStatus unnecessarily, as there is a price to pay. When you call it, the user gets only a brief glimpse of the confirmed menu item. You wiped out the confirmed menu item when you restored the screen bits. This cure is still better than the problem, however, as a mess on the screen is worse than wiping out the status quickly.

 A good way to ensure that you have implemented MenuEraseStatus when necessary is to use shortcut characters in your testing. This lets you determine when you need to make a call to MenuEraseStatus to clean up screen trash.

Note that forms that have unchanging buttons at the bottom are obviously not affected by this problem. For these forms, the automatic timed erasing works just fine. It's only forms with changing data at the bottom that are affected.

Handling Unusable Menu Items

The Menu Manager APIs don't provide a mechanism for visually disabling menu items (by graying them). As we said earlier, however, the 3.5 OS Menu Manager has added support for adding or deleting menu items dynamically. The question then becomes: "What you should do if there are menus or menu items that can't be used in certain situations?"

One possibility is to present an alert to the user explaining why it's not possible to do what was requested. That's the strategy used by the built-in To Do application when the user tries to delete an item and nothing is selected (see Figure 11-10).

Figure 11-10. Deleting an item in Expense when nothing is selected

This is certainly better than having the menu item appear and disappear as an item is selected and deselected—a tactic guaranteed to make users foam at the mouth. Disappearing and reappearing things make some folks doubt their sanity; they usually have no idea how to make a menu item reappear.

A good time to remove a menu item

There are cases, however, where you do want to remove menu items. For example, you may have a menu item that will never be present on a user's device. An obvious case of this is sending (using the Exchange Manager), which is available only if OS 4.0 is present. A well-designed application ought to figure out what OS it is running under and behave accordingly. It should have the Send item display only on 4.0 devices and hide it on pre-4.0 devices.

There are two different ways to implement this nice design: adding a Send item dynamically, or a rather simplistic solution—two menu bars, each with its own copy of the menus. One of the menus should have a Send item, the other shouldn't. We'll show you both ways—one in each form that supports Send.

 Applications built with CodeWarrior must have sequential item IDs within a menu. To make sure that menu items that are in both menu bars remain in the same position, put the Send menu item at the bottom of the 4.0 version.

Adding a menu item dynamically

First, we'll define the menu bar without the Send item (see Example 11-4).

Example 11-4. Menu bar for an Order form without the Send menu item

```
MENU ID OrderNoSendMenuBar
BEGIN
  PULLDOWN "Record"
  BEGIN
    MENUITEM "Delete Item..." ID RecordDeleteItem "D"
    MENUITEM "Delete Customer..." ID RecordDeleteCustomer
    MENUITEM "Customer Information..." ID RecordCustomerDetails "E"
    MENUITEM "Beam Customer" ID RecordBeamCustomer "B"
  END

  PULLDOWN "Edit"
  BEGIN
    MENUITEM "Undo" ID EditUndo "U"
    MENUITEM "Cut" ID EditCut "X"
    MENUITEM "Copy" ID EditCopy "C"
    MENUITEM "Paste" ID EditPaste "P"
    MENUITEM "Select All" ID EditSelectAll "S"
    MENUITEM "-" EditSeparator
    MENUITEM "Keyboard" ID EditKeyboard "K"
    MENUITEM "Grafitti Help" ID EditGrafitti "G"
```

```
  END

  PULLDOWN "Options"
  BEGIN
    MENUITEM "About Sales" ID OptionsAboutSales
  END
END
```

The 3.5 OS defines a new event, menuOpenEvent, that is sent when a menu bar is initialized. It is on receipt of this event that you should do any menu customization. In our form's event handler, we'll look for that event and, if needed, add a new menu item (sysGetROMVerMajor is a system macro that returns the major number of a ROM version; GetRomVersion is our own utility routine that returns the current ROM version). Notice that we are looking for 4.0 or later devices only:

```
case menuOpenEvent:
  // Send only supported on 4.0 and later.
  if (sysGetROMVerMajor(GetRomVersion()) >= 4) {
    MemHandle h = DmGetResource(strRsc, SendCustomerString);

    if (h) {
      MenuAddItem(RecordBeamCustomer, RecordSendCustomer, '\0',
        (Char *) MemHandleLock(h));
      MemHandleUnlock(h);
    }
  }
  handled = true;
  break;
```

Using a separate menu bar

The other approach is to use two menu bars, and switch from one to the other dynamically. Here are the two menu bars. The OS 4.0 or later menu bar is first (see Example 11-5).

Example 11-5. Menu bar for an Order form with the Send menu item

```
MENU ID CustomersWithSendMenuBar
BEGIN
  PULLDOWN "Customer"
  BEGIN
    MENUITEM "New Customer" ID CustomerNewCustomer "N"
    MENUITEM "Beam all Customers" ID CustomerBeamAllCustomers "B"
    MENUITEM "Send all Customers" ID CustomerSendAllCustomers
  END

  PULLDOWN "Options"
  BEGIN
    MENUITEM "About Sales" ID OptionsAboutSales
  END
END
```

Example 11-6 shows the menu bar for earlier system versions.

Example 11-6. Pre-4.0 menu bar for an Order form with the Send menu item

```
MENU ID CustomersNoSendMenuBar
BEGIN
  PULLDOWN "Customer"
  BEGIN
    MENUITEM "New Customer" ID CustomerNewCustomer "N"
    MENUITEM "Beam all Customers" ID CustomerBeamAllCustomers "B"
  END

  PULLDOWN "Options"
  BEGIN
    MENUITEM "About Sales" ID OptionsAboutSales
  END
END
```

Specify one menu bar of the form's menu bar as part of the resource (let's make it CustomersWithSendMenuBar, the one that does include the Send item). You may need to change the menu bar at runtime using FrmSetMenu, which changes the menu bar ID of a form. Make the change when you open the form with code like this:

```
if (sysGetROMVerMajor(GetRomVersion( )) < 4)
  FrmSetMenu(FrmGetActiveForm( ), CustomersNoSendMenuBar);
```

Adding to the Command Bar

For OS 3.5 and later, when the user enters the menu shortcut key, a menuCmdBarOpenEvent is sent, allowing you the opportunity to customize the command bar. To add to the command bar, use MenuCmdBarAddButton:

```
Err MenuCmdBarAddButton(UInt8 where, UInt16 bitmapID,
    MenuCmdBarResultType resultType, UInt32 result, Char *nameP);
```

Position your icon with either menuCmdBarOnLeft, to place it on the left of existing icons in the bar, or menuCmdBarOnRight, to place it to the right of any existing icons. The bitmapID is the resource ID of a bitmap (or bitmap family). The resultType specifies what to do when the icon is tapped (menuCmdBarResultMenuItem—specifying that result contains a menu item ID is the usual thing to specify). The result parameter specifies the data for the icon (usually a menu item ID). Finally, nameP specifies the name to display when the user taps the icon (NULL will cause it to grab the text from the associated menu).

The default behavior for the menuCmdBarOpenEvent is to add appropriate Cut, Copy, Paste, and Undo icons if there is a current field. If you need to add any icons to the left of these icons, you'll need to cause the Field Manager to add its icons first, and then add your own icons afterward. Do this by calling FldHandleEvent with the menuCmdBarOpenEvent within your own event handler. You then have to notify the system that the Field Manager has already added its icons, so that it doesn't do so twice (the preventFieldButtons in the event). Example 11-7 shows adding a beam icon before the appropriate Cut, Copy, Paste, and Undo icons, and a Trash icon afterward.

Example 11-7. Code that adds icons to the menu command bar

```
case menuCmdBarOpenEvent:
  field = GetCurrentField( );
  if (field)
    FldHandleEvent(field, event);
  // Add Beam and Delete.
  MenuCmdBarAddButton(menuCmdBarOnRight, BarDeleteBitmap,
    menuCmdBarResultMenuItem, RecordDeleteItem, 0);
  MenuCmdBarAddButton(menuCmdBarOnLeft, BarBeamBitmap,
    menuCmdBarResultMenuItem, RecordBeamCustomer, 0);

  // Field buttons have already been added.
  event->data.menuCmdBarOpen.preventFieldButtons = true;
  // Don't set handle to true; this event must fall through to the system.
  break;
```

Adding Menus to the Sample Application

Now it is time to add the menus to our Sales application. The menu bars are added first. Next, we set up our definitions for our menu items and menu bars. Once these are in place, we can create our code to handle common menu items and the functions we need to handle our forms. Our last step is to make sure the main event loop in our application calls our menu-handling function correctly.

The Menu Bars

The application has five menu bars, the first of which contains the Record, Edit, and Options menus (Figure 11-11). This menu bar is for the Order form. The Send Customer menu item is added dynamically on a 4.0 device.

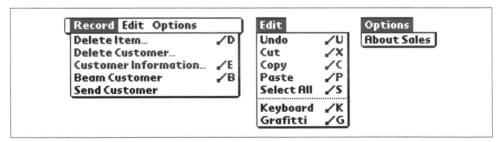

Figure 11-11. The Order menus on a 4.0 or later device

The second menu bar, DialogWithInputField, is used for dialog boxes that have textual input fields (see Figure 11-12). It contains just one menu, the Edit menu.

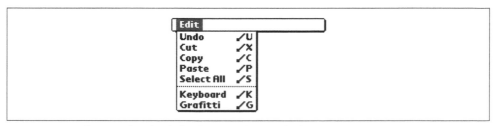

Figure 11-12. The menu bar for dialog boxes with input fields

The third and fourth menu bars are used separately, depending on whether the application is running on a 4.0 or earlier device. As you can see in Figure 11-13, the difference is whether sending shows up as a menu item. We have different menus for different devices so that a pre-4.0 user doesn't get confused about either the application's or device's capability.

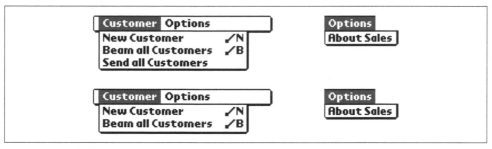

Figure 11-13. Different Customer menus for 4.0 and pre-4.0 devices

Menu Definitions

The first thing to do is get our menu definitions set up neatly. Example 11-8 shows part of the contents of *SalesRsc.h* that defines the constants for the menu bars, and for each menu item (the menu item constants will be used by both the *.rcp* file and the code for the event handlers).

Example 11-8. Portion of SalesRsc.h with constants relevant to menus

```
#define CustomersWithSendMenuBar       1000
#define CustomersNoSendMenuBar         1100
#define OrderWithSendMenuBar           1200
#define OrderNoSendMenuBar             1300
#define DialogWithInputFieldMenuBar    1400

#define CustomerNewCustomer            2001
#define CustomerBeamAllCustomers       2002
#define CustomerSendAllCustomers       2003

#define OptionsAboutSales              2101

#define RecordDeleteItem               2201
```

```
#define RecordDeleteCustomer            2202
#define RecordCustomerDetails           2203
#define RecordBeamCustomer              2204
#define RecordSendCustomer              2205

#define EditUndo                        10000
#define EditCut                         10001
#define EditCopy                        10002
#define EditPaste                       10003
#define EditSelectAll                   10004
#define EditSeparator                   10005
#define EditKeyboard                    10006
#define EditGrafitti                    10007
```

Example 11-9 shows the portion of *Sales.rcp* that defines the menu bars.

Example 11-9. Portion of Sales.rcp with menus

```
MENU ID OrderNoSendMenuBar
BEGIN
  PULLDOWN "Record"
  BEGIN
    MENUITEM "Delete Item..." ID RecordDeleteItem "D"
    MENUITEM "Delete Customer..." ID RecordDeleteCustomer
    MENUITEM "Customer Information..." ID RecordCustomerDetails "E"
    MENUITEM "Beam Customer" ID RecordBeamCustomer "B"
  END

  PULLDOWN "Edit"
  BEGIN
    MENUITEM "Undo" ID EditUndo "U"
    MENUITEM "Cut" ID EditCut "X"
    MENUITEM "Copy" ID EditCopy "C"
    MENUITEM "Paste" ID EditPaste "P"
    MENUITEM "Select All" ID EditSelectAll "S"
    MENUITEM "-" EditSeparator
    MENUITEM "Keyboard" ID EditKeyboard "K"
    MENUITEM "Grafitti Help" ID EditGrafitti "G"
  END

  PULLDOWN "Options"
  BEGIN
    MENUITEM "About Sales" ID OptionsAboutSales
  END
END

MENU ID DialogWithInputFieldMenuBar
BEGIN
  PULLDOWN "Edit"
  BEGIN
    MENUITEM "Undo" ID EditUndo "U"
    MENUITEM "Cut" ID EditCut "X"
    MENUITEM "Copy" ID EditCopy "C"
    MENUITEM "Paste" ID EditPaste "P"
```

Example 11-9. Portion of Sales.rcp with menus (continued)

```
    MENUITEM "Select All" ID EditSelectAll "S"
    MENUITEM "-" EditSeparator
    MENUITEM "Keyboard" ID EditKeyboard "K"
    MENUITEM "Grafitti Help" ID EditGrafitti "G"
  END
END

MENU ID CustomersWithSendMenuBar
BEGIN
  PULLDOWN "Customer"
  BEGIN
    MENUITEM "New Customer" ID CustomerNewCustomer "N"
    MENUITEM "Beam all Customers" ID CustomerBeamAllCustomers "B"
    MENUITEM "Send all Customers" ID CustomerSendAllCustomers
  END

  PULLDOWN "Options"
  BEGIN
    MENUITEM "About Sales" ID OptionsAboutSales
  END
END

MENU ID CustomersNoSendMenuBar
BEGIN
  PULLDOWN "Customer"
  BEGIN
    MENUITEM "New Customer" ID CustomerNewCustomer "N"
    MENUITEM "Beam all Customers" ID CustomerBeamAllCustomers "B"
  END

  PULLDOWN "Options"
  BEGIN
    MENUITEM "About Sales" ID OptionsAboutSales
  END
END

// Used in menu for 4.0 OS and above.
STRING ID SendCustomerString "Send Customer"
```

Example 11-10 shows the form definitions that specify a particular menu bar.

Example 11-10. Portion of Sales.rcp that uses the menu bars

```
FORM ID CustomersForm AT (0 0 160 160)
MENUID CustomersNoSendMenuBar
BEGIN
  // Form objects deleted.
END


FORM ID OrderForm AT (0 0 160 160)
MENUID OrderNoSendMenuBar
BEGIN
  // Form objects deleted.
```

Example 11-10. Portion of Sales.rcp that uses the menu bars (continued)

```
END

FORM ID ItemForm AT (2 40 156 kItemFormHeight)
MODAL
SAVEBEHIND
HELPID ItemHelpString
MENUID DialogWithInputFieldMenuBar
BEGIN
  // Form objects deleted.
END

FORM ID CustomerForm AT (2 20 156 138)
MODAL
SAVEBEHIND
HELPID CustomerHelpString
MENUID DialogWithInputFieldMenuBar
BEGIN
  // Form objects deleted.
END
```

Handling Common Menus

The Sales application has an About menu item in more than one of its menu bars. Rather than duplicating the code to handle that item, we handle it in AppHandleEvent (see Example 11-11), which is responsible for application-wide events.

Example 11-11. AppHandleEvent (emphasized code handles the About menu item)

```
Boolean AppHandleEvent(EventPtr event)
{
  FormPtr frm;
  UInt16  formId;
  Boolean handled = false;

  switch (event->eType) {
  case frmLoadEvent:
    // Load the form resource specified in event, then activate the form.
    formId = event->data.frmLoad.formID;
    frm = FrmInitForm(formId);
    FrmSetActiveForm(frm);

    // Set the event handler for the form.  The handler of the currently
    // active form is called by FrmDispatchEvent each time it receives
    // an event.
    switch (formId)
    {
    case OrderForm:
      FrmSetEventHandler(frm, OrderHandleEvent);
      break;

    case CustomersForm:
      FrmSetEventHandler(frm, CustomersHandleEvent);
```

```
      break;

    }
    handled = true;
    break;

  case menuEvent:
    if (event->data.menu.itemID == OptionsAboutSales) {
      FrmAlert(AboutBoxAlert);
      handled = true;
    }
    break;
  }
  return handled;
}
```

Regardless of which form is displayed, if a menu event arrives with the item ID of OptionsAboutSales, we display our About dialog box.

The Customers Form

Here's the event handler for the Customers form:

```
Boolean CustomersHandleEvent(EventPtr event)
{
  Boolean    handled = false;

  switch (event->eType)
    {
    case menuEvent:
      handled = CustomersHandleMenuEvent(event->data.menu.itemID);
      break;

    // Code deleted that handles other event types.
    }
    return handled;
  }
```

Note that it just delegates the handling for menu items to a different function. Example 11-12 shows that function.

Example 11-12. Function that handles menu events in the Customers form

```
Boolean CustomersHandleMenuEvent(UInt16 menuID)
{
  Boolean handled = false;

  switch (menuID) {
  case CustomerNewCustomer:
    // Code deleted that creates a new customer.
    handled = true;
    break;
```

```
  case CustomerBeamAllCustomers:
  case CustomerSendAllCustomers:
    SendAllCustomers(
      (menuID == CustomerBeamAllCustomers) ? exgBeamPrefix : exgSendPrefix);
    handled = true;
    break;
  }
  return handled;
}
```

The Customers form has two different menu bars, one with a Send item, one without. Here's where one is changed if we're running on a 4.0 or greater system:

```
    static void CustomersFormOpen(FormPtr form)
    {
      ListPtr list = (ListPtr) GetObjectFromForm(form, CustomersCustomersList);
      InitNumberCustomers();
      LstSetDrawFunction(list, DrawOneCustomerInListWithFont);

      if (sysGetROMVerMajor(GetRomVersion()) >= 4)
        FrmSetMenu(form,  CustomersWithSendMenuBar);
    }
```

The Order Form

The Order form is very similar to the Customers form. OrderHandleEvent delegates its menu items to OrderHandleMenuEvent (see Example 11-13).

Example 11-13. Function that handles menu events in the Order form

```
static Boolean OrderHandleMenuEvent(UInt16 menuID)
{
  Boolean handled = false;
  UInt16  zero = 0;

  switch (menuID) {
    case RecordDeleteItem:
      // Code deleted that deletes an item.
      handled = true;
      break;

    case RecordCustomerDetails:
      // Code deleted that puts up a Details dialog box.
      handled = true;
      break;

    case RecordBeamCustomer:
    case RecordSendCustomer:
      SendCustomer(GetRecordNumberForCustomer(
        gCurrentOrder->customerID),
        menuID == RecordBeamCustomer ? exgBeamPrefix : exgSendPrefix);
      handled = true;
      break;
```

```
    case RecordDeleteCustomer:
      // Code deleted that deletes this customer.
      break;
    }
  return handled;
}
```

In addition, the Order form adds a new menu item (if we're on a 4.0 or greater system) when the menu is initialized (see Example 11-14).

Example 11-14. When the menu is opened, we may add the Send item

```
Boolean OrderHandleEvent(EventPtr event)
{
  Boolean    handled = false;
  FormPtr    form;

  switch (event->eType)
    {
    case menuOpenEvent:
      // Send only supported on 4.0 and later.
      if (sysGetROMVerMajor(GetRomVersion()) >= 4) {
        MemHandle h = DmGetResource(strRsc, SendCustomerString);
        if (h) {
          MenuAddItem(RecordBeamCustomer, RecordSendCustomer, '\0',
            (Char *) MemHandleLock(h));
          MemHandleUnlock(h);
        }
      }
      handled = true;
      break;

    case menuEvent:
      handled = OrderHandleMenuEvent(event->data.menu.itemID);
    }
  return handled;
}
```

The Order form also adds a Beam and Delete icon if there is a currently selected item (see Example 11-15).

Example 11-15. Event handler from an Order form that customizes the menu command bar

```
case menuCmdBarOpenEvent:
  field = GetCurrentField();
  if (field)
    FldHandleEvent(field, event);
  if (gRowSelected) {
    // Add Beam and Delete.
    MenuCmdBarAddButton(menuCmdBarOnRight, BarDeleteBitmap,
      menuCmdBarResultMenuItem, RecordDeleteItem, 0);
```

Example 11-15. Event handler from an Order form that customizes the menu command bar

```
    MenuCmdBarAddButton(menuCmdBarOnLeft, BarBeamBitmap,
      menuCmdBarResultMenuItem, RecordBeamCustomer, 0);
}

// Field buttons have already been added.
event->data.menuCmdBarOpen.preventFieldButtons = true;
// Don't set handle to true; this event must fall through to the system.
break;
```

Summary

This is all the code and definitions necessary to make our menus work. You saw that our strategy for menus included a design preference for making menu items completely disappear if the application is present on a device that doesn't use the feature (as in sending). There was also a display problem with Graffiti shortcuts that you needed to work around in your code.

At this point, the Sales application is almost complete—you have all the essential UI elements and code in place. Just a few important bits are left. You still need to add support for Find and beaming.

CHAPTER 12

Extras

This chapter discusses two topics that are needed to make an application fully functional, but that are too small to warrant individual chapters: Palm's Find feature and the Exchange Manager.

Find

In this section, we discuss the Find feature of the Palm OS. First, we give you an overview of Find, the UI, and its intended goals. Second, we walk through the entire Find process from beginning to end. Third, we implement Find in our sample application and discuss important aspects of the code.

Overview of Find

The Palm OS UI supports a global Find—a user can find all the instances of a string in all applications. The operating system doesn't do the work, however. Instead, it orders each application, in turn, to search through its own databases and return the results.

There is much to be said for this approach. The most obvious rationale is that the operating system has no idea what's inside the records of a database: strings, numbers, or other data. Therefore, it's in no position to know what's a reasonable return result and what's nonsense. Indeed, the application is uniquely positioned to interpret the Find request and determine the display of the found information to the user.

Find requests are sent from the OS by calling the application's `PilotMain` (see "Other Times Your Application Is Called" in Chapter 5) with a specific launch code—`sysAppLaunchCmdFind`—along with parameters having to do with interpreting the Find.

The objectives of Find

Speed on the handheld is essential, so Find is intended to be a quick process. Here are some of the things the OS does to ensure this:

Does not create global variables
　An application's global variables are not created when it receives the `sysApp-LaunchCmdFind` launch code. Creating, initializing, and releasing every application's globals would be a time-consuming process.

Displays only one screenful of items at a time
　The Find goes on only long enough to fill one screen with items. If the user wants more results, the Find resumes where it left off until it has another screenful of found items, then stops again. This process continues until it runs out of results.

Makes long Finds easy to stop
　Applications check the event queue every so often to see whether an event has occurred. If so, the application prematurely quits the Find. Thus, a simple tap on the screen prevents a long search of a large database that would otherwise lock up the handheld.

Find minimizes memory use

Another goal is to minimize the amount of memory used. Remember that the Find request could well occur while an application other than yours is running. In such cases, it would be rude to suck away the application's dynamic heap. To prevent such bad manners, memory use is minimized in the following ways:

No global variables
　No global variables are created for applications doing a Find.

Minimal information about each found item is stored
　An application doesn't save much information about the items it finds. Rather, the application draws a summary of the found items and passes the Find Manager six pieces of information: the database, the record number, the field number, the card number, the position within the field, and an additional integer.

Only one screenful of items is stored
　Only one screenful of found items is maintained in memory. If the user requests more, the current information is thrown out and the search continues where it left off.

A Walkthrough of Finding Items

Following is a walkthrough of what happens when the user writes in a string to be found and taps Find. First, the currently running application is sent the launch code `sysAppLaunchCmdSaveData`, which requests that the application save any data that is currently being edited but has not yet been saved in a database. Then, starting with the open application, each application is sent the launch code `sysAppLaunchCmdFind`.

The application's response to a Find request

Each application responds with these steps:

1. The application opens its database(s) using the mode specified in its Find parameters. This can be specified as the read-only mode and may also (depending on the user's security settings) specify that secret records should be shown.

2. The application draws an application header in the Find Results dialog box. Figure 12-1 contains some examples of application headers as they appear in the dialog box. The application uses FindDrawHeader to retrieve the application header from the application's resource database. If FindDrawHeader returns true, there is no more space in the Find Results dialog box, and step 3 is skipped. If there is room in the dialog box, it is on to step 3.

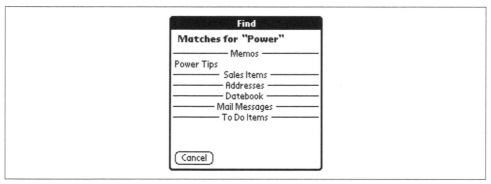

Figure 12-1. Find Results dialog box showing application headers

3. The application iterates through each of the records in its database. If it is sent a Find request and there is room to fit all the found items on the screen, the application iterates through the records, starting at record 0. If some records from the application have already been displayed, the application has the Find Manager store the record number of the last-displayed record and continues the iteration with the next record when the user taps the More button. Here is the process:

   - Most applications retrieve the next record by using DmQueryNextInCategory, which skips private records, if necessary. If an error occurs, the application exits the loop.

   - The application looks for a string that matches. An application should normally ignore case while determining a match. The application can use FindStrInStr (or an internationally savvy equivalent, TxFindString) to determine whether there is a match and where the match occurs.

   - If the application finds a match, it saves information about the match using FindSaveMatch. If FindSaveMatch returns true, no more items can be drawn in the Find Results dialog box. In this case, the application has finished iterating and goes to step 4. Otherwise, it draws a one-line summary of the matching item in the Find Results dialog box (FindGetLineBounds returns the rectangle in which to draw). The summary should, if possible, include the searched-for string, along with other contextual information.

In addition, the application increments the `lineNumber` field of the Find parameters.

- The application should check the event queue every so often (using `EvtSysEventAvail`). If an event has occurred, the application should set the More field of the Find parameters to true and go to step 4.

4. The application closes any databases it has opened and returns.

When the Find Results dialog box is displayed, the user can choose Find More. In this case, the Find Manager starts the process again, skipping any applications that have been completely searched.

In the documentation for Find as of mid-2001, the `lineNumber` field in the Find parameters is incorrectly documented as being for System use only. The `lineNumber` field is necessary to correctly support Find. You must increment this field every time you display a found match.

Handling a Find request with multiple databases

If your application supports searching in multiple databases, you must handle continuing a search (Find More) carefully. The Find parameters provide the last-matched record number (as saved by `FindSaveMatch`) but not the last-matched database. Because of this, your Find routine doesn't know which database was last searched.

Our recommendation is to store the name of the last-searched database in the system preferences. When you call `FindSaveMatch`, you can retrieve the information. When you receive the Find launch code, if the `continuation` field of the Find parameters is false, mark the last database as invalid and start the search with your first database. If the `continuation` field of the Find parameters is true, start your search with the saved database (if it is valid).

Remember that you can't store information in global variables, because when the `sysAppLaunchCmdFind` launch code is sent, your application's global variables don't get allocated.

Alternatively, you could use the record number field as a combination record number and database: you could store the indicated database (0, 1, 2, and so on) in the upper few bits, and the actual record number in the remaining bits.

Navigating to a found item

When the user taps on an item in the Find Results dialog box, that item's application is sent the `sysAppLaunchCmdGoTo` launch code. That application may or may not be the current application. If it is, the application just switches to displaying the found item. If it isn't, the application must call StartApplication and enter a standard event loop.

Some parameters are sent, along with the sysAppLaunchCmdGoTo launch code. These parameters are all the items that were passed to FindSaveMatch, along with an additional one: the length of the searched-for string. Your application should then display the found item, highlighting the searched-for string within the found item.

Displaying a found item from a running application

Here's the step-by-step process your open application will go through when it receives the sysAppLaunchCmdGoTo launch code:

1. Close any existing forms (using FrmCloseAllForms).
2. Open the appropriate form to display the found item (using FrmGotoForm).
3. Create a frmGotoEvent event record with fields initialized from the Go To parameters, and post it to the event queue (using EvtAddEventToQueue).
4. Respond to the frmGotoEvent event in your form's event handler by navigating to the correct record and highlighting the found contents (using FldSetScrollPosition and FldSetSelection).

 Note that you must find the unique ID of the specified recordNumber before you close all the forms. There are many cases that call for this. For example, the user might be viewing a blank form immediately prior to the Find request. Before displaying the found item, the application needs to delete the blank Customer record and close the form. If this occurs, however, the records in the database may no longer be numbered the same. Therefore, you need to find the unique ID of the found record. After closing the forms, you then find the record based on its unchanging, unique ID instead of the possibly compromised record number.

Displaying a found item from a closed application

If your application is closed when it receives the sysAppLaunchCmdGoTo launch code, you need to do a few more things:

1. As specified by the sysAppLaunchFlagNewGlobals launch flag, call AppStart.
2. Create a frmGotoEvent event record with fields initialized from the Go To parameters, and post it to the event queue (using EvtAddEventToQueue).
3. Enter your AppEventLoop.
4. Respond to the frmGotoEvent event in your form's event handler by navigating to the correct record and highlighting the found contents (using FldSetScrollPosition and FldSetSelection).
5. Call AppStop after the AppEventLoop is finished.

Find in the Sales Application

From the preceding description of Find, you can see that supporting it in your application requires handling a number of steps and possible situations. Let's look now at how we handle these steps in the Sales application. We'll also examine the code that implements Find.

Handling the Find request

PilotMain handles the save data and the Find launch codes. Here's the bit of code from PilotMain that shows the handling of these launch codes:

```
// Launch code sent to running application before sysAppLaunchCmdFind
// or other action codes that will cause data searches or manipulation.
else if (cmd == sysAppLaunchCmdSaveData) {
  FrmSaveAllForms();
}
else if (cmd == sysAppLaunchCmdFind) {
  Search((FindParamsPtr)cmdPBP);
}
```

Searching for matching strings

Example 12-1 shows the Search routine that actually handles searching through our customer database. The part of the code that's specific to our application is emphasized; the remaining code is likely to be standard for most applications.

Example 12-1. Search routine used for handling Find (emphasized code is specific to our application)

```
void Search(FindParamsPtr findParams)
{
  Err          err;
  UInt16       pos;
  UInt16       fieldNum;
  UInt16       cardNo = 0;
  UInt16       recordNum;
  Char         *header;
  Boolean      done;
  MemHandle    recordH;
  MemHandle    headerH;
  LocalID      dbID;
  DmOpenRef    dbP;
  RectangleType r;
  DmSearchStateType searchState;

  // Unless told otherwise, there are no more items to be found.
  findParams->more = false;

  // Find the application's datafile.
  err = DmGetNextDatabaseByTypeCreator(true, &searchState,
    kCustomerDBType, kSalesCreator, true, &cardNo, &dbID);
  if (err != errNone)
    return;
```

Example 12-1. Search routine used for handling Find (emphasized code is specific to our application)

```
// Open the database.
dbP = DmOpenDatabase(cardNo, dbID, findParams->dbAccesMode);
if (! dbP)
  return;

// Display the heading line.
headerH = DmGetResource(strRsc, FindHeaderString);
header = (Char *) MemHandleLock(headerH);
done = FindDrawHeader(findParams, header);
MemHandleUnlock(headerH);
if (done) {
  findParams->more = true;
}
else {
    // Search all the fields; start from the last record searched.
  recordNum = findParams->recordNum;
  for(;;) {
    Boolean match = false;
    Customer    customer;

    // Because applications can take a long time to finish a Find,
    // users like to be able to stop the Find. Stop the Find
    // if an event is pending. This stops if the user does
    // something with the device. Because this call slows down
    // the search, we perform it every so many records instead of
    // every record. The response time should still be short
    // without introducing much extra work to the search.

    // Note that in the implementation below, if the next 16th
    // record is secret the check doesn't happen. Generally
    // this shouldn't be a problem, since if most of the records
    // are secret the search won't take a long time anyway!
    if ((recordNum & 0x000f) == 0 &&       // every 16th record
      EvtSysEventAvail(true)) {
      // Stop the search process.
      findParams->more = true;
      break;
    }

    recordH = DmQueryNextInCategory(dbP, &recordNum,
      dmAllCategories);
    // Have we run out of records?
    if (! recordH)
      break;

    // Search each of the fields of the customer.

    UnpackCustomer(&customer, (PackedCustomer *) MemHandleLock(recordH));

    if ((match = FindStrInStr(customer.name,
      findParams->strToFind, &pos)) != false)
      fieldNum = CustomerNameField;
    else if ((match = FindStrInStr(customer.address,
```

```
        findParams->strToFind, &pos)) != false)
        fieldNum = CustomerAddressField;
    else if ((match = FindStrInStr(customer.city,
      findParams->strToFind, &pos)) != false)
        fieldNum = CustomerCityField;
    else if ((match = FindStrInStr(customer.phone,
      findParams->strToFind, &pos)) != false)
        fieldNum = CustomerPhoneField;

  if (match) {
    done = FindSaveMatch(findParams, recordNum, pos, fieldNum, 0,
      cardNo, dbID);
    if (!done) {
      //Get the bounds of the region where we will draw the results.
      FindGetLineBounds(findParams, &r);

      // Display the title of the description.
      DrawCharsToFitWidth(customer.name, &r);

      findParams->lineNumber++;
    }
  }
  MemHandleUnlock(recordH);
  if (done)
    break;
  recordNum++;
  }
 }
 DmCloseDatabase(dbP);
}
```

Displaying the found item

Here's the code from `PilotMain` that calls `AppStart`, `AppEventLoop`, and `AppStop`, if necessary:

```
// This launch code might be sent to the application when it's already running.
else if (cmd == sysAppLaunchCmdGoTo) {
  Boolean justLaunched;
  justLaunched = (Boolean) (launchFlags & sysAppLaunchFlagNewGlobals);

  if (justLaunched) {
    error = AppStart();
    if (!error) {
      GoToItem((GoToParamsPtr) cmdPBP, justLaunched);
      AppEventLoop();
      AppStop();
    }
  } else {
    GoToItem((GoToParamsPtr) cmdPBP, justLaunched);
  }
```

The GoToItem function (see Example 12-2) opens the correct form and posts a frmGotoEvent.

Example 12-2. GoToItem called in response to sysAppLaunchCmdGoTo launch code

```
static void GoToItem (GoToParamsPtr goToParams, Boolean launchingApp)
{
  EventType   event;
  UInt16     recordNum = goToParams->recordNum;

  // If the current record is blank it will be deleted, so we'll
  // save the record's unique id to find the record index again, after all
  // the forms are closed.
  if (! launchingApp) {
    UInt32    uniqueID;

    DmRecordInfo(gCustomerDB, recordNum, NULL, &uniqueID, NULL);
    FrmCloseAllForms();
    DmFindRecordByID(gCustomerDB, uniqueID, &recordNum);
  }

  FrmGotoForm(CustomersForm);

  // Send an event to select the matching text.
  MemSet (&event, 0, sizeof(EventType));

  event.eType = frmGotoEvent;
  event.data.frmGoto.formID = CustomersForm;
  event.data.frmGoto.recordNum = goToParams->recordNum;
  event.data.frmGoto.matchPos = goToParams->matchPos;
  event.data.frmGoto.matchLen = (UInt16) goToParams->searchStrLen;
  event.data.frmGoto.matchFieldNum = goToParams->matchFieldNum;
  event.data.frmGoto.matchCustom = goToParams->matchCustom;
  EvtAddEventToQueue(&event);
}
```

Remember that this code needs to take into account the possibility of records that change numbers in between closing open forms and displaying the found record. We do this using DmRecordInfo and DmFindRecordByID. DmRecordInfo takes the record and finds the unique ID associated with it; DmFindRecordByID returns a record based on the unique ID.

Note also that we're opening the CustomersForm, even though we really want the CustomerForm. We can't get to the CustomerForm directly—it's a modal dialog box that is displayed above the CustomersForm. Thus, the CustomersForm needs to be opened first, because it is that bit of code that knows how to open the CustomerForm. Here's the code from CustomersHandleEvent that opens the CustomerForm:

```
    case frmGotoEvent:
      EditCustomerWithSelection(event->data.frmGoto.recordNum, false,
       &deleted, &hidden, event);
      handled = true;
      break;
```

EditCustomerWithSelection (see Example 12-3) scrolls and highlights the correct text.

Example 12-3. Portion of EditCustomWithSelection responsible for highlighting the correct text

```
void EditCustomerWithSelection(UInt16 recordNumber, Boolean isNew,
  Boolean *deleted, Boolean *hidden, EventPtr event)
{
  // Code deleted that gets the customer record and initializes
  // the fields.

  FrmDrawForm(frm); // Must do now, because pre-3.5, focus needed to be set
                    // *after* a call to FrmDrawForm.
  // Select one of the fields.
  if (event && event->data.frmGoto.matchFieldNum) {
    FieldPtr selectedField =
      (FieldPtr) GetObjectFromForm(form, event->data.frmGoto.matchFieldNum);
    FldSetScrollPosition(selectedField, event->data.frmGoto.matchPos);
    FrmSetFocus(form,
      FrmGetObjectIndex(form, event->data.frmGoto.matchFieldNum));
    FldSetSelection(selectedField, event->data.frmGoto.matchPos,
      event->data.frmGoto.matchPos + event->data.frmGoto.matchLen);
  } else {
    FrmSetFocus(form, FrmGetObjectIndex(form, CustomerNameField));
    FldSetSelection(nameField, 0, FldGetTextLength(nameField));
  }

  // Code deleted that displays the dialog box and handles updates
  // when the dialog box is dismissed.
}
```

That's all there is to adding support for Find to our application. Indeed, the trickiest part of the code is figuring out the types of situations you might encounter that will cause Find to work incorrectly. The two most important of these are searching applications with multiple databases correctly and making sure that you don't lose the record in between closing forms and displaying results.

Exchange

In this section, we discuss the Exchange Manager. First, we give you a general overview of Exchange, describe the UI, and offer you a few useful tips. Next, we provide a checklist that you can use to implement Exchange in an application. Last, we implement Exchange in the Sales application.

The Exchange Manager

The Exchange Manager is in charge of exchanging information between Palm OS devices and other devices. This manager was introduced in Palm OS 3.0 and is built on industry standards.

In Palm OS 3.0, the Exchange Manager works only over an infrared link (although it was designed to be extensible to other transports). It was enhanced in Palm OS 4.0 to work over other links (including via cell phone and Bluetooth). The Exchange Manager uses the ObEx Infrared Data Association (IrDA) standard to exchange information. As a result, it should be possible to exchange information between Palm OS devices and other devices that implement this ObEx standard.

For information on IrDA standards, see *http://www.irda.org*. For Multipurpose Internet Mail Extensions (MIME), see *http://www.mindspring. com/~mgrand/mime.html* or *http://www.faqs.org/faqs/mail/mime-faq/*. For information on Bluetooth, see *http://www.bluetooth.com*.

Overview of Sending

Applications that support this feature usually allow sending of either a single item or an entire category. Since infrared is so common, applications should also have separate menu items for beaming. When the user chooses the Send menu item, she is presented with a list of available transports (other than infrared). If only one transport is available (other than infrared), that transport is used automatically. For infrared, a dialog box appears showing that the beam is being prepared. Then the device searches for another device using infrared. Once it finds the other device, it beeps and then starts sending the data. After the remote device receives all the data, it beeps and then presents to the user a dialog box that asks whether the user wants to accept the data. If the user decides to accept the data, it is put away; if not, it is thrown away. The item is matched to an appropriate application on the receiving device, which then displays the newly received data.

Prior to OS 3.5, newly received items are always placed in the Unfiled category. This is true even when both sending and receiving units have the same categories. While problematic for a few users, this is the right solution for most situations. Users will have one consistent interface for receiving items. After all, who's to say that a user wants beamed items filed in the same name category that the sending handheld uses? In Palm OS 3.5, the receiving application can allow the user to choose the incoming category.

The user can also send an entire category. When a category is sent, private records should be skipped regardless of the user's security setting (to avoid accidentally sending unintended records). Newly received items are placed in the Unfiled category.

A Programming Walkthrough of Sending and Receiving

'When a user sends an item, your application gets the request. You call `ExgPut` to start the process; you call `ExgSend` in a loop to continue sending data; and you call `ExgDisconnect` when you're finished.

For receiving, your `PilotMain` does the work. It can be sent up to three different launch codes:

sysAppLaunchCmdExgAskUser

> This launch code allows an application either to quietly accept or quietly reject incoming data (without asking the user), or (by default) to open a dialog box asking the user whether the incoming data should be accepted or rejected. For OS 3.5 and later, an application can call `ExgDoDialog` to open a dialog box that includes a category picker.

sysAppLaunchCmdExgPreview

> This launch code (new to OS 4.0) is sent for an application to preview exchange data. This option is typically used when a user needs more information before deciding whether or not to receive an item. An application can either return a short string or a long string, or draw into a specified area.

sysAppLaunchCmdExgReceiveData

> Once a user decides to receive the data, this launch code is sent to tell the application to actually receive the data. An application will call `ExgAccept` to start the process; then it will call `ExgReceive` in a loop to receive the data; and, finally, it will call `ExgDisconnect` when all the data has been read.

Implementing Exchange

This is a set of miscellaneous tips to help you implement beaming. The first tips are optimization suggestions, the next will help you when debugging your code, and the last are a grab bag of helpful ideas.

Optimization tips

Here are some tips for optimization:

- When calling `ExgSend`, avoid making a lot of calls containing only a few bytes each. It is much better to allocate a buffer and send the entire buffer, if necessary. Throughput is faster with fewer, larger calls.

- When a receive beam launch code is sent to your `PilotMain`, your application is not necessarily running. As a result, you can't allocate similarly large buffers for receiving data with `ExgReceive`. In fact, you should make as few and as small a set of allocations as possible, to avoid stressing the currently running application. It is quite proper, however, to allocate a large buffer if you are running the current application when a receive beam takes place.

Debugging tips

Here are a couple of tips for debugging:

- If you have textual data to send, you can send to the Memo Pad (set the name to end in *.txt*) even before you've written your receive code. If the text doesn't appear, you know you've got problems in the sending portion of the code.

- Set `localMode` (in the `ExgSocketType`) to true to begin with. This gives you a loop of the data back to the same device. Or use shortcut, tap, tap, **t** to force a global loopback.

General tips

Here are some general suggestions:

- If you set the `target` creator ID when sending, you make it difficult for any other application to receive the data on the other end.

  Prior to OS 4.0, in this case, there was no way for any other application to receive data. OS 4.0 allows an application to register for a creator ID not its own and then to set itself as the default handler for that creator ID. The built-in applications in OS 3.5 and earlier *do* set the `target` creator ID. They no longer do so in OS 4.0.

- You must call `ExgSend` in a loop, because it may not send all the bytes you instruct it to send.

- The MIME type is not sent over infrared prior to OS 4.0. Under 4.0, it is sent.

- Call `ExgRegisterData` in your `PilotMain` when you receive the `sysAppLaunch-CmdSyncNotify` (sent when the application itself is installed). If you wait until your `AppStart` routine to register with the system, users won't be able to beam to your application after it has been installed until it has actually been run once.

- Don't call any Exchange Manager routines if your application is running on OS 2.0 or earlier. In fact, your code should specifically check for the version of the OS and take the proper precautions.

- Try running your application on a 3.0-or-greater device that lacks IR capability (such as POSE emulating a Palm III) to make sure that it fails gracefully. Figure 12-2 shows the alert the pops up when a user attempts to beam on a device that has the beaming APIs (3.0 OS or greater), but no IR hardware.

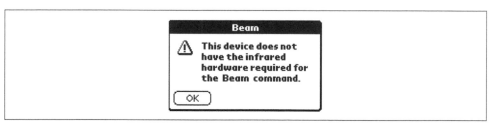

Figure 12-2. Alert shown when beaming on a device that has beaming APIs but no IR hardware

Step-by-Step Implementation Checklist

A checklist approach to implementation works well when you're adding exchange capability to your code. If you follow these steps in a cookbook-like fashion, you should get beaming and send your application up in a jiffy.

Determine data interchange format

You first need to decide whether you'll use a file extension or MIME type (or both). You also have to determine the format of the transmitted data, for both a single entry and a category.

Add user interface

Here is how to add a user interface:

1. Add a Beam menu item to beam the current entry.
2. Add a Beam Category item to the overview Record menu to beam the current category.
3. Add a Send menu item to send the current entry.
4. Add a Send Category item to the overview Record menu to send the current category.

Send an entry

Here is how to send an entry:

1. Add `<ExgMgr.h>` to your include files.
2. Declare an `ExgSocketType` and initialize it to 0.
3. Initialize the `description` field of the `ExgSocketType`.
4. Initialize type, target, and/or name. The name should be a URL that starts with:

    `_beam:` (or the constant `exgBeamPrefix`)
    > For infrared

    `_btobex:`
    > For Bluetooth

    `?_send:` (or the constant `exgSendPrefix`)
    > To have the user choose from all transports other than infrared

    `?_send;_beam:` (or the constant `exgSendBeamPrefix`)
    > To have the user choose from all transports including infrared

5. Initialize `localMode` to 1 (this is for testing with one device; it's optional).
6. Call `ExgPut` to begin the beam.
7. Call `ExgSend` in a loop to send the actual data.
8. Call `ExgDisconnect` to terminate the beam.

Receive an entry

Here is how to receive an entry:

1. Register for receiving based on the MIME type and/or file extension. This is optional; you'll have decided in step 1 what your type and/or extension is.

   In `PilotMain`, when a `sysAppLaunchCmdSyncNotify` launch code occurs, call `ExgRegisterData` with `exgRegExtensionID` and/or with `exgRegTypeID`.

   For OS 4.0, you can also call `ExgRegisterData` with `exgRegSchemeID` to register for a URL scheme or with `exgRegCreatorID` to register for a creator ID. This setup is optional, however.

   If a sender sends data specifying your target application creator ID, your application will be sent a launch code even if it hasn't registered for a specific extension and/or MIME type. You should register if there is a specific kind of data that you want to handle; senders of that data may not have a specific application in mind when they do the send.

2. Handle the receive beam launch code.

   In `PilotMain`, check for the `sysAppLaunchCmdExgReceiveData` launch code. You won't have global variables unless yours happens to be the open application.

3. Call `ExgAccept`.

4. Call `ExgReceive` repeatedly, until it returns 0. A zero is returned when no more data is being received or an error has occurred.

5. Call `ExgDisconnect` to hang up properly.

6. Set `gotoLaunchCode` and `gotoParams`.

   Set `gotoLaunchCode` to your creator's application. Set the following fields in `gotoParams` with the appropriate values: `uniqueID`, `dbID`, `dbCardNo`, and `recordNum`.

Display received item

This feature is a free gift, thanks to the work you did in supporting Find (handling the `sysAppLaunchCmdGoTo` launch code). If your application already correctly handles Find, displaying received items is no work.

Send an entire category

The code for sending an entire category is similar to the code for sending one item (the actual data you send will be different, of course). You must make sure that your data format allows you to distinguish between one item and multiple items. Here are the steps:

1. Declare an `ExgSocketType` and initialize it to 0.

2. Initialize the `description` field of the `ExgSocketType`.

3. Initialize `type`, `target`, and/or `name`.

4. Initialize `localMode` to 1 (this is for testing with one device; it's optional).

5. Call `ExgPut` to begin.

6. Call `ExgSend` in a loop to send the actual data.

7. Call `ExgDisconnect` when you're finished.

Receive an entire category

Receiving an entire category is similar to receiving one item:

1. Call `ExgAccept`.

2. Call `ExgReceive` repeatedly.

3. Call `ExgDisconnect`.

4. Set `gotoLaunchCode` and `gotoParams`.

Test all possibilities

You need to run a gamut of tests to make sure you haven't forgotten any of the details. Test every one of the following combinations of sending and receiving and run any other tests that come to mind:

1. Send a record while your application is open on the remote device.

2. Send a record while your application isn't open on the remote device.

3. Send a category with lots of records (so that the `ExgReceive` can't read all its data at one time).

4. Tap No when the Accept dialog box appears on the remote device.

5. Send a category with a private record. Verify that the private record isn't received.

6. Verify that sending an empty category does nothing.

7. Try the test on a 3.0 device that lacks IR capability (for example, POSE).

Sales Application

The Sales application doesn't have categories, so we don't have a Beam Category menu item; instead, we support Beam All Customers for times when the user wants to beam all the customer information. We also support beaming a single customer.

 We don't support beaming an entire order, although that would be a reasonable function to add to the application, particularly if it were a commercial product. Our interests are pedagogical rather than commercial, so we are skipping that bit; adding this support would not teach you anything new.

When sending a single customer, we send the customer record itself, with a name ending in *.CST*. When sending all customers, we send the following:

- A 2-byte record count indicating the number of total records we are beaming
- For each record, a 2-byte record length for the record and the customer record itself

Let's look at handling a single customer first and then turn to dealing with them all.

Sending a single customer

We add support for beaming/sending to OrderHandleMenuEvent, where we add the Beam and Send menu items:

```
case RecordBeamCustomer:
  SendCustomer(GetRecordNumberForCustomer(
    gCurrentOrder->customerID),  exgBeamPrefix);
  handled = true;
  break;

case RecordSendCustomer:
  SendCustomer(GetRecordNumberForCustomer(
    gCurrentOrder->customerID), exgSendPrefix);
  handled = true;
  break;
```

When the user selects the menu item, the SendCustomer routine we have created (see Example 12-4) is called into play to beam or send a single customer.

Example 12-4. SendCustomer sends or beams a single customer

```
void SendCustomer(UInt16 recordNumber, const Char *scheme)
{
  ExgSocketType s;
  MemHandle     theRecord = DmQueryRecord(gCustomerDB, recordNumber);
  PackedCustomer  *thePackedCustomer;
  Err      err;
  Char     name[50];

  thePackedCustomer = (PackedCustomer *) MemHandleLock(theRecord);
  MemSet(&s, sizeof(s), 0);
  s.description = thePackedCustomer->name;
  StrPrintF(name, "%s%s", scheme, "customer.cst");
  s.name = name;

  err = ExgPut(&s);
  if (err == errNone)
    err = SendBytes(&s, thePackedCustomer, MemHandleSize(theRecord));
  MemHandleUnlock(theRecord);
  err = ExgDisconnect(&s, err);
}
```

SendCustomer relies on SendBytes to actually send the data. Here is that code:

```
static Err SendBytes(ExgSocketPtr s, void *buffer, UInt32 bytesToSend)
{
  Err err = errNone;

  while (err == errNone && bytesToSend > 0) {
    UInt32 bytesSent = ExgSend(s, buffer, bytesToSend, &err);
    bytesToSend -= bytesSent;
    buffer = ((char *) buffer) + bytesSent;
  }
  return err;
}
```

That's all the code for beaming or sending one customer. Let's look at what we need to do to receive that information on the other end.

Receiving a record

First, we need to register with the Exchange Manager in PilotMain:

```
} else if (cmd == sysAppLaunchCmdSyncNotify) {
  DmOpenRef db;

  ExgRegisterData(kSalesCreator, exgRegExtensionID, "cst");

  // code deleted that resorts our databases
}
```

Next, we've got to handle the receive data launch code, which we also put into our PilotMain (see Example 12-5).

Example 12-5. Portion of PilotMain dealing with sysAppLaunchCmdReceiveData launch code

```
} else if (cmd == sysAppLaunchCmdExgReceiveData) {
  DmOpenRef dbP;

  // If our application is not active, we need to open the database.
  // The subcall flag is used to determine whether we are active.
  if (launchFlags & sysAppLaunchFlagSubCall) {
    dbP = gCustomerDB;

    // Save any data we may be editing.
    FrmSaveAllForms();

    error = ReceiveSentData(dbP, (ExgSocketPtr) cmdPBP);
  } else {
    dbP = DmOpenDatabaseByTypeCreator(kCustomerDBType, kSalesCreator,
      dmModeReadWrite);
    if (dbP) {
      error = ReceiveSentData(dbP, (ExgSocketPtr) cmdPBP);

      DmCloseDatabase(dbP);
    }
  }
}
```

We open the customer database if our application isn't already running. Then, we call FrmSaveAllForms to save any data currently being edited.

ReceiveSentData then does most of the real work. Note that since new customers need to have unique customer IDs, we assign a new customer ID to the newly received customer, just as we would if the user used the New Customer menu item.

The first version of ReceiveSentData (see Example 12-6) doesn't receive all customers yet. See "Receiving all customers" later in this chapter for the final version, which does.

Example 12-6. First version of ReceiveSentData that receives only a single customer

```
Err ReceiveSentData(DmOpenRef db, ExgSocketPtr socketPtr)
{
  Err    err;
  UInt16    index;
  Int32 newCustomerID = GetLowestCustomerID( ) - 1;

  err = ExgAccept(socketPtr);
  if (err == errNone) {
  // one customer
  err = ReadIntoNewRecord(db, socketPtr, 0xffffffff, &index);

  // must assign a new unique customer ID
  if (err == errNone) {
    MemHandle h = DmGetRecord(db, index);
    DmWrite(MemHandleLock(h), OffsetOf(Customer, customerID),
      &newCustomerID, sizeof(newCustomerID));
    MemHandleUnlock(h);
    DmReleaseRecord(db, index, true);
    }
    err = ExgDisconnect(socketPtr, err);
  }

  if (err == errNone) {
    DmRecordInfo(db, index, NULL, &socketPtr->goToParams.uniqueID,
      NULL);
    DmOpenDatabaseInfo(db, &socketPtr->goToParams.dbID,
      NULL, NULL, &socketPtr->goToParams.dbCardNo, NULL);
    socketPtr->goToParams.recordNum = index;
    socketPtr->goToCreator = kSalesCreator;
  }
  return err;
}
```

ReadIntoNewRecord (see Example 12-7) reads until there is no more to read (or up to the number of bytes specified, a feature we use when reading all customers). It returns the new record number in the indexPtr parameter.

Example 12-7. ReadIntoNewRecord reads from an exchange socket into a new record

```
// Read at most numBytes into a new record.
// Don't use very much dynamic RAM or stack space--another application is running.
```

```
static Err ReadIntoNewRecord(DmOpenRef db, ExgSocketPtr socketPtr,
  UInt32 numBytes, UInt16 *indexPtr)
{
  char  buffer[100];
  Err   err;
  UInt16  index = 0;
  UInt32  bytesReceived;
  MemHandle recHandle = NULL;
  Char  *recPtr;
  UInt32  recSize = 0;
  Boolean allocatedRecord = false;

  do {
    UInt32  numBytesToRead = sizeof(buffer);

    if (numBytesToRead > numBytes)
      numBytesToRead = numBytes;
    bytesReceived = ExgReceive(socketPtr, buffer, numBytesToRead, &err);
    numBytes -= bytesReceived;
    if (err == errNone) {
      if (!recHandle)
        recHandle = DmNewRecord(db, &index, bytesReceived);
      else
        recHandle = DmResizeRecord(db, index, recSize + bytesReceived);
      if (!recHandle) {
        err = DmGetLastErr();
        break;
      }
      allocatedRecord = true;
      recPtr = (Char *) MemHandleLock(recHandle);
      err = DmWrite(recPtr, recSize, buffer, bytesReceived);
      MemHandleUnlock(recHandle);
      recSize += bytesReceived;
    }
  } while (err == errNone && bytesReceived > 0 && numBytes > 0);

  if (recHandle) {
    DmReleaseRecord(db, index, true);
  }
  if (err != errNone && allocatedRecord)
    DmRemoveRecord(db, index);

  *indexPtr = index;
  return err;
}
```

That's all there is to sending and receiving a single customer. Next, let's look at what additional changes you need to make to send or receive all the customers at once.

Sending all customers

Once again, we add something to our CustomersHandleMenuEvent that handles sending all customers:

```
  case CustomerBeamAllCustomers:
    SendAllCustomers(exgBeamPrefix);
    handled = true;
    break;

  case CustomerSendAllCustomers:
    SendAllCustomers(exgSendPrefix);
    handled = true;
    break;
```

It calls SendAllCustomers (see Example 12-8), which sends the number of records, then the size of each record and the record itself.

Example 12-8. SendAllCustomers sends or beams all customers

```
void SendAllCustomers(const Char *scheme)
{
  DmOpenRef dbP = gCustomerDB;
  UInt16    mode;
  LocalID   dbID;
  UInt16    cardNo;
  Boolean   databaseReopened;
  UInt16    numCustomers;

  // If the database was opened to show secret records, reopen it to not
  // see secret records. The idea is that secret records are not sent when
  // a category is sent. They must be explicitly sent one by one.
  DmOpenDatabaseInfo(dbP, &dbID, NULL, &mode, &cardNo, NULL);
  if (mode & dmModeShowSecret) {
    dbP = DmOpenDatabase(cardNo, dbID, dmModeReadOnly);
    databaseReopened = true;
  } else
    databaseReopened = false;

  // We should send, because there's at least one record to send.
  if ((numCustomers = DmNumRecordsInCategory(dbP, dmAllCategories)) > 0) {
    ExgSocketType s;
    MemHandle     recHandle;
    Err           err;
    UInt16        index;
    Char          name[50];
    UInt16        i;

    MemSet(&s, sizeof(s), 0);
    s.description = "All customers";
    StrPrintF(name, "%s%s", scheme, kAllCustomersName);
    s.name = name;

    err = ExgPut(&s);
    if (err == errNone)
      err = SendBytes(&s, &numCustomers, sizeof(numCustomers));

    // Iterate backward through customers, because we know we'll be adding
    // them at the beginning of the database when they're received. This way,
    // they'll end up in the right order when received.
```

Example 12-8. SendAllCustomers sends or beams all customers (continued)

```
    for (i = 0,index = dmMaxRecordIndex; err == errNone && i < numCustomers;
      i++, index--) {
    UInt16  numberToSeek = 0;

      err = DmSeekRecordInCategory(dbP, &index, numberToSeek,
        dmSeekBackward, dmAllCategories);
      if (err == errNone) {
        UInt16 recordSize;

        recHandle = DmQueryRecord(dbP, index);
        ErrNonFatalDisplayIf(!recHandle, "Couldn't query record");
        recordSize = (UInt16) MemHandleSize(recHandle);
        err = SendBytes(&s, &recordSize, sizeof(recordSize));
        if (err == errNone) {
          PackedCustomer *theRecord;

          theRecord = (PackedCustomer *) MemHandleLock(recHandle);
          err = SendBytes(&s, theRecord, MemHandleSize(recHandle));
          MemHandleUnlock(recHandle);
        }
      }
    }
    err = ExgDisconnect(&s, err);
  } else
    FrmAlert(NoDataToBeamAlert);

  if (databaseReopened)
    DmCloseDatabase(dbP);
}
```

SendAllCustomers uses SendBytes, which we've already seen.

Receiving all customers

In order to receive all customers, ReceiveSentData must change just a bit (changes are emphasized).

Example 12-9. Final version of ReceiveSentData, which will receive multiple customers

```
Err ReceiveSentData(DmOpenRef db, ExgSocketPtr socketPtr)
{
  Err    err;
  UInt16     index;
  Boolean isSingleCustomer;
  Int32 newCustomerID = GetLowestCustomerID( ) - 1;

  // We have all customer if it has a name like
  // "foo:all customers"
  // Otherwise, it's a single customer.
  if (socketPtr->name) {
    Char *colonLocation;

    colonLocation = StrChr(socketPtr->name, ':');
```

```
    if (colonLocation &&
      StrCompare(colonLocation + 1, kAllCustomersName) == 0)
      isSingleCustomer = false;
  }
  err = ExgAccept(socketPtr);
  if (err == errNone) {
    if (isSingleCustomer) {
      // one customer
      err = ReadIntoNewRecord(db, socketPtr, 0xffffffff, &index);

      // must assign a new unique customer ID
      if (err == errNone) {
        MemHandle h = DmGetRecord(db, index);
        DmWrite(MemHandleLock(h), OffsetOf(Customer, customerID),
          &newCustomerID, sizeof(newCustomerID));
        MemHandleUnlock(h);
        DmReleaseRecord(db, index, true);
      }
    } else {
      // all customers
      UInt16  numRecords;

      ExgReceive(socketPtr, &numRecords, sizeof(numRecords), &err);
      while (err == errNone && numRecords-- > 0) {
        UInt16 recordSize;

        ExgReceive(socketPtr, &recordSize, sizeof(recordSize), &err);
        if (err == errNone) {
          err = ReadIntoNewRecord(db, socketPtr, recordSize, &index);
          // must assign a new unique customer ID
          if (err == errNone) {
            MemHandle h = DmGetRecord(db, index);
            DmWrite(MemHandleLock(h),
              OffsetOf(Customer, customerID),
                &newCustomerID, sizeof(newCustomerID));
            newCustomerID--;
            MemHandleUnlock(h);
            DmReleaseRecord(db, index, true);
          }
        }
      }
    }
    err = ExgDisconnect(socketPtr, err);
  }

  if (err == errNone) {
    DmRecordInfo(db, index, NULL, &socketPtr->goToParams.uniqueID, NULL);
    DmOpenDatabaseInfo(db, &socketPtr->goToParams.dbID,
      NULL, NULL, &socketPtr->goToParams.dbCardNo, NULL);
    socketPtr->goToParams.recordNum = index;
```

## CHAPTER 13

Communications

In this chapter, we discuss the types of communication available on the Palm OS. We go into detail about two of these types and show you how to write code for each type.

Palm OS supports three kinds of communication:

Serial

Serial communication occurs between the handheld and other devices using the cradle port. This is the most common form of communication on the Palm OS. For an example, we'll develop a special serial application that communicates (indirectly) with satellites.

TCP/IP

Currently, this communication standard is available only via a serial or modem connection. The future has no boundaries, however, so you may see built-in Ethernet or devices using wireless TCP/IP appear some day. To show you how to use TCP/IP, we'll create a small application that sends email to a server.

IrDA

This is an industry-standard hardware and software protocol for communicating over infrared. We won't discuss the details of communicating using IrDA in this chapter. We will, however, show you how to use the Exchange Manager to implement beaming (see the section entitled "Exchange" in Chapter 12). Beaming is a data-exchange method built on top of IrDA.

Serial Communications

The original version of the Serial Manager was a shared library that provided access to the one and only serial port on the device. The 3.3 OS introduced some important changes, including a new Serial Manager, which is no longer a shared library.

Your code no longer has to call SysLibFind to load the library before using it. The new Serial Manager provides the following:

- Support for multiple serial ports. You can specify either logical ports (such as the cradle port), physical ports (such as the port controlled by a particular UART), or virtual ports (such as an IrComm infrared pseudoserial connection). The Connection Manager provides a way for users to configure and specify ports.

- Support for serial drivers. These drivers can be either physical drivers that control some serial hardware, or virtual drivers that emulate serial drivers (by sending and receiving data in some fashion other than serial). The IrComm serial-over-IR is implemented using a virtual serial driver that handles sending and receiving using the Infrared Library APIs. We won't cover how to write serial drivers in this book.

 IrComm is an industry standard that defines a protocol for using infrared to emulate a serial port. It is used by legacy serial applications that haven't been rewritten to support infrared.

- Backward-compatibility for the old Serial Manager. Code that uses the old Serial Manager will work.

There is a great deal of similarity between the old and new Serial Managers. Most calls are similarly named and take the same parameters. The primary difference is the three-character prefix to the function names:

Ser
:   The old Serial Manager uses this prefix.

Srm
:   The new Serial Manager uses this prefix.

Rather than duplicating our discussions, we'll describe the new Serial Manager calls (with prefix Srm). Unless we note otherwise, there's also an associated Ser call that works the same way.

 In order to determine whether the new Serial Manager is available, call:

```
err = FtrGet(sysFileCSerialMgr, sysFtrNewSerialPresent,
    &value);
```

If err is 0 and value is nonzero, the new Serial Manager is present.

The Serial Manager is fairly straightforward. There are routines to do the following:

- Open and close the serial port
- Read and write data
- Query how many bytes are ready to be read

- Set options

Serial I/O can be done asynchronously (although it's not that common). You can arrange to be notified when data is received, instead of having your code poll to see whether the data has arrived.

Serial APIs

These are the most common APIs:

Err SrmOpen(UInt32 port, UInt32 baud, UInt16 *newPortIdP)
> This routine (defined only for the new Serial Manager) opens the given port at the given baud rate. The newPortIdP is filled in with a port ID: a 16-bit value that is used for all further calls to the new Serial Manager.
>
> Some examples of valid values for port are 0x8000 (to signify the cradle port) and 'ircm' (to signify the virtual IrComm port).
>
> If your code calls SrmOpen and it returns the error serErrAlreadyOpen, your open has succeeded, but some other code has already opened the port. Although it's possible to share the port, a sane person wouldn't normally want to do so. Sharing reads and writes with some other code is a recipe for mangled data. If you get this error, you should notify the user that the port is in use and gracefully call SrmClose.

Err SerOpen(UInt16 refNum, UInt16 port, UInt32 baud)
> This is the old Serial Manager call to open the serial port. The port parameter should always be 0. The refNum is the reference to the Serial Manager's shared library. It is obtained by calling SysLibFind as follows:
>
> ```
> err = SysLibFind("Serial Library", &refNum);
> ```
>
> The refNum is a 16-bit value that is used for all further calls to the old Serial Manager. Like SrmOpen, SerOpen can return serErrAlreadyOpen. Deal with it in the same way.
>
> In Versions 1.0 and 2.0 of the OS, the Serial Manager sends out a backspace character when the serial port is opened. There's no way to prevent this from occurring.

Err SrmClose(UInt16 portId)
> This routine closes the opened port.

UInt32 SrmSend(UInt16 portId, void *bufP, UInt32 count, Err *errP)
> This routine sends count bytes from the data pointed to by bufP. The bytes are sent out the given serial port. The return result is the number of bytes sent. errP is filled in with an error result.
>
> This routine is synchronous. It doesn't return until all the data has actually been transferred to the serial hardware buffers. Thus, this routine will take longer to send 1,000 bytes than it will to send 1 byte.

```
UInt32 SrmReceive(UInt16 portId, void *bufP, UInt32 count, Int32 timeout,
Err *errP)
```
SrmReceive receives count bytes into the buffer pointed to by bufP. It returns the number of bytes actually received. errP is filled in with an error result. The timeout is an inter-byte timeout (in ticks). If no bytes have been received for the specified number of ticks, the error serErrTimeOut is set, and SrmReceive returns the number of bytes actually received.

The old Serial Manager version, SerReceive, has a known bug: it doesn't return the correct number of bytes in the case of a timeout.

```
Err SrmReceiveWait(UInt16 portId, UInt32 count, Int32 timeout)
```
SrmReceiveWait is similar to SrmReceive, but it doesn't actually read any data. Instead, it just waits until the specified number of bytes are available to be read.

```
Err SrmSetReceiveBuffer(UInt16 portId, void *bufP,UInt16 bufSize)
```
This routine sets the incoming data buffer; it replaces the default 512-byte buffer. To restore the default, pass 0 as the bufSize.

Think of this receiving buffer as similar to a reservoir. The incoming data flows into the buffer, and reads from the buffer drain the data out the other side. As with a reservoir, too much incoming data causes the buffer to overflow, and data spills out and is lost. The error you get (on receiving) is serLineErrorSWOverrun.

If you expect a lot of data, it's best to adjust your buffer to accommodate greater inflows. You can set the size using SrmSetReceiveBuffer. When you're done, make sure to release the buffer before you close the port; do so by calling SrmSetReceiveBuffer with a size of 0. SrmClose won't release the buffer, so if you don't do it yourself, you'll leak memory.

```
Err SrmClearErr(UInt16 portId)
```
This routine clears any receive errors. The error serErrLineErr is sticky; it'll keep getting returned from the receive calls until you call SrmClearErr to clear it.

```
Err SrmReceiveFlush(UInt16 portId, Int32 timeout)
```
This routine flushes any data waiting to be received. It'll continue throwing away any incoming data until no data arrives for timeout ticks.

```
Err SrmSetWakeupHandler(UInt16 portId, WakeupHandlerProcPtr procP,
UInt32 refCon)
```
This routine is used for asynchronous data receiving. It establishes a wakeup handler with the port. This wakeup handler will be called (once you've primed with SrmPrimeWakeupHandler) when incoming data arrives and will be passed the refCon parameter (this parameter is used to provide some context to the wakeup handler). Note that the wakeup handler is called at interrupt time and therefore is extremely limited in what it can do: it has no access to global variables and can call very few OS routines. One OS routine it can call is EvtWakeup, which will cause the EvtGetEvent to wake up and return a nilEvent. If you've set a wakeup handler, you can't call SrmReceive or SrmReceiveWait; instead, you'll need to read data using SrmReceiveWindowOpen and SrmReceiveWindowClose.

`Err SrmPrimeWakeupHandler(UInt16 portId, UInt16 minBytes)`
This routine causes the wakeup handler (which must have already been set with `SrmSetWakeupHandler`) to be called when `minBytes` bytes have been received. You'll need to reprime the wakeup handler once it has been called.

`Err SrmReceiveWindowOpen(UInt16 portId, UInt8 **bufPP, UInt32 *sizeP)`
This routine provides direct access to the data in the Serial Manager's receive buffer (as opposed to `SrmReceive`, which copies the data from the receive buffer to some destination). Pass in a pointer to a buffer pointer, and a pointer to a size. On return, the buffer pointer will point to the beginning of the received data, and the size will specify the number of received bytes. You may read from the buffer, but you may not change the data in the buffer. After you've handled the received data, call `SrmReceiveWindowClose`.

Since the receive buffer is circular, there may be received data at the end of the buffer and (wrapped around) at the beginning. Thus, `SrmReceiveWindowOpen` may not return all the received data. You will need to call it a second time to return the (potential) data at the beginning of the buffer. If there is no such data, the size will be 0.

`Err SrmReceiveWindowClose(UInt16 portId, UInt32 bytesPulled)`
Call `SrmReceiveWindowClose` once you've finished reading from the buffer pointer `SrmReceiveWindowOpen` provided. The `bytesPulled` parameter specifies the number of bytes that you've consumed from the buffer (you could specify 0 as a way to peek at the data in the receive buffer without consuming any).

Connection Manager

The 3.3 OS adds a Connection Manager to accompany the new Serial Manager. This Connection Manager allows the user to configure profiles in the Connection panel of the Prefs application (see Figure 13-1). The user can specify a name for this profile, a port, a baud rate, handshaking, and information relevant to a modem connection (modem init string, touch-tone versus pulse, and so on).

An application can query the Connection Manager to find all the configured connections, which allows a user to set up a particular configuration and then to use that configuration in multiple applications. Here are the calls that will be the most useful:

`Err CncGetProfileList(Char *** nameListP, UInt16 *count)`
Pass in the address of a `Char **` for `nameListP`. When it returns, it will point to an array of null-terminated strings that are the names of the profiles. Pass in the address of a `UInt16` for `count`. It will be filled in with a count that represents the quantity of profiles available.

It is up to you to deallocate the memory associated with the array and with each of the null-terminated strings using `MemPtrFree`.

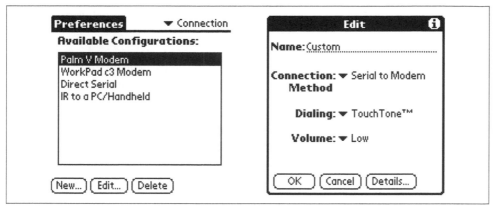

Figure 13-1. The Connection panel and the Edit dialog box that creates custom configurations

```
Err CncGetProfileInfo(Char *name, UInt32 *port, UInt32 *baud,
UInt16 *volume, UInt16 *handShake, Char *initString,
Char *resetString, Boolean *isModem, Boolean *isPulse)
```

This function returns information about the profile with the specified name. Pass pointers to variables to retrieve each of the pieces of information. Pass NULL for a parameter if you don't need that piece of information. You'll use the retrieved information to set up the connection in the way requested by the user.

Tips for Using the Serial Manager

Here are a bunch of miscellaneous tips that will help you when it's time to add serial functionality to an application:

Open the serial port only for short periods of time

Don't leave the serial port open any longer than absolutely necessary. If your application reads data from the serial port every five minutes, don't leave it open for that entire time. Instead, close the port, and reopen it after five minutes. As a rule of thumb, leave the serial port open for no longer than 30 seconds if it is not in use.

Similar advice is often given to drivers about stopped cars. If you will move again within a few minutes, leave the car idling; otherwise, shut the car off and restart it when you are ready to go. Just as an idling car wastes gas, an idle serial port wastes batteries by providing power to the serial chip. Such behavior will really annoy your users, who don't want an application that sucks all the life out of their batteries.

Prevent automatic sleep

If you don't want the Palm OS device to sleep while you are communicating, call EvtResetAutoOffTimer at least once a minute. This prevents the automatic sleep that happens when no user input occurs. If you have communication that shouldn't be interrupted, you certainly should do this, as you will lose the serial data when the device goes to sleep.

Know when there is data in the receive buffer

When reading data, it is best to do it in two steps. The first step is to call SrmReceiveWait, which blocks until the specified number of bytes are available in the buffer. To provide a timeout mechanism, SrmReceiveWait takes an interbyte tick timeout as a parameter. This timeout is used as a watchdog timer that is reset on every received byte. If the timer expires, the function returns with serErrTimeOut. Once SrmReceiveWait returns, the second step is to call SrmReceive to actually read the data from the receive buffer.

The timeout measures the time between successive bytes, not the time for all bytes. For example, if you call SrmReceiveWait waiting for 200 bytes with a 50-tick timeout, SrmReceiveWait returns either when 200 bytes are available, or when 50 ticks have passed since the last byte was received. In the slowest case, if bytes come 1 in every 49 ticks, SrmReceiveWait won't time out.

SrmReceiveWait is the preferred call, because it can put the processor into a low-power state while waiting for incoming data—another battery-saving technique that will make your users happy.

Handle user input properly during a serial event

Don't ignore user input while communicating. Wherever possible, you need to structure your application so that it deals with serial communication when the user isn't doing other stuff. Practically, this means you can do one of two things: your application can communicate every so often by calling EvtGetEvent with a timeout value; or, if your communication code is in a tight loop that doesn't call EvtGetEvent, you can call SysEventAvail every so often (certainly no less than once a second). Calling SysEventAvail allows you to see whether there's a user event to process. If there are user events, return to your event loop to process the event before attempting any more serial communication. Remember, a user who can't cancel will be very unhappy.

An alternative way to handle user input is to do your reading using a wakeup handler (see "Sample Asynchronous Receive" later in this chapter).

Clear errors

If SrmReceive, SrmReceiveWait, or SrmReceiveCheck returns srmErrLineErr, you need to clear the error using SrmClearErr. You should use SrmReceiveFlush if you also need to flush the buffer, since it will call SrmClearErr.

Use serial state machine

Serial protocols are often best written as though they are going to a state machine. You can do this by defining various states and the transitions that cause changes from one state to another. You use a global to contain information on the current state. While it might sound complicated, writing your serial code this way often makes it simpler and easier to maintain.

For example, if you use your Palm device to log into a Unix machine, you might send <CR><CR> and then enter the "Waiting for login:" state. In this state, you'd read until you got the characters "login:". You would then send your account name and enter the "Waiting for password:" state. In that state, you'd read until you got the characters "password:". Then you would send the password and enter yet another state.

Sample Serial Application

With these tips and the serial routines we have discussed, you now have enough information to look at an implementation of serial. As the Sales application doesn't have serial code in it, we've written a small application that communicates with a Global Positioning System (GPS) device over serial instead. A GPS device reads timestamped information sent by orbiting satellites; from that data, it determines the location of the device. In addition to the location (latitude, longitude, and altitude), the device obtains the Universal Time Coordinate (UTC) time.

Features of the sample application

Our sample application communicates with this GPS device using the industry-standard National Marine Electronics Association (NMEA) 0183 serial protocol.

We must use the old Serial Manager to support devices running OS versions earlier than 3.3. We use the new Serial Manager if OS 3.3 or higher is in use. If it is, we display the startup screen shown in Figure 13-2 to allow the user to choose a port.

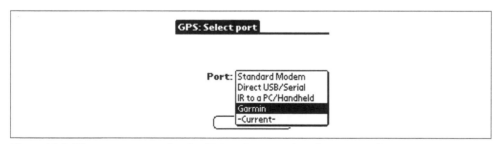

Figure 13-2. The startup screen for the GPS application when the new Serial Manager is present

Once the user selects a port and taps Open, the main screen is shown. If the device doesn't support the new Serial Manager, we skip the startup screen and go directly to the main screen.

The application's startup screen is shown in Figure 13-3.

As you can see, it is blank except for telling the user that it has no GPS information. The state changes as soon as the handheld has established communication with the GPS device and it, in turn, has acquired a satellite. Now it displays the time, latitude, and longitude, as shown in Figure 13-4.

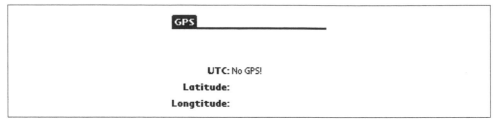

Figure 13-3. The GPS application when it is has not recently heard from the GPS device

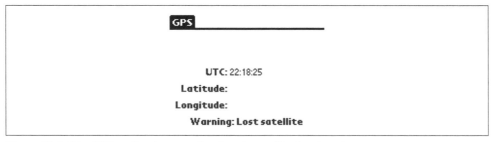

Figure 13-4. The GPS application displaying the current time, latitude, and longitude

The application updates these values every five seconds to make sure the location and time are up to date. If the GPS device loses contact with the satellite (as might happen when the user enters a building), the sample application warns the user (as shown in Figure 13-5).

Figure 13-5. The GPS application warning that the satellite has been lost

A GPS device hooked to a Palm OS handheld is a compact and useful combination. Imagine the versatile and convenient applications you could create that would use information augmented with exact location and precision timestamping. For example, a nature specialist could create a custom trail guide that other people could use to retrace the guide's path.

The GPS device

We' use a Garmin 12 GPS device purchased for under $200 from the sporting-goods section of a discount store. The serial connector on this device is custom, so we use a

Garmin-to-Handspring cable we obtained from Mark/Space Softworks (*http://www. markspace.com*). The Garmin is configured to send NMEA 0183 2.0 at 4800 baud.

The NMEA protocol

In our application, we want to update the time, latitude, and longitude every five seconds. Updating more often seems unnecessary and would reduce the battery life of the Palm OS device. The GPS device sends 10 lines of information every second; of the 50 that are sent over a 5-second period, we simply parse out the information we need. The rest we ignore. As a result, we don't have to understand the entire NMEA 0183 protocol, just the bit that pertains to our one line of interest.*

If we have valid satellite data, the relevant part will look similar to this string:

```
$GPRMC,204700,A,3403.868,N,11709.432,W,001.9,336.9,170698,013.6,E*6E
```

Let's look more closely at this example to see what each part means. Note that we care about only the first seven pieces of data. In Table 13-1, the important parts of the string are laid out with the definitions beside each item.

Table 13-1. NMEA string from GPS device

Sample string value	NMEA 0183 protocol	Description
$GPRMC		GPS-recommended minimum data.
204700	UTC_TIME	This comes in the form of a 24-hour clock, where the time uses HHMMSS as the format.
A	A or V	A means the data is OK; V is a warning.
3403.868	LAT	This comes in the form of a number such as ####.###.
N	LAT_DIR	This is (N)orth or (S)outh.
11709.432	LON	This comes in the form of a number such as #####.###.
W	LON_DIR	This is (W)est or (E)ast.

If we aren't receiving valid satellite data, the string is in the form:

```
$GPRMC,UTC_TIME,V,...
```

Here's a typical example:

```
$GPRMC,204149,V,,,,,,,170698,,*3A
```

Now that you have an idea of what we want to accomplish and the tools we are going to use, it is time to look at the code for the sample application.

---

* The NMEA 0183 protocol is a document that is available only in hard copy form. You can order it from NMEA at (252) 638-2626.

Opening the serial port

We are going to open the serial port in our `AppStart` routine (see Example 13-1).

Example 13-1. AppStart that opens the serial port

```
#define kBaudRate        4800

UInt16 gPortID;

Err AppStart(void)
{
  UInt32  value;

  gNewSerialManager = FtrGet(sysFileCSerialMgr,
    sysFtrNewSerialPresent, &value) == 0 && value != 0;

  if (gNewSerialManager) {
    FrmGotoForm(GPSPortForm);
  } else {
    Err err = SysLibFind("Serial Library", &gPortID);
    if (err == 0)
      err = SerOpen(gPortID, 0, kBaudRate);
    if (err == serErrAlreadyOpen) {
      FrmAlert(SerialInUseAlert);
    } else if (err)
      FrmAlert(CantOpenSerialAlert);
    else
      FrmGotoForm(GPSMainForm);
  }
  return 0;
}
```

We check to see whether the new Serial Manager is present (saving that information in a global variable). If it is, we go to the form to specify a port; otherwise, we find the serial library and open it. Note that we use the `gPortID` to hold either the old Serial Manager's library reference number or the new Serial Manager's port ID. This takes advantage of the fact that they are both 16-bit integers. We display an alert if the port is already in use and a different alert if we have some other problem opening the serial port.

Closing the serial port

In `AppStop`, we close the port if it is open:

```
    static void AppStop(void)
    {
      if (gPortID) {
        // restore the default buffer before closing the serial port
        DoSetReceiveBuffer(gPortID, NULL, 0);
        DoClose(gPortID);
      }
    }
```

Before closing, we reset the receive buffer, as our main form will take it out of the default setting.

Routines that work with the old and new Serial Managers

We've provided wrappers around all the functions that are common between the old and new Serial Managers. They all start with Do, and call either the Srm version of the routine or the Ser version, depending on whether the new Serial Manager is present. We'll give you one example; the others are similar:

```
Err DoSetReceiveBuffer(UInt16 portId, void *bufP, UInt16 bufSize)
{
  if (gNewSerialManager)
    return SrmSetReceiveBuffer(portId, bufP, bufSize);
  else
    return SerSetReceiveBuffer(portId, bufP, bufSize);
}
```

Allowing the user to choose a port

To allow the user to specify a port, we initialize a pop-up list with the list of profile names when our startup form opens (see Example 13-2).

Example 13-2. Initialization routine for Port form

```
Char **gProfiles;
UInt16 gNumProfiles;

void PortFormInit(FormPtr form)
{
  ListPtr list = (ListPtr) GetObjectFromForm(form, GPSPortList);
  Err     err;
  const UInt16 kMaxVisibleItems = 14;
  UInt16 numVisibleItems = kMaxVisibleItems;

  err = CncGetProfileList(&gProfiles, &gNumProfiles);
  LstSetListChoices(list, gProfiles, gNumProfiles);
  if (gNumProfiles < kMaxVisibleItems)
    numVisibleItems = gNumProfiles;
  LstSetHeight(list, numVisibleItems);
  LstSetSelection(list, noListSelection);
}
```

When the form closes, we free the memory for each profile name and for the array:

```
void PortFormDeinit( )
{
  if (gProfiles) {
    UInt16 i;

    for (i = 0; i < gNumProfiles; i++)
      if (gProfiles[i])
        MemPtrFree(gProfiles[i]);
```

```
        MemPtrFree(gProfiles);
        gProfiles = NULL;
    }
  }
```

Opening the port

When the user taps on the Open button, our form's event handler (see Example 13-3) finds the port and baud rate for that profile, then does the open.

Example 13-3. Portion of event handler that uses the new Serial Manager to open the port

```
case ctlSelectEvent:
  if (event->data.ctlSelect.controlID == GPSPortUsePortButton) {
    Err err;
    UInt32 portID;
    UInt32  baud;
    ListPtr list = (ListPtr) GetObjectFromActiveForm(GPSPortList);
    UInt16 listSelection = LstGetSelection(list);

    if (listSelection == noListSelection) {
      FrmAlert(NoProfileSelectedAlert);
      break;
    } else {
      err = CncGetProfileInfo(gProfiles[listSelection],
        &portID, &baud, 0, 0, 0, 0, 0, 0);
    }
    if (err == 0)
      err = SrmOpen(serPortCradlePort, kBaudRate, &gPortID);
    if (err == serErrAlreadyOpen) {
      FrmAlert(SerialInUseAlert);
      DoClose(gPortID);
    } else if (err)
      FrmAlert(CantOpenSerialAlert);
    else
      FrmGotoForm(GPSMainForm);
    handled = true;
  }
  break;
```

The Main form

Example 13-4 shows our form resource.

Example 13-4. Main form resource

```
FORM ID GPSMainForm AT (0 0 160 160)
BEGIN
  TITLE "GPS"
  LABEL "UTC:" AUTOID AT (RIGHT@60 53) FONT 1
  FIELD ID TimeField AT (PREVRIGHT+2 PREVTOP 50 AUTO) LEFTALIGN
    SINGLELINE MAXCHARS 10
```

Example 13-4. Main form resource (continued)

```
  LABEL "Latitude:" AUTOID AT (RIGHT@60 PREVBOTTOM+5) FONT 1
  FIELD ID LatitudeField AT (PREVRIGHT+2 PREVTOP 50 AUTO) LEFTALIGN
    SINGLELINE MAXCHARS 10
  LABEL "Longitude:" AUTOID AT (RIGHT@60 PREVBOTTOM+5) FONT 1
  FIELD ID LongitudeField AT (PREVRIGHT+2 PREVTOP 50 AUTO) LEFTALIGN
    SINGLELINE MAXCHARS 10
  LABEL "Warning: Lost satellite" LostSatelliteLabel AT
    (CENTER@80 PREVBOTTOM+5) NONUSABLE FONT 1
END
```

We have three labeled fields (one for time, one for latitude, and one for longitude). In addition, we have a warning label that, to begin with, is nonusable.

Setting the receive buffer to hold data

When the Main form opens (see Example 13-5), we set our own receive buffer so that we can hold an entire second's worth of data. We don't want to risk losing any data, so we give ourselves ample room. We also initialize some timeout values in ticks (we must convert from seconds to ticks).

Example 13-5. Initialization for Main form

```
char    gSerialBuffer[900]; // should be more than enough for one second of
                            // data: 10 lines @ 80 chars per line
UInt16 gTicksPerSecond;
// if we go this long without updating the time
// then update as soon as we get a valid time
// (without waiting for an even 5-second time)
UInt32 gMaxTicksWithoutTime;

// if we go this long without communicating with GPS,
// we've lost it and need to notify the user
UInt32  gTicksToLoseGPS;

Boolean gFormOpened = false;

void MainFormInit(void)
{
  Err     err;

  err = DoSetReceiveBuffer(gPortID, gSerialBuffer, sizeof(gSerialBuffer));
  gTicksPerSecond = SysTicksPerSecond( );
  gMaxTicksWithoutTime = 6 * gTicksPerSecond;
  gTicksToLoseGPS = 15 * gTicksPerSecond;
  gFormOpened = true;
}
```

We set gFormOpened in MainFormInit. We keep track of this because we don't want to start receiving nilEvents until the form has been opened and displayed.

We also need some globals to store information about timing:

```
// tickCount of last time we read data from GPS
UInt32    gLastSuccessfulReception = 0;

// tickCount of last time we displayed GPS data on the Palm device
UInt32    gLastTimeDisplay = 0;

// tickCount of the next scheduled read
UInt32    gNextReadTime = 0;
```

The event loop

In our event loop, instead of calling EvtGetEvent with no timeout, we call the function TimeUntilNextRead to obtain a timeout when we need it. Here's our EventLoop:

```
void EventLoop(void)
{
  EventType event;
  UInt16     error;

  do {
    EvtGetEvent(&event, TimeUntilNextRead( ));
    if (! SysHandleEvent(&event))
      if (! MenuHandleEvent(0, &event, &error))
        if (! ApplicationHandleEvent(&event))
          FrmDispatchEvent(&event);
  } while (event.eType != appStopEvent);
}
```

 EvtGetEvent, like SrmReceiveCheck, enters a low-power processor mode if possible.

Note that TimeUntilNextRead (see Example 13-6) returns the number of ticks until the next scheduled read.

Example 13-6. TimeUntilNextRead figures out when a read needs to occur next

```
long TimeUntilNextRead(void)
{
  if (!gFormOpened)
    return evtWaitForever;
  else {
    Int32 timeRemaining;

    timeRemaining = gNextReadTime - TimGetTicks( );

    if (timeRemaining < 0)
      timeRemaining = 0;
    return timeRemaining;
  }
}
```

The event handler

Example 13-7 shows our event handler.

Example 13-7. Event handler for Main form

```
Boolean MainFormHandleEvent(EventPtr event)
{
  Boolean   handled;
  Boolean   updatedDisplay;

  handled = false;
  switch (event->eType)
  {
  case nilEvent:
    handled = true;
    DoReceiveFlush(gPortID, 1); // throw away anything in the buffer--we want fresh data.

    // we loop until an event occurs, or until
    // we update the display
    do {
      updatedDisplay = ReadFromGPS( );
    } while (!updatedDisplay && !EvtSysEventAvail(false));
    break;

  case frmOpenEvent:
    MainFormInit( );
    FrmDrawForm(FrmGetActiveForm( ));
    handled = true;
    break;

  }
  return(handled);
}
```

Updating the display with new GPS data

Remember that the GPS device is spewing out data once a second. Since we are not going to update that often, we've settled on updating every five seconds as a happy medium. Normally, when we receive an idle event we have just been in the event loop, dozing for four seconds. Thus, our receive buffer could have old data in it or could have overflowed. Therefore, we flush the current receive buffer and then loop, reading from the GPS until either we've updated the display, or an event is waiting for us in the event queue.

The code that reads from the GPS in Example 13-8 returns true if the display has been updated and false otherwise.

Example 13-8. Routine that reads from the GPS device; returns true if display has been updated

```
Boolean ReadFromGPS(void)
{
  Err     err;
  Boolean updatedDisplay = false;
```

Example 13-8. Routine that reads from the GPS device; returns true if display has been updated

```
UInt32  numBytesPending;
UInt32  now = TimGetTicks();
char    theData[165]; // two lines (80 chars with <CR><LF>
                      //  + one for null byte

// If we've gone too long without hearing from the GPS
// tell the user.
WarnUserIfHaventHeardFromGPSRecently();

numBytesPending = WaitForData(sizeof(theData)-1);
if (numBytesPending > 0) {
  char    *startOfMessage;

  err = ReadAvailableData(theData, sizeof(theData) - 1, numBytesPending);
  if (err)
    return false;

  // Look for our magic string.
  if ((startOfMessage = StrStr(theData, "$GPRMC")) != NULL)
    updatedDisplay = HandleMessage(startOfMessage);
}
return updatedDisplay;
}
```

Note that `TimGetTicks` is a Time Manager call that returns the current number of ticks (since the last reset). It's often used for timing. We warn the user if we haven't read from the GPS recently, and then wait for a couple of lines of data. Once there's data present, we read it and then look for the $GPRMC that marks the start of the line we want (`StrStr` is a String Manager routine that finds one string within another). If we find it, we handle it with `HandleMessage`.

Alerting the user if GPS hasn't been heard from lately

The routine in Example 13-9 alerts the user if the application hasn't heard from the GPS recently.

Example 13-9. Routine that warns the user when GPS hasn't been heard from

```
void WarnUserIfHaventHeardFromGPSRecently(void)
{
  if ((TimGetTicks() - gLastSuccessfulReception) > gTicksToLoseGPS) {
    char  str[20];

    SysCopyStringResource(str, NoGPSString);
    SetFieldTextFromStr((FieldPtr) GetObjectFromActiveForm(TimeField),
      str, true);
    SetFieldTextFromStr((FieldPtr) GetObjectFromActiveForm(LatitudeField),
      "", true);
    SetFieldTextFromStr((FieldPtr) GetObjectFromActiveForm(LongitudeField),
      "", true);
  }
}
```

This routine displays "No GPS" in the time field and empties the latitude and longitude fields.

ReadFromGPS uses WaitForData (see Example 13-10) to wait until there's data to read.

Example 13-10. WaitForData waits until there's data to be read

```
UInt32 WaitForData(UInt32 bufferSize)
{
  UInt32 numBytesPending = 0;
  Err err;
  const Int32 kOneHalfSecond = gTicksPerSecond / 2;

  // We'll fill our read buffer, or 1/2 second between
  // bytes, whichever comes first.
  err = DoReceiveWait(gPortID, bufferSize, kOneHalfSecond);
  if (err == serErrLineErr) {
    DoReceiveFlush(gPortID, 1); // will clear the error
    return 0;
  }
  if (err != serErrTimeOut)
    ErrFatalDisplayIf(err != 0, "DoReceiveWait");
  err = DoReceiveCheck(gPortID, &numBytesPending);
  if (err == serErrLineErr) {
    DoReceiveFlush(gPortID, 1); // will clear the error
    return 0;
  }
  ErrFatalDisplayIf(err != 0, "DoReceiveCheck Fail");
  return numBytesPending;
}
```

This routine waits until the buffer is full, or until it's been half a second since a character has arrived. Also, if a line error occurs, we flush the buffer; this will clear the error. If some unknown error occurs, we display a fatal alert (probably not the best choice). The function returns the number of bytes waiting.

Reading the GPS data

Once ReadFromGPS knows there's data waiting, it calls ReadAvailableData (see Example 13-11) to read all waiting data.

Example 13-11. ReadAvailableData reads as much data as possible

```
Boolean ReadAvailableData(Char *data, UInt32 bufferSize,
  UInt32 numBytesPending)
{
  Err err;
  UInt32  numBytes;

  // Read however many bytes are waiting.
  if (numBytesPending > bufferSize)
    numBytesPending = bufferSize;
  numBytes = DoReceive(gPortID, data, numBytesPending, 0, &err);
```

Example 13-11. ReadAvailableData reads as much data as possible (continued)

```
    if (err == serErrLineErr) {
      DoReceiveFlush(gPortID, 1); // Will clear the error.
    } else
      data[numBytes] = '\0';  // Null-terminate the data.
    return 0;
}
```

ReadAvailableData null-terminates the string and flushes the receive buffer in case of a line error.

Finally, HandleMessage (see Example 13-12) will handle a line of data that starts with $GPRMC.

Example 13-12. HandleMessage will handle a GPRMC line

```
Boolean HandleMessage(Char *message)
{
  Char   s[11];
  UInt32  now = TimGetTicks();
  Boolean updatedDisplay = false;

  gLastSuccessfulReception = now; // We successfully read.
  if (GetField(message, 1, s)) {
    Boolean evenMultipleOf5Seconds = (s[5] == '0' || s[5] == '5');

    // Even multiple of five seconds OR it's been at
    // least kMaxTicksWithoutTime seconds since a display.
    // That way, if we lose 11:11:35, we won't have the
    // time go from 11:11:30 to 11:11:40. Instead, it'll go
    // 11:11:30, 11:11:36, 11:11:40
    if (evenMultipleOf5Seconds ||
      (now - gLastTimeDisplay) > gMaxTicksWithoutTime) {
      // change from HHMMSS to HH:MM:SS
      s[8] = '\0';
      s[7] = s[5];
      s[6] = s[4];
      s[5] = ':';
      s[4] = s[3];
      s[3] = s[2];
      s[2] = ':';

      // Most of the time, we'll be on a multiple of five.
      // Thus, we want to read in four and a half more seconds.
      // Otherwise, we want to read immediately.
      if (evenMultipleOf5Seconds)
        gNextReadTime = gLastSuccessfulReception +
          4*gTicksPerSecond + gTicksPerSecond / 2;
      else
        gNextReadTime = 0;

      // Update the time display.
      SetFieldTextFromStr((FieldPtr) GetObjectFromActiveForm(TimeField), s,
        true);
```

Example 13-12. HandleMessage will handle a GPRMC line (continued)

```
      gLastTimeDisplay = gLastSuccessfulReception;
      updatedDisplay = true;

      if (GetField(message, 2, s)) {
        if (s[0] == 'V')
          UpdateLostSatellite(true);
        else {
          UpdateLostSatellite(false);
          UpdateLatAndLon(message);
        }
      }
    }
  }
  return updatedDisplay;
}
```

Updating the display

Next, we parse out the time from the string (using `GetField` to retrieve the first field).
If it is a multiple of five or we've gone too long without updating the display, we do
all of the following:

1. Set the next time to read.

2. Parse out the remaining information.

3. Update our display with the new information (the current position or an indication that the link to the satellite is lost).

4. Return true, signifying that we've updated the display.

Otherwise, we return false, signifying that we haven't updated the display.

The utility routine `GetField` (see Example 13-13) will parse out a comma-delimited
field.

Example 13-13. GetField retrieves a field from a given string

```
// Returns n'th (0-based) comma-delimited field within buffer.
// True if field found, false otherwise.
static
Boolean GetField(const Char *buffer, UInt16 n, Char *result)
{
  int i;

  // Skip n commas.
  for (i = 0; i < n; i++) {
    while (*buffer && *buffer != ',')
      buffer++;
    if (*buffer == '\0')
      return false;
    buffer++;
  }
  while (*buffer && *buffer != ',')
    *result++ = *buffer++;
```

Example 13-13. GetField retrieves a field from a given string (continued)

```
  *result = '\0';
  return *buffer == ',' || *buffer == '\0';
}
```

UpdateLostSatellite (see Example 13-14) updates the display to signify whether the satellite is lost or not lost.

Example 13-14. Updates Lost Satellite label appropriately

```
void UpdateLostSatellite(Boolean satelliteIsLost)
{
  FormPtr     form = FrmGetActiveForm( );
  static Boolean gShowingLostSatellite = false;

  // update "Lost satellite" label
  if (satelliteIsLost) {
    if (!gShowingLostSatellite) {
      gShowingLostSatellite = true;
      FrmShowObject(form, FrmGetObjectIndex(form,
        LostSatelliteLabel));
    }
  } else {
    if (gShowingLostSatellite) {
      gShowingLostSatellite = false;
      FrmHideObject(form, FrmGetObjectIndex(form,
        LostSatelliteLabel));
    }
  }
}
```

UpdateLatAndLon (see Example 13-15) updates the latitude and longitude.

Example 13-15. Updates the latitude and longitude fields of the display

```
void UpdateLatAndLon(Char *message)
{
  Char  s[11];

  // 4 is N or S for Lat direction, 3 is lat
  if (GetField(message, 4, s) &&
    GetField(message, 3, s + StrLen(s)))
    SetFieldTextFromStr((FieldPtr) GetObjectFromActiveForm(LatitudeField),
      s, true);

  // 6 is E or W for Lon direction, 5 is lon
  if (GetField(message, 6, s) &&
    GetField(message, 5, s + StrLen(s)))
    SetFieldTextFromStr((FieldPtr) GetObjectFromActiveForm(LongitudeField),
      s, true);
}
```

That's all there is to our application. But as you can see from the discussion prior to the code, the difficulty with serial is not in the actual calls but in configuring your application to do the right thing. Much of the complexity is in being responsive to the user while doing communications and in conserving battery life by idling with EvtGetEvent and SerReceiveWait.

Sample Asynchronous Receive

We've created a very small application that implements another use of serial. This application demonstrates how asynchronous receiving can be done. As with the GPS sample, our code will use the new Serial Manager if present; otherwise, it reverts to the old Serial Manager. Users can choose a profile if the new Serial Manager is present.

This application simply displays any received data in a field. As you can see from Figure 13-6, the UI is nothing to write home about; the important point is that the data is received asynchronously. This allows you to use your normal event loop without changing the timeout, and without having to poll. This can lead to simpler code and longer battery life.

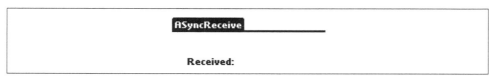

Figure 13-6. The Asynchronous application Main form

Now, let's look at the code that makes up the application.

The application's resource and global variable

Here is the application's form resource:

```
FORM ID MainForm AT (0 0 160 160)
BEGIN
  TITLE "ASyncReceive"
  LABEL "Received:" AUTOID AT (RIGHT@65 40) FONT 1
  FIELD ID MainField AT (PREVRIGHT+2 PREVTOP 80 100) LEFTALIGN
    MULTIPLELINE MAXCHARS kMaxCharsInField
END
```

Next, we define a global variable that will be true if there is data waiting to be read and false otherwise:

```
UInt16 gDataIsReady = false;  // non-zero if there is serial data ready
```

The wakeup handler

Next, we'll install the wakeup handler when the main form is opened. In addition to installing it, we've got to prime it (to be called after a byte arrives). This will ensure that the Serial Manager will call it when incoming data arrives:

```
void MainFormInit(void)
{
  DoSetWakeupHandler(gPortID, MyWakeupHandler, (UInt32) &gDataIsReady);
  DoPrimeWakeupHandler(gPortID, 1);
}
```

Note that we when we set the wakeup handler, we pass the address of the global variable; that will in turn be passed to the wakeup handler itself. This is necessary because wakeup handlers are called at interrupt time and can't *directly* access global variables. Here's the handler:

```
void MyWakeupHandler(UInt32 refCon)
{
  Boolean *dataIsReadyPtr = (Boolean *) refCon;

  *dataIsReadyPtr = true;
  EvtWakeup( );
}
```

The event handler

As well as setting the global variable (indirectly via the passed-in parameter), we need to make sure that our call to EvtGetEvent returns (we're likely to be sitting in a call to EvtGetEvent waiting for some event to happen). EvtWakeup will do that, causing EvtGetEvent to return with a nilEvent.

Example 13-16 shows our event handler, which handles the nilEvent.

Example 13-16. Event handler that reads on a nilEvent

```
Boolean MainFormHandleEvent(EventPtr event)
{
  Boolean    handled;

  handled = false;
  switch (event->eType)
  {
  case frmOpenEvent:
    MainFormInit( );
    FrmDrawForm(FrmGetActiveForm( ));
    handled = true;
    break;

  case nilEvent:
    if (gDataIsReady) {
      static UInt8   gBuffer[kMaxCharsInField];
      UInt32 amtRead;
```

Example 13-16. Event handler that reads on a nilEvent (continued)

```
      amtRead = ReadUsingWindow(gPortID, gBuffer, sizeof(gBuffer)-1);
      if (amtRead > 0) {
        FieldPtr  field;

        gBuffer[amtRead] = '\0';  // null-terminate the string

        field = (FieldPtr) GetObjectFromActiveForm(MainField);
        SetFieldTextFromStr(field, (Char *) gBuffer, true);
      }
      gDataIsReady = false;
      DoPrimeWakeupHandler(gPortID, 1);
    }
  }
  return handled;
}
```

We must check our global variable, gDataIsReady, because nilEvents can occur due not only to our wakeup handler, but to other parts of the OS as well. We read the data using ReadUsingWindow, then null-terminate it and display it in our field. Once we've done that, we set the global back to false, because we've consumed all the data, and then we reprime the wakeup handler.

Reading the data

ReadUsingWindow (see Example 13-17) actually reads the data. Recall that (for no good reason) we may not use SrmReceive or SrmReceiveCheck, but must use the window routines.

Example 13-17. Reads using window routines

```
// Reads into the given buffer. Returns the amount read and
// throws away any data beyond what will fit in the buffer.
UInt32 ReadUsingWindow(UInt16 portID, UInt8 *outBuf, UInt32 outSize)
{
  Err err;
  UInt8 *bytePtr;
  UInt32  size;
  UInt8 totalAmtRead = 0;

  do {
    err = DoReceiveWindowOpen(gPortID, &bytePtr, &size);
    if (err == 0) {
      UInt32 amtToMove = size;

      if (amtToMove > outSize)
        amtToMove = outSize;
      MemMove(outBuf, bytePtr, amtToMove);
      outBuf += amtToMove;
      outSize -= amtToMove;
      totalAmtRead += amtToMove;
      DoReceiveWindowClose(gPortID, size);
    }
```

Example 13-17. Reads using window routines (continued)

```
    } while (err == 0 && size > 0);
    return totalAmtRead;
}
```

Note that the routine loops, calling the WindowOpen and WindowClose routines until there is no longer any more data (or until an error occurs). This handles the case where the data has wrapped around the end of the circular buffer. When we call the WindowClose routine, we pass in the size returned from the WindowOpen routine, rather than just the amount we have copied out. Of course, this means we are throwing away data if there's more than will fit in our buffer. For this particular application that's OK, but other applications might not wish to lose any data. One way to avoid data loss is to dynamically allocate memory to hold the received data; we could also set a receive buffer smaller than the buffer to which we're copying, to guarantee that there's enough space.

TCP/IP Communications

Now it is time to look at TCP/IP. In this section, we will do the following:

- Discuss the API for networking on a Palm device
- Give you some programming tips for using TCP/IP
- Use TCP/IP in a small sample application that sends email to a Simple Mail Transfer Protocol (SMTP) server

Network API

The Palm OS (2.0 or later) contains a net library that provides network services, such as TCP/IP, to applications. With this library, an application on the Palm device can connect to any other machine on a network using standard TCP/IP protocols. The API for this library is a socket interface modeled closely on the Berkeley Sockets API.

 This section provides a brief introduction to network programming on the Palm OS. For more in-depth coverage, see *Palm OS Network Programming*, by Greg Winton (O'Reilly).

Berkeley Sockets API

Sockets are a communication mechanism. Information is sent into a socket on one machine and comes out of a socket on a remote machine (and vice versa). With a connection-oriented socket interface, you can establish the connection between the two machines prior to sending data. The connection stay opens whether or not data is sent. A good example of this is TCP. Sockets also allow a connectionless mode for sending datagrams. These can be sent to an address without any prior connection using a protocol such as the User Datagram Protocol (UDP).

 For a brief introduction to Berkeley Sockets and socket programming, see *http://www.ibrado.com/sock-faq/*. For a more detailed discussion, see *Unix Network Programming, Volume 1: Networking APIs—Sockets and XTI*, by W. Richard Stevens (Prentice Hall).

Palm OS NetLib API

The Networking library, NetLib, is a shared library; all the NetLib calls require a refNum to the library. You obtain that with the following call:

```
err = SysLibFind( "Net.lib", &libRefNum);
```

Here are the most important Palm OS Networking calls:

Err NetLibOpen (UInt16 libRefnum, UInt16 *netIFErrsP)

You pass in the refNum obtained from SysLibFind and a pointer to an error. NetLibOpen returns two different types of errors. The result of the function tells whether the high-level open succeeded or not. If it returns an error, do not call NetLibClose. The passed-in parameter returns a low-level interface error—on an interface error, you still must call NetLibClose.

Err NetLibClose (UInt16 libRefnum, UInt16 immediate)

The immediate parameter controls whether the network connection is closed immediately (if true) or after a delay. You'll normally want to pass false, so the user has time to switch to a different application and use the network connection.

NetSocketRef NetLibSocketOpen(UInt16 libRefnum, NetSocketAddrEnum domain, NetSocketTypeEnum type, Int16 protocol, Int32 timeout, Err *errP)

This creates a socket. The domain will normally be netSocketAddrINET. The type is usually either netSocketTypeStream (for a stream socket) or netSocketTypeDatagram (for a datagram socket). The protocol is normally 0. The routine will return with an error if the timeout (in ticks) is exceeded. Any error is returned in the passed-in error pointer, errP.

Int16 NetLibSocketClose(UInt16 libRefnum, NetSocketRef socket, Int32 timeout, Err *errP)

This closes the given socket. The libRefnum, timeout, and errP are the same as in other calls.

Int16 NetLibSocketConnect(UInt16 libRefnum, NetSocketRef socket, NetSocketAddrType *sockAddrP, Int16 addrLen, Int32 timeout, Err *errP)

This connects to the address given in sockAddrP (the length of the address is in addrLen). The libRefnum, timeout, and errP are the same as in the other calls.

```
Int16 NetLibReceive(UInt16 libRefNum, NetSocketRef socket,
void *bufP, UInt16 bufLen, UInt16 flags, void *fromAddrP,
UInt16 *fromLenP, Int32 timeout, Err *errP)
```

This reads data from the given socket into bufP (but no more than bufLen bytes). If the socket is a datagram socket, fromAddrP is filled in with the sender (fromLenP is the sender's address length). The flags can be used to do things like peek at the data without removing it from the incoming queue. The libRefnum, timeout, and errP are the same as in the other calls. The function returns the number of bytes read, which may be less than requested in bufLen. A return result of 0 means that the socket has been closed on the remote end. A return result of −1 signifies that an error occurred: the error is returned in the errP parameter.

```
Int16 NetLibDmReceive(UInt16 libRefNum, NetSocketRef socket, void *recordP,
UInt32 recordOffset, UInt16 rcvLen, UInt16 flags, void *fromAddrP,
UInt16 *fromLenP, Int32 timeout, Err *errP)
```

This is like NetLibReceive, except that it reads directly into a locked chunk in the storage heap. recordP is a pointer to a locked chunk, recordOffset is the offset that is used to determine where the reading starts.

```
Int16 NetLibSend(UInt16 libRefNum, NetSocketRef socket, void *bufP, UInt16
bufLen, UInt16 flags, void *toAddrP, UInt16 toLen, Int32 timeout, Err *errP)
```

This sends the data pointed to by bufP (of length bufLen) to the given socket. The flags can control whether the data is sent out-of-band. The toAddrP and toLen specify a destination address (used only if this is a datagram socket). The libRefnum, timeout, and errP are the same as in the other calls. The function returns the number of bytes sent (which may be less than the number requested). A result of 0 means the connection has been closed on the remote end. A result of −1 means an error occurred (the error is in the errP parameter).

Net library and the Berkeley Sockets API

The similarity between the Berkeley Sockets API and the net library is so close that you can compile Berkeley Sockets code for the Palm OS with minor—and sometimes no—changes. As a result, porting networking code to the Palm OS is simple.

The ported code works so well because the net library includes header files with macros that convert Berkeley Sockets calls to Palm OS calls. The net library accepts three additional parameters over and above what the Berkeley Sockets API expects; this is the main difference. These parameters are as follows:

A networking reference number
All calls to the net library need to use an integer reference to the net library. The Berkeley Sockets macros pass the global variable AppNetRefnum as their first parameter.

An error-code pointer
The Berkeley Sockets macros pass the address of the global variable errno.

A timeout
> The net library routines return if they haven't finished before the timeout. The Berkeley Sockets macros pass the global variable `AppNetTimeout`. Note that the default timeout (two seconds) may be too short for communicating by modem to busy servers.

To use the Berkeley Sockets APIs, you must include the following file:

```
#include <sys_socket.h>
```

In addition, you must define `errno` somewhere in your application:

```
Err errno
```

You must also declare `AppNetRefNum` (and initialize it, with a call to `SysLibFind`):

```
extern UInt16 AppNetRefNum;
```

And you may initialize the timeout, `AppNetTimeout`, if you wish:

```
AppNetTimeout = 3 * SysTicksPerSecond();
```

In addition, you'll need to link with the NetSocket library (add it to your project, or to your makefile).

Tips for Using TCP/IP

Here are some tips to help you implement TCP/IP in your Palm OS application:

Think about when to open a network connection
> Consider carefully when to open the net library and establish a connection. Your `AppStart` routine is usually not a good choice, as the Palm device would dial up for a connection as soon as the user tapped the application icon. A better way to handle this is to wait for some explicit user request to make the connection; for example, a mail application could wait until the user chooses to send or receive mail.

Be aware that send and receive may return less than requested
> When you send or receive, not all the requested bytes may be transmitted. This is not an error, but it is a common source of mistakes. If you need to send (or receive) a particular number of bytes you should loop, call the `NetLibSend` (or `NetLibReceive`) routine until all the bytes you need have been sent (or received).

Don't immediately close the connection
> When you close the net library with `NetLibClose`, pass `false` as the `immediate` parameter; the net library then remains open until the user-specified timer expires. As a result of the clever design of `NetLibClose`, the user can switch to another application that makes networking calls without having to redial. This ability can be useful to a user who is doing several network tasks in different applications. If you pass `true` as the `immediate` parameter, the connection closes immediately. In this case, the connection must be reestablished when the user switches to another application.

Imagine the situation of a user with three different network applications on the Palm device. The user might first check email, then read a newsgroup, and finally look at a few web sites—all with different applications. This is so common a situation that you should account for it in your code. If the email app, newsreader, and web browser each closed the network connection when they closed, the user would be quite rightly annoyed at the unnecessary waits to reestablish a connection.

A better solution is to let the network connection time out. While it is true that the net library, when open, sucks up a lot of memory and should be closed when not needed, it is also true that users often handle network tasks during discrete periods of time. Letting the network close after a timeout seems to be the best solution.

Use Berkeley Sockets

Use the Berkeley Sockets interface in preference to the Palm OS API. This gives you two advantages: your networking code is portable to other platforms, and programmers who are new to the Palm OS will find your code easier to read.

Use the Palm OS API if necessary

If you need to call networking code when your application globals aren't available, you must use the Palm OS API. You can't use the Berkeley Sockets API (which relies on the global variables errno, AppNetRefnum, and AppNetTimeout). Indeed, the only choice available to you is the Palm OS API, which allows—but doesn't require—globals.

Sample Network Application

As our Sales application does not use network services, we've created a custom sample application to show you how to use the net library to communicate over a network. As we said earlier, our example sends email to an SMTP server. The user fills in:

- The SMTP hostname (the host that's running the SMTP server)
- A "From" email address
- A "To" email address
- The subject
- The body of the message

When the user taps Send, we connect to the SMTP server and send the email message using the SMTP protocol.

The SMTP protocol is documented in RFC 821. Various sites contain the RFC documents; see *http://www.yahoo.com/Computers_and_Internet/Standards/RFCs/* for a list.

Creating the sample application on Linux

Following our own advice, we first created this sample application on another platform and then ported it to the Palm OS. The application was originally written on a Linux machine and tested with a simple command-line interface. Here's the header file that describes the interface to sendmail:

```
typedef void    (*StatusCallbackFunc)(char *status);
typedef void    (*ErrorCallbackFunc)(char *problem, char *extraInfo);

int sendmail(char *smtpHost, char *from, char *to, char *subject,
    char *data, StatusCallbackFunc statusFunc,
    ErrorCallbackFunc errorFunc);
```

The data parameter is the body of the mail message, with individual lines separated by newline characters ('\n'). The StatusCallbackFunc and ErrorCallbackFunc are used to provide status information (although sendmail doesn't currently provide status) and error information to the caller. These are abstracted from the sendmail routine itself, to make porting the program easier. A Linux command-line program has very different error reporting than a Palm OS application.

The Linux main program

Example 13-18 shows the Linux main program that operates as a test harness for sendmail.

Example 13-18. Linux user interface for sending mail

```
#include "sendmail.h"
#include <stdio.h>

void MyStatusFunc(char *status)
{
   printf("status: %s\n", status);
}

void MyErrorFunc(char *err, char *extra)
{
   if (extra)
      printf("error %s: %s\n", err, extra);
   else
      printf("error %s\n", err);
}

char    gMailMessage[5000];

int main(int argc, char **argv)
{
   if (argc != 5) {
      fprintf(stderr,
         "Usage: TestSendMail smtpServer fromAddress toAddres subject\n");
         exit(1);
```

Example 13-18. Linux user interface for sending mail (continued)

```
   }
   fread(gMailMessage, sizeof(gMailMessage), 1, stdin);
   sendmail(argv[1], argv[2], argv[3],
      argv[4], gMailMessage,
      MyStatusFunc, MyErrorFunc);
   return 0;
}
```

Linux include files and global definitions

Here are the include files and global definitions from *sendmail.c*:

```
#include <sys/socket.h>
#include <netdb.h>
#include <netinet/in.h>
#include <arpa/inet.h>

// Application headers

#include "sendmail.h"

static const int kLinefeedChr = '\012';
static const int kCrChr = '\015';

static StatusCallbackFunc gStatusFunc;
static ErrorCallbackFunc  gErrorFunc;
```

Sending the mail

Example 13-19 shows the sendmail function, which we used to send the data.

Example 13-19. The sendmail function

```
#define   kOK         '2'
#define   kWantMore   '3'

int sendmail(char *smtpHost, char *from, char *to, char *subject,
   char *data, StatusCallbackFunc statusFunc,
   ErrorCallbackFunc errorFunc)
{
   int success = 0;
   int   fd        = -1;      // Socket file descriptor

   gErrorFunc = errorFunc;
   gStatusFunc = statusFunc;

   // Open connection to the server.
   if ((fd = make_connection("smtp", smtpHost)) < 0 )
   {
      (*errorFunc)("Couldn't open connection", NULL);
      goto _Exit;
   }
```

Example 13-19. The sendmail function (continued)

```
    // Send and receive the data.
    if (!GotReply(fd, kOK))
       goto _Exit;

    if (!Send(fd, "HELO [", "127.0.0.1", "]"))
       goto _Exit;
    if (!GotReply(fd, kOK))
       goto _Exit;

    if (!Send(fd, "MAIL from:<", from, ">"))
       goto _Exit;
    if (!GotReply(fd, kOK))
       goto _Exit;

    if (!Send(fd, "RCPT to:<", to, ">"))
       goto _Exit;
    if (!GotReply(fd, kOK))
       goto _Exit;

    if (!Send(fd, "DATA", NULL, NULL))
       goto _Exit;
    if (!GotReply(fd, kWantMore))
       goto _Exit;

    if (!Send(fd, "Subject: ", subject, NULL))
       goto _Exit;

// Need empty line between headers and data.
    if (!Send(fd, NULL, NULL, NULL))
       goto _Exit;

    if (!SendBody(fd,data))
       goto _Exit;
    if (!Send(fd, ".", NULL, NULL))
       goto _Exit;

    if (!GotReply(fd, kOK))
       goto _Exit;

    if (!Send(fd, "QUIT", NULL, NULL))
       goto _Exit;

    success = 1;
    // Clean up the mess...

_Exit:

    if ( fd >= 0 ) close( fd );

    return success;
}
```

We make a connection to the SMTP server and alternate receiving status information and sending data. The entire conversation is in ASCII; every response from the SMTP server has a numeric code as the first three digits. We look at the first digit to determine whether a problem has occurred. A 2 signifies that everything is fine. A 3 signifies that more data is needed (the expected response when we send the DATA command; it's asking us to send the body of the email). Any other digit (for our purposes) represents an error.

The protocol specifies that each sent line ends with <CRLF> and that the body of the email ends with a period (.) on a line by itself. Any lines beginning with a period must have the period duplicated (for instance, ".xyz" is sent as "..xyz"); the SMTP server strips the extra period before processing the email.

Connecting to the server

The function make_connection (see Example 13-20) actually makes the connection to the SMTP server.

Example 13-20. The make_connection routine

```
/* This is a generic function to make a connection to a given server/port.
   service is the port name/number,
   netaddress is the hostname to connect to.
   The function returns the socket, ready for action.*/
static int make_connection(char *service, char *netaddress)
{
  /* First convert service from a string to a number. */
  int port = -1;
  struct in_addr *addr;
  int sock, connected;
  struct sockaddr_in address;

  port = atoport(service, "tcp");
  if (port == -1) {
  (*gErrorFunc)("make_connection:  Invalid socket type.\n", NULL);
    return -1;
  }
  addr = atoaddr(netaddress);
  if (addr == NULL) {
    (*gErrorFunc)("make_connection:  Invalid network address.\n", NULL);
    return -1;
  }

  memset((char *) &address, 0, sizeof(address));
  address.sin_family = AF_INET;
  address.sin_port = (port);
  address.sin_addr.s_addr = addr->s_addr;

  sock = socket(AF_INET, SOCK_STREAM, 0);

  connected = connect(sock, (struct sockaddr *) &address,
```

Example 13-20. The make_connection routine (continued)

```
    sizeof(address));
  if (connected < 0) {
    (*gErrorFunc)("connect", NULL);
    return -1;
  }
  return sock;
}
```

This function uses the Berkeley Sockets API calls socket and connect. Note that connect returns a file descriptor that is used in later read, write, and close calls.

Getting a port

To connect, we have to specify an address consisting of an IP address and a port number. We use atoport (see Example 13-21) to convert a well-known service name to a port number.

Example 13-21. atoport converts a service name to a port number

```
/* Take a service name and a service type, and return a port number.  The
   number returned is byte-ordered for the network. */
static int atoport(char *service, char *proto)
{
  int port;
  struct servent *serv;

  /* First try to read it from /etc/services */
  serv = getservbyname(service, proto);
  if (serv != NULL)
    port = serv->s_port;
  else {
      return -1; /* Invalid port address */
  }
  return port;
}
```

atoport uses the Berkeley Sockets API function getservbyname. Then atoaddr (see Example 13-22) converts a hostname (or string of the form "aaa.bbb.ccc.ddd") to an IP address.

Example 13-22. The atoaddr routine

```
/* Converts ASCII text to in_addr struct.  NULL is returned if the address
   cannot be found. */
static struct in_addr *atoaddr(char *address)
{
  struct hostent *host;
  static struct in_addr saddr;

  /* First try it as aaa.bbb.ccc.ddd. */
  saddr.s_addr = inet_addr(address);
```

Example 13-22. The atoaddr routine (continued)

```
  if (saddr.s_addr != -1) {
    return &saddr;
  }
  host = gethostbyname(address);
  if (host != NULL) {
    return (struct in_addr *) *host->h_addr_list;
  }
  return NULL;
}
```

Note that atoaddr uses the Berkley Sockets gethostbyname call that converts a domain name to an IP address.

Reading data character by character

Once the connection has been made, we need to start sending and receiving data. We use a utility routine, sock_gets (see Example 13-23), to read an entire <CRLF>-delimited line (note that it reads one character at a time).

Example 13-23. The sock_gets function (reads one line from a TCP/IP socket)

```
/* This function reads from a socket, until it receives a linefeed
   character.  It fills the buffer "str" up to the maximum size "count".
   This function will return -1 if the socket is closed during the read
   operation.

   Note that if a single line exceeds the length of count, the extra data
   will be read and discarded!  You have been warned. */
static int sock_gets(int sockfd, char *str, size_t count)
{
  int bytes_read;
  int total_count = 0;
  char *current_position;
  char last_read = 0;
  const char kLinefeed = 10;
  const char kCR = 13;

  current_position = str;
  while (last_read != kLinefeed) {
    bytes_read = read(sockfd, &last_read, 1);
    if (bytes_read <= 0) {
      /* The other side may have closed unexpectedly */
      return -1;
    }
    if ( (total_count < count) && (last_read != kLinefeed) &&
      (last_read != kCR) )
    {
      current_position[0] = last_read;
      current_position++;
      total_count++;
    }
```

Example 13-23. The sock_gets function (reads one line from a TCP/IP socket) (continued)

```
    }
    if (count > 0)
        current_position[0] = 0;
    return total_count;
}
```

The sendmail protocol specifies that the server may send us multiple lines for any reply. The last line will start with a three-digit numeric code and a space ("### "); any previous lines will have a "–" instead of the space ("###-"). We need to keep reading until we read the last line. ReadReply does that (see Example 13-24).

Example 13-24. ReadReply reads a response line and returns the numeric code

```
#define IsDigit(c) ((c) >= '0' && (c) <= '9')

// Reads lines until we get a non-continuation line.
static int ReadReply(int fd, char *s, unsigned int sLen)
{
    int     numBytes;
    do {
        numBytes = sock_gets(fd, s, sLen);
    } while (numBytes >= 0 && !(strlen(s) >= 4 && s[3] == ' ' &&
        IsDigit(s[0]) && IsDigit(s[1]) && IsDigit(s[2])));
    if (numBytes < 0)
        return numBytes;
    else
        return 0;
}
```

We use ReadReply in GotReply (see Example 13-25), which takes an expected status character and returns true if we receive that character and false otherwise.

Example 13-25. GotReply deals with the reply

```
#define kMaxReplySize 512

static int GotReply(int fd, char expectedLeadingChar)
{
    int     err;
    char    reply[kMaxReplySize];

    err = ReadReply(fd, reply, sizeof(reply));
    if (err != 0) {
        (*gErrorFunc)("Read error", NULL);
        return 0;
    }
    if (*reply != expectedLeadingChar) {
        (*gErrorFunc)("Protocol error", reply);
        return 0;
    }
    return 1;
}
```

The SMTP protocol specifies that no reply will exceed 512 characters (including the trailing <CRLF> characters); that's why we can safely define kMaxReplySize as we did. If the digit we read doesn't match the expected character, we call the error function, passing the line itself. This works well because the server usually provides a reasonable English error message with the numeric code. As a result, the user gets more than "Protocol error" for error information. That's all there is to reading data.

Sending data character by character

Having taken care of reading data, we now need to deal with sending it. Send (see Example 13-26) sends one line of data and tacks on a <CRLF> pair at the end.

Example 13-26. Send sends a single line of text

```
// Sends s1 followed by s2 followed by s3 followed by <CRLF>
static int Send(int fd, char *s1, char *s2, char *s3)
{
   if (s1 && nwrite(fd, s1, strlen(s1)) < 0)
      goto error;
   if (s2 && nwrite(fd, s2, strlen(s2)) < 0)
      goto error;
   if (s3 && nwrite(fd, s3, strlen(s3)) < 0)
      goto error;
   if (nwrite(fd, "\015\012", 2) < 0)
      goto error;
   return 1;

error:
   (*gErrorFunc)("Write error", NULL);
   return 0;
}
```

SendBody (see Example 13-27) sends the body of the email.

Example 13-27. SendBody sends the body, line by line

```
static int SendBody(int fd, char *body)
{
   char  *lineStart = body;
   int   result = 1;

   // Send all the newline-terminated lines.
   while (*body != '\0' && result == 1) {
      if (*body == '\n') {
         result = SendSingleBodyLine(fd, lineStart,
            body - lineStart);
         lineStart = body + 1;
      }
      body++;
   }

   // Send the last partial line.
```

Example 13-27. SendBody sends the body, line by line (continued)

```
   if (lineStart < body && result == 1)
      result = SendSingleBodyLine(fd, lineStart,
         body - lineStart);
   return result;
}
```

It relies on SendSingleBodyLine (see Example 13-28), which converts \n chars to <CRLF> and doubles "." characters that occur at the beginning of lines.

Example 13-28. SendSingleBodyLine sends a single line

```
 // Sends aLine, which is length chars long.
static int SendSingleBodyLine(int fd, char *aLine, int length)
{
   if (*aLine == '.') // double-up on '.' lines
      if (nwrite(fd, ".", 1) < 0)
         goto error;
   if (nwrite(fd, aLine, length) < 0)
      goto error;
   if (nwrite(fd, "\015\012", 2) < 0)
      goto error;
error:
   (*gErrorFunc)("Write error", NULL);
   return 0;
}
```

Both of these sending routines use nwrite, a utility routine that does our writing:

```
   static unsigned int nwrite(int fd, char *ptr, unsigned int nbytes)
   {
      unsigned int   nleft;
      int            chunk;
      int         nwritten;

      nleft = nbytes;
      while (nleft > 0) {

         if (nleft > 0x7000) chunk = 0x7000;
         else chunk = nleft;

         nwritten = write(fd, ptr, chunk);
         if (nwritten <= 0)
            return(nwritten);    /* error */

         nleft -= nwritten;
         ptr   += nwritten;
      }
      return(nbytes - nleft);
   }
```

This routine loops through, calling write over and over until all the data is sent. For sockets, the write routine may not send all the data you request. A lesser amount may be all that will fit in a packet.

Testing the Linux application

Testing was simplified because the Linux machine is on a network with a full-time connection to the Internet. Therefore, we have no time delays in making a connection. (If it hadn't had a full-time connection, we could have set up an SMTP server on the Linux machine and run it standalone, with no connection to the Internet.)

We used the Linux source-level debugger, GDB, to step through the original code. We also fixed some errors in our original attempt.

Porting the Linux application to Palm OS

Now let's take a look at what it will take to port the Linux application to the Palm OS world. Here are the changes we need to make:

1. *sendmail.c* requires only a small change to the headers in order to work under the Palm OS. We use *sys_socket.h* instead of *sys/socket.h*, and add a few headers that *sys_socket.h* requires:

   ```
   #ifdef linux
   #include <sys/socket.h>
   #include <netdb.h>
   #include <netinet/in.h>
   #include <arpa/inet.h>
   #else
   #include <StringMgr.h>
   #include <MemoryMgr.h>
   #include <sys_socket.h>
   #endif
   ```

2. Our main source file, *Main.c*, must include *NetMgr.h*, declare AppNetRefnum, and define errno:

   ```
   #include <NetMgr.h>
   extern UInt16 AppNetRefnum;
   Err errno;          // Needed for Berkeley Socket interfaces.
   ```

3. We add some fairly primitive error and status routines that put up an alert:

   ```
   void MyErrorFunc(char *error, char *additional)
   {
       FrmCustomAlert(ErrorAlert, error, additional ? additional : "", NULL);
   }

   void MyStatusFunc(char *status)
   {
       FrmCustomAlert(StatusAlert, status, NULL, NULL);
   }
   ```

4. We also need a new utility routine that returns the text in a field:

   ```
   // Returns (locked) text in a field object.
   char *GetLockedPtr(UInt16 objectID)
   {
     FormPtr frm = FrmGetActiveForm();
     FieldPtr fld = FrmGetObjectPtr(frm, FrmGetObjectIndex(frm, objectID));
   ```

```
      MemHandle h = FldGetTextHandle(fld);

      if (h)
        return MemHandleLock(h);
      else
        return 0;
    }
```

5. We need to add an event handler that handles the Send button:

```
    Boolean MainViewHandleEvent(EventPtr event)
    {
      Boolean   handled = false;

      switch (event->eType) {
      case ctlSelectEvent:
        if (event->data.ctlSelect.controlID == SendmailMainSendButton)
          HandleSendButton();
        handled = true;
        break;

      case frmOpenEvent:
        FrmDrawForm(FrmGetActiveForm());
        handled = true;
      }
      return handled;
    }
```

This in turn calls HandleSendButton to do the actual work:

```
    void HandleSendButton()
    {
      char  *smtpServer = GetLockedPtr(SendmailMainSmtpHostField);
      char  *to = GetLockedPtr(SendmailMainToField);
      char  *from = GetLockedPtr(SendmailMainFromField);
      char  *subject = GetLockedPtr(SendmailMainSubjectField);
      char  *body = GetLockedPtr(SendmailMainBodyField);

      if (!smtpServer)
        MyErrorFunc("Missing smtpServer", NULL);
      else if (!to)
        MyErrorFunc("Missing to", NULL);
      else if (!from)
        MyErrorFunc("Missing from", NULL);
      else if (!subject)
        MyErrorFunc("Missing subject", NULL);
      else if (!body)
        MyErrorFunc("Missing body", NULL);
      else
        OpenNetLibAndSendmail(smtpServer, to, from, subject, body);

      if (smtpServer)
        MemPtrUnlock(smtpServer);
      if (to)
        MemPtrUnlock(to);
      if (from)
```

```
    MemPtrUnlock(from);
  if (subject)
    MemPtrUnlock(subject);
  if (body)
    MemPtrUnlock(body);
}
```

As you can see, this routine retrieves the strings from the different fields and makes sure they aren't empty.

6. Now, we need to add a routine, OpenNetLibAndSendmail, to actually send:

```
OpenNetLibAndSendmail(char *smtpServer, char *to,
  char *from, char *subject, char *body)
{
  UInt16  interfaceError;
  Err error;

  if (SysLibFind( "Net.lib", &AppNetRefnum) == 0) {
    error = NetLibOpen(AppNetRefnum, &interfaceError);
    if (interfaceError != 0) {
      MyErrorFunc("NetLibOpen: interface error", NULL);
      NetLibClose(AppNetRefnum, true);
    } else if (error == 0 || error == netErrAlreadyOpen) {
      if (sendmail(smtpServer, from, to,
        subject, body, MyStatusFunc, MyErrorFunc))
        MyStatusFunc("Completed successfully");
      NetLibClose(AppNetRefnum, false);
    } else
      MyErrorFunc("netLibOpen error", NULL);
  } else
    MyErrorFunc("SysLibFind error", NULL);
}
```

We find the networking library, open it, and then call the same sendmail function that the Linux version calls. Note that when we're finished and call NetLibClose, it does not immediately close the network connection, but relies on a timeout to do so.

7. The other routines in *Main.c* are just the standard ones: PilotMain, EventLoop, and so on.

You can see from this example that writing code that uses network services on the Palm OS is fairly simple. A distinct advantage of Palm's implementation of the Berkeley Sockets API is that you can easily have code that ports to many platforms. In our example, this made it possible to write the data-sending portion of the email program—the sendmail function—on another platform, where testing was easier. Very little was required to get that email program up and running on the Palm platform after the Linux version was tested: we simply had to give the Palm application a UI, including error information, and put a new shell around the data-sending portion of the code.

Designing Conduits

CHAPTER 14

Getting Started with Conduits

It is time to discuss conduits—what they do and how to create them. In this chapter we'll describe the conduit development environment, important APIs, tricky little problems you might encounter when installing a conduit, conduit entry points, and information that gets sent to the HotSync log. Since it will also help if you understand (code-wise) what happens when a Palm device is plopped into a cradle and the user pushes the HotSync button, we'll show you those events too.

Understanding these events is useful if you want to know what happens when your conduit code is called and how it interacts with the Sync Manager to perform its tasks.

After all of this, we'll take a brief detour to discuss the types of applications that can profitably use the Backup conduit (a conduit that simply archives databases on the desktop). We'll also show you the code changes required in your application if you want to use the Backup conduit as your conduit solution.

Last of all, we'll create an actual conduit and show you how to use the Conduit Inspector and POSE to debug it. This conduit is for the Sales application and is built using *Visual C++*. It doesn't do much—it just writes a message to the log file—but it's still quite useful. This example will demonstrate what is involved in creating a minimal conduit and what it takes to get to the point where syncing is ready to begin.

Overview of Conduits

A conduit can be simple or complex, depending on the job it has to do. Regardless of its complexity, you create it in the same way: a conduit is a desktop plug-in made in a desktop development environment.

A conduit isn't code that runs on the Palm handheld, but an executable library that runs during the HotSync.

What Does a Conduit Do?

A conduit is responsible for the application's data during synchronization between the handheld and a desktop computer. The conduit needs to do the following:

- Open and close databases on the Palm device.
- Determine whether data should be moved to the handheld, from the handheld, or some combination of both.
- Appropriately add, delete, and modify records on the handheld and on the desktop.
- Be able to work within a multiuser environment in which more than one Palm handheld may be syncing to the same network or desktop computer (though not necessarily at the same time).
- Convert the data in the application's database records to appropriate data structures on the desktop computer.
- Compare records so that only modified records are synced (this is optional, though recommended).

Your conduit is responsible for saving the data on the desktop in whatever way makes sense. If your conduit syncs to a file for a desktop application, it needs to read and write data in that application's file format. Your conduit may read and write records from a database on the desktop or some database on the network. As a result, each conduit handles storing and retrieving desktop data differently.

There are two broad categories of conduits:

To- or from-handheld only
> Conduits that just copy databases to or from the handheld. The conduit for the Expense application is an example that copies expenses from the handheld and creates a spreadsheet on the desktop. A sales-force automation (SFA) solution might copy product lists to the handheld and copy orders from the handheld.

Mirror-image record synchronization
> Conduits that do a two-way synchronization. The conduits for Address Book, Memo Pad, and To Do are examples.

Conduit Development on Windows

When you are ready to develop a conduit, you use Palm's Conduit Development Kit (CDK). At the time this book was written, CDK 4.02 was the latest version on Windows. It contains a variety of useful tools and allows for a choice of languages for conduit development. Let's look at some of the most important things you need to know about CDK.

CDK versions and Palm Desktop

Certain new features of Palm Desktop 3.0 and later are supported only for conduits created with CDK 3.0 or CDK 4.0. One major feature is File Linking, which provides a way to copy information from an external file to a separate category. An example of this would be to copy entries from a company-wide address book to a special category on the handheld as part of syncing to a user's personal address book on the desktop. There are some other slight API changes in 3.0.

Conduits created with CDK 4.0 are generally backward-compatible with older versions of the desktop software, although the new API calls can't be called in earlier versions (your application can make a call to find out what version of the API is available).

Using C++

CDK 4.02 comes with a C-C++ Sync Suite that requires Visual C++ 6.0 or later running on Windows 95/NT or later. CDK 4.02 can also be used with Metrowerks's CodeWarrior Pro for Windows (which is a different product from CodeWarrior for Palm OS). We used Visual C++ 6.0 to create our Sales conduit.

When you install the CDK, you get a Conduit Wizard as a plug-in to Visual C++. The wizard is a nifty tool that allows you to create a new conduit by specifying a handful of choices about the kind of conduit you want. The wizard then generates a project, along with preliminary source code, that you can use as a starting point. We use the Conduit Wizard to generate the conduit examples we create in this and the next two chapters.

Using Java

CDK 4.02 also comes with a JSync Suite that you can use to create a conduit with everyone's favorite caffeinated development language.

The JSync Suite allows development using any Java development environment that supports the Java 2 Platform, Standard Edition, Version 1.3.

Conduits written using the JavaSync Suite can run not only on Windows, but also on Solaris 8 (Sun's Unix system). We expect to see the ability to run on Mac OS in the future.

We don't cover creating Java conduits in this book.

Using Visual Basic or other COM-creating environments

The COM Sync Suite from CDK 4.02 allows you to create a conduit from any COM-enabled development environment.

The COM Sync Suite is aimed primarily at programmers using Visual Basic, but it can also be used by any other COM-enabled development environment, such as Borland Delphi, Visual C++, and Borland C++ Builder.

We don't cover using the COM Sync Suite in this book.

Conduit Development on Macintosh

There is a Conduit Development Kit for Macintosh that allows creating conduits for Mac OS using CodeWarrior Pro for Macintosh.

The APIs between Mac OS and Windows are almost identical, and it is possible to write a conduit that shares 95 percent of its code between platforms. For example, the Generic Conduit Framework (see "Generic Conduit Framework" in Chapter 16) works on both Mac OS and Windows.

Our samples in this book discuss the Windows CDK, although Mac OS versions of the conduits from this book are available at the book's web site (*http://www.calliopeinc.com/palmprog2/*).

Required Elements in a Minimal Conduit

Later in this chapter, we will show you how to create a minimal conduit. That conduit will contain a few essential elements that we want to tell you about now:

A mechanism for registration
> A conduit won't run unless it has been registered. We'll talk at length about how to register your conduits.

Six C entry points
> One returns the conduit's name, another its version number, and another further information about the conduit. Two are used for configuring the conduit, and the last serves as an entryway into the syncing process.

Log messages
> You need to provide log messages to the user. Among other things, you must mention whether the sync was successful or not.

We will look at registration issues first, then discuss the entry points. Last, we will discuss log messages.

Using the Backup Conduit

You may have an application that doesn't require its own conduit. In such cases, you can rely on the Backup conduit. First, let's discuss the types of applications that can profitably use this approach. Then we'll tell you what you need to do to set this up on your application.

The Backup conduit works on any database that has the backup flag set and has been modified since the last sync, unless the database type is DATA and it has an associated conduit.

The Backup conduit will always back up non-DATA databases, but it will back up only those DATA databases that have no associated conduit. The built-in PIM applications use DATA as their database type; that way, if the associated conduit exists, it'll be responsible for backing up the database, but if the conduit isn't there, the Backup conduit will take over.

Whenever the Backup conduit is used, the data in the database is completely copied from the Palm device to the desktop and saved as a PDB (database) or PRC (application) file. Since each record is copied from the database, you don't want to use this as a solution for large databases that change often.

Applications That Might Use the Backup Conduit

The Backup conduit is well suited to the following types of applications:

Games
> Where you save top-score information

Utilities
> Where you save some user settings

Alarm clocks or other timers
> Where you save world clock information or other types of alarm settings

Electronic books
> Where you save display information, bookmarks, or the books themselves

Newsreaders
> Where you save newsgroup lists

Using System Prefs Instead

Another approach for these types of applications is to use the System Prefs database. This database contains a record for each application that stores preferences. These preferences are automatically backed up because the Systems Prefs database has the backup bit set.

> Actually, when you create system preferences you can specify whether you want them to be backed up or not (a true value for the saved parameter to PrefSetAppPreferences means you want the preferences backed up). If you've got some information that you want to save between calls to your application but that you don't need backed up, use the non-backed-up preferences (a false value for the saved parameter).
>
> A game might want the 512 bytes of high scores backed up (heaven forbid *they* get lost!), but not the 6K of information about what level the user was on, what weapons were in what hands, and so on.

Setting the Backup Bit for a Database

To set the backup bit, you can use the DmSetDatabaseInfo call on the handheld to change the attributes of a database. Example 14-1 shows code for the handheld that sets the backup bit given a specific type and creator.

Example 14-1. Setting the backup bit

```
Err SetBackupBitByTypeCreator(UInt32 type, UInt32 creator)
{
  LocalID theDBID;
  UInt16 theCardNum;
  UInt16 theAttrs;
  Err err;
  DmSearchStateType theSearchState;

  // Determine the DB ID and Card number of our database.
  err = DmGetNextDatabaseByTypeCreator(true, &theSearchState, type,
    creator, true, &theCardNum, &theDBID);
  if (err)
    return err;
  // Get the attributes for our database.
  err = DmDatabaseInfo(theCardNum, theDBID, NULL, &theAttrs, NULL, NULL,
    NULL, NULL, NULL, NULL, NULL, NULL, NULL);
  if (err)
    return err;

  // Set the backup flag.
  theAttrs |= dmHdrAttrBackup;

  // Set the attributes.
  err = DmSetDatabaseInfo(theCardNum, theDBID, NULL, &theAttrs, NULL, NULL,
    NULL, NULL, NULL, NULL, NULL, NULL, NULL);
  return err;
}
```

Note that the backup bit isn't reset automatically after a backup. With early versions of the HotSync application, as long as the backup bit of a database is set, the database is backed up every time the user syncs (unless the database is of type DATA and there is a conduit installed for it). With recent versions, the database is backed up only if it has been modified since the last sync.

Set the Backup Bit for Every Application

Your application itself should usually have the backup bit set. This will ensure that the application is backed up into the user's backup directory and thus will minimize user trauma in the case of data loss. If the user must restore everything from the desktop to the handheld (imagine a new handheld replacing a lost one), all data *and* applications are restored. Any applications whose backup bit isn't set will require individual installation.

The Install conduit will automatically set the backup bit for any applications (or databases) that it installs, but it still makes sense for you to explicitly set the backup bit when you build your application.

Registering and Unregistering

Before a conduit can be used, it needs to be registered. This is how the Sync Manager application knows that the conduit exists and knows which databases it is responsible for syncing. Depending on which version of the CDK you have, there are differences in what you do to register. We'll tell you about both the old, difficult way and the new, improved methods.

The Old, Ugly Way

In Version 2.1 (and earlier versions) of the CDK, conduit registration was done by adding entries to the Windows Registry. Unregistration required removing entries from the Registry (and possibly renaming existing entries). This was an ugly process. It was prone to error and incredibly fragile: if one developer modified the registry incorrectly, he could cause some or all of the other conduits to fail.

These troubles only increased during the acquisition-of-Palm frenzy of the late 1990s. During these times, the keys used for the Windows Registry by various versions of the Sync Manager and the Desktop Manager changed from Palm Computing to U.S. Robotics.*

As a result, conduits needed to be aware of various registry keys and needed to perform a careful set of steps when registering and an even more careful set when unregistering. As we said...ugly, ugly, ugly. The time was ripe for a better approach.

The New, Sleek Way

The Conduit Manager (part of Palm Desktop 3.0 and Version 3.0 of the CDK), contains an API for registration and unregistration. It knows about the various versions of HotSync, the different keys used in the Windows Registry, and the careful steps needed for registering and unregistering conduits.

This Conduit Manager functionality is provided in a dynamic link library (DLL) that ships with Palm Desktop. As we discuss later in "A Complicated Wrinkle—Finding the Correct DLL," you also need to include the DLL as part of your installer.

Version 3.0 of the Sync Manager continues to use the Windows Registry for the sake of older conduits that don't use the Conduit Manager. You should expect, however, that future versions of HotSync may not use the Windows Registry at all.

---

* Palm Computing was acquired by U.S. Robotics, which was in turn acquired by 3Com, which in turn spun off Palm as Palm, Inc.

As long as you use the Conduit Manager, you'll be shielded from any such changes to the underlying registry mechanism.

Conduit Entry Information Needed to Register

You need several pieces of information (*conduit entries*) to register a conduit. Some are required; others are optional.

Required conduit entries

These entries are required to register a conduit:

Conduit
> The name of the conduit DLL. If this entry doesn't include a directory, the name must be found in the HotSync directory or current PATH; otherwise, it should include the full pathname to the DLL. (Generally, you don't keep your DLLs in the HotSync directory.) If your conduit is written using the JSync Suite, this entry should be *JSync13.DLL*, a C++ shim that translates between C++ and Java. If your conduit is written using the COM Sync Suite, the entry should be *ComConduit.DLL*, a C++ shim that translates between C++ and COM.

Creator
> The four-character creator ID of the database(s) for which your conduit is responsible. Your conduit will be called during a HotSync only if an application with this creator ID exists on the handheld.

Directory
> The name of the conduit's directory. Each user has a subdirectory in the HotSync directory. Within each user's directory, each conduit has its own directory where it can store files. This string specifies the conduit's directory name.

Optional entries

The optional entries are more numerous. They include the following:

File
> A string specifying a file (if the string doesn't include a directory, it is assumed to be within the conduit's directory). This is intended to be the local file that the conduit will sync the handheld against. However, your conduit is not restricted to using just this file (some conduits may need to read or write multiple files on the desktop).

Information
> A string that provides information about your conduit. This string can be used to resolve conflicts. If more than one conduit wants to handle the same creator ID, an installation tool could display this string and ask the user which conduit

should be used for syncing. (To be honest, we've never seen a conduit that registers this information.)

Name
> The user-visible name of the conduit. If it's there, this string is used instead of calling the conduit's `GetConduitName` entry point.

Priority
> A value between 0 and 4 that controls the relative order in which conduits run. Conduits registered with a lower priority run before conduits registered with higher priorities. If you don't set this value, the Sync Manager uses a default value of 2 for your application. It's hard to think of a case in which the order matters, and we've never seen a conduit that specifies anything other than 2.

Remote DB
> A string specifying a database name on the handheld. This string is provided for you to use in your conduit when it runs; your conduit isn't required to use it, however.

Username
> The name of the user for which this conduit is installed. Note that this entry is not currently used.

JSync Suite entries

The following entries are relevant only if the conduit is written in Java:

Class name
> The name of the Java conduit class (including package)

Class path
> The directory that contains all the classes used by the Java conduit

COM Sync Suite entries

This entry is relevant only if the conduit is written using the COM Sync Suite:

COM Client
> The ProgID of your COM module

Registering and Unregistering Manually Using CondCfg

CondCfg is an application supplied in the CDK along with the Conduit Manager DLL. *CondCfg* uses the Conduit Manager. This application displays all the registered conduits and allows you to register conduits, change registration information, and delete conduits (see Figure 14-1).

During development, you'll use *CondCfg* to register your conduit. Note, however, that your end users won't use or even see *CondCfg* as you automate the conduit-registration process as part of installing and uninstalling it on the desktop.

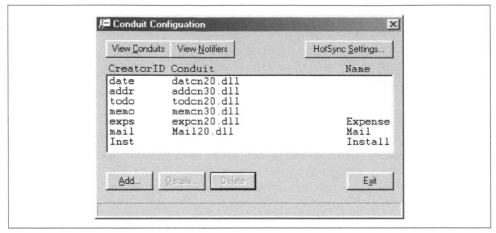

Figure 14-1. CondCfg—a developer utility for registering and unregistering conduits

Using Desktop APIs

Along with other things, the Conduit Development Kit provides three DLLs that provide functionality for desktop code. The three DLLs are used for:

- Registering and unregistering conduits
- Starting and stopping a HotSync
- Retrieving a list of Palm users and installing applications for any of those users

First, we'll look at the most common APIs from each of those DLLs, along with short samples of how to use them. Next, we'll talk about a complicated wrinkle involving finding the correct DLL at runtime. This complication requires slight changes to the samples. Finally, we'll discuss some of the most important issues involved in writing an installer for a conduit and/or Palm OS application.

Registering/Unregistering Conduit Manager APIs

A small command-line program (*ConduitInstall.exe*) is going to install and register our conduit. We use a separate program (*ConduitDeinstall.exe*) to uninstall it.

Installing the conduit

As *ConduitInstall.exe* executes, it makes calls to the Conduit Manager API to register our conduit. It needs to register the three required entries of the conduit (Conduit, Creator, and Directory) and any of the optional entries we want to set.

We are using *ConduitInstall.exe*—a simple command-line program—to avoid clouding the relevant issues with a lot of technical details concerning Windows application programming. A number of installation methods are available; we couldn't possibly cover them all. Here are just two possibilities: you could write a custom application to do the installation, or you could use the popular installer utility, InstallShield (the CDK contains a sample that uses this method). In any event, we keep things simple so that you will understand exactly what is necessary in order to install and register a conduit. We leave it up to you to choose an installation method.

The first call you make is one that registers the Creator entry point of the conduit:

```
int CmInstallCreator(const char *creatorString, int conduitType);
```

The conduitType is one of CONDUIT_APPLICATION or CONDUIT_COMPONENT. The latter constant is used only to register components added in to the Palm Desktop application; you'll use a type of CONDUIT_APPLICATION.

If that succeeds, you call a different CmSetCreator routine for all the rest of your entry points. Most of the CmSetCreator routines match the registration entry name and are easy to figure out (the two exceptions are CmSetCreatorName and CmSetCreatorTitle). Here are the routines we use and the information they register:

CmSetCreatorName
Sets the required Conduit entry

CmSetCreatorTitle
Sets the name entry

CmSetCreatorDirectory
Sets the required Directory entry

CmSetCreatorFile
Sets the file entry

CmSetCreatorPriority
Sets the priority entry

ConduitInstall.exe

Our simple command-line program, *ConduitInstall.exe*, registers a conduit (see Example 14-2).

Example 14-2. ConduitInstall.exe registers a conduit

```
#include <Windows.h>
#include "CondMgr.h"
#include <stdio.h>
```

Example 14-2. ConduitInstall.exe registers a conduit (continued)

```
int main(int argc, char **argv)
{
  const char *kCreator = "SLES";

  err = CmInstallCreator(kCreator, CONDUIT_APPLICATION);
  if (err == 0)
    err = CmSetCreatorName(kCreator, "C:\\Sales\\Debug\\Sales.DLL");
  if (err == 0)
    err = CmSetCreatorDirectory(kCreator, "Sales");
  if (err == 0)
    err = CmSetCreatorFile(kCreator, "Sales");
  if (err == 0)
    err = CmSetCreatorPriority(kCreator, 2);
  if (err == 0)
    printf("Registration succeeded\n");
  else
    printf("Registration failed %d\n", err);
  return err;
}
```

This application registers a conduit for the creator of "SLES" and then sets the conduit's path (using CmSetCreatorName), its directory, its file, and its priority (because 2 is the default priority, this was an optional setting).

Automatically uninstalling a conduit

Uninstalling is just as simple. Our little application *ConduitDeinstall.exe* (see Example 14-3) uses CmRemoveConduitByCreatorID, which removes all the conduits registered with a particular creator ID. It returns the number of conduits removed (or a negative number, in the case of an error). The application prints the number of conduits it unregistered.

Example 14-3. ConduitDeinstall.exe

```
#include <Windows.h>
#include "CondMgr.h"

int main(int argc, char **argv)
{
  const char *kCreator = "Sles";
  int numConduitsRemoved = CmRemoveConduitByCreatorID(kCreator);
  if (numConduitsRemoved >= 0)
    printf("Unregistration succeeded for %d conduits\n", numConduitsRemoved);
  else
    printf("Unregistration failed %d\n", numConduitsRemoved);
}
```

That's all there is to installing and uninstalling a conduit.

The HotSync APIs

The *HSAPI.DLL* contains a few entry points that are used to find out the status of the HotSync application, start it, and stop it. This is quite important when registering or unregistering a conduit, since *HotSync.exe* reads the registration information only when it starts. Thus, if HotSync is running when you register a conduit, you must quit and restart it in order for that registration to take effect.

Here are the most common routines you'll use:

long HsGetSyncStatus(DWORD *pdwStatus)

> This routine returns ERROR_HSAPI_HOTSYNC_NOT_FOUND if the HotSync application is not running. If it is running, it returns 0. The parameter returns one of these:
>
> - HOTSYNC_STATUS_SYNCING if it's in the middle of a sync
> - HOTSYNC_STATUS_IDLE if no sync is occurring

long HsSetAppStatus(HsStatusType statusType, DWORD dwStartFlags)

> You use this routine to stop, start, or restart HotSync. For the statusType, pass HsCloseApp, HsStartApp, or HsRestart. The dwStartFlags can contain different flags that affect how HotSync starts; you'll normally pass HSFLAG_NONE to specify the equivalent of starting the HotSync application by hand with no flags.

We have an example application that will either start, stop, or restart HotSync, depending on the command-line arguments (see Example 14-4).

Example 14-4. TestHSAPI stops, starts, or restarts HotSync

```
#include <stdio.h>
#include <Windows.h>
#include <HSAPI.h>

void Usage()
{
  fprintf(stderr,
    "usage: TestHSAPI -shutdown | -restart | -start\n");
  exit(1);
}

int main(int argc, char* argv[])
{
  long err = 0;

  if (argc != 2)
    Usage();
  else if (strcmp(argv[1], "-shutdown") == 0)
    err = HsSetAppStatus(HsCloseApp, HSFLAG_NONE);
  else if (strcmp(argv[1], "-restart") == 0)
    err = HsSetAppStatus(HsRestart, HSFLAG_NONE);
  else if (strcmp(argv[1], "-start") == 0)
```

Example 14-4. TestHSAPI stops, starts, or restarts HotSync (continued)

```
    err = HsSetAppStatus(HsStartApp, HSFLAG_NONE);
  else
    Usage( );
  if (err != 0)
    fprintf(stderr, "err: %d\n", err);
  return 0;
}
```

Retrieving Users and Installing Application APIs

These Install Aide APIs are the most commonly used functions from *InstAide.DLL*:

int PltGetUserCount(void)
> This routine returns the number of Palm users on this desktop machine.

int PltGetUser(unsigned int iIndex, TCHAR *pUserBuffer, short *psUserBufSize)
> Given iIndex, a number between 0 and PltGetUserCount( )-1, this routine returns the name of the user in the pUserBuffer. On input, psUserBufSize points to the size of the buffer. On output, psUserBufSize points to the number of characters copied into the buffer.

int PltInstallFile(TCHAR *pUser, TCHAR *pFileSpec)
> This routine queues up the file referenced by the full pathname pFileSpec to be installed for the given user, pUser, and copies the file into the user's *Install* directory in preparation for installation when that user next syncs.

InstallApp (see Example 14-5) is an example that will install the *Giraffe.prc* application to either a named user or, if there is only one user, that user. If passed the –l flag, it will list all the Palm users.

Example 14-5. InstallApp application installs, or lists users

```
#include <stdio.h>
#include <Windows.h>
#include <InstAide.h>

char *GetNthUserName(int n)
{
  static char userName[1024];
  int err;
  short size = sizeof(userName);

  err = PltGetUser(n, userName, &size);
  if (err < 0)
    fprintf(stderr, "err in PltGetUser: %d\n", err);
  return userName;
}

int main(int argc, char* argv[])
{
  char *kAppToInstall = "C:\\Palm\\Add-on\\Giraffe.prc";
  int err = 0;
```

Example 14-5. InstallApp application installs, or lists users (continued)

```
  if (argc == 2 && strcmp(argv[1], "-l") == 0) {
    int numUsers = PltGetUserCount( );

    for (int i = 0; i < numUsers; i++)
      printf("%s\n", GetNthUserName(i));
  } else if (argc == 1) {
    if (PltGetUserCount( ) > 1)
      fprintf(stderr, "too many users\n");
    else
      err = PltInstallFile(GetNthUserName(0), kAppToInstall);
  } else if (argc == 2)
    err = PltInstallFile(argv[1], kAppToInstall);
  else {
    fprintf(stderr, "usage: InstallApp -l\n"
                    "or: InstallApp \n"
                    "or: InstallApp user\n");
    exit(1);
  }
    if (err < 0)
    fprintf(stderr, "error installing: %d\n", err);
  return 0;
}
```

For example, if called as `InstallApp -l`, it prints (on our machine):

```
Neil Rhodes
POSE
POSE 2
Julie
```

If we call it as `InstallApp Julie`, it prints nothing (no news is good news). Checking with the Palm Install tool, however, we find that *Giraffe.prc* is now queued in Julie's application installation list.

This is all you need to know about the APIs used for installing or uninstalling conduits that are running the sync process or finding users and installing applications. Now it's time to look at a funny sort of problem.

A Complicated Wrinkle—Finding the Correct DLL

Palm provides these three DLLs, which we have just discussed:

CondMgr.DLL
> Used for conduit registration and unregistration

HSAPI.DLL
> Used for starting and stopping the HotSync application

InstAide.DLL
> Used for obtaining a list of Palm users, and modifying the list of files to install for those users

Having these DLLs is quite useful, as we are not required to recompile if the underlying implementation changes. For example, a new *CondMgr.DLL* could register in a different way, and our code won't need to know about it.

There is a problem, however, and it doesn't have a simple workaround. You might ask, if you were a cautious person, how it is possible for your installation code to use a new version of the Conduit Manager DLL.

You might assume that Palm would help you out here and ensure that *CondMgr.DLL* would always be found in the same place. For example, if *CondMgr.DLL* were installed in the *System* directory, it would be part of the path that the system searches to load DLLs and would automatically be found and loaded when your installation program ran. You probably know by now that things are not this simple.

CondMgr.DLL is not installed in the *System* directory when the user installs the Palm Desktop software (this is done so that the Palm Desktop can be installed without needing Administrator privileges on Windows NT/2000). Instead, it is put in the same directory as the Palm Desktop software. You might say that this is no big deal; you just need to know where the Palm Desktop software is. The folks at Palm are happy to provide that information—using the Conduit Manager APIs that are in the Conduit Manager DLL. It's a chicken-and-egg problem. The solution to the problem is described in the next section.

The solution to finding the correct DLL

Here are the steps:

1. Use a copy of *CondMgr.DLL* that you ship with your installation program to find the directory containing the HotSync executable (`CmGetHotSyncExecPath` returns the full pathname of the HotSync executable). Check in that directory for the desired DLL. If it's there, use it (it's the version that matches *HotSync.exe*, and may be newer than the version you are shipping in your installation program).

2. If the desired DLL is not in the Palm Desktop software, revert to using the version of the DLL that you ship along with your installation program.

Implementing the solution

In order to make the process of finding the right DLL as painless as possible, we've written a small shim (mediating DLL) called *PalmDLLShim.DLL* (available at *http://www.calliopeinc.com/palmprog2/*). It simplifies life by containing duplicates of the Palm entry points from all three DLLs. You initialize the DLL with the directory location containing our copy of the DLLs, and then, for each DLL, load the proper version. Each of the shim entry points will then find the corresponding entry point in the loaded DLL and use it.

An application that uses *CondMgr.DLL*, *HSAPI.DLL*, or *InstAide.DLL* will need to change in four ways:

- It will need to include *PalmDLLShim.h*.
- It will need to initialize the DLL by calling `PalmDLLShimInit`, passing the full path to the directory containing the real DLLs.
- It will need to uninitialize the DLL by calling `PalmDLLShimDeinit`.
- It will need to link with the *PalmDLLShim.lib* rather than the *.lib* files for the other three DLLs.

The elements in our solution

Our solution contains several DLLs found in two separate directories. One directory contains our shim and an application:

PalmDLLShim.DLL
> As described above, this file contains the same entry points found in each of the three Palm DLLs.

Executable
> This is an application that uses *PalmDLLShim.DLL*. It could also be any of the sample applications we saw earlier, as long as they added calls to `PalmDLLShimInit` and `PalmDLLShimDeinit`.

We've put the Palm DLLs in another directory, *C:\PalmDLLs*. We can actually put them in any directory we wanted (including the directory containing the executable), as long as we specify the location to the *PalmDLLShim*.

CondMgr.DLL
> This is called by *PalmDLLShim.DLL* at a minimum to find the HotSync path. It will be called for further routines if a version of *CondMgr.DLL* isn't found in the *HotSync* directory.

InstAide.DLL
> This will be called by *PalmDLLShim.DLL* if a version of *InstAide.DLL* isn't found in the *HotSync* directory.

HSAPI.DLL
> This will be called by *PalmDLLShim.DLL* if a version of *HSAPI.DLL* isn't found in the *HotSync* directory.

Modifying the application

Example 14-6 shows a copy of *ConduitInstall.c*, which is modified to work with the *PalmDLLShim*.

Example 14-6. ConduitInstall.c modified to use PalmDLLShim

```
#include <Windows.h>
#include "CondMgr.h"
#include <stdio.h>
#include "PalmDLLShim.h"
```

Example 14-6. ConduitInstall.c modified to use PalmDLLShim (continued)

```
int main(int argc, char **argv)
{
  const char *kCreator = "SLES";

  if (PalmDLLShimInitialize("C:\\PalmDLLs")) {
    fprintf(stderr, "Initialization failed\n");
    exit(1);
  }
  err = CmInstallCreator(kCreator, CONDUIT_APPLICATION);
  if (err == 0)
    err = CmSetCreatorName(kCreator, "C:\\Sales\\Debug\\Sales.DLL");
  if (err == 0)
    err = CmSetCreatorDirectory(kCreator, "Sales");
  if (err == 0)
    err = CmSetCreatorFile(kCreator, "Sales");
  if (err == 0)
    err = CmSetCreatorPriority(kCreator, 2);
  PalmDLLShimDeinitialize( );
  if (err == 0)
    printf("Registration succeeded\n");
  else
    printf("Registration failed %d\n", err);
  return err;
}
```

The code for PalmDLLShim

Let's look at the code for *PalmDLLShim*. First, here's the header file, *PalmDLLShim.h*, which declares our initialization and deinitialization routines (the declarations for the three DLLs remain in their respective header files):

```
// The following ifdef block is the standard way of creating macros, which
// make exporting from a DLL simpler. All files within this DLL are compiled
// with the PALMDLLSHIM_EXPORTS symbol defined on the command line. This
// symbol should not be defined on any project that uses this DLL. This way
// any other project whose source files include this file see
// PALMDLLSHIM_API functions as being imported from a DLL, whereas this DLL
// sees symbols defined with this macro as being exported.
#ifdef PALMDLLSHIM_EXPORTS
#define PALMDLLSHIM_API __declspec(dllexport)
#else
#define PALMDLLSHIM_API __declspec(dllimport)
#endif

PALMDLLSHIM_API bool WINAPI PalmDLLShimInit(char *dllDir);
PALMDLLSHIM_API void WINAPI PalmDLLShimDeinit(void);
```

Now, let's go to the source file, *PalmDLLShim.c*. First, we define globals:

```
#define kMaxPathName  1024
char   gDLLDir[kMaxPathName];
char   gHotSyncDir[kMaxPathName];
```

```
HINSTANCE gCondMgrLib;
HINSTANCE gHsapiLib;
HINSTANCE gInstAideLib;
```

We keep track of the directories in which we've provided our versions of the three
Palm DLLs, as well as the directory containing the HotSync application. In addition,
we keep references to the three libraries we've opened—they may be in our directory
or in the *HotSync* directory.

From our Conduit Manager DLL, our initialization routine (see Example 14-7)
obtains the path to the HotSync executable. Once it's found, we strip off the filename at the end, leaving a pure directory. Next, we try opening each of the three
DLLs from the *HotSync* directory (if the DLLs are present). Failing that, we open
them from our own directory. Note that LoadLibrary, GetProcAddress, and
FreeLibrary are Windows OS calls.

Example 14-7. PalmDLLShim's initialization routine

```
bool WINAPI PalmDLLShimInit(char *dllDir)
{
  strcpy(gDLLDir, dllDir);

  HINSTANCE ourCondMgrLib = LoadLibFromDirectory(dllDir, "CondMgr.DLL");
  if (!ourCondMgrLib)
    return false;

  typedef int  (WINAPI *ProcPtr)(TCHAR *pPath, int *piSize);
  ProcPtr procPtr;

  procPtr = (ProcPtr) GetProcAddress(ourCondMgrLib, "CmGetHotSyncExecPath");
  if (!procPtr){
    FreeLibrary(ourCondMgrLib);
    return false;
  }
  int size = sizeof(gHotSyncDir);
  (*procPtr)(gHotSyncDir, &size);

  StripTrailingSlashAndName(gHotSyncDir);

  FreeLibrary(ourCondMgrLib);
  gCondMgrLib = LoadProperLib("CondMgr.DLL");
  gHsapiLib = LoadProperLib("HSAPI.DLL");
  gInstAideLib = LoadProperLib("InstAide.DLL");

  if (!gCondMgrLib || !gHsapiLib || !gInstAideLib) {
    if (gCondMgrLib)
      FreeLibrary(gCondMgrLib);
    gCondMgrLib = NULL;
    if (gHsapiLib)
      FreeLibrary(gHsapiLib);
    gHsapiLib = NULL;
    if (gInstAideLib)
```

Example 14-7. PalmDLLShim's initialization routine (continued)

```
      FreeLibrary(gInstAideLib);
    gInstAideLib = NULL;
  }
  return true;
}
```

Our deinitialization routine simply closes all three of the loaded libraries:

```
void WINAPI PalmDLLShimDeinit(void)
{
  if (gCondMgrLib)
    FreeLibrary(gCondMgrLib);
  gCondMgrLib = NULL;
  if (gHsapiLib)
    FreeLibrary(gHsapiLib);
  gHsapiLib = NULL;
  if (gInstAideLib)
    FreeLibrary(gInstAideLib);
  gInstAideLib = NULL;
}
```

There are some utility routines. The first one loads a library from a given directory:

```
HINSTANCE LoadLibFromDirectory(char *dllDir, char *dllName)
{
  char fullPathName[kMaxPathName];

  sprintf(fullPathName, "%s\\%s", dllDir, dllName);
  return LoadLibrary(fullPathName);
}
```

Another utility routine loads a DLL from either the *HotSync* directory or, failing that, from our directory:

```
HINSTANCE LoadProperLib(char *dllName)
{
  HINSTANCE lib;

  lib = LoadLibFromDirectory(gHotSyncDir, dllName);
  if (lib)
    return lib;
  return LoadLibFromDirectory(gDLLDir, dllName);
}
```

A final utility routine strips off the trailing filename from a full pathname:

```
void StripTrailingSlashAndName(char *s)
{
  char *locationOfLastSlash;

  locationOfLastSlash = strrchr(s, '\\');
  if (locationOfLastSlash)
    *locationOfLastSlash = '\0';
}
```

Now, we need a shim entry point for each of the entry points in each of the three DLLs. Here's an example of what we want:

```
PALMDLLSHIM_API int WINAPI PltInstallFile(TCHAR *pUser, TCHAR *pFileSpec)
{
  typedef int (WINAPI *ProcPtr)(TCHAR *pUser, TCHAR *pFileSpec);
  ProcPtr func = (ProcPtr) GetProcAddress(gCondMgrLib, "PltInstallFile");
  if (!func) {
    return -1;  // maybe return some other error?
  } else
    return (*func)(puser, pFileSpec);
}
```

The PltInstallFile function loads the function from the appropriate library, then calls it indirectly. It would be quite a bit of copying, pasting, and typing to write the above nine-line function for every single entry point. Instead, we take advantage of the similarity of the basic structure of the routines. We define a macro that parameterizes the return result of the function, the name of the function, the declaration, how to call it, and the library it is in. Here's that macro:

```
#define DeclareShimFunction(returnResult, name, apiDecl, apiCall, library) \
PALMDLLSHIM_API returnResult WINAPI name   apiDecl \
{ \
  typedef returnResult (WINAPI *ProcPtr)apiDecl; \
  ProcPtr func = (ProcPtr) GetProcAddress(library, #name); \
  if (!func) {\
    return -1;\
  } else\
    return (*func)apiCall;\
}
```

It calls the previous macro as:

```
DeclareShimFunction(int, PltInstallFile, (TCHAR *pUser, TCHAR *pFileSpec), \
  (pUser, pFileSpec), gCondMgrLib)
```

which yields exactly the same PltInstallFile function we defined earlier, but with only two lines of code rather than nine.

We'll declare another macro for each of the three libraries, so we don't have to repeat the reference to the global library:

```
#define DeclareCMShimFunction(returnResult, name, apiDecl, apiCall) \
  DeclareShimFunction(returnResult, name, apiDecl, apiCall, gCondMgrLib)

#define DeclareHSShimFunction(returnResult, name, apiDecl, apiCall) \
  DeclareShimFunction(returnResult, name, apiDecl, apiCall, gCondMgrLib)

#define DeclareIAShimFunction(returnResult, name, apiDecl, apiCall) \
  DeclareShimFunction(returnResult, name, apiDecl, apiCall, gCondMgrLib)
```

Then, we have calls to the macro as shown in Example 14-8 (we'll show you only a few from each of the DLLs, to avoid boredom due to repetition).

Example 14-8. Shim functions as created by macros

```
DeclareCMShimFunction(int, CmGetHotSyncExecPath, \
  (TCHAR *pPath, int *piSize), (pPath, piSize))

DeclareCMShimFunction(WORD, CmGetLibVersion, (void), ())

DeclareCMShimFunction(int, CmInstallCreator, \
  (const char *creatorString, int conduitType),
  (creatorString, conduitType))

DeclareCMShimFunction(int, CmSetCreatorName, \
  (const char *pCreatorID, const TCHAR * pConduitName),
  (pCreatorID, pConduitName))

DeclareCMShimFunction(int, CmRemoveConduitByCreatorID, \
  (const char *pCreatorID),
  (pCreatorID))
...

DeclareHSShimFunction(long, HsGetSyncStatus, (DWORD *pdwStatus), (pdwStatus))

enum HsStatusType; // must define since we don't include HSAPI.h
DeclareHSShimFunction(long, HsSetAppStatus,
  (HsStatusType statusType, DWORD dwStartFlags),
  (statusType, dwStartFlags))
...

DeclareIAShimFunction(int, PltGetUserCount, (void), ())

DeclareIAShimFunction(int, PltInstallFile, \
  (TCHAR *pUser, TCHAR *pFileSpec), \
  (pUser, pFileSpec))

DeclareIAShimFunction(int, PltGetUser, \
 (unsigned int iIndex, TCHAR *pUserBuffer, short *psUserBufSize), \
  (iIndex, pUserBuffer, psUserBufSize))
...
```

With this solution, you need never worry again about where to find the relevant DLLs. Instead, you can focus on creating an installer for your conduit and handheld application.

Important Issues for Creating an Installer

An installer is required for a conduit and is desirable even if you have only a handheld application. The biggest argument in favor of an installer is that it gives your user a pleasant experience. An installer simplifies the installation process by running one application that automatically causes a conduit to be installed and registered, and/or adds a handheld application to the installation list for the next sync.

What the installer needs to do

If the installer is installing a conduit, it must do the following:

1. Check to make sure the HotSync application is present. If it isn't, it must warn the user to install Palm Desktop and abort the installation process.
2. Copy the conduit(s) to an application-specific location on the desktop (often in *Program Files*). It's better not to install your conduit directly into the *HotSync* folder; that way, the user can upgrade to a new version of Palm Desktop without affecting your conduit.
3. Register the conduit(s).
4. If the HotSync application is running, restart it (so that it will be aware of the newly registered conduits).

If the installer is installing a handheld application or database, it must do the following:

1. Check to make sure the HotSync application is present. If it isn't, it must warn the user to install Palm Desktop and abort the installation process.
2. Obtain the list of Palm users on the desktop. If there are no Palm users, notify the user and abort the installation process. If there is more than one Palm user, display the list of Palm users and have whoever is running the installer choose a user.
3. Install the application(s) and/or database(s) for the Palm user from step 2.
4. Tell the user that the application(s) will be installed the next time a sync is done.

If the user has installed a conduit, an uninstaller must be available that will do the following:

1. Unregister the conduit(s).
2. Remove the conduit(s) from the desktop machine.
3. If the HotSync application is running, restart it (so it will be aware that the conduits are no longer registered).

How the installer will work

If your installer won't be installing a conduit, it's fairly easy. Your installer will ship with the three Palm DLLs, along with the *PalmDLLShim*.

If you're installing a conduit, you must not only use these DLLs temporarily, but you must also save them somewhere so that your uninstall will work successfully.

 Palm's Knowledge Base article 2129 contains sample code for a Conduit Installer DLL that will install or uninstall a conduit. It is provided with a command-line application that uses the DLL (for testing), along with instructions for creating an InstallShield installer that uses the DLL.

Conduit Entry Points

In our initial discussion of conduits, we told you that a conduit has three required entry points. There are also some optional ones (including some that are only for CDK 3.0 or later). Now it is time to look at these entry points in greater detail.

Required Entry Points

The required entry points are as follows:

`long GetConduitName(char* pszName, WORD nLen)`

> This function returns the conduit's name in `pszName`. The length of the passed-in buffer is the second parameter. A conduit should truncate the conduit's name, if needed, rather than writing past the end of the buffer.
>
> Like all the entry points, the return value is 0 for no error, or nonzero for an error.

`DWORD GetConduitVersion( )`

> This function returns the version of the conduit as a 4-byte value. The minor version is in the low byte. The major version is in the next byte. The upper two bytes are unused. A conduit with version 1.5 would return 0x15.

`long OpenConduit(PROGRESSFN progress, CSyncProperties &sync)`

> It is from this entry point that the conduit actually does its syncing. The first parameter, `progress`, is a pointer to a function. Although most conduits don't use this function, you can call it with a status string to display that status in the HotSync Progress dialog box. The second parameter is a structure with information about the sync. The most important fields in the structure are shown in Table 14-1.

Table 14-1. Important fields in CSyncProperties

Field	What it does
m_SyncType	An enumeration describing the type of synchronization to be performed: • Copy handheld to PC • Copy PC to handheld • Fast sync • Slow sync • Do nothing We'll discuss fast sync and slow sync in Chapter 16.
m_PathName	A string containing the full path to the conduit's directory within the user's directory.
m_LocalName	The value of the `File` registration entry.
m_UserName	The name of the user on the handheld.
m_RemoteName	An array of database names. This array is populated with databases whose creator matches those of the conduit and whose type is `DATA`. If there are no such databases, the array has one entry, copied from the `RemoteDB` registration entry.

Table 14-1. Important fields in CSyncProperties (continued)

Field	What it does
m_RemoteDBList	A list of all the databases on the handheld whose creator matches those of the conduit and whose type is DATA.
m_nRemoteCount	A count of all the databases in the m_RemoteName array.

Optional Entry Points

The optional entry points give you customization capabilities (and File Linking in 3.0 or later):

```
long GetConduitInfo(ConduitInfoEnum infoType, void *pInArgs,
void *pOut, DWORD *pdwOutSize)
```

This entry point is an extensible way to return information from the conduit, as an alternative to continuing to add more entry points. It is called by the Sync Manager to return the name of the conduit (as an alternative to GetConduitName); the version of Microsoft Foundation Classes (MFC), if any, used to build the conduit; and the default action of the conduit (the choices being no action, sync, handheld overwrites desktop, or desktop overwrites handheld). Its parameters are:

infoType

One of eConduitName, eMfcVersion, or eDefaultAction. There may be more options in the future.

pInArgs

Used to pass information into this routine. Its value is dependent on the infoType.

pOut

Used to return information from the routine. Its value is dependent on the infoType.

pdwOutSize

The size of the pOut buffer; don't write past the end of it.

`long ConfigureConduit(CSyncPreference& pref)`

This is called when the user wants to customize the conduit by pressing Change in the Custom HotSync dialog box (see Figure 14-2). The conduit is responsible for displaying a dialog box and saving user choices. A mirror-image synchronization conduit is responsible for displaying the dialog box shown in Figure 14-3. The user chooses what action should happen when a sync occurs (unchecking the permanent checkbox in the dialog box specifies that the dialog box setting should affect only the next sync).

This entry point has been superseded by CfgConduit. For backward-compatibility, however, you should provide both of them; if the user uses this conduit with a pre-3.0 version of HotSync, ConfigureConduit will be used.

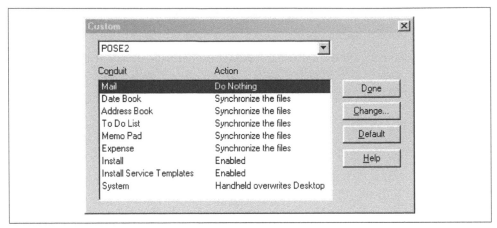

Figure 14-2. HotSync dialog box for customizing conduits

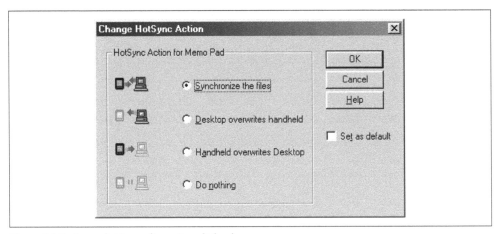

Figure 14-3. A conduit's configuration dialog box

Specific conduits may also have different things the user can configure. In any case, conduit configuration should always allow the user the option to do nothing. This way, the user can pick and choose which conduits are active (for example, to expedite syncing just the Address Book before rushing to a meeting).

If this entry point isn't present in your conduit, pressing the Change button does nothing—an action guaranteed to be confusing and annoying to users. Even if you are unwilling to provide a way for the user to configure your conduit to do nothing, you should provide this entry point and have it tell the user that the conduit can't be configured.

 Our reasoning relies on an age-old adage of good design: every allowable user action should produce a visible effect. Words to warm a designer's heart.

The parameter is a structure with the following fields that you'll often use:

m_SyncType
> Describes what type of operation the user has chosen: `eFast`, `eSlow`, `eHHtoPC`, `ePCtoHH`, `eInstall`, `eBackup`, `eDoNothing`, or `eProfileInstall`

m_SyncPref
> Describes whether this operation applies to just the next sync (`eTemporaryPreference`), or all syncs from now on (`ePermanentPreference`)

`long CfgConduit(ConduitCfgEnum cfgType, void *pArgs, DWORD *pdwArgsSize)`
> This is a newer entry point that replaces `ConfigureConduit`. Its purpose is the same as that of `ConfigureConduit`, but it receives more information when called. `CfgConduit` is extensible; more information could be provided in the future since it is passed a variable-size argument block.
>
> It's called by Sync Manager 3.0 and later. If this entry point isn't there, Sync Manager 3.0 reverts to calling `ConfigureConduit`.

 Support for calling `ConfigureConduit` may be phased out in future versions of the Sync Manager.

> Currently, the `cfgType` will be `eConfig1`, which signifies that the `pArgs` is a pointer to a `CfgConduitInfoType` structure. `CfgConduit` is also provided with the username for which the conduit is being configured (this is not provided to `ConfigureConduit`).

Optional File Linking entry points

These are the entry points used only for File Linking. (File Linking is provided in HotSync 3.0 or later and is not implemented in a conduit in this book):

`long SubscriptionSupported();`
> If this entry point exists and returns 0, File Linking is supported by the conduit.

`long ConfigureSubscription(SubProperties*& subProps)`
> This is called to provide information necessary for File Linking.

`long ImportData(CSubInfo*& subInfo)`
> This imports data from a linked file and displays it to the user.

`long UpdateTables(SubProperties* subProps)`
> This is called to update desktop files when File Linking information changes.

The HotSync Log

The CDK provides routines that add to a HotSync log. There are several of them that are quite useful; the main one is `LogAddEntry`.

long LogAddEntry(LPCTSTR logString, Activity act, BOOL timestamp)

You will continually use this routine to add entries to the HotSync log. Here are the parameters:

logstring

> The string displayed in the log.

timestamp

> This is a Boolean. True means that the log entry will be timestamped.

act

> This is an enumerated type. Many different enumeration constants are available for your use. The enumerated types used most often as a value for activity are as follows:
>
> slSyncStarted
>
> > Tells the log that your conduit is beginning synchronization. Call the following when you begin the sync process:
> >
> > ```
> > LogAddEntry("", slSyncStarted, false)
> > ```
>
> slSyncAborted
>
> > Tells the log that your conduit is done and that there was an error. Call:
> >
> > ```
> > LogAddEntry("your conduit name",
> >     slSyncAborted, false)
> > ```
> >
> > when you finish syncing with an error.
>
> slSyncFinished
>
> > Tells the log that your conduit is done without errors. Call:
> >
> > ```
> > LogAddEntry("your conduit name", slSyncFinished, false)
> > ```
> >
> > when you finish syncing without an error.
>
> slWarning
>
> > Adds the specified logString to the log and tells the user at the end of the HotSync that there are messages in the log.
>
> slText
>
> > Adds the specified logString to the log, but doesn't tell the user about the message.

long LogAddFormattedEntry(Activity act, BOOL timestamp, const char* dataString, ...)

Another useful routine is LogAddFormattedEntry. It acts as a combination of sprintf and LogAddEntry. It is especially helpful if you need to construct the log string from numbers or other strings. Here's an example of its use:

```
LogAddFormattedEntry(slText, false, "The number (%d) is bad", myNumber)
```

This is all you need to know about installation, entry points, and log messages. Next, we discuss the events that occur when the user does a sync.

LogAddFormattedEntry works by doing a sprintf into a buffer, and then calling LogAddEntry. Note that the buffer is not very big (it seems to be about 256 bytes) and can overflow if you pass too long a string.

The workaround is to just call sprintf yourself into your own (large enough) buffer, and then call LogAddEntry with that buffer.

When the HotSync Button Is Pressed

Let's go through a step-by-step sequence of the events that occur when the user pops a Palm device into the cradle and pushes the HotSync button. From this sequence (started here and continued in the next chapter), you can see exactly when and how the code in your conduit interacts with the desktop, the Palm device, and the Sync Manager.

For the purposes of this example, you should assume that our sample application has been successfully installed and contains no problems. Table 14-2 contains a description on the left of what the user does or what activity is occurring; the right column indicates what's going on programmatically in your conduit or on the desktop.

For now, we are just going to wave our hands around when we get to a description of moving data to and from the handheld. We'll fill in these gaps in the next chapter. The whole grand system should be clear by that point.

Table 14-2. What happens when a synchronization occurs

Action (by the user or by the system)	What is happening programmatically
The user pushes the HotSync button.	The handheld sends an "Are you there" message out the serial port until the Sync Manager on the desktop notices that someone is knocking.
HotSync synchronizing starts.	The Sync Manager negotiates a baud rate with the handheld and begins communication. It reads the user ID and name from the handheld and tries to find a corresponding HotSync user. If it doesn't find one, it prompts on the desktop for the user to select one or to create a new one.
The user gets the message: "Connecting with the desktop." HotSync retrieves from the handheld a list of all databases and their creators.	For each database on the handheld, the Sync Manager tries to find a conduit registered for that creator.
	Databases that have the backup bit set (unless they are of type DATA and have a conduit) are added to the list to be backed up by the Backup conduit. Remaining databases are ignored.
3.0 or later—Sync Manager installs new databases.	**The Install conduit is called to install databases.**
The Sync Manager determines if a fast sync is possible (if this is the same desktop machine last synced with) or if a slow sync is required (if it is different).	Conduits can take advantage of a fast sync by reading only from the handheld records marked as modified; nonmarked records won't have changed since the last sync.

Table 14-2. What happens when a synchronization occurs (continued) (continued)

Action (by the user or by the system)	What is happening programmatically
The user is notified that syncing has now started.	The Install conduit is run and new applications are installed.
	The Sync Manager starts the iteration through its list of conduits based on their priority codes (as specified when the conduit was registered).
The Sync Manager finishes with the conduit prior to ours.	
The Sync Manager prepares to sync.	Our conduit is loaded.
The Sync Manager checks the conduit's version number.	`GetConduitVersion` is called and returns the conduit's version number.
The Sync Manager gets the conduit name so that is can display information in the Status dialog box.	`GetConduitName` is called and returns the name of the conduit.
The Sync Manager prepares to sync by passing the synchronization off to the conduit.	`OpenConduit` is called, and the conduit's DLL gets loaded into memory. It is told whether to do a fast sync, a slow sync, a copy from handheld to desktop, a copy from desktop to handheld, or nothing. When `OpenConduit` returns, it has completed the task.
The Sync Manager runs the remaining conduits.	
The Sync Manager backs up modified databases that require backup.	The Backup conduit is called.
2.0 or earlier—Sync Manager installs new databases.	**The Install conduit is called to install databases.**
The handheld notifies applications whose conduits have run that their database(s) have been synced.	Your handheld application gets a `sysAppLaunch-CmdSyncNotify` launch code if any of its databases have been modified during the sync.
Syncing is complete.	

Using Conduit Inspector to Verify Your Conduit

Now it's time to tell you what to do if you have problems with your conduit: use the Conduit Inspector, which is part of the CDK. With the Conduit Inspector, you can examine a conduit DLL and verify that it:

- Is registered correctly
- Has the right entry points
- Implements those entry points correctly

You can run the Conduit Inspector manually, or from the HotSync application.

Running the Conduit Inspector Manually

To run the Conduit Inspector manually, you should execute:

```
C:\CDK402\Common\Bin\C4.02\ConduitInspector.exe
```

From the File menu, choose Open and select your conduit.

The Conduit Inspector will display information about the conduit and will also open Dependency Walker, a third-party tool that is included with Visual Studio (this tool shows what DLLs the conduit depends on—see *http://www.dependencywalker.com* for full details). You can use Dependency Walker to verify that all the needed DLLs are present. This is especially important because HotSync will silently ignore your conduit if it depends on a missing DLL.

 When you first open the Conduit Inspector, it may be unable to find the Dependency Walker. To fix this problem, run the Dependency Walker by hand once (using Start → Programs → Microsoft Visual C++ → Microsoft Visual C++ Tools → Depends). Having run it once, the Conduit Inspector seems to be able to find it from then on when necessary.

Running the Conduit Inspector from the HotSync Application

You can also run the Conduit Inspector automatically if you use the developer version of HotSync, which is found in:

```
C:\CDK401\Common\Bin\C4.02\HotSync.exe
```

It has a command-line flag, -ic, that will automatically launch the Conduit Inspector when a sync begins. HotSync will also print out lots of debugging information to a log window with Conduit Inspector as the sync occurs. Example 14-9 shows a short excerpt.

Example 14-9. Excerpt from Conduit Inspector log window using HotSync -ic

```
...
    Backup job added: Name: Graffiti ShortCuts, Type: 1835098994, Creator graf, CardNum 0,
Flags 32793
    Backup job added: Name: System MIDI Sounds, Type: 1936549490, Creator psys, CardNum 0,
Flags 8
    Backup job added: Name: Saved Preferences, Type: 1936749158, Creator psys, CardNum 0,
Flags 9
Associating and running General Sync Conduits
    Current conduit: Name: datcn20.dll, Creator ID date
        Found task and attempting to load conduit.
SyncReadSystemInfo( )
SyncRegisterConduit( )
SyncOpenDB( )
SyncReadDBAppInfoBlock( )
SyncWriteDBAppInfoBlock( )
SyncReadNextModifiedRec( )
SyncPurgeDeletedRecs( )
SyncGetDBRecordCount( )
SyncGetDBRecordCount( )
SyncResetSyncFlags( )
```

Example 14-9. Excerpt from Conduit Inspector log window using HotSync -ic (continued)

```
SyncCloseDB( )
SyncCloseDBEx( )
OK Date Book
SyncUnRegisterConduit( )
    Current conduit: Name: addcn30.dll, Creator ID addr
        Found task and attempting to load conduit.
SyncReadSystemInfo( )
SyncRegisterConduit( )
SyncOpenDB( )
SyncReadDBAppInfoBlock( )
SyncWriteDBAppInfoBlock( )
SyncReadNextModifiedRec( )
SyncPurgeDeletedRecs( )
SyncGetDBRecordCount( )
SyncGetDBRecordCount( )
SyncResetSyncFlags( )
SyncCloseDB( )
SyncCloseDBEx( )
OK Address Book
SyncUnRegisterConduit( )
    Current conduit: Name: todcn20.dll, Creator ID todo
        Found task and attempting to load conduit.
...
```

As you can see, the log shows the steps the Sync Manager goes through while load-ing a conduit, as well as showing all the calls that the conduit makes.

Syncing from POSE

In order to sync directly from POSE, you'll need to do so over TCP/IP. This pro-cess—while simple—requires some setup on the desktop and also on the emulated handheld. Note that you need to do one version of the setup or the other, depending on which version of Palm OS you are running.

If You Are Using Palm OS 3.3 or Later

Here are the steps you'll need to follow if you're using Palm OS 3.3 or later (contain-ing the new Serial Manager).

On the desktop:

1. Right-click on the HotSync icon in the system tray.
2. Make sure the Network menu item is checked.

In POSE:

1. Right-click on the POSE window and choose Settings → Properties. Make sure the Redirect NetLib calls to host TCP/IP checkbox is checked.
2. From within POSE, open the HotSync application.

3. Choose the Modem Sync Prefs menu item.

4. Tap on the Network push button, and tap OK.

5. Choose the Primary PC Setup menu item.

6. Enter **!!** for Primary PC Name (this special name causes the address to remain at 127.0.0.1 rather than updating it to the real IP address; this is important for a desktop whose IP address changes dynamically).

7. Enter **127.0.0.1** for Primary PC Address (this specifies the local host).

8. Tap OK.

9. Tap the Modem push button in the main form.

10. Tap the Select Service trigger.

11. Tap the Done button.

12. Tap the HotSync bitmap button to sync.

If You Are Using Palm OS 3.0 to 3.2

Here are the steps you'll need to follow if you're using Palm OS 3.0 to 3.2 (containing TCP/IP but the old Serial Manager).

On the desktop:

1. Right-click on the HotSync icon in the system tray.

2. Make sure the Network menu item is checked.

In POSE:

1. Right-click on the POSE windows and Settings → Properties. Make sure the Redirect NetLib calls to host TCP/IP checkbox is checked.

2. Open the HotSync application within POSE.

3. In POSE, install *netsync.prc*. Download *nhssetup.exe* from *http://www.palm.com/support/downloads/netsync.html*. Then, run *nhssetup.exe* to extract *setupex.exe*. Finally, run *setupex.exe* to extract *netsync.prc*.

4. Choose the Modem Sync Prefs menu item.

5. Tap on the Network push button, and tap OK.

6. Choose the Primary PC Setup menu item.

7. Enter **!!** for Primary PC Name.

8. Enter **127.0.0.1** for Primary PC Address (this specifies the local desktop).

9. Tap OK.

10. Tap the Select Service trigger (beneath Modem Sync).

11. Tap the Done button.

12. Tap the Modem Sync bitmap button.

Creating a Minimal Sales Conduit

When you use Visual C++ and the development kit, only a few steps are required to create a minimal conduit. We assume that you've installed the 4.02 CDK in its default location: the *C:\CDK402* folder. Let's walk through the steps:

1. Create a new project of type Palm Conduit Wizard (dll) (see Figure 14-4).
2. Specify that you want Conduit entry points only (no sync logic), as shown in Figure 14-5.
3. Specify that you want a Sync action configuration dialog box (see Figure 14-6).
4. Verify the filenames that the Wizard will create (see Figure 14-7).

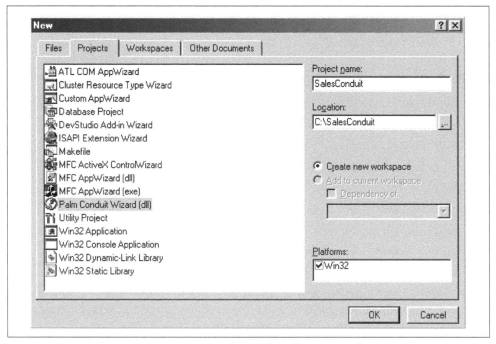

Figure 14-4. A new MFC AppWizard project for our do-nothing minimal conduit

Code for the Sales Conduit

As we said before, this is a conduit that does very little—it considers itself successful if it writes a message to the log file. It's great, however, at distilling the process you use for creating the outer shell of a conduit. First, let's show you the code. Then we'll look at what is involved in registering and testing the conduit.

The Conduit Wizard has generated the source code for a conduit that includes almost everything. It includes code for the following entry points: OpenConduit, GetConduitName, GetConduitVersion, ConfigureConduit, GetConduitInfo, and CfgConduit. Furthermore, all of this code is quite functional, with the exception of

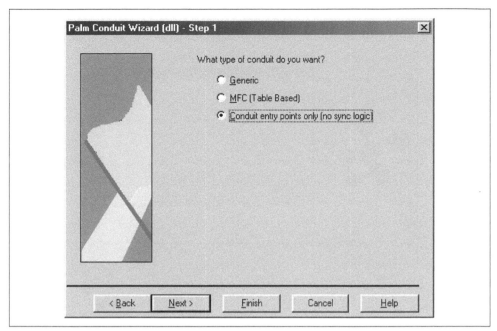

Figure 14-5. Selecting the type of conduit

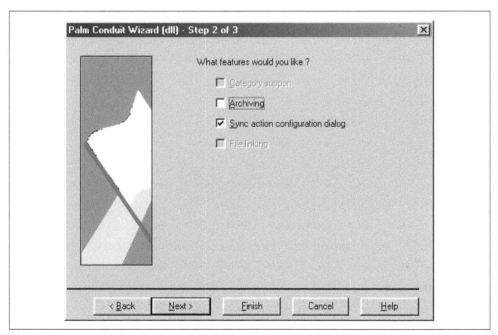

Figure 14-6. Specifying the features for the conduits

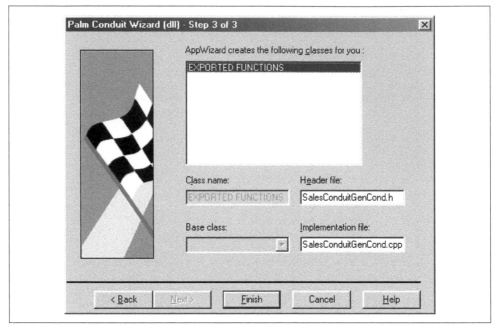

Figure 14-7. Verifying the Wizard's filenames

OpenConduit. Here's the rather useless bit of code that the Wizard generates for OpenConduit:

```
ExportFunc long OpenConduit(PROGRESSFN pFn, CSyncProperties& rProps)
{
  long retval = -1;
  if (pFn)
  {
    // TODO - create your own custom sync class, and run it
  }
  return(retval);
}
```

Unfortunately, if you use this, the sync will generate an error and display the following problem in the log:

```
Conduit 'Sales' Error: Unknown error.  (FFFF)
```

We have to do a few things, and OpenConduit needs some additional code in order to do nothing effectively. We need to do these three things:

- Add an include file.
- Modify OpenConduit and write some messages to the log.
- Change some strings in our resource file.

Let's look at these tasks in order:

1. Add an include file.

First, we add an include file that declares the APIs for the HotSync log:

```
#include <HSLog.h>
```

2. Modify OpenConduit.

OpenConduit is passed a class, CSyncProperties, which contains information about the sync that will take place. We're interested in the m_SyncType field of that class, which tells us what type of sync we have. The only type of sync we can handle is eDoNothing. In that case, we write an appropriate message to the log and then return.

For any other type of sync, we begin the sync process by calling SyncRegisterConduit (if that fails, we return the error), then we write to the log that we've begun. When we finish, we write to the log that we've finished (or, if an error had occurred, that we've aborted).

The following code shows our code changes for OpenConduit:

```
ExportFunc long OpenConduit(PROGRESSFN progress,
    CSyncProperties &sync)
{
  long err = 0;
  CONDHANDLE myConduitHandle = (CONDHANDLE) 0;
  char  conduitName[100];

  GetConduitName(conduitName, sizeof(conduitName));
  if (!progress)
    return -1;
  else if (sync.m_SyncType == eDoNothing) {
    LogAddFormattedEntry(slText, false,
      "%s - sync configured to Do Nothing", conduitName);
    return 0;
  } else if ((err = SyncRegisterConduit(myConduitHandle)) == 0) {
    LogAddEntry("", slSyncStarted, false);

    LogAddEntry(conduitName, err ? slSyncAborted : slSyncFinished,
        false);
    SyncUnRegisterConduit(myConduitHandle);
    return err;
  } else
    return err;
}
```

3. Update strings in the resource file.

There are a couple of strings that must be changed in *Sales.rc*. We open *Sales.rc* and the string table and make the changes shown in Table 14-3.

Table 14-3. Updating strings in the resource file

String ID	Change from	Change to
IDS_CONDUIT_NAME	TODO - Put conduit name	Sales
IDS_SYNC_ACTION_TEXT	TODO - Put conduit action string here	HotSync action for Sales

Registering the Conduit

Now that we have made the necessary changes to make our DoNothing Conduit work, we can register it. We run CondCfg and add a new entry. Figure 14-8 shows the settings we use.

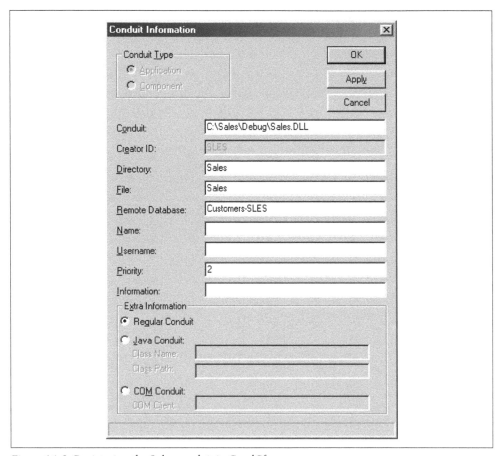

Figure 14-8. Registering the Sales conduit in CondCfg

Source-Level Debugging

Once we've registered the conduit, we can do some source-level debugging of it. Here are the necessary steps:

1. Quit the HotSync application (choose Exit from the HotSync menu in the system tray).

2. From Visual C++, use the menu item Build → Start Debug → Go.

3. When prompted for an executable to debug (see Figure 14-9), enter:

   `C:\Palm\HotSync.exe`

In order for Visual C++ to debug a DLL, it needs to start the application. This will, in turn, call the DLL. Visual C++ will remember this executable name; you won't have to enter it each time.

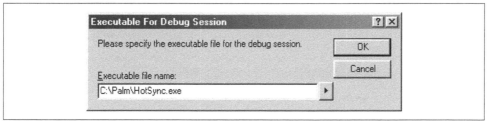

Figure 14-9. Visual C++ asking for the name of an executable to debug

4. When notified that HotSync doesn't contain debugging symbols (see Figure 14-10), check Do not prompt in the future, and click OK. Visual C++ is warning us that HotSync itself can't be debugged; this is not a problem, as we're not trying to debug it. We will be debugging our DLL, which does have debugging symbols.

Figure 14-10. Visual C++ warning that HotSync doesn't have debugging symbols

5. Now, we set a breakpoint at some point (e.g., within OpenConduit) by right-clicking on a source line and choosing Insert/Remove breakpoint. When execution reaches this line, it'll stop, allowing us to debug (single-step, examine data, and so on).

Testing

Having successfully learned how to debug our DoNothing Conduit, it is time to test it. To do so, we must first choose Custom from the HotSync menu. You should see the Sales conduit in the list of conduits (see Figure 14-11).

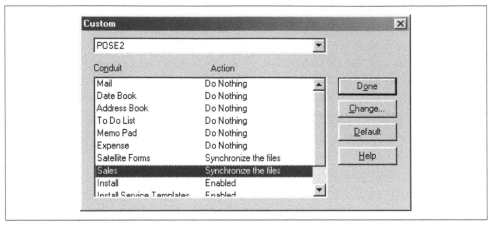

Figure 14-11. The Custom dialog box of HotSync showing the list of registered conduits

Proving that CfgConduit works

Now we need to select the Sales application and click the Change button. You should see the dialog box shown in Figure 14-12. Displaying this dialog box proves that our conduit's CfgConduit function has been called.

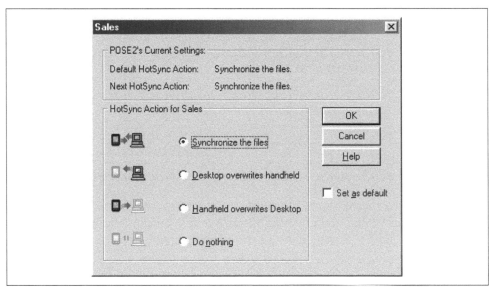

Figure 14-12. Changing the HotSync settings of the Sales conduit

Next, it's time to test syncing. First, we make sure that the Sales application has been installed on the handheld (otherwise, the Sales conduit won't be invoked).

Seeing the conduit in the HotSync log

When we sync, we should get the message "Synchronizing Sales" in the HotSync Progress dialog box. Once a sync has been completed, we will open the HotSync log for that user. Information that includes a line about the Sales conduit should show up in the log. It should look something like this:

```
HotSync started 07/30/98 11:59:53
OK Date Book
OK Address Book
OK To Do List
OK Memo Pad
OK Sales
OK Expense
```

Setting the conduit to Do nothing

Now we need to change the HotSync settings for the Sales conduit from Synchronize the files to Do nothing (see Figure 14-12).

After you sync, the log should show the following:

```
HotSync started 07/30/98 12:02:37
OK Date Book
OK Address Book
OK To Do List
OK Memo Pad
Sales - sync configured to Do Nothing
OK Expense
```

Now that we have a conduit shell that has been tested and works correctly, we can continue adding functionality to it. We will do so in the next chapter by moving data to and from the handheld.

## CHAPTER 15

Moving Data to and from the Handheld with a Conduit

Now we are going to show you how to move data back and forth between the desktop and the handheld. To do this, we need to discuss quite a few Sync Manager functions. We'll show you the functionality required in a conduit to support data transfers as well as some useful additional features. After we discuss these topics, we'll return to our walkthrough of what happens when the HotSync button gets pressed.

Next, we'll discuss portability issues and, finally, we'll turn to conduit creation. We'll rewrite our DoNothing Sales application conduit so that it handles moving data to and from the handheld. We'll show you how to move the sales orders and customers from the handheld, and move the products and customers to the handheld. We'll also handle deleted records in the customer database.

Conduit Requirements

At a bare minimum, a conduit that handles data moving to and from the handheld has to do all of the following:

- Register and unregister the conduit with the Sync Manager
- Open and close databases
- Read and write records
- Deal with categories (if the application supports categories)

Where to Store Data

There is an important demarcation to remember when deciding where to store data on the desktop. Data specific to a particular user should be stored in a private location, whereas data shared among many users should be stored in a group location.

For example, in our Sales application each salesperson has her own list of customers but should get the product list from a general location. The first set of data is specific to a particular user; the second type is general. They should be stored in separate locations.

Specific data
> Store this data in your conduit folder in the user's folder in the *HotSync* folder.

General data
> Store this data in your application's *Desktop* folder.

Also keep in mind that data doesn't necessarily need to be stored locally. While it may be stored on a particular desktop, it is just as likely to be stored on a server or a web site.

Creating, Opening, and Closing Databases

Database management during synchronization is handled completely by the conduit.

Creating a Database

There is a standard database call used by the Sync Manager to create a database:

```
long SyncCreateDB(CDbCreateDB& rDbStats)
```

Like all the Sync Manager routines, SyncCreateDB returns SYNCERR_NONE if no error occurs; otherwise, it returns an error code. SyncCreateDB creates a new record or resource database on the handheld and then opens it. You have the same control over database creation from within the conduit that you have on the handheld.

The rDbStats parameter is of the type CDbCreateDBClass and contains the following important fields:

m_FileHandle
> Output field. On a successful return, this contains a handle to the created database with read or write access.

m_Creator
> Database creator ID. This should typically match the creator ID of the application.

m_Flags
> The database attributes. Choose one of the following: eRecord for a standard database or eResource for a resource database. Another flag within which you can do a bitwise-or is eBackupDB (this sets the backup bit of the database).

m_Type
> The 4-byte database type.

m_CardNo
> Memory card where the database is located. Use 0, since no Palm OS device has (or will likely have) more than one writable memory card.

m_Name
> The database name.

m_Version
> The version of the database.

m_dwReserved
> Reserved for future use. Must be set to 0.

Opening a Database

The Sync Manager call to open a remote database is:

```
long SyncOpenDB(char *pname, int nCardNum, Byte& rHandle, Byte openMode)
```

The values for the four parameters are:

pName
> Name of the database.

nCardNum
> Memory card where the database is located. Use 0, unless you're trying to open a database on a read-only Handspring Springboard module.

rHandle
> Output parameter. On a successful return, this contains a handle to the open database.

openMode
> Use (eDbRead | eDbShowSecret) to read all records, including private ones. Use (eDbRead | eDbWrite | eDbShowSecret) to be able to write and/or delete records.

You need to close any database you open; and only one can be open at a time. An error results if you try to open a new database without closing the prior one.

Closing the Database

The Sync Manager call to close a remote database should come as no surprise. It is SyncCloseDB, and it takes only one parameter: the handle you created when you opened or created the database:

```
long SyncCloseDB(Byte fHandle)
```

SyncCloseDBEx provides slightly more sophisticated results. This function also allows you to modify the database's backup and modification dates. Both functions close databases that have been opened with either SyncCreateDB or SyncOpenDB.

Moving Data to the Handheld

As we discussed earlier, there are several different ways to move data around during a synchronization. Let's look at what is involved in moving data from the desktop to the handheld. This is commonly done with databases that are updated exclusively on the desktop and are routinely moved to handhelds where they aren't modified, but may also occur when the user chooses "Desktop overwrites handheld" in the HotSync Settings dialog box (see Figure 14-12).

You need to create the database if it doesn't already exist. You should delete any existing records before moving the ones from the desktop because you won't want the old ones; all you'll want are the newly moved ones.

Deleting Existing Records

There are a few different routines from which to choose for removing records from the handheld:

SyncDeleteRec
> Removes one specific record

SyncPurgeAllRecs
> Removes all records from a database

SyncPurgeAllRecsInCategory
> Removes all records from the specified category

SyncPurgeDeletedRecs
> Removes all records that have been marked as deleted or archived

For no terribly good reason, one API uses the term "delete," while others use "purge." All of them remove records (completely) from the database. In our particular case, SyncPurgeAllRecs is the call we want to use.

Writing Records

Once you have a nice, empty database, you can fill it up with fresh records from the desktop. You can add or replace records with the Sync Manager call, SyncWriteRec:

```
long SyncWriteRec(CRawRecordInfo &rInfo)
```

The parameter rInfo (of class CRawRecordInfo) contains several important fields:

m_FileHandle
> Handle to the open database.

m_RecId
> Input/output field; the record's unique ID. To add a new record, set this field to 0; on return, the field contains the new record's unique ID. To modify an existing record, set this field to the unique ID of one of the records in the database. An error occurs if this field doesn't match an existing unique record ID. Note that when you add a new record, it's the handheld that assigns the unique record ID.

m_Attribs
> The attributes of the record. See "Working with Records" in Chapter 10 for a complete discussion.

m_CatId

    The record's category index. Use values from 0 to 14.

m_RecSize

    The number of bytes in the record.

m_TotalBytes

    The number of bytes of data in the m_pBytes buffer. It should be set to the number of bytes in the record to work around bugs in some versions of the Sync Manager.

 Unique record IDs are not perfect. A record maintains its unique ID until a hard reset occurs. Prior to HotSync 3.0, after a hard reset, HotSync would generate new unique IDs for the records when it restored the database. Only HotSync 3.0 or later restores the unique record IDs correctly.

On the handheld, when you create a database record you specify the location in the database of that record. When using a conduit, on the other hand, you have no way to specify the record's exact location. SyncWriteRec always adds new records at the end of the database. In addition, if you modify an existing record, that record is moved to the end of the database.

Your application may expect records in a sorted order. If the conduit is writing records to an empty database, it can add them in sorted order. If it is modifying records though, they won't stay in or end up in sorted order. In such cases, the sysAppLaunchCmdSyncNotify launch code for Palm OS applications comes to the rescue. After a sync occurs for a database with a specific creator, that database's application is called with the sysAppLaunchCmdSyncNotify launch code. This launch code tells the application that its database has changed, and gives the application a chance to sort it.

Writing the AppInfo Block

You commonly use the AppInfo block of a database to store categories and other information relevant to the database as a whole. The Sync Manager call that you use to write the AppInfo block is:

```
long SyncWriteDBAppInfoBlock (BYTE fHandle, CDbGenInfo &rInfo)
```

The parameter rInfo is an object of the type CdbGenInfo and contains the following fields:

m_pBytes

    A pointer to the data you want copied to the AppInfo block.

m_TotalBytes

The number of bytes of data in the m_pBytes buffer. This should be set to the number of bytes in the record to work around bugs in some versions of the Sync Manager.

m_BytesRead

To work around bugs in some versions of the Sync Manager, set this to m_TotalBytes.

m_dwReserved

Reserved for the future. Set this field to 0.

Moving Data to the Desktop

When you send data from the handheld to the desktop you have to read through the records of the remote database and translate them into appropriate structures on the desktop. Here is the step-by-step process, starting with the choices you have in how you read through the records.

Finding the Number of Records

SyncGetDBRecordCount finds the number of records in a database:

```
long SyncGetDBRecordCount(BYTE fHandle, WORD &rNumRecs);
```

Call it with:

```
WORD numRecords;
err = SyncGetDBRecordCount(rHandle, numRecords);
```

Reading Records

You can read records in a remote database using any of the following strategies:

- Iterate through each record, locating the next altered record.
- Look up exact records via unique record ID.
- Read the *n*th record in the database.

We employ the last strategy for reading the records from our Sales order databases and the first strategy when we fully synchronize our customer list. There are a few points worth mentioning about each strategy.

Iterating through each record, stopping only for altered ones

If you want to iterate through the records and stop only on the ones that have been modified, use SyncReadNextModifiedRec. It retrieves a record from the remote database if the dirty bit in the record has been set.

A variation of this routine is `SyncReadNextModifiedRecInCategory`, which also filters based on the record's category. This function takes the category index as an additional parameter.

Looking up exact records via unique record ID

Sometimes you want to read records based on their unique record IDs. In such cases, use `SyncReadRecordByID`.

Iterating through the records of a database from beginning to end

Use `SyncReadRecordByIndex` to get a record based on the record number. Use this when you want to read through a database from beginning to end. This function takes one parameter, `rInfo`, which has the record index as one of its fields.

The CRawRecordInfo class

Each of these read routines takes as a parameter an object of the `CRawRecordInfo` class. The needed fields in the `CRawRecordInfo` class are:

`m_FileHandle`
> A handle to the open database.

`m_pBytes`
> A pointer that you allocate into which the record will be copied.

`m_TotalBytes`
> The size of the `m_pBytes` pointer. This is the number of bytes that can be copied into `m_pBytes` without it overflowing.

`m_BytesRead`
> Output field; the number of bytes read. If `m_BytesRead` is greater than `m_TotalBytes`, the record is too large. Sync Manager 2.1 or later copies the first `m_totalBytes` of record data to `m_pBytes`. Previous versions of the Sync Manager copy nothing.

`m_catId`
> Input field for `SyncReadNextRecInCategory` and `SyncReadNextModifiedRecIn-Category`. Output field for the other read routines. This contains the category, as a number between 0 and 14.

`m_RecIndex`
> Input field for `SyncReadRecordByIndex`. Output field for other read routines for Sync Manager 2.1 or later (earlier versions of Sync Manager don't write to this field).

`m_Attribs`
> The attributes of the record.

`m_dwReserved`
> Reserved for the future. Set this field to 0.

Beware of modifying the records in a database while iterating with SyncReadNextModifiedRec or SyncReadNextModifiedRecInCatgegory. In pre-2.0 versions of the Palm OS, the iteration routines don't work properly. In Palm OS 2.0, a modified record is read again by the iteration routines. In Palm OS 3.0, the modified record isn't reread.

If the record you read is larger than the space you've allocated, the sync read routines will not return an error. You need to explicitly check for this problem. If after the read, m_BytesRead is greater than m_TotalBytes, you haven't allocated enough space. For Palm OS 4.0 and earlier, no record can be more than 65,505 bytes.

Reading the AppInfo Block

There are times when you need to read information from the AppInfo block. For example, if the AppInfo block contains category names, you'll need to read it to get them. The Sync Manager call to use is SyncReadDBAppInfoBlock.

This function takes two parameters: a handle to the open record or database on the handheld, and the object, rInfo, which contains information about the database header.

The parameter rInfo is an object of type CdbGenInfo with the following fields:

m_pBytes
> A pointer to memory you've allocated into which you are going to copy the AppInfo block.

m_TotalBytes
> The number of bytes allocated for the m_pBytes field.

m_BytesRead
> Output field; the number of bytes read. If m_BytesRead is greater than m_TotalBytes, the AppInfo block is too large. Sync Manager 2.1 or later copies the first m_totalBytes of AppInfo block data to m_pBytes. Previous versions of the Sync Manager copy nothing.

m_dwReserved
> Reserved for the future. Set this field to 0.

Deleted/Archived Records

For databases that will be two-way synced, the handheld application doesn't completely remove a deleted record; it marks it as deleted, instead. When a sync occurs, those marked records need to be deleted from the desktop database.

There are a couple of ways that you can delete marked records and a few pitfalls to avoid. First, note that you have two different ways in which to remove records from a database: completely delete them or just archive them. Figure 15-1 shows the two possible dialog box settings that a user can select when given the option to delete a record. Choosing Save archive copy on PC means the record is marked as deleted until the next sync, at which point it is saved in an archive file and then deleted from the database. Not checking Save archive copy on PC means the record is marked as deleted until the next sync and then completely deleted from the database. See Chapter 10 for further details.

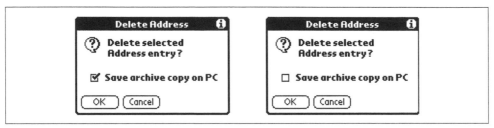

Figure 15-1. Saving or not saving an archive copy when deleting a record

Archiving records

You should create a separate archive file and append archived records there. This is for situations in which the user doesn't want the records cluttering up the handheld or the normal desktop application, but does want the record available if needed. It's customary to create a separate archive file for each category.

Deleting records

Once any archived records have been archived, and any deleted records have been removed from the corresponding desktop file, those records should be completely deleted from the handheld. SyncPurgeDeletedRecs is the call you should use:

```
err = SyncPurgeDeletedRecs(rHandle);
```

Keeping the HotSync Progress Dialog Box Alive

If your conduit does lengthy calculations or operations between calls to the Sync Manager, you will cause the HotSync Progress dialog box to stop functioning: the moving arrows that show progress will stop moving and the Cancel button will no longer work.

The Sync Manager provides a call to make during lengthy operations:

```
long SyncYieldCycles(WORD wMaxMilliSecs)
```

This keeps the user interface alive so that you can let the user know what is happening if necessary. The parameter, wMaxMilliSecs, is unused: pass 1.

You should call this routine at least every second or so. If you are calling other Sync Manager routines often, you do not need to call this one, as any call to the Sync Manager will keep the Progress dialog box alive.

Prior to HotSync 3.0, this call was also needed to prevent the communications link between the desktop and the handheld from timing out. This is no longer needed; the communications link won't be lost even if your conduit is carrying out a lengthy operation.

When the HotSync Button Is Pressed

We left off in the previous discussion ready to exchange information between the conduit on the desktop and the handheld unit. Let's continue walking through the chain of events (see Table 15-1).

Table 15-1. When the HotSync button is pressed

Action (by the user or by the system)	What is happening programmatically
The Sync Manager gets the conduit name so that it can display information in the Status dialog box.	GetConduitName is called and returns.
The Sync Manager prepares to sync by passing the synchronization off to the conduit.	The conduit's DLL is loaded into memory and its OpenConduit is called. It is told whether to do a fast sync, a slow sync, a copy from handheld to desktop, a copy from desktop to handheld, or to do nothing. When OpenConduit returns, it will have completed the task.
The conduit registers with the Sync Manager.	SyncRegisterConduit returns a handle.
The conduit notifies the log that syncing is about to start.	Conduit calls LogAddEntry("", slSyncStarted, false).
The conduit opens the remote order database on the handheld.	Conduit calls SyncOpenDB, which returns a handle to the remote order database.
The user sees that the Sales application is being synced.	All the data is written from the handheld to the desktop.
The conduit closes the remote database.	Conduit calls SyncCloseDB to close the Sales order database.
	Conduit calls SyncOpenDB, which returns a handle to the product database.
The conduit closes the remote database.	Conduit calls SyncCloseDB, which destroys the handle opened earlier for that database.
The Sync Manager backs up other stuff.	The Backup conduit is called.

Portability Issues

There are two important portability issues to take into account when moving data back and forth from the handheld to the desktop: byte ordering and structure packing.

Byte Ordering

The Palm OS currently runs on a Motorola platform, which stores bytes differently from Windows running on an Intel platform. This crucial difference can mess up data transfers royally if you are not careful.

It's been announced that a future version of the OS will run on the ARM processor in little-endian mode (which will match the Intel ordering). Right now, it's not clear what the implication will be for conduits. To be safe, use the Sync Manager routines for swapping rather than writing your own.

On the handheld, the 16-bit number 0x0102 is stored with the high byte, 0x01, first, and the low byte, 0x02, second. In the conduit on Windows, the same number is stored with the low byte, 0x02, first, and the high byte, 0x01, second. As a result, any 2-byte values stored in your records or in your AppInfo block must be swapped when transferred between the two systems. (If you fail to swap, a simple request for 3 boxes of toys on the handheld would be processed on the desktop as a request for 768 boxes!) A similar problem occurs with 4-byte values; they are also stored in switched forms (see Table 15-2).

Table 15-2. Comparison of byte orderings for the 4-byte value 0x01020304

Palm handheld byte order	Wintel byte order
0X01	0X04
0X02	0X03
0X03	0X02
0X04	0X01

The Sync Manager provides routines for converting 2- and 4-byte values from the handheld to host byte ordering:

```
Word SyncHHToHostWord(Word value)
DWord SyncHHToHostDWord(DWord value)
```

and for the opposite conversion:

```
Word SyncHostToHHWord(Word value)
DWord SyncHostToHHDWord(DWord value)
```

Here are the return values:

- SyncHHtoHostWord(0x0102) returns 0x0201
- SyncHostToHHWord(0x0201) returns 0x0102
- SyncHHToHostDWord(0x01020304) returns 0x04030201
- SyncHostToHHDWord(0x04030201) returns 0x012020304

 Strings are not affected by this byte ordering. On both platforms, the string abc is stored in the order a, b, c, \0.

Structure Packing

Sometimes the compiler leaves holes in structures between successive fields. This is done so that fields can begin on specific byte, word, or double-word boundaries. As a result, you need to lay out the structures carefully. You must define your records and/or the AppInfo block in the same way for both the compiler you use to create your handheld application and the compiler you use to create your conduit.

For Visual C++, we've found that the pragma pack can be used to change the packing rules to match that of CodeWarrior:

```
#pragma pack(2)

structure declarations for structures that will be read from the handheld

#pragma pack
```

The Sales Conduit

With all this information on hand regarding the conduit's role of moving data to and from the handheld, it is time to return to the Sales conduit. We will extend it so that our shell from the previous chapter also supports "Desktop overwrites handheld" and "Handheld overwrites desktop." We are postponing full syncing until Chapter 16.

For our conduit, we've got to define what it means to do each type of overwriting. Here's the logic that we think makes sense for the Sales application:

Desktop overwrites handheld
> The products database and the customers database are completely overwritten from the desktop; nothing happens to the orders database.

Handheld overwrites database
> The products are ignored (since they can't have changed on the handheld). The customers and orders databases are copied to the desktop. Any archived customers are appended to a separate file; deleted customers are removed from the handheld.

The end result is that the customer database is moved both to and from the handheld. The product database is sent to the handheld and the order database is sent to the desktop. Figure 15-2 shows you where each type of data is moving.

Format Used to Store Data on the Desktop

We store data on the desktop as tab-delimited text files.

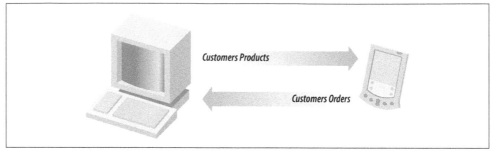

Figure 15-2. Where data is moving between the desktop and the handheld

The customers will be stored in a file named *Customers.txt* in the user's directory within the Sales conduit directory. Each line in the file is of the form:

```
Customer ID<tab>Name<tab>Address<tab>City<tab>Phone
```

The orders will be stored in a file named *Orders.txt* in the same directory. Each order is stored as:

```
ORDER Customer ID
quantity<tab>Product ID
quantity<tab>Product ID
...
qauntity<tab>Product ID
```

Orders follow one another in the file.

The products are stored in a *Products.txt* file and start with the categories, followed by the products:

```
Name of Category 0
Name of Category 1
...
Name of last Category
<empty line>
Product ID<tab>Name<tab>Category Number<tab>Price in dollars and cents
...
Product ID<tab>Name<tab>Category Number<tab>Price in dollars and cents
```

Modifying OpenConduit

Example 15-1 shows our modifications to OpenConduit to handle copying from handheld to desktop (eHHtoPC) and from desktop to handheld (ePCtoHH).

Example 15-1. OpenConduit supports moving to and from a handheld

```
ExportFunc long OpenConduit(PROGRESSFN progress, CSyncProperties &sync)
{
  long err = 0;
  CONDHANDLE myConduitHandle = (CONDHANDLE) 0;
  char  conduitName[100];

  GetConduitName(conduitName, sizeof(conduitName));
```

```
  if (!progress)
    return -1;
  else if (sync.m_SyncType == eDoNothing) {
    LogAddFormattedEntry(slText, false,
      "%s - sync configured to Do Nothing", conduitName);
    return 0;
  } else if ((err = SyncRegisterConduit(myConduitHandle)) == 0) {
    LogAddEntry("", slSyncStarted, false);

    if (sync.m_SyncType == eHHtoPC) {
      if ((err = CopyOrdersFromHH(sync)) != 0)
        goto exit;
      if ((err = CopyCustomersFromHH(sync)) != 0)
        goto exit;
    } else if (sync.m_SyncType == ePCtoHH) {
      if ((err = CopyProductsAndCategoriesToHH(sync)) != 0)
        goto exit;
      if ((err = CopyCustomersToHH(sync)) != 0)
        goto exit;
    } else if (sync.m_SyncType == eFast || sync.m_SyncType == eSlow) {
      LogAddEntry("Sales conduit doesn't (yet) support fast or slow. Choose "
        "Desktop overwrites Handheld or Handheld overwrites Desktop "
        "from the Custom menu", slWarning, false);
    }
exit:
    LogAddEntry(conduitName, err ? slSyncAborted : slSyncFinished,
        false);
    SyncUnRegisterConduit(myConduitHandle);
    return err;
  } else
    return err;
}
```

We copy in one direction if the request is from HH to PC, and to the other if the request is PC to HH. If we're asked to do a fast or slow (two-way) sync, we just note in the log that we aren't able to do so. Next chapter we'll add support for two-way syncing.

General Code

We have some other code to add, as well. We need to define our databases, create a global variable, and add some data structures.

Database defines

We have defines for the databases (these can be copied directly from the code for the handheld application):

```
#define salesCreator    'SLES'
#define salesVersion    0
#define customerDBType  'DATA'
```

```
#define customerDBName   "Customers-SLES"
#define orderDBType      'Ordr'
#define orderDBName      "Orders-SLES"
#define productDBType    'Prod'
#define productDBName    "Products-SLES"
```

Globals

We read and write records using a global buffer. We size it to be bigger than any possible record (at least on Palm OS 4.0 or earlier):

```
#define kMaxRecordSize  65535
char    gBigBuffer[kMaxRecordSize];
```

Data structures

We have structures (see Example 15-2) that need to correspond exactly to structures on the handheld (thus, we use the pragma pack). We then use these structures to read and write data on the handheld.

Example 15-2. Structure declarations for data structures on the handheld

```
// On the Palm handheld, the items array in PackedOrder starts at offset 6.
// Natural alignment on Windows would start it at offset 8.
#pragma pack(2)

struct Item {
    unsigned long   productID;
    unsigned long   quantity;
};

struct PackedOrder {
    long            customerID;
    unsigned short  numItems;
    Item            items[1];
};

struct PackedCustomer{
    long customerID;
    char name[1];
};

struct PackedProduct {
    unsigned long   productID;
    unsigned long   price;  // in cents
    char    name[1];
};

#define kCategoryNameLength 15
typedef char    CategoryName[kCategoryNameLength + 1];

struct PackedCategories {
```

```
    unsigned short   numCategories;
    CategoryName     names[1];
};

#pragma pack( )
```

Next, we've got some structures that we use to store data in memory in the conduit (see Example 15-3). Since we're using C++, we have constructors and destructors to make our lives easier:

Example 15-3. Conduit structures for in-memory use

```
struct Customer {
    Customer( ) { name = address = city = phone = 0;}
    ~Customer( ) {delete [] name; delete [] address; delete [] city;
        delete [] phone; };
    long customerID;
    char *name;
    char *address;
    char *city;
    char *phone;
};

struct Categories {
    Categories(int num) { numCategories = num;
        names = new CategoryName[num];}
    ~Categories( ) {delete [] names;};
    unsigned short numCategories;
    CategoryName *names;
};

struct Order {
    Order(unsigned short num) { numItems = num;
        items = new Item[numItems];};
    ~Order( ) { delete [] items;};
    long            customerID;
    unsigned short  numItems;
    Item            *items;
};

struct Product {
    Product( ) {name = 0;};
    ~Product( ) {delete [] name;};

    unsigned long   productID;
    unsigned long   price;  // in cents
    unsigned char   category:4;
    char    *name;
};
```

Moving Data to the Handheld

To move data to the handheld, we have to take care of a number of things:

1. We need to copy the customers to the handheld. If the database doesn't exist, we need to create it.

2. Once the database is open, we need to read through the records.

3. We need to repeat these steps for products.

Moving customers to the handheld

We copy the customers to the handheld in `CopyCustomersToHH` (see Example 15-4).

Example 15-4. CopyCustomersToHH copies customers from desktop to handheld

```
int CopyCustomersToHH(CSyncProperties &sync)
{
    FILE *fp = NULL;
    BYTE rHandle;
    int err;
    bool dbOpen = false;

    if ((err = SyncOpenDB(customerDBName, 0, rHandle, eDbWrite | eDbRead
        | eDbShowSecret)) != 0) {
        LogAddEntry("SyncOpenDB failed", slWarning, false);
        if (err == SYNCERR_FILE_NOT_FOUND)
        {
            CDbCreateDB dbInfo;
            memset(&dbInfo, 0, sizeof(dbInfo));
            dbInfo.m_Creator  = salesCreator;
            dbInfo.m_Flags    = eRecord;
            dbInfo.m_CardNo   = 0;
            dbInfo.m_Type     = customerDBType;
            strcpy(dbInfo.m_Name, customerDBName);

            if ((err = SyncCreateDB(dbInfo)) != 0)
            {
                LogAddEntry("SyncCreateDB failed", slWarning, false);
                goto exit;
            }
            rHandle = dbInfo.m_FileHandle;
        } else
            goto exit;
    }
    dbOpen = true;

    char    buffer[BIG_PATH *2];
    strcpy(buffer, sync.m_PathName);
    strcat(buffer, "Customers.txt");

    if ((fp = fopen(buffer, "r")) == NULL) {
        err = 1;
```

```
            LogAddFormattedEntry(slWarning, false, "fopen(%s) failed",
                buffer);
            goto exit;
        }

        if ((err = SyncPurgeAllRecs(rHandle)) != 0) {
            LogAddEntry("SyncPurgeAllRecs failed", slWarning, false);
            goto exit;
        }

        Customer *c;
        while (c = ReadCustomer(fp)) {
            CRawRecordInfo recordInfo;
            recordInfo.m_FileHandle = rHandle;
            recordInfo.m_RecId = 0;
            recordInfo.m_pBytes = (unsigned char *) gBigBuffer;
            recordInfo.m_Attribs = 0;
            recordInfo.m_CatId = 0;
            recordInfo.m_RecSize = CustomerToRawRecord(gBigBuffer,
                sizeof(gBigBuffer), c);
            recordInfo.m_dwReserved = 0;

            if ((err = SyncWriteRec(recordInfo)) !=0) {
                delete c;
                LogAddEntry("SyncWriteRec failed", slWarning, false);
                goto exit;
            }

            delete c;
        }

exit:
    if (fp)
        fclose(fp);
    if (dbOpen)
        if ((err = SyncCloseDB(rHandle)) != 0)
            LogAddEntry("SyncDBClose failed", slWarning, false);
    return err;
}
```

We try to open the customers database on the handheld. If it doesn't exist, we create it using SyncCreateDB. Next, we open *Customers.txt*, the file with the customers. We delete all the existing records from the customers database on the handheld. Then, we start reading each customer (using ReadCustomer) and writing the customer (using SyncWriteRec) to the database.

 You probably noticed that we added a couple of log entries to this code. These were not intended for users, but to help in our debugging. We are notified via the log if the code failed to properly open *Customers.txt* or if we failed to delete all the existing records.

ReadCustomer (see Example 15-5) reads a customer from a text file, returning 0 if there are no more customers.

Example 15-5. ReadCustomer reads all customers from the given file

```
Customer *ReadCustomer(FILE *fp)
{
    const char *separator = "\t";
    if (fgets(gBigBuffer, sizeof(gBigBuffer), fp) == NULL)
        return 0;
    char *customerID = strtok(gBigBuffer, separator);
    char *name = strtok(NULL, separator);
    char *address = strtok(NULL, separator);
    char *city = strtok(NULL, separator);
    char *phone = strtok(NULL, separator);

    if (!address)
        address = "";
    if (!city)
        city = "";
    if (!phone)
        phone = "";
    if (customerID && name) {
        Customer *c = new Customer;
        c->customerID = atol(customerID);
        c->name = new char[strlen(name) + 1];
        strcpy(c->name, name);
        c->address = new char[strlen(address) + 1];
        strcpy(c->address, address);
        c->city = new char[strlen(city) + 1];
        strcpy(c->city, city);
        c->phone = new char[strlen(phone) + 1];
        strcpy(c->phone, phone);
        return c;
    } else
        return 0;
}
```

CustomerToRawRecord writes a customer to the passed-in buffer in the format the handheld expects (see Example 15-6). It returns the number of bytes it has written. Note that it must swap the 4-byte customerID to match the byte ordering on the handheld.

Example 15-6. CustomerToRawRecord converts an in-memory customer to a handheld record

```
int CustomerToRawRecord(void *buf, int bufLength, Customer *c)
{
    PackedCustomer *cp = (PackedCustomer *) buf;
    cp->customerID = SyncHostToHHDWord(c->customerID);
    char *s = cp->name;
    strcpy(s, c->name);
    s += strlen(s) + 1;
    strcpy(s, c->address);
```

```
    s += strlen(s) + 1;
    strcpy(s, c->city);
    s += strlen(s) + 1;
    strcpy(s, c->phone);
    s += strlen(s) + 1;
    return s - (char *) buf;
}
```

Moving products to the handheld

The CopyProductsAndCategoriesToHH function updates the products database on the handheld from the *Products.txt* file on the PC (see Example 15-7).

Example 15-7. CopyProductsAndCategoriesToHH copies from desktop

```
int CopyProductsAndCategoriesToHH(CSyncProperties &sync)
{
    FILE *fp = NULL;
    BYTE rHandle;
    int err;
    bool dbOpen = false;

    char    buffer[BIG_PATH *2];
    strcpy(buffer, sync.m_PathName);
    strcat(buffer, "Products.txt");

    if ((fp = fopen(buffer, "r")) == NULL) {
        err = 1;
        LogAddFormattedEntry(slWarning, false, "fopen(%s) failed",
            buffer);
        goto exit;
    }

    if ((err = SyncOpenDB(productDBName, 0, rHandle,
        eDbWrite | eDbRead | eDbShowSecret)) != 0) {
        if (err == SYNCERR_FILE_NOT_FOUND)
        {
            CDbCreateDB dbInfo;
            memset(&dbInfo, 0, sizeof(dbInfo));
            dbInfo.m_Creator  = salesCreator;
            dbInfo.m_Flags    = eRecord;
            dbInfo.m_CardNo   = 0;
            dbInfo.m_Type     = productDBType;
            strcpy(dbInfo.m_Name, productDBName);

            if ((err = SyncCreateDB(dbInfo)) != 0)
            {
                LogAddEntry("SyncCreateDB failed", slWarning, false);
                goto exit;
            }
            rHandle = dbInfo.m_FileHandle;
        } else
```

```
            goto exit;
    }
    dbOpen = true;

    if ((err = SyncPurgeAllRecs(rHandle)) != 0) {
        LogAddEntry("SyncPurgeAllRecs failed", slWarning, false);
        goto exit;
    }

    Categories *c;
    if (c = ReadCategories(fp)) {
        CDbGenInfo   rInfo;

        rInfo.m_pBytes = (unsigned char *) gBigBuffer;
        rInfo.m_TotalBytes = CategoriesToRawRecord(gBigBuffer,
            sizeof(gBigBuffer), c);
        rInfo.m_BytesRead = rInfo.m_TotalBytes; // Because older versions
                   // of the sync manager looked in the wrong field for
                   // the total size, the documented API of
                   // SyncWriteDBAppInfoBLock is that both m_TotalBytes
                   // and m_BytesRead should be filled in with the total.
        rInfo.m_dwReserved = 0;
        if ((err = SyncWriteDBAppInfoBlock(rHandle, rInfo)) !=0) {
            delete c;
            LogAddEntry("SyncWriteDBAppInfoBlock failed", slWarning,
              false);
            goto exit;
        }
        delete c;
    }

    Product *p;
    while (p = ReadProduct(fp)) {
        CRawRecordInfo recordInfo;
        recordInfo.m_FileHandle = rHandle;
        recordInfo.m_RecId = 0;
        recordInfo.m_pBytes = (unsigned char *) gBigBuffer;
        recordInfo.m_Attribs = 0;
        recordInfo.m_CatId = p->category;
        recordInfo.m_RecSize = ProductToRawRecord(gBigBuffer,
            sizeof(gBigBuffer), p);
        recordInfo.m_dwReserved = 0;

        if ((err = SyncWriteRec(recordInfo)) !=0) {
            delete p;
            LogAddEntry("SyncWriteRec failed", slWarning, false);
            goto exit;
        }
        delete p;
    }

exit:
```

```
    if (fp)
        fclose(fp);

    if (dbOpen)
        if ((err = SyncCloseDB(rHandle)) != 0)
            LogAddEntry("SyncDBClose failed", slWarning, false);
    return err;
}
```

You probably noticed that this routine has almost exactly the same structure as the previous CopyCustomersToHH. One difference is that the categories are written to the AppInfo block using SyncWriteDBAppInfoBlock instead. It uses ReadCategories to read the categories from the *Products.txt* file (see Example 15-8). The function continues reading categories, one per line, until it reaches an empty line.

Example 15-8. ReadCategories reads the categories file and creates an in-memory object

```
#define kMaxCategories  15
Categories *ReadCategories(FILE *fp)
{
    const char *separator = "\n";
    int numCategories = 0;
    Categories *c = new Categories(kMaxCategories);
    for (int i = 0; i < kMaxCategories ; i++) {
        if (fgets(gBigBuffer, sizeof(gBigBuffer), fp) == NULL)
            break;
        // Strip newline.
        if (gBigBuffer[strlen(gBigBuffer) - 1] == '\n')
            gBigBuffer[strlen(gBigBuffer) - 1] = '\0';
        if (gBigBuffer[0] == '\0')
            break;
        // Copy it.
        strncpy(c->names[i], gBigBuffer, kCategoryNameLength);
        c->names[i][kCategoryNameLength] = '\0';
    }

    c->numCategories = i;
    return c;
}
```

ReadProduct reads the products that follow in the file (see Example 15-9).

Example 15-9. ReadProduct reads a single product from the text file

```
Product *ReadProduct(FILE *fp)
{
    const char *separator = "\t";
    if (fgets(gBigBuffer, sizeof(gBigBuffer), fp) == NULL)
        return 0;

    char *productID = strtok(gBigBuffer, separator);
```

Example 15-9. ReadProduct reads a single product from the text file (continued)

```
    char *name = strtok(NULL, separator);
    char *categoryNumber = strtok(NULL, separator);
    char *price = strtok(NULL, separator);

    if (productID && name && categoryNumber) {
        Product *p = new Product;
        p->productID = atol(productID);
        p->name = new char[strlen(name) + 1];
        strcpy(p->name, name);
        p->category = (unsigned char) atoi(categoryNumber);
        p->price = (long) (atof(price) * 100);  // Convert to cents.
        return p;
    } else
        return 0;
}
```

CategoriesToRawRecord, shown in Example 15-10, writes the categories in the format the handheld expects (therefore, the numCategories 2-byte field must be swapped).

Example 15-10. CategoriesToRawRecord converts to handheld format

```
int CategoriesToRawRecord(void *buf, int bufLength, Categories *c)
{
    PackedCategories *pc = (PackedCategories *) buf;
    pc->numCategories = SyncHostToHHWord(c->numCategories);
    char *s = (char *) pc->names;
    for (int i = 0; i < c->numCategories; i++) {
        memcpy(s, c->names[i], sizeof(CategoryName));
        s += sizeof(CategoryName);
    }
    return s - (char *) buf;
}
```

ProductToRawRecord is similar, but must swap both the productID and the price (see Example 15-11).

Example 15-11. ProductToRawRecord converts to handheld format

```
int ProductToRawRecord(void *buf, int bufLength, Product *p)
{
    PackedProduct *pp = (PackedProduct *) buf;
    pp->productID = SyncHostToHHDWord(p->productID);
    pp->price = SyncHostToHHDWord(p->price);
    strcpy(pp->name, p->name);
    return offsetof(PackedProduct, name) + strlen(pp->name) + 1;
}
```

That completes the conduit code for moving data to the handheld. Remember, however, that the order in which SyncWriteRec adds new records to the database isn't defined. As a result, the handheld must resort the databases (to be sorted by ID). Example 15-12 shows the code in our PilotMain handheld function that does this.

Example 15-12. Excerpt from the Sales application's PilotMain

```
} else if (cmd == sysAppLaunchCmdSyncNotify) {
    DmOpenRef    db;

    // code for beaming removed

// After a sync, we aren't guaranteed the order of any changed databases.
// We'll just resort the products and customer which could have changed.
// We're going to do an insertion sort because the databases
// should be almost completely sorted (and an insertion sort is
// quicker on an almost-sorted database than a quicksort).
// Since the current implementation of the Sync Manager creates new
// records at the end of the database, our database are probably sorted.
    db= DmOpenDatabaseByTypeCreator(customerDBType, salesCreator,
        dmModeReadWrite);
    if (db) {
        DmInsertionSort(db, (DmComparF *) CompareIDFunc, 0);
        DmCloseDatabase(db);
    } else
        error = DmGetLastErr();
    db= DmOpenDatabaseByTypeCreator(productDBType, salesCreator,
        dmModeReadWrite);
    if (db) {
        DmInsertionSort(db, (DmComparF *) CompareIDFunc, 0);
        DmCloseDatabase(db);
    } else
        error = DmGetLastErr();
}
```

Moving Data to the Desktop

We need to handle the same sorts of things when we are moving data to the desktop instead of to the handheld. Here is our list of tasks:

1. Copy orders from the handheld to the desktop by opening the database and reading the records.

2. Do the proper conversion.

3. Send them along their merry way to the desktop.

4. Repeat these steps for the customers.

Moving orders to the desktop

We've got to copy the orders from the handheld to the desktop (see Example 15-13).

Example 15-13. CopyOrdersFromHH copies orders in order database to desktop

```
int CopyOrdersFromHH(CSyncProperties &sync)
{
    FILE *fp = NULL;
    BYTE rHandle;
```

Example 15-13. CopyOrdersFromHH copies orders in order database to desktop (continued)

```
    int err;
    bool dbOpen = false;
    int i;

    if ((err = SyncOpenDB(orderDBName, 0, rHandle,
        eDbRead | eDbShowSecret )) != 0) {
        LogAddEntry("SyncOpenDB failed", slWarning, false);
        goto exit;
    }
    dbOpen = true;

    char    buffer[BIG_PATH *2];
    strcpy(buffer, sync.m_PathName);
    strcat(buffer, "Orders.txt");

    if ((fp = fopen(buffer, "w")) == NULL) {
        LogAddFormattedEntry(slWarning, false, "fopen(%s) failed",
            buffer);
        goto exit;
    }

    WORD recordCount;
    if ((err = SyncGetDBRecordCount(rHandle, recordCount)) !=0) {
        LogAddEntry("SyncGetDBRecordCount failed", slWarning, false);
        goto exit;
    }

    CRawRecordInfo recordInfo;
    recordInfo.m_FileHandle = rHandle;

    for (i = 0; i < recordCount; i++) {
        recordInfo.m_RecIndex = i;
        recordInfo.m_TotalBytes = (unsigned short) sizeof(gBigBuffer);
        recordInfo.m_pBytes = (unsigned char *) gBigBuffer;
        recordInfo.m_dwReserved = 0;

        if ((err = SyncReadRecordByIndex(recordInfo)) !=0) {
            LogAddEntry("SyncReadRecordByIndex failed", slWarning, false);
            goto exit;
        }

        Order *o = RawRecordToOrder(recordInfo.m_pBytes);
        if ((err = WriteOrderToFile(fp, o)) != 0) {
            LogAddEntry("WriteOrderToFile failed", slWarning, false);
            delete o;
            goto exit;
        }
        delete o;
    }
exit:
    if (fp)
        fclose(fp);
```

```
    if (dbOpen)
        if ((err = SyncCloseDB(rHandle)) != 0)
            LogAddEntry("SyncDBClose failed", slWarning, false);
    return err;
}
```

The code opens the orders database (read-only, since it won't change the database). Then it creates the *Orders.txt* file. It finds the number of records in the database with SyncGetDBRecordCount. Then it reads record by record using SyncReadRecordByIndex. RawRecordToOrder reads the raw record and converts it to an in-memory record. Finally, the order is written to the file with WriteOrderToFile.

Example 15-14 shows the code that converts a record to an order (again, byte-swapping is necessary).

Example 15-14. RawRecordToOrder converts from handheld format to desktop format

```
Order *RawRecordToOrder(void *p)
{
    PackedOrder *po = (PackedOrder *) p;
    unsigned short numItems = SyncHHToHostWord(po->numItems);
    Order *o = new Order(numItems);
    o->customerID = SyncHHToHostDWord(po->customerID);
    for (int i = 0; i < o->numItems; i++) {
        o->items[i].productID = SyncHHToHostDWord(po->items[i].productID);
        o->items[i].quantity = SyncHHToHostDWord(po->items[i].quantity);
    }
    return o;
}
```

Finally, Example 15-15 shows the code that writes the order to the file.

Example 15-15. WriteOrderToFile writes to a text file

```
int WriteOrderToFile(FILE *fp, const Order *o)
{
    int result;

    if ((result = fprintf(fp, "ORDER %ld\n", o->customerID)) < 0)
        return result;
    for (int i = 0; i < o->numItems; i++) {
        if ((result = fprintf(fp, "%ld %ld\n", o->items[i].quantity,
            o->items[i].productID)) < 0)
            return result;
    }
    return 0;
}
```

Moving customers to the desktop

Moving customers to the desktop is slightly more complicated than moving orders, because the handheld supports deleting and archiving customers.

Example 15-16 shows the routine that moves the customers database to the desktop.

Example 15-16. CopyCustomersFromHH copies customers to the desktop

```
int CopyCustomersFromHH(CSyncProperties &sync)
{
    FILE *fp = NULL;
    FILE *archivefp = NULL;
    BYTE rHandle;
    int err;
    bool dbOpen = false;
    int i;

    if ((err = SyncOpenDB(customerDBName, 0, rHandle,
        eDbWrite | eDbRead | eDbShowSecret)) != 0) {
        LogAddEntry("SyncOpenDB failed", slWarning, false);
        goto exit;
    }
    dbOpen = true;

    char    buffer[BIG_PATH *2];
    strcpy(buffer, sync.m_PathName);
    strcat(buffer, "Customers.txt");

    if ((fp = fopen(buffer, "w")) == NULL) {
        LogAddFormattedEntry(slWarning, false, "fopen(%s) failed",
            buffer);
        goto exit;
    }

    strcpy(buffer, sync.m_PathName);
    strcat(buffer, "CustomersArchive.txt");

    if ((archivefp = fopen(buffer, "a")) == NULL) {
        LogAddFormattedEntry(slWarning, false, "fopen(%s) failed",
            buffer);
        goto exit;
    }

    WORD recordCount;
    if ((err = SyncGetDBRecordCount(rHandle, recordCount)) !=0) {
        LogAddEntry("SyncGetDBRecordCount failed", slWarning, false);
        goto exit;
    }

    CRawRecordInfo recordInfo;
    recordInfo.m_FileHandle = rHandle;

    for (i = 0; i < recordCount; i++) {
```

```
        recordInfo.m_RecIndex = i;
        recordInfo.m_TotalBytes = (unsigned short) sizeof(gBigBuffer);
        recordInfo.m_pBytes = (unsigned char *) gBigBuffer;
        recordInfo.m_dwReserved = 0;

        if ((err = SyncReadRecordByIndex(recordInfo)) !=0) {
            LogAddEntry("SyncReadRecordByIndex failed", slWarning, false);
            goto exit;
        }

        FILE *fileToWriteTo;
        if (recordInfo.m_Attribs & eRecAttrArchived)
            fileToWriteTo = archivefp;
        else if (recordInfo.m_Attribs & eRecAttrDeleted)
            continue;    // Skip deleted records.
        else
            fileToWriteTo = fp;

        Customer *c = RawRecordToCustomer(recordInfo.m_pBytes);
        if ((err = WriteCustomerToFile(fileToWriteTo, c)) != 0) {
            delete c;
            LogAddEntry("WriteCustomerToFile failed", slWarning, false);
            goto exit;
        }
        delete c;
    }

    if ((err = SyncPurgeDeletedRecs(rHandle)) != 0)
        LogAddEntry("SyncPurgeDeletedRecs failed", slWarning, false);

exit:
    if (fp)
        fclose(fp);

    if (archivefp)
        fclose(archivefp);

    if (dbOpen)
        if ((err = SyncCloseDB(rHandle)) != 0)
            LogAddEntry("SyncDBClose failed", slWarning, false);
    return err;
}
```

After reading each record with SyncReadRecordByIndex, we examine the record attributes (m_Attribs). If the archive bit is set, we write the record to a different file (appending to *CustomersArchive.txt*):

```
    FILE *fileToWriteTo;

    if (recordInfo.m_Attribs & eRecAttrArchived)
      fileToWriteTo = archivefp;
```

If the delete bit is set, we skip this record:

```
else if (recordInfo.m_Attribs & eRecAttrDeleted)
            continue;   // Skip deleted records.
```

Once we're done iterating through the records, we remove the deleted and archived records from the handheld (using SyncPurgeDeletedRecs). In order to change the database in this way, we have to open the database with write permission (eDbWrite).

Now we need to put the customer records where they belong. The following routine appends a customer to the given file:

```
int WriteCustomerToFile(FILE *fp, const Customer *c)
{
    int result;

    if ((result = fprintf(fp, "%d\t%s\t%s\t%s\t%s\n", c->customerID, c->name,
        c->address, c->city, c->phone)) < 0)
        return result;
    return 0;
}
```

Example 15-17 shows the code that converts a record to a customer.

Example 15-17. RawRecordToCustomer converts from handheld format

```
Customer *RawRecordToCustomer(void *rec)
{
    Customer *c = new Customer;
    PackedCustomer *pc = (PackedCustomer *) rec;
    c->customerID = pc->customerID;
    char * p = (char *) pc->name;
    c->name = new char[strlen(p)+1];
    strcpy(c->name, p);
    p += strlen(p) + 1;
    c->address = new char[strlen(p)+1];
    strcpy(c->address, p);
    p += strlen(p) + 1;
    c->city = new char[strlen(p)+1];
    strcpy(c->city, p);
    p += strlen(p) + 1;
    c->phone = new char[strlen(p)+1];
    strcpy(c->phone, p);
    return c;
}
```

With this code in place, we have a conduit that can move data to and from the handheld as needed. Now we are ready to move to the next chapter and tackle full two-way data syncing.

## CHAPTER 16

Two-Way Syncing

We'll look at the logic involved in two-way, mirror-image syncing, and then investigate the particulars of the Generic Conduit Framework, Palm's C++ framework for creating a two-way syncing conduit. Having discussed the important points of Generic Conduit Framework, we then use the framework in our Sales conduit. From this, we get a working conduit that can send data back and forth between the handheld and the desktop; it's a two-way syncing conduit. We also make sure this two-way syncing conduit continues to support sending data to and from the handheld.

The Logic of Syncing

Because handhelds can be synced to more than one desktop machine, there are two different forms of syncing. These two forms are:

Fast sync

> This occurs when the handheld is being synced to the same desktop machine that it was synced to the previous time.

Slow sync

> This occurs when a handheld is synced to a different machine from its previous sync. In such cases, a set of problems arise in determining what changes have been made.

Before discussing either type of syncing, however, we need to explain some of the difficulties that can arise in situations in which the same record can be modified in more than one location. After we give you some rules for handling these conflicts, we discuss fast syncing and then turn to the more difficult slow syncing.

Thorny Comparisons—Changes to the Same Records on Both Platforms

There are some very thorny cases of record conflicts we have to consider. When you give users the capability of modifying a record in more than one location, some twists result. The problem occurs when you have a record that can be changed simultaneously on the handheld and on the local database, but in different ways. For example, a customer record in our Sales application has its address changed on the handheld database and its name changed on the local database. Or a record was deleted on one platform and changed on another. The number of scenarios is so great that some formal rules are required to govern cases of conflict.

The rule—first, do no harm

The Palm philosophy concerning such problems is that no data loss should occur, even at the price of a proliferation of records with only minor differences. Thus, in the case of a record whose name is changed to "Smith" on the handheld and to "Smithy" on the local file, the end result is two records, each present in both places. Here are the various possibilities and how this philosophy plays out into rules for actual data conflicts.

A record is deleted on one database and modified on the other

The deleted version of the record is killed, and the changed one is copied to the other platform.

A record is archived on one database and changed on the other

The archived version of the record is put in the archive database, and the changed version is copied to the other platform.

A record is archived on one database and deleted on the other

The record is put in the archive database.

A record is changed on one database and changed differently on the other

The result is two records. This is true for records with the same field change, such as our case of "Smith" and "Smithy." It is also true for a record where the Name field is changed on one record and the Address field on the other. In this case, you also end up with two records. Thus, the following initial records:

Handheld database	Desktop
Name: Smith	Name: Smithy
Address: 120 Park Street	Address: 100 East Street
City: River City	City: River City

yield these records in fully synced mirror image databases:

Handheld Database	Desktop
Name: Smith	Name: Smith
Address: 120 Park Street	Address: 120 Park Street
City: River City	City: River City
Name: Smithy	Name: Smithy
Address 100 East Street	Address 100 East Street
City: River City	City: River City

Of course, if your conduit has some way of doing field-by-field synchronization, feel free to do so. However, the Palm's Data Manager has no built-in support to help you do this; it just contains a single dirty bit that specifies that the entire record has changed.

A record is changed on one database and changed identically on the other

If a record is changed in both places in the same way (the record ends up identical in both places); the result is one record in both places.

This can get tricky, however. While it may be clear that "Smith" is not "Smithy," it is not so obvious that "Smith" is not "smith" or even worse that "LaVerne" is not "Laverne." Depending on the nature of your record fields, you may need to make case-by-case decisions about the meaning of *identical*.

Fast Sync

A fast sync occurs when a handheld syncs to the same desktop as it last did (the handheld keeps track of the ID of the last desktop to which it has synced). In such cases, you can be assured that the deleted, archived, and dirty bits from the handheld are accurate—that is, they accurately reflect the changes that have occurred on the handheld since the last sync to this desktop. In this event, the conduit needs to do the following:

- Examine the handheld data
- Examine the local desktop data
- Dispose of the old data
- Save a backup file

Let's look at each of these tasks in turn.

Examine the handheld data

For each changed record on the handheld, the conduit needs to do the activities shown in Table 16-1.

Table 16-1. Conduit duties for changed records on the handheld

Activity	How it works
Archive	If the record is archived, it adds the record to an archived file on the desktop and marks it in the local file as a pending delete. It deletes the archived record from the handheld.
Delete	If deleted, it marks the record in the local file as a pending delete and removes it from the handheld. (Remember, user-deleted records aren't actually deleted until a sync occurs; the user may not see them, but your application keeps them around for this very occasion.)
Modify	If modified, it modifies it in the local file and clears the dirty bit.
New	If the handheld has a new record that doesn't exist in the desktop file, the conduit adds it.

Examine the local desktop data

The conduit must also handle modified records in the local desktop file by comparing them to the handheld records. The conduit's tasks for the local desktop file are shown in Table 16-2.

Table 16-2. Conduit duties for changed records in a desktop file

Activity	How it works
Archive	If the desktop record is archived, it removes the record from the handheld, puts it in the archived file, and marks it as a pending delete in the local file.
Delete	If a desktop record is deleted, the conduit removes it from the handheld and marks it as a pending delete in the local file.
Modify	If it is modified, it copies the modifications to the handheld and clears the modification flag from the record in the local file.
New	If a new record is present, it copies the record to the handheld and clears the added flag from the record in the local file.

Dispose of the old data

Now the conduit deletes all records in the local database that are marked for deletion. At this point, all the records in the local database should match those on the handheld.

Save a backup file

A copy of the local file is also saved as a backup file—you will be using this for a slow sync.

This is all that is involved in a fast sync between a handheld and a desktop machine.

Slow Sync

A slow sync takes place when the last sync of the handheld was not with this desktop. Commonly, this occurs when the user has more recently synced to another desktop machine. Less frequently, this happens because this is the first sync of a handheld. If the last sync of the handheld was not with this desktop, the dirty, archived, and deleted bits are not accurate with respect to this desktop. They may be accurate with the desktop last synced to, but this doesn't help with the current sync scenario.

Since the modify, archive, and delete bits aren't accurate, we need to figure out how the handheld database has changed from the desktop file since the last sync. We can't just compare the records currently on the handheld to those currently on the desktop. For example, what if a record's contents are different? This could be caused by a modification on the handheld, or on the desktop, or on both. The action we want to carry out is different in all three cases.

In order to accurately determine what's changed since the last sync, we need an accurate copy of the local file at the time of the last sync. This is complicated by the possibility that the local database may have changed since the last sync. The solution to this problem is to use the backup copy that we made after the last sync between these two machines—the last point at which these two matched. Since this backup, both the handheld and the desktop records may have diverged.

While it is true that all the changes to the desktop have been marked (dirty, new, deleted, archived), this is not true for the handheld. Some or all of the changes to the handheld data were lost when the intervening sync took place; the deleted or archived records were removed, and the modified records were unmarked.

Comparing the backup record to the current records

To deal with this problem, we use a slow sync. As the name implies, a slow sync looks at every record from the handheld. It copies these records into an in-memory database on the desktop (the Remote Records database) and compares them to the backup file records.

The possibilities that need to be taken into account by the conduit are shown in Table 16-3.

Table 16-3. Comparing the backup record to the current record

Scenario	What it means and what you do
The remote record matches a record in the backup file.	Nothing has changed, so you don't do anything.
The remote record isn't present in the backup file.	The record is new and is marked as modified.

Scenario	What it means and what you do
The backup record isn't present in the remote record database.	The remote record has been deleted (it could have been archived, in which case it has been archived on a different desktop). The record is marked as deleted.
The backup record and the remote record are different.	The remote record has been modified. The record is marked as changed.

At this point, we've got a copy of the remote records database where each record has been left alone, marked as modified (due to being new or changed), or marked as deleted. Now the conduit can carry out the rest of the sync. Thus, the difference between the two syncs is the initial time required to mark records so that the two databases agree. It is a slow sync because every record from the handheld had to be copied to the desktop.

Now that you know what to do with records during a sync, let's discuss how to do it.

MFC Conduit Framework

The original support that Palm provided for two-way mirror-image synchronization was an MFC (Microsoft Foundation Classes) Conduit framework. These classes are sometimes called basemon and basetabl because of the filenames in which they are located.

These classes worked very well for the standard conduits (for example, the conduits for Palm Desktop are built with the MFC Conduit framework). There are some limitations that make them more difficult for third parties to use, however:

- First, they do require MFC, which means that your conduit must provide information on what version of MFC is used. This can make debugging somewhat more difficult.

- Second, the file format they write is MFC-serialized objects; that's handy for Palm Desktop, since Palm Desktop is an MFC-application. It is quite difficult to write other formats, however.

- In addition, there's no easy way to port a conduit based on the MFC Conduit framework to the Mac OS.

For these reasons, we don't recommend using this framework.

Generic Conduit Framework

Generic Conduit Framework is the other approach to creating a conduit that handles two-way syncing. It is a framework that Palm set up to make it easier for developers to create a conduit.

The Generic Conduit Framework is a set of classes that work together to carry out the functions of a conduit. As might be expected, you subclass some of the classes and use others as is.

Advantages of Using Generic Conduit

There are some persuasive advantages to basing a conduit on this framework:

In some cases, you don't need to write any code
> The Generic Conduit Framework contains everything, including `CfgConduit`, `GetConduitName`, and so on. If you compile and register it without writing any code, it'll be happy to two-way sync your Palm database to a file on the desktop. This approach requires the use of its own file format, however. If you don't like that format, you need to customize the Generic Conduit Framework classes to some extent.

If you do have to write code, it might not be much
> The number of classes and the number of methods is much less daunting than those found in the MFC Conduit framework. The other alternative—writing directly to the Sync Manager APIs—would require a great deal more code.

All the source code is available
> The entire source code is provided (unlike the MFC Conduit framework); if you so desire, you can change any or all of it.

Generic Conduit Classes

There are eight classes that affect your use of Generic conduit. As might be expected, each has a different responsibility. Figure 16-1 shows the inheritance relationship.

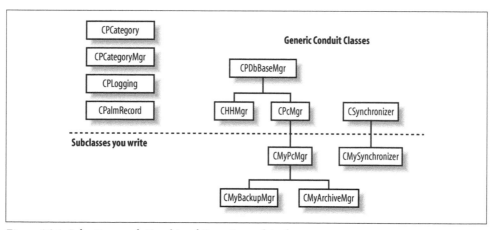

Figure 16-1. Inheritance relationship of Generic conduit classes

Table 16-4 contains a quick look at each class, in the order we discuss them in this chapter.

Table 16-4. Generic conduit classes

Class	What it does	Use
CPalmRecord	Represents a record (including attributes, ID, category number, length, and a pointer to data).	As is
CPCategory	Represents a category on the handheld.	As is
CPCategoryMgr	Represents a set of categories.	As is
CPDbBaseMgr	Defines database methods for iterating, adding and deleting records, and so on.	Classes derived from
CHHMgr	Subclass of CPDbBaseMgr; implements those routines by using Sync Manager.	As is
CPcMgr	Subclass of CPDbBaseMgr; implements the CDbManager member functions for a file on the desktop.	Derive own class from
CPLogging	Reports errors to the sync log.	As is
CSynchronizer	Handles the sync logic and control flow.	Derive own class from

Now let's examine each class in detail.

CPalmRecord

This represents a Palm record; it stores attributes, a unique ID, a category number, a record length, and a pointer to the raw record data. The CPalmRecord, just like a record on the handheld, has no concept of fields; to determine whether two records are identical, it just compares the attributes, the category number, the record length, and the raw data. *You normally use this class as is.*

Here are the member functions you'll commonly use:

CPalmRecord( )
> The constructor creates a new empty record.

long SetRawData(DWORD dwDataSize, BYTE *pData)
> This sets the data of the record (in handheld format). It makes a copy of the incoming pData.

long GetRawData(BYTE *pData, DWORD *pdwDataSize)
> This returns the data of the record (in handheld format). Pass in a buffer, and a pointer to the buffer size. On return, pdwDataSize will be set to the size of the record. If the buffer is too small for the data, GEN_ERR_BUFFER_TOO_SMALL is returned.

void SetID(DWORD dwID)
> This sets the record's unique ID.

```
DWORD GetID(void)
```
This returns the unique ID of the record.
```
void SetCategory(DWORD dwCatIndex)
```
This sets the category to the given category number.
```
DWORDGetCategory(void)
```
This returns the category number of the record.
```
void SetPrivate(BOOL bSet=TRUE)
```
This sets (or unsets) the private bit of the record.
```
void SetDeleted(BOOL bSet=TRUE)
```
This sets (or unsets) the deleted bit of the record.
```
void SetArchived(BOOL bSet=TRUE)
```
This sets (or unsets) the archived attribute of the record.
```
void SetUpdate(BOOL bSet=TRUE)
```
This sets (or unsets) the dirty bit of the record.
```
void SetNew(BOOL bSet=TRUE)
```
The Generic Conduit Framework distinguishes between new records and existing records that are modified (that distinction doesn't exist on the handheld). This routine sets (or unsets) that attribute.
```
void ResetAttribs(void)
```
This clears the private, deleted, archived, dirty, and new attributes.
```
BOOL IsPrivate(void)
```
This returns true if the record is private.
```
BOOL IsDeleted(void)
```
This returns true if the record is deleted.
```
BOOL IsArchived(void)
```
This returns true if the record is archived.
```
BOOL IsUpdate(void)
```
This returns true if the record is dirty.
```
BOOL IsNew(void)
```
This returns true if the record is new.

CPCategory

This represents a single category on the handheld. A category has a name, a 1-byte ID, and a modified bit. Unlike records, in which ID numbers are always assigned on the handheld, category IDs are segmented:

0–127 IDs
　　Reserved for categories created on the handheld

128–255 IDs
　　Reserved for those created on the desktop

You will use this class as is. Here are the member functions you'll normally use:

CPCategory( )
> This constructor creates an empty category.

void SetID(DWORD dwID)
> This sets the ID of the category. Although it's defined to take a DWORD, the ID is only a single byte on the handheld.

long SetName(TCHAR *pName)
> This sets the name of the category. It returns an error if the name is too long (more than 16 bytes).

void SetDirty(BOOL bSet = TRUE)
> This sets (or unsets) the modified bit.

DWORD GetID(void)
> This returns the ID of the category.

char *GetName(void)
> This returns the name of the category.

BOOL IsDirty(void)
> This returns true if the modified attribute is set.

CPCategoryMgr

This represents a set of categories. It can be converted to and from the category structure stored in the app info block on the handheld. *You will use this class as is.*

Here are the member functions you'll normally use:

CPCategoryMgr( )
> This constructor creates an empty set of categories.

DWORD GetCount(void)
> This returns the number of categories.

CPCategory *FindFirst(void)
> This returns the first category in the set. It resets the iteration provided by FindNext.

CPCategory *FindNext(void)
> This iterator function returns the next category in the set. If there are no more categories, it returns NULL.

BOOL IsChanged(void)
> This returns true if any of the categories in this set have changed.

long Add(CPCategory &cat)
> This adds a copy of the given category to the set.

CPDbBaseMgr

This is the class that is responsible for a database. It defines methods for iterating through the records, adding and deleting records, etc. It is an abstract class. There are two derived classes that implement these methods: one for the handheld and one for the desktop. *This class isn't used as is: the derived classes are used.*

You may need to read from the following data members:

CPalmRecord**m_pRecordList
> This holds the array of record objects; note that some records may be NULL.

DWORD m_dwMaxRecordCount
> This contains the number of entries in the m_pRecordList array.

If you support categories, you may need to set the following data member:

CPCategoryMgr *m_pCatMgr
> This holds the Category Manager (if any) for the database.

CHHMgr

This class is derived from CDbManager and implements the CDbManager member functions by using the Sync Manager. This concrete subclass uses the interface of the abstract class. It can be used just like any other database, but its implementation is different. For example, its method to add a record is implemented using SyncWriteRec. *This class is normally used as is.* Furthermore, you don't usually directly use this class; instead, it is instantiated and used by CSynchronizer as the interface to the handheld database.

CPcMgr

This class implements CDbManager member functions for a file on the desktop. When a file is opened, it reads all the records into memory and stores them in a list. Changes to the database are reflected in memory until the database is closed; at that point, the records are rewritten to the database.

You normally create your own derived class from CPcMgr and override the functions RetrieveDB and StoreDB to read and write your own file formats.

There are two member functions that you'll override. They are used for reading and writing your data from memory to your file:

long StoreDB(void)
> This stores the in-memory records to your file format. The default version of this routine writes out the data as MFC-style serialized objects.

```
long RetrieveDB(void)
```
This reads the data from your file format into in-memory (handheld-style) records. The default version of this routine reads data from a file containing MFC-style serialized objects.

Here are the member functions you'll normally use:

```
CPcMgr(CPLogging *pLogging, DWORD dwGenericFlags, char *szDbName, TCHAR
*pFileName = NULL, void *pFileUInfo = NULL, eSyncTypes syncType = eDoNothing)
```
This constructor is used to create a new PC manager. Parameters include the logging object, flags about whether to support the app info block and categories, the name of the remote database, the name of the local file, the path to the conduit-specific directory, and the sync type.

```
long Open(void)
```
This opens the file within the conduit's directory (by creating the file if necessary). It'll use read or read/write mode depending on the type of synchronization.

```
long Close(BOOL bDontUpdate=FALSE)
```
This closes the open desktop file. The parameter is ignored.

```
long AddRec(CPalmRecord &palmRec)
```
This adds a copy of the given record to the list of records held by the PC Manager.

```
long ExtractCategories(void)
```
This creates a Category Manager from the AppInfo block held in the m_pAppInfo data member. This routine should be called automatically. On a "Handheld overwrites PC" sync, however, it hasn't been called, so you must call it.

In addition, you will need to override this routine to do nothing if you are saving your data in anything other than the handheld format (see "Handling Categories," later in this chapter for a more detailed discussion).

```
CPCategoryMgr *GetCatMgr(void)
```
This returns the Category Manager associated with the PC Manager.

```
long WriteOutData(LPVOID pBuffer, DWORD dwNumberOfBytesToWrite)
```
This writes data to the (currently-open) file.

```
long ReadInData(LPVOID pBuffer, DWORD dwNumberOfBytesToRead)
```
This reads data from the (currently-open) file. You should pass in the size of the butter as the second parameter.

Here are the data members you'll commonly use:

```
BOOL m_bNeedToSave
```
This will be true if there are any changes that require saving, false if nothing has changed. You'll need to read this, as well as set it, after storing your database.

```
TCHAR m_szDataFile[256]
```
You'll check this before storing your database, and return an error if it is empty.
```
HANDLE m_hFile
```
You'll check this before storing your database, and return an error if it is NULL.

CPLogging

This class is responsible for logging when any type of failure occurs during syncing. *You normally use this class as is.*

The routines you'll use are:
```
void LogInfo(const char *pMessage)
```
This writes the given message to the log.
```
void LogWarning(const char *pMessage)
```
This writes the given message to the log, marking it as a warning.

CSynchronizer

This class is responsible for handling the actual synchronization. It creates the database classes and manages the entire process. It is this class that handles the fast sync/slow sync logic and deals with the difficulties when a record has been modified in both places. You normally create your own derived class from CSynchronizer and override three of its member functions. You create your own class derived from CPcMgr; this is responsible for your main data file, backup file, and archive files.

Here are the member functions you'll override:
```
long CreatePCManager(void)
```
This creates the subclass of CPcMgr that is responsible for reading and writing your main data file. The CDK Wizard normally generates this subclass, as well as this routine.
```
long CreateBackupManager(void)
```
This creates the subclass that is responsible for reading and writing your backup file. The CDK Wizard normally generates this subclass, as well as this routine.
```
CPDbBaseMgr *CreateArchiveManager(TCHAR *pFilename)
```
This creates the subclass that is responsible for reading and writing your archive file. The parameter is the filename to use. The CDK Wizard normally generates this subclass, as well as this routine.

Here are the member functions you'll commonly use:
```
CSynchronizer(CSyncProperties& rProps, DWORD dwDatabaseFlags =
GENERIC_FLAG_CATEGORY_SUPPORTED | GENERIC_FLAG_APPINFO_SUPPORTED)
```
This creates a CSynchronizer object. The parameters are the CSyncProperties passed into OpenConduit and the flags that specify whether your database on the handheld has an AppInfo block, and, if so, whether it has categories stored in it.

```
long Perform(void)
```
This carries out the entire synchronization process.

This covers all the classes and routines that make up the Generic Conduit Framework. Now that you know what comprises the framework, we can look at what is involved in actually creating a conduit. Remember, we'll use the Conduit Wizard, which will make it easier to get our conduit up and running.

Using the Wizard to Create a Minimal Generic Conduit

You can use the Conduit Wizard to generate the entry points for a conduit, or to create a full-fledged conduit based on the Generic Conduit Framework. We are going to use it to create a full-fledged two-way syncing conduit. Once we show you the shell that the Wizard creates, we will register it and add support for custom file formats and categories. Having described this process, we'll use it again to create a Sales conduit.

First, let's look at the few easy steps required to create a Generic conduit using the Conduit Wizard. You should be pleasantly surprised by the simplicity of the process:

1. Choose New from the File menu. In the resulting dialog box (see Figure 16-2), select Palm Conduit Wizard (dll).

2. Enter the desired project name and click OK. (Use "SalesGen" and "C:\SalesGen" if you wish.)

3. In the next dialog box (see Figure 16-3), specify that you'd like a Generic conduit and select Next.

4. In the next dialog box, choose the features you'd like (see Figure 16-4) and then select Next. Here is some advice about the choices:

   Category support
   > Check this if your handheld application supports categories (and stores category names in the `AppInfo` block, as standard).

   Archiving
   > If your handheld application supports archiving, choose this.

   Sync Action Configuration dialog box
   > You'll almost always want a Configuration dialog box.

   The Sales application doesn't support categories, so we won't request category support.

5. The next two dialog boxes are Confirmation dialog boxes that verify what you are creating. Once you click through those, the Wizard will actually make your project.

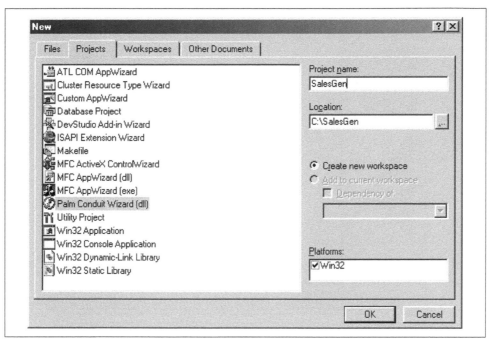

Figure 16-2. First step to creating a generic conduit from the Wizard

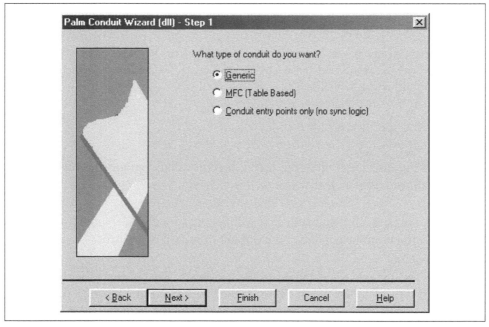

Figure 16-3. Specifying the type of conduit

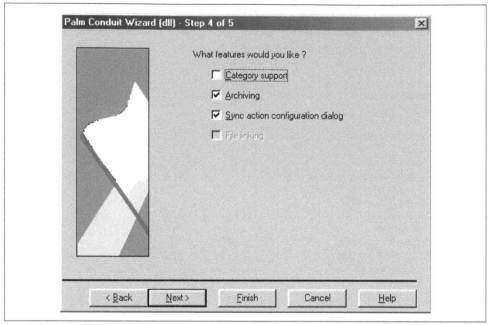

Figure 16-4. Specifying the features

Registering the Conduit

At this point, you can register the conduit.

The Generic conduit needs the type of your database to be DATA. This is because in the "PC overwrites Handheld" case, the conduit creates a database on the handheld. The creator and name of the database are specified when you register, but the type is DATA.

Make sure you specify correctly the following in CondCfg:

Directory

> This is the directory within the user's directory that contains the files the conduit will read from and write to.

File

> This is the name of the datafile that will be synced with the conduit—it receives the records from the handheld. If it doesn't exist, it'll be created.

Remote database

> This is the name of the database on the handheld. The registered name will only be used if the database doesn't exist on the handheld (if for instance, the application has never run). The Generic conduit will use the name as the name of the database to create.

What the Conduit Does

Do a sync. When you do, you'll find that your conduit runs and that it creates two files in the conduit directory within the user's directory:

- One has the name of the "File:" entry in CondCfg. It holds the user's data file (the records from the handheld).

- The other has the same name but a different suffix: (*.bak*). This is the backup file that will be used in case of a slow sync.

If any records on the handheld have been archived, there will be additional files created (one per category) containing the archived records.

The file format the Generic conduit uses is that of MFC-style streamed objects. You can see the data in your file by dragging it into Visual C++. It will do a hex dump of the data that will allow you to see, at the very least, the strings from your data.

Custom File Formats

If you are going to support your own file format in your conduit, then you'll need to override two routines in your subclass of CPcMgr: StoreDB and RetrieveDB. The first will save the in-memory list of records to your format. The second will read from your format, creating records and adding them to the in-memory list.

We'd always suggest writing StoreDB first, if for no other reason than you can test it without having written RetrieveDB. This is because the Generic Conduit Framework won't call your RetrieveDB routine if there's no file in the user's directory. Therefore, as long as you keep deleting the file between syncs, you can test your StoreDB to your heart's content.

Note that when StoreDB is called, the sync has already taken place and all of the following actions have occurred:

- Modified records have been copied between the handheld and the in-memory list (maintained by the Generic conduit).

- Records whose deleted bits were set have been deleted.

- All the records are clean (the dirty and deleted bits are not set).

The StoreDB Routine

Example 16-1 shows the outline of a StoreDB routine.

Example 16-1. A typical StoreDB (emphasized code is specific to your conduit)

```
long CMyConduitPcMgr::StoreDB(void)
{
  if ( !m_bNeedToSave) { // If no changes, don't waste time saving.
    return 0;
  }
}
```

```
  long err = Open( );
  if (err)
    return GEN_ERR_UNABLE_TO_SAVE;

  for (DWORD dwIndex = 0;
    (dwIndex < m_dwMaxRecordCount) && (!err); dwIndex++) {
    if (!m_pRecordList[dwIndex])
      continue;
    err = WriteRecord(m_pRecordList[dwIndex]);
  }
  Close( );
  if (err == 0) {
    m_bNeedToSave = FALSE;
    return 0;
  } else
    return GEN_ERR_UNABLE_TO_SAVE;
}
```

We check the m_bNeedToSave data member; if it isn't set, there's no reason to do anything more. At the end of the routine, assuming everything has completed successfully, we set m_bNeedToSave to false.

We call Open to open our desktop file and Close when we are finished with the desktop file. While the file is open, we iterate through m_pRecordList, which is an array of records. For each non-NULL record, we must write it out (our code assumes something like WriteRecord).

To obtain information about the record, use the CPalmRecord functions GetRawData, GetCategory, GetID, and IsPrivate. To actually write to the file, use WriteOutData.

Example 16-2 shows an example of writing out a record.

Example 16-2. Outline of a routine to write out a record

```
long CMyPcMgr::WriteRecord(CPalmRecord *pPalmRec)
{
    const int   kMaxRecordSize = 65535;
    char    record[kMaxRecordSize];
    char    buf[kMaxRecordSize];
    DWORD   recordSize = kMaxRecordSize;
    long    retval;

    retval = pPalmRec->GetRawData((unsigned char *) record, &recordSize);
    if (retval)
        return retval;
    // Add code to use WriteOutData to write out data in desired format.

    DWORD uniqueID = pPalmRec->GetID( );
    // Add code to use WriteOutData to write out uniqueID in desired format.
```

Example 16-2. Outline of a routine to write out a record (continued)

```
    BOOL isPrivate = pPalmRec->IsPrivate( );
    // Add code to use WriteOutData to write out isPrivate in desired format.

    return 0;
}
```

The RetrieveDB Routine

For reading information in, you'll need RetrieveDB (see Example 16-3).

Example 16-3. Typical RetrieveDB routine (emphasized code is specific to your conduit)

```
long CMyConduitPcMgr::RetrieveDB(void)
{
    long err = 0;

    if (!_tcslen(m_szDataFile))
        return GEN_ERR_INVALID_DB_NAME;

    if (m_hFile == INVALID_HANDLE_VALUE)
        return GEN_ERR_INVALID_DB;

    CPalmRecord newRecord;

    while ((ReadRecord(newRecord, err) && err == 0)
        AddRec(newRecord);

    m_bNeedToSave = FALSE;
    return err;
}
```

We check to make sure there is a filename (m_szDataFile), and that the file is open (m_hFile). Next, we need to read from our file into a CPalmRecord. For each one, we add it to the list with AddRec, which will duplicate the given record.

In order to read from our datafile, we will use the member function ReadInData.

Our code that reads in a record will need to set the following:

- The data with SetRawData
- The category number with SetCategory
- The unique ID with SetID (if the record is new on the desktop, the unique ID should be 0)
- The private bit (with SetPrivate)
- The new bit (with SetNew)
- The dirty bit (with SetModified)
- The deleted bit (with SetDeleted)

Example 16-4 shows an example that reads in a record.

Example 16-4. Outline of a routine to read in a record

```
bool CMyPcMgr::ReadRecord(CPalmRecord &rec, long &err)
{
    unsigned char *recordData;
    DWORD recordLength;
    DWORD uniqueID;
    BOOL  isPrivate;
    BOOL  isNew;
    BOOL  isUpdated;
    BOOL  isDeleted;

    // Add code to:
    //   Read data in from the desktop file using ReadInData
    //   Set local variables to correct values based on read-in data
    //   If (there are no more records)
    //       return false.

    rec.SetRawData(recordLength, recordData);
    rec.SetCategory(0);
    rec.SetID(isNew ? 0 : uniqueID);
    rec.ResetAttribs();
    rec.SetPrivate(isPrivate);
    rec.SetNew(isNew);
    rec.SetUpdate(isUpdated);
    rec.SetDeleted(isDeleted);
    return true;
}
```

Handling Categories

The Generic Conduit Framework handles categories oddly—it expects that the category data will be stored on the desktop in the same way it is stored in the AppInfo block. Most applications won't use this strategy, but instead will probably choose to store categories by saving the following:

- The category name
- The category ID (a number from 0 to 255, where 128 and above are reserved for categories created on the desktop)
- A dirty bit (showing that the category has been edited on the desktop since the last sync)

To begin with, you'll need to notify the Generic Conduit Framework that you'll be using categories. You can do this in OpenConduit (see Example 16-5) by changing the last parameter in the constructor from the 0 value that signifies that you don't use categories.

Example 16-5. OpenConduit that supports categories

```
ExportFunc long OpenConduit(PROGRESSFN pFn, CSyncProperties& rProps)
{
    long retval = -1;
    if (pFn)
    {
        CMemopadConduitWithCategoriesSync* pGeneric;
        pGeneric = new CMemopadConduitWithCategoriesSync(rProps,
            GENERIC_FLAG_CATEGORY_SUPPORTED| GENERIC_FLAG_APPINFO_SUPPORTED);
        if (pGeneric){
            retval = pGeneric->Perform( );

            delete pGeneric;
        }
    }
    return(retval);
}
```

In order to deal with categories, you'll need to write out the category ID of each record when you write out your file. In addition, you'll need to write out the categories themselves. Example 16-6 shows a modified StoreDB, with emphasized lines showing the changes that were necessary for categories.

Example 16-6. StoreDB that supports categories

```
 long CMyConduitPcMgr::StoreDB(void)
{
    if ( !m_bNeedToSave) { // If no changes, don't waste time saving.
        if ((!GetCatMgr()) || (!GetCatMgr()->IsChanged( )))
            return 0;
    }

    long retval = Open( );
    if (retval)
      return GEN_ERR_UNABLE_TO_SAVE;

    if (!GetCatMgr( ))  // On a HH->PC copy, the PC category mgr isn't created.
        CPcMgr::ExtractCategories( );
    CPCategoryMgr *catMgr = GetCatMgr( );
    if (retval == 0 && catMgr) {
        for (CPCategory *category = catMgr->FindFirst( );
            retval == 0 && category != NULL;
            category = catMgr->FindNext( )){
            // Add code to write out category->GetID( )
            // and category->GetName( ).
        }
    }
    for (DWORD dwIndex = 0;
      (dwIndex < m_dwMaxRecordCount) && (!retval); dwIndex++) {
      if (!m_pRecordList[dwIndex])
        continue;
```

Example 16-6. StoreDB that supports categories (continued)

```
    retval = WriteRecord(m_pRecordList[dwIndex]);
  }
  Close();
  if (retval == 0)
   m_bNeedToSave = FALSE;
  return retval;
}
```

Next, in your `RetrieveDB`, you'll need to create a Category Manager and populate it with the categories that you read:

```
long CMyConduitPcMgr::RetrieveDB(void)
{
    long err = 0;

    if (!_tcslen(m_szDataFile))
        return GEN_ERR_INVALID_DB_NAME;

    if (m_hFile == INVALID_HANDLE_VALUE)
        return GEN_ERR_INVALID_DB;

    m_pCatMgr = new CPCategoryMgr;
    CPCategory *category;
    while ((category = ReadCategory(err)) && err == 0) {
       m_pCatMgr->Add(*category);
    }
    for (;;) {
        CPalmRecord newRecord;

        if (ReadRecord(newRecord, err) && err == 0) {
            AddRec(newRecord);
         } else
            break;
    }
    m_bNeedToSave = FALSE;
    return err;
}
```

Example 16-7 shows the appropriate code for `ReadCategory`.

Example 16-7. Outline of a routine to read in a category

```
CPCategory *CMyPcMgr::ReadCategory(long &err)
{
    CPCategory *cat = new CPCategory;

    char *categoryName;
    BOOL isDirty;
    DWORD categoryID;

    // Add code to use ReadInData to read categoryName,
```

Example 16-7. Outline of a routine to read in a category (continued)

```
    // categoryID, and isDirty.

    cat->SetID(categoryID);
    cat->SetName(categoryName);
    cat->SetDirty(isDirty);
    return cat;
}
```

The last thing you must do is override `ExtractCategories` (see Example 16-8). Normally, this is called after `RetrieveDB`. It converts the binary category information into a set of category objects managed by a Category Manager. Since you create a Category Manager and populate it within your `RetrieveDB`, you don't want anything to happen in `ExtractCategories`. Thus, declare the overridden member function in your class declaration.

Example 16-8. Declaring override of ExtractCategories

```
class CMyPcMgr : public CPcMgr
{
public:
    CMyPcMgr(CPLogging *pLogging, DWORD dwGenericFlags, char *szDbName,
        TCHAR *pFileName = NULL, TCHAR *pDirName = NULL,
        eSyncTypes syncType = eDoNothing);
    virtual ~CMyPcMgr();
    virtual long RetrieveDB(void);
    virtual long StoreDB(void);
protected:
    long ExtractCategories(void);

};
```

And then, write that routine to do nothing:

```
    long CMyPcMgr::ExtractCategories(void)
    {
        // When we read in the data in our RetrieveDB,
        // we create the Category Manager there.
        return 0;
    }
```

Sales Conduit Based on Generic Conduit

Now that we have walked through the creation of a mirror-image conduit created with a Generic conduit, it is time to apply our knowledge to our own Sales example. We will use the conduit we just created, named `SalesGen`, and add support for two-way syncing of the Customers database. Next, we'll extend the conduit to upload the orders and download the products. Remember, our conduit will support everything except categories (since we don't use them for our Customers).

We'll be storing the customers in a tab-delimited text file named *Customers.txt*. It'll have one line for each customer. Private customers will have a P in the third from the last field whereas nonprivate customers will have an empty string instead:

```
Cust ID<tab>Name<tab>Addr<tab>City<tab>Phone<tab>P<tab>unique ID<tab>attrs
Cust ID<tab>Name<tab>Addr<tab>City<tab>Phone<tab><tab>unique ID<tab>attrs
```

The unique ID is the record unique ID (as opposed to our separate customer ID). The attrs field is composed of a number of characters:

N   New, added on the desktop

M   Modified since the last sync to the handheld (M and N are exclusive)

A   Archived

D   Deleted

CSalesGenPCMgr

Part of our conduit includes the custom class derived from CPcMgr (the Wizard created it). We will add three new member functions (ReadString, ReadRecord, WriteRecord) to it as well (see Example 16-9).

Example 16-9. CSalesGenPcMgr (emphasized code has been added)

```
class CSalesGenPcMgr : public CPcMgr
{
public:
  CSalesGenPcMgr(CPLogging *pLogging, DWORD dwGenericFlags, char *szDbName,
    TCHAR *pFileName = NULL, TCHAR *pDirName = NULL,
    eSyncTypes syncType = eDoNothing);
  virtual ~CSalesGenPcMgr( );
  virtual long RetrieveDB(void);
  virtual long StoreDB(void);
protected:
  long ReadString(char *buffer, long size);
  bool ReadRecord(CPalmRecord &rec, long &err);
  long WriteRecord(CPalmRecord *pPalmRec);
};
```

CSalesGenPCMgr constructor

Our constructor is unchanged from what the Wizard created; it just initializes the base class:

```
CSalesGenPcMgr::CSalesGenPcMgr(CPLogging *pLogging, DWORD dwGenericFlags, char
*szDbName, TCHAR *pFileName, TCHAR *pDirName, eSyncTypes syncType)
: CPcMgr(pLogging, dwGenericFlags, szDbName, pFileName, pDirName, syncType)
{

  // TODO - Put your own class initalization here.

}
```

CSalesGenPCMgr destructor

The destructor is just as uninteresting:

```
CSalesGenPcMgr::~CSalesGenPcMgr( )
{
    TRACE0("CSalesGenPcMgr Destructor\n");
}
```

StoreDB function

Our StoreDB routine writes the list of records in text-delimited format (see Example 16-10).

Example 16-10. StoreDB for the Sales conduit

```
long CSalesGenPcMgr::StoreDB(void)
{
  if (!m_bNeedToSave) { // If no changes, don't waste time saving.
    return 0;
  }

  long err = Open( );
  if (err)
    return GEN_ERR_UNABLE_TO_SAVE;

  for (DWORD dwIndex = 0; (dwIndex < m_dwMaxRecordCount) && (!err);
    dwIndex++){
    if (!m_pRecordList[dwIndex]) // If there is no record, skip ahead.
      continue;
    err = WriteRecord(m_pRecordList[dwIndex]);
  }

  Close( );
  if (err == 0) {
    m_bNeedToSave = FALSE;
    return 0;
  } else
    return GEN_ERR_UNABLE_TO_SAVE;
}
```

It calls WriteRecord, one of our new member functions, which writes a single record line by line (see Example 16-11).

Example 16-11. WriteRecord for Sales conduit

```
long CSalesGenPcMgr::WriteRecord(CPalmRecord *pPalmRec)
{
  unsigned long len;
  const int     kMaxRecordSize = 1000;
  char      buf[kMaxRecordSize];
  char      rawRecord[kMaxRecordSize];
  DWORD     recordSize = kMaxRecordSize;
  long      retval;
```

Example 16-11. WriteRecord for Sales conduit (continued)

```
  retval = pPalmRec->GetRawData((unsigned char *) rawRecord, &recordSize);
  if (retval)
    return retval;

  Customer *aCustomer = RawRecordToCustomer(rawRecord);

  // Write the record to the file as (if private):
  // <customerID>\t<name>\t<address>\t<city>\t<phone>\tP\t<recID>\t
  //    or, if not private:
  // <customerID>\t<name>\t<address>\t<city>\t<phone>\t\t<recID>\t
  sprintf(
    buf,
    "%d\t%s\t%s\t%s\t%s\t%s\t%d\t\r\n",
    aCustomer->customerID,
    aCustomer->name,
    aCustomer->address,
    aCustomer->city,
    aCustomer->phone,
    pPalmRec->IsPrivate( ) ? "P": "",
    pPalmRec->GetID( )
  );
  len = strlen(buf);
  retval = WriteOutData(buf, strlen(buf));

  delete aCustomer;

  return retval;
}
```

WriteRecord, in turn, calls RawRecordToCustomer, which converts the bytes in a record to a customer (see Example 16-12).

Example 16-12. RawRecordToCustomer converts from handheld format

```
Customer *RawRecordToCustomer(void *rec)
{
    Customer *c = new Customer;
    PackedCustomer *pc = (PackedCustomer *) rec;
    c->customerID = SyncHHToHostDWord(pc->customerID);
    char * p = (char *) pc->name;
    c->name = new char[strlen(p)+1];
    strcpy(c->name, p);
    p += strlen(p) + 1;
    c->address = new char[strlen(p)+1];
    strcpy(c->address, p);
    p += strlen(p) + 1;
    c->city = new char[strlen(p)+1];
    strcpy(c->city, p);
    p += strlen(p) + 1;
    c->phone = new char[strlen(p)+1];
    strcpy(c->phone, p);
    return c;
}
```

Retrieving a database

We also have a function, RetrieveDB, that reads a text file and creates records from it (see Example 16-13).

Example 16-13. RetrieveDB for Sales conduit

```
long CSalesGenPcMgr::RetrieveDB(void)
{
  long err = 0;

  m_bNeedToSave = FALSE;
  if (!_tcslen(m_szDataFile))
    return GEN_ERR_INVALID_DB_NAME;

  if (m_hFile == INVALID_HANDLE_VALUE)
    return GEN_ERR_INVALID_DB;

  CPalmRecord newRecord;
  while (ReadRecord(newRecord, err) && err == 0)
    AddRec(newRecord);

  return err;
}
```

Reading customer information

The previous routine relies on a utility routine that we will also need to write. ReadRecord (see Example 16-14) simply reads in a line from the tab-delimited text file and turns it into a Palm record.

Example 16-14. ReadRecord reads a record from a text file

```
bool CSalesGenPcMgr::ReadRecord(CPalmRecord &rec, long &err)
{
  static char gBigBuffer[4096];

  if ((err = ReadString(gBigBuffer, sizeof(gBigBuffer))) != 0) {
    if (err == GEN_ERR_STORAGE_EOF) // No problem, we hit the last record.
      err = 0;
    return false;
  }

  char *p = gBigBuffer;
  char *customerID = FindUpToNextTab(&p);
  char *name = FindUpToNextTab(&p);
  char *address = FindUpToNextTab(&p);
  char *city = FindUpToNextTab(&p);
  char *phone = FindUpToNextTab(&p);
  char *priv = FindUpToNextTab(&p);
  char *uniqueID = FindUpToNextTab(&p);
  char *attributes = FindUpToNextTab(&p);

  if (!address)
```

Example 16-14. ReadRecord reads a record from a text file (continued)

```
      address = "";
  if (!city)
    city = "";
  if (!phone)
    phone = "";
  if (!priv)
    priv = "";
  if (!attributes)
    attributes = "";
  if (!uniqueID)
    uniqueID = "0";
  if (customerID && name) {
    rec.SetID(atol(uniqueID));
    rec.SetCategory(0);

    rec.SetPrivate(*priv == 'P');

    // 'N' -- new, 'M' -- modify, 'D'-- delete, 'A' -- archive
    // 'N' and 'M' are exclusive.
    rec.ResetAttribs( );
    if (strchr(attributes, 'N'))
      rec.SetNew( );
    else if (strchr(attributes, 'M'))
      rec.SetUpdate( );
    if (strchr(attributes, 'D'))
      rec.SetDeleted( );
    if (strchr(attributes, 'A'))
      rec.SetArchived( );

    static char buf[4096];
    Customer c;
    PackedCustomer *pc = (PackedCustomer *) buf;
    pc->customerID = SyncHostToHHDWord(atol(customerID));
    char *p = (char *) pc->name;
    strcpy(p, name);
    p += strlen(p) + 1;
    strcpy(p, address);
    p += strlen(p) + 1;
    strcpy(p, city);
    p += strlen(p) + 1;
    strcpy(p, phone);
    p += strlen(p) + 1;

    rec.SetRawData(p - buf, (unsigned char *) buf);

    return true;
  } else
    return false;
}
```

The ReadRecord routine itself relies on a couple of utility routines. The first is ReadString, which reads a string from the datafile (see Example 16-15).

Example 16-15. ReadString reads a string from a text file

```
long CSalesGenPcMgr::ReadString(char *buffer, long size)
{
  long err;
  long  i;
  for (i = 0; i < size-1; i++) {
    err = ReadInData((unsigned char *) buffer + i, 1);
    if (err)
      break;
    if (i > 0 && buffer[i-1] == '\r' && buffer[i] == '\n') {
      buffer[i-1] = '\0';
      return 0;
    }
  }
  buffer[i] = '\0';

  // Last line may not be null-terminated.
  if (err == GEN_ERR_STORAGE_EOF && i > 0)
    err = 0;
  return err;
}
```

The other utility routine finds characters up to a tab, and also replaces the tab it finds with a null-byte:

```
char *FindUpToNextTab(char **p)
{
  char *orig = *p;
  while (**p != '\0' && **p != '\t')
    (*p)++;
  if (**p == '\t') {
    **p = '\0'; // Kill the trailing tab.
    (*p)++;
  }
  return orig;
}
```

Customizing resources

There are a couple of string resources we must change. In *SalesGen.rc*, open the string table, and change the strings shown as in Table 16-5.

Table 16-5. What to change in the SalesGen.rc string table.

String	From	To
ID IDS_CONDUIT_NAME	Generic conduit	Sales
ID IDS_SYNC_ACTION_TEXT	HotSync action for Generic conduit	HotSync action for Sales

Registering the conduit

Once we've written this, we must register the conduit with the following settings:

Conduit
```
C:\SalesGen\Debug\SalesGen.DLL
```
Creator
```
SLES
```
Directory
```
Sales
```
File
```
Customers.txt
```
Remote Database
```
Customers-SLES
```

Testing the conduit

At this point, we can run the conduit, and it correctly does a two-way mirror-image synchronization of the Customers database.

You can now use all of the following steps to test the conduit:

- Delete, add, modify, and archive records on the handheld, and verify that the changes propagate to the desktop.

- Test by deleting, adding, modifying, and archiving records on the desktop (make sure to set the appropriate attributes in the last field of changed records). Verify that the changes propagate to the handheld.

- Try "Handheld overwrites Desktop" and "Desktop overwrites Handheld". For real thrills, verify that "Do Nothing" works!

CSalesGenSynchronizer

In the last chapter, we saw code to upload the Orders database and download the Products database. Now, we've got to add support for these to our two-way syncing conduit.

We modify the Wizard-generated CSalesGenSynchronizer in order to add the ability to copy our Orders database from the handheld and our Products database to the handheld.

Class definition

Example 16-16 shows our class declaration of CSalesGenSynchronizer (our change is emphasized).

Example 16-16. CSalesGenSynchronizer declaration

```
class CSalesGenSync : public CSynchronizer
{
public:
  CSalesGenSync(CSyncProperties& rProps, DWORD dwDatabaseFlags);
  virtual ~CSalesGenSync( );
```

Example 16-16. CSalesGenSynchronizer declaration (continued)

```
  virtual long Perform(void);

protected:
  virtual CPDbBaseMgr *CreateArchiveManager(TCHAR *pFilename);
  virtual long CreatePCManager(void);
 virtual long CreateBackupManager(void);
};
```

Modifying Perform to add uploading and downloading products and orders

Perform is a fairly large routine that does many things: it opens the conduit, does the appropriate kind of syncing, and closes the conduit. This is where we need to insert our Products and Orders database copying code.

There is an interesting code design issue here. We think it would have been easier had there been one method to open the database, one to do the syncing, and one to close the conduit. This way, we could have just augmented the behavior of the method that did the syncing. We have one big routine to work with instead. As a result, we've got to copy it and add our desired code to a large, instead of a small, routine. Example 16-17 shows that copied routine with our code.

Example 16-17. Our override of Perform (emphasized code has been added)

```
#define MAX_PROD_ID_TEXT 255

long CSalesGenSync::Perform(void)
{
  long retval = 0;
  long retval2 = 0;

  if (m_rSyncProperties.m_SyncType > eProfileInstall)
    return GEN_ERR_BAD_SYNC_TYPE;


  if (m_rSyncProperties.m_SyncType == eDoNothing) {
    return 0;
  }
  // Obtain system information.
  m_SystemInfo.m_ProductIdText = (BYTE*) new char [MAX_PROD_ID_TEXT];
  if (!m_SystemInfo.m_ProductIdText)
    return GEN_ERR_LOW_MEMORY;
  m_SystemInfo.m_AllocedLen = (BYTE) MAX_PROD_ID_TEXT;
  retval = SyncReadSystemInfo(m_SystemInfo);
  if (retval)
    return retval;

  retval = RegisterConduit();
  if (retval)
    return retval;

  for (int iCount=0; iCount < m_TotRemoteDBs && !retval; iCount++) {
    retval = GetRemoteDBInfo(iCount);
```

Example 16-17. Our override of Perform (emphasized code has been added) (continued)

```
    if (retval) {
      retval = 0;
      break;
    }

    switch (m_rSyncProperties.m_SyncType) {
      case eFast:
        retval = PerformFastSync( );
        if ((retval) && (retval == GEN_ERR_CHANGE_SYNC_MODE)){
            if (GetSyncMode( ) == eHHtoPC)
                retval = CopyHHtoPC( );
            else if (GetSyncMode( ) == ePCtoHH)
                retval = CopyPCtoHH( );
        }
        break;
      case eSlow:
        retval = PerformSlowSync( );
        if ((retval) && (retval == GEN_ERR_CHANGE_SYNC_MODE)){
          if (GetSyncMode( ) == eHHtoPC)
            retval = CopyHHtoPC( );
          else if (GetSyncMode( ) == ePCtoHH)
            retval = CopyPCtoHH( );
        }
        break;
      case eHHtoPC:
      case eBackup:
          retval = CopyHHtoPC( );
          break;
      case eInstall:
      case ePCtoHH:
      case eProfileInstall:
          retval = CopyPCtoHH( );
          break;
      case eDoNothing:
          break;
        default:
          retval = GEN_ERR_SYNC_TYPE_NOT_SUPPORTED;
          break;
    }

    DeleteHHManager( );
    DeletePCManager( );
    DeleteBackupManager( );
    CloseArchives( );
  }

  // Added here for sales conduit.
  if (retval == 0 && m_rSyncProperties.m_SyncType == eHHtoPC ||
    m_rSyncProperties.m_SyncType == eFast ||
    m_rSyncProperties.m_SyncType == eSlow)
    retval = CopyOrdersFromHH(m_rSyncProperties);
  if (retval == 0 && m_rSyncProperties.m_SyncType == ePCtoHH ||
    m_rSyncProperties.m_SyncType == eFast ||
```

Example 16-17. Our override of Perform (emphasized code has been added) (continued)

```
    m_rSyncProperties.m_SyncType == eSlow)
    retval = CopyProductsAndCategoriesToHH(m_rSyncProperties);
  // Done added here for sales conduit.

  // Unregister the conduit.
    retval2 = UnregisterConduit((BOOL)(retval != 0));

    if (!retval)
        return retval2;
    return retval;
}
```

From the last chapter, we use the routines CopyOrderFromHH (see "Moving orders to the desktop") and CopyProductsAndCategoriesToHH (see "Moving products to the handheld").

Testing the Conduit

Here are some good tests you can perform to ensure that the conduit is working properly:

Do a sync without having ever run your application
> Your database(s) won't exist yet. This is a good simulation of what occurs when a user syncs after installing your software but before using it. If your conduit performs correctly, any data from the desktop should be copied to the handheld.

Do a sync having run your application once
> (Do this test after first deleting your last test's databases on the desktop.) This simulates a user syncing after installing your software and using it. If everything works as expected, data from the handheld should be copied to the desktop.

Add a record on the handheld and sync
> Make sure the new record gets added to the desktop.

Add a record on the desktop and sync
> Make sure the new record gets added to the handheld.

Delete a record on the handheld and sync
> Make sure the record gets deleted from the desktop.

Delete a record on the desktop and sync
> Make sure the record gets deleted from the handheld.

Archive a record on the handheld
> Make sure the record gets deleted from the main desktop file and added to the archive file.

Of course, there are other tests you can use, but these provide a good starting place.

As you can see, Generic conduit makes the task of supporting two-way mirror-image syncing fairly easy. It involves, for the most part, simply converting from the handheld record format to some other file format and vice versa.

PART IV

Appendixes

Where to Go from Here

We have put all the Palm developer resources we could think of into this location as a handy reference guide.

Palm Programming Book Web Site

Any updates to the source code in this book are located at:

http://www.calliopeinc.com/palmprog2

You will also find helpful links to other Palm programming locations.

The Official Palm Developer Site

Palm's official Palm OS developer site is *http://www.palmos.com/dev*.

This is the place you should go to check for the most recent versions of the SDK, CDK, and information on updates to the operating system. There are also a lot of other resources at this site—everything from white papers on various topics to Palm's FAQ for developers.

Getting Your Application Creator ID

Palm's developer site is also where you go to register your application and obtain your application's unique creator ID. A creator ID is a four-ASCII-character ID that each application needs to distinguish itself from all other applications. This is an essential part of application development and you shouldn't leave it until the last minute.

Knowledge Base

Palm's developer site has a knowledge base containing a collection of articles, documentation, and sample code. A query engine allows easy search of the collection.

Resource Pavilion

The Resource Pavilion is a private area for members of the Palm Alliance program. It contains technical and marketing information, prerelease development tools, a hardware purchase discount program, and other opportunities available to program members. This is also where you can download ROM files.

There's no charge to become a member of the Palm Alliance program and you can apply online.

Palm-Powered Compatible Solution

You can have your application tested to be eligible for a special logo (Palm's way of notifying a consumer that an application has undergone stringent testing). Applications that pass this compatibility testing receive the right to use the Palm-Powered Compatible Solution logo and some marketing and developer support from Palm.

This testing is administered by a third-party provider, Quality Partners, which has a web site (*http://www.qpqa.com*) where you can get information about testing standards and a free developer's testing kit. The testing kit contains detailed descriptions of their entire test suite.

No matter what, you should look over the testing cycle that Quality Partners uses on an application and do what is necessary to ensure that your application meets those guidelines. Their tests include important checks such as:

- Proper Graffiti and shortcut support
- Design consistency with Palm UI guidelines
- Proper handling of errors and use of alerts
- Successful handling of one million Gremlin events

Palm Programming Mailing Lists

The following mailing lists are hosted by Palm, and it's common to see Palm employees answering questions. While these lists are not officially supported, they serve as a good self-support mechanism and are constantly used by developers to answer each other's questions.

Palm's developer web site has forms to subscribe to any of these lists:

Palm Developer Forum
General Palm OS development

Conduit Forum
Development of conduits, for both Windows and Mac OS

Emulator Forum
Discussion of Palm OS Emulator

Communication Developer Forum
Discussion of communications (TCP/IP, serial, Bluetooth, IrDA)

Tools Forum
Discussion of development tools

Java Forum
Java development (both native and conduit)

Web Clipping Forum
Development of Web Clipping applications

Web Clipping Announcements
Announcements (no posting allowed) of interest to all Web Clipping developers

There are also forums for each of the licensees (IBM, Symbol, and so on).

Almost all the messages from the first two lists (Palm Developer Forum and Conduit Forum) have been archived at Yahoo! Groups (*http://groups.yahoo.com/group/palm-dev-forum/* and *http://groups.yahoo.com/group/conduit-dev-forum/*). Less comprehensive archives for those groups, as well as archives for all the other groups, can be found at *http://www.escribe.com*.

Palm OS Developer Exchange

In conjunction with HotDispatch, Palm has established this marketplace for support. You can post questions along with a price you're willing to pay for the answer. Knowledgeable people respond to your questions; if you're satisfied with the answer, you pay for it.

Basically, it's community peer-to-peer support, with a capitalist twist.

Third-Party Palm Programming Resources

Third parties have lots of useful information.

Newsgroups

Currently there are no Palm programming newsgroups distributed on Usenet. However, *Falch.net* hosts a newsgroup server with some different newsgroups:

news://news.falch.net/pilot.programmer
> General Palm programming questions

news://news.falch.net/pilot.programmer.gcc
> Discussion about using the GNU PalmPilot SDK

news://news.falch.net/pilot/programmer.codewarrior
> Discussion about using CodeWarrior

news://news.falch.net/pilot.programmer.pila
> Discussion about programming in Motorola 68000 assembly language

news://news.falch.net/pilot.programmer.jump
> Discussion about programming in Java

news://news.falch.net/pilot.programmer.jump
> Discussion about programming in Waba

Palm Programming FAQ

This site, *http://www.cyberport.com/~tangent/palm/faq/*, is an FAQ containing answers to common Palm OS programming questions.

Sales Source Code

This is a complete listing of all the source code for the Sales application. It is for your reference.

To get a copy for use in your programs, go to our web site. Although this code was up-to-date when the book was written, there may have been later changes. To get the most up-to-date version, you should also check our web site:

http://www.calliopeinc.com/palmprog2

Source Code

Customer.c

```
/*
  Copyright (c) 1998-2001, Neil Rhodes and Julie McKeehan
     neil@pobox.com
  All rights reserved.

From the book "Palm OS Programming (2nd edition)"
by O'Reilly.

Permission granted to use this file however you see fit.
*/
#define DO_NOT_ALLOW_ACCESS_TO_INTERNALS_OF_STRUCTS
#include <BuildDefines.h>
#ifdef DEBUG_BUILD
#define ERROR_CHECK_LEVEL ERROR_CHECK_FULL
#endif
#include <PalmOS.h>
#include "Customer.h"
#include "Utils.h"
```

```
#include "SalesRsc.h"
#include "Common.h"

Boolean      gSaveBackup = true;

Boolean AskDeleteCustomer(void)
{
  FormPtr form = FrmInitForm(DeleteCustomerForm);
  UInt16  hitButton;
  UInt16  ctlIndex;

  // Set the "save backup" checkbox to its previous setting.
  ctlIndex = FrmGetObjectIndex(form, DeleteCustomerSaveBackupCheckbox);
  FrmSetControlValue(form, ctlIndex, gSaveBackup);

  hitButton = FrmDoDialog(form);
  if (hitButton == DeleteCustomerOKButton)
    gSaveBackup = (Boolean) FrmGetControlValue(form, ctlIndex);
  FrmDeleteForm(form);
  return (Boolean) (hitButton == DeleteCustomerOKButton);
}

static Boolean CustomerHandleEvent(EventPtr event)
{
  if (event->eType == ctlSelectEvent &&
    event->data.ctlSelect.controlID == CustomerDeleteButton) {
    if (!AskDeleteCustomer())
      return true;  // Don't bail out if they cancel the Delete dialog box.
  }
  return false;
}

// isNew is true if this is a brand-new customer.
void EditCustomerWithSelection(UInt16 recordNumber, Boolean isNew,
  Boolean *deleted, EventPtr event)
{
  FormPtr    form;
  UInt16     hitButton;
  Boolean    dirty = false;
  Boolean    isEmpty = false;
  ControlPtr privateCheckbox;
  UInt16     attributes;
  Boolean    isSecret;
  FieldPtr   nameField;
  FieldPtr   addressField;
  FieldPtr   cityField;
  FieldPtr   phoneField;
  Customer   theCustomer;
  UInt16     offset = OffsetOf(PackedCustomer, name);
  MemHandle  customerHandle;

#ifdef DEBUG_BUILD
  CheckDatabases(true);
#endif
```

```
customerHandle = DmGetRecord(gCustomerDB, recordNumber);
*deleted = false;
DmRecordInfo(gCustomerDB, recordNumber, &attributes, NULL, NULL);
isSecret = (Boolean) ((attributes & dmRecAttrSecret) == dmRecAttrSecret);

form = FrmInitForm(CustomerForm);
FrmSetEventHandler(form, CustomerHandleEvent);

UnpackCustomer(&theCustomer,
  (PackedCustomer *) MemHandleLock(customerHandle));

nameField    = (FieldPtr) GetObjectFromForm(form, CustomerNameField);
addressField = (FieldPtr) GetObjectFromForm(form, CustomerAddressField);
cityField    = (FieldPtr) GetObjectFromForm(form, CustomerCityField);
phoneField   = (FieldPtr) GetObjectFromForm(form, CustomerPhoneField);

SetFieldTextFromStr(nameField,    theCustomer.name, false);
SetFieldTextFromStr(addressField, theCustomer.address, false);
SetFieldTextFromStr(cityField,    theCustomer.city, false);
SetFieldTextFromStr(phoneField,   theCustomer.phone, false);

FrmDrawForm(form); // Must do now, because pre-3.5, focus needed to be set
                   //  *after* a call to FrmDrawForm.
// Select one of the fields.
if (event && event->data.frmGoto.matchFieldNum) {
  FieldPtr selectedField =
    (FieldPtr)  GetObjectFromForm(form, event->data.frmGoto.matchFieldNum);
  FldSetScrollPosition(selectedField, event->data.frmGoto.matchPos);
  FrmSetFocus(form,
    FrmGetObjectIndex(form, event->data.frmGoto.matchFieldNum));
  FldSetSelection(selectedField, event->data.frmGoto.matchPos,
    event->data.frmGoto.matchPos + event->data.frmGoto.matchLen);
} else {
  FrmSetFocus(form, FrmGetObjectIndex(form, CustomerNameField));
  FldSetSelection(nameField, 0, FldGetTextLength(nameField));
}

// Unlock the customer.
MemHandleUnlock(customerHandle);

privateCheckbox =
  (ControlPtr) GetObjectFromForm(form, CustomerPrivateCheckbox);
CtlSetValue(privateCheckbox, isSecret);

hitButton = FrmDoDialog(form);

if (hitButton == CustomerOKButton) {
  dirty = FldDirty(nameField) || FldDirty(addressField) ||
    FldDirty(cityField) || FldDirty(phoneField);
  if (dirty) {
    theCustomer.name = FldGetTextPtr(nameField);
    if (!theCustomer.name)
      theCustomer.name = "";
    theCustomer.address = FldGetTextPtr(addressField);
```

```
      if (!theCustomer.address)
        theCustomer.address = "";
      theCustomer.city = FldGetTextPtr(cityField);
      if (!theCustomer.city)
        theCustomer.city = "";
      theCustomer.phone = FldGetTextPtr(phoneField);
      if (!theCustomer.phone)
        theCustomer.phone = "";
    }
    isEmpty = StrCompare(theCustomer.name, "") == 0 &&
      StrCompare(theCustomer.address, "") == 0 &&
      StrCompare(theCustomer.city, "") == 0 &&
      StrCompare(theCustomer.phone, "") == 0;
    if (dirty)
      PackCustomer(&theCustomer, customerHandle);
    if (CtlGetValue(privateCheckbox) != isSecret) {
      dirty = true;
      if (CtlGetValue(privateCheckbox)) {
        attributes |= dmRecAttrSecret;
        // Tell user how to hide or mask private records.
        if (gPrivateRecordStatus == showPrivateRecords)
          FrmAlert(privateRecordInfoAlert);
      } else
        attributes &= (UInt8) ~dmRecAttrSecret;
      DmSetRecordInfo(gCustomerDB, recordNumber, &attributes, NULL);
    }
  }
  FrmDeleteForm(form);

  DmReleaseRecord(gCustomerDB, recordNumber, dirty);
  if (hitButton == CustomerDeleteButton) {
    *deleted = true;
    if (isNew && !gSaveBackup)
      DmRemoveRecord(gCustomerDB, recordNumber);
    else {
      if (gSaveBackup)  // Need to archive it on PC.
        DmArchiveRecord(gCustomerDB, recordNumber);
      else
        DmDeleteRecord(gCustomerDB, recordNumber);
      // Deleted records are stored at the end of the database.
      DmMoveRecord(gCustomerDB, recordNumber, DmNumRecords(gCustomerDB));
    }
  }
  else if (hitButton == CustomerOKButton && isNew && isEmpty) {
    *deleted = true;
    DmRemoveRecord(gCustomerDB, recordNumber);
  }
  else if (hitButton == CustomerCancelButton && isNew) {
    *deleted = true;
    DmRemoveRecord(gCustomerDB, recordNumber);
  }
#ifdef DEBUG_BUILD
  CheckDatabases(true);
#endif
}
```

```
// Returns true if the customer was changed/deleted.
void EditCustomer(UInt16 recordNumber, Boolean isNew, Boolean *deleted)
{
  EditCustomerWithSelection(recordNumber, isNew, deleted, NULL);
}
```

Customers.c

```
/*
 Copyright (c) 1998-2001, Neil Rhodes and Julie McKeehan
    neil@pobox.com
 All rights reserved.

From the book "Palm OS Programming (2nd edition)"
by O'Reilly.

Permission granted to use this file however you see fit.
*/
#define DO_NOT_ALLOW_ACCESS_TO_INTERNALS_OF_STRUCTS
#include <BuildDefines.h>
#ifdef DEBUG_BUILD
#define ERROR_CHECK_LEVEL ERROR_CHECK_FULL
#endif
#include <PalmOS.h>
#include <TxtGlue.h>
#include "Customers.h"
#include "Utils.h"
#include "Common.h"
#include "Customer.h"
#include "Exchange.h"
#include "SalesRsc.h"

static Int32 GetCustomerIDForNthCustomer(UInt16 itemNumber)
{
  Int32          customerID;
  UInt16         index = 0;
  MemHandle      h;
  PackedCustomer *packedCustomer;

  // Must do seek to skip over secret records.
  DmSeekRecordInCategory(gCustomerDB, &index, itemNumber, dmSeekForward,
    dmAllCategories);
  h = DmQueryRecord(gCustomerDB, index);
  ErrNonFatalDisplayIf(!h,
    "can't get customer in GetCustomerIDForNthCustomer");
  packedCustomer = (PackedCustomer *) MemHandleLock(h);
  customerID = packedCustomer->customerID;
  MemHandleUnlock(h);

  return customerID;
}
```

```
static void DrawOneCustomerInListWithFont(Int16 itemNumber, RectanglePtr bounds, Char
**text)
{
#pragma unused(text)
  MemHandle h;
  UInt16   index = 0;

  // Must do seek to skip over secret records.
  DmSeekRecordInCategory(gCustomerDB, &index,  (UInt16) itemNumber,
    dmSeekForward, dmAllCategories);
  if (gPrivateRecordStatus == maskPrivateRecords) {
    UInt16 attr;

    DmRecordInfo(gCustomerDB, index, &attr, NULL, NULL);
    if (attr & dmRecAttrSecret) {
      // Show gray rectangle.
      const CustomPatternType grayPattern =
        {0xAA, 0x55, 0xAA, 0x55, 0xAA, 0x55, 0xAA, 0x55};
      CustomPatternType origPattern;
      MemHandle bitmapHandle;
      RectangleType grayBounds = *bounds;

      // Draw lock icon.
      grayBounds.extent.x -= SecLockWidth;
      bitmapHandle = DmGetResource(bitmapRsc, SecLockBitmap);
      if (bitmapHandle) {
        BitmapPtr bitmap = (BitmapPtr) MemHandleLock(bitmapHandle);

          // Right-hand side, centered vertically.
        WinDrawBitmap(bitmap, grayBounds.topLeft.x + grayBounds.extent.x,
          grayBounds.topLeft.y + ((grayBounds.extent.y - SecLockHeight) / 2));
        MemHandleUnlock(bitmapHandle);
        DmReleaseResource(bitmapHandle);
      }

      // Draw gray box.
      WinGetPattern(&origPattern);
      WinSetPattern(&grayPattern);
      WinFillRectangle(&grayBounds, 0);
      WinSetPattern(&origPattern);
      return;
    }
  }
  h = DmQueryRecord(gCustomerDB, index);
  if (h) {
    FontID   curFont;
    Boolean setFont = false;
    PackedCustomer   *packedCustomer = (PackedCustomer *) MemHandleLock(h);

    if (!OrderExistsForCustomer(packedCustomer->customerID)) {
      setFont = true;
      curFont = FntSetFont(boldFont);
    }
    DrawCharsToFitWidth(packedCustomer->name, bounds);
    MemHandleUnlock(h);
```

```
      if (setFont)
        FntSetFont(curFont);
  }
}

static void InitNumberCustomers(void)
{
  ListPtr list = (ListPtr) GetObjectFromActiveForm(CustomersCustomersList);
    // If we use DmNumRecords, we'll count the deleted records too.
  UInt16  numCustomers =
    DmNumRecordsInCategory(gCustomerDB, dmAllCategories);

  LstSetListChoices(list, NULL, (Int16) numCustomers);
}

static
void RedrawCustomersAfterChange(void)
{
  ListPtr list = (ListPtr) GetObjectFromActiveForm(CustomersCustomersList);

  LstEraseList(list); // Erase list *before* updating num items.
  InitNumberCustomers();
  LstDrawList(list);  // Draw list *after* updating num items.
}


static
void CustomersFormOpen(FormPtr form)
{
  ListPtr list = (ListPtr) GetObjectFromForm(form, CustomersCustomersList);

  InitNumberCustomers();
  LstSetDrawFunction(list, DrawOneCustomerInListWithFont);
  LstSetSelection(list, noListSelection);

  if (sysGetROMVerMajor(GetRomVersion()) >= 4)
    FrmSetMenu(form,  CustomersWithSendMenuBar);
}

static
Boolean CustomersHandleMenuEvent(UInt16 menuID)
{
  Boolean handled = false;
  UInt16  recordNumber = 0; // Add at beginning. Will maintain sorting by
                            // customer ID because temporary customer IDs are
                            // assigned more and more negative.
  MemHandle customerHandle;
  Int32 newCustomerID;

  switch (menuID) {
  case CustomerNewCustomer:
    newCustomerID = GetLowestCustomerID( ) - 1;
    customerHandle = DmNewRecord(gCustomerDB, &recordNumber, 1);
    if (!customerHandle) {
      FrmAlert(DeviceIsFullAlert);
```

```
      } else {
        Customer   theCustomer;
        Boolean    deleted;

        theCustomer.customerID = newCustomerID;
        theCustomer.name = theCustomer.address = theCustomer.city =
          theCustomer.phone = "";
        PackCustomer(&theCustomer, customerHandle);
        DmReleaseRecord(gCustomerDB, recordNumber, 1);
        EditCustomer(recordNumber, true, &deleted);
        RedrawCustomersAfterChange();
      }
      handled = true;
      break;

    case CustomerBeamAllCustomers:
      SendAllCustomers(exgBeamPrefix);
      handled = true;
      break;

    case CustomerSendAllCustomers:
      SendAllCustomers(exgSendPrefix);
      handled = true;
      break;
  }
  return handled;
}

Boolean CustomersHandleEvent(EventPtr event)
{
  Boolean    handled = false;
  Boolean    deleted;
  FormPtr    form;
  UInt16     listIndex;

  switch (event->eType)
  {
  case lstSelectEvent:
    listIndex = (UInt16) event->data.lstSelect.selection;

      LstSetSelection(event->data.lstSelect.pList, noListSelection);
    if (gPrivateRecordStatus == maskPrivateRecords) {
      UInt16 attr;
      UInt16   index = 0;

        // Must do seek to skip over deleted records.
        DmSeekRecordInCategory(gCustomerDB, &index,  listIndex,
          dmSeekForward, dmAllCategories);
        DmRecordInfo(gCustomerDB, index, &attr, NULL, NULL);
      if (attr & dmRecAttrSecret) {
        if (!SecVerifyPW (showPrivateRecords)) {
            handled = true;
            break;
          } else {
            // We only want to unmask this one record, so restore the preference.
```

```
                PrefSetPreference (prefShowPrivateRecords, maskPrivateRecords);
             }
          }
       }
     OpenCustomerWithID(GetCustomerIDForNthCustomer(listIndex));
     handled = true;
     break;

  case menuEvent:
     handled = CustomersHandleMenuEvent(event->data.menu.itemID);
     break;

  case keyDownEvent:
     if (TxtGlueCharIsVirtual(event->data.keyDown.modifiers,
        event->data.keyDown.chr) &&
        event->data.keyDown.chr == vchrPageUp ||
        event->data.keyDown.chr == vchrPageDown) {
        ListPtr list = (ListPtr)
GetObjectFromActiveForm(CustomersCustomersList);
        WinDirectionType   d;

        if (event->data.keyDown.chr == vchrPageUp)
          d = winUp;
        else
          d = winDown;
        LstScrollList(list, d, 1);
     }
     handled = true;
     break;

 case frmOpenEvent:
    form = FrmGetActiveForm( );
    CustomersFormOpen(form);
    FrmDrawForm(form);
    handled = true;
    break;

  case frmGotoEvent:
     EditCustomerWithSelection(event->data.frmGoto.recordNum, false,
        &deleted, event);
     RedrawCustomersAfterChange( );
     handled = true;
     break;

  case frmCloseEvent:
#ifdef DEBUG_BUILD
     CheckDatabases(true);
#endif
     handled = false;
     break;


  }
  return handled;
}
```

Data.c

```
/*
 Copyright (c) 1998-2001, Neil Rhodes and Julie McKeehan
    neil@pobox.com
 All rights reserved.

From the book "Palm OS Programming (2nd edition)"
by O'Reilly.

Permission granted to use this file however you see fit.
*/
#define DO_NOT_ALLOW_ACCESS_TO_INTERNALS_OF_STRUCTS
#include <BuildDefines.h>
#ifdef DEBUG_BUILD
#define ERROR_CHECK_LEVEL ERROR_CHECK_FULL
#endif
#include <PalmOS.h>
#include "Data.h"

DmOpenRef    gCustomerDB;
DmOpenRef    gOrderDB;
DmOpenRef    gProductDB;

#ifdef DEBUG_BUILD
void CheckDatabases(Boolean justCustomer)
{
  UInt8 highest;
  UInt32  count;
  UInt32  busy;

  return;
  DmGetDatabaseLockState(gCustomerDB, &highest, &count, &busy);
  if (highest || busy)
    ErrFatalDisplay("customer db not quiescent");
  if (justCustomer)
    return;
  DmGetDatabaseLockState(gOrderDB, &highest, &count, &busy);
  if (highest || busy)
    ErrFatalDisplay("order db not quiescent");
  DmGetDatabaseLockState(gProductDB, &highest, &count, &busy);
  if (highest || busy)
    ErrFatalDisplay("product db not quiescent");
}
#endif

Int16 CompareIDFunc(Int32 *p1, Int32 *p2, Int16 i,
  SortRecordInfoPtr s1, SortRecordInfoPtr s2, MemHandle appInfoH)
{
#pragma unused(i, s1, s2, appInfoH)
  // Can't just return *p1 - *p2 because that's a Int32 which may overflow
  // our return type of Int16.  Therefore, we do the comparison ourselves.
  // and check
  if (*p1 < *p2)
```

```
      return -1;
    else if (*p1 > *p2)
      return 1;
    else
      return 0;
}

void PackCustomer(Customer *customer, MemHandle customerDBEntry)
{
  // Figure out necessary size.
  UInt16    length = 0;
  Char      *s;
  UInt16    offset = 0;

  length = (UInt16) (sizeof(customer->customerID) + StrLen(customer->name) +
    StrLen(customer->address) + StrLen(customer->city) +
    StrLen(customer->phone) + 4); // 4 for string terminators.

  // Resize the MemHandle.
  if (MemHandleResize(customerDBEntry, length) == 0) {
    // Copy the fields.
    s = (Char *) MemHandleLock(customerDBEntry);
    offset = 0;
    DmWrite(s, offset, &customer->customerID,
      sizeof(customer->customerID));
    offset += sizeof(customer->customerID);
    DmStrCopy(s, offset, customer->name);
    offset += (UInt16) StrLen(customer->name) + 1;
    DmStrCopy(s, offset, customer->address);
    offset += (UInt16) StrLen(customer->address) + 1;
    DmStrCopy(s, offset, customer->city);
    offset += (UInt16) StrLen(customer->city) + 1;
    DmStrCopy(s, offset, customer->phone);
    MemHandleUnlock(customerDBEntry);
  }
}

// packedCustomer must remain locked while customer is in use.
void UnpackCustomer(Customer *customer,
  const PackedCustomer *packedCustomer)
{
  const char *s = packedCustomer->name;
  customer->customerID = packedCustomer->customerID;
  customer->name = s;
  s += StrLen(s) + 1;
  customer->address = s;
  s += StrLen(s) + 1;
  customer->city = s;
  s += StrLen(s) + 1;
  customer->phone = s;
  s += StrLen(s) + 1;
#ifdef DEBUG_BUILD
  if (StrLen(customer->name) > 80 || StrLen(customer->address) > 80 ||
      StrLen(customer->city) > 80 || StrLen(customer->phone) > 80)
      ErrFatalDisplay("field too long");
```

```
#endif
}

// Returns a customer ID no higher than any existing one.
// This is used so that new customers get negative customer IDs.
Int32 GetLowestCustomerID( )
{
  UInt16      cardNo;
  LocalID     dbID;
  UInt16      mode;
  DmOpenRef dbP = gCustomerDB;
  Boolean     databaseReopened;
  Int32     result;

  DmOpenDatabaseInfo(dbP, &dbID, NULL, &mode, &cardNo, NULL);

  // Want *all* customers.
  if (!(mode & dmModeShowSecret))
  {
    dbP = DmOpenDatabase(cardNo, dbID, dmModeReadOnly | dmModeShowSecret);
    databaseReopened = true;
  } else
    databaseReopened = false;

  // We must use categories so we don't count deleted.
  if (DmNumRecordsInCategory(dbP, dmAllCategories) == 0)
    result = 0;
  else {
    // The first record won't be deleted because deleted are at the end.
    MemHandle h = DmQueryRecord(dbP, 0);
    PackedCustomer *c;

    c = (PackedCustomer *) MemHandleLock(h);
    result = c->customerID;
    if (result > 0)
      result = 0;
    MemHandleUnlock(h);
  }
  if (databaseReopened)
    DmCloseDatabase(dbP);
  return result;
}

void PackProduct(Product *product, MemHandle productDBEntry)
{
  // Figure out necessary size.
  UInt16      length = 0;
  Char      *s;
  UInt16      offset = 0;

  length = (UInt16) (sizeof(product->productID) + sizeof(product->price) +
    StrLen(product->name) + 1);

  // Resize the MemHandle.
```

```
    if (MemHandleResize(productDBEntry, length) == errNone) {
      // Copy the fields.
      s = (Char *) MemHandleLock(productDBEntry);
      DmWrite(s, OffsetOf(PackedProduct, productID), &product->productID,
        sizeof(product->productID));
      DmWrite(s, OffsetOf(PackedProduct, price), &product->price,
        sizeof(product->price));
      DmStrCopy(s, OffsetOf(PackedProduct, name), product->name);
      MemHandleUnlock(productDBEntry);
    }
}

// packedProduct must remain locked while product is in use.
void UnpackProduct(Product *product,
  const PackedProduct *packedProduct)
{
  product->productID = packedProduct->productID;
  product->price = packedProduct->price;
  product->name = packedProduct->name;
}

// If successful, returns the product, and the locked MemHandle.
MemHandle GetProductFromProductID(UInt32 productID, Product *theProduct, UInt16
*indexPtr)
{
  UInt16       index;
  MemHandle    foundHandle = 0;
  PackedProduct findRecord;

  findRecord.productID = productID;
  index = DmFindSortPosition(gProductDB, &findRecord, NULL, (DmComparF *)
CompareIDFunc, 0);
  if (index > 0) {
    PackedProduct *p;
    MemHandle      h;

    index--;
    h = DmQueryRecord(gProductDB, index);
    p = (PackedProduct *) MemHandleLock(h);
    if (p->productID == productID) {
      if (theProduct)
        UnpackProduct(theProduct, p);
      else
        MemHandleUnlock(h);
      if (indexPtr)
        *indexPtr = index;
      return h;
    }
    MemHandleUnlock(h);
  }
  return NULL;
}

void GetProductNameFromProductID(UInt32 productID, Char *productName)
```

```
{
  Product p;
  MemHandle h = GetProductFromProductID(productID, &p, NULL);

  *productName = '\0';
  ErrNonFatalDisplayIf(!h, "can't get product");
  if (h) {
    ErrNonFatalDisplayIf(StrLen(p.name) >= kMaxProductNameLength, "product name too
long");
    StrCopy(productName, p.name);
    MemHandleUnlock(h);
  }
}

// Open a database. If it doesn't exist, create it.
Err OpenOrCreateDB(DmOpenRef *dbP, UInt32 type, UInt32 creator,
  UInt16 mode, UInt16 cardNo, char *name, Boolean *created)
{
  Err err = errNone;

  *created = false;
  *dbP = DmOpenDatabaseByTypeCreator(type, creator, mode);
  if (! *dbP)
  {
    err = DmGetLastErr( );
    if (err == dmErrCantFind)
      err = DmCreateDatabase(cardNo, name, creator, type, false);
    if (err != errNone)
      return err;
    *created = true;

    *dbP = DmOpenDatabaseByTypeCreator(type, creator, mode);
    if (! *dbP)
      return DmGetLastErr( );
  }
  return err;
}
```

Exchange.c

```
/*
 Copyright (c) 1998-2001, Neil Rhodes and Julie McKeehan
    neil@pobox.com
 All rights reserved.

From the book "Palm OS Programming (2nd edition)"
by O'Reilly.

Permission granted to use this file however you see fit.
*/
#define DO_NOT_ALLOW_ACCESS_TO_INTERNALS_OF_STRUCTS
#include <BuildDefines.h>
#ifdef DEBUG_BUILD
#define ERROR_CHECK_LEVEL ERROR_CHECK_FULL
```

```
#endif
#include <PalmOS.h>
#include "Exchange.h"
#include "Common.h"

#define kAllCustomersName "All.cst"

// Read at most numBytes into a new record.
// Don't use very much dynamic RAM or stack space--another application is running.
static Err ReadIntoNewRecord(DmOpenRef db, ExgSocketPtr socketPtr,
  UInt32 numBytes, UInt16 *indexPtr)
{
  char    buffer[100];
  Err     err;
  UInt16  index = 0;
  UInt32  bytesReceived;
  MemHandle recHandle = NULL;
  Char    *recPtr;
  UInt32  recSize = 0;
  Boolean allocatedRecord = false;

  do {
    UInt32   numBytesToRead = sizeof(buffer);

    if (numBytesToRead > numBytes)
      numBytesToRead = numBytes;
    bytesReceived = ExgReceive(socketPtr, buffer, numBytesToRead, &err);
    numBytes -= bytesReceived;
    if (err == errNone) {
      if (!recHandle)
        recHandle = DmNewRecord(db, &index, bytesReceived);
      else
        recHandle = DmResizeRecord(db, index, recSize + bytesReceived);
      if (!recHandle) {
        err = DmGetLastErr();
        break;
      }
      allocatedRecord = true;
      recPtr = (Char *) MemHandleLock(recHandle);
      err = DmWrite(recPtr, recSize, buffer, bytesReceived);
      MemHandleUnlock(recHandle);
      recSize += bytesReceived;
    }
  } while (err == errNone && bytesReceived > 0 && numBytes > 0);

  if (recHandle) {
    DmReleaseRecord(db, index, true);
  }
  if (err != errNone && allocatedRecord)
    DmRemoveRecord(db, index);

  *indexPtr = index;
  return err;
}
```

```
Err ReceiveSentData(DmOpenRef db, ExgSocketPtr socketPtr)
{
  Err    err;
  UInt16    index;
  Boolean isSingleCustomer = true;
  Int32 newCustomerID = GetLowestCustomerID( ) - 1;

  // We have all customers if it has a name like:
  // "foo:all customers"
  // Otherwise, it's a single customer.
  if (socketPtr->name) {
    Char *colonLocation;

    colonLocation = StrChr(socketPtr->name, ':');
    if (colonLocation &&
      StrCompare(colonLocation + 1, kAllCustomersName) == 0)
      isSingleCustomer = false;
  }
  err = ExgAccept(socketPtr);
  if (err == errNone) {
    if (isSingleCustomer) {
      // One customer.
      err = ReadIntoNewRecord(db, socketPtr, 0xffffffff, &index);

      // Must assign a new unique customer ID.
      if (err == errNone) {
        MemHandle h = DmGetRecord(db, index);
        DmWrite(MemHandleLock(h), OffsetOf(Customer, customerID),
          &newCustomerID, sizeof(newCustomerID));
        MemHandleUnlock(h);
        DmReleaseRecord(db, index, true);
      }
    } else {
      // All customers.
      UInt16    numRecords;

      ExgReceive(socketPtr, &numRecords, sizeof(numRecords), &err);
      while (err == errNone && numRecords-- > 0) {
        UInt16 recordSize;

        ExgReceive(socketPtr, &recordSize, sizeof(recordSize), &err);
        if (err == errNone) {
          err = ReadIntoNewRecord(db, socketPtr, recordSize, &index);
          // Must assign a new unique customer ID.
          if (err == errNone) {
            MemHandle h = DmGetRecord(db, index);
            DmWrite(MemHandleLock(h),
              OffsetOf(Customer, customerID),
              &newCustomerID, sizeof(newCustomerID));
            newCustomerID--;
            MemHandleUnlock(h);
            DmReleaseRecord(db, index, true);
          }
        }
      }
    }
```

```
    }
    err = ExgDisconnect(socketPtr, err);
  }

  if (err == errNone) {
    DmRecordInfo(db, index, NULL, &socketPtr->goToParams.uniqueID, NULL);
    DmOpenDatabaseInfo(db, &socketPtr->goToParams.dbID,
      NULL, NULL, &socketPtr->goToParams.dbCardNo, NULL);
    socketPtr->goToParams.recordNum = index;
    socketPtr->goToCreator = kSalesCreator;
  }
  return err;
}

static Err SendBytes(ExgSocketPtr s, void *buffer, UInt32 bytesToSend)
{
  Err err = errNone;

  while (err == errNone && bytesToSend > 0) {
    UInt32 bytesSent = ExgSend(s, buffer, bytesToSend, &err);
    bytesToSend -= bytesSent;
    buffer = ((char *) buffer) + bytesSent;
  }
  return err;
}

void SendCustomer(UInt16 recordNumber, const Char *scheme)
{
  ExgSocketType s;
  MemHandle      theRecord = DmQueryRecord(gCustomerDB, recordNumber);
  PackedCustomer  *thePackedCustomer;
  Err       err;
  Char       name[50];

  thePackedCustomer = (PackedCustomer *) MemHandleLock(theRecord);
  MemSet(&s, sizeof(s), 0);
  s.description = thePackedCustomer->name;
  StrPrintF(name, "%s%s", scheme, "customer.cst");
  s.name = name;

  err = ExgPut(&s);
  if (err == errNone)
    err = SendBytes(&s, thePackedCustomer, MemHandleSize(theRecord));
  MemHandleUnlock(theRecord);
  err = ExgDisconnect(&s, err);
}

void SendAllCustomers(const Char *scheme)
{
  DmOpenRef dbP = gCustomerDB;
  UInt16     mode;
  LocalID    dbID;
  UInt16     cardNo;
  Boolean    databaseReopened;
  UInt16     numCustomers;
```

```
// If the database was opened to show secret records, reopen it to not
// see secret records. The idea is that secret records are not sent when
// a category is sent. They must be explicitly sent one by one.
DmOpenDatabaseInfo(dbP, &dbID, NULL, &mode, &cardNo, NULL);
if (mode & dmModeShowSecret) {
  dbP = DmOpenDatabase(cardNo, dbID, dmModeReadOnly);
  databaseReopened = true;
} else
  databaseReopened = false;

// We should send because there's at least one record to send.
if ((numCustomers = DmNumRecordsInCategory(dbP, dmAllCategories)) > 0) {
  ExgSocketType s;
  MemHandle     recHandle;
  Err           err;
  UInt16        index;
  Char          name[50];
  UInt16        i;

  MemSet(&s, sizeof(s), 0);
  s.description = "All customers";
  StrPrintF(name, "%s%s", scheme, kAllCustomersName);
  s.name = name;

  err = ExgPut(&s);
  if (err == errNone)
    err = SendBytes(&s, &numCustomers, sizeof(numCustomers));

  // Iterate through customers backward because we know we'll be adding
  // them at the beginning of the database when received. This way,
  // they'll end up in the right order when received.
  for (i = 0,index = dmMaxRecordIndex; err == errNone && i < numCustomers;
    i++, index--) {
    UInt16  numberToSeek = 0;

    err = DmSeekRecordInCategory(dbP, &index, numberToSeek,
      dmSeekBackward, dmAllCategories);
    if (err == errNone) {
      UInt16 recordSize;

      recHandle = DmQueryRecord(dbP, index);
      ErrNonFatalDisplayIf(!recHandle, "Couldn't query record");
      recordSize = (UInt16) MemHandleSize(recHandle);
      err = SendBytes(&s, &recordSize, sizeof(recordSize));
      if (err == errNone) {
        PackedCustomer *theRecord;

        theRecord = (PackedCustomer *) MemHandleLock(recHandle);
        err = SendBytes(&s, theRecord, MemHandleSize(recHandle));
        MemHandleUnlock(recHandle);
      }
    }
  }
  err = ExgDisconnect(&s, err);
```

```
      } else
        FrmAlert(NoDataToBeamAlert);

    if (databaseReopened)
      DmCloseDatabase(dbP);
  }
```

Item.c

```
/*
 Copyright (c) 1998-2001, Neil Rhodes and Julie McKeehan
    neil@pobox.com
 All rights reserved.

From the book "Palm OS Programming (2nd edition)"
by O'Reilly.

Permission granted to use this file however you see fit.
*/
#define DO_NOT_ALLOW_ACCESS_TO_INTERNALS_OF_STRUCTS
#include <BuildDefines.h>
#ifdef DEBUG_BUILD
#define ERROR_CHECK_LEVEL ERROR_CHECK_FULL
#endif

#include <PalmOS.h>
#include "Item.h"
#include "Common.h"
#include "Utils.h"
#include "SalesRsc.h"

static Item        *gItem;
static UInt32       gEditedProductID;
static Char         gProductName[kMaxProductNameLength];

static
void ItemFormOpen(void)
{
  ListPtr list;
  FormPtr form = FrmGetFormPtr(ItemForm);
  ControlPtr  control;
  FieldPtr field = (FieldPtr) GetObjectFromForm(form, ItemQuantityField);
  char  quantityString[kMaxNumericStringLength];

  // Initialize quantity.
  StrIToA(quantityString, (Int32) gItem->quantity);
  SetFieldTextFromStr(field, quantityString, false);

  // Select entire quantity (so it doesn't have to be selected before
  // writing a new quantity).
  FrmSetFocus(form, FrmGetObjectIndex(form, ItemQuantityField));
  FldSetSelection(field, 0, (UInt16) StrLen(quantityString));
```

```
      list = (ListPtr) GetObjectFromForm(form, ItemProductsList);
      LstSetDrawFunction(list, DrawOneProductInList);

      gEditedProductID = gItem->productID;
      control = (ControlPtr) GetObjectFromForm(form, ItemProductPopTrigger);
      if (gItem->productID) {
        Product p;
        MemHandle h;

        h = GetProductFromProductID(gItem->productID, &p, NULL);
        ErrNonFatalDisplayIf(!h, "can't get product for existing item");

        ErrNonFatalDisplayIf(StrLen(p.name) >= kMaxProductNameLength,
          "product name too long");
        StrCopy(gProductName, p.name);
        CtlSetLabel(control, gProductName);
        MemHandleUnlock(h);
      } else
        CtlSetLabel(control, kUnknownProductName);
    }

    static
    Boolean ItemHandleEvent(EventPtr event)
    {
      Boolean   handled = false;
      FieldPtr  fld;

      switch (event->eType) {
        case ctlSelectEvent:
          switch (event->data.ctlSelect.controlID) {
          case ItemOKButton:
            {
              char   *textPtr;
              UInt32  quantity;

              fld = (FieldPtr) GetObjectFromActiveForm(ItemQuantityField);
              textPtr = FldGetTextPtr(fld);
              ErrNonFatalDisplayIf(!textPtr, "No quantity text");
              quantity = (UInt32) StrAToI(textPtr);
              gItem->quantity = quantity;
              gItem->productID = gEditedProductID;
            }
            break;

          case ItemCancelButton:
            break;

          case ItemDeleteButton:
            if (FrmAlert(DeleteItemAlert) != DeleteItemOK)
              handled = true; // Don't allow further processing.
            break;
          }
          break;
```

```
          case ctlEnterEvent:
            if (event->data.ctlEnter.controlID == ItemProductPopTrigger)
              HandleProductPopupEnter(ItemProductPopTrigger, ItemProductsList,
                gEditedProductID);
            // handled = false;
            break;

          case popSelectEvent:
            if (event->data.ctlEnter.controlID == ItemProductPopTrigger){
              if (HandleProductPopupSelect(event, &gEditedProductID,
                gProductName))
                CtlSetLabel(event->data.popSelect.controlP, gProductName);
              handled = true;
              break;
            }
            break;
      }
    return handled;
}

// Returns true if modified.
Boolean EditItem(Item *item, Boolean *deleted)
{
  FormPtr frm = FrmInitForm(ItemForm);
  UInt16  hitButton;

  gItem = item;
  FrmSetEventHandler(frm, ItemHandleEvent);
  ItemFormOpen();

  hitButton = FrmDoDialog(frm);
  FrmDeleteForm(frm);
  if (hitButton == ItemCancelButton)
    return false;
  else {
    *deleted = (Boolean) (hitButton == ItemDeleteButton);
    return true;
  }
}
```

Order.c

```
/*
 Copyright (c) 1998-2001, Neil Rhodes and Julie McKeehan
    neil@pobox.com
 All rights reserved.

From the book "Palm OS Programming (2nd edition)"
by O'Reilly.

Permission granted to use this file however you see fit.
*/
//#define DO_NOT_ALLOW_ACCESS_TO_INTERNALS_OF_STRUCTS
```

```
#include <BuildDefines.h>
#ifdef DEBUG_BUILD
#define ERROR_CHECK_LEVEL ERROR_CHECK_FULL
#endif
#include <PalmOS.h>
#include <TxtGlue.h>
#include "Order.h"
#include "Item.h"
#include "Common.h"
#include "Utils.h"
#include "SalesRsc.h"
#include "Customer.h"
#include "Exchange.h"

// Columns in the table
#define kProductIDColumn     0
#define kProductNameColumn   1
#define kQuantityColumn      2


static Char gProductNames[OrderItemLastPopup - OrderItemFirstPopup +
1][kMaxProductNameLength];
static UInt16      gTopVisibleItem;      // Which item is in the first row
static Boolean     gRowSelected = false; // True if something is selected
static UInt16      gCurrentSelectedItemIndex;  // Which item  is selected
                                        // (meaningful only if
                                        // gRowSelected is true).
static Boolean     gCurrentOrderChanged;
static Char        *gFormTitle = NULL;

// Returns record number for order, if it exists, or where it
// should be inserted.
UInt16 OrderRecordNumber(Int32 customerID, Boolean *orderExists)
{
  Order    findRecord;
  UInt16   recordNumber;

  *orderExists = false;
  findRecord.customerID = customerID;
  recordNumber = DmFindSortPosition(gOrderDB, &findRecord, 0,
    (DmComparF *) CompareIDFunc, 0);

  if (recordNumber > 0) {
    Order *order;
    MemHandle theOrderHandle;
    Boolean foundIt;

    theOrderHandle = DmQueryRecord(gOrderDB, recordNumber - 1);
    ErrNonFatalDisplayIf(!theOrderHandle, "DMGetRecord failed!");

    order = (Order *) MemHandleLock(theOrderHandle);
    foundIt = (Boolean) (order->customerID == customerID);
    MemHandleUnlock(theOrderHandle);
    if (foundIt) {
```

```
      *orderExists = true;
      return recordNumber - 1;
    }
  }
  return recordNumber;
}

void OpenCustomerWithID(Int32 customerID)
{
  if ((gCurrentOrder =  GetOrCreateOrderForCustomer(
    customerID, &gCurrentOrderIndex)) != NULL)
    FrmGotoForm(OrderForm);
}

Boolean OrderExistsForCustomer(Int32 customerID)
{
  Boolean orderExists;

  OrderRecordNumber(customerID, &orderExists);
  return orderExists;
}

// Returns true if successful. itemNumber is location at which it was
// added
static
Boolean AddNewItem(UInt16 *itemNumber)
{
  MemHandle theOrderHandle;
  UInt16  numItems;
  Item  newItem = {0, 0};
  MemHandle oldHandle;

  ErrFatalDisplayIf(!gCurrentOrder, "no current order");
  theOrderHandle = MemPtrRecoverHandle(gCurrentOrder);
  MemHandleUnlock(theOrderHandle);

  oldHandle = theOrderHandle;
  theOrderHandle = DmResizeRecord(gOrderDB, gCurrentOrderIndex,
    MemHandleSize(theOrderHandle) + sizeof(Item));
  if (!theOrderHandle) {
    gCurrentOrder = (Order *) MemHandleLock(oldHandle);
    FrmAlert(DeviceIsFullAlert);
    return false;
  }
  gCurrentOrder = (Order *) MemHandleLock(theOrderHandle);
  numItems = gCurrentOrder->numItems + 1;
  DmWrite(gCurrentOrder, OffsetOf(Order, numItems), &numItems,
    sizeof(numItems));
  *itemNumber = gCurrentOrder->numItems - 1;
  DmWrite(gCurrentOrder, OffsetOf(Order, items[*itemNumber]), &newItem,
    sizeof(newItem));
  gCurrentOrderChanged = true;
  return true;
}
```

```
Order *GetOrCreateOrderForCustomer(Int32 customerID,
  UInt16 *recordNumPtr)
{
  MemHandle theOrderHandle;
  Order    *order;
  Boolean exists;

  *recordNumPtr = OrderRecordNumber(customerID, &exists);
  if (exists) {
    theOrderHandle = DmGetRecord(gOrderDB, *recordNumPtr);
    ErrNonFatalDisplayIf(!theOrderHandle, "DMGetRecord failed!");
    order = (Order *) MemHandleLock(theOrderHandle);
  } else {
    Order o;
    theOrderHandle = DmNewRecord(gOrderDB, recordNumPtr, sizeof(Order));
    if (!theOrderHandle) {
      FrmAlert(DeviceIsFullAlert);
      return NULL;
    }
    o.numItems = 0;
    o.customerID = customerID;
    order = (Order *) MemHandleLock(theOrderHandle);
    DmWrite(order, 0, &o, sizeof(o));
  }
  return order;
}

static UInt16 GetRecordNumberForCustomer(Int32 customerID)
{
  UInt16       recordNumber;
  PackedCustomer  findRecord;
  PackedCustomer  *packedCustomer;
  MemHandle     theCustomerHandle;

  findRecord.customerID = customerID;
  recordNumber = DmFindSortPosition(gCustomerDB, &findRecord, 0,
    (DmComparF *) CompareIDFunc, 0);

  ErrNonFatalDisplayIf(recordNumber == 0, "Can't find customer");

  theCustomerHandle = DmQueryRecord(gCustomerDB, recordNumber - 1);
  ErrNonFatalDisplayIf(!theCustomerHandle, "DMGetRecord failed!");

  packedCustomer = (PackedCustomer *) MemHandleLock(theCustomerHandle);
  ErrNonFatalDisplayIf(packedCustomer->customerID != customerID,
    "Can't find customer");
  MemHandleUnlock(theCustomerHandle);
  return recordNumber - 1;
}

static
void ShowHideIndex(FormPtr form, UInt16 objIndex, Boolean show)
{
  if (show)
```

```
      FrmShowObject(form, objIndex);
    else
      FrmHideObject(form, objIndex);
}

static
void ShowHideRow(FormPtr form, UInt16 row, Boolean show)
{
  ShowHideIndex(form, FrmGetObjectIndex(form, row + OrderItemFirstField),
    show);
  ShowHideIndex(form, FrmGetObjectIndex(form, row + OrderItemFirstPopup),
    show);
}

FieldPtr  *gFields;
UInt16    gNumRows;
UInt16    gNumVisibleRows;

static
FieldPtr GetFieldForRow(UInt16 row)
{
  return gFields[row];
}


static
UInt16 RowNumberToPopupID(UInt16 rowNumber)
{
  return rowNumber + OrderItemFirstPopup;
}


static
ControlPtr GetPopupForRow(UInt16 rowNumber)
{
  return (ControlPtr) GetObjectFromActiveForm(RowNumberToPopupID(rowNumber));
}

static void SetPopupName( )
{
}

static
void InitRow(UInt16 row, UInt16 itemIndex, Boolean redraw)
{
  Char    buffer[kMaxNumericStringLength + 1];
  ControlPtr  popup;
  UInt32     productID;

  StrIToA(buffer, (Int32) gCurrentOrder->items[itemIndex].quantity);
  SetFieldTextFromStr(GetFieldForRow(row), buffer, redraw);

  popup = GetPopupForRow(row);
```

```
  productID = gCurrentOrder->items[itemIndex].productID;
  if (productID)
    GetProductNameFromProductID(productID, gProductNames[row]);
  else
    StrCopy(gProductNames[row], kUnknownProductName);
  CtlSetLabel(popup, gProductNames[row]);
}

static UInt16 ItemNumberToRowNumber(UInt16 itemNumber)
{
  return itemNumber - gTopVisibleItem;
}

static UInt16 RowNumberToItemNumber(UInt16 rowNumber)
{
  return rowNumber + gTopVisibleItem;
}

static
FieldPtr GetCurrentField(void)
{
  if (gRowSelected) {
    FieldPtr field =
GetFieldForRow(ItemNumberToRowNumber(gCurrentSelectedItemIndex));
    ErrNonFatalDisplayIf(field == NULL, "row selected, but no current field");
    return field;
  }
  else
    return NULL;
}
static void SaveCurrentField(void)
{
  FieldPtr field;
  Boolean  dirty;

  ErrNonFatalDisplayIf(!gRowSelected, "a row should be selected!");

  field = GetCurrentField( );

  dirty = FldDirty(field);

  if (dirty) {
    Char  *textP = FldGetTextPtr(field);
    UInt32 newQuantity = 0;

    if (textP)
      newQuantity = (UInt32) StrAToI(textP);
    DmWrite(gCurrentOrder,
      OffsetOf(Order, items[gCurrentSelectedItemIndex].quantity),
      &newQuantity, sizeof(newQuantity));
    gCurrentOrderChanged = true;
  }
}

static UInt16 GetLastPossibleTopItem( )
```

```
{
  if (gCurrentOrder->numItems > gNumRows)
    return gCurrentOrder->numItems - gNumRows;
  else
    return 0;
}

static
void DeselectRow(Boolean removeFocus)
{
  if (removeFocus)
    FrmSetFocus(FrmGetActiveForm( ), noFocus);
  gRowSelected = false;
}

static void SelectItem(UInt16 itemNumber);

static
void LoadFields(Boolean redraw)
{
  FormPtr    form = FrmGetActiveForm( );
  UInt16     row;
  UInt16     lastPossibleTopItem = GetLastPossibleTopItem( );
  Boolean    hadFocus = false;
  UInt16     focusedItem;

  // If we have a currently selected item, make sure that it is visible.
  if (gRowSelected)
    if (gCurrentSelectedItemIndex < gTopVisibleItem ||
      gCurrentSelectedItemIndex >= gTopVisibleItem + gNumRows) {

      hadFocus = true;
      focusedItem = RowNumberToItemNumber(gCurrentSelectedItemIndex);
      DeselectRow(true);
      gTopVisibleItem = gCurrentSelectedItemIndex;
  }

  // Scroll up as necessary to display an entire page of info.
  if (gTopVisibleItem > lastPossibleTopItem)
    gTopVisibleItem = lastPossibleTopItem;

  gNumVisibleRows = gCurrentOrder->numItems - gTopVisibleItem;
  if (gNumVisibleRows > gNumRows)
    gNumVisibleRows = gNumRows;
  for (row = 0; row < gNumVisibleRows; row++) {
      ShowHideRow(form, row, true);
      InitRow(row, row + gTopVisibleItem, redraw);
  }
  for (row = gNumVisibleRows; row < gNumRows; row++)
      ShowHideRow(form, row, false);
  SclSetScrollBar(
    (ScrollBarPtr) GetObjectFromForm(form, OrderScrollbarScrollBar),
    (Int16) gTopVisibleItem, 0, (Int16) lastPossibleTopItem,
    (Int16) gNumRows - 1);
```

```
  if (hadFocus)
    SelectItem(focusedItem);
}

static
UInt16 RowNumberToFieldID(UInt16 rowNumber)
{
  return rowNumber + OrderItemFirstField;
}

static
void SelectItem(UInt16 itemNumber)
{
  FormPtr form;
  UInt16  fieldIndex;
  FieldPtr  field;

  ErrFatalDisplayIf(gRowSelected, "row already selected");
  gRowSelected = true;
  gCurrentSelectedItemIndex = itemNumber;
  if (itemNumber < gTopVisibleItem ||
    itemNumber >= gTopVisibleItem + gNumVisibleRows) {
    UInt16    lastPossibleTopItem = GetLastPossibleTopItem( );

    gTopVisibleItem = itemNumber;
    if (gTopVisibleItem < lastPossibleTopItem)
      gTopVisibleItem = lastPossibleTopItem;
    LoadFields(true);
  }
  form = FrmGetActiveForm( );
  fieldIndex = FrmGetObjectIndex(form,
    RowNumberToFieldID(ItemNumberToRowNumber(itemNumber)));
  FrmSetFocus(form, fieldIndex);
  field = GetCurrentField( );
    // Select all the text for easy typing.
  FldSetSelection(field, 0, FldGetTextLength(field));
}

static
Boolean OrderDeselectRowAndDeleteIfEmptyHelper(Boolean removeFocus)
{
  Boolean    empty;

  if (!gRowSelected)
    return false;

  SaveCurrentField( );

  // If the item ID is 0, delete the item.
  empty = (Boolean)
    (gCurrentOrder->items[gCurrentSelectedItemIndex].productID == 0);

  if (empty) {
    gCurrentOrderChanged = true;
    DeleteNthItem(gCurrentSelectedItemIndex);
```

```
      LoadFields(true);
    }
    DeselectRow(removeFocus);

    return empty;
}

// Returns true if some item (other than that in index) matches the
// given product ID. If true, return sthe index that matches.
static Boolean ProductIDExistsInOrder(UInt32 productID, UInt16 *index)
{
    UInt16  i;

    for (i = 0; i < gCurrentOrder->numItems; i++) {
        if (gCurrentOrder->items[i].productID == productID && i != *index) {
            *index = i;
            return true;
        }
    }
    return false;
}

static Boolean OrderDeselectRowAndDeleteIfEmpty(void)
{
    return OrderDeselectRowAndDeleteIfEmptyHelper(true);
}

static Boolean OrderDeselectRowAndDeleteIfEmptyButDontRemoveFocus(void)
{
    return OrderDeselectRowAndDeleteIfEmptyHelper(false);
}

static void OrderScrollRows(Int16 numRows)
{
    Int32 newVisible = gTopVisibleItem + (Int32) numRows;

    if (newVisible < 0)
        gTopVisibleItem = 0;
    else
        gTopVisibleItem = (UInt16) newVisible;
    LoadFields(true);
}

static void OrderSetTitle()
{
    MemHandle customerHandle;
    Customer  theCustomer;
    FormPtr   form = FrmGetActiveForm();
    Char      *newTitle;
    MemHandle titleParamHandle;

    customerHandle = DmQueryRecord(gCustomerDB,
        GetRecordNumberForCustomer(gCurrentOrder->customerID));
    UnpackCustomer(&theCustomer,
        (PackedCustomer *) MemHandleLock(customerHandle));
```

```
    titleParamHandle = DmGetResource(strRsc, OrderTitleString);
    newTitle = TxtGlueParamString((Char *) MemHandleLock(titleParamHandle),
      theCustomer.name, NULL, NULL, NULL);
    MemHandleUnlock(titleParamHandle);
    ErrFatalDisplayIf(!newTitle, "can't allocate memory");
    MemHandleUnlock(customerHandle);
    FrmSetTitle(form, newTitle);
    // Don't free until *after* calling FrmSetTitle
    // (because until then form still has the old title).
    if (gFormTitle)
      MemPtrFree(gFormTitle);
    gFormTitle = newTitle;
}

static
void OrderFormOpen(FormPtr form)
{
  UInt16    i;

  gNumRows = OrderItemLastField - OrderItemFirstField + 1;

  gFields = (FieldPtr *) MemPtrNew(sizeof(FieldPtr) * gNumRows);
  ErrFatalDisplayIf(!gFields, "can't allocate memory");
  for (i = 0; i < gNumRows; i++)
    gFields[i] = (FieldPtr) GetObjectFromForm(form, OrderItemFirstField + i);
  gRowSelected = false;
  gCurrentOrderChanged = false;
  gTopVisibleItem = 0;
  LoadFields(false);
  LstSetDrawFunction((ListPtr) GetObjectFromForm(form, OrderProductsList),
    DrawOneProductInList);

  OrderSetTitle( );
}

static void OrderFormClose(void)
{
  UInt16    numItems;
  MemHandle theOrderHandle;
  OrderDeselectRowAndDeleteIfEmpty( );
  numItems = gCurrentOrder->numItems;
  // Unlock the order.
  theOrderHandle = MemPtrRecoverHandle(gCurrentOrder);
  MemHandleUnlock(theOrderHandle);

  // Delete order if it is empty; release it back to the database otherwise.
  if (numItems == 0)
    DmRemoveRecord(gOrderDB, gCurrentOrderIndex);
  else
    DmReleaseRecord(gOrderDB, gCurrentOrderIndex, gCurrentOrderChanged);

  MemPtrFree(gFields);

  // Free parameterized handle.
```

```
  MemPtrFree(gFormTitle);
  gFormTitle = NULL;
#ifdef DEBUG_BUILD
  CheckDatabases(false);
#endif
}

static Boolean OrderHandleMenuEvent(UInt16 menuID)
{
  Boolean handled = false;
  UInt16  zero = 0;

  switch (menuID) {
  case RecordDeleteItem:
    if (!gRowSelected)
      FrmAlert(NoItemSelectedAlert);
    else {
      UInt16 itemNumToDelete = gCurrentSelectedItemIndex;
      MenuEraseStatus(0); // Because we'll turn off insertion point when
                          // deselecting; command bar will then restore it!
      if (OrderDeselectRowAndDeleteIfEmpty()) {
        // It was an empty row anyway, don't bother them.
      } else if (FrmAlert(DeleteItemAlert) == DeleteItemOK) {
        DeleteNthItem(itemNumToDelete);
        gCurrentOrderChanged = true;
        LoadFields(true);
      }
    }
    handled = true;
    break;

  case RecordCustomerDetails:
    {
      Boolean deleted;

      EditCustomer(GetRecordNumberForCustomer(gCurrentOrder->customerID),
        false, &deleted);
      if (deleted) {
        // OrderCloseForm will remove order associated with this customer as
        // long as we set the numItems to 0.
        OrderDeselectRowAndDeleteIfEmpty(); // This may decrement numItems.
        DmWrite(gCurrentOrder, OffsetOf(Order, numItems), &zero,
          sizeof(zero));
          FrmGotoForm(CustomersForm);
      }
      else
        OrderSetTitle();
    }
    handled = true;
    break;

  case RecordBeamCustomer:
    SendCustomer(GetRecordNumberForCustomer(
      gCurrentOrder->customerID),  exgBeamPrefix);
```

```
        handled = true;
        break;

      case RecordSendCustomer:
        SendCustomer(GetRecordNumberForCustomer(
          gCurrentOrder->customerID), exgSendPrefix);
        handled = true;
        break;

      case RecordDeleteCustomer:
        if (AskDeleteCustomer( )) {
          UInt16   recordNumber =
            GetRecordNumberForCustomer(gCurrentOrder->customerID);

          if (gSaveBackup) {   // Archive it on PC.
            DmArchiveRecord(gCustomerDB, recordNumber);
          } else {
            DmDeleteRecord(gCustomerDB, recordNumber);
          }
          // Deleted records are stored at the end of the database.
          DmMoveRecord(gCustomerDB, recordNumber, DmNumRecords(gCustomerDB));

          // OrderCloseForm will remove order associated with this customer as
          // long as we set the numItems to 0.
          OrderDeselectRowAndDeleteIfEmpty( ); //  This may decrement numItems.
          DmWrite(gCurrentOrder, OffsetOf(Order, numItems), &zero,
            sizeof(zero));
          FrmGotoForm(CustomersForm);
        }
        break;
    }
    return handled;
}


static Boolean OrderHandleKey(EventPtr event)
{
  UInt16   c = event->data.keyDown.chr;
  Boolean handled = false;

  if (TxtGlueCharIsVirtual(event->data.keyDown.modifiers,
    event->data.keyDown.chr)) {
    // Bottom-to-top screen gesture can cause this, depending on
    // configuration in Prefs/Buttons/Pen.
    if (c == vchrSendData)
      handled = OrderHandleMenuEvent(RecordBeamCustomer);
    else if (c == vchrPageUp || c == vchrPageDown) {
      Int16 numRowsToScroll = (Int16) gNumRows;

      OrderDeselectRowAndDeleteIfEmpty( );
      if (c == vchrPageUp)
        numRowsToScroll = -numRowsToScroll;
      OrderScrollRows(numRowsToScroll);
      handled = true;
    }
```

```
    } else if (c == linefeedChr) {
      // The return character takes us out of edit mode.
      OrderDeselectRowAndDeleteIfEmpty();
      handled = true;
    } else if (!gRowSelected && TxtGlueCharIsAlNum(c) &&
      !TxtGlueCharIsAlpha(c)) {
      // We can't use TxtGlueCharIsDigit(c) in 4.0 SDK
      // because the macro is broken.
      UInt16  itemNumber;

      if (AddNewItem(&itemNumber)) {
        SelectItem(itemNumber);
        // handled = false; // Pass it through to the field.
      }
    }
  }
  return handled;
}

Boolean OrderHandleEvent(EventPtr event)
{
  Boolean   handled = false;
  FormPtr   form;
  FieldPtr  field;
  Char      productName[kMaxProductNameLength];

  switch (event->eType) {
  case ctlEnterEvent:
    if (event->data.ctlSelect.controlID >= OrderItemFirstPopup &&
      event->data.ctlSelect.controlID <= OrderItemLastPopup) {
      UInt16 row = event->data.ctlSelect.controlID - OrderItemFirstPopup;
      if (! (gRowSelected && RowNumberToItemNumber(row) ==
gCurrentSelectedItemIndex)) {
        OrderDeselectRowAndDeleteIfEmpty();
        SelectItem(RowNumberToItemNumber(row));
      }
      HandleProductPopupEnter(event->data.ctlSelect.controlID, OrderProductsList,
        gCurrentOrder->items[gCurrentSelectedItemIndex].productID);
      //handled = false;  // Still want the pop-up to occur.
    }
    break;

  case popSelectEvent:
    if (event->data.popSelect.controlID >= OrderItemFirstPopup &&
      event->data.popSelect.controlID <= OrderItemLastPopup) {
      UInt32  productID;
      UInt16  row;
      Char    newProductName[kMaxProductNameLength];

      row = event->data.popSelect.controlID - OrderItemFirstPopup;
      if (HandleProductPopupSelect(event, &productID, newProductName)) {
        UInt16  oldItemIndex = RowNumberToItemNumber(row);
        UInt16  itemIndex = oldItemIndex;

        SaveCurrentField();
```

```
    if (ProductIDExistsInOrder(productID, &itemIndex)) {
      GetProductNameFromProductID(productID,
        productName);
      if (FrmCustomAlert(ProductExistsAlert, productName, NULL, NULL)
        != ProductExistsCancel) {
        UInt32  newItemTotal;
        DeselectRow(true);

        newItemTotal = gCurrentOrder->items[itemIndex].quantity +
          gCurrentOrder->items[oldItemIndex].quantity;
        DmWrite(gCurrentOrder, OffsetOf(Order, items[itemIndex].quantity),
          &newItemTotal, sizeof(newItemTotal));
        DeleteNthItem(oldItemIndex);
        LoadFields(true); // Remove deleted row from screen.
        if (oldItemIndex < itemIndex)
          itemIndex--;  // Because we've removed an item before this one.
        SelectItem(itemIndex);
      }
    } else {
      DmWrite(gCurrentOrder,
        OffsetOf(Order,
        items[gCurrentSelectedItemIndex].productID),
        &productID,
        sizeof(productID));
      StrCopy(gProductNames[row], newProductName);
      CtlSetLabel(event->data.popSelect.controlP, gProductNames[row]);
    }
    gCurrentOrderChanged = true;
  }
  handled = true;
  }
  break;

case menuCmdBarOpenEvent:
  field = GetCurrentField();
  if (field)
    FldHandleEvent(field, event);
  if (gRowSelected) {
    // Add Beam and delete.
    MenuCmdBarAddButton(menuCmdBarOnRight, BarDeleteBitmap,
      menuCmdBarResultMenuItem, RecordDeleteItem, 0);
    MenuCmdBarAddButton(menuCmdBarOnLeft, BarBeamBitmap,
      menuCmdBarResultMenuItem, RecordBeamCustomer, 0);
  }
  // Field buttons have already been added.
  event->data.menuCmdBarOpen.preventFieldButtons = true;
  // Don't set handled to true; this event must fall through to the system.
  break;

case ctlSelectEvent:
  switch (event->data.ctlSelect.controlID) {
    case OrderNewButton:
    {
      UInt16  itemNumber;
```

```
        OrderDeselectRowAndDeleteIfEmpty( );
        if (AddNewItem(&itemNumber)) {
          SelectItem(itemNumber);
        }
      }
      handled = true;
        break;
      case OrderDoneButton:
        FrmGotoForm(CustomersForm);
      handled = true;
        break;
      case OrderDetailsButton:
        if (!gRowSelected)
          FrmAlert(NoItemSelectedAlert);
        else {
          UInt16  indexToShow = gCurrentSelectedItemIndex;
          Boolean deleteItem;
          Item    item;

          SaveCurrentField( );
          item = gCurrentOrder->items[gCurrentSelectedItemIndex];
          if (EditItem(&item, &deleteItem)) {
            gCurrentOrderChanged = true;
            if (deleteItem) {
              DeleteNthItem(gCurrentSelectedItemIndex);
              DeselectRow(true);
              LoadFields(true);
            } else {
              UInt16  oldItemIndex = gCurrentSelectedItemIndex;
              UInt16  itemIndex = oldItemIndex;

              if (ProductIDExistsInOrder(item.productID, &itemIndex)) {
                GetProductNameFromProductID(item.productID,
                  productName);
                if (FrmCustomAlert(ProductExistsAlert, productName, NULL, NULL)
                  != ProductExistsCancel) {
                  UInt32  newItemTotal;

                  DeselectRow(true);
                  newItemTotal = gCurrentOrder->items[itemIndex].quantity +
                    item.quantity;
                  DmWrite(gCurrentOrder, OffsetOf(Order, items[itemIndex].quantity),
                    &newItemTotal, sizeof(newItemTotal));
                  DeleteNthItem(oldItemIndex);
                  LoadFields(true); // Remove deleted row from screen.
                  if (oldItemIndex < itemIndex)
                    itemIndex--;  // Because we've removed an item before this one
                  SelectItem(itemIndex);
                }
              } else {
                DmWrite(gCurrentOrder, OffsetOf(Order,
                  items[gCurrentSelectedItemIndex]), &item,
                  sizeof(item));
```

```
            LoadFields(true);
        }
      }
    }
  }
  handled = true;
  break;
}
break;

case fldEnterEvent:
{
    // We can't remove the focus because the focus has already changed!
    // However, if item is already selected, do nothing.
    UInt16 itemNumber =
      RowNumberToItemNumber(event->data.fldEnter.fieldID - OrderItemFirstField);
    if (! (gRowSelected && gCurrentSelectedItemIndex == itemNumber)) {
      OrderDeselectRowAndDeleteIfEmptyButDontRemoveFocus( );
      SelectItem(itemNumber);
    }
}
break;

case keyDownEvent:
  handled = OrderHandleKey(event);
  break;

case sclRepeatEvent:
  OrderDeselectRowAndDeleteIfEmpty( );
  OrderScrollRows(event->data.sclRepeat.newValue -
    event->data.sclRepeat.value);
  handled = false;   // Scrollbar needs to handle the event too.
  break;

case frmOpenEvent:
  form = FrmGetActiveForm( );
  OrderFormOpen(form);
  FrmDrawForm(form);
  handled = true;
  break;

case frmCloseEvent:
  OrderFormClose( );
  handled = false;
  break;

case menuOpenEvent:
  // Send only supported on 4.0 and later.
  if (sysGetROMVerMajor(GetRomVersion( )) >= 4) {
    MemHandle h = DmGetResource(strRsc, SendCustomerString);
    if (h) {
      MenuAddItem(RecordBeamCustomer, RecordSendCustomer, '\0',
        (Char *) MemHandleLock(h));
```

```
      MemHandleUnlock(h);
    }
  }
  handled = true;
  break;

case frmSaveEvent:
  OrderDeselectRowAndDeleteIfEmpty( );
  handled = false;

case menuEvent:
  handled = OrderHandleMenuEvent(event->data.menu.itemID);
}
return handled;
}
```

Sales.c

```
/*
 Copyright (c) 1998-2001, Neil Rhodes and Julie McKeehan
    neil@pobox.com
 All rights reserved.

From the book "Palm OS Programming (2nd edition)" by O'Reilly.

Permission granted to use this file however you see fit.
*/
#define DO_NOT_ALLOW_ACCESS_TO_INTERNALS_OF_STRUCTS
#include <BuildDefines.h>
#ifdef DEBUG_BUILD
#define ERROR_CHECK_LEVEL ERROR_CHECK_FULL
#endif
#include <PalmOS.h>

#include "Utils.h"
#include "Exchange.h"
#include "Customers.h"
#include "Customer.h"
#include "Common.h"
#include "Item.h"
#include "Order.h"
#include "SalesRsc.h"
#include "Data.h"


#define kSalesPrefID      0x00
#define kSalesVersion     0x00
#define kCustomerDBType   'DATA'
#define kCustomerDBName   "Customers-SLES"
#define kOrderDBType      'Ordr'
#define kOrderDBName      "Orders-SLES"
#define kProductDBType    'Prod'
#define kProductDBName    "Products-SLES"
```

```
Order        *gCurrentOrder;
UInt16       gCurrentOrderIndex;
UInt16       gCurrentCategory = 0;
UInt16       gNumCategories;
privateRecordViewEnum    gPrivateRecordStatus;

typedef struct {
  Boolean      saveBackup;
} SalesPreferenceType;

// gCurrentOrder changes after this routine. gCurrentItem is no longer valid.
void DeleteNthItem(UInt16 itemNumber)
{
  UInt16     newNumItems;

  ErrNonFatalDisplayIf(itemNumber >= gCurrentOrder->numItems,
    "bad itemNumber");

  // Move items from itemNumber+1..numItems down 1 to:
  // itemNumber .. numItems - 1
  if (itemNumber < gCurrentOrder->numItems - 1)
    DmWrite(gCurrentOrder,
      OffsetOf(Order, items[itemNumber]),
      &gCurrentOrder->items[itemNumber+1],
      (gCurrentOrder->numItems - itemNumber - 1) * sizeof(Item));

  // Decrement numItems;
  newNumItems = gCurrentOrder->numItems - 1;
  DmWrite(gCurrentOrder,
    OffsetOf(Order, numItems), &newNumItems, sizeof(newNumItems));

  // Resize the pointer smaller. We could use MemPtrRecoverHandle,
  // MemHandleUnlock, MemHandleResize, MemHandleLock.
  // However, MemPtrResize will always work
  // as long as your are making a chunk smaller.  Thanks, Bob!
  MemPtrResize(gCurrentOrder,
    OffsetOf(Order, items[gCurrentOrder->numItems]));
}

static void InitializeCustomers(void)
{
  Customer  c1 = {1, "Joe's toys-1", "123 Main St." ,"Anytown",
    "(123) 456-7890"};
  Customer  c2 = {2, "Bucket of Toys-2", "" ,"", ""};
  Customer  c3 = {3, "Toys we be-3", "" ,"", ""};
  Customer  c4 = {4, "a", "" ,"", ""};
  Customer  c5 = {5, "b", "" ,"", ""};
  Customer  c6 = {6, "c", "" ,"", ""};
  Customer  c7 = {7, "d", "" ,"", ""};
  Customer *customers[7];
  UInt16  numCustomers = sizeof(customers) / sizeof(customers[0]);
  UInt16  i;

  customers[0] = &c1;
  customers[1] = &c2;
```

```
    customers[2] = &c3;
    customers[3] = &c4;
    customers[4] = &c5;
    customers[5] = &c6;
    customers[6] = &c7;
    for (i = 0; i < numCustomers; i++) {
      UInt16  index = dmMaxRecordIndex;
      MemHandle h = DmNewRecord(gCustomerDB, &index, 1);
      if (h) {
        PackCustomer(customers[i], h);
        DmReleaseRecord(gCustomerDB, index, true);
      }
    }
}

static void InitializeProducts(void)
{
#define kMaxPerCategory 4
#define kNumCategories 3
    Product prod1 = {125, 253 ,"GI-Joe"};
    Product prod2 = {135, 1122 ,"Barbie"};
    Product prod3 = {145, 752 ,"Ken"};
    Product prod4 = {9,   852 ,"Skipper"};
    Product prod5 = {126, 253 ,"Kite"};
    Product prod6 = {127, 350 , "Silly-Putty"};
    Product prod7 = {138, 650 ,"Yo-yo"};
    Product prod8 = {199, 950 ,"Legos"};
    Product prod9 = {120, 999 ,"Monopoly"};
    Product prod10= {129, 888 , "Yahtzee"};
    Product prod11= {10, 899 ,  "Life"};
    Product prod12= {20, 1199 ,"Battleship"};
    Product *products[kNumCategories][kMaxPerCategory];
    UInt16  i;
    UInt16  j;
    MemHandle h;

    products[0][0] = &prod1;
    products[0][1] = &prod2;
    products[0][2] = &prod3;
    products[0][3] = &prod4;
    products[1][0] = &prod5;
    products[1][1] = &prod6;
    products[1][2] = &prod7;
    products[1][3] = &prod8;
    products[2][0] = &prod9;
    products[2][1] = &prod10;
    products[2][2] = &prod11;
    products[2][3] = &prod12;
    for (i = 0; i < kNumCategories; i++) {
      for (j = 0; j < kMaxPerCategory && products[i][j]->name; j++) {
        UInt16       index;
        PackedProduct findRecord;
        MemHandle    h;
```

```
      findRecord.productID = products[i][j]->productID;
      index = DmFindSortPosition(gProductDB, &findRecord, 0,
        (DmComparF* ) CompareIDFunc, 0);
      h = DmNewRecord(gProductDB, &index, 1);
      if (h) {
        UInt16  attr;
        // Set the category of the new record to the category it
        // belongs in.
        DmRecordInfo(gProductDB, index, &attr, NULL, NULL);
        attr &= (UInt16) ~dmRecAttrCategoryMask;
        attr |= (UInt16) i;      // Category is kept in low bits of attr.

        DmSetRecordInfo(gProductDB, index, &attr, NULL);
        PackProduct(products[i][j], h);
        DmReleaseRecord(gProductDB, index, true);
      }
    }
  }

  h = DmNewHandle(gProductDB,
    OffsetOf(CategoriesStruct, names[kNumCategories]));
  if (h) {
    char  *categories[] = {"Dolls", "Toys", "Games"};
    CategoriesStruct  *c = (CategoriesStruct *) MemHandleLock(h);
    LocalID      dbID;
    LocalID      appInfoID;
    UInt16       cardNo;
    UInt16       num = kNumCategories;
    Err          err;

    DmWrite(c, OffsetOf(CategoriesStruct, numCategories), &num,
      sizeof(num));
    for (i = 0; i < kNumCategories; i++)
      DmStrCopy(c,
        OffsetOf(CategoriesStruct, names[i]), categories[i]);
        MemHandleUnlock(h);
    appInfoID = MemHandleToLocalID( h);
    err = DmOpenDatabaseInfo(gProductDB, &dbID, NULL, NULL,
      &cardNo, NULL);
    if (err == errNone) {
      err = DmSetDatabaseInfo(cardNo, dbID, NULL, NULL, NULL, NULL,
        NULL, NULL, NULL, &appInfoID, NULL, NULL, NULL);
      ErrNonFatalDisplayIf(err, "DmSetDatabaseInfo failed");
    }
  }
}

static void InitializeOrders(void)
{
  Item item1 = {125, 253};
  Item item2 = {145, 999};
  Item item3 = {135, 888};
  Item item4 = {9, 777};
  Item item5 = {10, 6};
```

```
    Item item6 =  {20, 5};
    Item item7 =  {120, 5};
    Item item8 =  {126,  3};
    Item item9 =  {127,   45};
    Item item10 = {129, 66};
    Item item11 = {138, 75};
    Item item12 = {199, 23};
    Item items[12];
    MemHandle h;
    Order   *order;
    UInt16  recordNum;
    UInt16  numItems = sizeof(items) / sizeof(items[0]);

    items[0] =   item1;
    items[1] =   item2;
    items[2] =   item3;
    items[3] =   item4;
    items[4] =   item5;
    items[5] =   item6;
    items[6] =   item7;
    items[7] =   item8;
    items[8] =   item9;
    items[9] =   item10;
    items[10] = item11;
    items[11] = item12;

    order= GetOrCreateOrderForCustomer(1, &recordNum);

    // Write numItems.
    DmWrite(order, OffsetOf(Order, numItems), &numItems, sizeof(numItems));

    // Resize to hold more items.
    h = MemPtrRecoverHandle(order);
    MemHandleUnlock(h);
    MemHandleResize(h, OffsetOf(Order, items) + sizeof(Item) * numItems);
    order = (Order *) MemHandleLock(h);

    // Write new items.
    DmWrite(order, OffsetOf(Order, items), items, sizeof(items));

    // Done with it.
    MemHandleUnlock(h);
    DmReleaseRecord(gOrderDB, recordNum, true);
}

static Err AppStart(void)
{
    SalesPreferenceType prefs;
    UInt16              prefsSize;
    UInt16              mode = dmModeReadWrite;
    Err                 err = errNone;
    CategoriesStruct    *c;
    Boolean             created;
```

```
  // Read the preferences / saved-state information. There is only one
  // version of the preferences, so don't worry about multiple
  // versions.
  prefsSize = sizeof(SalesPreferenceType);
  if (PrefGetAppPreferences(kSalesCreator, kSalesPrefID, &prefs,
    &prefsSize, true) == noPreferenceFound) {
    // POSE doesn't send sysAppLaunchCmdSyncNotify launch code, so
    // we may not already be registered.
    ExgRegisterData(kSalesCreator, exgRegExtensionID, "cst");
  } else {
     gSaveBackup = prefs.saveBackup;
  }

  // Determmime if secret records should be shown.
  if (Has35FeatureSet())
    gPrivateRecordStatus =
      (privateRecordViewEnum) PrefGetPreference(prefShowPrivateRecords);
  else {
    if (PrefGetPreference(prefHidePrivateRecordsV33))
      gPrivateRecordStatus = hidePrivateRecords;
   else
      gPrivateRecordStatus = showPrivateRecords;
  }
  if (gPrivateRecordStatus != hidePrivateRecords)
    mode |= dmModeShowSecret;

  // Find the Customer database. If it doesn't exist, create it.
  OpenOrCreateDB(&gCustomerDB, kCustomerDBType, kSalesCreator, mode,
    0, kCustomerDBName, &created);
  if (created)
    InitializeCustomers();

  // Find the Order database. If it doesn't exist, create it.
  OpenOrCreateDB(&gOrderDB, kOrderDBType, kSalesCreator, mode,
    0, kOrderDBName, &created);
  if (created)
    InitializeOrders();

  // Find the Product database. If it doesn't exist, create it.
  OpenOrCreateDB(&gProductDB, kProductDBType, kSalesCreator, mode,
    0, kProductDBName, &created);
  if (created)
    InitializeProducts();

  c = (CategoriesStruct *) GetLockedAppInfo(gProductDB);
  if (c) {
    gNumCategories = c->numCategories;
    MemPtrUnlock(c);
  }

  return err;
}

static void AppStop(void)
```

```
{
  SalesPreferenceType prefs;

  // Write the preferences / saved-state information.
  prefs.saveBackup = gSaveBackup;

  PrefSetAppPreferences(kSalesCreator, kSalesPrefID, kSalesVersion, &prefs,
    sizeof(SalesPreferenceType), true);

  // Close all open forms. This will force any unsaved data to
  // be written to the database.
  FrmCloseAllForms();

#ifdef DEBUG_BUILD
  CheckDatabases(false);
#endif
  // Close the databases.
  DmCloseDatabase(gCustomerDB);
  DmCloseDatabase(gOrderDB);
  DmCloseDatabase(gProductDB);
}

void SelectACategory(ListPtr list, UInt16 newCategory)
{
  UInt16    numItems;

  gCurrentCategory = newCategory;
  numItems = DmNumRecordsInCategory(gProductDB, gCurrentCategory) +
    (gNumCategories + 1);
  LstSetHeight(list, (Int16) numItems);
  LstSetListChoices(list, NULL, (Int16) numItems);
}


void DrawOneProductInList(Int16 itemNumber, RectanglePtr bounds,
  Char **text)
{
#pragma unused(text)
  void *p = NULL;
  FontID  curFont;
  Boolean setFont = false;
  const char  *toDraw = "";
  Int16   seekAmount = itemNumber;
  UInt16  index = 0;

  if (itemNumber == gCurrentCategory) {
    curFont = FntSetFont(boldFont);
    setFont = true;
  }
  if (itemNumber == gNumCategories)
    toDraw = "---";
  else if (itemNumber < gNumCategories) {
    CategoriesStruct *c = (CategoriesStruct *) GetLockedAppInfo(gProductDB);
```

```
    if (c) {
      toDraw = c->names[itemNumber];
      p = c;
    }
  } else {
    MemHandle h;
    DmSeekRecordInCategory(gProductDB, &index,
      seekAmount - (gNumCategories + 1), dmSeekForward, gCurrentCategory);
    h = DmQueryRecord(gProductDB, index);
    if (h) {
      PackedProduct *packedProduct = (PackedProduct *) MemHandleLock(h);
      Product s;
      UnpackProduct(&s, packedProduct);
      toDraw = s.name;
      p = packedProduct;
    }
  }
  DrawCharsToFitWidth(toDraw, bounds);
  if (p)
    MemPtrUnlock(p);
  if (setFont)
    FntSetFont(curFont);
}

// Returns false if no product selected, true if one is selected
// (in which case productID and name are set).
Boolean HandleProductPopupSelect(EventPtr event, UInt32 *newProductID,
  Char *productName)
{
  ListPtr     list = event->data.popSelect.listP;
  ControlPtr  control = event->data.popSelect.controlP;

  ErrNonFatalDisplayIf(event->eType != popSelectEvent,
    "wrong kind of event");
  if (event->data.popSelect.selection < (gNumCategories + 1)) {
    if (event->data.popSelect.selection < gNumCategories)
      SelectACategory(list, (UInt16) event->data.popSelect.selection);
    LstSetSelection(list, (Int16) gCurrentCategory);
    CtlHitControl(control);
    return false;
  } else {
    UInt16          index = 0;
    MemHandle       h;
    PackedProduct   *packedProduct;
    Product         s;

    DmSeekRecordInCategory(gProductDB, &index,
      event->data.popSelect.selection - (gNumCategories + 1),
      dmSeekForward, gCurrentCategory);
    ErrNonFatalDisplayIf(DmGetLastErr( ), "Can't seek to product");
    h = DmQueryRecord(gProductDB, index);

    ErrNonFatalDisplayIf(!h, "Can't get record");
    packedProduct = (PackedProduct *) MemHandleLock(h);
```

```
    UnpackProduct(&s, packedProduct);
    ErrNonFatalDisplayIf(StrLen(s.name) >= kMaxProductNameLength,
      "product name too long");
    StrNCopy(productName, s.name, kMaxProductNameLength);
    productName[kMaxProductNameLength-1] = '\0';  // Just in case too long.
    MemHandleUnlock(h);
    *newProductID = s.productID;
    return true;
  }
}

void HandleProductPopupEnter(UInt16 controlID, UInt16 listID,
  UInt32 productID)
{
  FormPtr form = FrmGetActiveForm();
  UInt16 listIndex = FrmGetObjectIndex(form, listID);
  ListPtr list = (ListPtr) FrmGetObjectPtr(form, listIndex);

  if (productID == 0) {
    SelectACategory(list, gCurrentCategory);
    LstSetSelection(list, (Int16) gCurrentCategory);
  } else {
    MemHandle h;
    Product   p;
    UInt16    attr;
    UInt16    index;
    Coord     dontCare;
    Coord     x;
    Coord     y;

    h = GetProductFromProductID(productID, &p, &index);
    ErrNonFatalDisplayIf(!h, "can't get product for existing item");
    DmRecordInfo(gProductDB, index, &attr, NULL, NULL);
    MemHandleUnlock(h);

    SelectACategory(list, attr & dmRecAttrCategoryMask);
    LstSetSelection(list,
      (Int16) (DmPositionInCategory(gProductDB, index, gCurrentCategory) +
      gNumCategories + 1));

    // Make list top match trigger top.
    FrmGetObjectPosition(form, listIndex, &x, &dontCare);
    FrmGetObjectPosition(form, FrmGetObjectIndex(form, controlID),
      &dontCare, &y);
    FrmSetObjectPosition(form, listIndex, x, y);
  }
}

static void Search(FindParamsPtr findParams)
{
  Err         err;
  UInt16      pos;
  UInt16      fieldNum;
  UInt16      cardNo = 0;
```

```
UInt16        recordNum;
Char          *header;
Boolean       done;
MemHandle     recordH;
MemHandle     headerH;
LocalID       dbID;
DmOpenRef     dbP;
RectangleType r;
DmSearchStateType searchState;

// Unless told otherwise, there are no more items to be found.
findParams->more = false;

// Find the application's data file.
err = DmGetNextDatabaseByTypeCreator(true, &searchState,
  kCustomerDBType, kSalesCreator, true, &cardNo, &dbID);
if (err)
  return;

// Open the expense database.
dbP = DmOpenDatabase(cardNo, dbID, findParams->dbAccesMode);
if (! dbP)
  return;

// Display the heading line.
headerH = DmGetResource(strRsc, FindHeaderString);
header = (Char *) MemHandleLock(headerH);
done = FindDrawHeader(findParams, header);
MemHandleUnlock(headerH);
if (done) {
  findParams->more = true;
}
else {
    // Search all the fields; start from the last record searched.
  recordNum = findParams->recordNum;
  for(;;) {
    Boolean match = false;
    Customer    customer;

    // Because applications can take a long time to finish a find,
    // users like to be able to stop the find.  Stop the find
    // if an event is pending. This stops if the user does
    // something with the device.  Because this call slows down
    // the search, we perform it every so many records instead of
    // every record.  The response time should still be short
    // without introducing much extra work to the search.

    // Note that in the implementation below, if the next 16th
    // record is secret, the check doesn't happen.  Generally
    // this shouldn't be a problem since if most of the records
    // are secret the search won't take long anyway!
    if ((recordNum & 0x000f) == 0 &&      // Every 16th record.
      EvtSysEventAvail(true)) {
      // Stop the search process.
```

```
        findParams->more = true;
        break;
      }

      recordH = DmQueryNextInCategory(dbP, &recordNum,
        dmAllCategories);
      // Have we run out of records?
      if (! recordH)
        break;

      // Search each of the fields of the customer.

      UnpackCustomer(&customer, (PackedCustomer *) MemHandleLock(recordH));

      if ((match = FindStrInStr(customer.name,
        findParams->strToFind, &pos)) != false)
        fieldNum = CustomerNameField;
      else if ((match = FindStrInStr(customer.address,
        findParams->strToFind, &pos)) != false)
        fieldNum = CustomerAddressField;
      else if ((match = FindStrInStr(customer.city,
        findParams->strToFind, &pos)) != false)
        fieldNum = CustomerCityField;
      else if ((match = FindStrInStr(customer.phone,
        findParams->strToFind, &pos)) != false)
        fieldNum = CustomerPhoneField;

      if (match) {
        done = FindSaveMatch(findParams, recordNum, pos, fieldNum, 0,
          cardNo, dbID);
        if (!done) {
          // Get the bounds of the region where we will draw the results.
          FindGetLineBounds(findParams, &r);

          // Display the title of the description.
          DrawCharsToFitWidth(customer.name, &r);

          findParams->lineNumber++;
        }
      }
      MemHandleUnlock(recordH);
      if (done)
        break;
      recordNum++;
    }
  }
  DmCloseDatabase(dbP);
}

static void GoToItem (GoToParamsPtr goToParams, Boolean launchingApp)
{
  EventType   event;
  UInt16      recordNum = goToParams->recordNum;
```

```
  // If the current record is blank, it will be deleted, so we'll
  // save the record's unique id to find the record index again,
  // after all the forms are closed.
  if (! launchingApp) {
    UInt32    uniqueID;

    DmRecordInfo(gCustomerDB, recordNum, NULL, &uniqueID, NULL);
    FrmCloseAllForms();
    DmFindRecordByID(gCustomerDB, uniqueID, &recordNum);
  }

  FrmGotoForm(CustomersForm);

  // Send an event to select the matching text.
  MemSet (&event, 0, sizeof(EventType));

  event.eType = frmGotoEvent;
  event.data.frmGoto.formID = CustomersForm;
  event.data.frmGoto.recordNum = goToParams->recordNum;
  event.data.frmGoto.matchPos = goToParams->matchPos;
  event.data.frmGoto.matchLen = (UInt16) goToParams->searchStrLen;
  event.data.frmGoto.matchFieldNum = goToParams->matchFieldNum;
  event.data.frmGoto.matchCustom = goToParams->matchCustom;
  EvtAddEventToQueue(&event);
}

static
Boolean AppHandleEvent(EventPtr event)
{
  FormPtr frm;
  UInt16    formId;
  Boolean handled = false;

  switch (event->eType) {
  case frmLoadEvent:
    // Load the form resource specified in event, then activate the form.
    formId = event->data.frmLoad.formID;
    frm = FrmInitForm(formId);
    FrmSetActiveForm(frm);

    // Set the event handler for the form. The handler of the currently
    // active form is called by FrmDispatchEvent each time it receives
    // an event.
    switch (formId)
    {
    case OrderForm:
      FrmSetEventHandler(frm, OrderHandleEvent);
      break;

    case CustomersForm:
      FrmSetEventHandler(frm, CustomersHandleEvent);
      break;

    }
```

```
      handled = true;
      break;

    case menuEvent:
      if (event->data.menu.itemID == OptionsAboutSales) {
        FrmAlert(AboutBoxAlert);
        handled = true;
      }
      break;
  }
  return handled;
}

static void AppEventLoop(void)
{
  EventType event;
  UInt16     error;

  do {
    EvtGetEvent(&event, evtWaitForever);
    if (! SysHandleEvent(&event))
      if (! MenuHandleEvent(0, &event, &error))
        if (! AppHandleEvent(&event))
          FrmDispatchEvent(&event);
  } while (event.eType != appStopEvent);
}

UInt32 PilotMain(UInt16 cmd, MemPtr cmdPBP, UInt16 launchFlags)
{
  Err error = errNone;

  error = RomVersionCompatible(sysMakeROMVersion(3, 0, 0, 0, 0),
    launchFlags);
  if (error)
    return error;

  if (cmd == sysAppLaunchCmdNormalLaunch)
  {
    error = AppStart();
    if (error == errNone)
    {
      FrmGotoForm(CustomersForm);
      AppEventLoop();

      AppStop();
    }
  }
  // Launch code sent to running application before sysAppLaunchCmdFind
  // or other action codes that will cause data searches or manipulation.
  else if (cmd == sysAppLaunchCmdSaveData) {
    FrmSaveAllForms();
  }
  else if (cmd == sysAppLaunchCmdFind) {
    Search((FindParamsPtr)cmdPBP);
  }
```

```
  // This launch code might be sent to the application when it's already running.
  else if (cmd == sysAppLaunchCmdGoTo) {
    Boolean launched;
    launched = (Boolean) (launchFlags & sysAppLaunchFlagNewGlobals);

    if (launched) {
      error = AppStart( );
      if (error == errNone) {
        GoToItem((GoToParamsPtr) cmdPBP, launched);
        AppEventLoop( );
        AppStop( );
      }
    } else {
      GoToItem((GoToParamsPtr) cmdPBP, launched);
    }
  } else if (cmd == sysAppLaunchCmdExgReceiveData) {
    DmOpenRef dbP;

    // If our application is not active, we need to open the database.
    // The subcall flag is used to determine whether we are active.
    if (launchFlags & sysAppLaunchFlagSubCall) {
      dbP = gCustomerDB;

      // Save any data we may be editing.
      FrmSaveAllForms( );

      error = ReceiveSentData(dbP, (ExgSocketPtr) cmdPBP);
    } else {
      dbP = DmOpenDatabaseByTypeCreator(kCustomerDBType, kSalesCreator,
        dmModeReadWrite);
      if (dbP) {
        error = ReceiveSentData(dbP, (ExgSocketPtr) cmdPBP);

        DmCloseDatabase(dbP);
      }
    }
  } else if (cmd == sysAppLaunchCmdSyncNotify) {
    DmOpenRef db;

    ExgRegisterData(kSalesCreator, exgRegExtensionID, "cst");

    // After a sync, we aren't guaranteed the order of any changed databases.
    // We'll just resort the products and customer which could have changed.
    // We're going to do an insertion sort because the databases
    // should be almost completely sorted (and an insertion sort is
    // quicker on an almost-sorted database than a quicksort).
    // Since the current implementation of the Sync Manager creates new
    // records at the end of the database, our databases are probably sorted.
    db= DmOpenDatabaseByTypeCreator(kCustomerDBType, kSalesCreator,
      dmModeReadWrite);
    if (db) {
      DmInsertionSort(db, (DmComparF *) CompareIDFunc, 0);
      DmCloseDatabase(db);
    } else
```

```
      error = DmGetLastErr( );
    db= DmOpenDatabaseByTypeCreator(kProductDBType, kSalesCreator,
      dmModeReadWrite);
    if (db) {
      DmInsertionSort(db, (DmComparF *) CompareIDFunc, 0);
      DmCloseDatabase(db);
    } else
      error = DmGetLastErr( );
  }

  return error;
}
```

Utils.c

```
/*
 Copyright (c) 1998-2001, Neil Rhodes and Julie McKeehan
    neil@pobox.com
 All rights reserved.

From the book "Palm OS Programming (2nd edition)"
by O'Reilly.

Permission granted to use this file however you see fit.
*/
#define DO_NOT_ALLOW_ACCESS_TO_INTERNALS_OF_STRUCTS
#include <BuildDefines.h>
#ifdef DEBUG_BUILD
#define ERROR_CHECK_LEVEL ERROR_CHECK_FULL
#endif
#include <PalmOS.h>
#include "Utils.h"
#include "Common.h"
#include "SalesRsc.h"

Err SetFieldTextFromStr(FieldPtr field, const Char *s, Boolean redraw)
{
   MemHandle       h;

   h = FldGetTextHandle(field);
   if (h) {
     Err   err;

     FldSetTextHandle(field, NULL);
     err = MemHandleResize(h, StrLen(s) + 1);
     if (err != errNone) {
       FldSetTextHandle(field, h);   // Restore handle.
       return err;
     }
   } else {
     h = MemHandleNew(StrLen(s) + 1);
     if (!h)
       return memErrNotEnoughSpace;
   }
```

```
      // At this point, we have a handle of the correct size.

      // Copy the string to the locked handle.
      StrCopy((Char *) MemHandleLock(h), s);
      // Unlock the string handle.
      MemHandleUnlock(h);

      FldSetTextHandle(field, h);
      if (redraw)
        FldDrawField(field);
      return errNone;
}

// Draw strings at top of rectangle r, but don't overwrite
// right-edge of r.
void DrawCharsToFitWidth(const Char *s, RectanglePtr r)
{
  Int16 stringLength = StrLen(s);
  Int16 pixelWidth = r->extent.x;
  Boolean truncate;

  // FntCharsInWidth will update stringLength to the
  // maximum without exceeding the width.
  FntCharsInWidth(s, &pixelWidth, &stringLength, &truncate);
  WinDrawChars(s, stringLength, r->topLeft.x, r->topLeft.y);
}

void *GetLockedAppInfo(DmOpenRef db)
{
  UInt16  cardNo;
  LocalID dbID;
  LocalID appInfoID;
  Err     err;

  if ((err = DmOpenDatabaseInfo(db, &dbID, NULL, NULL,
    &cardNo, NULL)) != errNone)
    return NULL;
  if ((err = DmDatabaseInfo(cardNo, dbID, NULL, NULL, NULL, NULL, NULL,
    NULL, NULL, &appInfoID, NULL, NULL, NULL)) != errNone)
    return NULL;
  return MemLocalIDToLockedPtr(appInfoID, cardNo);
}

UInt32 GetRomVersion()
{
  UInt32 romVersion;

  // The system records the version number in a feature.  A feature is a
  // piece of information that can be looked up by a creator and feature
  // number.
  FtrGet(sysFtrCreator, sysFtrNumROMVersion, &romVersion);
  return romVersion;
}
```

```
Err RomVersionCompatible(UInt32 requiredVersion, UInt16 launchFlags)
{
  UInt32 romVersion = GetRomVersion();

  // See if we're on minimum required version of the ROM or later.
  if (romVersion < requiredVersion)
    {
    // If the user launched the application from the launcher, explain
    // why the application shouldn't run. If the application was contacted for
    // something else, for example, it was asked to find a string by the
    // system find, don't bother the user with a warning dialog box.
    // These flags tell how the application was launched to decide if a
    // warning should be displayed.
    if ((launchFlags &
      (sysAppLaunchFlagNewGlobals | sysAppLaunchFlagUIApp))
      == (sysAppLaunchFlagNewGlobals | sysAppLaunchFlagUIApp)) {
      FrmAlert(RomIncompatibleAlert);

      // Pilot 1.0 will continuously relaunch this application unless we switch
      // to another safe one. The sysFileCDefaultApp is considered "safe".
      if (sysGetROMVerMajor(romVersion) < 2) {
        AppLaunchWithCommand(sysFileCDefaultApp,
          sysAppLaunchCmdNormalLaunch, NULL);
      }
    }
    return sysErrRomIncompatible;
  }
  return errNone;
}

Boolean Has35FeatureSet()
{
  return (Boolean) (GetRomVersion() > 0x03503000);  // From Palm OS Reference.
}

UInt16 GetObjectIndexInActiveForm(UInt16 objectID)
{
  return FrmGetObjectIndex(FrmGetActiveForm(), objectID);
}

void *GetObjectFromForm(FormPtr form, UInt16 objectID)
{
  return FrmGetObjectPtr(form,
    FrmGetObjectIndex(form, objectID));
}

void *GetObjectFromActiveForm(UInt16 objectID)
{
  return GetObjectFromForm(FrmGetActiveForm(), objectID);
}
```

Headers

Common.h

```
/*
 Copyright (c) 1998-2001, Neil Rhodes and Julie McKeehan
    neil@pobox.com
 All rights reserved.

From the book "Palm OS Programming (2nd edition)"
by O'Reilly.

Permission granted to use this file however you see fit.
*/
#ifndef __COMMON_H__
#define __COMMON_H__

#include <PalmOS.h>
#include "Data.h"

#define kMaxNumericStringLength    6
#define kSalesCreator    'SLES'
#define kUnknownProductName "-Product-"

extern privateRecordViewEnum       gPrivateRecordStatus;
extern UInt16        gCurrentCategory;
extern UInt16        gNumCategories;
extern Order         *gCurrentOrder;
extern UInt16        gCurrentOrderIndex;

void OpenCustomerWithID(Int32 customerID);
Boolean OrderExistsForCustomer(Int32 customerID);
Boolean HandleProductPopupSelect(EventPtr event,
  UInt32 *newProductID, Char *productName);
void HandleProductPopupEnter(UInt16 triggerID, UInt16 listID, UInt32 productID);

void SelectACategory(ListPtr list, UInt16 newCategory);
void DrawOneProductInList(Int16 itemNumber, RectanglePtr bounds,
  Char **text);
void DeleteNthItem(UInt16 itemNumber);

#endif
```

Customer.h

```
/*
 Copyright (c) 1998-2001, Neil Rhodes and Julie McKeehan
    neil@pobox.com
 All rights reserved.

From the book "Palm OS Programming (2nd edition)"
by O'Reilly.
```

```
   Permission granted to use this file however you see fit.
   */
   #ifndef __CUSTOMER_H__
   #define __CUSTOMER_H__

   #include <PalmOS.h>

   extern Boolean      gSaveBackup;

   // Returns true if the customer was changed/deleted.
   void EditCustomer(UInt16 recordNumber, Boolean isNew, Boolean *deleted);
   void EditCustomerWithSelection(UInt16 recordNumber, Boolean isNew,
     Boolean *deleted, EventPtr event);
   Boolean AskDeleteCustomer(void);

   #endif
```

Customers.h

```
   /*
    Copyright (c) 1998-2001, Neil Rhodes and Julie McKeehan
       neil@pobox.com
    All rights reserved.

   From the book "Palm OS Programming (2nd edition)"
   by O'Reilly.

   Permission granted to use this file however you see fit.
   */
   #ifndef __CUSTOMERS_H__
   #define __CUSTOMERS_H__

   #include <PalmOS.h>

   Boolean CustomersHandleEvent(EventPtr event);

   #endif
```

CWDebugDefines.h

```
   /* CWDebugDefines.h */
   #define DEBUG_BUILD
```

Data.h

```
   /*
    Copyright (c) 1998-2001, Neil Rhodes and Julie McKeehan
       neil@pobox.com
    All rights reserved.

   From the book "Palm OS Programming (2nd edition)" by O'Reilly.
```

```
  Permission granted to use this file however you see fit.
*/
#ifndef __DATA_H__
#define __DATA_H__

/*
Three databases:
  Customer: (sorted by order to visit. New customers added at beginning).
    customer ID # (unique. Permanent assignment by desktop (positive values). If the
      Handheld creates a customer, it assigns a temporary negative unique #
    name: null-terminated string
    address: null-terminated string
    city: null-terminated string
    phone: null-terminated string

  Order: (sort order irrelevant)
    customerID
    numProducts
    products: array of
      product ID #
      quantity

  Product each product has a category (sorted by product id #)
    Product ID # (assigned by desktop, unique)
    Price
    ProductName: null-terminated string

  In the app info block of the product database:
    Num categories: short
    array of
      category names
*/
typedef struct {
  UInt32  productID;
  UInt32  quantity;
} Item;

typedef struct {
  Int32 customerID;
  UInt16 numItems;
  Item  items[1]; // This array will actually be numItems long.
} Order;

typedef struct {
  Int32   customerID;
  const char *name;
  const char *address;
  const char *city;
  const char *phone;
} Customer;
```

```
typedef struct {
  Int32 customerID;
  char  name[1];  // May actually be longer than 1.
} PackedCustomer;

#define kMaxProductNameLength 40

typedef struct {
  UInt32  productID;
  UInt32  price; // In cents.
  const char  *name;
} Product;

typedef struct {
  UInt32  productID;
  UInt32  price; // In cents.
  char  name[1]; // May actually be longer than 1, but no more than
            //  kMaxProductNameLength (including null terminator).
} PackedProduct;

typedef char  CategoryName[16];

typedef struct {
  UInt16      numCategories;
  CategoryName  names[1];
} CategoriesStruct;


extern DmOpenRef     gCustomerDB;
extern DmOpenRef     gProductDB;
extern DmOpenRef     gOrderDB;

Int16 CompareIDFunc(Int32 *p1, Int32 *p2, Int16 i,
  SortRecordInfoPtr s1, SortRecordInfoPtr s2, MemHandle appInfoH);
MemHandle GetProductFromProductID(UInt32 productID, Product *theProduct, UInt16
*indexPtr);
void GetProductNameFromProductID(UInt32 productID, Char *productName);
void PackCustomer(Customer *customer, MemHandle customerDBEntry);
void UnpackCustomer(Customer *customer,
  const PackedCustomer *packedCustomer);
void PackProduct(Product *product, MemHandle productDBEntry);
void UnpackProduct(Product *product,
  const PackedProduct *packedProduct);
Int32 GetLowestCustomerID( );
Err OpenOrCreateDB(DmOpenRef *dbP, UInt32 type, UInt32 creator,
  UInt16 mode, UInt16 cardNo, char *name, Boolean *created);

#ifdef DEBUG_BUILD
void CheckDatabases(Boolean justCustomer);
#endif
#endif
```

Exchange.h

```
/*
 Copyright (c) 1998-2001, Neil Rhodes and Julie McKeehan
    neil@pobox.com
 All rights reserved.

From the book "Palm OS Programming (2nd edition)"
by O'Reilly.

Permission granted to use this file however you see fit.
*/
#ifndef __EXCHANGE_H__
#define __EXCHANGE_H__


#include <PalmOS.h>

void SendCustomer(UInt16 recordNumber, const Char *scheme);
void SendAllCustomers(const Char *scheme);
Err ReceiveSentData(DmOpenRef db, ExgSocketPtr socketPtr);

#endif
```

Item.h

```
/*
 Copyright (c) 1998-2001, Neil Rhodes and Julie McKeehan
    neil@pobox.com
 All rights reserved.

From the book "Palm OS Programming (2nd edition)"
by O'Reilly.

Permission granted to use this file however you see fit.
*/
#ifndef __ITEM_H__
#define __ITEM_H__

#include <PalmOS.h>
#include "Data.h"

// Return true if edited, false otherwise.
Boolean EditItem(Item *item, Boolean *deleted);

#endif
```

Order.h

```
/*
 Copyright (c) 1998-2001, Neil Rhodes and Julie McKeehan
    neil@pobox.com
 All rights reserved.
```

```
  From the book "Palm OS Programming (2nd edition)"
  by O'Reilly.

  Permission granted to use this file however you see fit.
*/
#ifndef __ORDER_H__
#define __ORDER_H__

#include <PalmOS.h>
#include "Common.h"

Boolean OrderHandleEvent(EventPtr event);
UInt16 OrderRecordNumber(Int32 customerID, Boolean *orderExists);
Boolean OrderExistsForCustomer(Int32 customerID);
Order *GetOrCreateOrderForCustomer(Int32 customerID,
  UInt16 *recordNumPtr);

#endif
```

SalesRsc.h

```
/*
 Copyright (c) 1998-2001, Neil Rhodes and Julie McKeehan
    neil@pobox.com
 All rights reserved.

 From the book "Palm OS Programming (2nd edition)"
 by O'Reilly.

 Permission granted to use this file however you see fit.
*/
#define CustomersForm                       1000
#define CustomersCustomersList              1002


#define OrderForm                           1100
#define OrderNewButton                      1102
#define OrderDetailsButton                  1103
#define OrderDoneButton                     1104
#define OrderProductsList                   1106
#define OrderScrollbarScrollBar             1105
#define OrderItemsTable                     1101
#define OrderItemFirstField                 1111
#define OrderItem1Field                     1111
#define OrderItem2Field                     1112
#define OrderItem3Field                     1113
#define OrderItem4Field                     1114
#define OrderItem5Field                     1115
#define OrderItem6Field                     1116
#define OrderItem7Field                     1117
#define OrderItemLastField                  1117

#define kFirstFieldTop                      20
```

```
#define OrderItemFirstPopup                 1121
#define OrderItem1Popup                     1121
#define OrderItem2Popup                     1122
#define OrderItem3Popup                     1123
#define OrderItem4Popup                     1124
#define OrderItem5Popup                     1125
#define OrderItem6Popup                     1126
#define OrderItem7Popup                     1127
#define OrderItemLastPopup                  1127

#define ItemForm                            1200
#define ItemOKButton                        1204
#define ItemDeleteButton                    1205
#define ItemCancelButton                    1206
#define ItemQuantityField                   1203
#define ItemProductsList                    1210
#define ItemProductPopTrigger               1209


#define DeleteCustomerForm                  1400
#define DeleteCustomerOKButton              1404
#define DeleteCustomerCancelButton          1405
#define DeleteCustomerSaveBackupCheckbox    1403

#define CustomerForm                        1300
#define CustomerOKButton                    1303
#define CustomerCancelButton                1304
#define CustomerDeleteButton                1305
#define CustomerPrivateCheckbox             1310
#define CustomerNameField                   1302
#define CustomerAddressField                1307
#define CustomerCityField                   1309
#define CustomerPhoneField                  1313

#define RomIncompatibleAlert                1001

#define DeleteItemAlert                     1201
#define DeleteItemOK                        0
#define DeleteItemCancel                    1

#define NoItemSelectedAlert                 1000

#define AboutBoxAlert                       1100

#define ProductExistsAlert                  1200
#define ProductExistsAdd                    0
#define ProductExistsCancel                 1
#define DeviceIsFullAlert                   1300

#define DeleteCustomerHelpString            1400
#define FindHeaderString                    1000
#define ItemHelpString                      1001
#define CustomerHelpString                  1003
#define SendCustomerString                  1004
#define OrderTitleString                    1005
```

```
#define CustomersWithSendMenuBar              1000
#define CustomersNoSendMenuBar                1100
#define OrderWithSendMenuBar                  1200
#define OrderMenuBar                          1300
#define DialogWithInputFieldMenuBar           1400

#define CustomerNewCustomer                   2001
#define CustomerBeamAllCustomers              2002
#define CustomerSendAllCustomers              2003

#define OptionsAboutSales                     2101

#define RecordDeleteItem                      2201
#define RecordDeleteCustomer                  2202
#define RecordCustomerDetails                 2203
#define RecordBeamCustomer                    2204
#define RecordSendCustomer                    2205

#define EditUndo                              10000
#define EditCut                               10001
#define EditCopy                              10002
#define EditPaste                             10003
#define EditSelectAll                         10004
#define EditSeparator                         10005
#define EditKeyboard                          10006
#define EditGrafitti                          10007

#define kDefaultButtonHeight 12
#define kInterButtonWidth 6
#define kDefaultButtonBottom   159
#define kDefaultButtonLeft     1
#define kDefaultButtonInModalLeft 5
#define kDefaultButtonInModalBottomMargin 5
#define kGSIFromBottom   10
#define kGSIInModalLeft        148
#define kGSILeft   152
#define kGSITop        150

#define kItemFormHeight 118
#define kDeleteCustomerFormHeight 95
#define kCustomerFormHeight        120
```

Utils.h

```
/*
 Copyright (c) 1998-2001, Neil Rhodes and Julie McKeehan
     neil@pobox.com
 All rights reserved.

From the book "Palm OS Programming (2nd edition)"
by O'Reilly.

Permission granted to use this file however you see fit.
```

```
*/
#ifndef __UTILS_H__
#define __UTILS_H__

#include <PalmOS.h>
Err SetFieldTextFromStr(FieldPtr field, const Char *strP, Boolean redraw);

void DrawCharsToFitWidth(const Char *s, RectanglePtr r);

void *GetLockedAppInfo(DmOpenRef db);

Err RomVersionCompatible(UInt32 requiredVersion, UInt16 launchFlags);

Boolean Has35FeatureSet();

UInt32 GetRomVersion();
UInt16 GetObjectIndexInActiveForm(UInt16 objectID);

void *GetObjectFromActiveForm(UInt16 objectID);
void *GetObjectFromForm(FormPtr form, UInt16 objectID);

#endif
```

Resources

Sales.rcp

```
/*
 Copyright (c) 1998-2001, Neil Rhodes and Julie McKeehan
    neil@pobox.com
 All rights reserved.

From the book "Palm OS Programming (2nd edition)"
by O'Reilly.

Permission granted to use this file however you see fit.
*/
#include "SalesRsc.h"


FORM ID CustomersForm AT (0 0 160 160)
MENUID CustomersNoSendMenuBar
BEGIN
  TITLE "Sales"
  LIST "" ID CustomersCustomersList AT (0 15 160 132) ENABLED FONT 0
END

FORM ID OrderForm AT (0 0 160 160)
MENUID OrderMenuBar
BEGIN
  TITLE "Order"
  POPUPTRIGGER "" ID OrderItem1Popup AT (5 kFirstFieldTop 90 AUTO) RIGHTANCHOR
    FONT 0
```

```
POPUPLIST ID OrderItem1Popup OrderProductsList
POPUPTRIGGER "" ID OrderItem2Popup
  AT (PREVLEFT PREVBOTTOM+3 PREVWIDTH PREVHEIGHT) RIGHTANCHOR FONT 0
POPUPLIST ID OrderItem2Popup OrderProductsList
POPUPTRIGGER "" ID OrderItem3Popup
  AT (PREVLEFT PREVBOTTOM+3 PREVWIDTH PREVHEIGHT) RIGHTANCHOR FONT 0
POPUPLIST ID OrderItem3Popup OrderProductsList
POPUPTRIGGER "" ID OrderItem4Popup
  AT (PREVLEFT PREVBOTTOM+3 PREVWIDTH PREVHEIGHT) RIGHTANCHOR FONT 0
POPUPLIST ID OrderItem4Popup OrderProductsList
POPUPTRIGGER "" ID OrderItem5Popup
  AT (PREVLEFT PREVBOTTOM+3 PREVWIDTH PREVHEIGHT) RIGHTANCHOR FONT 0
POPUPLIST ID OrderItem5Popup OrderProductsList
POPUPTRIGGER "" ID OrderItem6Popup
  AT (PREVLEFT PREVBOTTOM+3 PREVWIDTH PREVHEIGHT) RIGHTANCHOR FONT 0
POPUPLIST ID OrderItem6Popup OrderProductsList
POPUPTRIGGER "" ID OrderItem7Popup
  AT (PREVLEFT PREVBOTTOM+3 PREVWIDTH PREVHEIGHT) RIGHTANCHOR FONT 0
LIST "" ID OrderProductsList
  AT (PREVRIGHT-67 25 67 99) NONUSABLE DISABLED FONT 0
POPUPLIST ID OrderItem7Popup OrderProductsList

FIELD ID OrderItem1Field AT (103 kFirstFieldTop 40 13)
  RIGHTALIGN NUMERIC FONT 0 UNDERLINED SINGLELINE MAXCHARS 20
FIELD ID OrderItem2Field AT (PREVLEFT PREVBOTTOM+2 PREVWIDTH PREVHEIGHT)
  RIGHTALIGN NUMERIC FONT 0 UNDERLINED SINGLELINE MAXCHARS 20
FIELD ID OrderItem3Field AT (PREVLEFT PREVBOTTOM+2 PREVWIDTH PREVHEIGHT)
  RIGHTALIGN NUMERIC FONT 0 UNDERLINED SINGLELINE MAXCHARS 20
FIELD ID OrderItem4Field AT (PREVLEFT PREVBOTTOM+2 PREVWIDTH PREVHEIGHT)
  RIGHTALIGN NUMERIC FONT 0 UNDERLINED SINGLELINE MAXCHARS 20
FIELD ID OrderItem5Field AT (PREVLEFT PREVBOTTOM+2 PREVWIDTH PREVHEIGHT)
  RIGHTALIGN NUMERIC FONT 0 UNDERLINED SINGLELINE MAXCHARS 20
FIELD ID OrderItem6Field AT (PREVLEFT PREVBOTTOM+2 PREVWIDTH PREVHEIGHT)
  RIGHTALIGN NUMERIC FONT 0 UNDERLINED SINGLELINE MAXCHARS 20
FIELD ID OrderItem7Field AT (PREVLEFT PREVBOTTOM+2 PREVWIDTH PREVHEIGHT)
  RIGHTALIGN NUMERIC FONT 0 UNDERLINED SINGLELINE MAXCHARS 20
SCROLLBAR ID OrderScrollbarScrollBar
  AT (PREVRIGHT+4 kFirstFieldTop 7 PREVBOTTOM- kFirstFieldTop)
  VALUE 0 MIN 0 MAX 0 PAGESIZE 0

BUTTON "New" ID OrderNewButton
  AT (kDefaultButtonLeft BOTTOM@kDefaultButtonBottom
  AUTO kDefaultButtonHeight)
  LEFTANCHOR FRAME FONT 0
BUTTON "Details..." ID OrderDetailsButton
  AT (PREVRIGHT + kInterButtonWidth PREVTOP 40 kDefaultButtonHeight)
  LEFTANCHOR FRAME FONT 0
BUTTON "Done" ID OrderDoneButton
  AT (PREVRIGHT + kInterButtonWidth PREVTOP 36 kDefaultButtonHeight)
  LEFTANCHOR FRAME FONT 0
GRAFFITISTATEINDICATOR AT (kGSILeft kGSITop)
END

FORM ID ItemForm AT (2 158 - kItemFormHeight 156 kItemFormHeight)
```

```
MODAL
SAVEBEHIND
HELPID ItemHelpString
MENUID DialogWithInputFieldMenuBar
BEGIN
  TITLE "Item"
  LABEL "Quantity:" AUTOID AT (RIGHT@60 53) FONT 1
  FIELD ID ItemQuantityField AT (PREVRIGHT+2 PREVTOP 50 12) LEFTALIGN FONT 0
    UNDERLINED NUMERIC MULTIPLELINES MAXCHARS 20
  LABEL "Product:" ID 1201 AT (RIGHT@60 27) FONT 1
  POPUPTRIGGER "" ID ItemProductPopTrigger AT (PREVRIGHT+2 PREVTOP 32 12)
    LEFTANCHOR FONT 0
  POPUPLIST ID ItemProductPopTrigger ItemProductsList
  LIST "" ID ItemProductsList AT (PREVLEFT PREVTOP 94 11) NONUSABLE FONT 0
  BUTTON "OK" ID ItemOKButton
    AT (kDefaultButtonInModalLeft
    BOTTOM@(kItemFormHeight-kDefaultButtonInModalBottomMargin)
    36 kDefaultButtonHeight) LEFTANCHOR FRAME FONT 0
  BUTTON "Delete" ID ItemDeleteButton
    AT (PREVRIGHT + kInterButtonWidth PREVTOP 36 kDefaultButtonHeight)
    LEFTANCHOR FRAME FONT 0
  BUTTON "Cancel" ID ItemCancelButton
    AT (PREVRIGHT + kInterButtonWidth PREVTOP 36 kDefaultButtonHeight)
    LEFTANCHOR FRAME FONT 0
  GRAFFITISTATEINDICATOR
    AT (kGSIInModalLeft kItemFormHeight - kGSIFromBottom)
END

FORM ID CustomerForm AT (2 158 - kCustomerFormHeight 156 kCustomerFormHeight)
MODAL
SAVEBEHIND
HELPID CustomerHelpString
MENUID DialogWithInputFieldMenuBar
BEGIN
  TITLE "Customer Information"
  BUTTON "OK" ID CustomerOKButton AT
    (kDefaultButtonInModalLeft
    BOTTOM@(kCustomerFormHeight - kDefaultButtonInModalBottomMargin)
    36 kDefaultButtonHeight) LEFTANCHOR FRAME
    FONT 0
  BUTTON "Cancel" ID CustomerCancelButton
    AT (PREVRIGHT + kInterButtonWidth PREVTOP 36 kDefaultButtonHeight)
    LEFTANCHOR FRAME FONT 0
  BUTTON "Delete" ID CustomerDeleteButton
    AT (PREVRIGHT + kInterButtonWidth PREVTOP 36 kDefaultButtonHeight)
    LEFTANCHOR FRAME FONT 0
  LABEL "Name:" AUTOID AT (RIGHT@51 19) FONT 1
  LABEL "Address:" AUTOID AT (RIGHT@PREVRIGHT PREVBOTTOM+4) FONT 1
  LABEL "City:" AUTOID AT (RIGHT@PREVRIGHT PREVBOTTOM+4) FONT 1
  LABEL "Phone:" AUTOID AT (RIGHT@PREVRIGHT PREVBOTTOM+4) FONT 1
  LABEL "Private:" AUTOID AT (RIGHT@PREVRIGHT PREVBOTTOM+4) FONT 1
  FIELD ID CustomerNameField AT (54 19 97 13) LEFTALIGN FONT 0 UNDERLINED
    MULTIPLELINES MAXCHARS 80 AUTOSHIFT
  FIELD ID CustomerAddressField AT (54 PREVBOTTOM+3 97 13) LEFTALIGN FONT 0
    UNDERLINED MULTIPLELINES MAXCHARS 80 AUTOSHIFT
```

```
    FIELD ID CustomerCityField AT (54 PREVBOTTOM+3 97 13) LEFTALIGN FONT 0
      UNDERLINED MULTIPLELINES MAXCHARS 80 AUTOSHIFT
    FIELD ID CustomerPhoneField AT (54 PREVBOTTOM+3 97 13) LEFTALIGN FONT 0
      UNDERLINED  MULTIPLELINES MAXCHARS 80
    CHECKBOX "" ID CustomerPrivateCheckbox AT (54 PREVBOTTOM + 3 19 12)
      LEFTANCHOR FONT  0 GROUP 0
    GRAFFITISTATEINDICATOR
      AT (kGSIInModalLeft kCustomerFormHeight - kGSIFromBottom)
END


FORM ID DeleteCustomerForm
  AT (2 158 - kDeleteCustomerFormHeight  156 kDeleteCustomerFormHeight)
MODAL
SAVEBEHIND
HELPID DeleteCustomerHelpString
BEGIN
  TITLE "Delete Customer"
  FORMBITMAP AT (13 19) BITMAP 10005
  LABEL "Delete selected\ncustomer?" ID 1402 AT (42 20) FONT 1
  CHECKBOX "Save backup copy on PC?" ID DeleteCustomerSaveBackupCheckbox
    AT (12 53 140 12) LEFTANCHOR  FONT 1 GROUP 0 CHECKED
  BUTTON "OK" ID DeleteCustomerOKButton AT (kDefaultButtonInModalLeft
    BOTTOM@(kDeleteCustomerFormHeight - kDefaultButtonInModalBottomMargin)
      36 kDefaultButtonHeight)
    LEFTANCHOR FRAME
    FONT 0
  BUTTON "Cancel" ID DeleteCustomerCancelButton
    AT (PREVRIGHT + kInterButtonWidth PREVTOP 36 kDefaultButtonHeight)
    LEFTANCHOR FRAME FONT 0
END

MENU ID OrderMenuBar
BEGIN
  PULLDOWN "Record"
  BEGIN
    MENUITEM "Delete Item..." ID RecordDeleteItem "D"
    MENUITEM "Delete Customer..." ID RecordDeleteCustomer
    MENUITEM "Customer Information..." ID RecordCustomerDetails "E"
    MENUITEM "Beam Customer" ID RecordBeamCustomer "B"
  END

  PULLDOWN "Edit"
  BEGIN
    MENUITEM "Undo" ID EditUndo "U"
    MENUITEM "Cut" ID EditCut "X"
    MENUITEM "Copy" ID EditCopy "C"
    MENUITEM "Paste" ID EditPaste "P"
    MENUITEM "Select All" ID EditSelectAll "S"
    MENUITEM "-" EditSeparator
    MENUITEM "Keyboard" ID EditKeyboard "K"
    MENUITEM "Grafitti Help" ID EditGrafitti "G"
  END
```

```
    PULLDOWN "Options"
    BEGIN
      MENUITEM "About Sales" ID OptionsAboutSales
    END
  END

MENU ID DialogWithInputFieldMenuBar
BEGIN
  PULLDOWN "Edit"
  BEGIN
    MENUITEM "Undo" ID EditUndo "U"
    MENUITEM "Cut" ID EditCut "X"
    MENUITEM "Copy" ID EditCopy "C"
    MENUITEM "Paste" ID EditPaste "P"
    MENUITEM "Select All" ID EditSelectAll "S"
    MENUITEM "-" EditSeparator
    MENUITEM "Keyboard" ID EditKeyboard "K"
    MENUITEM "Grafitti Help" ID EditGrafitti "G"
  END
END


MENU ID CustomersWithSendMenuBar
BEGIN
  PULLDOWN "Customer"
  BEGIN
    MENUITEM "New Customer" ID CustomerNewCustomer "N"
    MENUITEM "Beam all Customers" ID CustomerBeamAllCustomers "B"
    MENUITEM "Send all Customers" ID CustomerSendAllCustomers
  END

  PULLDOWN "Options"
  BEGIN
    MENUITEM "About Sales" ID OptionsAboutSales
  END
END


MENU ID CustomersNoSendMenuBar
BEGIN
  PULLDOWN "Customer"
  BEGIN
    MENUITEM "New Customer" ID CustomerNewCustomer "N"
    MENUITEM "Beam all Customers" ID CustomerBeamAllCustomers "B"
  END

  PULLDOWN "Options"
  BEGIN
    MENUITEM "About Sales" ID OptionsAboutSales
  END
END

// Used in menu for 4.0 OS and above.
STRING ID SendCustomerString "Send Customer"

STRING ID FindHeaderString "\tSales Items"
```

STRING ID ItemHelpString "You can edit the product and the quantity. To choose a product, tap on the product picklist. Then, choose the appropriate category. Finally, choose the correct product."

STRING ID CustomerHelpString "Edit the information about a customer here. To delete the customer, tap Deleted. To cancel any changes you've made, tap Cancel."

STRING ID DeleteCustomerHelpString "The Save Backup Copy option will " \
    "store deleted records in an archive file on your desktop computer at " \
    "the next HotSync. Some records will be hidden but not deleted until then."

STRING ID OrderTitleString "Order: ^0"

ALERT ID NoItemSelectedAlert
INFORMATION
BEGIN
  TITLE "Select Item"
  MESSAGE "You must have an item selected to perform this command. " \
    "To select an item, tap on the product name of the item."
  BUTTONS "OK"
END

ALERT ID ProductExistsAlert
CONFIRMATION
BEGIN
  TITLE "Product Exists"
  MESSAGE "You've already got an item with the product ^1. " \
    "Delete this item and add to the existing one?"
  BUTTONS "Add to Existing" "Cancel"
END

ALERT ID RomIncompatibleAlert
ERROR
BEGIN
  TITLE "System Incompatible"
  MESSAGE "System Version 3.0 or greater is required to run this " \
    "application."
  BUTTONS "OK"
END

ALERT ID DeviceIsFullAlert
ERROR
BEGIN
  TITLE "Device Full"
  MESSAGE "The data storage of the device is full."
  BUTTONS "OK"
END

ALERT ID DeleteItemAlert
CONFIRMATION
BEGIN
  TITLE "Delete Item"
  MESSAGE "Delete selected order item?"
  BUTTONS "OK" "Cancel"
END

```
ALERT ID AboutBoxAlert
INFORMATION
BEGIN
  TITLE "Sales v. 2.0"
  MESSAGE "This application is from the book \"Palm OS Programming\", " \
    "2nd edition, by Neil Rhodes and Julie McKeehan."
  BUTTONS "OK"
END

VERSION ID 1000 "2.0"

ICONFAMILY "Sales1.bmp" "Sales2.bmp" "Sales4.bmp" "Sales8.bmp" TRANSPARENTINDEX 0

SMALLICONFAMILY "Sales1.bmp" "Sales2.bmp" "Sales4.bmp" "Sales8.bmp" TRANSPARENTINDEX
0

APPLICATIONICONNAME ID 1000 "Sales"
```

PRC-Tools Build Files

Makefile

```
CC = m68k-palmos-gcc
DEBUGCFLAGS= -g -DDEBUG_BUILD
RELEASECFLAGS= -O2
# Change the following from DEBUGCFLAGS to RELEASECFLAGS for a no-debug build.
CFLAGS = -palmos4.0 -lPalmOSGlue $(DEBUGCFLAGS)
# Change the following line to change the name of the built project.
# Make sure you also change the name of the .def file to match.
APP=Sales

SRCDIR=Src/
OUTPUTDIR=GCC/
RCPFILE=Sales.rcp

OBJS=$(OUTPUTDIR)Customer.o \
     $(OUTPUTDIR)Customers.o \
     $(OUTPUTDIR)Data.o \
     $(OUTPUTDIR)Exchange.o \
     $(OUTPUTDIR)Item.o \
     $(OUTPUTDIR)Order.o \
     $(OUTPUTDIR)Sales.o \
     $(OUTPUTDIR)Utils.o


$(OUTPUTDIR)$(APP).prc: $(OUTPUTDIR)$(APP) $(OUTPUTDIR)bin.stamp $(APP).def
        build-prc $(APP).def $(OUTPUTDIR)$(APP) -o $(OUTPUTDIR)$(APP).prc
$(OUTPUTDIR)*.bin

$(OUTPUTDIR)$(APP): $(OBJS)
        $(CC) -o $@ $(OBJS) $(CFLAGS)
```

```
$(OUTPUTDIR)%.o: $(SRCDIR)%.c
        $(CC) $(CFLAGS) -c $< -o $@

$(OBJS): $(SRCDIR)SalesRsc.h $(SRCDIR)Utils.h $(SRCDIR)Common.h $(SRCDIR)Data.h

$(OUTPUTDIR)Customer.o: \
      $(SRCDIR)Customer.h

$(OUTPUTDIR)Customers.o: \
      $(SRCDIR)Customer.h  \
      $(SRCDIR)Customers.h  \
      $(SRCDIR)Exchange.h

$(OUTPUTDIR)Exchange.o: \
      $(SRCDIR)Exchange.h

$(OUTPUTDIR)Item.o: \
      $(SRCDIR)Item.h

$(OUTPUTDIR)Order.o: \
      $(SRCDIR)Customer.h  \
      $(SRCDIR)Exchange.h  \
      $(SRCDIR)Item.h

$(OUTPUTDIR)Sales.o: \
      $(SRCDIR)Customer.h  \
      $(SRCDIR)Customers.h  \
      $(SRCDIR)Exchange.h  \
      $(SRCDIR)Item.h  \
      $(SRCDIR)Order.h


$(OUTPUTDIR)bin.stamp: $(SRCDIR)$(RCPFILE) $(SRCDIR)SalesRsc.h \
    $(SRCDIR)Sales1.bmp $(SRCDIR)Sales2.bmp $(SRCDIR)Sales4.bmp \
    $(SRCDIR)Sales8.bmp
        ( cd $(OUTPUTDIR); rm *.bin; pilrc -allowEditID -I \
           ../$(SRCDIR) ../$(SRCDIR)$(RCPFILE))
        touch $(OUTPUTDIR)/bin.stamp


clean:
        rm -f $(OBJS) $(OUTPUTDIR)$(APP) $(OUTPUTDIR)$(APP).prc \
          $(OUTPUTDIR)*.bin $(OUTPUTDIR)bin.stamp
```

Sales.def

```
application { "Sales-SLES" "SLES" backup }
```

APPENDIX C
PilRC Manual

This appendix has been included to help you use PilRC. *This manual is not our work*; it is by Aaron Ardiri and it is the PilRC Version 2.8 User Manual, 1 May 2001. While we have looked over the manual and can in general recommend it to help you use PilRC, we have made no modifications to it.

If you are not using PilRC with your development environment then there is no reason beyond intellectual curiosity for you to read through this appendix. The manual is organized loosely as follows:

- PilRC syntax and usage.
- Understanding usage and terminology within the manual.
- A reference for using the resource language. This includes syntax and code examples for all supported forms and form objects.
- How to add international support to an application.
- Known problems in PilRC Version 2.8

Usage

```
pilrc   [-L LANGUAGE] [-I INCLUDE PATH] [-D MACRO(=VAL)] [-R RESFILE]
  [-q] [-V] [-Fh] [-Fj] [-F5] [-Fg] [-Fkm] [-Fkt] [-allowEditID] [-LE32]
  file.rcp [output path]
pilrcui [-L LANGUAGE] file.rcp
```

 Command-line switches are not supported in the PilRC plug-in. The plug-in is executed with the switches -L ENGLISH -allowEditID.

-L LANGUAGE

Generate resource files for a target language, LANGUAGE.

-I INCLUDE PATH

Search INCLUDE PATH when looking for include or bitmap files.

Note: multiple paths be repeating the -I option.

-D MACRO[=VAL]

Define a preprocessor symbol with an optional value.

The macros defined with the -D option can be referenced in #ifdef statements in the resource file for conditional compilation.

Note: if no value is specified, the symbol will be given the value of 1.

-R RESFILE

Output a *.res* file specifying all the resources emitted by PilRC.

-H INCFILE

Output a *.h* file containing auto-generated resource item IDs for resource items that were defined without an ID previously.

Note: if -H is not specified then undefined IDs are considered errors.

-q

Less noisy output, for you minimalists.

-V

Generate Microsoft (VS-style) warning/error output (default is GNU-style).

-Fh

Use Hebrew font widths for AUTO width calculations.

-Fj

Use Japanese font widths for AUTO width calculations.

-F5

Use Chinese (Big5) font widths for AUTO width calculations.

-Fg

Use Chinese (GB) font widths for AUTO width calculations.

-Fkm

Use Korean font widths for AUTO width calculations (Hanme font).

-Fkt

Use Korean font widths for AUTO width calculations (Hantip font).

-allowEditID

Allow the use of "Edit menu" ID values (10000-10007 inclusive).

-LE32

Generate little-endian 32-bit compatible resources (ARM, NT).

file.rcp
> Input file describing the resources to be emitted. Each resource is written as a separate file in the output path directory. The output filename is constructed by appending the hexcode resource ID to the four-character resource type.

output path
> Directory where *.bin* files should be generated.

Examples

```
pilrc myprogram.rcp
pilrc -I c:\resources -L FRENCH myprogram.rcp
pilrc -I c:\resources -L BIG5 -F5 -R myprogram.res myprogram.rcp c:\output
```

Understanding the Manual

Syntax

- Items in all CAPS appear as literals in the file.
- Items enclosed in "<" and ">" are required fields.
- Items enclosed in "[" and "]" are optional fields.
- **Bold** items are default.
- Each field's required type is indicated by a suffix after the field name (see below for types).

Types

.i Identifier

> Example: kFoo

.c Character (may contain normal C style character escapes)

> Example: "0"

.s String (may contain normal C-style character escapes)

> Example: "Click Me"

.ss Multiline string

> PilRC will concatenate strings on separate lines.

> Example:

```
"Now is the time for all good " \
"men to come and aid of their country"
```

.*n*   Number

Defined constant or simple arithmetic expression. Valid operators are "+", "-", "*" and "/". Precedence is left to right, unless changed with the use of parenthesis.

Note: Math calculations are integer based.

Example:

```
23
12+3+1
12*(2+3)
'PALM'
```

.*p*   Position coordinate

May be a number, expression, or one of the following keywords.

AUTO
 Automatic width or height.

 Value is computed based on the text in the item.

CENTER
 Centers the item either horizontally or vertically.

CENTER@<coord.n>
 Centers the item at the coordinate that follows.

RIGHT@<coord.n>
 Aligns the item at the right coordinate that follows.

BOTTOM@<coord.n>
 Aligns the item at the bottom coordinate that follows.

PREVLEFT
 Previous item's left coordinate.

PREVRIGHT
 Previous item's right coordinate.

PREVTOP
 Previous item's top coordinate.

PREVBOTTOM
 Previous item's bottom coordinate.

PREVWIDTH
 Previous item's width.

PREVHEIGHT
 Previous item's height.

Example:

```
PREVRIGHT+2
CENTER@80/2
```

Note: AUTO and CENTER are not valid in arithmetic expressions.

Comments

- Single-line comments begin with //.
- Block comments exist betweenthe /* and */ tokens.
- Note that // comments within the definitions of objects are treated as errors.

Include Files

The *.rcp* file may contain #include directives. This allows a programmer to have one header file for their project containing predefined resource IDs. Source code can reference the symbols as can PilRC.

PilRC understands three include file formats.

.h

```
#define <Symbol.i> <Value.n>
```

.inc

```
<Symbol.i> equ <Value.n>
```

.java, .jav

```
package <PackageName>
public class <ClassName> {
  public static final short <Symbol.i> = <Value.n>;
}
```

Once defined, a symbol can be used in place of any number.

Note: #ifdef derivatives are ignored by PilRC.

Resource Language Reference

The *.rcp* file may contain the following object definitions:

FORM
    Form resource

MENU
    Form menu bar

ALERT
    Alert dialog box resource

VERSION
    Version string

STRING
    String resource

STRINGTABLE
    String list resource

CATEGORIES
   Default category names
APPLICATIONICONNAME
   Application icon name
APPLICATION
   Application creator ID
LAUNCHERCATEGORY
   Default launcher category name
ICON
ICONFAMILY
   Icon bitmap resource
SMALLICON
SMALLICONFAMILY
   Small icon bitmap resource
BITMAP
BITMAPGREY
BITMAPGREY16
BITMAPCOLOR16
BITMAPCOLOR
BITMAPCOLOR16K
BITMAPCOLOR24K
BITMAPCOLOR32K
BITMAPFAMILY
BITMAPFAMILYSPECIAL
BOOTSCREENFAMILY
   Bitmap resource
TRAP
   HackMaster trap resource
FONT
   User-defined font resource
FONTINDEX
   Font Index table for font resource
HEX
   Binary resource (hex/string based)
DATA
   Binary resource (datafile based)

INTEGER
> 2-byte integer value

BYTELIST
> 1-byte integer value list

WORDLIST
> 2-byte integer value list

LONGWORDLIST
> 4-byte integer value list

PALETTETABLE
> Color list resource

FEATURE
> System reserved

GRAFFITIINPUTAREA
> System reserved

COUNTRYLOCALISATION
> System reserved

KEYBOARD
> System reserved

MIDI
> Copy *.aif* to a Palm midi resource

TRANSLATION
> Language string translation resource

FORM (tFRM)

```
FORM ID <FormResourceId.n> AT (<Left.p> <Top.p> <Width.p> <Height.p>)

    [FRAME] [NOFRAME]
    [MODAL]
    [SAVEBEHIND] [NOSAVEBEHIND]
    [USABLE]
    [HELPID <HelpId.n>]
    [DEFAULTBTNID <BtnId.n>]
    [MENUID <MenuId.n>]
BEGIN
  <OBJECTS>
END
```

Where `<OBJECTS>` is one or more of the following:

TITLE
> `<Title.s>`

BUTTON
> `<Label.s> ID <Id.n> AT (<Left.p> <Top.p> <Width.p> <Height.p>)`
> > `[USABLE] [NONUSABLE] [DISABLED] [LEFTANCHOR] [RIGHTANCHOR]`
> > `[FRAME] [NOFRAME] [BOLDFRAME]  [<FontId.n>]`
> > `[GRAPHICAL] [BITMAPID <BitmapId.n>] [SELECTEDBITMAPID <BitmapId.n>]`

PUSHBUTTON
>   <Label.s> ID <Id.n> AT (<Left.p> <Top.p> <Width.p> <Height.p>)
>   [**USABLE**] [NONUSABLE] [DISABLED] [LEFTANCHOR] [RIGHTANCHOR]
>   [FONT <FontId>] [GROUP <GroupId.n>]
>   [GRAPHICAL] [BITMAPID <BitmapId.n>] [SELECTEDBITMAPID <BitmapId.n>]

CHECKBOX
>   <Label.s> ID <Id.n> AT (<Left.p> <Top.p> <Width.p> <Height.p>)
>   [**USABLE**] [NONUSABLE] [DISABLED] [LEFTANCHOR] [RIGHTANCHOR]
>   [FONT <FontId.n>] [GROUP <GroupId.n>] [CHECKED]

POPUPTRIGGER
>   <Label.s> ID <Id.n> AT (<Left.p> <Top.p> <Width.p> <Height.p>)
>   [**USABLE**] [NONUSABLE] [DISABLED] [LEFTANCHOR] [RIGHTANCHOR]
>   [FONT <FontId.n>]
>   [GRAPHICAL] [BITMAPID <BitmapId.n>] [SELECTEDBITMAPID <BitmapId.n>]

SELECTORTRIGGER
>   <Label.s> ID <Id.n> AT (<Left.p> <Top.p> <Width.p> <Height.p>)
>   [**USABLE**] [NONUSABLE] [DISABLED] [LEFTANCHOR] [RIGHTANCHOR]
>   [FONT <FontId.n>]
>   [GRAPHICAL] [BITMAPID <BitmapId.n>] [SELECTEDBITMAPID <BitmapId.n>]

REPEATBUTTON
>   <Label.s> ID <Id.n> AT (<Left.p> <Top.p> <Width.p> <Height.p>)
>   [**USABLE**] [NONUSABLE] [DISABLED] [LEFTANCHOR] [RIGHTANCHOR]
>   [**FRAME**] [NOFRAME] [BOLDFRAME] [FONT <FontId.n>]
>   [GRAPHICAL] [BITMAPID <BitmapId.n>] [SELECTEDBITMAPID <BitmapId.n>]

LABEL
>   <Label.s> ID <Id.n> AT (<Left.p> <Top.p>)
>   [**USABLE**] [NONUSABLE] [FONT <FontId.n>]

FIELD
>   ID <Id.n> AT (<Left.p> <Top.p> <Width.p> <Height.p>)
>   [**USABLE**] [NONUSABLE] [DISABLED] [**LEFTALIGN**] [RIGHTALIGN]
>   [FONT <FontId.n>] [**EDITABLE**] [NONEDITABLE] [UNDERLINED]
>   [**SINGLELINE**] [MULTIPLELINES] [DYNAMICSIZE] [MAXCHARS <MaxChars.n>]
>   [AUTOSHIFT] [NUMERIC] [HASSCROLLBAR]

POPUPLIST
>   ID <Id.n> <ControlId.n> <ListId.n>

LIST
>   <Item.s> ... <Item.s>
>   ID <Id.n> AT (<Left.p> <Top.p> <Width.p> <Height.p>)
>   [**USABLE**] [NONUSABLE] [DISABLED]
>   [VISIBLEITEMS <NumVisItems.n>]
>   [FONT <FontId.n>]

FORMBITMAP
>   AT (<Left.p> <Top.p>)
>   [BITMAP <BitmapId.n>]
>   [**USABLE**] [NONUSABLE]

GADGET
>   ID <Id.n> AT (<Left.p> <Top.p> <Width.p> <Height.p>) [**USABLE**] [NONUSABLE]

TABLE
>   ID <Id.n> AT (<Left.p> <Top.p> <Width.p> <Height.p>)
>   [ROWS <NumRows.n>] [COLUMNS <NumCols.n>]
>   [COLUMNWIDTHS <Col1Width.n> ... <ColNWidth.n>]

SCROLLBAR
>   ID <Id.n> AT (<Left.p> <Top.p> <Width.p> <Height.p>)
>   [**USABLE**] [NONUSABLE] [VALUE <Value.n>] [MIN <MinValue.n>]
>   [MAX <MaxValue.n>] [PAGESIZE <PageSize.n>]

GRAFFITISTATEINDICATOR
>   AT (<Left.p> <Top.p>)

SLIDER
>   ID <Id.n> AT (<Left.p> <Top.p> <Width.p> <Height.p>)
>   [>**USABLE**] [NONUSABLE] [DISABLED] [VERTICAL] [FEEDBACK]
>   [THUMBID <BitmapId.n>] [BACKGROUNDID <BitmapId.n>]

Notes

- ID <Id.n> can be replaced with AUTOID. PilRC will assign an identifier for each control that specifies AUTOID. This is useful for controls that you won't refer to within the application (for example, LABEL's). Auto IDs begin at 9000 and increase sequentially.
- The bitmap referenced by the FORMBITMAP tag must appear as a separate resource in the *.rcp* file via the BITMAP tag.
- MAXCHARS is required for the FIELD tag to work properly.
- Any user-defined fonts defined by FONT 128 and FONT 255 must be before the FORM definition using the FONT tag.
- Any translations defined must be declared before the FORM definition using the TRANSLATION tag.

Example

```
FORM ID 1 AT (2 2 156 156)
  USABLE MODAL
  HELPID 1
  MENUID 1
BEGIN
  TITLE "AlarmHack"
  LABEL "Repeat Datebook alarm sound" AUTOID AT (CENTER 16)
  PUSHBUTTON "1" ID 2001 AT (20 PrevBottom+2 12) AUTO GROUP 1
  PUSHBUTTON "2" ID 2002 AT (PrevRight+1 PrevTop PrevWidth PrevHeight)
    GROUP 1
  PUSHBUTTON "3" ID 2003 AT (PrevRight+1 PrevTop PrevWidth PrevHeight)
    GROUP 1

  LABEL "times. Ring again every" AUTOID AT (CENTER PrevBottom+2) FONT 0

  PUSHBUTTON "never" ID 3000 AT (13 PrevBottom+2 32 12) GROUP 2
  PUSHBUTTON "10 sec" ID 3001 AT (PrevRight+1 PrevTop PrevWidth PrevHeight)
    GROUP 2
  PUSHBUTTON "30 sec" ID 3002 AT (PrevRight+1 PrevTop PrevWidth PrevHeight)
    GROUP 2
  PUSHBUTTON "1 min" ID 3003 AT (PrevRight+1 PrevTop PrevWidth PrevHeight)
    GROUP 2

  LABEL "Alarm sound:" AUTOID AT (24 PrevBottom+4)
  POPUPTRIGGER "" ID 5000 AT (PrevRight+4 PrevTop 62 AUTO) LEFTANCHOR
```

```
    LIST "Standard" "Bleep" ID 6000 AT (PrevLeft PrevTop 52 1) VISIBLEITEMS 2
        NONUSABLE
    POPUPLIST ID 5000 6000

    BUTTON "Test" ID 1202 AT (CENTER 138 AUTO AUTO)
    GRAFFITISTATEINDICATOR AT (100 100)
END
```

MENU (MBAR)

```
MENU ID <MenuResourceId.n>
BEGIN
  <PULLDOWNS>
END
```

Where <PULLDOWNS> is one or more of the following:

```
    PULLDOWN <PullDownTitle.s>
    BEGIN
      <MENUITEMS>
    END
```

Where <MENUITEMS> is one or more of the following:

```
    MENUITEM <MenuItem.s> ID <MenuItemId.n> [AccelChar.c]
    MENUITEM SEPARATOR
```

Notes

- For the PilRC CodeWarrior plug-in, the menu item IDs must be sequential within a menu (for example, 1001, 1002, and 1003 are valid, but 1003, 1005, and 1015 are not).

Example

```
    MENU ID 100
    BEGIN
      PULLDOWN "File"
      BEGIN
        MENUITEM "Open..." ID 100 "O"
        MENUITEM SEPARATOR
        MENUITEM "Close..." ID 101 "C"
      END
      PULLDOWN "Options"
      BEGIN
        MENUITEM "Get Info..." ID 200 "I"
      END
    END
```

ALERT (Talt)

```
ALERT ID <AlertResrouceId.n>
  [HELPID <HelpId.n>]
  [DEFAULTBUTTON <ButtonIdx.n>]
  [INFORMATION] [CONFIRMATION] [WARNING] [ERROR]
BEGIN
  TITLE <Title.s>
  MESSAGE <Message.ss>
  BUTTONS <Button.s> ... <Button.s>
END
```

Notes

- The DEFAULTBUTTON tag can be used to specify the button number to select if the user switches to another application without pressing any button in the alert. The argument is the index of the button, where the leftmost button is at index '0'.

Example

```
ALERT ID 1000
  HELPID 100
  DEFAULTBUTTON 1
  CONFIRMATION
BEGIN
  TITLE "AlarmHack"
  MESSAGE "Continuing will cause you 7 years of bad luck\n" \
          "Are you sure?"
  BUTTONS "Ok" "Cancel"
END
```

VERSION

```
VERSION ID <VersionResourceId.n> <Version.s>
VERSION <Version.s>
```

Notes

- The ID can be 1 or 1000—either will be accepted by the default launcher.

Example

```
VERSION ID 1 "1.0 beta"
VERSION "1.0 beta"
```

STRING (tSTR)

```
STRING ID <StringResourceId.n> <String.ss>
STRING ID <StringResourceId.n> FILE <StringFile.s>
```

Example

```
STRING ID 100 "This is a very long string that shows escape characters \n" \
              "as well as continued .ss syntax strings"
STRING ID 101 FILE "string.txt"
```

STRINGTABLE (tSTL)

STRINGTABLE ID <StringTableResourceId.n> <PrefixString.ss> ... <String.ss>

Notes

- Using the tSTL resource in a LIST:

```
[source.rcp]
STRINGTABLE stringTableMetric
  "" "Litres" "Meters" "Celsius" "Newtons" "Kilograms"

[source.c]
MemHandle memHandle, memStringList;
MemPtr    ptrTable;
UInt16    count;

memHandle = DmGetResource('tSTL', stringTableMetric);
ptrTable  = (MemPtr)MemHandleLock(memHandle);

// get the string count <-- "messy"
count    =
  (*((UInt8 *)(ptrTable + StrLen((Char *)ptrTable) + 1)) << 8) |
   *((UInt8 *)(ptrTable + StrLen((Char *)ptrTable) + 2)));

// get the handle to an array of strings
memStringList =
  SysFormPointerArrayToStrings(ptrTable+StrLen((Char *)ptrTable) + 3, count);

// Note: the "prefix" is ignored here
...

MemHandleUnlock(memHandle);
DmReleaseResource(memHandle);
```

Using the tSTL resource to get a single string:

```
[source.rcp]
STRINGTABLE stringTableTypes "Units are:" "Metric" "Imperial"

[source.c]
Char string[32];
SysStringByIndex(stringTableTypes, 0, string, 32);
```

Notes

- A limitation of 384 strings applies.

Example

```
STRINGTABLE ID 100 "" "One" "Two" "Three" "Four"
STRINGTABLE ID 100 "-" "One" "Two" "Three" "Four"
```

CATEGORIES (tAIS)

CATEGORIES ID <CategoryResourceId.n> <Category1.s> ... <Category2.s>

Notes

- The CATEGORIES tag can be used to specify the default category names for the application. This resource can then be passed to the CategoryInitialize API function to create the category strings in the AppInfo block.

Example

CATEGORIES ID 100 "Unfiled" "Business" "Personal"

APPLICATIONICONNAME (tAIN)

APPLICATIONICONNAME ID <AINResourceId.n> <ApplicationName.s>

Example

APPLICATIONICONNAME ID 100 "AlarmHack"

APPLICATION (APPL)

APPLICATION ID <ApplResourceId.n> <APPL.s>

Notes

- <APPL.s> must be four characters long.
- <APPL.s> represents the creator ID for the application, which can be registered at *http://www.palmos.com*.

Example

APPLICATION ID 1 "PALM"

LAUNCHERCATEGORY (taic)

LAUNCHERCATEGORY [ID <LaunchCatResourceId.n>] <APPL.s>

Example

LAUNCHERCATEGORY "Games"
LAUNCHERCATEGORY ID 1000 "Games"

ICON (tAIB)

ICON [ID <IconResourceId.n>] <IconFileName.s>
ICONFAMILY [ID <IconResourceId.n>]
        <BitmapFileName.s> ... <BitmapFileName.s>

```
[NOCOLORTABLE] [COLORTABLE]
[TRANSPARENT r g b] [TRANSPARENTINDEX index]
```

Notes

- The bitmap must be 32×32, 32×22 or 22×22 in dimension.
- Compression is not available for ICONS.
- A tAIB resource with ID 1000 is created unless an alternate ID is specified.
- ICON creates a monochrome icon resource.
- ICONFAMILY creates a multibit (1bpp, 2bpp, 4bpp and 256 color) icon resources.
- The inclusion of the bitmap color table is *not* recommended as it slows down system performance. PilRC implements a simple color table matching algorithm to match the bitmaps color table to the system palette.
- When an alternate ID is used for the ICON resource, bitmap size is not checked.

Example

```
ICON "myicon.bmp"
ICONFAMILY "icon1bpp.bmp" "icon2bpp.bmp"
ICONFAMILY "icon1bpp.bmp" "icon2bpp.bmp" "icon4bpp.bmp" "icon8bpp.bmp"
ICONFAMILY "icon1bpp.bmp" "" "" "icon8bpp.bmp" TRANSPARENTINDEX 255
```

SMALLICON (tAIB)

```
SMALLICON [ID <IconResourceId.n>] <IconFileName.s>
SMALLICONFAMILY [ID <IconResourceId.n>]
                <BitmapFileName.s> ... <BitmapFileName.s>
                [<font color="#0000ff">NOCOLORTABLE] [COLORTABLE]
                [TRANSPARENT r g b] [TRANSPARENTINDEX index]
```

Notes

- The bitmap must be 15×9 in dimension.
- Compression is not available for SMALLICONS.
- A tAIB resource with ID 1001 is created unless an alternate ID is specified.
- SMALLICON creates a monochrome icon resource.
- SMALLICONFAMILY creates multibit (1bpp, 2bpp, 4bpp, and 256 color) icon resources.
- The inclusion of the bitmap color table is *not* recommended as it slows down system performance. PilRC implements a simple color table matching algorithm to match the bitmaps color table to the system palette.
- When an alternate ID is used for the SMALLICON resource, bitmap size is not checked.

Example

```
SMALLICON "mysmicon.bmp"
SMALLICONFAMILY "smic1bpp.bmp" "smic2bpp.bmp"
SMALLICONFAMILY "smic1bpp.bmp" "smic2bpp.bmp" "smic4bpp.bmp" "smic8bpp.bmp"
SMALLICONFAMILY "smic1bpp.bmp" "" "" "smic8bpp.bmp" TRANSPARENTINDEX 255
```

BITMAP (Tbmp) (tbsb)

```
BITMAP        [<ResType.s>] ID <BitmapResourceId.n> <BitmapFileName.s>
              [NOCOMPRESS] [COMPRESS] [FORCECOMPRESS]
BITMAPGREY    [<ResType.s>] ID <BitmapResourceId.n> <BitmapFileName.s>
              [NOCOMPRESS] [COMPRESS] [FORCECOMPRESS]
BITMAPGREY16  [<ResType.s>] ID <BitmapResourceId.n> <BitmapFileName.s>
              [NOCOMPRESS] [COMPRESS] [FORCECOMPRESS]
BITMAPCOLOR16 [<ResType.s>] ID <BitmapResourceId.n> <BitmapFileName.s>
              [NOCOMPRESS] [COMPRESS] [FORCECOMPRESS]
BITMAPCOLOR   [<ResType.s>] ID <BitmapResourceId.n> <BitmapFileName.s>
              [NOCOLORTABLE] [COLORTABLE]
              [TRANSPARENT r g b] [TRANSPARENTINDEX index]
              [NOCOMPRESS] [COMPRESS] [FORCECOMPRESS]
BITMAPCOLOR16K [<ResType.s>] ID <BitmapResourceId.n> <BitmapFileName.s>
              [TRANSPARENT r g b] [<font color="#0000ff">NOCOMPRESS] [COMPRESS]
[FORCECOMPRESS]
BITMAPFAMILY  [<ResType.s>] ID <BitmapResourceId.n>
              <BitmapFileName.s> ... <BitmapFileName.s>
              [NOCOLORTABLE] [COLORTABLE]

              [TRANSPARENT r g b] [TRANSPARENTINDEX index]
              [NOCOMPRESS] [COMPRESS] [FORCECOMPRESS]
BITMAPFAMILYSPECIAL [<ResType.s>] ID <BitmapResourceId.n>
              <BitmapFileName.s> ... <BitmapFileName.s>
              [NOCOLORTABLE] [COLORTABLE]
              [TRANSPARENT r g b] [TRANSPARENTINDEX index]
              [NOCOMPRESS] [COMPRESS] [FORCECOMPRESS]
BOOTSCREENFAMILY [<ResType.s>] ID <BitmapResourceId.n>
              <BitmapFileName.s> ... <BitmapFileName.s>
              [NOCOLORTABLE] [COLORTABLE]
              [TRANSPARENT r g b] [TRANSPARENTINDEX index]
              [NOCOMPRESS] [COMPRESS] [FORCECOMPRESS]
```

Notes

- BITMAP creates a monochrome bitmap resource.
- BITMAPGREY creates a 2bpp (4 color grayscale) bitmap resource.
- BITMAPGREY16 creates a 4bpp (16 color grayscale) bitmap resource.
- BITMAPCOLOR16 creates a 4bpp (16 color) bitmap resource.
- BITMAPCOLOR creates a 256 color bitmap resource.
- BITMAPFAMILY creates multibit (1bpp, 2bpp, 4bpp, and 256 color) icon resources.
- BITMAPFAMILYSPECIAL creates multibit (1bpp, 2bpp, 4bpp color, and 256 color) icon resources.
- BOOTSCREENFAMILY creates multibit (1bpp, 2bpp, 4bpp color, and 256 color) icon resources. In the header we found a size, a checksum and a BITMAPFAMILY. The Resource created is a 'tbsb'.
- BOOTSCREENFAMILY is system reserved.

- The inclusion of the bitmap color table is *not* recommended as it slows down system performance. PilRC implements a simple color table matching algorithm to match the bitmaps color table to the system palette.
- A new exiting graphics mode is available for application developers who wish to use only a standard 16 color palette (running at 4bpp means half as much memory to copy). BITMAPCOLOR16 and BITMAPFAMILYSPECIAL can be used with the following code:

```
{
  UInt32      depth;
  RGBColorType palette[] = {
                              {  0, 0xff, 0xff, 0xff },
                              {  1, 0x80, 0x80, 0x80 },
                              {  2, 0x80, 0x00, 0x00 },
                              {  3, 0x80, 0x80, 0x00 },
                              {  4, 0x00, 0x80, 0x00 },
                              {  5, 0x00, 0x80, 0x80 },
                              {  6, 0x00, 0x00, 0x80 },
                              {  7, 0x80, 0x00, 0x80 },
                              {  8, 0xff, 0x00, 0xff },
                              {  9, 0xc0, 0xc0, 0xc0 },
                              { 10, 0xff, 0x00, 0x00 },
                              { 11, 0xff, 0xff, 0x00 },
                              { 12, 0x00, 0xff, 0x00 },
                              { 13, 0x00, 0xff, 0xff },
                              { 14, 0x00, 0x00, 0xff },
                              { 15, 0x00, 0x00, 0x00 }
                            };

  // change to 4bpp grayscale
  depth = 4;
  WinScreenMode(winScreenModeSet,NULL,NULL,&amp;depth,NULL);

  // and tweak to the 16 color palette
  WinPalette(winPaletteSet,0,16,palette);
}
```

Example

```
BITMAP       ID 1 "bitmap.bmp" COMPRESS
BITMAPGREY   ID 2 "bmp2bpp.bmp" COMPRESS
BITMAPGREY16 ID 3 "bmp4bpp.bmp" COMPRESS
BITMAPCOLOR16 ID 4 "bmp4bpc.bmp" COMPRESS
BITMAPCOLOR  ID 4 "bmp8bpp.bmp" COMPRESS COLORTABLE
BITMAPFAMILY ID 5 "bmp1bpp.bmp" "bmp2bpp.bmp" COMPRESS
BITMAPFAMILY ID 6 "bmp1bpp.bmp" "bmp2bpp.bmp" "bmp4bpp.bmp" "bmp8bpp.bmp"
  COMPRESS
BITMAPFAMILY ID 7 "bmp1bpp.bmp" "" "" "bmp8bpp.bmp" COMPRESS
BITMAPFAMILY ID 8 "bmp1bpp.bmp" "" "" "bmp8bpp.bmp" COMPRESS
  TRANSPARENT 255 255 255
BITMAPFAMILY ID 9 "bmp1bpp.bmp" "" "" "bmp8bpp.bmp" COMPRESS TRANSPARENTINDEX 255
```

TRAP (TRAP)

```
TRAP ID <TrapId.n> <TrapNumber.n>
```

Notes

- DaggerWare's HackMaster (*http://www.daggerware.com/hackmstr.htm*) is required.
- `<TrapId.n>` must be greater than 1000.

Example

```
TRAP ID 1000 367
```

FONT (NFNT)

```
FONT ID <FontResourceId.n> FONTID <FontId.n> <FontFileName.s>
```

FONT file format

The file containing the font information is plain ASCII. To understand how it works it is first necessary to understand how a font is arranged in memory. A font consists of four main parts: a header, a bitmap image, a bitmap location table, and an offset/width table. The bitmap image and location table are generated for you automatically.

The ASCII file consists of two parts: the header and the font data (glyph objects). A full font file is provided with the PilRC distribution.

The FONT header has the following fields:

fontType
>   The purpose of this field is unknown. The ROM fonts define this value to be 36864.

maxWidth
>   Defined as "maximum character width." If not set, it is automatically set to the width of the widest character.

kernMax
>   Defined as "negative of maximum kern value." The purpose of this field is unknown.

nDescent
>   Defined as "negative of descent." The purpose of this field is unknown, and is not used in the ROM fonts.

fRectWidth
>   Defined as "width of font rectangle." If not set, it is automatically set to the width of the widest character.

fRectHeight
>   Defined as "height of font rectangle." If not set, it is automatically set when the first glyph is defined.
>
>   All characters must be exactly this height.

ascent
>   The number of rows that make up the ascending part of the glyphs. Ascent plus descent equals fRectHeight. This value should be set.

descent

The number of rows that make up the descending part of the glyphs. Descent plus ascent equals fRectHeight. This value should be set.

leading

The purpose of this field is unknown.

Each glyph has a bitmap, offset, and a width associated with it. The width can be overridden, however, it is not recommended as it is set automatically.

Notes

- FONT declarations must be defined before the font is used.
- *All* font declaration must have the following as a last glyph:

```
GLYPH -1
-----
-----
-----
-----
#####
#---#
#---#
#---#
#---#
#---#
#---#
#####
-----
-----
-----
```

- <FontId.n> must be between 128 and 255.
- Custom FONT declarations can only be used on Palm OS 3.0 and later.
- Palm OS 2.0 and before.

```
[source.rcp]
FONT ID 1000 FONTID 128 "font.txt"

[source.c]
void *font128;
font128=MemHandleLock(DmGetResource('NFNT', 1000));
UICurrentFontPtr = font128;
```

- Palm OS 3.0+

```
[source.rcp]
FONT ID 1000 FONTID 128 "font.txt"

[source.c]
FontPtr font128;
font128=MemHandleLock(DmGetResource('NFNT', 1000));
FntDefineFont(128, font128);
```

- FONT support in PilRC is not complete, and has been reverse engineered.

FONTINDEX

```
FONTINDEX ID <ResId.n>
BEGIN
    <FontType.s> <ResId.n>
    ...
END
```

Notes

- This resource is system reserved.

Example

```
FONTINDEX ID 1000
BEGIN
    "NFNT" 9001
    "NFNT" 9002
    "NFNT" 9003
END
```

HEX

```
HEX <ResType.s> ID <ResId.n> <Byte.n> | <String.s>
```

Notes

- String values within the data *do not* have implicit null termination. You must add a 0×00 hex value after the string, if needed.

Example

```
HEX "junk" ID 1000
    0x00 0x00 0x00 0x23 "String" 0x00 "String2"
    0x00 0x00 0x00 0x00 0x00 0x00 0x00 0x00 0x00
```

DATA

```
DATA <ResType.s> ID <ResId.n> <FileName.s>
```

Example:

```
DATA "junk" ID 1000 "binary.bin"
```

INTEGER (tint)

```
INTEGER ID <ResId.n> <Value.n>
```

Notes

- ResLoadConstant API can be used to load the 'tint' resource.

Example

```
INTEGER ID 1000 1974
```

BYTELIST (BLST)

```
BYTELIST ID <ResId.n>
BEGIN
   <Value.n>
   ...
END
```

Example

```
BYTELIST ID 1000
BEGIN
    23
    3
    205
    55
END
```

WORDLIST (wrdl)

```
WORDLIST ID <ResId.n>
BEGIN
   <Value.n>
   ...
END
```

Example

```
WORDLIST ID 1000
BEGIN
    23
    1303
    2505
    2055
END
```

LONGWORDLIST (DLST)

```
LONGWORDLIST ID <ResId.n>
BEGIN
   <Value.n>
   ...
END
```

Example

```
LONGWORDLIST ID 1000
BEGIN
    123456789
    130300
    78005
    200055
END
```

PALETTETABLE (tclt)

```
PALETTETABLE ID <ResId.n>
BEGIN
    <index.n> <red.n> <green.n> <blue.n>
    ...
END
```

Example

```
    PALETTETABLE ID 1000
    BEGIN
       0x00 0xFF 0xFF 0xFF
       0x01 0x00 0x00 0x00
    END
```

FEATURE (tfea)

```
FEATURE ID <ResId.n>
BEGIN
    [CREATOR <creator.s>]
    BEGIN
       [ENTRY] [NUMBER<number.n>] [VALUE<value.n>]
       ...
    END
END
```

Example

```
    FEATURE ID 1000
    BEGIN
      [CREATOR <creator.s>]
      BEGIN
         ENTRY NUMBER 5 VALUE 0
         ENTRY NUMBER 6 VALUE 0
      END
    END
```

GRAFFITIINPUTAREA (silk)

```
GRAFFITIINPUTAREA ID <GraffitiInputAreaId.n>
  [VERSION <version.n>]
  [CREATOR <creator.s>]
  [LANGUAGE <language.s>]
  [COUNTRY <conutry.s>]
BEGIN
  <OBJECTS>
END
```

Where <OBJECTS> is one or more of the following:

```
    AREA<AT (<Left.p> <Top.p> <Width.p> <Height.p>)
      [SCREEN] [GRAFFITI] [INDEX <index.n>]
```

```
BUTTON  AT (<Left.p> <Top.p> <Width.p> <Height.p>)
    [KEYDOWNCHR <keydownchr.n>]
    [KEYDOWNKEYCODE <keydownkeycode.n>]
    [KEYDOWNMODIFIERS <keydownmodifiers.n>]
```

Notes

- This resource is system reserved.
- LANGUAGE is one of the following: "English," "French," "German," "Italian," "Spanish," "Japanese."
- COUNTRY is one of the following: "Australia," "Austria," "Belgium," "Brazil," "Canada," "Denmark," "Finland," "France," "Germany," "HongKong," "Iceland," "Ireland," "Italy," "Japan," "Luxembourg," "Mexico," "Netherlands," "NewZealand," "Norway," "Spain," "Sweden," "Switzerland," "UnitedKingdom," "UnitedStates," "India," "Indonesia," "Korea," "Malaysia," "RepChina," "Philippines," "Singapore," "Thailand," "Taiwan."

Example

```
GRAFFITIINPUTAREA ID 10000
  VERSION 1
  CREATOR "psys"
  LANGUAGE "English"
  COUNTRY "UnitedStates"
BEGIN
  AREA AT (0 0 160 160) SCREEN INDEX 0
  AREA AT (27 164 62 56) GRAFFITI INDEX 0
  AREA AT (89 164 44 56) GRAFFITI INDEX 1
  BUTTON AT (27 206 18 14) KEYDOWNCHR 272 KEYDOWNKEYCODE 0
    KEYDOWNMODIFIERS 8
  BUTTON AT (115 206 18 14) KEYDOWNCHR 273 KEYDOWNKEYCODE 0
    KEYDOWNMODIFIERS 8
  BUTTON AT (0 164 27 28) KEYDOWNCHR 264 KEYDOWNKEYCODE 0
    KEYDOWNMODIFIERS 8
  BUTTON AT (0 192 27 28) KEYDOWNCHR 261 KEYDOWNKEYCODE 0 KEYDOWNMODIFIERS 8
  BUTTON AT (133 164 27 28) KEYDOWNCHR 267 KEYDOWNKEYCODE 0
    KEYDOWNMODIFIERS 8
  BUTTON AT (133 192 27 28) KEYDOWNCHR 266 KEYDOWNKEYCODE 0
    KEYDOWNMODIFIERS 8
END
```

COUNTRYLOCALISATION (cnty)

```
COUNTRYLOCALISATION ID <ResId.n>
BEGIN
  BEGIN
    [NUMBER <number.n>]
    [NAME <name.s>]
    [DATEFORMAT <dateformat.n>]
    [LONGDATEFORMAT <longdateformat.n>]
    [WEEKSTARTDAY <weekstartday.n>]
```

```
      [TIMEFORMAT <timeformat.n>]
      [NUMBERFORMAT <numberformat.n>]
      [CURRENCYNAME <currencyname.s>]
      [CURRENCYSYMBOL <currencysymbol.s>]
      [CURRENCYUNIQUESYMBOL <currencyuniquesymbol.s>]
      [CURRENCYDECIMALPLACES <currencydecimalplaces.n>]
      [DAYLIGHTSAVINGS <daylightsavings.n>]
      [MINUTESWESTOFGMT <minuteswestofgmt.n>]
      [MEASUREMENTSYSTEM <measuresystem.n>]
   END
   BEGIN
   ...
   END
END
```

Notes

- This resource is system reserved.

Example

```
   COUNTRYLOCALISATION ID 10000
   BEGIN
      BEGIN
         NUMBER 7
         NAME "France"
         DATEFORMAT 1
         LONGDATEFORMAT 8
         WEEKSTARTDAY 1
         TIMEFORMAT 2
         NUMBERFORMAT 2
         CURRENCYNAME "Franc"
         CURRENCYSYMBOL "F"
         CURRENCYUNIQUESYMBOL "FRF"
         CURRENCYDECIMALPLACES 2
         DAYLIGHTSAVINGS 3
         MINUTESWESTOFGMT 60
         MEASUREMENTSYSTEM 1
      END
      BEGIN
         NUMBER 23
         NAME "United States"
         DATEFORMAT 0
         LONGDATEFORMAT 7
         WEEKSTARTDAY 0
         TIMEFORMAT 1
         NUMBERFORMAT 0
         CURRENCYNAME "US Dollar"
         CURRENCYSYMBOL "$"
         CURRENCYUNIQUESYMBOL "$US"
         CURRENCYDECIMALPLACES 2
         DAYLIGHTSAVINGS 1
         MINUTESWESTOFGMT 1140
         MEASUREMENTSYSTEM 0
      END
   END
```

KEYBOARD (tkbd)

KEYBOARD ID <ResId.n> <Value.n>

Notes

- Supported values are as follows:
    - If the keyboard is for the United States, then the value = 0.
    - If the keyboard is for France, then the value = 1.
    - If the keyboard is for Germany, then the value = 2.
- This resource is system reserved.

Example

    KEYBOARD ID 1000 0

MIDI (MIDI)

MIDI ID <ResId.n> <string.s>

Notes

- This does not convert the file to a midi resource. The *.aif* file must be Palm midi compliant.

Example

    MIDI ID 1000 "trompette.aif"

International Support

PilRC supports a limited form of international tokenization. It works by substituting strings in the resource definitions with replacements specified in a TRANSLATION section. Multiple translation blocks may be specified in a resource script. The active language is specified with the -L flag to PilRC.

Positioning of controls is a *large* problem if absolute values are used. It is recommended that you use AUTO, CENTER, and PREVRIGHT, and others when defining the contents of your forms.

Example

    pilrc -L FRENCH myscript.rcp res

TRANSLATION

    TRANSLATION <Language.s>
    BEGIN
      <STRINGTRANSLATIONS>
    END

Where <STRINGTRANSLATIONS> is one or more of:

```
<Original.s> = <Translated.ss>
```

Notes:

- Declare a short keyword for long strings, and define native and foreign translations for it.

Example

</u>

```
TRANSLATION "FRENCH"
BEGIN
  "Repeat Datebook alarm sound" = "Répétitions Alarme Agenda"
  "Ring again every" = "Rappel tous les"
END
```

Known Bugs

- LIST
  - — DISABLED does not work.
  - — VISIBLEITEMS may be required for list objects to show properly.
- FIELD
  - — MAXCHARS required for field control to accept characters to work.
  - — NUMERIC doesn't work in the Palm OS prior to 3.0.
- FORM
  - — Using NOSAVEBEHIND on the Palm OS prior to 3.0 may cause errors.
- FONT
  - — Developed based on reverse-engineering. The complete operation of how Palm handles FONT manipulation is unknown.

Index

Symbols

: (colon), 49
! (exclamation point icon), 42
? (question mark icon), 42
... (ellipses), 44

Numbers

64 KB memory chunk limit, 176
80/20 rule, 57
   DateBk4, 64
   Datebook+, 61

A

About menu, 377
   item, 370
active forms, 232
alerts, 42, 140, 237–239, 242–245
   APIs, 238
   creating, tips for, 239
   customizing, 237
   effective design, 74–75
   example, 238
   types, 237
AllocateFeatureMemory( ), 185, 194
allocating
   memory, 190
   pseudorecord as chunks, 347
APIs (application program interfaces)
   alerts, for, 238
   Berkeley Sockets, 440
   controls, 261
   for desktop functionality, 468–481

form objects, 23
form objects, for, 251–254
form-level, 235
Install Aide, 472
memory addressing, 189
Palm OS, network, 440
serial ports, 418
AppEventLoop( ), 145
   exit on command, 168
   modified not to call SysHandleEvent, 166
   non-exiting, 168
AppForge, 36
AppHandleEvent( ), 148, 170, 236, 318, 375
   common menu bars, handling with, 388
AppInfo block, structure packing, handheld
      and conduit, 511
AppInfoType, 330
Apple Newton, 4
application creator ID, web site for
      registration, 565
application design
   functionality and complexity, 64
application development
   development environments, 26–39
   for Palm platform, 9
   tools, available from Palm, 30
   (see also designing applications)
application icons, 256
application info blocks, 322, 329
AppNetRefnum, 454
appointments, scheduling, 58, 60, 61
AppStart( ), 144, 327, 354
AppStdio.c, 181
AppStop( ), 144

We'd like to hear your suggestions for improving our indexes. Send email to *index@oreilly.com*.

About the Authors

Neil Rhodes and **Julie McKeehan** are the principals of Calliope Enterprises, Inc., (*http://www.calliopeinc.com*), a consulting firm specializing in custom programming and instruction for the Palm OS. Calliope's clients include companies such as Palm, Symbol, and other Palm OS licensees, as well as firms requiring individualized Palm solutions.

Along with their numerous programming books, Neil and Julie have developed three Palm OS programming classes for Palm that are used by Palm, Symbol, and others to teach Palm OS programming to developers worldwide. Neil enjoys teaching Palm OS programming and is available to teach at corporate facilities worldwide.

Neil and Julie have been involved in handheld development for eight years and are recognized experts in the field.

Colophon

Our look is the result of reader comments, our own experimentation, and feedback from distribution channels. Distinctive covers complement our distinctive approach to technical topics, breathing personality and life into potentially dry subjects.

The bird on the cover of *Palm OS Programming: The Developer's Guide,* Second Edition, is a rock dove. There are 14 subspecies of rock dove, including the domestic pigeon. These birds are widely distributed throughout the world. In their native environment, rock doves live on rocky cliffs, building their nests in crevices and caves. In the urban environment that most domestic pigeons inhabit, nests are built on the ledges of buildings. Rock doves are not migratory birds; they establish permanent residences. Domestic pigeons often have a range as small as 500 square meters. The rock doves' diet consists mainly of grains containing meal and oil. They also feed on insects and snails, and they supplement this diet with stones, sand, and clay. There is a considerably less savory aspect of their diet, as well: rock doves often satisfy their salt requirements by feeding at dung heaps, or near refuse or human waste sites.

The rock dove population has exploded as many of their natural predators, such as the falcon, hawk, and owl, have decreased in number. This population increase is also helped along by humans, who feed the birds.

Linley Dolby was the production editor and proofreader for *Palm OS Programming: The Developer's Guide*, Second Edition. Mark Nigara was the copyeditor. Rachel Wheeler, Sada Preisch, Mary Anne Weeks Mayo, and Claire Cloutier provided quality control. John Bickelhaupt wrote the index. Edie Shapiro, Jeffrey Holcomb, Derek Di Matteo, Ann Schirmer, Tatiana Apandi Diaz, and Sarah Sherman provided production support.

Edie Freedman designed the cover of this book using a 19th-century engraving from the Dover Pictorial Archive. Emma Colby produced the cover layout with Quark-XPress 4.1 using Adobe's ITC Garamond font.

Melanie Wang designed the interior layout, based on a series design by David Futato. Neil Walls converted the files from Microsoft Word to FrameMaker 5.5.6 using tools created by Mike Sierra. The text font is Linotype Birka; the heading font is Adobe Myriad Condensed; and the code font is LucasFont's TheSans Mono Condensed. The illustrations that appear in the book were produced by Robert Romano and Jessamyn Read using Macromedia FreeHand 9 and Adobe Photoshop 6. The tip and warning icons were drawn by Christopher Bing. This colophon was written by Clairemarie Fisher O'Leary.

Whenever possible, our books use a durable and flexible lay-flat binding.

Get even more for your money.

Join the O'Reilly Community, and register the O'Reilly books you own. It's free, and you'll get:

- $4.99 ebook upgrade offer
- 40% upgrade offer on O'Reilly print books
- Membership discounts on books and events
- Free lifetime updates to ebooks and videos
- Multiple ebook formats, DRM FREE
- Participation in the O'Reilly community
- Newsletters
- Account management
- 100% Satisfaction Guarantee

Signing up is easy:

1. Go to: oreilly.com/go/register
2. Create an O'Reilly login.
3. Provide your address.
4. Register your books.

Note: English-language books only

To order books online:
oreilly.com/store

For questions about products or an order:
orders@oreilly.com

To sign up to get topic-specific email announcements and/or news about upcoming books, conferences, special offers, and new technologies:
elists@oreilly.com

For technical questions about book content:
booktech@oreilly.com

To submit new book proposals to our editors:
proposals@oreilly.com

O'Reilly books are available in multiple DRM-free ebook formats. For more information:
oreilly.com/ebooks

O'REILLY®

Spreading the knowledge of innovators | oreilly.com

Lightning Source UK Ltd.
Milton Keynes UK
UKHW030146070619
343999UK00005B/811/P